Poverty, Progress, and Po

By the early nineteenth century England was very different from its continental neighbours. It was wealthier, growing more rapidly, more heavily urbanised, and far less dependent upon agriculture. A generation ago it was normal to attribute these differences to the 'industrial revolution' and to suppose that this was mainly the product of recent change. No longer. Current estimates suggest only slow growth during the period from 1760 to 1840. This implies that the economy was much larger and more advanced by 1760 than had previously been supposed and suggests that growth in the preceding century or two must have been decisive in bringing about the 'divergence' of England. Sir Tony Wrigley, a leading historian of industrial Britain, here examines the issues which arise in this connection from three viewpoints: economic growth; the transformation of the urban–rural balance; and demographic change in the seventeenth and eighteenth centuries.

PROFESSOR SIR TONY WRIGLEY is Emeritus Professor of Economic History at the University of Cambridge and former Master of Corpus Christi College, Cambridge and President of the British Academy. His previous books include *Continuity, chance and change* (1988), described by the *Economic History Review* as 'an intellectual breakthrough which, like it or not, will influence all our thinking in the future', and *The population history of England and Wales 1541–1871* (1989) with R. S. Schofield.

Poverty, Progress, and Population

E. A. Wrigley

CAMBRIDGE
UNIVERSITY PRESS

PUBLISHED BY THE PRESS SYNDICATE OF THE UNIVERSITY OF CAMBRIDGE
The Pitt Building, Trumpington Street, Cambridge, United Kingdom

CAMBRIDGE UNIVERSITY PRESS
The Edinburgh Building, Cambridge, CB2 2RU, UK
40 West 20th Street, New York, NY 10011-4211, USA
477 Williamstown Road, Port Melbourne, VIC 3207, Australia
Ruiz de Alarcón 13, 28014 Madrid, Spain
Dock House, The Waterfront, Cape Town 8001, South Africa

http://www.cambridge.org

First published 2004

Printed in the United Kingdom at the University Press, Cambridge

Typeface Plantin 10/12 pt   *System* LATEX 2ε   [TB]

A catalogue record for this book is available from the British Library

Library of Congress Cataloguing in Publication data

Wrigley, E. A. (Edward Anthony), 1931-
    Poverty, progress, and population / E. A. Wrigley.
        p. cm.
    Includes articles previously published or soon to be published in
    scholarly journals.
    Includes bibliographical references and index.
    ISBN 0 521 82278 5 – ISBN 0 521 52974 3 (pb.)
    1. England – Economic conditions. 2. Industrial revolution –
    England.   3. Cities and towns – England – Growth – History.
    4. England – Population – History.   I. Title.
HC255.W833   2003
330.942′07 – dc21   2003048472

ISBN 0 521 82278 5 hardback
ISBN 0 521 52974 3 paperback

To my past and present colleagues at
the Cambridge Group for the History of
Population and Social Structure

Contents

Figures

Tables

Acknowledgements

The essays in this volume which have been published previously (or are about to be published) are the following. They are listed in the order in which they were published.

'Men on the land and men in the countryside: employment in agriculture in early nineteenth-century England', in L. Bonfield, R. M. Smith, and K. Wrightson, eds., *The world we have gained: histories of population and social structure* (Oxford: Basil Blackwell, 1986), pp. 295–336.

'No death without birth: the implications of English mortality in the early modern period', in R. Porter and A. Wear, eds., *Problems and methods in the history of medicine* (London: Croom Helm, 1987), pp. 133–50.

'Two kinds of capitalism, two kinds of growth', *LSE Quarterly*, 2 (1988), pp. 97–121.

'Malthus on the prospects for the labouring poor', *Historical Journal*, 31 (1988), pp. 813–29.

'Why poverty was inevitable in traditional societies', in J. A. Hall and I. C. Jarvie, eds., *Transition to modernity: essays on power, wealth and belief* (Cambridge: Cambridge University Press, 1991), pp. 91–110.

'City and country in the past: a sharp divide or a continuum?', *Historical Research*, 64 (1991), pp. 107–20.

'"The great commerce of every civilized society": urban growth in early modern Europe', *Scottish Economic and Social History*, 12 (1992), pp. 5–23.

'The effect of migration on the estimation of marriage age in family reconstitution studies', *Population Studies*, 48 (1994), pp. 81–97.

'Explaining the rise in marital fertility in England in the "long" eighteenth century', *Economic History Review*, 51 (1998), pp. 435–64.

'Corn and crisis: Malthus on the high price of provisions', *Population and Development Review*, 25 (1999), pp. 121–8.

'The divergence of England: the growth of the English economy in the seventeenth and eighteenth centuries', *Transactions of the Royal Historical Society*, 6th ser., 10 (2000), pp. 117–41.

'Country and town: the primary, secondary, and tertiary peopling of England in the early modern period', in P. Slack (ed.), *The peopling of Britain*, The Linacre Lectures 1999 (Oxford: Oxford University Press, 2001), pp. 217–42.

'The quest for the industrial revolution', will also be published in *Proceedings of the British Academy, 2002 Lectures* (Oxford: Oxford University Press, 2003).

Introduction

The essays published in this volume reflect my main research interests over the past dozen years. They fall under three main heads: economic history, urban history, and population history. Described in this fashion, it might seem that they must be disparate, and indeed it is true that, say, investigations into the reasons for a rise in marital fertility in the eighteenth century must seem to have little in common with Malthus's discussion of the causes of the high price of provisions in England in 1800–1, or the latter with the nature of the relationship between urban systems and their rural hinterlands. Yet, though some of the essays may, like planets towards the edge of the solar system, seem far removed from its centre, it remains the case that all are subject to the pull of a single central force. Since my days as a research student, I have always been ultimately more preoccupied with the wish to achieve a better understanding of the industrial revolution than with any other issue, with gaining a clearer insight into the circumstances in which the world learned how to produce goods and services on a scale which would have astonished and bemused anyone born before the nineteenth century. This is an issue to intrigue an historian in any country, but with a particular fascination for one living in England since, although every continent was rapidly suffused by some or all of the changes which ensued, much of the early story was played out in an English setting.

Gauging the relevance of a given topic to the central theme of the industrial revolution is bound to be heavily influenced by the dominant interests of whoever makes the judgement. A conviction that the industrial revolution was essentially a supply-side phenomenon, for example, will be associated with a different view of the key issues from those of greatest concern to someone whose view of its nature suggests a focus on institutional structures. Different emphases do not necessarily conflict in the sense that adopting one means rejecting another, but they will enforce different priorities in identifying what is most relevant. It may help to justify the claim that all the essays in this volume are ultimately serving a common purpose, if I stress that it is my conviction that the significance

1

of the changes which made for accelerated growth can only be appreciated properly if attention is paid to the reasons why bursts of growth in other periods and places had always previously died away. The 'heroic' view of the industrial revolution, still prominent half a century ago, laid emphasis on a period of marked acceleration in the growth rate in real output per head, the step change which Rostow termed 'take-off', before which it was conventional to see any gains as slow and halting. But this view is now almost impossible to maintain. Any overall acceleration was modest to a degree until the middle decades of the nineteenth century, while the scale of the success of the English economy in the seventeenth and early eighteenth centuries was until recently undervalued.

Although Rostow was sufficiently cautious to characterise his take-off dates as 'tentative, approximate', he located the take-off phase in Britain as the period 1783–1802.[1] His vision of the circumstances typical of a society before take-off occurred was divided between two alternatives. One was that of 'a reasonably stable and traditional society containing an economy mainly agricultural, using more or less unchanging production methods'. The other was that of a country in which take-off was delayed 'not by political, social, and cultural obstacles but by the high (and even expanding) levels of welfare that could be achieved by exploiting land and natural resources'.[2] He went on to give the United States, Australia, and perhaps Sweden as examples of the second possibility. Neither of the two prior situations sketched by Rostow describe the English case even approximately well. Rostow's was an idiosyncratic formulation of the characteristics of the industrial revolution, but he had much in common with many other economic historians in the decades immediately following the Second World War, at least so far as the timing and distinctiveness of the sudden surge of growth were concerned. Ashton was, perhaps, the bellwether figure amongst those with a particular interest in the industrial revolution half a century ago. He did not make use of the term 'industrial revolution' frequently, and was ambivalent about its appropriateness even in a book carrying that title,[3] but his analysis did not run counter to the view that a major acceleration occurred towards the end of the eighteenth century. Take, for example, the following passage:

When Arnold Toynbee gave currency to the term 'industrial revolution' he set the beginnings of the movement at 1760; and the tendency of later scholars has been to seek an earlier *terminus a quo*. The roots of modern industrial society can be traced back indefinitely into the past, and each historian is at liberty to select

[1] Rostow, *The process of economic growth*, p. 282.
[2] Ibid., p. 277.
[3] Ashton, *Industrial revolution*, p. 2.

his own starting point. If, however, what is meant by the industrial revolution is a sudden quickening of the pace of output we must move the date forward, not backward, from 1760. After 1782 almost every statistical series of production shows a sharp upward turn.[4]

Even Clapham, notoriously reluctant to use the term 'industrial revolution' and very effective in demonstrating its limited impact before the era of railway construction, was willing to use the term occasionally and to attach to it a meaning not greatly dissimilar to that then widely current. He wrote, 'That the industrial revolution, with the attendant changes in agriculture and transport, rendered the maintenance of a rapidly growing population possible, without resort to the cabin-and-potato standard of life, is beyond question.'[5]

In recent decades a focus on the aggregate performance of the economy as a whole and the use of national income accounting techniques to measure it have nourished the conviction that in the half century before c.1830 growth was little, if any, faster than in the preceding decades, and that the rise in output per head may even have been slower than beforehand.[6] Estimates of the size of the gross national product in the mid-nineteenth century, however, have scarcely changed. This, coupled with the evidence of slow growth in the preceding century, implies a recognition that the divergence of England occurred much earlier than was once supposed and greatly increases the implicit importance of understanding the circumstances which brought about growth before the accession of George III. If the English economy was so productive and successful at the time of the Great Exhibition, but had been growing relatively slowly during the previous century, it must already have been well clear of its main rivals in 1750. Growth rates in output per head on this view probably fluctuated within the same range throughout the

---

[4] Ashton, *Economic history of England*, p. 125.

[5] Clapham, *Economic history of modern Britain*, I, p. 54.

[6] See below pp. 18–9. Not surprisingly, those who have reservations about the capacity of national income accounting to capture many of the most important developments taking place in the century before 1850 remain unimpressed by the new consensus. The counter-view was put vigorously and effectively by Berg and Hudson, 'Rehabilitating the industrial revolution'. They write (p. 34): 'Finally, the national accounts framework and productivity calculations cannot measure that qualitative improvement in the means of production which can yield shorter working hours or less arduous or monotonous work routines. Clearly, a broader concept of technological change and of innovation is required than can be accommodated by national income accounting. If the most sensible way to view the course of economic change is through the timing and impact of innovation, it is arguable that the use of national accounting has frustrated progress. Emphasis has been placed on saving and capital formation at the expense of science, economic organization, new products and processes, market creativity, skills, dexterity, the knacks and work practices of manufacture, and other aspects of economic life which may be innovative but have no place in accounting categories.'

quarter-millennium before 1850, without any distinctive acceleration towards the end of the eighteenth century. For the first three-quarters of the period growth stemmed chiefly from a notably successful exploitation of the possibilities inherent in an organic economy, one in which the productivity of the land ultimately determined all else since almost all the material artefacts useful to man were made from animal or vegetable raw materials. Towards the end of the quarter-millennium, however, the continuance of growth came to depend on breaking free from the constraints always experienced by expanding organic economies. Therefore, both to identify the changes which facilitated first the maintenance and later the acceleration of growth, and to appreciate the nature of the developments which had already taken England ahead of other European countries apart from the Dutch Republic *before* the conventional period of the industrial revolution, it is essential to pay as much attention to the earlier part of the period as to the decades towards its end.

The range of issues discussed in the first section of the book reflects these considerations. They are intended, on the one hand, to explore the problems which faced all organic communities in their attempts to make the best of the limited opportunities available to them, and, on the other, to describe the developments which enabled England gradually to overcome these constraints. The second and third sections of the book, take up particular aspects of this range of topics, those which arise in the context of urban history and population history.

Population history must figure prominently in the economic and social history of all organic economies for reasons which were articulated with notable clarity by Malthus. In such economies the tension between population and production can never be far from the surface of economic life, nor can the imminence of poverty and its attendant sufferings be evaded by a substantial part, often the bulk, of the population. The rate of growth of population and the level of individual real incomes tended to be inversely correlated. The other classical economists shared Malthus's view of the depressing implications of this tension. Adam Smith, for example, regarded it as clear, almost as self-evident, that the supply of labour, like that of any other commodity, was regulated by the demand for labour and that, although the existence of a conventional view of the minimum acceptable standard of living might prevent wages being pushed down to bare subsistence, there was no credible prospect of a secular improvement in living standards.[7] In this, like the other classical economists, he was to prove a poor prophet, but the process by which population and production accommodated to each other could not fail to be a fundamental

---

[7] A. Smith, *Wealth of nations*, I, p. 89.

feature of all organic economies, and the change in this relationship made possible by the escape from the constraints of an organic economy is a key feature of the industrial revolution. It was the industrial revolution which for the first time made poverty problematic, in the sense that it became capable of cure. Previously there had been no option but to endure it.

Similarly, the relationship between town and country was crucial to economic success, as, again, Adam Smith recognised. If the value systems of peasant societies emphasised the importance of avoiding all but a very limited dependence on the market for goods and services, there could be no foundation for a flourishing urban sector and little chance of exploiting the possibilities of raising output per head by the division of labour. In favourable circumstances, in contrast, there was mutual benefit to town and country from exchange between them; positive feedback might flourish. For this to be possible, however, the market had to enter the everyday life of those working the land no less than the life of town dwellers. The spread of capitalist values and practices proved an effective way of securing this change in attitudes. England followed the Netherlands in benefiting from the development of a capitalist agriculture and from the increasing volume of rural–urban interchange which this facilitated.

The essays in the first section, 'The wellsprings of growth', fall into three main groups. The first three chapters of the book are concerned with the transformation of the productive power of the English economy between the reigns of Elizabeth and Victoria. They are placed first because they represent, so to speak, the centre of the imaginary solar system to which reference was made earlier. They deal with the distinctive features of the English economy during the quarter-millennium between the two reigns. During this period England changed from being largely dependent upon her continental neighbours for the acquisition of best practice in the techniques of both agricultural and industrial production, a comparatively minor power whether judged in military or wider political terms, and a country whose population was dwarfed by that of France, to having the most advanced and dynamic economy, the soundest and strongest financial base, formidable naval might, and a population which placed it roughly on a par with the major states of western Europe, France, Spain, Italy, and Germany. That part of this transformation which sprang from economic advance was once depicted as concentrated differentially in the conventional period of the industrial revolution. What was once regarded as compressed into half a century, however, is now understood to have been in train for a period three or four times as long. And what was once treated as the product of a unitary process now seems better understood as two distinct types of growth which overlapped each other in time, one associated with the achievement of an optimum use of resources within a 'traditional' economy, the other, which very gradually increased in importance, enabling the momentum of growth to be maintained when the stimuli which had previously been effective were beginning to lose their power.

The second group of chapters (chapters 4 and 5) presents and discusses census information about occupational structure, drawn chiefly from the censuses of 1831, 1841, and 1851. In due course I hope it may prove possible to extend this analysis backward for a further century in the first instance, and eventually, if all goes well, to cover a still earlier period, though less thoroughly. The idea underlying these chapters is that the character of a country's economy at a point in time and of any changes in its economy taking place over time are necessarily reflected in its occupational structure. Employment is shaped by demand. The structure of aggregate demand in turn is largely determined by the level of disposable income among consumers. Demand for the basic necessities will always predominate where most members of a population are poor and it is not therefore surprising that agriculture provides employment for three-quarters or more of the labour force where poverty is deep and widespread. Food is invariably the first necessity. But the income elasticity of demand for necessities is less than unity and therefore if and when real incomes rise there is a disproportionately rapid rise in the percentage of the workforce which is employed in secondary and tertiary occupations. Reliable data about occupational structure and change, therefore, provide information which directly reflects the structure of demand and the economic activity of the day, and indirectly reflects the living standards of the population. Change over time is very instructive in this regard. If, in due course, it proves possible to reconstruct the history of changing occupational structure throughout the early modern period, and particularly if regional differences can be identified, this will go far towards resolving many of the present uncertainties about the nature and phasing of change in the centuries preceding the conventional dating of the industrial revolution. The two essays included in this collection deal only with the end of the quarter-millennium in question, but, in addition to revealing the frailty of much census data, they underline some features of the English scene in the early nineteenth century which run counter to widespread assumptions: for example, they reveal that 'traditional' occupations, such as carpenters, tailors, or butchers still afforded far more employment than 'new' occupations and were still increasing substantially in number; that employment in such occupations was remarkably evenly spread over the country as whole; and that, despite the rapid growth in employment in occupations associated with factory industry and distant markets, tertiary employment was growing much faster than secondary employment in the middle decades of the century.

Two of the remaining three chapters in the first section deal with poverty. Given the nature of all economies before the industrial revolution, poverty was unavoidable. Not only was all food either animal or vegetable in origin, so also were almost all the raw materials from which the material artefacts of use to man were made. Therefore the productivity of the land set limits to the volume of production which it was possible to attain, and, since the supply of land, in contrast to the supply of labour or of capital, could not be expanded, organic economies were in the unfortunate position that each increase in output beyond a certain level made the next such step harder to take. The productivity of labour and of capital was certain to tend to decline both at the intensive and extensive margins of agricultural production. Technical ingenuity and inventiveness might serve to offset this for a time, but ultimately there could be no escape from the law of diminishing returns. This issue is explored in the last two chapters of the first section, chapters 7 and 8. In one it is treated generally, in the other discussed in relation to the writings of Robert Malthus. Malthus added a particular urgency to the discussion of poverty by pointing in his first publication, the *Essay on population*, to an additional force tending to ensure widespread poverty – the tendency of population, if its growth were unchecked, to outstrip any conceivable increase in output. He laid to rest the easy assumption that, since with every new mouth there came a pair of hands, population growth would, so to speak, take care of itself. For this reason he was a forceful opponent of the poor law, which, in his view, by encouraging improvident marriages and their attendant offspring, could only have the effect of exacerbating the problem which it sought to alleviate. Yet it should not be overlooked that Malthus's views changed substantially from those which he expressed as a young man of 32 in 1798 when the *Essay on population* was published. As his knowledge grew, and especially as evidence accumulated that marriage in many European societies suggested the exercise of greater 'prudence' than he had once supposed; that the 'nuptiality valve' was sometimes effective in restraining growth, he came to adopt in his mature years a much more shaded, at times guardedly optimistic view of future prospects.

Chapter 6 is brief. It is a reconsideration of the argument advanced by Malthus in the second of his publications, a short essay concerned with identifying the reasons for the high price of corn in England in 1800–1. Malthus had recently undertaken an extensive tour of Scandinavia where he had witnessed at first hand the grave suffering in a large tract of western Sweden in the aftermath of a poor harvest. He was greatly struck by the fact that the price of the main bread grain in Värmland, rye, had risen much less than the price of wheat in England, which was causing so much public concern at the time of his return to England, although the absolute shortage was far greater in western Sweden. His essay is striking for two reasons. First, his discussion anticipates many of the strands in the analysis of food shortage, price movements, and deprivation which Sen developed in his recent review of the issue.[8] Second, it is a notable illustration of his characteristic willingness to allow empirical evidence to outweigh theory if the two were in conflict, for in spite of his general, and principled dislike of the English poor law, he emphasised its importance in transferring to those most in need sufficient additional purchasing power to enable them to obtain a substantially larger fraction of the available supply of food than they would have been able to secure without such assistance.

The second section, 'Town and country', is devoted to two themes within urban history broadly interpreted. One of the three, chapter 10, is, in effect, a commentary upon Adam Smith's well-known remark that the exchange taking place between town and country is 'the great commerce of every civilized society'. Smith's discussion is in part an elaboration of a relatively straightforward point – that in an organic economy all the raw materials used by the craftsmen and artisans in a town must be derived from the surplus produce of the countryside, and that if those living and working on the land were to be successfully encouraged to provide such raw materials, the town must make available in return wares which were better made, cheaper, or more fashionable than those available from rural craftsmen. Once this commerce was in being, however, it held out the hope of what, in today's jargon, is termed positive feedback. The increasing range and sophistication of urban produce might serve to induce farmers to invest in improved practices to generate the additional income which would enable them to satisfy wants newly awakened by their close contact with urban life. This process was a principal mechanism by which the benefits of the division of labour and an increasing investment of capital could be realised in practice. But Smith went well beyond the exposition of this issue, important though it was in explaining the nature and scale of economic growth in England in the seventeenth and eighteenth centuries. He included a substantial historical section in book III of the *Wealth of nations* in which he advanced reasons to suppose that urban growth was the chief cause of the development of a capitalist economic system because it was so closely associated with the establishment of security of the person and of property, the replacement of custom

---

[8] Sen, *Poverty and famines.*

by enforceable contract, and more generally with the securing of personal freedoms. Furthermore, he gave a very clear account, later developed to telling effect by von Thünen, of the impact of the presence of a town on the intensity of land use in its vicinity.[9]

The other two chapters in the second section deal with a distinct, if related topic – the character of urban systems and in particular the relationship between urban systems and the rural hinterlands in which they were set. Chapter 9 tackles the question in general terms, exploring such issues as, for example, the relationship between the proportion of a population living in towns and the structure of aggregate demand. This is a topic which has, perhaps, attracted less than its fair share of attention in the past. If one starts from the platitude that commodities and services are only produced if there is an effective demand for them, it is self-evident that if, say, a community is so poor that three-quarters of all income is devoted to the purchase of food, a broadly comparable proportion of the labour force will work on the land. No doubt the reason why textile and clothing industries were so often the largest employment sector in towns in the past is associated with the fact that clothing is one of the four necessities of life, together with food, housing, and fuel, and that a substantial demand for clothing is therefore to be found even in relatively poor communities; but whereas the other three necessities were principally supplied to country dwellers from local sources, clothing was often more conveniently produced in an urban setting where a finer product could be manufactured, a product moreover which was readily transportable even when roads were primitive and goods moved overland either on horseback or by cart.

The final chapter in the second section covers a similar topic historically rather than thematically. The distinction between primary, secondary, and tertiary output is analytically convenient in many contexts. In relation

---

[9] Von Thünen, *The isolated state*. Smith had written, for example: 'The greater the number and revenue of the inhabitants of the town, the more extensive is the market which it affords to those of the country; and the more extensive that market, it is always the more advantageous to a great number. The corn which grows within a mile of the town sells therefore for the same price with that which comes from twenty miles distance. But the price of the latter must generally, not only pay the expence of raising and bringing it to market, but afford too the ordinary profits of agriculture to the farmer. The proprietors and cultivators of the country, therefore, which lies in the neighbourhood of the town, over and above the ordinary profits of agriculture, gain, in the price of what they sell, the whole value of the like produce that is brought from more distant parts, and they save, besides, the whole value of the carriage in the price of what they buy. Compare the cultivation of the lands in the neighbourhood of any considerable town, with that of those which lie at some distance from it, and you will easily satisfy yourself how much the country is benefited by the commerce of the town.' A. Smith, *Wealth of nations*, I, pp. 401–2.

to the history of the peopling of England, it is attractive to use it as a device for giving coherence to secular change. The income elasticity of demand for the products of these three sectors of the economy is very different. As a simplifying generalisation it is fair to say that the elasticity is less than unity for primary products and that it is highest for the products of tertiary industries, with secondary industry somewhere in between. It follows that as incomes rise the primary sector will decline in importance, while expansion is always likely to be swiftest in the tertiary sector, even though it may initially be far smaller than either of the other two. Two hundred years ago well over half, in some countries more than three-quarters, of all employment was in the primary sector, whereas today in advanced economies more than three-quarters of all men and women in gainful employment work in the tertiary sector. Chapter 11 discusses population growth in England in the early modern period using this set of concepts. Since the share of secondary and tertiary employment in the national whole increased greatly between *c.*1550 and *c.*1850, and since secondary and tertiary employment is far more concentrated spatially than primary employment, this altered the regional and local patterning of the distribution of population substantially.

The third and final section, 'The numbers game', consists of chapters dealing with population history. It is convenient to begin by referring to the last chapter in the book, chapter 15. It is reasonable to claim that in the past forty years knowledge of the population history of England has been transformed more radically than that of any other aspect of her history which is capable of quantification. There is a plethora of detailed information about almost every aspect of fertility, mortality, and nuptiality for the whole of the 'parish register' period from 1538 to 1837. Much of the information has been set out in tabular form with an exactness that invites suspicion, if not derision. Who can suppose that when the population of England is said to be 4,161,784 in 1601,[10] the quoted total is dependable to the last digit, or even to the last five or six digits? Plainly, such totals and many of the vast array of rates of various kinds associated with them are subject to significant margins of error. Scepticism about precise totals and exact rates is fully justified. The key question is the margin of uncertainty surrounding the published results. This chapter employs a range of tests designed to expose any weaknesses in the published results and concludes that, in the main, they survive such tests successfully. Although this conclusion is likely to provoke a response similar to the well-known remark attributed to Mandy Rice-Davies, I trust that the chapter will serve to lend effective support to the view that the published findings are

---

[10] Wrigley *et al.*, *English population history*, tab. A9.1, pp. 614–5.

broadly dependable and therefore that the conclusions which have been drawn from them, for example about the proximate causes of the accelerated growth of population in the eighteenth century, are to be relied upon.

The penultimate chapter is taken up with an aspect of the question of the reliability of demographic estimates derived from family reconstitution which is especially intriguing, and merits separate consideration. Ruggles has shown that, on certain assumptions about the timing and nature of migratory movements, reconstitution-based estimates of marriage age must be substantially and systematically inaccurate.[11] His logic is impeccable provided that his assumptions are justified, and if this were the case, reconstitution-based estimates of marriage age would need to be corrected significantly to approximate to the true position. His fundamental point is very simple. Those who marry late, *ceteris paribus*, are more likely to have migrated away from their parish of origin than those who marry early and so, if the aim of the exercise is to measure the average age at marriage of a rising generation of young men and women in a given parish, migration will cause the average to be underestimated.[12] The greater the rate of migration, the greater the distortion involved. In England there was an exceptionally high level of mobility among parish populations, so that the issue is of greater significance than in most of continental Europe where a larger proportion of young people married and settled in the parish in which they had been born. It transpires, however, that the 'Ruggles effect' is so slight as to be negligible in the case of early modern England (and indeed, where it has been tested, elsewhere also).[13] It is abundantly clear that Ruggles has identified a possibility that must always be taken seriously, but equally that the assumptions associated with his argument were often either unjustified or offset by other factors.

The rapidity of population growth in eighteenth-century England set it apart from any of the larger countries of continental western Europe. It can be shown that, in accounting for the acceleration which took place, the rise in fertility which occurred was about twice as important as the fall in mortality.[14] Although the most important single cause of the rise

---

[11] See below pp. 368–70.

[12] For those unfamiliar with family reconstitution, it should be pointed out that the age at marriage of men and women migrating into a given parish cannot normally be calculated, since they were born elsewhere, and it is the difference between the date of an individual's baptism and his or her marriage which enables age at marriage to be calculated. Therefore, ages at marriage of immigrants to the parish cannot be used to offset the loss of ages at marriage of those who leave the parish before marrying.

[13] See below, pp. 370–93.

[14] See below, pp. 431–2.

in fertility was a substantial fall in marriage age, there was also a significant rise in marital fertility. Chapter 12 seeks to demonstrate that the rise in marital fertility was chiefly due to a marked fall in the stillbirth rate. There seems no reason to suppose that the tempo of conception changed but the percentage of conceptions which were carried successfully to term rose. If conception rather than parturition is regarded as the beginning of life, in other words, there was no rise in fertility but a big fall in mortality in the subsequent nine months before birth (there was also a large fall in mortality in the first few days and weeks after birth, a parallel change which was to be expected since the causes of death in the weeks immediately before and after birth have much in common).

Chapter 13, 'No death without birth', is intended as a stimulant to discussion rather than a contribution to empirical knowledge. The argument stems from a necessary feature of all organic, or pre-industrial societies. In such societies population growth was bound to be slow in general. True, in areas of recent settlement where there was new land to be taken up, or in the exceptional circumstances which followed a major loss of population, there might for a time be many more births than deaths. But in general, and over any but the short term, births and deaths were bound to be in rough balance. For example a very modest surplus of births over deaths of 3 per 1,000 (the situation which would obtain if the crude birth rate were 33 per 1,000 and the crude death rate 30 per 1,000) will cause population to rise twentyfold in a thousand years, a comparatively brief span of time in human history. Clearly for most of the past 5,000 years birth and death rates must have been far closer together. In some places death rates were unavoidably high because, say, of a very unfavourable disease environment, and in such areas birth rates must have been equally high or the population would have disappeared. But where death rates were not unavoidably high but birth rates were nonetheless high because, say, of conventions about age at marriage or because the normal duration of breastfeeding was relatively short, death rates would necessarily climb to the same level because rapid population growth was not possible. The chapter discusses the implications of the fact that, because the two rates were necessarily of similar magnitude, in principle and in fact death rates might often be high because of high birth rates rather than the reverse.

Of the fifteen chapters in this book, twelve have been published previously.[15] It should be noted, however, that, in addition to converting all footnote references to a standard form, I have taken the opportunity to amend the text of all twelve. Sometimes this has involved little more

---

[15] A thirteenth, chapter 1, will be published in a briefer version elsewhere at much the same time as this volume.

than correcting minor errors, rephrasing cumbersome sentences, clarifying passages which now seem to me have been obscurely phrased, and deleting redundancies, but on occasion the changes were somewhat more substantial. In some cases the revised version is shorter than the original. Where this is the case, the reason is usually to do with the wish to minimise repetition; this also often explains the occasional cross-references between chapters.

Adam Smith remarked, memorably, that 'I am always willing to run some hazard of being tedious in order to be sure that I am perspicuous': an admirable sentiment.[16]

---

[16] A. Smith, *Wealth of nations*, I, p. 33.

Part I

The wellsprings of growth

1   The quest for the industrial revolution

The paradox

When Deane and Cole published their pathbreaking study of the growth of the British economy between the late seventeenth and mid-twentieth centuries, they concluded, in effect, that the term 'industrial revolution' was meaningful and that the conventional chronology was broadly correct – that over a period of half a century or so beginning in the last decades of the eighteenth century there was a marked acceleration in the rate of growth of the national product, an acceleration so marked that, in spite of the fact that population grew faster in this period than at any earlier or subsequent time, output per head also rose more quickly than previously. 'At the end of the century, however, there was a crucial change. After 1785, both total output and population were growing much faster than before, but the former now began to draw decisively ahead of the latter. For the first time, per capita output started to increase – at more than three times the average rate for the rest of the period under review [the eighteenth century].'[1]

In one sense it is almost impossible to quarrel with the use of the term 'industrial revolution'. We live in a world in which it is difficult for people in wealthy countries to see the point of the plea in the Lord's Prayer that we should each day be given our daily bread. Relative deprivation may be severe even in the wealthiest of countries, but few lack the ability to buy as much bread as they can eat. Yet for most people in every generation before the industrial revolution the plea made perfect sense. When there was a poor harvest, the few with surplus grain to sell might prosper; others, with few exceptions, suffered.[2] The industrial revolution resolved a tension which had haunted all organic economies, those economies in which

---

This chapter is a modified version of the sixth British Academy Lecture delivered on 12 November 2002.
[1] Deane and Cole, *British economic growth*, p. 80.
[2] The continued reality of the widespread misery which followed in the wake of serious harvest failure is vividly brought home by Goubert's study of the Beauvaisis in the early modern period: Goubert, *Beauvais et le Beauvaisis*.

almost all the material artefacts of value to man were derived from animal or vegetable products, and whose production was therefore constrained by the productivity of the land. This was the tension to which Malthus gave classical expression when he called attention to the tendency of population when unchecked to grow geometrically, while the supply of food could at best be expected to rise arithmetically.[3] By one of the more striking ironies of intellectual history, however, Malthus published his *Essay on population* just at the time when, with the benefit of hindsight, it is clear that his strictures were ceasing to be applicable, and it is additionally ironical that the changes which made his analysis obsolete were happening in the country in which he was living.

Yet there is another sense in which the use of the term industrial revolution poses a severe problem. The work of Deane and Cole was pathbreaking in that they made a determined effort to quantify the size and rate of growth of the national economy as a whole, to parallel earlier qualitative or partial descriptions of the industrial revolution by an exercise which would integrate estimates of growth rates in individual industries into a comprehensive account covering the economy as whole and which would allow the relative importance of the different components of the whole to be identified.[4] How significant within the overall national picture was agriculture, the cotton industry, the iron industry, and so on? Was expansion widespread and uniform, or disproportionately concentrated in a few sectors of the economy? How localised was any growth spurt?

Deane and Cole recognised, indeed emphasised, that many of the estimates which they incorporated in their analysis were fragile because the available data were fragmentary or even completely lacking, forcing them to make assumptions which were open to question. Others following in the footsteps of Deane and Cole reconsidered their assumptions and were also able to take advantage of fuller or more reliable data. In particular, twenty years after the publication of Deane and Cole's *British economic growth*, Crafts published a book with the same short title which reviewed all that had happened in the interim and concluded that the spurt in the growth rate after *c*.1785 was an illusion. If measured per caput, the growth rate of the national economy at the end of the eighteenth century was no greater than at its beginning and any further acceleration was so modest

---

[3] 'Population, when unchecked, increases in a geometrical ratio. Subsistence increases only in an arithmetical ratio. A slight acquaintance with numbers will show the immensity of the first power in comparison of the second.' Malthus, *Essay on population* [1798], p. 9.

[4] The radical nature of the contrast between the approach of Deane and Cole and that of their predecessors is well illustrated by comparing their *British economic growth* with Ashton's *Economic history of England*, a widely acclaimed work, which had been published only seven years earlier.

as to call in question its reality; even if measured in aggregate, growth was only moderately faster, at least before the 1830s.[5] Subsequent work has confirmed, even reinforced scepticism about acceleration during the classical period of the industrial revolution.[6] Like the grin on the face of the Cheshire cat, it might be said, the industrial revolution has faded from the face of the economic history of Britain in the later eighteenth and early nineteenth centuries. The term itself has not lost currency, but its traditional meaning has few remaining advocates.

This claim needs some qualification, or at least further exposition. By 'traditional meaning' I have in mind the view that there was an abrupt acceleration in the overall rate of growth of the economy in the period *c*. 1780 to *c*. 1840. There are many historians who would agree that, expressed in this fashion, the claim is valid, but who retain a belief that fundamental changes were in train in the late eighteenth and early nineteenth centuries, and that the term industrial revolution remains a proper designation for these changes. Even supposing that national income accounting methods are appropriate for certain purposes, it is argued, they fail to capture the phenomena which justify the use of the term industrial revolution. The fish that matter slip through the net. This alternative viewpoint can take many different forms. It can be argued that crucial technological changes occurred in this period even though their ability to affect national aggregates only appeared at a later date; or that the problem with national income accounting lies with the adjective 'national' since in certain regions of the country dramatic and fundamental change occurred but for a time its overall impact was limited; or that focusing on a few eye-catching industries which grew rapidly but which remained too small to affect national aggregates has led to the neglect of less dramatic changes in long-established industries whose size meant that relatively modest gains in individual productivity had a marked, but unnoticed impact on national aggregates. The list could be much extended. It is also possible to call in question some of the assumptions embodied in the national income calculations themselves which jointly appear to prohibit

[5] Crafts estimated the rate of growth of national product per head in 1700–60 as 0.31 per cent per annum; in 1780–1801 as 0.35 per cent per annum, while the comparable rates of growth in the aggregate national product were 0.69 and 1.32: Crafts, *British economic growth,* tab. 2.11, p. 45.

[6] In a measured review of recent scholarship, Deane noted, 'The results so far published now point, still tentatively, to two conclusions: first that such acceleration as occurred in the national rate of British economic growth during the late eighteenth and early nineteenth centuries represented the culmination of a long-drawn-out process, an evolutionary rather than a revolutionary development; and second that the British experience of industrialization differed in significant respects from that of any other of the countries which industrialized subsequently.' Deane, 'The British industrial revolution', p. 15.

the retention of the traditional view of the industrial revolution. For example, the size and especially the rate of growth of industries in the tertiary sector are notoriously difficult to measure, and different assumptions about these parameters can reasonably be made which would restore, partially at least, the traditional view.[7] Despite the significance of some of these counter-claims, the importance of what might be termed the Crafts revision remains.

How best, then, to resolve the apparent paradox posed by these two senses in which the term 'industrial revolution' is used? Is it possible either, on the one hand, to restore to it a meaning which would allow it to be located clearly in time and space once more, or, on the other, to show reason to replace it with a term or a concept which would 'save the phenomena' in a way which the old term no longer succeeds in doing?

England and the Netherlands: urbanisation, occupational structure, and real income

The first step, in my view, is to consider further the implications of the Crafts revision.[8] Note, first, what has not changed significantly since the work of Deane and Cole. Estimates of the size of the national economy in the middle decades of the nineteenth century are little different now from those of 40 years ago. In the middle of the nineteenth century, output per head and average real incomes were higher in Britain than in any other country.[9] The 1851 Exhibition symbolised what all well-informed

[7] See, for example, Hoppit, 'Counting the industrial revolution'; Mokyr, *The lever of riches*; Jackson, 'The rate of economic growth during the industrial revolution'; Berg and Hudson, 'Rehabilitating the industrial revolution'.
[8] Not that it has been Crafts's work alone which has brought about the change.
[9] Maddison offers the following estimates of GDP per caput (1990 international $s):

	1820	1870
United Kingdom	1,707	3,191
United States	1,257	2,445
France	1,230	1,876
The Netherlands	1,821	2,753

In considering these estimates, it should be borne in mind that GDP per caput was much higher in England and Wales than in the UK as a whole. Maddison offers estimates for England and Wales and for the UK as a whole for 1801. Assuming that his estimates are reliable and that the same ratio obtained later in the century, the figures for England and Wales in 1820 and 1870 would be 2,169 and 4,056. The 1801 ratio should be approximately valid for 1820 but not for 1870 since the Irish fraction of the total UK population fell precipitately in the wake of the great famine of the 1840s. Maddison, *The world economy*, tab. B-13, p. 247 and tab. B-21, p. 264.

observers agreed to be the case, that Britain possessed the most productive economy to be found anywhere in the world. Pollard recently noted that Britain at that time 'was able to produce, in a whole series of key sectors, as much as the rest of the world put together'; an astonishing, if necessarily transient, phenomenon.[10] Those countries which had successfully challenged Britain's position by the close of the century, such as Germany and the United States, were still adrift at the century's midpoint. The significance of this fact, however, in the light of the Crafts revision, is arguably greater in relation to 1750 than it is to 1850. If the rate of growth of the economy during the classic period of the industrial revolution was radically slower than was once assumed and yet estimates of its size at the end of that period have not changed, it follows that its size at the beginning of the period must be markedly larger than was previously supposed. If the slope of a line inclining up to a fixed point is reduced, the point representing the other end of the line will necessarily rise higher.

The scale of the change implied by the Crafts revision is substantial. His estimates of growth rates between 1760 and 1831 imply that national output in 1760 must have been approximately 60 per cent larger than supposed by Deane and Cole. Similarly, whereas they estimated that output per head rose by 87 per cent over this period, he put the comparable figure at only 29 per cent.[11] Precision is, of course, beyond reach in this connection, but what is indisputable is that the Crafts revision enforces the view that the economy was much larger in the mid-eighteenth century than it was once conventional to assume, and, even more important, that output per head was only modestly lower at that time than in the early years of Victoria's reign, a massive contrast with the near doubling in individual productivity per head which Deane and Cole had supposed in 1962. If it is both true that in the mid-nineteenth century the British lead was clear-cut and also true that a century earlier individual productivity was not far short of its mid-nineteenth century level, interest shifts from the classic period of the industrial revolution to the centuries which preceded it. The gap between Britain and her neighbours, which was once assumed to have been largely the product of an exceptional surge in growth taking place during the reigns of George III and his sons, must now appear to have opened up much earlier.[12]

---

[10] Pollard, 'The industrial revolution', p. 376.

[11] The figures quoted were derived by chaining the growth rate percentages in Crafts, *British economic growth*, tab. 2.11, p. 45.

[12] It is important in this connection to distinguish clearly between the rate of growth of aggregate output and the rate of growth of output per head. Because the classic period of the industrial revolution coincided with the period in which the rate of population

It is one of the great strengths of Crafts's discussion of growth during the industrial revolution period that he went to much trouble to compare the British experience with that of her continental neighbours. He had no difficulty in showing that the latter had more in common with each other than they had with Britain. At similar levels of economic advance, as measured by real income per head, Britain was much more urbanised and far less dependent upon agriculture than her neighbours, and, whereas on the continent the value of the annual product per head of those engaged in agriculture fell far below that found elsewhere in the economy, in Britain productivity in agriculture, measured in this fashion, equalled the national average. Change was also much slower in Britain than elsewhere. Crafts estimated, for example, that continental countries moved from an average income per head of $400 to an average of $550 (in 1970 US dollars) in about one-third of the time taken by Britain (he regarded an income level of $550 as representing a point at which rapid change was well under way).[13]

The comparisons made by Crafts are both valid and valuable, but the conclusion that Britain was very different from her neighbours is essentially a matter of perspective. Viewed from the early twenty-first century, it may ring true. Viewed from the late eighteenth century, it would have seemed odd to treat the British experience in this fashion. It should be remembered that by this date, in the light of the Crafts revision, output per head in Britain must be regarded as already well above the European norm. There was, in other words, already something to explain. The divergence of England did not lie in the future; it was already a fact. But the British advance was not seen by Adam Smith, for example, as out of line with experience elsewhere; on the contrary, in Smith's view, Britain was treading the path long trodden by the Netherlands. In many key respects what was happening in England, and to a lesser degree elsewhere in Britain, resembled what had happened in the Netherlands a century or so earlier. Adam Smith, in my view, was right. Consider three closely inter-related variables which illustrate the point: urbanisation, occupational structure, and real income per head.

It is one of the most remarkable, though often least remarked, paradoxes of early modern Europe that although in a Braudelian world

---

growth accelerated sharply to reach a height never exceeded before or since, aggregate output could only have failed to accelerate substantially if there had been a fall in output per head, but in the context of the present discussion the key variable is output per head rather than total output, and in the light of the Crafts revision output per head was rising by only about 0.35 per cent per annum between 1760 and 1831 (Crafts gives the rate of growth in product per head during the periods 1760–80, 1780–1801, and 1801–31 as 0.01 per cent per annum, 0.35, and 0.52 respectively: ibid., tab. 2.11, p. 45).

[13] Ibid., p. 61.

capitalism and urbanisation are strongly linked, and the capitalist system is regarded as having made great advances between the sixteenth and eighteenth centuries, continental Europe was little more urbanised in 1800 than it had been in 1600. The growth of towns and cities can be quantified with greater confidence than most other aspects of social and economic development in the early modern period. It has recently been the subject of extensive study by de Vries. His critical collation of the available evidence led him to conclude that 10.8 per cent of the total population of Europe lived in cities with 5,000 or more inhabitants in 1600 rising to 13.0 per cent in 1800. However, if England, whose urban growth was exceptionally vigorous, is removed from the European totals, the picture changes: the percentages are then 10.9 and 11.9, suggesting only marginal growth in continental Europe.[14] At much the same time as de Vries, Bairoch undertook a similar study of urban growth in Europe. His estimates produce a still more striking result. Using the same criterion, that a settlement counted as urban if its population was 5,000 or more, his urban percentages for Europe as a whole in 1600 and 1800 were 12.9 and 13.8, but if England is excluded from the calculation, there is a slight *fall* in the urban percentage between the two dates from 13.1 to 13.0.[15]

Urban growth in England in the second half of the eighteenth century was so notable and elsewhere so modest that about 70 per cent of all the urban growth in Europe as a whole occurred in England alone, even though the English share of the total European population was only 8 per cent.[16] But the remarkable surge of urban growth in England in the seventeenth and eighteenth centuries did no more than parallel earlier developments in the Netherlands. Since the Netherlands was a substantially smaller country than England, the absolute increase in urban population totals was comparatively modest, but the proportional changes were similar. Steady urban growth in the sixteenth century meant that the Netherlands in 1600 was already almost as urbanised as England in 1800 (24.7 and 27.5 per cent respectively), and a century later 33.9 per cent of

---

[14] De Vries, *European urbanization*, tab. 3.6, pp. 36–7 and tab. 4.13, p. 72; Wrigley, 'Urban growth', tab. 7.4, p. 170.

[15] Bairoch, Batou, and Chèvre, *La population des villes*, tab. B2, p. 255. Bairoch's definition of 'Europe', though excluding Russia in this tabulation, covers a wider area than that of de Vries, who excluded most of eastern Europe. Bairoch does not provide estimates of total population, but the table gives both urban percentages and urban totals, so that the implied total populations can be calculated with only an insignificant margin of error. The English population totals were again taken from Wrigley, 'Urban growth', tab. 7.4, p. 170.

[16] Ibid., tab. 7.7, p. 179.

the Dutch population lived in cities with 5,000 or more inhabitants.[17] By 1700, therefore, the Netherlands was significantly more urbanised than England a hundred years later, though during the eighteenth century the Dutch economy was becalmed and the urban percentage slipped from 33.9 to 29.5 per cent. In 1800 the two countries were roughly equal in this regard.[18]

The extent of the contrast between the occupational structure of the labour force in England and that on the continent in 1800 has often been stressed. At that date only about 40 per cent of the male labour force in England was employed on the land, at a time when the comparable percentage characteristically lay between 65 and 80 per cent on the continent, a contrast which implies, of course, that a far higher percentage of the English labour force was engaged in secondary or tertiary occupations.[19] Here again, however, England was doing no more than mirror the position reached a century earlier in the Netherlands. In the 1670s approximately 40 per cent of the Dutch labour force was engaged in agriculture, 32 per cent in industry, and the remaining 28 per cent in service employments.[20] More than a century later, in 1800, the comparable English percentage in agriculture was identical and the other two percentages were closely similar.[21] The high level of output per head in English agriculture was one of the characteristics to which Crafts rightly drew attention. It was this which made possible such a considerable release of labour into activities other than agriculture. The agricultural labour force in 1800 was probably little if any larger than it had been in 1600 and yet in 1800 England was still largely self-sufficient in foodstuffs, even though the population was more than twice as large as it had been at the end of Elizabeth's reign.[22] Once again, however, the Netherlands was beforehand. Urban need created a large and expanding market for agricultural products and Dutch agriculture proved as adept as English in responding

[17] De Vries, *European urbanization*, tab. 3.6, pp. 36–7 and app. 1, p. 271; Wrigley, 'Urban growth', tab. 7.4, p. 170.

[18] There are interesting points of similarity between London and Amsterdam, the primate cities in the two countries. Each grew roughly fourteen-fold between 1500 and 1700, and in both the growth rate declined sharply in the eighteenth century, though more markedly in Amsterdam than in London, but Amsterdam did not dominate the Dutch urban system to the astonishing, almost bizarre degree that London overshadowed other cities in England; de Vries, *European urbanization*, app. 1, pp. 270–1.

[19] See tab. 4.12, p. 124; and tab. 11.2, p. 297 and associated discussion.

[20] De Vries and van der Woude, *The first modern economy*, p. 527.

[21] Deane and Cole, *British economic growth*, tab. 30, p. 142; tab. 4.12, p. 124.

[22] Jones estimated that British agricultural output covered 90 per cent of the country's food needs *c*. 1800. Overton's recent discussion of this and cognate questions results in a similar or somewhat higher figure. Jones, 'Agriculture 1700–80', tab. 4.1, p. 68; Overton, *Agricultural revolution in England*, pp. 74–6.

flexibly to market demand, in economising in the use of labour, in raising output per head, and in identifying where its comparative advantage lay; and it did so at an earlier date.[23]

The acid test of the productiveness of an economy is the level of real income which it will support. Few contemporaries doubted that the Netherlands led the way in this respect throughout the early modern period.[24] England probably remained in arrears until well into the eighteenth century, and the same was true *a fortiori* of Britain as a whole. The estimates made by de Vries and van der Woude suggest that any crossover occurred only sometime in the third quarter of the eighteenth century. Maddison's comparative data on real incomes place England slightly ahead of the Netherlands at the end of the eighteenth century, but suggest a very marked Dutch advantage a hundred years earlier, thus broadly paralleling the conclusions of De Vries and van der Woude.[25]

Evidence that England was treading a path beaten earlier by Holland would have come as no surprise to Adam Smith. He often turned to events in Holland as a guide to what might be expected to occur in England in the future, and it is therefore instructive to note his conclusions about the prospects facing Holland in the immediate future and other countries in due course.

When in 1776 he published *An inquiry into the nature and causes of the wealth of nations* he was clear about the continued superiority of the Dutch economy over its rivals. 'The province of Holland, on the other hand, [that is, in contrast to France] in proportion to the extent of its territory and the number of its people, is a richer country than England.'[26] But it was not this bald assertion that is intriguing about Smith's use of the example of Holland, but his subsequent discussion of economic growth and its limits, for it provides a useful clue in the quest for

---

[23] In the sixteenth and seventeenth centuries the Dutch agricultural labour force was broadly unchanging in number: output per head roughly doubled. De Vries, 'Dutch economic growth', p. 456. See also Allen, 'Economic structure and agricultural productivity', esp. pp. 18–22.

[24] Though Gregory King was inclined to view the difference as relatively minor. He estimated that in 1695 income per head in England was £7-16-0, in Holland £8-2-9, and in France £5-18-0: King, *Natural and political observations*, p. 68.

[25] De Vries and van der Woude, *The first modern economy*, fig. 13.1, p. 707; Maddison, *The world economy*, tab. B-13, p. 247 and tab. B-21, p. 264 (it is important to note that Maddison's estimates for England and Wales are substantially higher than for the United Kingdom). De Vries and van der Woude suggest that the Dutch advantage in the later seventeenth century may have been between 30 and 40 per cent. Indeed they estimate that in the period of the Anglo-Dutch wars the gross national product of the Dutch Republic was probably 40–5 per cent of that of England, though by 1800 it was only 20 per cent of the English total: ibid., p. 710. See also de Vries, 'Dutch economic growth'.

[26] A. Smith, *Wealth of nations*, I, p. 102. He added, 'The wages of labour are said to be higher in Holland than in England.' Ibid., p. 102.

the industrial revolution. His reference to Holland occurs in a chapter entitled 'Of the profits of stock'. He begins by noting that it is very difficult to measure what he referred to as 'the average profit of all the different trades carried on in a great kingdom',[27] or what might now be termed the rate of return on investment, but added: 'though it may be impossible to determine with any degree of precision, what are or were the average profits of stock, either in the present, or in ancient times, some notion may be formed of them from the interest of money'.[28] He then went on to develop an argument which related the rate of interest to the scale of the opportunities for profitable investment, noting that the rate was higher in Scotland and France than in England because of their relative backwardness, but was higher in England than in Holland. In England the government was able to borrow at 3 per cent in peacetime and people of good credit at between 3.5 and 4.5 per cent, but in Holland the comparable rates were 2 per cent for the government and 3 per cent for private individuals.[29] The rate declined *pari passu* with economic success because opportunities for profitable investment were not unlimited. Present growth must always come at the cost of future deceleration with unpleasant attendant circumstances both for labour and capital, or as Smith put it:

In a country which had acquired that full complement of riches which the nature of its soil and climate, and its situation with respect to other countries, allowed it to acquire; which could, therefore, advance no further, and which was not going backwards, both the wages of labour and the profits of stock would probably be very low.[30]

A little later he repeated the same initial phrase 'In a country which had acquired its full complement of riches' and drew out some further implications of this tendency, adding that 'The province of Holland seems to be approaching near this state.'[31] England was a little further from the same sad fate, but Smith saw no prospect of escape from it.

Capitalism

I have drawn attention to Adam Smith's views partly because doing so affords an opportunity to view the eighteenth-century world through an acute and well-informed contemporary eye, but also because his analysis

[27] Ibid., I, p. 98.
[28] Ibid., I, p. 99.
[29] Ibid., I, pp. 100, 102.
[30] Ibid., I, p. 106.
[31] Ibid., I, p. 108.

is a convenient introduction to two further issues which deserve discussion in attempting to cover the range of matters relevant to the reconsideration of the industrial revolution: capitalism and the nature of the limits to growth in a pre-industrial world.

Smith was a keen advocate of the market as a vehicle for the efficient allocation of resources and for the identification of opportunities for growth. He favoured what is now conventionally referred to as the capitalist system, though his support was far from uncritical, but, as we have already seen, he did not suppose that the adoption of capitalism would prove a guarantee of indefinite growth, merely that it was the best institutional form to ensure that the good use was made of the opportunities offered by a country's situation and resources. During the phase of expansion, before a country had exhausted the opportunities for profitable growth, those who were dependent on wages could benefit substantially, even as those who drew their income from the deployment of capital found their return declining.

Since the time of Henry VIII the wealth and revenue of the country have been continually advancing, and, in the course of their progress, their pace seems rather to have been gradually accelerated, than retarded. They seem not only to have been going on, but to have been going on faster and faster. The wages of labour have been continually advancing during the same period, and in the greater part of the different branches of trade and manufactures the profits of stock have been diminishing.[32]

Ultimately the latter trend would arrest further growth as the incentive to invest decreased to the point where no further advance was feasible. As investment declined for lack of profitable outlets, employment opportunities would shrivel, leaving labour in a sorry state. His view of the possibilities of growth was, to use modern jargon, asymptotic rather than exponential. In view of this, and of his belief that the future for other countries was etched in the past experience of Holland, it is striking that in their recent study of Dutch economic history, entitled in its English version *The first modern economy*, de Vries and van der Woude may be said to re-express Adam Smith's views in the terminology of the late twentieth century. They offer a definition of a modern economy which, in its essentials, is one which might equally well be employed to define a capitalist economy.[33] The Netherlands in the early modern period, they argue, was a modern, that is a capitalist, economy. It was also an economy which, towards the end of the seventeenth century, lost momentum, reaching

[32] Ibid., I, p. 100.
[33] De Vries and van der Woude, *The first modern economy*, p. 693. Their four criteria are set out fully below, p. 61.

what might be termed a plateau of economic achievement, bearing a close resemblance to that described by Adam Smith when he referred to what would happen when a country had acquired its 'full complement of riches', a condition sometimes termed 'the stationary state'.[34] Having analysed the reasons for the loss of growth momentum and having shown that these were characteristic of a modern economy rather than a pre-industrial economy, de Vries and van der Woude went on to make explicit what was already implied by their analysis: 'This formulation harbors an implicit claim about modern economic growth. It is not self-sustained, exponential, and unbounded.'[35] The capitalist system, in other words, may promote growth and increase productive efficiency, but there is nothing in its nature to guarantee the long continuance of these features.[36]

It is perhaps over simple to treat 'modern' and 'capitalist' as interchangeable adjectives. Certainly it would be possible, without doing violence to either term, to define them in ways which endowed them with somewhat different meanings. De Vries and van der Woude listed the four key characteristics of a modern economy as: (1) free markets for both commodities and factors of production; (2) a sufficiently high level of agricultural productivity to sustain a complex social and economic structure with extensive division of labour; (3) a state willing and able to support property rights, freedom of movement and contract, and concerned to advance the material conditions of life of its population; (4) a level of technology and organisation able to support a sufficiently sophisticated material culture to sustain market-orientated consumer behaviour.[37] Capitalism might be defined in more restricted terms. The final part of the third element in their definition would in some eyes be at odds with the nature of capitalism. In a more extended discussion,

---

[34] Even as late as the middle of the nineteenth century when the economy was greatly changed from the days of Adam Smith, John Stuart Mill, the dominant economic thinker of his day, remained troubled by this issue: 'The materials of manufacture being all drawn from the land, and many of them from agriculture, which supplies in particular the entire material of clothing; the general law of production from the land, the law of diminishing return, must in the last resort be applicable to manufacturing as well as to agricultural history. As population increases, and the power of the land to yield increased produce is strained harder and harder, any additional supply of material as well as of food, must be obtained by a more than proportionally increasing expenditure of labour'. Mill, *Principles of political economy*, I, p. 182. Mill, however, also found reasons to take a less pessimistic stand, but one of his reasons for advocating restraint upon fertility was his concern about the dangers of over-rapid population growth: ibid., I, pp. 345–6.
[35] De Vries and van der Woude, *The first modern economy*, p. 720.
[36] These issues are explored at greater length below, pp. 62–3.
[37] Ibid., p. 693.

it would be profitable to pursue these issues further.[38] In the present context, however, it is only necessary to note that the example of the Netherlands illustrates the point that neither the process of modernisation nor the presence of a capitalist economic system was capable of guaranteeing sustained growth in an organic economy though both could help to ensure that the possibilities for growth offered by such economies were exploited effectively.

The limits to growth in organic economies

What was it that constrained expansion, which promised at best asymptotic growth in the early modern world? Why did there appear to be limits to growth? Gaining clearer understanding of this issue is of great consequence in the quest for the industrial revolution because it serves to make clear why England, having followed the Dutch example so closely for so long, did not lose the momentum of growth, but made a successful transition from an asymptotic to an exponential growth curve. The answer was given starkly and trenchantly by the third of the triumvirate of the great economists of the era later generations have labelled the industrial revolution, David Ricardo. It was Ricardo who gave clearest expression to what is usually termed the law of diminishing returns.[39] He recognised the possibility that in benign circumstances wages might rise but accepted the conclusion already drawn both by Adam Smith and Malthus that improved living standards would provoke more rapid population growth which in turn would drive labourers' wages back towards some conventional minimum. But the last state was likely to be worse than the first because the productivity of labour and of capital would both fall at the intensive and extensive margins of cultivation, and yet the very process of growth would enforce a move to these margins. The fall in the return to capital would discourage investment and bring growth to a halt. Both labour and capital must suffer from the fact that the supply of land was limited. He concluded, significantly: 'This [that is the reduced reward both to labour and to capital] will necessarily be rendered permanent by the laws of nature, which have limited the productive powers of the land.'[40]

Ricardo's essential insight can be restated in a manner which helps to explain how, at the very time when Smith, Ricardo, and Malthus were writing, the problem which all three viewed as ineluctable was slowly

---

[38] I have attempted to provide such a discussion in Wrigley, 'The process of modernization'.
[39] Though Malthus expressed the same idea at much the same time in *The nature and progress of rent.*
[40] Ricardo, *Principles of political economy*, pp. 125–6.

ceasing to trouble the English economy. Ricardo referred to the laws of nature, and was right to do so, since it was a combination of physical, chemical, and biological processes which formed the key constraint. Both the sustenance of life and the production of all the material artefacts of value to man must involve the consumption of energy. Food is the fuel of all living organisms, but man, once no longer living in hunter/gatherer communities, unlike other animals, was also a voracious consumer of energy for purposes other than personal subsistence. Each advance in material culture involved the production of an increasing range of material artefacts. At some point in the sequence of activities which converts raw materials into finished products for human consumption or use, both heat energy and mechanical energy must be expended.

The ultimate source of almost all energy available on the surface of the earth is the sun. The scale of energy transfer from the sun in the form of insolation in the course of a year is enormous, but organic economies could only hope to tap a tiny fraction of this inflow of energy. Overwhelmingly the most important accessible energy source for such societies was the process of photosynthesis by which plants use sunlight to generate the vegetable growth. Mankind shared the need for food with other animals and satisfied that need from the products of photosynthesis. But photosynthesis did not only provide food to sustain human life. It also provided the energy used in all productive processes. It fuelled all secondary production, providing the heat energy used by organic economies in the form of wood, and most of the mechanical energy which they used in the form of human or animal muscle power. The inflow of solar energy, of course, also provided an additional source of mechanical power because of the energy potential of moving wind and water, but in most contexts this was of minor importance compared with muscle power.[41] Nor should it be overlooked that most of the raw materials which entered production processes were organic, of either vegetable or animal origin. Even in the production of metals, although the raw materials were mineral, their smelting meant the expenditure of heat energy on a large scale, and this energy came from the burning of wood or charcoal.

---

[41] Authoritative estimates of the relative importance of different energy sources for the period covered in this essay are lacking. However, the pioneering work of Kander is suggestive in this regard. She has published detailed annual estimates of all the main types of energy production in Sweden from 1800 onwards. She summarised her findings as showing that in the nineteenth century 'direct working water and wind energy, although important sources of motive energy for specific tasks, were rather insignificant compared to firewood consumption or muscle energy.' Kander, *Economic growth, energy consumption*, p. 50. English circumstances were very different, but there seem few grounds for supposing that English data, if they existed, would point to a different conclusion.

Unhappily for the inhabitants of the pre-industrial world, photosynthesis is not an efficient process. The conversion efficiency of natural vegetation has been variously estimated at between one and four parts in one thousand. The natural plant cover, in other words, captures only a tiny fraction of what is potentially available. Cultivated plants have a slightly higher conversion ratio on average, but remain within the same range. Thus, to indicate the severity of the constraint which is inherent in this situation, although the annual solar energy receipt of the United Kingdom has been estimated at more than 22 billion tons of coal equivalent a year, a truly colossal total,[42] the theoretical maximum available to the country in a pre-industrial era via the process of photosynthesis was only at most roughly 40 million tons of coal equivalent. Of this, however, a very substantial fraction was unavailable for human use because of the energy loss in moving up the food chain and because of the claims of other forms of life.[43] All pre-industrial economies were organic in the sense that they were dependent upon animal and vegetable resources for almost all their energy, whether expressed as food for men and women, as fodder for draught animals, or as fuel for heating a house, baking bread, making bricks, boiling dyes, brewing beer, smelting metal, or heating salt pans. All such societies had to work within an energy budget which made many of the activities and processes which became basic to economic life in later centuries physically impossible. It would be impossible, for example, within the constraints of an organic economy to produce iron and steel on a scale sufficient to construct a modern rail network or an oil tanker, still less the tens of millions of cars which are manufactured every year. Symbolically, one might describe the change wrought by the lifting of the energy constraint as the difference between a Toledo blade and a battle tank.

As long as the great bulk of aggregate demand was devoted to the purchase of the products of primary and secondary industry, there was necessarily a close relationship between the level of real incomes per head and the scale of energy consumption per head. Even as late as the middle of the twentieth century this relationship is clear. Kindleberger assembled data from *c*.1960 relating to countries all over the world, from the richest to the poorest, and showed that there was a broadly linear relationship between the two variables when the log of income per head was plotted against energy consumption per head.[44] More recently, with the

---

[42] At its peak in 1913 the coal output of British collieries was 287 million tons, or only about 1.5 per cent of the solar energy receipt.

[43] See White and Plaskett, *Biomass as fuel*, pp. 2, 12; Pimentel, 'Energy flow', p. 2.

[44] Kindleberger, *Economic development*, fig. 4.4, p. 70.

steady rise in the proportion of income devoted to the products of tertiary industry, this relationship has weakened. In the circumstances of an organic economy, however, any rise in living standards associated with a phase of growth would be highly likely to exacerbate the energy problem, tightening the ligature which cramped growth.

The escape from the constraints of an organic economy

Stating the problem in this fashion points to the developments which made escape from these constraints feasible. Only by finding a way round the energy barrier which had always limited growth could poverty cease to be an inescapable element in the human condition and become problematic for the first time in human history. Nothing could be done to alter the flow of energy from the sun, nor to change the nature of the process of photosynthesis. The annual quantum of available useful energy could not be enlarged. But in certain circumstances the annual quantum was, so to speak, stored and might be tapped to meet human needs. The possibility was already familiar to those living within the confines of an organic economy, if only on a small scale. Mature standing timber represents the product of a century of photosynthesis, where a hayfield represents the product of only a year. Little wonder that reckless eldest sons on inheriting an estate would sell off the oaks their great grandfathers had planted, thus realising instantly a credit line which had been accumulating over several generations.[45]

In favourable circumstances, however, the annual quantum of energy secured by photosynthesis can be stored over far more than a century. One reason for the outstanding success of the Dutch economy during its golden age in the sixteenth and seventeenth centuries was the presence of large and accessible supplies of peat.[46] Many of the industries which flourished in the Netherlands in this period were energy-intensive activities: salt and sugar refineries, breweries, distilleries, brick kilns, tanneries, and so on. Peat represents the product of photosynthesis accumulated over thousands of years, where a mature forest is limited to a single century of accumulation. The potential of peat, however, is dwarfed in turn by

---

[45] In 1870, at the time when the United States was about to replace Britain as the world's leading economy, it has been estimated that more than half its total energy consumption still consisted of the use of fuel wood. The early days of settlement in a new country may permit energy consumption per head from organic sources to balloon well above the level which could be sustained in the country of origin: Fisher, *Energy crises*, tab. A2.2, pp. 160–1.

[46] De Zeeuw, 'Peat and the Dutch Golden Age'; Unger, 'Energy sources'; de Vries and van der Woude, *The first modern economy*, pp. 37–40.

the energy potential of coal seams where energy accumulated over millions of years rather than millennia is stored. Other energy sources could offer only a temporary escape from the constraints of an organic economy. Coal held out the promise of a solution which might prove long lasting, at least on the time-scale of human history.

Throughout the early modern period the British economy was gradually reducing its dependence upon organic energy sources. Coal displaced wood as a source of heat energy in a steadily widening range of industries, initially those, like the boiling of salt, where the source of heat and the object to be heated were separated by a physical barrier which prevented chemical contamination, or in the heating of houses where pollution was tolerated because coal was cheap, but extending in time across many other industries – brickmaking, pottery manufacture, glassmaking, and brewing, for example; and culminating in finding a solution to the use of coal in the smelting of iron, the development which has rightly attracted the greatest subsequent attention. Coal output and consumption in Britain were on a different scale from the continent. As late as the early decades of the nineteenth century, British coal output, which was already over 20 million metric tons per annum, exceeded the output of the whole of continental Europe by a factor of seven.[47]

The benefit gained from the substitution of coal for traditional energy sources was to be seen in many facets of life in England. For example, the possibility of substituting brick for wood as the most important structural material in the building of houses and the fact that windows were glazed in the houses not just of the elite but of a broad swathe of society in contrast to what was true of, say, France, depended upon the existence of a cheap source of heat energy.[48] The timing of the change from wood to brick in the building industry underlines the point that much had happened well before the period which once attracted disproportionate attention. Brick became the dominant urban constructional material in the period from *c.*1650 to *c.*1730 in southern England.[49] London was in the vanguard of change partly because of the coastal coal trade. After the Great Fire brickworks in the capital greatly expanded their output to meet the much-increased demand for bricks, and it is symbolic of the strategic importance of cheap coal in making this possible that the price of bricks rose steeply only once during the rebuilding, when the Dutch fleet temporarily stopped the collier vessels from reaching London from

[47] Wrigley, *Continuity, chance and change*, p. 29, n. 38.
[48] Arthur Young's comments about the absence of window glass as he journeyed through France in the years immediately before the revolution are instructive: Young, *Travels in France and Italy*, pp. 22, 25, 30, 101, 103, 105, 208, 213.
[49] Falkus and Jones, 'Urban improvement', graph 1, p. 204 and accompanying text.

Tyneside.[50] The benefits to health of living in brick-built rather than wooden-framed lath and plaster houses were substantial, and there were major capital savings because the frequency and severity of urban conflagrations diminished spectacularly when brick and tile replaced wood and thatch.[51] But the benefits created by the increasing use of coal were not simply those of conferring a competitive advantage on a growing range of industries. More fundamental was the erosion of the organic constraint.

In the past expansion had always brought about its own nemesis. Each successive step taken made the next step harder to take. If land were devoted to forest cover to supply wood for fuel and for construction, it could not also be used as arable to meet the food needs of a growing population. An expanding iron industry implied devoting an increasing acreage to trees, at the expense, at least symbolically, of the food supply of the iron workers. If a growing economy was built upon the division of labour, the process which Adam Smith described in his secular parable about the pinmakers, it must, among other things, raise the demand for transport by increasing the separation between producer and consumer, and this must, by the same token, exacerbate the problem that land given over to the feeding of draught animals could not also be used to produce milk and cheese. One by one such constraints were reduced or eliminated as coal use suffused an increasing proportion of the productive economy. The laws of nature to which Ricardo referred were not contravened, but they were circumvented. The land was the source of a steadily declining proportion of the raw materials used in the English economy as mineral raw materials increasingly supplemented or displaced vegetable and animal raw materials, but the disappearance of the energy constraint was the key development.[52] Whereas organic economies were

---

[50] Ibid., p. 202.

[51] Jones brought home the nature of the contrast by pointing to the contrast in Devon between the county's stone-built towns and those like Crediton, Cullompton, Honiton, or Tiverton which had been repeatedly subject to widespread fire loss and where in consequence few buildings have survived from before the eighteenth century. He summarised the significance of the new situation in a pithy sentence: 'It was the spread of brick-and-tile which brought the non-stone areas out of the middle ages.' Jones, 'Fire damage', p. 149.

[52] It is interesting to note that English coal was gradually transforming the energy budgets of other countries, thereby alleviating a range of ecological problems, and helping to reverse environmental degradation. See, for example, Kjaergaard, *The Danish revolution*, pp. 120–1, 130. He commented at one point: 'Denmark was faced with this catastrophic situation in the eighteenth century [severe energy shortage]. But after teetering on a knife's edge, the Danish energy balance was saved by ever-larger supplies of energy from Europe's subterranean forests of coal' (p. 128). The coal in question was predominantly imported from England.

dominated by negative feedback, escape from the energy constraint carried with it the possibility of positive feedback as growth continued in England.

The use of coal provided an obvious solution to the *heat* energy problem but not, initially, to that of *mechanical* energy. It was at first simply a cheap and dirty substitute for wood but not for horses or oxen. Hence the immense importance of the development of the steam engine as a prime mover. Although initially only a tiny proportion of the energy in the steam was converted into useful power, the coal-fired steam engine, allied to suitable machinery, could increase individual productivity dramatically. Furthermore, an increasing proportion of the material needs of mankind could be satisfied without increasing the consumption of organic raw materials. Inorganic raw materials were disproportionately important in the new mineral-based energy-intensive economy which was developing. Inside the chrysalis of an organic economy a new and very different economy was slowly taking shape in England in the seventeenth and eighteenth centuries.

Even though the early stages of a radical transformation of the English economy were in train, however, the older, organic system remained dominant throughout this period. The scope for growth and change was largely determined by the vigour of agriculture.

The centrality of agriculture

I noted earlier that the best estimates now available suggest no acceleration in the rate of growth of national product per head in the later eighteenth and early nineteenth centuries, and that one of the implications of this revision of the previous orthodoxy is that the English economy, indeed presumptively the economy of Britain as a whole, was much more productive in the middle of the eighteenth century than was once supposed. It is not yet possible to attempt a convincing estimate of the comparable situation in Elizabethan times, but it is unlikely that England enjoyed any advantage over her neighbours in this regard in the sixteenth century. It would be a major surprise, therefore, if the revised view of the situation *c*.1750 did not imply that the rate of growth of national product per head for a century or more before 1750 was as high as, or higher than, it was in the century next following.

This turns the spotlight on agriculture, whose centrality to all organic economies is clear by definition. It must figure prominently in any quest for the industrial revolution, despite its apparent exclusion by the oddities of nomenclature. Before 1750, and indeed for many decades thereafter, progress in the organic sector of the economy, which was, of course, largely underpinned by agriculture, was far more important than any developments in the inorganic sector in determining the level of output per head. Until well into the nineteenth century agriculture was much the largest single industry and the largest employer of labour. Productivity trends in agriculture were, therefore, the single most important influence on overall productivity trends. The fact that a steadily increasing proportion of the labour force could find a living outside agriculture was made possible only because output per head in agriculture was rising *pari passu*.[53] England was probably the only country in western Europe, other than the Netherlands, in which the number of men working on the land scarcely changed in the course of the seventeenth and eighteenth centuries, even though the English population, and hence the labour force, was growing faster than in any other large country in western Europe. Elsewhere numbers in agriculture rose, if not as rapidly as the overall increase in population, then nevertheless substantially. The result was the remarkable contrast emphasised by Crafts between output per head in agriculture in England where it was close to the average for the economy as a whole and the comparable ratio in continental countries. In nineteenth-century France, for example, the average worker in agriculture contributed only half as much to national income as the average worker in the rest of the economy.[54]

In a peasant society it is normally the case that people leave the land with great reluctance. Individuals may remain on the family plot even though they are contributing less to the output of the farm than they are receiving from it. Development economists are familiar with the generalisation, which is perhaps over-simple, that in an archetypal peasant society an individual will leave the family holding only when his or her presence causes the *average* level of income to fall below some conventionally accepted minimum, whereas in a capitalist, market-orientated society, this will happen as soon as the *marginal* individual's contribution falls below this level. English agriculture became increasingly capitalist in nature in the early modern period.

> Ill fares the land, to hastening ills a prey,
> Where wealth accumulates, and men decay:

[53] As Deane recently remarked, 'In the last analysis, then, the most distinctive feature of British agriculture's role in the development of the first industrial revolution stemmed from its ability to meet all or most of the food needs of a fast-growing and urbanizing population using a steadily diminishing proportion of the national workforce.' Deane, 'The British industrial revolution', p. 31.

[54] This is implied by the estimate that in 1870 50.6 per cent of the male labour force was in agriculture, but agriculture contributed only 33.5 per cent of national income: Crafts, *British economic growth*, tab. 3.4, p. 57.

Princes and lords may flourish, or may fade;
A breath can make them, as a breath hath made;
But a bold peasantry, their country's pride,
When once destroyed, can never be supplied.

By the time Oliver Goldsmith wrote *The deserted village* as a heartfelt protest against enclosure and the grasping landlord, the picture which he drew, though moving, was already archaic, the product of a charming, but unconvincing nostalgia. But it was what he went on to say which gives the game away.

A time there was, ere England's griefs began,
When every rood of ground maintained its man;
For him light labour spread her wholesome store,
Just gave what life required, but gave no more:
His blest companions, innocence and health;
And his best riches, ignorance of wealth.

Goldsmith's peasants would have fitted well into what de Vries termed his 'peasant model', men who 'strive to avoid market dependence',[55] resulting in a situation which frustrated the development of mutually beneficial exchange between town and country of the type which Adam Smith regarded as fundamental to growth and prosperity.[56] The peasants of the western Netherlands transformed themselves into market-orientated specialist producers of those products which yielded the highest return on their capital. Their enhanced income and changed life-style made them a significant market for urban products. In England events took a different turn. In many areas the characteristic agrarian structure of landlord, capitalist farmer, and landless labourer became dominant, but the upshot in economic terms was not dissimilar. Specialisation progressed; new crops, breeds of livestock, tools, and working practices were widely adopted; and the mutual dependence of town and country deepened and extended. In both Holland and England labour left the land readily and was largely successful in finding employment in secondary and tertiary occupations both in urban areas and in the countryside.

'When Henry VIII died, full of years and sin, some of the main characteristics, which were to distinguish it till the advent of steam-power and machinery, could already, though faintly, be descried', Tawney remarked.[57] Whether the changes which took place in English rural society in the early modern period should be welcomed or deplored will depend

---

[55] De Vries, *Dutch rural economy*, p. 6.
[56] See, for example, the chapter 'How the commerce of towns contributed to the improvement of the country' in A. Smith, *Wealth of nations*; also ch. 10 below.
[57] Tawney, *Religion and the rise of capitalism*, pp. 70–1.

upon the set of values of the observer. But the peasant society of which Goldsmith wrote, though having all the virtues which he claimed for it, could never have been a suitable launch pad for a society seeking to break free from the constraints of an organic economy. The doubling of output per head in agriculture which took place in England between 1600 and 1800 was a necessary, though not a sufficient cause of the complex of changes which gave birth to the modern world. An economy whose rural sector conformed to the 'peasant model' sketched by de Vries,[58] as many did in Europe in the centuries before the French revolution, stood no chance of achieving such a notable feat. Indeed, in an era in which population was rising, productivity per head in agriculture was more likely to fall than to rise.

The industrial revolution: a revised perspective

The quest for the industrial revolution should lead, in my view, to the following conclusions about the nature of the changes taking place in England between the sixteenth and nineteenth centuries:

1. In seeking to understand what occurred, it is just as important to pay attention to the period prior to 1750 as to the classic period of the industrial revolution. It is unlikely that the rate of growth of production per head changed much between a date which might provisionally be located in the early seventeenth century and the mid-nineteenth century. It may even have been higher before c.1750 than thereafter until the middle decades of the nineteenth century.

2. What was extraordinary about the rate of growth of product per head in the century between 1750 and 1850 was not that it was so low but that it did not turn negative. An increase in the rate of population growth as great as that experienced in this period might have been expected in the light of earlier experience to have reduced output per head and depressed living standards substantially.[59] In the later seventeenth century the intrinsic growth rate of the English population was zero. By the early decades of the nineteenth century it had reached about 1.7 per cent per annum, sufficient to cause the population to double in only just over 40 years, a rate almost without precedent in European experience.[60] That output per head did not turn negative in a land long fully settled,

---

[58] The peasant model is described in de Vries, *Dutch rural economy*, pp. 4–7.

[59] Wrigley and Schofield, *Population history of England*, fig. 10.4, p. 410 and associated discussion.

[60] Wrigley *et al.*, *English population history*, tab. A9.1, pp. 614–5. Growth rates reached a peak during the period 1806–25.

in these circumstances, is persuasive evidence that remarkable developments were in train.

3. Before the later eighteenth century growth in England strongly resembled what had already occurred in the Netherlands. As in the Netherlands it may be viewed as the product of establishing a 'modern', 'capitalist', or 'market-orientated' economy which facilitated making optimum use of the possibilities afforded by an advanced organic economy with an increasingly productive agriculture.

4. Growth of this sort, however well conducted, could not continue indefinitely. If it had not been for the emergence of some radically new features in the economy, the example of the Netherlands would in all probability have been followed by England in this respect also, as Adam Smith expected. This would have occurred because of the necessary constraints upon growth in all organic economies, constraints which, as Ricardo noted, were imposed, as he put it, by the laws of nature.

5. To escape from this danger, to avoid the growth curve becoming asymptotic, it was essential to break free from the constraint imposed by the energy budgets of organic economies, which depended almost exclusively upon annexing as much as possible of the annual inflow of energy from the sun trapped by plants through photosynthesis. Such economies were incapable of sustaining growth over a prolonged period since the maximum quantity of heat and mechanical energy which could be secured in this fashion was modest. The close correspondence between the rates of growth of output and the consumption of energy ensured that expansion must be limited.

6. Escape was possible because of the circumstances of plant life during the Carboniferous era which resulted in a part of the photosynthetic products of hundreds of millions of years of plant growth being 'frozen' in geological strata.[61] Some of these strata were readily accessible in England, and began to be exploited on an increasingly significant scale from the sixteenth century onwards. A succession of technical innovations made coal applicable in a widening range of applications where heat energy was needed, and at a later stage, because of the ingenuity and perseverance of men such as Newcomen and Watt, the burning of coal could be made to overcome bottlenecks in the use of mechanical energy also.

---

[61] Sieferle illustrated this idea elegantly when he entitled his monograph about the characteristics of historical energy systems and the significance of the advent of coal as a dominant energy source, *The subterranean forest* (its title in the original German edition was *Der unterirdische Wald*). He provides a handy ready reckoner of the land saving effect of the use of coal by noting that 'an annual use of 1 ton of coal makes 1 hectare of land available that would otherwise have been required as fuel plantation': Sieferle, *The subterranean forest*, p. 103.

7. The significance of the gradual circumventing of the energy bottleneck was not that it suddenly produced a marked acceleration in the rate of the growth of the economy or in the level of individual productivity. It was that it removed a barrier which would otherwise have tended slowly to constrict growth. Only at a much later stage in the process by which the organic economy gave way to a mineral-based energy-intensive economy did the full benefit emerge in the form of a significantly higher rate of economic growth both in aggregate and per head. In England this occurred during the middle decades of the nineteenth century, and then only because of a series of technological advances which enabled the new possibilities to begin to be realised. An abrupt acceleration in the early stages of the process was never a plausible possibility.[62]

Conclusion

The manner in which a question is posed determines the kind of answer which can be offered. Since it is possible to define what is meant by the industrial revolution in innumerable, different ways, and the question posed often includes or implies a particular definition, it is not surprising that so many differing opinions have been proposed concerning its nature, origins, and timing, often plausible enough in their own terms. At one extreme, it has been argued that the term is vacuous and should no longer be given currency.[63] At another, it is asserted that the industrial revolution was the culmination of a comparatively simple cumulative process which had been in train for a millennium before reaching fruition.[64] My case is no different. I have expounded the nature of the problem in a manner which foreshadowed the type of discussion which ensued and indeed the conclusions reached. Therefore, it may be appropriate to say a few words about the logical status of this essay. Its prime purpose was not to attempt to explain why or how the industrial revolution occurred, though some aspects of these issues are covered directly or by implication. It was to identify the *explicandum*. I revert to the paradox with which I began. On the one hand, it is impossible to doubt the fundamental

---

[62] That the process was, in effect, certain to be gradual is well illustrated by a calculation which Mokyr made for a somewhat similar purpose. He pointed out that if there were a sector of an economy which was growing at 4 per cent per annum but which initially comprised only 10 per cent of the whole (the 'modern' sector), and another sector comprising the remaining 90 per cent of the economy growing at 1 per cent per annum (the 'traditional' sector), it would take 74 years for the two sectors to become equal in size and that even then the overall growth rate would be no more than 2.5 per cent per annum. Mokyr, 'Editor's introduction', p. 12.

[63] Cameron, 'The industrial revolution: a misnomer'.

[64] Snooks, 'Great waves of economic change'.

nature of the difference between the ease with which modern economies can flood the world with material goods and a host of related services and the desperate difficulty experienced by most communities in earlier centuries in meeting the most basic needs of their inhabitants for food, shelter, clothing, and fuel. It is absurd not to accord this change a title which symbolises its significance. On the other hand, inasmuch as the term revolution connotes abrupt change, it seems bizarre to apply it to a period in which there is little reason to think that change, as measured by the yardsticks commonly employed to describe economic activity, was unusually rapid.

To be paradoxical in turn, one might say that the revolution was not economic so much as physical, chemical, and biological, or at least that viewing it principally as an economic phenomenon and neglecting other attributes of production processes, and above all their energy require-ments, will result in an incomplete and unbalanced picture. Although the industrial revolution involved a profound economic transformation, the conventional tools of economic description and analysis fail to ex-pose much that was fundamental to its character. The analytic frame-work erected by Adam Smith works splendidly in explaining the growth process which characterised the Dutch Republic in its golden age and England a little later. The accumulation of capital, the division of labour, symbolised in the pinmaker parable, and such linked developments as improved transport facilities and the creation of mutually beneficial ex-change between town and country; what is often, indeed, referred to simply as 'Smithian' growth, accounts satisfactorily for the changes asso-ciated with the suffusion of Dutch and later English society by capitalist practices and a market economy. But neither classical nor neo-classical economics accounts well for what came later unless reference is made to other developments which played no part in the thinking of the clas-sical economists and have often been ignored subsequently. The classi-cal economists expected growth to grind to a halt. Capital and labour might both increase virtually without limit in favourable circumstances but the third of the trinity of factors needed to secure material output, land, was in fixed supply. Hence, even allowing for human ingenuity in squeezing an increased output from a given area, there was no prospect of exponential growth. But their gloomy prognostications, though logi-cal, proved unfounded. In the quest for the industrial revolution, both the growth which took place in the early modern period, and its fail-ure to die away thereafter must be taken into account. Coupled with a 'Smithian' analysis of early success, there must be a satisfactory expla-nation of why growth did not die away, why the stationary state did not supervene.

If England had remained, as all countries previously had remained, an organic economy, the comparative paucity of energy supplies would have exercised the same restraining influence on growth which it had always done. But a means of escape was found, by happenstance rather than conscious design initially, and once the nature of the escape route became clear, it proved, of course, irresistibly attractive, whatever the pains of the initial transition. The industrial revolution was not a unitary process. If it had been, the pessimistic forebodings of the classical economists would have proved justified. Its nature was essentially dual. In parallel with 'Smithian' growth, there was a slow transformation of what had previously been a purely organic economy into one which was less and less dependent on the products of the earth, on the current yield of photosynthesis.

The economy became capitalist not only in the sense which is reflected in Adam Smith's writings, but also in a second sense. An expanding economy necessarily requires a rising expenditure of energy, broadly in parallel with the curve of growth. No organic economy could meet a rising demand of this sort indefinitely. To avoid deceleration, it was essential to begin to tap the energy capital which had been locked up in coal deposits 300 million years previously. The annual *flow* of solar energy could not sustain continued growth; only by tapping a vast capital *stock* of energy could it be sustained and enhanced. The current inflow of energy from the sun was insufficient to permit exponential growth, but a way was found to tap the inflow which had reached the land surface of Britain geological ages before there were first men on earth. To revert to the issue of the logical status of this essay, it would be equally apposite to define it as focusing on one *necessary* condition for an industrial revolution. It will probably never be possible to secure agreement about what constituted *sufficient* conditions for the changes which took place, but, in my view, it is demonstrable that, without the gradual substitution of inorganic for organic sources of energy, substantial and sustained growth would have proved beyond reach.

Viewed in this light the key feature of the industrial revolution consisted less in an acceleration in growth than in the absence of any deceleration. It is easy to be blinded by the growth rates achieved in the last 150 years and so fail to note the remarkable nature of the growth rates achieved in early modern England. Set against earlier experience output per head was rising at breakneck speed. A very crude calculation will put the achievements of the seventeenth and eighteenth centuries in perspective. Between 1600 and 1800 the population of England rose from 4.2 to 8.7 millions.[65] The agricultural labour force changed very little over

---

[65] Wrigley *et al.*, *English population history*, tab. A9.1, pp. 614–5.

this period.[66] Since the country remained largely self-sufficient in food-stuffs and the scale of agricultural output for purposes other than food and drink (fodder for draught animals, wool, hair, leather, straw, reeds, flax, etc.) probably grew at least commensurately, it is likely that output per head rather more than doubled over these two centuries. Agriculture was by far the largest single industry, so that output per head overall may well also have doubled. In some other industries, there is tolerably clear evidence to support the presumption that manpower productivity was rising substantially.[67] A doubling in output per head over a 200-year period implies an average rate of growth per annum of about 0.35 per cent per annum. By comparison with the comparable rates of growth from the middle of the nineteenth century onwards, this is a very modest figure but by comparison with such rates in organic economies generally, it is exceptionally high.[68] Such a rate of growth sustained over a period of 500 years, for example, implies a sixfold increase in individual productivity, which would have transformed living standards beyond recognition if it had ever obtained. It is a measure of the economic success of England between the time of the Spanish armada and the struggle with Napoleon that such a rate of growth was achieved. But even the most advanced organic economy was still certain to be faced in due course by an energy barrier which it could not breach if it continued to expand, and would meet the barrier more rapidly if it grew quickly than if it grew slowly. More production necessarily meant more energy consumption. Only by gradually ceasing to depend upon the products of photosynthesis as an energy source could the problem be overcome.

What might seem an exaggerated claim to the title of a revolution if judged using the conventional tools of economic measurement, therefore, none the less seems fully justified when attention is paid to the physical and biological character of the production process and to the changes therein. Perhaps, in short, the apparent paradox is not beyond resolution.

---

[66] Wrigley, 'Urban growth', tab. 7.4, p. 170.

[67] This was true of shipping, for example: Ville, 'English shipping industry'.

[68] Once again, however, developments in Holland anticipated those in England. De Vries and van der Woude estimate that output tripled between *c.* 1500 and *c.* 1800 while the agricultural labour force grew by only 50 per cent. Most of the increase was concentrated in the first half of the period when output was rising by 0.6–0.7 per cent per annum: de Vries and van der Woude, *The first modern economy*, p. 232.

The divergence of England: the growth of the
     English economy in the seventeenth and
     eighteenth centuries

That something remarkable was happening in England in the quarter-millennium separating the late sixteenth from the early nineteenth century is plain. In Elizabeth I's reign the Spanish armada was perceived as a grave threat: the English ships were scarcely a match for the Spanish, and the weather played a major part in the deliverance of the nation. By the later eighteenth century the Royal Navy was unchallenged by the naval forces of any other country, and during the generation of war which followed the French revolution, it proved capable of controlling the seas in the face of the combined naval forces mustered by Napoleon in an attempt to break the British oceanic stranglehold.[1] Growing naval dominance was a symbol of a far more pervasive phenomenon. In the later sixteenth century England was not a leading European power and could exercise little influence over events at a distance from its shores. The Napoleonic wars showed that, even when faced by a coalition of countries occupying the bulk of Europe west of Russia and led by one of the greatest of military commanders, Britain possessed the depth of resources to weather a very long war, enabling her to outlast her challenger and ultimately secure a victory.[2] The combination of a large and assertive navy and dominant financial and commercial strength meant that, in the early decades of the nineteenth century, Britain was able to impose her will over large tracts

---

This chapter was originally given as the Prothero Lecture to the Royal Historical Society on 7 July 1999.

[1] Or, as Brewer put it, 'From its modest beginnings as a peripheral power – a minor, infrequent almost inconsequential participant in the great wars that ravaged sixteenth and seventeenth-century Europe – Britain emerged in the late seventeenth and early eighteenth centuries as the military *Wunderkind* of the age.' Brewer, *Sinews of power*, p. xiii. What was true in the early eighteenth century was true *a fortiori* by its end.

[2] The fact that it is accurate to refer to England when describing events in the sixteenth century, but to Britain when attention is transferred to the eighteenth and nineteenth centuries is, of course, itself highly significant. I shall be less than punctilious in this regard in this essay, normally referring to England when it might be more accurate to refer to Britain or even to the British Isles, but since much of my discussion is concerned with long periods of time, I hope it is an acceptable simplification to write of England rather than to attempt greater precision.

of every continent. But her dominance did not grow out of the barrel of a gun. It derived chiefly from exceptional economic success: it grew out of the corn sack, the cotton mill, and the coal mine.

In a long-settled area which largely shares a common culture and technology it is unusual for one political entity substantially to increase its relative 'weight' compared with other political units unless it expands territorially in the manner of the Chinese or Roman empires. This is likely to be especially true of pre-industrial political entities because every such economy had an 'organic' base.[3] The land provided almost all material products of value to man. Density of settlement and ability to produce material goods were closely linked to the productivity of the soil. Hence the tendency on the part of a rising power to seek territorial expansion both to symbolise and to consolidate a temporary advantage: Prussia in the late seventeenth and eighteenth centuries is an example of this mode of expansion. There will be exceptions to any generalisation of this kind but few more striking than the experience of England in the early modern period. The remarkable relative increase in English power sprang principally from what might be described as an intensification rather than an extensification of her territory.[4]

My intention in this essay is to draw attention to some features of English history between the later sixteenth and the early nineteenth century which exemplify the exceptional character of English development relative to that of most neighbouring continental countries. Economic success was at the heart of the differential success of England and it is with this aspect of the period that I shall be chiefly concerned, though I shall also touch on wider questions about capitalism and modern economic growth.

To provide a perspective for subsequent discussion, consider the following crude calculation of changing relative gross national product. The population of England almost quadrupled between 1550 and 1820 while the population of western Europe minus England less than doubled.[5]

---

[3] The concept of an organic economy is described in Wrigley, *Continuity, chance and change*, pp. 17–32.

[4] In a more extended discussion of this question, it would be necessary to take into account the complex issues associated with the extension of English power within the British Isles and, especially towards the end of the period, the acquisition of colonies on other continents. Hence the qualification implied by using the adverb 'principally'.

[5] The English population rose by about 280 per cent during this period; that of the rest of western Europe by about 80 per cent, with little variation between the different countries. Wrigley, 'Growth of population', pp. 121–5. Countries such as Italy or Germany were not, of course, united political entities in this period. Even those, such as France, which were already nation states in the sixteenth century experienced boundary changes during the early modern period. The estimated growth rates are intended to refer to the areas now occupied by the states in question, though all are subject to significant margins of error.

Attempting to estimate changes in output per head over the same period is subject to much wider uncertainties than the estimate of population change, but it seems certain that the pace of increase was higher
in England than elsewhere. Maddison's calculations suggest that in 1820
English output per head was about 40 per cent higher than that of France
or Holland and even further ahead of that of continental Europe as a
whole.[6] If, for argument's sake, we assume that there was little difference
between England and the continent in the mid-sixteenth century, the implication of this exercise is that the gross national product of England
was three times larger relative to that of continental countries by the end
of the period than it had been at its beginning.[7] An exercise of this kind
is subject to many uncertainties, and can make no claim to precision.
The result, however, is as likely to understate as to overstate the relative
economic advance of England. In any case it leaves no room for doubt
that her relative advance was exceptional. How did it come about?

An advanced organic economy

A first point to stress is that the relative advance was in train long before
the period which has conventionally been assigned to the industrial revolution. The change was cumulative and progressive rather than abrupt. It
was largely the product of developments within the period often termed
pre-industrial; the period when the land was the source not simply of

[6] At first sight his work does not suggest large differences between England and advanced
continental countries at the beginning of the nineteenth century. For example, his estimates of gross domestic product per head in 1820 for France, the Netherlands, and the
United Kingdom fall within quite a narrow range: that for France (expressed in 1970
US dollars) is $377, for the Netherlands $400, and for the United Kingdom $454. But
the UK figure includes Ireland and Maddison estimated Irish output per head at only
half the British figure. Since Irish population was 32.6 per cent of the UK total in 1821,
this implies that the British figure for GDP per head would be $542 rather than $454,
or 36 per cent higher than the Dutch and 44 per cent higher than the French, rather
than 14 and 20 per cent as suggested by a comparison using UK GDP estimates. Since
Scottish output per head was lower than English, a figure for England only would be
still higher and the advantage over France and the Netherlands, therefore, still more pronounced: Maddison, *Phases of capitalist development*, tab. 1.4, pp. 8 and 167; Mitchell,
British historical statistics, tab. 1.2, pp. 9–10. If data for European countries other than
France and the Netherlands were available, the contrast would, in general, be still more
pronounced.

[7] To be more concrete, by way of illustration, suppose that output per head in a 'typical'
continental country rose by one-third between 1550 and 1820 and that its population
increased by 80 per cent, then its gross national product would have risen by about 140
per cent ($1.33 \times 1.8 \times 100 = 239$). Over the same period the English population rose by
280 per cent and we have made the assumption that its output per head moved from parity
with a continental average in 1550 to an advantage of 40 per cent by 1820. Therefore
gross national product would have risen by about 600 per cent ($(1.33 \times 1.4) \times 3.8 \times
100 = 708$). And $708/239 = 2.96$, or approximately a threefold relative increase.

the food of the nation but of the great bulk of its raw materials also, and when therefore the productivity of the land was the key to the possibility of increasing the output of material goods; the period when the economy was still organic.

Since an almost exclusive emphasis on the land as the source of the material products needed to satisfy human wants is an unfamiliar idea today, it may be helpful to exemplify the point somewhat. Many of the largest industries of the twentieth century are freed from any dependence on animal or vegetable raw materials. Capital goods are constructed predominantly from metal, concrete, and bricks. Most consumer durables are made from metal or plastics. Ceramics and glass are widely used and are produced in great quantity. Transport vehicles – ships, planes, trains, lorries, and cars – are made of metal, plastics, and glass. Even articles of clothing, once made exclusively from vegetable or animal raw materials, are now often made from nylon, polyester, or similar materials. Footwear is no longer exclusively made from leather. The supply of mineral ores, clays, oil, and coal, the raw materials from which so many products are manufactured, is not unlimited. Some may become exhausted in the foreseeable future. All must eventually be worked out or at least become increasingly inaccessible. Converting them for human use entails expending huge quantities of energy. This, too, in time may give rise to grave difficulties, either because no cheap and effective alternative to fossil fuels is developed, or because of the pollution to which their use gives rise. But all such problems are quite different from those which faced organic economies.

The nature of such economies is immediately suggested by their employment structures. In England the most numerous employment groups outside agriculture even as late as 1831 were trades such as shoemakers, carpenters, tailors, blacksmiths, masons, butchers, bricklayers, and bakers, or service occupations such as publicans and shopkeepers.[8] A couple of centuries earlier, if equivalent information were available, it is unlikely that shopkeepers or bricklayers would have been so prominent but the other occupations, though many fewer in absolute number, would have retained much the same relative positions. With the exception of masons, all these were occupations which depended on animal or vegetable raw materials either as inputs into the production process or, in the case of the service occupations, as the ultimate source of the material goods which they were making available to the public. Blacksmiths and bricklayers

---

[8] These ten occupations were the largest in the general category 'handicraft and trade' at the taking of the 1831 census: tab. 4.2, pp. 92–3. The lists of trades are given in descending order of size. If all ten occupations were to be treated as a single list, publicans would rank fourth and shopkeepers fifth in size.

were only apparent exceptions to the rule since the smelting of metals and the baking of bricks were traditionally dependent upon wood as a fuel source, and this was the reason for the modest scale of the output from iron foundries or brickworks in the pre-industrial era. The first stirrings of change in regard to fuel supply, however, were already taking place in early modern England, a harbinger of the future which was to prove highly significant.

If, for simplicity's sake, and as a first approximation, it is agreed that England for most of the early modern period may be regarded as an organic economy, then the nature of the limitation imposed upon it, in common with all other such economies, is clear. All animal and vegetable life is ultimately dependent upon photosynthesis, the process by which a small fraction of the incident energy pouring down upon the earth each year from the sun is converted into a form which either itself constitutes life or affords a basis for other life forms. Animate life is normally in a sense a zero sum game. A square kilometre of forest occupied by pine trees cannot also sustain oaks. A tribe of Neanderthals who succeed in securing the bulk of the annual 'crop' of deer will put pressure on a local wolf population which had been heavily dependent upon deer for its food. Symbiosis greatly complicates any such over-simple picture but there is none the less a substantial element of truth in viewing competition for the finite products of photosynthesis as a defining feature of animate life. Organic economies constantly juggled with the same problem. Fodder for livestock represented the product of land which might otherwise have been used to grow food for people. The woollen industry could not expand indefinitely without limiting wheat output.

This point underlies the well-known principle, formulated to great effect by Ricardo, which has come to be known as the law of diminishing returns. This principle follows directly from the nature of any organic economy. If the base of all material production lies in the process of photosynthesis and the land surface is finite, there must be limits to the expansion of the quantity of raw materials which can be made available to mankind. The neolithic food revolution, by substituting plants of use to man for the natural vegetation cover, vastly increased the proportion of the products of photosynthesis annexed by man for his own use at the expense of those plants and animals which did not serve his purposes. But once the limits of convenient cultivation had been reached, additional output had either to be won from soils rendered relatively infertile by altitude, steep slope, or poor drainage; or from the more intensive farming of land already in cultivation. In either case, so Ricardo argued, each additional unit of output could be secured only by an increasing proportional input of labour, or capital, or both. As a result the returns to capital and labour must both fall and, at some point, further expansion would become impossible.[9]

All organic economies faced these difficulties, but England proved exceptionally adept at overcoming them. It is a crude but convincing measure of the extent of her achievement to note that by the beginning of the nineteenth century, when the country was still largely self-sufficient in food, only about 40 per cent of the adult male labour force was engaged in agriculture, whereas in continental Europe the comparable figure characteristically ranged between 60 and 80 per cent.[10] An unusually small proportion of the labour force in agriculture, of course, also implies an unusually large proportion in secondary industry and tertiary occupations. Or again, in 1800 England was the most heavily urbanised country in Europe other than Holland, even though in the mid-sixteenth century she had been amongst the least urbanised.[11] London became the largest city in Europe during the seventeenth century.[12] Urban growth in England accelerated so dramatically that during the second half of the eighteenth century 70 per cent of all the urban growth taking place in Europe as a whole occurred in England alone, even though the population of England was only about 8 per cent of that of Europe.[13] Gregory King had been concerned about the ability of England to provide a strong enough tax base to sustain a prolonged conflict with France or Holland, the two countries whose power gave most concern to Englishmen in his day.[14] Yet the course of events in the eighteenth century showed that the English economy was able to cope with a substantially heavier tax burden, both in times of peace and war, than that imposed by the French government. Moreover, the weight of taxation did not prevent a continued

---

[9] For a fuller discussion of the treatment of this issue by the classical economists, Adam Smith, Ricardo, and Malthus, see Wrigley, 'The classical economists'.

[10] In Finland in 1805 82.1 per cent of the total labour force was engaged in agriculture. In Italy in 1871 61.2 per cent of the male labour force was in agriculture, and the comparable percentages in Ireland (1841) and Sweden (1860) were 68.5 and 64.6. The percentages for Italy, Ireland, and Sweden would certainly have been higher at the beginning of the nineteenth century. In England in 1800 comparable percentage was only about 38 per cent. Mitchell, *European historical statistics*, tab. C1, pp. 161–73; tab. 4.12, p. 124.

[11] De Vries, *European urbanization*, tab. 3.2, p. 30; tab. 3.6, pp. 36–7. Also Wrigley, 'Urban growth'.

[12] The population of London in 1600, 1700, and 1800 was approximately 200,000; 575,000; and 865,000: the population of Paris, her chief rival in size, at the same three dates was 220,000; 430,000; and 581,000: de Vries, *European urbanization*, app. 1, pp. 269–78.

[13] Wrigley, 'Urban growth', tab. 7,7, p. 179.

[14] See, for example, King, *Natural and political observations*, pp. 227–30. His concern with this issue surfaces repeatedly in the many calculations reproduced from his notebooks in this work.

and sustained expansion of the economy contrary to the fears expressed by King and many others.[15]

Although no comprehensive agricultural production statistics are available until well into the nineteenth century, it may be taken as certain not only that there was a very large rise in the output of English agriculture between the late sixteenth and the early nineteenth century, but also that output per head increased greatly.[16] The first point follows directly from the fact that the population tripled while the country remained broadly self-sufficient in basic foodstuffs.[17] The second follows from the first if combined with the probability that the workforce engaged in agriculture increased only slightly between 1600 and 1800.[18] The second point is the more remarkable of the two since it signifies that for a quarter-millennium England succeeded in escaping from the ineluctable pressures which Ricardo had described.[19]

[15] An extended discussion of the scale of the tax burden in England, of its nature, and of the relation between the tax yield and military success, together with a comparison of England and her main rivals, France and the Dutch Republic, in these respects, may be found in Brewer, *Sinews of power*. See also O'Brien, 'The political economy of British taxation' and Mathias and O'Brien, 'Taxation in England and France'.

[16] Official series for agricultural acreages and livestock numbers for Great Britain began in 1867, though production series are available only from 1885. Mitchell, *British historical statistics*, section III.

[17] Nor was the population ill nourished. There is persuasive evidence that the English population was better nourished than populations in continental Europe at the end of the eighteenth century, though much less well fed than those who lived in the newly independent United States. Fogel, *Conquest of high mortality*, tab. 4, p. 30 and fig. 5, p. 38.

[18] Wrigley, 'Urban growth', tab. 7.4, p. 170.

[19] It is relevant to note in this connection, however, that, unlike many other European countries, the population of England in 1600 was probably still substantially smaller than it had been at its medieval peak at the beginning of the fourteenth century. In 1600 the population was approximately 4.2 million; c.1300 it is widely thought to have exceeded 6 million. The pressure of population on agricultural resources may therefore have been significantly less pronounced in early seventeenth-century England than in many other countries and population growth may have been accommodated more easily. For the population in 1600: Wrigley et al., *English population history*, tab. A9.1, pp. 614–5. The size of the population 300 years earlier is subject to much wider margins of uncertainty, but Smith concluded, after a critical review both of the available empirical evidence and of the views of leading scholars, that they strongly suggested 'that the English population total prior to 1310 is very unlikely to have been less than 5.0 million and most probably exceeded 6.0 million': R. M. Smith, 'Demographic developments in rural England', p. 49. He noted that this may imply that not until the 1760s was the medieval peak exceeded (p. 50). There are, however, those who stand out against the consensus. Campbell et al., for example, basing their view on the area sown to grain crops each year, net yield per acre, and assumptions about average calorie intake, conclude that the population of England may have been no higher than between 3.4 and 5.6 million and make it clear that their sympathies lie with a figure towards the lower end of the range: B. M. S. Campbell et al., *A medieval capital and its grain supply*, p. 43, and, more generally, pp. 37–45.

How should one seek to explain this phenomenon? In an extended discussion of this issue it would be natural to begin by reviewing in detail the changes which occurred. For example, there is clear evidence that cereal yields doubled between *c*.1600 and *c*.1800. This change, combined with the fact that new rotational systems made it possible to reduce the proportion of the land which was fallowed from perhaps 30 per cent of the arable area at the beginning of the period to a figure of about 12 per cent at its end, goes far towards establishing the proximate reasons for the country's ability to cope with a growing population without any large percentage increase in the area in cultivation.[20] Indeed, since these assumptions imply that cereal output per unit area of arable land increased 2.5 times, whereas population rose only 2.1 times, the area needed to meet the cereal needs of the nation may actually have fallen.[21] Or again, the nitrogen content of the soil is now widely seen as the key immediate determinant of crop yields. The introduction of leguminous plants into crop rotations helped in this connection both directly by the fixing of nitrogen in their root systems and indirectly by enabling a larger livestock population to be sustained and hence a larger quantity of nitrogen in the form of animal manure to be returned to the soil. Since there is a trade-off between the number of draught animals available on the farm and the number of men whom it is necessary to employ, and it is demonstrable that the ratio of draught animals to men in agricultural employment was substantially higher in England than in France, a part of the rise of manpower productivity taking place in England can probably be attributed to an increase in this ratio.[22] An abundance of draught animals also makes it more readily possible to perform the large number of ton-miles of effort needed if lime and marl are to be applied assiduously

[20] The figure of 30 per cent for the sixteenth century is probably an underestimate. In different parts of the country arable land was fallowed every second, every third, or every fourth year. The overall figure is therefore a function of the relative importance of the three different predominant rotations. The position is much clearer for the beginning of the nineteenth century when the data available in the county surveys suggests that the ratio of fallow to crops was about 1:7. Holderness, 'Prices, productivity, and output', p. 133.

[21] The population of England rose from 4.162 to 8.671 million; Wrigley *et al.*, *English population history*, tab. A9.1, pp. 614–5. If 100 acres of arable land produced 700 bushels in 1600 (a yield of 10 bushels per acre on the 70 per cent of the land not in fallow), the same acreage in 1800 would have produced 1,760 bushels (20 bushels per acre on the 88 per cent of land not in fallow). This seriously understates the true proportionate gain, however, since it was not gross output per acre but net output which mattered. Roughly 2 bushels per acre would have been reserved from current use at both dates to provide seed for the next harvest. Therefore the net yield would have risen from 560 (700 − (70 × 2)) to 1,594 bushels (1760 − (88 × 2)), or 2.85 times.

[22] Wrigley, 'Energy availability'.

to improve soil quality.[23] However, since this discussion must be brief, I intend to concentrate upon some wider issues that are repeatedly raised when attempting to account for the marked advantage over neighbouring countries which England enjoyed for a time.

England and the Netherlands

The first point to consider is whether what happened in England was *sui generis*, or whether there were precedents for it. The question can be made more explicit. In what respects, if any, were developments in England in the seventeenth and eighteenth centuries different from those which took place in Holland in the sixteenth and seventeenth centuries? Was English success merely Dutch success writ large because of greater resources and a bigger population? Holland in its heyday had developed a productive commercial agriculture; had urbanised to the same extent as that attained by England about 1800; had achieved dominance of the international oceanic carrying trade; had succeeded in raising Dutch real incomes to a level substantially higher than that of her rivals; and had enjoyed technical superiority in many branches of manufacture. Yet the momentum of growth in the Dutch republic had faded before the end of the seventeenth century, giving way during the eighteenth to a lengthy period of virtual stagnation. Alone among the nations of western Europe the population of Holland failed to grow during the eighteenth century and her economy ceased to expand.[24] The standard of living did not plummet. Real wages fell moderately during the eighteenth century, but they remained higher than those of most other European countries.[25] The Dutch economy, however, ceased to display what is often taken as a defining characteristic of a modern economy, that over any considerable period both gross output and output per head will rise. In this respect, English experience was different since the two centuries of expansion before 1800 were followed not by stagnation but by a further acceleration in the rate of growth. Focusing on this feature of English experience compared with Dutch points to a distinctive aspect of the divergence of England. It also makes it possible to approach a question of fundamental importance in shaping our view of the nature of the modern world, since it is inextricably intertwined with the related question of the propriety of treating the development of capitalism as a valid explanation of the unprecedented economic dynamism of west European countries in this period.

[23] Wrigley, *Continuity, chance and change*, pp. 43–4.
[24] De Vries and van der Woude, *The first modern economy*, pp. 665–93.
[25] Ibid., pp. 627–32.

The question at issue is whether the very nature of the capitalist system ensured that growth would be constant and progressive, if at times productive of severe hardship and social tension, or whether capitalist economies, on the model of eighteenth-century Holland, might enter a phase of stagnation, which might prove long lasting or even possibly indefinite. If the former were the case, the whole sequence of growth from Tudor times to Edwardian England and beyond may be seen as a unitary phenomenon, each phase a natural, even an inevitable development from earlier phases. If the Dutch case is not treated simply as an aberration, however, the advent of capitalism is not in itself a sufficient explanation of the course of events. Since the chances of securing exponential growth may appear very differently *ex prae facto* from *ex post facto*, it is illuminating both to consider the views of contemporaries and of more recent scholarship in this connection.

Adam Smith considered the sources of growth and the limits to growth at length, often turning to Holland in the course of his discussion of the question. He opened the *Wealth of nations* by analysing with great clarity the possibilities for increasing productivity per head afforded by the division of labour, and then explained the close connection between gains achieved in this fashion, the extent of the market, and the scale of capital accumulation. The example which he chose to illustrate the scope for productivity gains has subsequently acquired the status of a secular parable. He asserted that 20 pinmakers combining to maximise the efficiency of pin production were capable of raising productivity per head 240 times when compared with what a single pinmaker could achieve operating on his own.[26] Even when allowance is made for the fact that he regarded the comparable opportunities in agriculture, by far the largest employer of labour, as slighter,[27] the world which he depicts might appear to offer immense opportunities for progressive gains in productivity, intimately connected with capitalist enterprise. But Adam Smith himself saw matters differently. He was convinced that opportunities for raising production per head were finite and limited, remarking:

In a country which had acquired that full complement of riches which the nature of its soil and climate, and its situation with respect to other countries, allowed it to acquire; which could, therefore, advance no further, and which was not going backwards, both the wages of labour and the profits of stock would probably be very low.[28]

[26] A. Smith, *Wealth of nations*, I, pp. 8–9.
[27] Ibid., I, pp. 9–10.
[28] Ibid., I, p. 106.

Although Smith did not suppose that any country had yet reached this state, it is clear that he believed that Holland was close to it. It had largely exhausted the range of opportunities for profitable local investment. Smith, using the prevailing interest rate as a surrogate measure of the return on capital, noted that in Holland the government could borrow at 2 per cent and individuals of good credit at 3 per cent and remarked that 'the diminution of profit is the natural effect of its prosperity [that is, the prosperity of Holland], or of a greater stock being employed in it than before'.[29] With investment opportunities so limited close to home, and capital abundant and cheap, Dutch capitalists increasingly turned to other countries and to the carrying trade.[30] Smith, in other words, in common with the other great classical economists, Malthus and Ricardo, envisaged growth as giving way eventually to the stationary state, an unpromising situation in which neither those who depended on their labour for a livelihood, nor those who depended on capital, were well rewarded for their contributions to the production process.[31] In short, Adam Smith not only regarded it as possible that the advent of capitalism might, after a period of growth and prosperity, be followed by a much darker situation, but expected that the very dynamism of the capitalist system in seeking out opportunities for profitable investment must eventually bring about the stationary state. On this view, what happened subsequently in England was against all expectation.

That Smith's pessimism was unjustified is plain. Rather than deceleration occurring, later generations experienced rates of growth without precedent. Before the nineteenth century the low level of productivity per head universally experienced in fully settled countries meant that the idea of abolishing poverty was a utopian dream. By the end of the century, this possibility no longer seemed out of reach. The outrage expressed by Marx that the productive capacity existed to enable poverty to be abolished, but that the vastly increased flow of wealth was being concentrated in fewer and fewer hands, fired socialist politics for several generations. The classical economists proved mistaken in their forebodings, but perhaps they were mistaken, not from any flaw in their logic, but because, as

---

[29] Ibid., I, p. 102.

[30] 'The carrying trade', he remarked, 'is the natural effect and symptom of great national wealth; but it does not seem to be the natural cause of it.' Ibid., I, p. 395. See also ibid., I, p. 108.

[31] Labour and capital could both enjoy good returns during the phase of expansion made possible by the division of labour, an extensive market, and a steadily rising supply of capital, but this would not last. Smith wrote, 'It is in the progressive state, while the society is advancing to the further acquisition, rather than when it has acquired its full complement of riches, that the condition of the labouring poor, of the great body of the people, seems to be the happiest and most comfortable. It is hard in the stationary, and miserable in the declining state.' Ibid., I, pp. 90–1.

so often in history, events took a turn for which there was no precedent and which was therefore impossible to foresee.

The other classical economists followed Adam Smith's lead, adducing additional arguments in reaching the same conclusion. Malthus, though in his later years less pessimistic than Smith about the future, was nevertheless oppressed by the thought of what must follow if a rising population pressed harder and harder on a fixed and limited supply of land.[32] Ricardo, in formulating the doctrine of declining marginal returns, was the most categorical of all in ruling out any possibility of a prosperous future for mankind, insisting that the problem arose ultimately from the laws of nature rather than the dispositions of man.[33]

Capitalist growth: Marx and others

The event which escaped contemporary notice was the coming into existence alongside the organic economy of a new and different economy based not on the produce of the land, and thus ultimately on the limits set by the annual quantum of photosynthesis, but on minerals and on fossil fuels which, in contrast to output derived from the soil, were often not subject to declining marginal returns, at least on a time scale of centuries. Production in this mode could be expanded immensely, and often enjoyed increasing marginal returns. Negative feedback could be replaced by positive feedback. But was the course taken by events implied by the

---

[32] Malthus's model of the characteristic behaviour of an economy included long-term 'oscillations' during which for considerable periods of time the secular tendency of real wages might be either upwards or downwards. During an upswing, as he envisaged the matter, one of two results were possible: 'one, that of a rapid increase in population, in which case the high wages are chiefly spent on the maintenance of large and frequent families; and the other, that of a decided improvement in the modes of subsistence, and the conveniences and comforts enjoyed, without a proportionate acceleration in the rate of increase.' In the latter case, the benefits accruing were not necessarily dissipated by excessive population growth but might facilitate the establishment of a new and higher plateau of living standards. Malthus, *Principles of political economy*, p. 183.

[33] He wrote: 'Whilst the land yields abundantly, wages may temporarily rise, and the producers may consume more than their accustomed proportion; but the stimulus which will thus be given to population will speedily reduce the labourers to their usual consumption. But when poor lands are taken into cultivation, or when more capital and labour are expended on the old land, with a less return of produce, the effect must be permanent. A greater proportion of that part of the produce which remains to be divided, after paying rent, between the owners of stock and the labourers, will be apportioned to the latter. Each man may, and probably will, have a less absolute quantity; but as more labourers are employed in proportion to the whole produce retained by the farmer, the value of a greater proportion of the whole produce will be absorbed by wages, and consequently the value of a smaller proportion will be devoted to profits. This will necessarily be rendered permanent by the laws of nature, which have limited the productive powers of the land.' Ricardo, *Principles of political economy*, pp. 125–6.

very nature of the new economic system, the capitalist system, which had grown up in the past two or three centuries, or might capitalist economies, as Adam Smith supposed, pass from growth to stagnation? To express the same idea using differing terminology, was capitalist growth intrinsically exponential or might it equally well be asymptotic?

There can be no final resolution of this issue, given its nature and the uncertainties which surround it. Yet, since the answer to these questions must affect our appreciation of the nature of capitalism, they cannot be ignored. Marx, whose influence has been pervasive both among those who have shared his political views and among those who have not, may be taken as the weightiest advocate of the former view. A capitalist economy, in his analysis, moved inevitably from the handicraft period through manufacture to modern industry. Manufacture developed out of the handicraft system either 'from the union of various independent handicrafts, which become stripped of their independence and specialised to such an extent as to be reduced to mere supplementary partial processes in the production of one particular commodity' or because it split up a 'particular handicraft into its various detail operations, isolating, and making these operations independent of one another up to the point where each becomes the exclusive function of a particular labourer . . . But whatever may have been its particular starting point, its final form is invariably the same – a productive mechanism whose parts are human beings.'[34] During the manufacturing period machinery played only a subordinate role to the division of labour in securing more efficient production.[35] It was an organisational form rather than a particular embodied technology which defined manufacture. Such an organisational form required the concentration of larger and larger amounts of capital in the hands of capitalist entrepreneurs, converting the labourer into what Marx termed 'a crippled monstrosity'.[36] 'As the chosen people bore in their features the sign manual of Jehovah', he concluded, allowing himself a flight of fancy, 'so division of labour brands the manufacturing workman as the property of capital'.[37]

The critical difference between the era of manufacture and the era of modern industry, in Marx's eyes, lay in the nature of the machine. The capitalist strives constantly to reduce production costs because, by

[34] Marx, *Capital*, I, p. 329.
[35] 'But, on the whole, machinery played that subordinate part which Adam Smith assigns to it in comparison with the division of labour.' What Marx termed the 'collective labourer, formed by the combination of a number of detail labourers' was 'the machinery specially characteristic of the manufacturing period'. Ibid., I, p. 341.
[36] Ibid., I, p. 354.
[37] Ibid., I, p. 355.

shortening that fraction of the working day in which the labourer works for himself, that is to supply his maintenance, the fraction of the day during which he works for the capitalist is increased.[38] 'In short', as Marx put it, 'it is a means of producing surplus-value.'[39] The emphasis shifts from labour power itself to the instruments of labour. The crucial distinction between the two eras, in his view, was that between a tool and a machine. 'The machine proper is therefore a mechanism that, after being set in motion, performs with its tools the same operations that were formerly done by the workman with similar tools. Whether the motive power is derived from man, or from some other machine, makes no difference in this respect. From the moment that the tool proper is taken from man, and fitted into a mechanism, a machine takes the place of a mere implement.'[40] He explicitly rejected the view that the crucial distinction had to do with motive power. He noted that it had been argued that in the case of a tool the motive power was supplied by the worker himself whereas in the case of a machine the motive power was supplied by an animal, the wind, or a waterfall, but he suggested, as an insuperable obstacle to this view, that it would entail accepting that production by machinery preceded production by handicraft since animals had been used to provide mechanical energy in the production process from a very early date.[41] Elaborating the same point, he wrote:

The steam engine itself, such as it was at its invention, during the manufacturing period at the close of the 17th century, and as it continued to be down to 1780, did not give rise to any industrial revolution. It was on the contrary, the invention of machines that made a revolution in the form of steam engines necessary. As soon as man, instead of working with an implement on the subject of his labour, becomes merely the motive power of an implement-machine, it is a mere accident that motive power takes the disguise of human muscle; it may equally well take the form of wind, water or steam.[42]

For Marx, therefore, the transition between manufacture and modern industry was unproblematic. The nature of capitalism determines the characteristics of both economic systems and ensures that there will be a transition from one to the other. The technological changes which

---

[38] Ibid., II, p. 365.
[39] Ibid., II, p. 366.
[40] Ibid., II, p. 368.
[41] Ibid., II, p. 366.
[42] Ibid., II, p. 370. Finally, in summary, he wrote, 'The machine, which is the starting point of the industrial revolution, supersedes the workman, who handles a single tool, by a mechanism operating with a number of similar tools, and set in motion by a single motive power, whatever the form of that power may be.' Ibid., II, pp. 370–1.

occurred were equally unproblematic since they were induced by the necessities of the two systems. Capitalism, unlike any earlier socio-economic form, brought into being a dominant class whose nature committed them to promoting changes which tended to increase productivity. 'The bourgeoisie', he wrote, 'cannot exist without constantly revolution-ising the instruments of production, and thereby the relations of production, and with them the whole relations of society. Conservation of the old modes of production in unaltered form, was, on the contrary, the first condition of existence for all earlier industrial classes.'[43] There was a continuum between the forces which had first turned independent craftsmen into what would now be termed a proto-industrial workforce and those which substituted powered machinery for hand-held tools.[44]

Marx's conviction that development was essentially continuous has been echoed by many others. One of the two economic historians to be awarded a Nobel prize in 1993, Douglass North, for example, comes to the same conclusion, though by a different route. Since he regards change in institutional structures as the key development which made possible a capitalist economy and facilitated rapid and persistent economic growth, he focuses on the importance of the appearance of a legal framework within which rational decisions can be taken and implemented and treats the subsequent growth, whether occurring before or after the changes which we term the industrial revolution, as essentially downstream from the creation of such a framework. 'The technological change associated with the industrial revolution required the *prior* development of a set of property rights, which raised the private rate of return on invention and innovation.'[45] Further, 'our stereotyped views of the industrial revolution are in need of revision. The period that we have come to call the industrial revolution was not the radical break with the past that we sometimes believe it to have been. Instead, – it was the evolutionary cul-mination of a series of prior events.'[46] Or again, 'The most convincing explanation for the industrial revolution as an acceleration in the rate of innovation is one drawn from straightforward neoclassical theory in which a combination of better specified and enforced property rights and

[43] Marx and Engels, *The Communist manifesto*, p. 16.
[44] Marx's manufacturing phase closely resembles the proto-industrial period as defined by Mendels, who coined the term. Mendels, 'Proto-industrialization'.
[45] North, *Structure and change*, p. 147. The same, he argued, had been true of the earlier growth surge in the Netherlands. 'The merchants of the Low Countries in recognition of this situation paid their rulers through the States General to establish and enforce property rights and end restrictive practices. The Netherlands as a result became the first country to achieve sustained economic growth.' Ibid., p. 154.
[46] Ibid., p. 162.

increasingly efficient and expanding markets directed resources into new channels.'[47]

The list of those taking a similar view of the continuity in the nature of change before, during, and after the industrial revolution could be extended almost indefinitely. The increasingly clear consensus amongst economic historians intent on measuring aggregate economic growth that any acceleration which took place during the classic period of the industrial revolution was minor has tended to underwrite this viewpoint.[48]

The traditional view that the industrial revolution represented a marked discontinuity with the past and that it occurred during the later decades of the eighteenth century and the early decades of the nineteenth century has not, however, disappeared from recent literature on the subject. Few scholars have taken a more wide-ranging interest in the question than Mokyr. He leaves no doubt about his view of the importance of the industrial revolution. 'Examining British economic history in the period 1760–1830 is a bit like studying the history of the Jewish dissenters between 50 BC and 50 AD. At first provincial, localised, even bizarre, it was destined to change the life of every man and woman in the West beyond recognition and to affect deeply the lives of others'.[49] And Mokyr is explicit that capitalism alone is no guarantee of change as fundamental as that which occurred in Britain in this period. 'Holland', he pointed out, 'was an urban, capitalist, bourgeois society, indicating that having the "right kind of society" is not a sufficient condition for a successful

[47] Ibid., p. 166. Further, 'Particularly significant to the developing of more efficient markets, however, is the better specification and enforcement of property rights over goods and services; and in many cases much more was involved than simply removing restrictions on the mobility of capital and labour – important as those changes were. Private and parliamentary enclosures in agriculture, the Statute of Monopolies establishing a patent law, and the immense development of a body of common law to better specify and enforce contracts are also part of the story.' Ibid., p. 167. Or again, 'an increase in the rate of technological progress will result from either an increase in the size of the market or an increase in the inventor's ability to capture a larger share of the benefits created by his invention.' Ibid., pp. 165–6.

[48] There is an enormous literature on this issue and a substantial remaining dispute about the weights to be attached to individual output series and the best methods of dealing with sectors of the economy, such as services, for which the direct empirical evidence is very limited. It is symptomatic of the scale of the revision which has taken place that Crafts, who has been a leading figure in urging the case for much more modest estimates of growth rates, concluded that in none of the four sub-periods into which he divided the period 1700–1830 did the rate of growth of national product per head exceed 0.5 per cent per annum and in one period (1760–80) he estimated that there was no increase at all in this figure, a very marked contrast with the earlier estimates of Deane and Cole. Crafts, *British economic growth*, tab. 2.11, p. 45. On the potential significance of the services sector in this context, see Jackson, 'Government expenditure'.

[49] Mokyr, 'Editor's introduction', p 131.

Industrial Revolution.'[50] Nor does he accept the kind of argument advanced by North, once again by drawing attention to the Dutch case.[51]

To dispose of one common source of misunderstanding about the industrial revolution, and to underline its transformative power, Mokyr undertook two simple modelling exercises. The first relates to the absence of a sharp acceleration in *aggregate* growth rates during the 'classic' period of the industrial revolution. If there is a small 'modern' sector of the economy with a very high growth rate and a much larger 'traditional' sector where the growth rate is low, it will take a long time for the former to contribute sufficiently to the overall growth rate to produce a marked general acceleration. For example, if, at a given date, the modern sector comprises 10 per cent of the whole and is growing at 4 per cent per annum, while the remainder, the traditional sector, is growing at 1 per cent per annum, the combined growth rate will be 1.3 per cent per annum. Assuming that both sectors continue to grow at the stated rates, it will take 74 years for the two sectors to become of equal size, at which point the overall growth rate will have increased to no more than 2.5 per cent per annum.[52] The second exercise was designed to establish what might have happened to living standards if growth had continued within the constraints obtaining before the cluster of technological changes which Mokyr regards as the key to explaining what happened. He addressed the question by means of a counterfactual exercise assuming that there were no technological advances, that labour and resources changed at their actual historical rates, and that productivity growth was constrained to zero. He then made three different assumptions about the rate of capital accumulation. The result on the most optimistic assumption was an estimated fall in real income per head of 6 per cent between 1760 and 1830. On the least optimistic assumption the fall was 19 per cent. Mokyr gives reasons to suppose that his calculations probably understate the fall which would have taken place in the absence of an industrial revolution.[53] Both these econometric exercises and the more conventional arguments which he also deployed, therefore, confirmed Mokyr in his view that something exceptional took place in late eighteenth-century England.

It is noteworthy that the Dutch experience should have attracted attention both in Adam Smith's time and still today. To Adam Smith the history of the Dutch Republic was his warrant for expecting growth rates generally to falter. To Mokyr it supplied good reasons to look for a feature peculiar to England to account for the industrial revolution. Recently

---

[50] Ibid., p. 39.
[51] Ibid., pp. 44–5.
[52] Ibid., p. 12.
[53] Ibid., pp. 119–20.

two distinguished economic historians have returned to the issue of the 'modernity' of the early modern Dutch economy and have delivered a clear verdict. Their work bears closely on the 'divergence of England' question, since de Vries and van der Woude are intent on demonstrating that in her 'golden age' Holland was subject to opportunities and constraints essentially similar to those which determine the behaviour of advanced economies in more recent centuries; that it was indeed, in their phrase, the 'first modern economy'.

Four main criteria were employed by de Vries and van der Woude in deciding whether or not a 'modern' economy existed. They were:

1. that markets both for commodities and for the three factors of production, land, labour, and capital, should be reasonably free and cover the bulk of productive activity.
2. that agricultural productivity should be sufficiently high to support a complex social and occupational structure, thus making possible an extensive division of labour.
3. that the state should be attentive to property rights and freedom of movement and contract, while not neglecting the material needs of the bulk of the population.
4. that a level of technology and organisation should exist capable of supporting a material culture of sufficient variety to sustain market-oriented consumer behaviour.[54]

The defining characteristics of what de Vries and van der Woude term a modern economy, therefore, are essentially those which might equally well be employed to define a capitalist economy, though they prefer to conduct their discussion in terms of modernity.[55] It is convenient briefly to summarise their key findings. Enumerating them will also underline the closeness of the parallels between the Dutch experience and events in England a century or so later.

That the economy of the Netherlands made extraordinary progress between the middle decades of the sixteenth century and $c.1680$ has never been in dispute. De Vries and van der Woude emphasise that, although the achievements of the Dutch Republic in commerce and industry have attracted more attention, agriculture was an equally dynamic sector of the economy. The physical output of Dutch agriculture was increasing on average by between 0.7 and 0.8 per cent per annum during the sixteenth and early seventeenth centuries.[56] Yields rose sharply, especially in the maritime zone where they were double the continental norm.[57] Output

---

[54] De Vries and van der Woude, *The first modern economy*, p. 693.
[55] I have discussed a very similar range of issues in Wrigley, 'The process of modernization'.
[56] De Vries and van der Woude, *The first modern economy*, p. 232.
[57] Ibid., p. 230.

per worker engaged in agriculture was far in excess of the European average and this was the basis for a beneficial relationship between the agricultural sector and the rest of the economy.[58] These developments were a prerequisite for the rapid urban growth which took place in the Republic and for the transformation of the occupational structure of the country which anticipated that found in England by 150 years.[59] They insist on the immense benefits conferred on the Dutch economy through the creation of an excellent transport infrastructure and the availability of an abundance of cheap energy, again pointing to two of the main stimuli to growth in England at a later date.[60] The role of cheap and abundant energy supply in the Dutch golden age is of particular interest.[61] It is noteworthy, however, that energy use in the Netherlands had already peaked before the end of the seventeenth century and thereafter declined irregularly down to the beginning of the nineteenth century.[62]

De Vries and van der Woude seek to demonstrate the modernity of the early modern Dutch economy, by showing that the same influences which shape the success or failure of a twentieth-century economy were dominant in the seventeenth-century Netherlands, and that the same modes of analysis which can throw light on these issues today are applicable to the Dutch economy three centuries ago. They insist that the period of stagnation which began before the end of the seventeenth century and lasted for a century-and-a-half must also be understood as modern in nature. 'To suggest that the Republic suffered a "modern decline"', they

---

[58] They refer to 'the integral part it played through interaction with   commercial and industrial activity in creating the dynamic qualities of the seventeenth-century economy'. Ibid., p. 195.

[59] The percentages in agriculture, industry, and other forms of employment in the Netherlands in the eighteenth century are given by de Vries and van der Woude as 41, 32, and 27 which may   be compared with figures of 36, 30, and 34 for England for the same categories in 1801. Ibid., tab. 11.5, p. 528. Since if anything agriculture increased in relative importance in the Netherlands in the   eighteenth century, it is probable that if comparable data existed for the mid-seventeenth   century, they would show a lower percentage in agriculture and higher percentages in the other two   categories.

[60] Ibid., p. 338.

[61] De Vries and van der Woude note that in the seventeenth century many of the   export-orientated industries, including bricks, tiles and ceramics, pipes, beer, spirits, sugar, salt, soap, whale oil, and glass 'shared a pronounced energy intensity, which suggest their common debt to the Republic's uniquely low-cost energy supplies. It appears that energy use in the Republic, both household and industrial, stood far above the levels common to the rest of Europe until the end of the eighteenth century.' Ibid., pp. 338–9. They remark that the foundation of the Republic's 'technological superiority was its effective utilisation of energy supplies (peat, wind, and water), which took expression in the development of specific applications of the available energy sources to the needs of the economy', and note that 'The Republic's peat deposits provided a uniquely large supply of heat energy – in excess even of England's coal output until well in to the eighteenth century'. Ibid., pp. 344, 694. See also de Zeeuw, 'Peat and the Dutch Golden Age'.

[62] De Vries and van der Woude, *The first modern economy*, p. 710.

write, 'must seem perverse, but this is our argument. The economy did not suffer a Malthusian crisis, nor did it revert to some pre-industrial norm after a brief, "accidental" boom. In sector after sector . . . the economy struggled with the modern problems of profit, employment, market access, and costs.'[63] They then go on to make explicit the conclusions implicit in their earlier analysis: 'This formulation harbors an implicit claim about modern economic growth. It is not self-sustained, exponential, and unbounded.'[64] The view that an economy having the hallmarks of modern capitalism is not *ipso facto* assured of exponential growth is persuasive, both in the form to be found in Adam Smith and in its most recent guise, as expounded by de Vries and van der Woude. Accepting it implies that because English growth continued unchecked, explaining her success entails directing attention to some features of English experience not represented in the history of the Dutch Republic. This issue is the focus of the balance of this article.

Why England diverged and what brought her relative success to an end

I start with a platitude. The answer to any question is heavily conditioned by the way in which it is posed. I propose to discuss the divergence of England by treating the secular trend in output per head as the most important single measure of economic growth, a trend which is likely to be roughly paralleled by that in real income per head. If this definition is adopted, there is a clear and vitally important distinction between the period since the industrial revolution and any earlier period in capitalist societies. Even though the early decades of the industrial revolution brought terrible hardship and uncertainty for many people, thereafter, and as a result of its occurrence, a larger and larger fraction of the population of the world has enjoyed a degree of freedom from material deprivation, from malnourishment, and from disease which has no earlier precedent. Pre-industrial capitalism, for reasons which have never been more clearly expressed than in the *Wealth of nations*, was capable of leading to a more effective deployment of capital and labour than alternative systems, and, since it facilitated the division of labour, it could give rise to substantial improvements in output per man hour. Yet, again for reasons which were spelled out by Adam Smith, this did not imply that progress in this regard would be prolonged, or universal. Rather, with the exhaustion of opportunities for the profitable employment of capital, it was likely that

[63] Ibid., p. 711.
[64] Ibid., p. 720.

the stationary state would supervene and that 'corn wages', that is the purchasing power of the average worker, would be driven down to a low level. This is a realistic assessment of the possibilities open to an organic economy, but not to an economy which has ceased to be organic.

It was in early modern England that a new base for economic activity began to appear for the first time on a substantial scale, but initially it emerged so inconspicuously that the classical economists mistook England still for what all societies had previously been, a country constrained by the limitations from which an organic economy cannot free itself. The key to initial success lay in the achievements of the agricultural sector, a development in accord with Adam Smith's growth model.[65] English agriculture succeeded not only in raising food output to keep pace with population increase at rates much higher than those found on the continent; output of animal and vegetable raw materials to sustain a rapid growth of industry; and output of energy in the form of fodder for a rising population of draught animals to bolster both agriculture and transport, but achieved this with little or no increase in the agricultural labour force. Thus for several centuries there was a benign conjunction of rising aggregate output and rising output per head in agriculture which both permitted and fostered a great expansion in the demand for the products of secondary industry and for the services supplied by the tertiary sector, paralleled by major changes in the occupational structure of the labour force. The same developments also underpinned a notable surge in urban growth.

These changes would have sufficed to bring about a major reordering of England's rank within the nations of Europe, economically, politically, and militarily, as indeed they had already done in the case of the Dutch Republic. They would not, however, have sufficed on their own to engender an industrial revolution. England was not simply successful in making the most of the possibilities of an organic economy; the first beginnings of a more radical change were in train. No matter how assiduously Icarus may strive, human flight is not possible if the energy employed in the attempt is derived from human muscle. Yet what will always elude the flapping of artificial wings is feasible with the assistance of mechanical power. An organic economy suffers from certain necessary limitations

---

[65] He wrote: 'The capital employed in agriculture, therefore, not only puts into motion a greater quantity of productive labour than any equal capital employed in manufactures, but in proportion too to the quantity of productive labour which it employs, it adds a much greater value to the annual produce of the land and labour of the country, to the real wealth and revenue of its inhabitants. Of all the ways in which a capital can be employed, it is by far the most advantageous to the society.' A. Smith, *Wealth of nations*, I, p. 385.

which are, as Ricardo asserted, ultimately related to physical and more especially biological constraints. An economy which is increasingly based on inorganic raw materials is not so constrained. Its advantages spring partly from the fact that harnessing the stored energy of innumerable past millennia of insolation in the form of coal, oil, and natural gas places at the disposal of mankind vastly greater quantities of energy than can be secured when the annual quantum of energy is limited by the process of photosynthesis. But the change also confers the further advantage that the rising input of raw materials into the production process, which in an organic economy always creates competition for the use of land, can be achieved from the mouth of a mine rather than from a cultivated field.

Between Elizabethan and Victorian times England moved gradually from dependence upon a purely organic base to a mixed economy in which a steadily increasing fraction of the output of secondary industry was based on minerals. In so doing she also eased herself clear of the problems which would otherwise have led to growing difficulties. The fact that in 1800 British coal output was providing as much energy as would otherwise have required the devotion of perhaps 15 million acres to the production of wood for fuel on a sustained yield basis is a telling instance of the scale of the changes which had been taking place.[66] When Arthur Young travelled the length and breadth of France in the years 1787, 1788, and 1789 he frequently remarked upon the absence of glazing from the windows even of houses which were otherwise well-built. This was something which was, as he put it, an 'extraordinary spectacle for English eyes' at the time.[67] The fact that sheet glass had become a commonplace in England reflected the availability of cheap thermal energy. Brick became the normal building material for the same reason. Similarly, once a means had been found to use the thermal energy of coal to smelt iron ore without introducing unwanted impurities in the process, the output of iron could reach a multiple of what had previously been possible, given the extravagant amount of heat needed to produce iron or steel and the limited area of forest available as a source of charcoal.

---

[66] Wrigley, *Continuity, chance and change*, pp. 54–5.
[67] 'Pass an extraordinary spectacle for English eyes, of many houses too good to be called cottages, without any glass windows.' Young, *Travels in France and Italy*, p. 22. He was referring to houses encountered en route between Limoges and Brive. He made similar remarks about cottages near Pont-de-Rodez in the Dordogne and about 'a large village of well-built houses, without a single glass window' near St Gaudens (ibid., pp. 25, 30). Brittany provoked a rash of comparable comments when he passed through Combourg, Guingamp, and Auray (ibid., pp. 101, 103, 105); and again at Aix-en-Provence (ibid., p. 208) and at Cuges-les-Pins near Toulon (ibid., p. 213). In the last he complained that there was no glass in the windows of his room in the *auberge* even though he had one of the best rooms.

A tree may store the energy acquired from the sun by photosynthesis for a century. A coal mine can tap the stored energy of the sun accumulated in forests over millions of years. Further illustrations of the same point abound. The history of the advent of the steam engine, the blast furnace, the railway, the steamship, and of power-driven machinery of all types, for example, has been told many times and from many viewpoints. In the context of this essay the significance of these developments can be simply expressed. The move away from an exclusively organic economy was a *sine qua non* of achieving a capacity for exponential growth. As a result of the advent of energy-intensive and mineral-based sectors in the economy, poverty became problematic for the first time in human history, problematic because the *capacity* to satisfy human material needs was transformed, leaving uncertain only the question of whether the will and the institutional structure existed to banish it. These changes were largely an English phenomenon in their early stages, and the same changes which were transforming her productive potential were also reinforcing the divergence of England from other countries.

The gradual emergence of a new kind of economy in England during the period between the late sixteenth and the mid-nineteenth century raises many questions which remain controversial. Why, for example, should access to coal as a source of energy have led to the progressive transformation of so many sectors of industrial production in England but not in China where coal usage was common in certain areas as early as the fourth century and may have reached a peak about the eleventh century?[68] But for present purposes the significance of these developments lies in the additional impetus which they gave to the divergence of England and the part which they played in ensuring that the growth process did not lose momentum in England as it had done in Holland. It is idle to speculate about what might have been the course of events if, for example, there had not happened to be abundant coal close to the surface in England, but it would be rash to assume that in its absence an alternative base would have been found to sustain the momentum of growth. Seventeenth-century Holland was a highly successful capitalist economy, enjoying rapid growth. But the Dutch economy lost its earlier momentum in the eighteenth century. For well over a century it trod water. It did not fulfil the worst fears expressed by Adam Smith. But on the other hand, when growth resumed it was not generated by a renewed domestic dynamism but rather as part of the process by which the whole of western Europe began to conform to the new path of economic growth first traced out by England. Indeed de Vries and van der Woude regard earlier

---

[68] Golas, *Mining*, pp. 186–201, esp. 195–6.

success as having been an obstacle to the adoption of new production technology, arguing that the 'nineteenth-century industrial development of the Netherlands was not held back by its backwardness but rather by its very modernity'.[69]

There is an instructive irony about the industrial revolution in England. The great bulk of the advance made relative to continental countries before 1800 was due to much the same causes as had earlier allowed a much smaller country to achieve a brilliant period of commercial and economic dominance and a notable degree of naval and military success. It sprang from expertise in making the most of the possibilities of an advanced organic economy. In this period, the sources of increased economic efficiency were in the main institutional rather than technological, and institutional structures are often difficult to transfer to different political and social environments. Other countries both admired and feared the growth of English power, as they had earlier admired and feared Dutch success, without finding it easy to emulate. But when the sources from which growth derived themselves changed; when the new mineral-based and energy-intensive sector of the economy became the driving force of the economy as a whole; when the attention of the world was drawn to the steam engine, the puddling furnace, the railway, gas lighting, the mule, and the power loom; when, in other words, the sources of growth were technological rather than institutional, other countries found it far less difficult to recover lost ground. England's continental neighbours soon narrowed the gap between themselves and their island rival. Before the end of the nineteenth century, it was England which was observing German industrial, technological, and educational excellence with increasing concern, rather than the reverse. The same developments which had allowed England to escape the constraints of an organic economy also made it comparatively easy for others to match and later to surpass her achievements. As a result, the divergence of England rapidly came to an end.

---

[69] De Vries and van der Woude, *The first modern economy*, p. 713. They note that the country possessed a large stock of capital but that this was invested in obsolete plant, equipment, and skills. Ibid., p. 712.

3   Two kinds of capitalism, two kinds of growth

In his *An inquiry into the nature and causes of the wealth of nations* Adam Smith set out an analytic scheme which has proved immensely influential in deciding the framework within which later generations have discussed economic growth, and in associating capitalism with that growth. At the beginning of the first chapter of the book Adam Smith told the parable of the pinmakers. It was intended to drive home the huge scale of the gain in output per man that could be attained by a suitable division of labour. Having described the way in which pin manufacture could be broken down in eighteen distinct operations, and having referred to his visit to a small manufactory employing ten men capable of producing a total of 48,000 pins or more each day, he concluded:

> But if they had all wrought separately and independently, and without any of them having been educated to this peculiar business, they certainly could not each of them have made twenty, perhaps not one pin in a day; that is, certainly not the two hundred and fortieth, perhaps not the four thousand eight hundredth part of what they are at present capable of performing, in consequence of a proper division and combination of their different operations.[1]

Adam Smith went on to make it clear that what held true for pin manufacture also applied to 'every other art and manufacture', though he was careful to stress that it applied only to a much lesser degree in agriculture where 'the ploughman, the harrower, the sower of seed, and the reaper of the corn' were perforce one and the same and there was therefore less opportunity to specialise.[2]

The increase in capital and the division of labour

Division of labour was thus the key to enhanced output per head but it implied that 'the produce of a man's own labour [could] supply but a

[1] A. Smith, *Wealth of nations*, I, p. 9.
[2] Ibid., I., pp. 9–10.

very small part of his occasional wants'.[3] This in turn meant that every man must depend upon the produce of many others, each a specialist like himself. He must be able to purchase both the raw materials for his work and many of the necessities of life from others. 'But this purchase cannot be made till such time as the produce of his own labour has not only been completed, but sold. A stock of goods of different kinds, therefore, must be stored up somewhere sufficient to maintain him, and to supply him with the materials and tools of his work, till such time, at least, as both these events can be brought about.'[4] Hence the intimate connection between the accumulation of capital and the division of labour. 'As the accumulation of stock must, in the nature of things, be previous to the division of labour, so labour can be more and more subdivided in proportion only as stock is previously more and more accumulated';[5] or again, 'The quantity of industry, therefore, not only increases in every country with the increase of the stock which employs it, but, in consequence of that increase, the same quantity of industry produces a much greater quantity of work.'[6]

Adam Smith's assertion of a close link between the deployment of capital and rising productivity has remained a commonplace of economics. The association between the two phenomena is also reflected in discussions of capitalism as an economic system. It is possible to view the concentration of larger and larger accumulations of capital in a limited number of hands either as a benign development tending to improve the lot of all members of society, or as repugnant in that it enriches a minority at the expense of the rest of the community. But both advocates and enemies of the capitalist system are apt to see it as possessing previously unparalleled, almost demonic powers of galvanising an economy into the path of growth. In Smithian terms this is true almost by definition since the rapid accumulation of capital is synonymous with the transformation of the scale of total output and of the level of output per worker.

The classical economists on the prospects for real wages

Even before telling the parable of the pinmakers, in the second paragraph of the introduction to the *Wealth of nations*, Adam Smith offered a definition of the economic health of a nation broadly similar to the modern concept of real income per head. 'According therefore, as this produce [the annual output of the country], or what is purchased with

[3] Ibid., I, p. 291.
[4] Ibid., I, p. 291.
[5] Ibid., I, pp. 291–2.
[6] Ibid., I, p. 292.

it, bears a greater or smaller proportion to the number of those who are
to consume it, the nation will be better or worse supplied with all the
necessaries and conveniencies for which it has occasion.'[7] It is curious,
therefore, that having drawn attention to the significance of the ratio between production and population, and having exemplified the enormous
percentage increase in output per head that could be secured by the division of labour made possible by the accumulation of capital, he should,
none the less, have taken such a pessimistic view of the prospects for the
mass of the labouring poor.

Smith considered that what he termed 'the real recompense of labour'
had improved substantially in the course of the eighteenth century, and
he was an advocate of high wages both because well-fed workmen are
capable of heavier labour than those who are half-starved, and because
high wages are an inducement to diligent work.[8] But his view of the
prospects for growth in general led him to discount the possibility of a
prolonged or substantial improvement in real wages, and to fear that the
last state of the labourer would prove to be worse than the first, a view
that was reinforced by his anticipation of some of the arguments to which
Malthus was later to give the classic formulation.

Smith drew a distinction between the scale of a country's wealth and
its rate of change. However great national wealth might be, if it were not
increasing, the condition of the labourer was likely to be moderate at best:

It deserves to be remarked, perhaps, that it is in the progressive state, while the
society is advancing to the further acquisition, rather than when it has acquired
its full complement of riches, that the condition of the labouring poor, of the
great body of the people, seems to be the happiest and the most comfortable. It
is hard in the stationary, and miserable in the declining state.[9]

He was led to this conclusion by the conviction that the poor were very
prolific and that their numbers were restrained only by misery and its
accompanying afflictions. 'Every species of animals naturally multiplies in
proportion to their means of subsistence, and no species can ever multiply
beyond it', he wrote: in this respect mankind was an animal species like
any other. Thus, 'the demand for men, like that for any other commodity,
necessarily regulates the production of men; quickens it when it goes on
too slowly, and stops it when it advances too fast'.[10] Hence scope for
increasing wages existed only when the stock of capital was rising so
rapidly that demand for labour outstripped supply.

---

[7] Ibid., I, p. 1.
[8] Ibid., I, pp. 87, 91.
[9] Ibid., I, pp. 90–1.
[10] Ibid., I, p. 89.

Holding these views Adam Smith might still have taken a sanguine view of the prospects for real wages, were it not also his view that the characteristic trajectory of national economic growth tended to be asymptotic rather than exponential. He held that the scope for profitable investment was limited. Taking the rate of interest at which money could be borrowed as a proxy for the rate of return on investment,[11] he noted that in the most advanced country in Europe, Holland, the rate of interest was lower than anywhere else, and supposed England to be approaching a similar state, whereas the higher rates prevailing in Scotland and France were evidence of the greater profits to be made in these countries, of their greater development potential.[12] The progressive tendency for the rate of return on capital to fall signified the steady exhaustion of the finite opportunities for investment that would yield an attractive return. Brief periods of improved real wages came to an end as investment slowed down for lack of an adequate stimulus.

In a country which has acquired that full complement of riches which the nature of its soil and climate, and its situation with respect to other countries, allowed it to acquire; which could, therefore, advance no further, and which was not going backwards, both the wages of labour and the profits of stock would probably be very low.[13]

The two greatest of Adam Smith's successors among the classical economists, Malthus and Ricardo, developed arguments that served to reinforce the pessimism that Smith displayed about the secular prospects for real wages. Malthus examined the implications of his two 'postulata' about 'the passion between the sexes' and the necessity for food to sustain life. In essence his argument was that since improved wages tended both to encourage earlier marriage, and thus to raise fertility, and simultaneously to reduce mortality, prosperity raised population growth rates. Economic growth was matched *pari passu* by demographic growth. Only, therefore, if economic growth in general and the expansion of food production in particular could be raised to a rate that exceeded the maximum rate of population growth that could reasonably be expected, would real wages show a rising trend. Malthus himself did not express his conclusion in this form, but it is implicit in his argument. He had no doubt, as he showed by his well-known contrast of geometric and arithmetic growth rates (for population and food production respectively), that rates of economic growth would tend to decline.

[11] Ibid., I, p. 99.
[12] Ibid., I, pp. 101–3.
[13] Ibid., I, p. 106.

Malthus, and more particularly Ricardo, later found an argument that appeared to clinch the matter, the concept of declining marginal returns on the land. The two men formulated broadly similar expressions of the concept at much the same time, though it was Ricardo's exposition that came to be regarded as the *locus classicus* of the idea.[14] If all, or almost all, forms of material production require the combination of three basic factors of production, land, labour, and capital, and if one of the three, land, is in fixed supply, it must be the case that at some point, as agricultural production expands, larger and larger inputs of capital and labour will be needed in order to secure a unit increase in output both at the intensive and at the extensive margins of production. Improvements in agricultural techniques might postpone the evil day, but it was idle to hope for more than a temporary reprieve. Ricardo's conclusion was unequivocal:

Whilst the land yields abundantly, wages may temporarily rise, and the producers may consume more than their accustomed proportion; but the stimulus which will thus be given to population, will speedily reduce the labourers to their usual consumption. But when poor lands are taken into cultivation, or when more capital and labour are expended on the old land, with a less return of produce, the effect must be permanent. A greater proportion of that part of the produce which remains to be divided, after paying rent, between the owners of stock and the labourers, will be apportioned to the latter. Each man may, and probably will, have a less absolute quantity; but as more labourers are employed in proportion to the whole produce retained by the farmer, the value of a greater proportion of the whole produce will be absorbed by wages, and consequently the value of a smaller proportion will be devoted to profits. This will necessarily be rendered permanent by the laws of nature, which have limited the productive powers of the land.[15]

The prospects for the mass of mankind were bleak.

It is instructive that the classical economists, who between them constructed such valuable tools for the analysis of economic growth; who threw so much light on the ways in which legal systems, institutional forms, and political and social organisation could foster or hinder development; and who were such persuasive advocates of the market as the regulator of economic activity and of capitalism as an economic system, should have been so keenly alive to the improbability that the mass of the population would benefit from following their precepts, at least in the way and to the degree that has in practice occurred. They did not, of course, suppose that competition in the labour market would drive down wages to the level of bare subsistence. Each expounded the importance of the distinction between a conventional minimum standard of living and

[14] Malthus, *Inquiry into the nature and progress of rent*; Ricardo, *Principles of political economy.*
[15] Ibid., pp. 125–6.

a physiological minimum,[16] and would have assented to the proposition that for the labouring poor living standards in 1800 were better than they had been in 1500. But, looking to the future, they saw no likelihood of significant further advance and some danger of regression.

Yet later generations have often seen a substantial and sustained rise in real income as the key distinguishing characteristic of the industrial revolution, at least after its early decades. They have placed those early decades in the period spanning the years between the publication of the *Wealth of nations* in 1776 and the appearance of the second edition of Malthus's *Principles of political economy* shortly after his death in 1834. Here then is an intriguing paradox. The capitalism described by the classical economists was not expected by them to produce the changes now termed the industrial revolution. Indeed they unanimously and explicitly denied the possibility of the change now regarded as its most important single feature, and perhaps as its great redeeming feature – the substantial and largely continuous rise in the standard of living that it has occasioned. The contrast between expectation and event is instructive. If the classical economists were correct, there is a close connection between the advent of capitalism as an economic system and an increase in productive efficiency, but no necessary link between its advent and a rise in the standard of living of the bulk of the population. Or, to put the same point in a different way, Adam Smith and his successors envisaged a substantial rise in the wealth of nations in the sense of large increases in aggregate output, but they expected them to be broadly matched by increases in population, leaving the ratio between the two little changed. Production might rise but population would keep pace: only in the periods when the rate of growth in production was at its height might there be a temporary, golden interlude when demand for labour outstripped supply and wages rose in consequence.[17]

The constraints on growth in an organically based economy

To convince oneself that the views of the classical economists were not unreasonable in the circumstances of the day, it is important to consider

---

[16] Adam Smith's account of the standard of living of the Canton boat people illustrates vividly his consciousness of this point. 'The subsistence they find is so scanty that they are eager to fish up the nastiest garbage thrown overboard from any European ship. Any carrion, the carcase of a dead dog or cat, for example, though half putrid and stinking, is as welcome as the most wholesome food to the people of other countries'. A. Smith, *Wealth of nations*, I, p. 81. Malthus and Ricardo were equally clear on this point.

[17] Of the three great classical economists, contrary to the prevailing view, Malthus was the least pessimistic about the secular prospects for real wages: see ch. 8.

the constraints upon growth that existed in the world with which they were familiar and that seemed to be permanent and ineradicable. Two in particular deserve to be emphasised. In all economies before the nineteenth century the land was not merely the source of almost all food, it was also the source of almost all raw materials needed to supply other human wants. Fuel, shelter, and clothing, no less than food were provided from the products of the land. A rise in population increased pressure on the land not only by causing a rise in the demand for food, but also by boosting the demand for a wide range of other material goods produced from animal or vegetable raw materials. A prosperous cloth industry, by raising the demand for wool, made it necessary to find grazing for more sheep, and land used for wool could not simultaneously grow wheat. A flourishing iron industry was as likely to fail for lack of coppice woodland as from the exhaustion of local ores. In general wool, flax, leather, hops, barley, reeds, straw, fur, bone, horn, and above all wood supplied the raw materials for those engaged in manufacture – the weavers, spinners, tailors, shoemakers, coopers, carpenters, hatters, brewers, thatchers, bakers, and butchers who comprised the bulk of the industrial labour force; but even brickmakers, smiths, potters, and glassmakers, most of whose raw materials were mineral, were dependent upon a source of heat to enable production to take place, and turned to wood to provide it. The productivity of the soil set limits to every form of economic activity. Well might Adam Smith assert that:

The capital employed in agriculture, therefore, not only puts into motion a greater quantity of productive labour than any equal capital employed in manufactures, but in proportion too to the quantity of productive labour which it employs, it adds a much greater value to the annual produce of the land and labour of the country, to the real wealth and revenue of its inhabitants. Of all the ways in which a capital can be employed, it is by far the most advantageous to the society.[18]

The second, powerful constraint upon growth in general, and growth in productivity per head in particular, had always been the very limited scale of energy availability. In all forms of material production energy had to be expended, whether in the form of heat when boiling dye in a vat, smelting ore, or baking bread; or in the form of mechanical energy when cutting, pulling, pressing, lifting, turning, beating, stamping, and so on. And after the primary production process was complete, further energy was needed to transport the product to market. Two examples may serve to illustrate the nature of the problem. Von Thünen, the father of locational economics, who had an extensive practical experience of the operations

---

[18] A. Smith, *Wealth of nations*, I, p. 385.

of a large estate in the early nineteenth century, noted that a four-horse team, making a round trip of 46 miles (that is, 23 in each direction) could haul 2,400 Hamburg lb. of grain to market in Rostock from his estate at Tellow, but the team needed 300 lb. of grain as fodder to do it.[19] A similar problem arose with the marketing of animals for slaughter. A Norfolk farmer told James Caird that the advent of the railway saved him £600 a year because he no longer had to drive his fatstock to London. The journey had taken a fortnight and reduced the weight of a bullock by 28 lb. and of a sheep by 7 lb.[20]

Before the industrial revolution, heat energy came principally from burning wood and mechanical energy was chiefly muscular, whether supplied by men or by animals. As a result, in many fields of productive endeavour there was a relatively low upper limit to the level of productivity that could be achieved. The stoutest woodman makes slow work of felling a tree with an axe. A man with a horse and cart can move goods much more readily than with a wheelbarrow since a horse has ten times his strength, but, even on a well-made road, the number of ton-miles he and his team can perform in a day's work is small and cannot readily be increased in the energy circumstances of a traditional economy.

Both the two proximate constraints just described are in turn a function of a more general feature of all economies before the industrial revolution. To be dependent upon organic products, a dependency reflected both in the problems of expanding the supply of food and raw materials and in the meagre quantities of energy that could be harnessed, ultimately meant that all economic activity had to be geared to the annual inflow of energy from the sun. All animal and vegetable production depended upon the scale of the process of photosynthesis which harnessed insolation to the constitution of vegetable matter, and so established the base of the pyramid of life whose upper levels were linked by the food chain to its photosynthetic foundation. The total annual inflow of energy from the sun is gigantic. Even the surface of a small island like Britain receives an energy input equivalent to about 20,000 million tons of coal each year. But photosynthesis can capture only a very small fraction of the total inflow, in round terms between one tenth and two tenths of 1 per cent. In the case of Britain, therefore, only about 20–40 million tons of coal equivalent could be harnessed annually to meet the needs of an organically based economy.[21] Although they did not couch their discussion of

---

[19] Von Thünen, *The isolated state*, p. 13.
[20] Chambers, *The workshop of the world*, p. 54.
[21] White and Plaskett, *Biomass as fuel*, pp. 2, 12; Pimentel, 'Energy flow', p. 2. The capacity of different plant species to capture the sun's energy varies substantially so that this calculation is inevitably illustrative rather than precise.

the limits to growth in these terms, the classical economists recognised the reality and severity of the constraints inherent in all organic economies. Food, the raw materials of industry, and the bulk of all forms of useful energy were drawn from the same source – the annual yield of the soil brought into being by the annual quantum of incident sunlight.

Before the industrial revolution, therefore, advance in material culture had consisted in successive technological changes whose effect was to enable an increasing fraction of the annual product of the soil to be put to human use. Thus, controlling fire made available the heat energy of wood; cultivating particular plants ensured that the products of photo-synthesis were increasingly those vegetable species of greatest value for food, clothing, shelter, or fuel; domesticating animals both reduced the effort needed to obtain a pound of meat (though at the cost of the loss of the excitement and ritual of the hunt) and greatly increased the me-chanical energy available for agricultural and industrial operations since oxen and horses possess far greater muscular power than men. But these triumphs all consisted of a more effective exploitation of an unvarying *flow* of energy arriving annually at the earth's surface. There was little or no element of *stock* in the process overall.

It is true that the standing timber of a virgin forest area may repre-sent the stock of, say, a century of growth, with corresponding benefits to the first settlers in a heavily wooded area; and some large animals are fairly long-lived, and therefore represent a living store of the product of several years' grazing. But in general the annual quantum of vegetable growth set a limit both to the material production and to the energy bud-get of any pre-industrial society. Such societies were therefore much at risk to any variations in that annual quantum, and the fortunes of the har-vest were the fortunes of the whole economy.[22] Ingenuity and investment might alleviate the problem. Both what might be termed chronological risk-spreading through the storage of the less perishable crops such as grain, and geographical risk-spreading through the concatenation of local economies with varying harvest fortunes by trading networks, could sub-stantially reduce the exposure of a community to the vagaries of harvest. But the difficulties inherent in an organically based economy appeared ineluctable, and coloured the views of governments, casual commenta-tors, and even the most penetrating of observers, such as the classical economists.

---

[22] The conviction that this was the case was still prevalent during the 'classic' period of the industrial revolution. This attitude is strongly reflected, for example, in the writings of one of the most influential contemporary commentators on the economic fluctuations of the period. Tooke, *History of prices*.

The situation changed fundamentally, however, with the advent of a major stock element in what had previously been a flow-dominated economic scene. I shall use the term 'capitalism' to denote this new and profoundly influential feature of the economic landscape, even though it is at odds with the normal usage of the word, both because it captures an important aspect of its nature and to suggest by implication its central role in transforming economic life. It was this second kind of capitalism, what may be termed resource capitalism, that made possible the growth that has occurred over the past two centuries, and that enabled the gloomy prognostications of the classical economists about the trend of real wages to be falsified by events.

The significance of the new developments is perhaps most easily gauged by reverting to the two major constraints upon growth in any organically based economy, but in reverse order, taking energy first.

The mineral-based energy economy: resource capitalism

All organic economies were severely constrained by the limited availability of energy. If four hectares of forest were needed to produce a ton of iron,[23] horseshoes and ploughshares might figure among productive equipment in use, but not, say, iron vessels displacing thousands of tons, let alone railway track systems involving the laying of millions of tons of steel. The large-scale production of bricks, glass, salt, and beer all involved the use of much heat and were subject to severe restrictions of scale if producers were dependent upon wood as a source of heat. The supply of mechanical energy posed equally pressing difficulties. Many production processes can be carried out only if mechanical energy is applied on a large scale. Since the sod is heavy and refractory, for example, the land cannot be cultivated without much effort. A farmer with a hoe will necessarily be unable, therefore, to achieve a high level of output per head. A farmer with a horse and plough can do much better, but the 'fuel' needs of a horse mean that about five acres of land must be devoted to the maintenance of each horse.[24] Simple arithmetic quickly shows the limitations that this implies for the use of animal power in agriculture, industry, and transport. Water and wind power offered relief for certain types of industry but once again the total power available was limited, often inconveniently sited, sometimes intermittently available, and subject to the disadvantage that the best sites were used first so that additions to the power supply involved higher unit costs.

---

[23] Benaerts, *La grande industrie allemande*, p. 454.
[24] McCulloch, *Statistical account*, I, pp. 489–90.

If the *flow* of energy available was inconveniently slight, however, huge capital *stocks* could be tapped in favourable circumstances. In the carboniferous period of geological history the timber yield of countless millennia was preserved and ultimately became fossilised in the coal seams that date from that period. The heat energy thus locked away accumulated on such a vast scale that countries well-endowed with coal, and possessing the mining skill to extract it, could dispose of energy in quantities to dwarf the total that could be secured by traditional methods from the annual inflow of energy from the sun. Already by about 1810 the annual output of coal in Britain, at about 20 million tons, was roughly equivalent to the quantity of energy theoretically available for capture from the sun's rays by photosynthesis each year.[25]

The immense benefits enjoyed by an economy that could turn capitalist in this second sense are indisputable. This was sure to be true even if the new source of energy were used only to supply heat. There were many industries whose production horizons were transformed by gaining freedom from dependence upon wood as a source of heat energy. But the transformation of the economy as a whole would have been incomplete unless the supply of mechanical energy had undergone a comparable revolution. Hence the importance of the Newcomen engine and later the Watt engine since these were devices that converted heat into mechanical energy, though initially in a very wasteful fashion. The steam engine relieved society from the biblical curse that a man could eat only by the sweat of his brow. As long as human muscle was the predominant source of mechanical energy the assertion was virtually a truism, but steam power proved adaptable to almost every application previously performed by the hand or foot. And the new source of mechanical energy made any earlier source seem puny by comparison. Increasingly, labour meant not so much the provision of energy as its oversight. Freed from the necessity of supplying the primary power himself a weaver could tend half a dozen looms each operating at a higher speed than the single loom at which he had once sat.

The capitalism that Adam Smith described identified the division of labour as the proximate agent of increased productivity per head. Its capital was the embodied labour of earlier periods visible in the stocks needed to set men on work and to bridge the interval in time between initial production and ultimate sale. This capital was accumulated by the hand of man. The hand of nature over a very different time scale had also accumulated capital, and in massive quantities, and this capital, too, could be used to enhance productivity. Levasseur once used the analogy of the

[25] Flinn, *British coal industry*, tab. 1.2, p. 26.

employment of slaves to suggest the way in which the economy benefited from the use of steam engines. Writing in the 1880s, and reviewing the changes that had taken place over the previous forty years, Levasseur remarked that in 1840 French industry had at its disposal the equivalent of the labour of 1 million men in this new form, 'true slaves, the most sober, docile and tireless that could be imagined'. By the mid-1880s their number had risen to 98 millions, 'deux esclaves et demi par habitant de France'.[26] There was no definable limit to the possible increase in average mechanical energy employed per worker, and in consequence no ceiling to the rise in productivity per head that could be secured. In the absence of such expansible energy supplies, however, there were often severe limits to productivity gains because energy needs for productive purposes were so often inflexible for physical reasons.

The rise in importance of capitalism of the second type implied great danger no less than great opportunity. The traditional sources of heat energy and mechanical energy were modest in scale but indefinitely available; the flow continued year after year. The switch to dependence on energy capital allowed production to be expanded enormously, but this capital, unlike the man-made variety, could not be replaced. Every ton of coal dug was a ton less left for future needs. It has been a singular blessing to the process of economic growth over the last two centuries that reserves of fossil fuels have proved sufficiently large to sustain the huge growth in energy consumption that has taken place. To appreciate the significance of England's good fortune in this respect, one has only to turn to the example of Holland in the seventeenth and eighteenth centuries. The striking success of the Dutch economy in the seventeenth century appears also to have been due to a substantial extent to cheap heat energy in the form of a capital stock. But the stock in question was peat and the ratio of annual consumption to total accessible reserves was such that severe problems emerged within about a century and a half of the start of heavy usage.[27]

The second major constraint upon growth in an organically based economy yielded to changes logically similar to those just described. Dependence on animal and vegetable raw materials implied a pressing danger of rising marginal costs of supply because the area of fertile land was virtually fixed. But if mineral raw materials could be substituted for organic raw materials, and on the assumption that the capital stock of the minerals in question was adequately large, an immense growth in output could

---

[26] Levasseur, *La population française*, III, p. 74.
[27] De Zeeuw, 'Peat and the Dutch Golden Age'; Unger, 'Energy sources'; Wrigley, *Continuity, chance and change*, ch. 2.

occur without provoking the problems that had accompanied growth in the past.

Most of the major industries that have developed during and after the industrial revolution, with the notable exception of the food industry and the textile industry, are mineral-based. The metal industries; chemicals; pottery, ceramics, glass, and bricks; plastics; the building industry; even, in recent decades, some parts of the textile industry, have all come to depend largely or exclusively upon mineral raw materials. Today the large items among durable consumption goods – cars, television sets, freezers, microwave ovens – are mineral in their constitution. The change began modestly – pottery for wooden platters, iron girders for timber beams, iron wagons for wooden carts, tiles for thatch, and so on – but each such change cleared the way in a new sector of production for a growth that would no longer add to the strain upon a resource in fixed supply: or to express the change in different terms, it meant that expansion no longer entailed a call upon a flow whose scale could be enlarged only with much difficulty, but was accommodated instead by increasing calls upon a capital stock that was often large enough to pose no problems even when demand grew to unprecedented levels.[28] Sometimes the story of Dutch peat was repeated, as with South American guano, but, even when this occurred, abundant energy combined with increasing chemical and physical knowledge often enabled a substitute to be found. Abundant energy proved to be rather like the alchemist's stone in making it feasible to transmute unpromising substances into forms that met the needs of society.

The new mineral-based, energy-rich economy not only meant avoiding dependence on the land but also the overcoming of the traditional constraints on agricultural output. Previously farms had been ecologically self-sufficient units. In energy terms they were large net exporters, producing in the form of food and fodder many times the quantity of energy used in the agricultural production process. In time farms came to be very large net importers of energy, using several times as much energy in the form of oil for tractors, fertilisers, herbicides, and so on, as was represented in the output of the farm.[29] But this reversal of energy ratios, which would have spelt imminent disaster in the past, could be sustained because of the huge stocks of energy capital available. The scale of agricultural output was in consequence transformed; farms increasingly became outdoor chemical and biological factories.

[28] In the case of coal, use meant total and final consumption, but in the case of many other minerals, such as iron or copper, recycling was feasible, so that the stock was not necessarily depleted each year by a quantity equal to the amount produced.
[29] Grigg, *Dynamics of agricultural change*, pp. 78–80.

The English economy began to benefit substantially from what might be termed resource capitalism from the sixteenth century onward, principally through the development of coal production on a substantial scale. By 1800, when their annual rate of output was well over 10 million tons, English coalfields were making available as much heat as would otherwise have required the annual timber yield of an area of at least 10 million acres of woodland.[30] English coal output was several times larger than the whole of the rest of the world at that time and about half the heat derived from burning the coal was used by industry.[31]

Over the period between 1550 and 1820 the population of England increased by about 280 per cent while that of the rest of western Europe rose by about 80 per cent.[32] It may be taken as virtually certain that output per head rose more steeply in England than elsewhere over the same period. If, purely by way of illustration, we assume that it rose by 50 per cent in England and 20 per cent elsewhere (probably an underestimate of the extent of the contrast) then the index of aggregate output which had stood at 100 in England in 1550 would have reached 570 by 1820; the comparable figure for 1820 for the rest of western Europe would have been 216. This represents an enormous disparity in relative annual growth rates (0.65 per cent and 0.29 per cent respectively). That it was feasible in England to sustain such a high rate of growth was partly due to the lessening of pressure on the provision of energy and raw materials in the wake of the rapid expansion of coal output. To have supplied heat energy on the scale of consumption obtaining in England in 1800, or even a century earlier, from wood, the traditional source, would have been far beyond the capacity of local sources, even when supplemented by import. Not to have been able to command a large and rising source of heat energy, on the other hand, would have frustrated growth.

Full benefit from resource capitalism, however, only came when the provision of mechanical energy was transformed as radically as the provision of energy in the form of heat. It is entirely appropriate that Watt's steam engine should capture so much of the limelight in 'heroic' accounts of the industrial revolution. To be able to annex larger and larger quantities of power to assist, or sometimes to replace, the human hand opened the prospect of virtually unlimited rises in output per head wherever the limited strength of human and animal muscle had been a constraint on productivity, a condition that applied in a high proportion of the tasks

---

[30] Flinn, *British coal industry*, tab. 1.2, p. 26; White and Plaskett, *Biomass as fuel*, tab. 1, p. 12, and p. 125.
[31] Flinn, *British coal industry*, tab. 1.2, p. 26 and tab. 7.13, pp. 252–3; Mitchell, *European historical statistics*, tab. E2, pp. 381–91; Wrigley, *Continuity, chance and change*, pp. 54–5.
[32] Wrigley, 'Growth of population', pp. 121–4.

discharged in agriculture, transport, and manufacturing industry. The new possibilities could not, of course, be exploited immediately in all situations. Where the application of energy had to be controlled with precision; where the movement to be duplicated was intricate; where it was important that the power should be dispersed widely and in small amounts, steam engines and the machines they powered were useless in their early forms. But the ingenuity of men, increasingly guided by more accurate knowledge of basic physical and chemical processes, could be relied upon to overcome most such problems, once the potential value of the steam engine had become obvious. The fossilised remnants of car- boniferous forests made available the energy of millions of annual cycles of insolation. For a time at least, having found a hoard beyond his earlier imagination, the peasant could live like a prince.

There is an irony about the central importance of coal in fostering radical change in the productive system, since the production of coal itself throughout the formative decades of the industrial revolution, in- deed until the early twentieth century, remained a remarkably primitive, labour-intensive business. Although the drainage of mines was the first task to which steam power was applied, in the form of the Newcomen engine, and steam winding of men and coal up and down the pit shaft later became common, the winning of coal at the face and its transport to the shaft bottom long remained at a technical level equivalent in mining practice to hoe-and-wheelbarrow agriculture. Lumps of coal were hacked free with picks, shovelled into tubs, and trundled by hand or with the help of pit ponies through the mine galleries. Even so, immense quantities of energy were made available to the economy as a whole by these labori- ous and dangerous methods. But the way in which coal was mined may have helped to obscure its critical importance to transforming productive horizons in industry.

From negative to positive feedback

In their essential nature traditional economies were negative feedback systems. At some point the growth process itself provoked changes which caused growth to decelerate and grind to a halt. Success in a partic- ular round of growth implied difficulty at a later stage. A flourishing iron industry denuded the local forests; a surge in the output of woollen cloth required that more land should become sheep pasture; expansion in brewing was conditional upon more land being devoted to barley. A generalised expansion meant simultaneous extra demands being im- posed from many directions on a limited resource; and since economic expansion almost always meant a rising population, each pressure felt because output was rising, was further exacerbated by an increased demand for food. Rising marginal production costs could not be avoided, though they might be moderately postponed by technological advance in agriculture. The classical economists were pessimistic in their discussion of growth prospects because they recognised the reality and omnipresence of negative feedback, though they employed less ugly terms with which to describe the phenomenon. The gradual exhaustion of opportunities for profitable investment, however, which they described, was the working out in a given economy of the kind of general constraint whose nature is today identified by the term negative feedback. Local triumphs were possible, proximately due to the division of labour, but a sustained advance across a broad front was not.

To pass from negative to positive feedback, from a state in which expansion bred problems to one in which each step taken made the next easier, required the conjunction of two capitalisms. Specialisation of function through the division of labour promised substantial but often finite gains in some sectors of the economy, though by no means all. Agriculture was expected to remain refractory, for example, while even in Adam Smith's paradigm case of pinmaking, once sufficient workmen had been drawn together to enable individual specialists in each of the eighteen distinct operations to collaborate, his argument suggests that further gains in output per head would be slight or non-existent. The gains in productivity obtainable by the application of power were in principle pervasive and almost indefinitely extensible, provided that the source from which the power was derived was not tightly bounded, nor liable to sharply rising marginal costs of production, and provided that the raw materials, to whose processing and transport the power was applied, were also free from the same limitation. The switch from an organically based economy to one that was largely mineral-based and blessed with abundant energy, from a flow-based to a capital-based economy, opened up new and much wider horizons.

Escape from the Malthusian tension between production and reproduction could come either from the circumstances of production changing so radically that it too could rise exponentially and at a faster rate than population, or from population losing its tendency to rise exponentially unless checked, or from some combination of the two. Initially relief came from the unexampled power of growth conferred by the gradual escape from the constraints of an organically based economy. Later, with the rapid spread of contraceptive practices among married couples, the old buoyancy of population growth weakened despite the dramatic fall in mortality rates. Indeed, in the twentieth century, it has become normal to associate rapid population growth with poverty rather than prosperity, a reversal that would have astonished the classical economists.

Inability to conduct controlled experiments necessarily limits the conclusiveness of discussion of historical change, and of the nature of interlinkage between elements of change. In conventional discussions of raw material supply and energy provision during the industrial revolution, it has been normal to accept their importance but to treat them as unproblematic developments brought about by vigorous expansion, and to discuss the latter in terms that still owe much to Adam Smith's treatment of economic growth, and hence to the characteristics of the capitalist economic system. For example, Dobb, in an orthodox Marxist treatment of the industrial revolution, remarked, 'The inventions which ushered in the modern world were not only closely linked with one another in their progress: they were also interlocked with the state of industry and of economic resources, with the nature of its problems and the character of its personnel in the earlier period of capitalism from the soil of which they grew.'[33] Very similar views have also frequently been expressed by non-Marxists. But since Adam Smith's treatment of economic growth, and still more that of his two great successors, Malthus and Ricardo, laid so much emphasis on the limits of growth, and especially on the implausibility of any belief that the growth of production could outstrip reproduction (and thus permit a secular rise in real wages), the kind of growth that took place is problematic, even given the establishment of capitalist relations of production.

A revised view of proto-industrialisation

In this connection recent discussions of the concept of proto-industrialisation are of interest since they identify an important phenomenon but then tend to misinterpret its significance. Take, for example, the description and analysis of the process of what has been termed 'industrial involution'.[34] The immiseration that is depicted as a common fate of episodes of proto-industrial expansion, using long-established techniques of domestic production, and organised by capitalist entrepreneurs who knit together local producers and distant markets, is seen as a painful intermediate stage between an earlier, largely pre-capitalist mode of production and the apotheosis of industrial capitalism in a world of large factories and wage-paid labour. Yet to the classical economists what is now

---

[33] Dobb, *Development of capitalism*, p. 271.
[34] Levine, *Family formation*, pp. 33–4.

termed proto-industrial organisation of manufacturing output would it-self have been regarded as a final stage. They understood well both its capacity substantially to increase aggregate output and output per head, and the fragility of any gains achieved, especially when population growth was rapid. Regions which experienced this type of industrial growth were sometimes forced into crisis by the rise of factory industry, as in Lancashire, Flanders, and Silesia, but similar difficulties also occurred even in the absence of such rivalry. The cottage textile industry in Over-ijssel is a case in point.[35]

A capitalist system of production (in the conventional meaning of the term) is consonant either with a rise or fall in living standards. The changes in the organisation of production which it connotes are likely to increase output per head in some sectors of the economy, and this in turn may generate a rise in living standards. But the final upshot is likely to depend on the relative growth rates of production and population, and therefore to be uncertain *a priori*. Even in the event of a favourable res-olution of the tension between production and reproduction, however, there is no serious prospect of a sustained and substantial rise in living standards.

Conclusion

Within the context of an organically based economy, sustained and sub-stantial growth sufficient to transform the standard of living was a utopian dream, whatever the prevailing economic system. To make the dream come true there had to be an escape to an economy not dependent on the annual product of the earth for all supplies of raw materials and en-ergy. Such a regime involved a shift to mineral sources of supply and meant dependence upon a different kind of capital. It may seem an in-vitation to confusion to use the term capitalism a second time and in a different sense to describe the switch that occurred. Yet a good purpose is served by doing so if this causes some prevailing assumptions to be questioned. In particular, it is debatable whether the habit of associating the advent of the capitalist system with the industrial revolution is jus-tifiable, certainly if the former is regarded as a sufficient, as opposed to a necessary condition of the latter. It may be wiser to view the capitalist system as the classical economists did and to pay more heed to the Dutch experience in the seventeenth and eighteenth centuries.[36] Using the term

---

[35] Slicher van Bath, *Een samenleving onder spanning.*

[36] Since writing this essay the publication of *The first modern economy* by de Vries and van der Woude has provided weighty support for the view that the existence of a sophisticated capitalist economy is no guarantee of sustained economic expansion.

resource capitalism to describe another, different change that released a previously unparalleled growth potential points to a feature that contrasts sharply with the comparable functioning of any earlier economy and at the same time makes an implicit claim about its significance in relation to the acceleration in the rate of economic growth that occurred.

If the validity of this claim is admitted, a further question naturally suggests itself. Were the two kinds of capitalism whose conjunction resulted in the industrial revolution, and so determined many of the salient features of the modern world, causally or only casually related? It will be clear from the argument of this essay that it is my conviction that each type of capitalism may reasonably be regarded as a necessary condition of an industrial revolution, and that institutional capitalism was not by itself a sufficient condition. It is incautious to assume that once institutional capitalism was established, the energy and ingenuity to which it gave rise must necessarily have solved the negative feedback problems that haunted the discussions of the classical economists when they turned their attention to growth. Institutional capitalism was no guarantee of the exponential growth that occurred. Ultimately the point is not demonstrable beyond reasonable doubt, and a full discussion of it is outside the scope of the present exercise, but it deserves further debate. For those who find the notion of two capitalisms persuasive and who regard their connection as contingent, the course of modern economic history must appear substantially different from the picture presented in conventional accounts of the industrial revolution and its aftermath.

4   Men on the land and men in the countryside: employment in agriculture in early nineteenth-century England

The main purpose of this essay is to re-examine the census evidence about the size of the agricultural labour force in England in the first half of the nineteenth century. Because of the limitations of the census data, the review is conducted chiefly in terms of the totals of adult males engaged in agriculture. It reinforces the conclusions of others who have considered the same evidence – that there was very little expansion of employment on the farm in this period.[1] Indeed, taken in conjunction with my more conjectural estimates of agricultural employment in earlier centuries, it seems reasonable to suggest that in the quarter-millennium between 1600 and 1850 employment on the land rose by no more than a third, although the population of England rose more than fourfold and remained very largely home fed.[2]

However, there is a subsidiary theme, as the title suggests. Although employment in agriculture rose so modestly, by perhaps a tenth between 1811 and 1851 (table 4.12), the population of rural England continued to grow vigorously during most of the first half of the century. It was only after 1850 that stagnation set in. Men on the land may have increased very little, but the number of men in the countryside grew by roughly a half between 1811 and 1851, and employment outside agriculture but in rural areas therefore grew faster still.

It has occasionally been supposed that the rapidly rising English labour force of the period, no longer able to find work on the land, turned principally to industrial employment as a means of support, whether in the new form of the factory or in the older form of domestic industry. In either case

I am grateful to the editors of *The world we have gained*, and especially to Richard Smith, for advice about how to improve the organisation of this essay: also to Keith Snell, who drew upon his exceptional knowledge of many matters related to the lives of the labouring poor to provide me with much helpful comment and information.

[1] Notably Deane and Cole, *British economic growth 1688–1959*, tab. 31, p. 143.
[2] See table 4.12 for estimates of the male agricultural labour force in the first half of the nineteenth century, and Wrigley, 'Urban growth', tab. 7.4, p. 170 for the period 1600–1800. The population of England rose from 4.110 to 16.736 million between 1601 and 1851. Wrigley and Schofield, *Population history of England*, tab. 7.8, pp. 208–9.

those concerned are pictured as making products sold mainly in distant markets, serving either national or international demand; they are seen as wage-paid proletarians, or moving rapidly towards that state.[3] Even a cursory examination of the census material, however, shows vividly how mistaken it would be to give credence to the view that factory or domestic industry of this type was the chief source of new employment in the first half of the nineteenth century. It also reveals some features of comparative occupational change in rural and non-rural England that are thought provoking. Since these aspects of the subsidiary theme serve to complement the absence of significant growth in agricultural employment, it is convenient to begin by briefly treating the wider issue.

The English male labour force 1811–1851

English population growth rates reached their highest level ever in the early decades of the nineteenth century, and labour force growth rates followed suit.[4] Between 1811 and 1851 the adult male labour force rose by 77 per cent, or by 1.4 per cent annually. The number of adult males employed in agriculture, however, grew by only 11 per cent over the same period, representing an annual growth rate of only 0.26 per cent. In 1811 agriculture employed 39 per cent of the total adult male labour force; by 1851 only 25 per cent. Employment outside agriculture, of course, expanded dramatically, rising from 1,405,000 to 3,090,000 in the 40-year period, or by 120 per cent. Non-agricultural male employment was expanding by 2.0 per cent per annum, a rate significantly higher than the comparable rate in the second half of the century.[5] In the early censuses there is little information of value in identifying the relative rates of growth in different types of employment outside agriculture. But the 1831 census contains much of value in this regard, and over the next two decades some interesting trends may be sketched in with fair confidence.

[3] For example, in the course of an exposition of the contrast between peasant and proletarian demographic systems, Levine argues that between 1700 and 1850 'the proletariat mushroomed from about 2.5 million to nearly 14 million. Both the agricultural and industrial sectors and the rural and urban areas grew. Clearly, however, the dramatic gains were in the proto-industrial, industrial and urban spheres . . . The crucial point is that wage work in agriculture had a limited scope for growth, whereas proto-industry and factory industry had practically insatiable appetites for new recruits'. Levine, 'Production, reproduction and the proletarian family', p. 114.

[4] In the three quinquennia between 1811 and 1826 the English population was rising by more than 1.5 per cent annually, and over the first 50 years of the century the average annual growth rate was 1.33 per cent, an appreciably higher rate than in the preceding or succeeding period. Wrigley and Schofield, *Population history of England*, tab. 7.9, p. 213.

[5] For the data underlying these calculations, see tab. 4.12. The male labour force figures are taken from col. 2 of the table. Employment outside agriculture was taken as the difference between the totals in cols. 1 and 2 at a given date.

When Rickman made provision for more extensive occupational returns of males over 20 in the 1831 census, the distinction which he drew between manufacturing on the one hand, and retail trade and handicraft on the other, corresponded closely with the distinction between the production of goods for a large, dispersed, national or international market and the production of goods or the provision of services for a local market. For the retail trade and handicraft category, though not for any other group, detailed returns were required from each overseer.[6] An additional form was distributed listing what Rickman believed to be the 100 largest occupations within the retail trade and handicraft category, and overseers were instructed to add as many additional occupations as might be necessary to cover any other local occupations not on the printed list. As a result the occupations in this category which afforded most employment can be specified; and the claim that those recorded within the retail trade and handicraft category were serving a local market almost exclusively can be substantiated. Analysis of the geographical dispersion of employment in retail trade and handicraft and of its near-constant share of total employment, down often to the level of the individual hundred, further underlines it.

In 1831 adult male employment in manufacturing constituted only 10 per cent of total adult male employment, whereas retail trade and handicraft comprised 32 per cent (or 15 and 47 per cent of non-agricultural employment).[7] Manufacturing employment was very heavily concentrated still in two counties, Lancashire and the West Riding of Yorkshire, which jointly provided 55 per cent of all such jobs. If they are excluded, in the rest of England the proportion of adult males employed in manufacture falls to just under 6 per cent.[8] Since manufacturing included employment both in the new factory industry and in those types of domestic manufacture, such as framework knitting or nailing, which were dependent on mass markets at a distance, the census provides striking evidence of the predominantly 'traditional' nature of employment outside agriculture at this date.

---

[6] The parish was the basic unit used for census purposes, and the overseers of the poor in each parish were responsible for making up the returns.

[7] There were 314,106 males over 20 employed in manufacture, compared with 964,177 in retail trade or handicraft. The total of males over 20 was taken as 3,010,595 (that is, 'other males' were excluded as being predominantly out of the active labour force: see next section). Those in the army, navy, and merchant marine were also excluded (see notes to tab. 4.12). *1831 Census*, Enumeration abstract, I, Preface, pp. xii–xiii.

[8] *1831 Census*, Enumeration abstract, II, pp. 832–3. Excluding Lancashire and the West Riding, manufacturing employed only 141,920 out of 2,487,427 (calculated on the same basis as the figures quoted in n. 7 above).

The sheer scale of the contrast in employment totals in 'new' and 'old' forms of employment outside agriculture is revealing. Although space constraints prohibit further inquiry into many related aspects of the phenomenon as a whole, a consideration of two points may serve to illustrate the nature of the developments in train.

The first concerns rates of growth, as opposed to the absolute scale of employment, in manufacturing and in retail trade and handicraft. The radical redesign of the categorisation of employment in 1851 makes for difficulties in comparing the general categories of the 1831 census with those for 1851 or any later census. The relative rates of growth in manufacturing and retail trade and handicraft between 1831 and 1841, however, can be established approximately from an *ad hoc* tabulation made in the 1841 census, in which an attempt was made to mirror the same two general categories used in 1831. For England and Wales combined, including islands in the British seas (no other breakdown was published), employment in manufacturing rose from 320,743 to 479,774; in retail trade and handicraft from 1,015,092 to 1,282,128.[9] The totals refer to males aged 20 or more. Predictably the annual rate of growth was substantially higher in the former than the latter category, 4.1 per cent compared with 2.4 per cent; but of the overall growth in employment in the two categories combined, 63 per cent was in retail trade and handicraft. In absolute terms many more additional jobs were still being found in 'traditional' forms of employment meeting the needs of local markets.

The second point extends the first by examining some of the trades within the retail trade and handicraft sector which were providing so many new jobs, and at the same time serves to show how rural England was faring in comparison with the rest of the country in this respect. In these trades comparison between 1831 and 1851 is feasible. To provide a setting for the comparison between rural England and the rest, table 4.1 provides summary population data for 17 rural counties and for the country as a whole (England is defined as including Monmouth, following the convention observed in the first five censuses: this definition is used throughout this essay). Between 1811 and 1851 population in rural England grew by 49 per cent; in England as a whole by 77 per cent; while in non-rural England, that is in the remaining 25 counties, population rose by 88 per cent.[10] In the next 40 years, between 1851 and 1891, the comparable percentages were 12, 62, and 78 respectively. The two final

---

[9] *1841 Census*, Occupation abstract, Preface, p. 26. The 1831 totals were obtained from *1831 Census*, Enumeration abstract, II, pp. 925 and 1059.

[10] If the three ridings of Yorkshire are treated as separate counties, there were 42 English counties at this date.

Table 4.1 *Population totals and growth rates in the rural counties of England (totals in 000s)*

| | | | | Annual growth rates (per cent per annum) | |
	Rural counties (1)	England (2)	(1) as percentage of (2) (3)	Rural counties (4)	England (5)
1811	2,628	9,553	27.5	1.49	1.68
1821	3,046	11,282	27.0	1.08	1.50
1831	3,391	13,090	25.9	0.80	1.37
1841	3,671	15,003	24.5	0.62	1.21
1851	3,904	16,922	23.1	0.28	1.22
1891	4,362	27,484	15.9		

Notes: The 17 rural counties are Bedfordshire, Berkshire, Buckinghamshire, Cambridgeshire, Cumberland, Devon, Dorset, Herefordshire, Huntingdonshire, Lincolnshire, Norfolk, Oxfordshire, Rutland, Somerset, Suffolk, Westmorland and Wiltshire. The growth rates in cols. 4 and 5 each refer to the period between the date on the line in question and the date on the next line: thus the rate of 1.49 on the first line in col. 4 refers to 1811–21; that of 0.28 on the fifth line to 1851–91.
Source: Mitchell and Deane, *British historical statistics,* ch. 1, tabs. 2 and 7

columns of the table show that in the first decade, 1811–21, there was little difference in growth rates between the rural counties and the whole country, though thereafter growth rates fell away steadily and quickly in the former until after 1851 there was little further growth, whereas in the latter the fall in growth rates was modest; indeed by the mid-century it had ceased.

Given that farming took on very few new hands between 1811 and 1851, it is obvious that other forms of adult male employment must have grown rapidly in the rural counties down to the mid-century. Table 4.2 provides some details of the fortunes over a 20-year period of the ten occupations within the retail trade and handicraft category which employed the largest number of men in 1831. Between them in 1831 the ten trades provided a livelihood for 17 per cent of all males aged 20 to 64 (for reasons explained later, having to do with the treatment of those too old for regular employment, it is appropriate to relate totals of adult males in employment to the population aged 20–64).[11] They accounted for

[11] See next section.

Table 4.2 Employment in ten major retail and handicraft employments 1831–1851 (males aged 20 and over)

	In the ten trades			Male population 20–64			Percentage of male population 20–64 in the ten trades			Ratio of employment in the ten trades	Ratio of population
	1831	1841	1851	1831	1841	1851	1831	1841	1851	1851/1831	1851/1831
Rural counties	134,189	151,525	164,418	779,000	842,000	906,527	17.2	18.0	18.1	1.225	1.164
Rest of England	382,790	495,149	555,907	2,246,000	2,805,000	3,193,158	17.0	17.7	17.4	1.452	1.422
England	516,979	646,674	720,325	3,025,000	3,647,000	4,099,685	17.1	17.7	17.6	1.393	1.355

The ten trades

	Rural counties				Rest of England				England			
	1831	1841	1851	1851/1831	1831	1841	1851	1851/1831	1831	1841	1851	1851/1831
Baker	6,603	7,413	8,627	1.307	17,127	21,327	25,629	1.496	23,730	28,740	34,256	1.444
Blacksmith	13,233	15,966	16,436	1.242	32,172	47,524	50,132	1.558	45,405	63,490	66,568	1.466
Bricklayer	6,468	7,674	10,114	1.564	22,471	27,746	44,579	1.984	28,939	35,420	54,693	1.890
Butcher	7,811	8,946	9,752	1.248	23,215	29,287	34,926	1.504	31,026	38,233	44,678	1.440
Carpenter	23,847	30,325	29,731	1.247	59,963	82,547	86,374	1.440	83,810	112,872	116,105	1.385
Mason	9,983	14,584	15,134	1.516	21,648	34,954	41,190	1.903	31,631	49,538	56,324	1.781
Publican	13,869	11,628	11,370	0.820	38,752	33,147	36,866	0.951	52,621	44,775	48,236	0.917
Shoemaker	27,671	29,866	34,489	1.246	82,451	114,735	118,843	1.441	110,122	144,601	153,332	1.392
Shopkeeper	11,405	7,487	11,414	1.001	38,124	39,942	48,767	1.279	49,529	47,429	60,181	1.215
Tailor	13,299	17,636	17,351	1.305	46,867	63,940	68,601	1.464	60,166	81,576	85,952	1.429
Total	134,189	151,525	164,418	1.225	382,790	495,149	555,907	1.452	516,979	646,674	720,325	1.393

The ten trades: employment per 10,000 of the adult male labour force

	Rural counties			Rest of England			England		
	1831	1841	1851	1831	1841	1851	1831	1841	1851
Baker	85	88	95	76	76	80	78	79	84
Blacksmith	170	190	181	143	169	157	150	174	162
Bricklayer	83	91	112	100	99	140	96	97	133
Butcher	100	106	108	103	104	109	103	105	109
Carpenter	306	360	328	267	294	270	277	309	283
Mason	128	173	167	96	125	129	105	136	137
Publican	178	138	125	173	118	115	174	123	118
Shoemaker	355	355	380	367	409	372	364	396	374
Shopkeeper	146	89	126	170	142	153	164	130	147
Tailor	171	209	191	209	228	215	199	224	210
Total	1,723	1,800	1,814	1,704	1,765	1,741	1,709	1,773	1,757

Notes: For a list of the 17 rural counties, see notes to tab. 4.1. Most of the occupational totals were taken directly from the census returns but the census categories and definitions varied from census to census in two cases, making some amalgamation of groups necessary. The term shopkeeper was taken to comprise the following groups. In 1831: grocer, greengrocer, shopkeeper. In 1841: greengrocer and fruiterer: grocer and tea dealer; shopkeeper and general dealer. In 1851: shopkeeper; greengrocer; grocer. For the elements combined under the term publican at the three censuses, see note 13 in this chapter. The totals in each occupational group were all males over 20 in 1831 and 1841 when the census included categories for the infirm, the 'superannuated', etc., but males aged 20–64 in 1851 when there was no such provision. For the derivation of the totals of men aged 20–64 at the three census dates, see the notes to tab. 4.12.

Sources: 1831 Census, Enumeration abstract, I; *1841 Census*, Occupation abstract, pt I; *1851 Census*, Population tables, II, Ages, civil condition, occupations and birth place of the people, I and II.

25.5 per cent of all non-agricultural employment, and these ten occupations alone engaged five men for every three in the whole of the
manufacturing category. The ten trades comprised an almost identical
fraction of the adult male labour force in both the rural counties and the
rest of the country.

In the two classes of employment where inter-censal comparison is
particularly difficult (publicans and shopkeepers: see notes to table 4.2),
there was apparently either a slight fall in employment (publicans) or a
more modest rise than in other occupations (shopkeepers). This may be
a function of 'leakage' into other occupational heads, though if so it is
not immediately obvious from the census. Equally, there may be similar
distortions concealed within some of the other eight occupations which
appear less vulnerable to this difficulty. Nevertheless, the overall impression of vigorous expansion in the group as a whole is not misleading: nor is
the differentially rapid growth in the two major building categories, bricklayers and masons, whose numbers came close to doubling nationally in
the 20-year period.

The fraction of total adult male employment comprised in the ten occupations in the rural counties was strikingly similar to that in the rest
of the country, and, equally, the relevant percentages changed little over
time. If anything, employment in these occupations was growing slightly
faster than the population of working age (though the differences are too
slight to be significant), yet these were all occupations in which there had
been little change from earlier generations in methods of work or organisation. And a large proportion of all the men employed in these trades
were independent small masters rather than wage-paid proletarians. Table 4.2 strongly underlines the falsity of the belief that manufacturing
employment related to distant markets, whether in the home or the factory, was the dominant source of new jobs for the rising generations of
young men in these decades.[12]

The absence of employment growth in agriculture proved no bar to
employment gains elsewhere in the local rural communities. The number
of men aged 20–64 grew by 127,000 in the rural counties between 1831
and 1851, while employment in the ten trades alone rose by 30,000.

[12] Failure to appreciate the relatively modest size of total employment in all the newer forms
of employment has led at times to the posing of false problems. Pollard, for example,
noting that there was 'plentiful labour supply or labour surplus', especially in the period c.1814–50, went on to ask: 'How could this easy labour supply be maintained at
a time when new industries and occupations were voraciously absorbing labour at unprecedented rates? How did the Industrial Revolution manage to have its cake and eat it
too?' Industries which have only 10 per cent of the labour force, however voracious their
appetites, can have only a limited impact on the overall labour market. Pollard, 'Labour
in Great Britain', p. 148.

Since these trades formed only 59 per cent of the employment in retail trade and handicraft generally in 1831, it is likely that the retail trades and handicraft were providing two-fifths or more of all new employment in the countryside in the second quarter of the century.

When the proportionate shares of the individual trades are examined (final part of table 4.2), the similarity between rural England and the rest of the country is as striking as in their combined totals. Everywhere, for example, about 1 per cent of the adult male labour force were butchers, 3 per cent carpenters, 3.5 per cent shoemakers. Such similarities are suggestive. The remarkably even spread of butchers across the country, for example, does not appear to be consonant with great differences in this important aspect of diet between rural England and the rest. Often the evidence of the table raises questions as well as suggesting conclusions. The apparent ebbing of employment in the drink trade is an instance of this. It may possibly be a misleading result of the long list of synonyms for publican used in the successive censuses rather than evidence of a declining enthusiasm for drink, but there are also grounds for supposing it to be genuine.[13] It is one of several issues which would warrant further attention.

Tables 4.1 and 4.2 clearly show that rural England retained sufficient economic momentum in the first half of the nineteenth century to permit notable increases in employment in many classes of occupation which could only flourish if the local economy were healthy, since they depended on a local market. Yet employment in agriculture, the prime industry of rural England, was almost at a standstill. It is time to turn first to the question of the evidence for near stagnation in agricultural employment, which has so far been asserted rather than demonstrated; and, in a final

---

[13] In 1831 there was a single category: publican; hotel or innkeeper; retailer of beer. In 1841 under the general heading of tavern-keeper there were subheads for beershop-keeper; hotel and innkeeper; publican and victualler; and spirit merchant (of these the last was excluded from the total in table 4.2 since both spirit merchant and wine dealer were separate categories in 1831). In 1851 innkeeper; licenced victualler; beershop-keeper; and wine and spirit merchant were distinct categories. The first was in class VI; the other two in class XIII. In this case the first two were included but the third was not. It would not be surprising, however, if there were a fall in the number of publicans. Pressure from the magistrates against small front-room beershops; high taxes on malt and hops; and the spread of tea-drinking may all have played a part. Some contemporaries much regretted the decline in beer drinking. See, for example, Cobbett, *Cottage economy*, pp. 20, 22, 42. Per caput consumption of beer fell substantially over the period. In the successive decades 1820–9 to 1850–9 the totals run (in gallons per annum) 28.70, 22.40, 19.45, and 21.55 (the first figure refers to England and Wales, the others to the UK). Consumption of spirits changed little. The comparable data are (in gallons) 0.89, 1.14, 0.93, and 1.04 (all UK). But tea consumption rose sharply: (in pounds) 1.29, 1.37, 1.55 and 2.25 (all UK). Mathias, *First industrial nation*, tab. 5, p. 200.

section, to the place of agriculture in the wider changes going forward in the English economy at the time.

Agricultural employment 1831–1851

In 1851 there was a radical overhaul of the system of occupational classification in the English census, which thereafter changed little during the rest of the century. After 1851 the total number of men employed in agriculture fell. The total stood at 1,129,841 in 1851; by 1861 it had fallen to 1,120,310, a minor change, but one which was to herald uninterrupted decline.[14] Before 1851 the census occupational data were both less detailed and given in a form which varied substantially. It is not therefore possible to say whether 1851 represented a peak of agricultural employment, the edge of a plateau, or part of a downward slope, without probing the available data with some care.[15]

In attempting to survey the first half of the nineteenth century it is convenient to move backwards in time from 1851 and to pay particular attention to the 1831 census, since it is both a notably informative source in itself and a bridge into the tabulations published in still earlier censuses. Three points need be noted initially: that the 1831 census was the last to be based on returns made by the overseers in each parish, rather than on individual household schedules; that the data refer almost exclusively to males aged 20 years and over; and that, in addition to six main employment categories for adult males, there was a seventh category for the elderly and infirm and those not included elsewhere under other heads.[16]

Table 4.3 shows the census totals of agricultural employment in 1831 and 1851. They relate to males over 20 in both cases. At first sight it seems evident there had been a growth in employment in agriculture over the 20-year period, even though the increase, at 15 per cent, is only about half the overall population growth of the period (the total population of males aged 20–64 rose from 3,025,000 to 4,099,685 over the period, or by

---

[14] The totals relate to England only (including Monmouth) and refer to men aged 20 years or over. The apparent small drop in numbers from 1851 to 1861 may well not be significant because of the changing treatment of the sub-categories within agriculture. For example, the male relatives of farmers resident on the farm were treated differently. See p. 98.

[15] This issue is discussed further below, pp. 120–5.

[16] The question put to the overseers were phrased as follows: 'How many other males upwards of twenty years old . . . have not been included in any of the foregoing classes? Including, therefore, in answer to this question, retired tradesmen, superannuated labourers, and males diseased or disabled in body or mind.' *1831 Census*, Enumeration abstract, I, p. vi.

Table 4.3 *Agricultural employment in England in 1831 and 1851 (males aged 20 and over)*

1831	
Occupiers employing one or more labourers or farm servants	141,460
Occupiers employing no labour other than their own family	94,883
Labourers and farm servants employed by the first class of occupiers	744,407
Total	980,750
1851	
Landed proprietors	16,098
Farmers and graziers	192,968
Farmers' and graziers' sons, grandsons, brothers, and nephews residing on the farm	60,971
Bailiffs	9,966
Agricultural labourers (outdoors)	693,925
Shepherds	9,926
Farm servants (indoors)	72,982
Others (in agriculture)	3,103
Woodmen	6,774
Gardeners, nurserymen	63,128
Total	1,129,841

Notes: The totals refer to England including Monmouth. The 1831 data are for ancient counties, those for 1851 are for registration counties, and the national totals are therefore not exactly comparable as Monmouth was not the same entity on the two occasions. In their returns for agriculture, overseers in 1831 were instructed to include graziers, cowkeepers, shepherds, and other farm servants, gardeners (other than those taxable as servants), and nurserymen. In 1851 farmers and graziers were separately tabulated but the latter were few in number and have not been separately distinguished. Similarly, gardeners and nurserymen were separately stated but have been amalgamated. The full occupational breakdown also included returns for 'others' in arboriculture and horticulture, but the totals involved were very small and they have in each case been included with the related main category.
Sources: See sources to tab. 4.2.

36 per cent).[17] On further consideration, however, the difference between the two totals narrows sharply.

First, the scope of the 1851 total is broader in that landed proprietors were included in agriculture. In 1831 there was a category covering capitalists and professional men. This was defined to include the following: 'wholesale merchants, bankers, capitalists, professional persons, artists, architects, teachers, clerks, surveyors and other educated men'. In addition, the overseers were told: 'You will include generally persons maintaining themselves otherwise than by manufacture, trade or bodily

[17] See tab. 4.12.

labour.'[18] Landed proprietors should therefore be excluded from the 1851 total for purposes of comparison.

Second, some adjustment is called for to reflect the fact that the later census placed those who were no longer able to work, or who were out of work, in the same category as those currently in work, whereas in 1831 there was a separate, if vaguely defined, category for such men. This category of 'other males' comprised 189,389 men, or 5.92 per cent of the total of males over 20 (3,199,984).[19] If it is assumed that agriculture was affected in the same way as other industries by decrepitude and disease among its workforce, the 1851 total should be reduced proportionately to facilitate comparison with 1831. The combined effect of adjusting the original total to allow for these two factors is to reduce the discrepancy between the two totals significantly. Removing the landed proprietors (16,098) brings down the original total from 1,129,841 to 1,113,743, while deducting 5.92 per cent from the latter total results in a figure of 1,047,809.

Third, in 1851 there was a category consisting of the male relatives of farmers, living on the farm and not known to have been otherwise employed. All sons and grandsons, brothers and nephews of farmers were required to be placed in this category in the process of census tabulation, unless specifically returned on the householder's schedule as otherwise employed. Proceeding in this fashion was an arbitrary way of dealing with a difficult problem, since it meant that a census official rather than the individual concerned determined occupation. It must tend to maximise apparent agricultural occupation. Farmers' male relatives were numerous, comprising, 60,971 individuals in 1851. It is interesting to note that the comparable totals in the next two censuses declined sharply to 49,489 and 38,994 respectively. Since the number of farmers was virtually constant (table 4.4), and therefore the number of resident male relatives is very unlikely to have changed other than marginally, it is evident that attribution of employment by census officials was carried out with greater discretion after the first introduction of the practice. The *Reports* of the censuses of 1861 and 1871 do not comment on the sharp contraction in the size of this group, but the regional patterning of change suggests that the original blanket instruction to include all male relatives was interpreted with increasing care.[20] In a group of contiguous counties in the

[18] *1831 Census*, Enumeration abstract, I, p. vi.

[19] The total of males over 20 excludes those in the army, navy, and merchant marine. For a discussion of the problems of estimating the number of men missed for this reason, see notes to tab. 4.12.

[20] In the 1851 census the strictness of the procedure followed in allocating male relatives of farmers to agriculture as an occupation is suggested by the insertion of a footnote in each

Table 4.4 *Occupiers of land in England 1831 to 1871 (males aged 20 and over)*

	1831
Occupiers employing one or more labourers or farm servants	141,460
Occupiers employing no labour other than their own family	94,883
All occupiers	236,343

	1841	1851	1861	1871
Farmers and graziers	194,596	192,968	193,355	191,947
Gardeners, nurserymen	42,364	63,128	69,104	87,506
Farmers' and graziers' sons, grandsons, brothers, and nephews		60,971	49,489	38,994

Notes: For definition of England see notes to tab. 4.3. In 1841 florists were included with gardeners and nurserymen.
Sources: For 1831, 1841, and 1851 see source notes to tab. 4.2. *1861 Census*, Population tables, II, Ages, civil condition, occupations, and birthplace of the people, pts I and II; *1871 Census*, III, Civil condition, occupations, and birthplace of the people, pt I.

west midlands the total of relatives either rose between 1851 and 1861 (Shropshire and Hereford) or did not materially alter (Worcestershire and Warwickshire), whereas in a band of counties in the south-east the fall was precipitous (in Suffolk, Essex, Kent, and Sussex the percentage fall in the totals in this subgroup was 39, 26, 26, and 24 respectively). While any adjustment to assist comparability between 1831 and 1851 must be arbitrary, the evidence of later censuses suggests that the 1851 total in agriculture should be reduced by, say, 15,000 if the number of men engaged in agriculture is not to be exaggerated.

Fourth and finally, the existence of a considerable discrepancy between the total of occupiers of land in 1831 and the total of farmers and graziers in 1851 calls for comment. There were 236,343 of the former but only 192,968 of the latter, yet there can be no reasonable doubt that the number of farmers in 1831 was almost the same as later in view of the stability in the size of the group over the next four censuses (table 4.4). Given the very limited breakdown of total agricultural employment made in 1831, it might seem at first sight difficult to determine whether the reasons for the discrepancy can be identified, or even whether it is a 'real' problem related to changes in classification or simply a result of haphazard and

county tabulation specifying that 'the "sons", "grandsons", "brothers", and "nephews" (not otherwise described) of farmers and graziers, being 15 years of age and upwards, and resident on the farm, etc., are separately returned in Class IX in connection with agriculture, as they are usually engaged in the business of the farm'.

unreliable estimation. Fortunately, however, the use of county-level data discloses patterns which appear to resolve the problem of reconciling the totals in question.

There are two possibilities to be investigated. As will be clear from table 4.4, the number of gardeners in 1841, when added to the total of farmers, results in a figure very similar to the total of occupiers in 1831. In the 1831 census only those gardeners who were not taxable as male servants were to be included in the return for agriculture. It is conceivable, therefore, if improbable, that many were occupiers of land and would be included in the 1831 returns in that category. The alternative and more plausible possibility is that the adult male relatives of farmers who were resident on the farm were returned within the 'occupiers of land' category, though they were placed in a separate category in 1851 and later. Again, the numbers involved are of the right order of magnitude to account for the difference. As will become apparent this explanation is almost certainly correct.

That the returns of 1831 and 1851 in general bear an intelligible and consistent relationship to each other is strongly suggested by the information set out in table 4.5. The division between occupiers employing labour and those using only family labour in 1831 is shown for each county together with a wider range of information from the 1851 census: the number of farms which employed men, the number employing no men (or failing to specify the number employed), the number of farmers and graziers, the number of gardeners and nurserymen, the number of farmers' resident male relatives (the totals here refer to 1861, not 1851) and, finally, a derived total. It should be noted that the number of farms making a return of the number of men employed (column 6) does not equal the number of farmers (column 7). The lack of agreement arises from several causes, as is made clear by the notes to the tables in the census volumes. On the one hand, some farmers made no return of acreage and numbers employed, and the census category of farmers included many who had retired and no longer occupied a farm. On the other hand, some returns were obtained from men who engaged in farming but whose principal occupation lay outside farming and who were not therefore included in the main census tabulations as farmers. Further, it should be remembered that there was a tiny number of farmers under 20 years of age (709 in all), whereas the totals relating to farms (columns 4 to 6) make no distinction as to the age of the farmer.

Perhaps the first point to note is the generally excellent accord between the totals in columns 1 and 2 on the one hand and those in columns 4 and 5 on the other. In the country as a whole there were about four-fifths as many farms employing labour in 1851 as occupiers employing labour in 1831 (columns 4 and 1), and the same holds good for farms employing no labour and occupiers employing no labour (columns 5 and 2). The ratio between farms employing labour and those employing none in 1851, however, varied enormously from county to county. In some eastern counties where farms were large there were seven or eight times as many of the former as of the latter, while at the other extreme there were four counties where farms employing no labour were in a majority.[21] The totals in columns 1 and 4, and 2 and 5, can be compared for the 42 counties, making 84 comparisons in all; in only three instances are the 1851 totals larger than the 1831 equivalents, in each case by a tiny margin.[22] Given the great variations in the proportions of employing to non-employing units, and the fact that the overall totals in 1851 were roughly four-fifths of those in 1831, this is impressive testimony to the consistency with which the two sets of returns were collected and compiled. It is equally clear that some factor or combinations of factors was at work to cause the earlier sets of totals to exceed the later. What does the county evidence suggest about the relative importance of farmers' male relatives and gardeners in causing the observed differences?

Undoubtedly many of the male relatives of farmers resident on the farm were engaged in farming; nor is there any reasonable doubt that the overseers in 1831 would have included such men among the occupiers of land rather than as farm labourers. There is persuasive indirect evidence that in 1851, when male relatives of farmers were separately distinguished, they were initially over-counted, and that the totals in later censuses were probably more accurate.[23] It is for this reason that the totals in the category in column 9 are taken from the 1861 rather than the 1851 census. The pattern of relationship between the totals in columns 1 and 2 and those in columns 4 and 5, already noted, strongly suggests that the former exceed the latter by a fairly stable ratio. This creates a strong presumption that male relatives represented the bulk of the difference since they varied only moderately as a proportion of farmers (columns 7 and 9), whereas the totals of gardeners fluctuated widely in this respect, ranging from under 10 per cent in Cornwall, Cumberland, Herefordshire, Westmorland, and the North Riding of Yorkshire, to over 70 per cent in Hampshire, Hertfordshire, and Kent (ignoring the special cases of Middlesex and Surrey).

A simple test can be made of the hypothesis that men who would have been classed as farmers or male relatives of farmers in 1851 and later

[21] Derbyshire, Lancashire, Westmorland, and the West Riding of Yorkshire.
[22] Durham (cols. 2 and 5); Hertfordshire (cols. 1 and 4); West Riding, Yorkshire (cols. 2 and 5).
[23] See p. 98.

Table 4.5 Testing the consistency of the 1831 and 1851 county totals for farmers and related categories

| | 1831 | | | 1851 | | | | | | |
	Occupiers with labour (1)	Occupiers without labour (2)	Total (1) + (2) (3)	Farms with labour (4)	Farms without labour or not stated (5)	Total (4) + (5) (6)	Farmers and graziers (7)	Gardeners and nurserymen (8)	Farmers' male relatives (1861) (9)	Derived total (10)
Bedfordshire	1,330	474	1,804	1,288	161	1,449	1,409	797	330	1,698
Berkshire	1,711	458	2,169	1,655	184	1,839	1,994	1,327	472	2,408
Buckinghamshire	2,152	453	2,605	1,598	212	1,810	1,868	788	399	2,218
Cambridgeshire	2,421	1,266	3,687	2,220	1,071	3,291	3,409	790	680	4,005
Cheshire	4,374	4,059	8,433	3,357	3,326	6,683	6,372	1,517	2,157	8,263
Cornwall	4,608	3,613	8,221	4,063	3,154	7,217	7,523	736	1,784	9,087
Cumberland	3,617	2,839	6,456	2,517	2,444	4,961	4,687	363	2,151	6,572
Derbyshire	3,320	4,257	7,577	1,834	2,955	4,789	5,051	747	1,367	6,249
Devonshire	9,328	3,356	12,684	7,414	3,013	10,427	11,413	1,990	3,354	14,353
Dorset	2,243	967	3,210	1,860	471	2,331	2,842	658	677	3,435
Durham	2,229	1,544	3,773	1,839	1,586	3,425	3,705	820	1,097	4,166
Essex	4,561	888	5,449	3,670	446	4,116	4,025	2,026	788	4,716
Gloucestershire	3,675	1,846	5,521	2,640	946	3,586	3,883	2,305	989	4,750
Hampshire	2,774	1,234	4,008	2,485	595	3,080	3,117	2,246	692	3,724
Herefordshire	2,505	1,679	4,184	1,684	850	2,534	2,623	41	651	3,194
Hertfordshire	1,518	399	1,917	1,561	182	1,743	1,660	1,164	403	2,013

Huntingdonshire	857	397	1,254	764	189	953	1,001	278	204	1,180
Kent	4,361	2,152	6,513	3,767	954	4,721	4,938	3,597	1,106	5,907
Lancashire	6,658	9,714	16,372	5,865	9,585	15,450	15,959	3,690	4,938	20,287
Leicestershire	2,656	2,145	4,801	2,507	1,237	3,744	3,462	793	654	4,035
Lincolnshire	6,901	6,204	13,105	5,922	5,095	11,017	10,225	1,152	2,046	12,018
Middlesex	1,050	490	1,540	836	168	1,004	1,300	6,878	164	1,444
Monmouthshire	1,648	1,143	2,791	1,276	1,118	2,394	2,418	461	666	3,002
Norfolk	5,229	2,718	7,947	4,868	1,664	6,532	6,463	1,894	1,069	7,400
Northamptonshire	3,015	1,117	4,132	2,438	382	2,820	2,761	780	591	3,279
Northumberland	2,376	1,268	3,644	1,875	946	2,821	2,935	834	1,210	3,996
Nottinghamshire	2,643	2,414	5,057	2,526	1,867	4,393	3,871	909	816	4,586
Oxfordshire	2,054	458	2,512	1,939	295	2,234	2,249	712	594	2,770
Rutland	429	424	853	412	314	726	677	102	150	808
Shropshire	3,832	2,139	5,971	3,357	1,578	4,935	4,797	963	1,503	6,114
Somerset	6,032	3,731	9,763	5,254	1,936	7,190	7,988	2,098	1,995	9,737
Staffordshire	3,781	3,649	7,430	3,128	2,898	6,026	5,856	1,559	1,370	7,057
Suffolk	4,526	1,121	5,647	4,353	749	5,092	5,180	1,409	784	5,867
Surrey	1,873	727	2,600	1,563	376	1,939	1,955	5,452	502	2,395
Sussex	3,160	1,330	4,490	3,153	719	3,872	3,961	1,752	853	4,709
Warwickshire	2,838	1,142	3,980	2,467	949	3,416	3,611	1,583	906	4,405
Westmorland	1,435	1,685	3,120	939	1,425	2,364	2,328	175	823	3,049
Wiltshire	3,387	1,239	4,626	2,563	517	3,080	3,176	1,202	791	3,869
Worcestershire	2,636	1,260	3,896	1,985	859	2,844	2,810	1,586	655	3,384
Yorkshire, East Riding	3,671	1,914	5,585	2,683	1,451	4,134	4,252	1,059	1,109	5,224

(cont.)

Table 4.5 (*cont.*)

	1831			1851						
	Occupiers with labour (1)	Occupiers without labour (2)	Total (1) + (2) (3)	Farms with labour (4)	Farms without labour or not stated (5)	Total (4) + (5) (6)	Farmers and graziers (7)	Gardeners and nurserymen (8)	Farmers' male relatives (1861) (9)	Derived total (10)
Yorkshire, North Riding	4,950	4,334	9,284	3,535	3,272	6,807	6,710	566	2,045	8,502
Yorkshire, West Riding	7,096	10,636	17,732	6,602	10,783	17,385	16,504	2,959	3,954	19,970
England	141,460	94,883	236,343	118,232	72,922	191,154	192,968	63,128	49,489	236,343

Notes: The data for 1831 relate to ancient counties, other data relate to registration counties. For the importance of the changed basis of tabulation, see n. 25 in this chapter. In 1851 and thereafter parts of the counties of Kent, Surrey, and Middlesex were included in the county of London. The county totals for the three counties in cols. 7 and 8 are nonetheless accurate because the breakdown by registration district within London enables the county totals to be reconstructed. Those in cols. 4, 5, 6, and 9 were estimated on the assumption that the totals in question for London were split between the three counties in the same proportion as was to be found in the London total of farmers in 1851. For derivation of col. 10 totals, see main text.

Sources: See sources to tab.4.2.

censuses formed the two classes of occupiers of land in 1831, and that gardeners were either never included among them or, if so, in numbers so small as to make only a negligible difference. If we assume that the number of farmers in 1831 was identical to the number in 1851 and that all others in the 'occupiers' class were their male relatives, the number of such relatives is easily calculated (43,375 = 236,343 − 192,968). They comprised a smaller number than in 1861 (49,489), though the discrepancy is not large. If the county totals of male relatives in column 9 of the table are in each case reduced in the ratio 43,375/49,489, and the resulting totals are added to the totals of farmers in 1851, the sum of the resulting county totals (column 10) is constrained by the method adopted to equal the national total in the two classes of occupiers in 1831. Comparison of the county totals at the two dates (columns 3 and 10) then affords a test of the propriety of the assumption that those who were not themselves farmers in the 1831 occupiers' totals were their male relatives. If other elements, such as gardeners, were contributing significantly to the 1831 county totals, there would be a poor correspondence between the 1831 and 1851 totals for many counties. The mean difference is 9.5 per cent (that is, if the 1831 figure is taken to be 100, the 1851 figure differs on average by 9.5). It is some indication of the generally satisfactory closeness of the two series that if comparison is made between the county totals of farmers in 1851 and 1871, another interval of 20 years, the mean difference is 6.5 per cent.[24] Since this is a simpler comparison involving only one category rather than two, and avoids the substantial distortions involved in the earlier comparison in moving from ancient to registration counties, it seems fair to regard the comparison of 1831 and 1851 as broadly confirming the assumptions made and as suggesting also that the underlying operations undertaken at the two censuses were consistent with each other.[25]

---

[24] The overall totals of farmers in 1851 and 1871 were almost identical.

[25] The goodness of fit between the county totals in 1831 and 1851 is considerably better than appears in the calculation above, and probably as good as that between 1851 and 1871. The mean difference of 9.5 per cent exaggerates the 'true' position because the 1831 data refer to ancient counties while those for 1851 refer to the new registration counties. Since the differences were sometimes pronounced, the effect is important. For example, there were 17 counties whose 1831 and 1851 totals differed by more than 10 per cent. Of these, three – Lancashire, Warwickshire, and the West Riding of Yorkshire – experienced a major expansion in agriculture during the period so that their totals 'should' have risen sharply (see pp. 108–9). In the remaining 14 counties the mean difference between the 1831 and 1851 totals was 14.7 per cent. If the 1851 totals of farmers and their male relatives in each of these counties is adjusted in the ratio of the population of the ancient county to that of the registration county in 1851, the mean figure drops quite sharply to 9.6 per cent.

It is time to take stock. To make a fair comparison between the numbers engaged in agriculture in 1831 and 1851, the gross total at the latter date must be reduced because it includes landed proprietors, because both those currently employed in the industry and those formerly employed but now retired or incapacitated were included, and because there is strong evidence to suggest that the number of those returned in 1851 as farmers' male relatives engaged in agriculture was substantially exaggerated. The successive corrections made to offset these sources of discrepancy reduced the original total of 1.130 million by roughly 16,000, 75,000, and 15,000 respectively, leaving a revised total of 1.024 million, a figure only 4.4 per cent larger than the 1831 total of 0.981 million. Investigation of the apparent differences between the 1831 total of occupiers of land and the 1851 total of farmers proved on examination to be reassuring rather than otherwise as to the accuracy of the two censuses.

If the revised total for 1851 is accurate there would remain an increase of just over 40,000 between 1831 and 1851 in the labour force engaged in agriculture. The increase is more likely to be overstated than the reverse. Men engaged in silviculture were included in agriculture in 1851, but in 1831 they were not specifically mentioned by Rickman in his instructions to overseers, and it is quite likely that some or all of them were placed in the 'other labourers' group, as fishermen, for example, were required to be. In 1851 woodmen numbered some 7,000 (table 4.3). Again it is possible that the total of farmers in 1851 should be reduced by more than 5.92 per cent. Farmers were in general an elderly body of men. In 1851 35,308 out of a total of 192,968 were over 65, and 10,923 were over 75, or 18.3 and 5.7 per cent respectively (the comparable national percentages for all males were 7.9 and 2.3). The 1861 census report remarked: 'It should be borne in mind . . . that many of the farmers by profession are superannuated, or have given up their farms.'[26] It is thus possible that a further element in the remaining difference between the census totals would disappear if this point were capable of testing.[27]

Notwithstanding these additional considerations, which might reduce any increase in agricultural employment between 1831 and 1851 almost to vanishing point, there was clearly a marked rise in one element within the agricultural labour force between 1831 and 1851 which is both intriguing and instructive. Elsewhere in England farm employment was probably at best static and may even have been in slight decline,

---

[26] *1861 Census*, General report, pt 1, p. 29.
[27] Later work has reinforced the view that a lower total of men employed in agriculture in 1851 is plausible: see pp. 151–8 below.

Table 4.6 *Agricultural growth in the metropolitan and industrial counties 1831–1851*

	1831					1841				1851							
	Occupiers with labour (1)	Occupiers without labour (2)	All occupiers (3)	Labourers (4)	Total (5)	Farmers (6)	Gardeners (7)	Labourers (8)	Total (9)	Farmers (10)	Farmer's male relatives (1861) (11)	Gardeners (12)	Others in agriculture (13)	Total (14)	Farms with labour (15)	Farms without labour (16)	Total farms (17)
Surrey	1,873	727	2,600	16,761	19,361	1,892	3,734	15,865	21,491	1,955	502	4,980	15,039	22,476	1,563	376	1,939
Middlesex	1,050	490	1,540	11,376	12,916	1,118	4,761	9,627	15,506	1,300	164	6,254	7,860	15,578	836	168	1,004
Metropolitan counties	2,923	1,217	4,140	28,137	32,277	3,010	8,495	25,492	36,997	3,255	666	11,234	22,899	38,054	2,399	544	2,943
Lancashire	6,658	9,714	16,372	20,949	37,321	14,740	2,195	24,761	41,696	15,959	4,938	3,287	27,602	51,786	5,865	9,585	15,450
Yorkshire, West Riding	7,096	10,636	17,732	24,502	42,234	15,327	2,038	24,615	41,980	16,504	3,954	2,614	26,993	50,065	6,602	10,783	17,385
Warwickshire	2,838	1,142	3,980	15,644	19,624	3,461	1,105	15,914	20,480	3,611	906	1,404	16,205	22,126	2,467	949	3,416
Industrial counties	16,592	21,492	38,084	61,095	99,179	33,528	5,338	65,290	104,156	36,074	9,798	7,305	70,800	123,977	14,934	21,317	36,251
Metropolitan and industrial counties (A)	19,515	22,709	42,224	89,232	131,456	36,538	13,833	90,782	141,153	39,329	10,464	18,539	93,699	162,031	17,333	21,861	39,194
England (B)	141,460	94,883	236,343	744,407	980,750	194,596	42,364	724,625	961,585	192,968	49,489	55,822	724,355	1,022,634	118,232	72,922	191,154
(B) − (A)	121,945	72,174	194,119	655,175	849,294	158,058	28,531	633,843	820,432	153,639	39,025	37,283	630,656	860,603	100,899	51,061	151,960
(A) as percentage of (B)	13.8	23.9	17.9	12.0	13.4	18.8	32.7	12.5	14.7	20.4	21.1	33.2	12.9	15.8	14.7	30.0	25.8

Sources: See source note to tab.4.2.

but in the neighbourhood of great cities and near the areas of greatest industrial expansion it grew rapidly. The data set out in table 4.6 show both the scale of the growth and the contrast between the metropolitan and industrial counties and the rest of England. The 1831 totals represent the straightforward division between occupiers of land and labourers already described in connection with table 4.3. Those for 1851 require more explanation. To assist comparability with occupiers in 1831, and for reasons discussed earlier, the total for farmers is supplemented by that for male relatives in 1861. For the same reason males over 65 have been deleted from the totals in the columns for gardeners and for others. The last category (others in agriculture) includes all who formed part of the return for agriculture in 1851, excluding farmers and their relatives, landed proprietors and gardeners, and therefore consists principally of labourers.

The difference between the 1831 and 1851 national totals comes to about 42,000. Of this over 30,000 relates to the industrial and metropolitan counties. The increase taking place elsewhere in England was no larger than the several uncertainties involved in comparing 1831 and 1851, but the growth in the industrial and metropolitan counties was far too great to be accounted for in this way (the percentage rises in the former and the latter were 1.3 and 23.3 respectively). So far from the high level of wages in the urban and industrial areas of England drawing labour out of agriculture in their vicinity, the strength of their demand for food stimulated more intensive agricultural activity. Von Thünen's model concerning the intensity of land use is strongly vindicated.[28]

The most spectacular growth took place in Lancashire and the West Riding of Yorkshire, where the overall growth in agricultural employment was 39 per cent and 19 per cent respectively. In the London metropolitan counties the rise was 18 per cent and in Warwickshire 13 per cent. The bulk of the expansion was in small-scale farming and in market gardening. The metropolitan and industrial counties in 1851 contained 13 per cent of all English farm labourers (treating column 13 totals as consisting essentially of labourers), 20 per cent of all farmers, and 33 per cent of all gardeners, which immediately suggests the prominence of small farms and market gardening in the agriculture of these counties. The percentage figure for gardening is especially striking. However, it should not be overlooked that even in the metropolitan and industrial counties gardeners formed only 11 per cent of the total employed in agriculture. In the London metropolitan counties alone the figure was much higher at 30 per cent; in the industrial counties as a group (Lancashire, the

---

[28] Von Thünen, *The isolated state.*

West Riding, and Warwickshire) 6 per cent; in the rest of England only 4 per cent. Though only a small element in the agricultural total even in some of the counties most likely to attract expansion in market gardening, the number of market gardeners had risen rapidly. The 1841 census material in table 4.6 suggests that during the 1840s gardening employment rose by 32 per cent.

Agricultural growth in the urban and industrial counties was not confined to market gardening, however. Indeed, only in the vicinity of London does it appear to have been the dominant element in the expansion. In Surrey and Middlesex, if it is safe to assume that the number of gardeners grew as fast in the 1830s as in the 1840s, almost all the gross rise in agricultural employment could be attributed to market gardening. In the industrial counties, in contrast, where overall agricultural employment rose by about 25,000 men, the same assumption would cover less than a sixth of the increase. Small farming by men employing no labour accounted for the bulk of the growth. Comparison of the percentages at the foot of columns 1, 2, 15, and 16 in table 4.6 shows this very clearly. In the 20 years between 1831 and 1851, the proportion of farms employing labour found in the industrial and metropolitan counties rose from 13.8 to 14.7 per cent of the national total. This is a substantial rise, but it was dwarfed by the massive rise in the comparable percentage share for farms employing no labour, which rose from 23.9 to 30.0. Both the scale of the rise and the fact that the absolute percentage for the small farm category was so much higher than for larger farms are eloquent testimony to the history of farming in these counties. In the industrial counties alone the shares for large farms were 11.7 and 12.6 per cent in 1831 and 1851; and for small farms 22.7 and 29.2 per cent.

Absolute totals in these categories for the two dates cannot be calculated on a basis which affords an accurate comparison, because in 1831 the two categories of occupiers included many resident male relatives of the farmers concerned. However, making a crude allowance for this, it is reasonable to suppose that the number of farms in the three industrial counties rose by 11 and 23 per cent respectively for the two categories of those which did and those which did not employ labour. In the rest of England, as we have seen, there are no grounds for supposing that the number of farms increased at all over the same period. In the metropolitan counties there was a very sharp drop in the number of small farms (columns 2 and 16), and it seems possible that in these counties, if not elsewhere, there was some transposition into the category of gardeners to account for so marked a change. The same tendency to transposition into the gardening category probably lies behind most of the drop in the number of labourers in these counties (columns 4 and 13). Both

Table 4.7 *Occupational distribution of families in England 1811–1831*

	Agriculture		Trade, manufacture, handicraft		Other		Total	
	Total	Per cent	Total	Per cent	Total	Per cent	Total	Per cent
1811	697,353	34.7	923,588	45.9	319,450	19.5	2,012,391	100.0
1821	773,732	33.0	1,118,295	47.7	454,690	19.4	2,346,717	100.0
1831	761,348	27.7	1,182,912	43.1	801,076	29.2	2,745,336	100.0

Sources: 1811 Census, Enumeration abstract, p. 427; *1821 Census*, Enumeration abstract, p. 427; *1831 Census*, Enumeration abstract, II, p. 832.

nationally and in the industrial counties the number of labourers showed little change between 1831 and 1851.

Agricultural employment 1811–1831

Before 1831 the problems involved in making estimates of the trend in agricultural employment change in nature. The first three censuses asked only very general questions about occupation, dividing the population as a whole into those engaged in agriculture; those in trade, manufacture, and handicraft; and the rest. In 1801 the information was requested for individuals but, since this gave rise to much confusion, in 1811 and 1821 it was requested for families. When Rickman greatly expanded the scope of his enquiries about occupation in 1831, he reverted to individuals as the basis for the returns to be made, concentrating principally on men aged 20 or over. However, he also asked word for word the same questions about occupation by families as had been asked ten years earlier, expecting that the result would facilitate comparison with earlier censuses.[29] Rickman's expectation was disappointed, as is clear from table 4.7. Between 1821 and 1831 there was a slight fall in the total of agricultural families, only a marginal increase in those engaged in trade, manufacture, and handicraft, but a massive rise in the total of families engaged in other occupations. It was clear to him that, though the wording of the questions had been unchanged, the overseers had interpreted them differently. He gave the following explanation:

[29] The question ran, 'What number of families in your parish, township, or place are chiefly employed in and maintained by agriculture; or by trade, manufacture, or handicraft; and how many families are not comprised in either of the two preceding classes?'

Table 4.8 *Adult males and families in major occupational categories in 1831*

	Men aged 20 and over (1)	Families (2)	(1)/(2) (3)
Agriculture	980,750	761,348	1.288
Trade, manufacture, handicraft	1,278,283	1,182,912	1.081
Other	940,951	801,076	1.175
Total	3,199,984	2,745,336	1.166

Sources: See sources to tabs.4.2 and 4.7.

The overseer in England, who knew that many industrious labourers in his parish were employed in mines, or in road-making, and otherwise during the larger proportion of the twelvemonth, but were occasionally employed in harvest, or in the cultivation of their gardens, was heretofore induced to class these as agricultural rather than in the column which *seemed* to denote idleness or no employment at all; but when (as in 1831) a distinct column was assigned to useful labour of whatever kind, he placed them in it, and having so classed them, he could not consistently class their families in the agricultural column, which was thereby lessened in amount, and the seemingly non-productive column of families proportionally increased.[30]

He believed a parallel set of considerations had also influenced overseers in ways which caused the total in trade, manufacture and handicraft to be similarly reduced relative to earlier censuses.

Rickman's explanation, though plausible, was misconceived, as may be seen in figures 4.1 and 4.2. In order to grasp the implications of the figures it is first necessary to note that in the 1831 census there was a marked asymmetry between the total of males over 20 years old employed in the three great occupational subdivisions of the early censuses and the totals of families in the three categories. Table 4.8 sets out the totals in question. The ratio of the former total to the latter was far higher in agriculture than in either of the other two categories.

A priori there seems no reason why the ratio for agriculture should have been much higher than in the other groups. The high ratio suggests that in the case of agriculture either the numerator was too high, the denominator too low, or both distorting influences were present. Moreover, the existence of such large variations in the ratio counts against Rickman's view that overseers in 1831 were induced to make the old-style returns by families consistent with the new-style returns by the occupation of

[30] *1831 Census*, Enumeration abstract, I, p. xii.

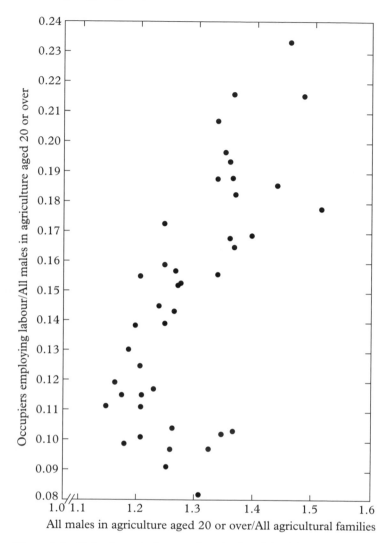

Figure 4.1. Males in agriculture and agricultural families: I
Source: 1831 Census. Enumeration abstract

males over 20. If they had been consistent, the ratios would have been less widely spread.

Figures 4.1 and 4.2 provide a strong hint about the source of the distortion in the ratio for agriculture. Figure 4.1 shows that when the ratio of all males over 20 engaged in agriculture to all agricultural families is plotted for each county against the ratio of occupiers employing labour (the larger

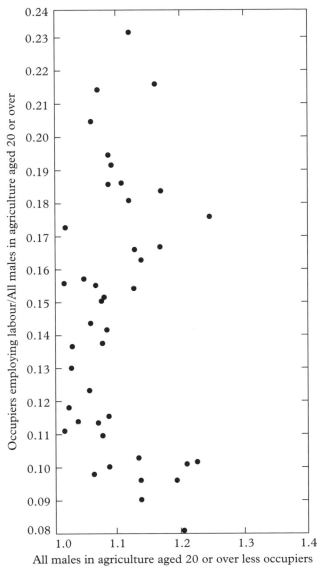

Figure 4.2. Males in agriculture and agricultural families: II
Source: As fig. 4.1.

farmers) to the total agricultural labour force of males over 20, a distinct pattern is visible. Where one ratio was low the others tended to be low also, and high ratios were similarly associated with each other. However, if the larger farmers are removed from the total of males over 20 in agriculture in the numerator of the ratio plotted on the horizontal scale, leaving all the other totals unchanged, the relationship disappears (figure 4.2).[31] Of course, in the latter case the ratios plotted on the horizontal axis are all lower because some individuals are lost from the numerator in every county, but the reduction is naturally far greater where the larger farmers were a substantial element in the agricultural labour force as a whole than where they were only a small minority. This suggests that the families of the big farmers employing hired labour were not included in the totals of families in agriculture even though they were counted in agriculture in the new-style individual occupational count in 1831. If such families had been included it would be natural to expect no relationship between the ratios represented on the horizontal axis to those on the vertical axis in figure 4.1. The disappearance of a relationship between the variables plotted in figure 4.2 leaves little doubt that this is the explanation of the change between the two figures.[32]

This explanation amounts to assuming that the overseers normally did not choose to regard the larger farmers as 'chiefly employed and maintained by agriculture' when classifying families, even though they were happy to include them as 'occupiers of land who constantly employ and pay one or more labourer or farm servant in husbandry' when classifying them as individuals. The apparent inconsistency is less quixotic than

---

[31] It may be worth noting that in both figures three of the four 'outliers' in the 'south-east' corner of the figure were the metropolitan counties of Middlesex, Surrey, and Kent, where the circumstances of agriculture in the period were unusual (see pp. 108–10). If these are disregarded the uniformity of pattern is in both cases enhanced.

[32] The same effect might be found if it were not the denominator which was artificially depressed but the numerator which was artificially raised. This possibility deserves to be considered but proves to be hard to entertain. The notion that the presence of resident servants in the households of the larger farmers might explain the high ratios can be dismissed. Such men were required to be included with farm labourers. An alternative explanation may also warrant brief attention. If farmers' male relatives were included in the case of the larger farmers but not in the case of others employed in agriculture, then conceivably this might produce an inflation in the numerator; their removal as part of the total for occupiers employing labour might be sufficient to produce the change visible between the two figures. This is intrinsically improbable since the households of labourers and small farmers must have contained equivalent members who would have been included in the occupational totals, and thus render it unlikely that the removal of the larger farmers from the ratio calculation would produce the relative changes observed. Moreover, experimental calculation shows that if a notional allowance is made for the male relatives of the larger farmers and they are removed from the overall agricultural total, the pattern found in fig. 4.1 still appears in a slightly muted form.

might appear, given that it might seem odd to classify a man as simultaneously employed and an employer, even though the imprecisions of English usage do not prohibit such an interpretation.[33] The same difficulty does not of course arise, at least with the same acuteness, with occupiers employing no labour. The ratios plotted against the horizontal axis of figure 4.2 suggest that they were normally included among agricultural families. Otherwise in counties where they were relatively numerous the ratios would have been aberrantly high. In fact, however, in the 16 counties where farmers employing no labour formed 10 per cent or more of the total male agricultural labour force, the average of the ratio was virtually identical to the average in the other counties (1.100 and 1.098 respectively). In these 16 counties small farmers were 18.2 per cent of the total of males in agriculture aged 20 or more: in the remaining 26 counties they were only 5.3 per cent, so that the similarity in the ratio in the two categories is probably meaningful. Finally, the absolute level of the ratio is significant. At 1.102 for England as a whole it was slightly higher than that found in trade, manufacture, and handicraft, and only a little below the national average (table 4.8). This further strengthens the view that the larger farmers were missing from the returns for families in agriculture. Had any significant number been included, the denominator would have been higher and the resulting ratio lower.

It follows from this train of argument that the total of families in agriculture needs to be increased if a 'true' figure is to be obtained for comparison with earlier censuses (though it does not follow, of course, that the totals in 1821 or earlier were free from distortions and therefore directly comparable with any revised figure for 1831).

Precision is beyond reach. If, however, one were to assume that the families of the larger farmers were indeed usually excluded from the count of farming families, then one might further assume that the relationship between the number of adult males per family in this category was the same as the national average (1.166) and that therefore the total of such families was 121,321 (141,460/1.166) – a total very close to the total of farms employing labour returned as part of the 1851 census (118,232). This in turn would increase the total of families engaged in agriculture from the census total of 761,348 to 882,669. In 1821 the total of farming families recorded in the census was 773,732, suggesting a substantial

---

[33] Rickman showed himself to be aware of the ambiguous position of the larger farmers. In wrestling with the problem of reconciling the returns for families with those relating to men aged 20 or more, he noted: 'Strictly speaking a large number of occupiers of land who employ labourers may be said not to subsist by *manual* labour; but they are so nearly allied to it and in such various degrees, that no computation of the exempted number can be hazarded.' *1831 Census*, Enumeration abstract, I, p. xi, note.

rise in agricultural employment in the 1820s. Indeed, if the 1821 census total were directly comparable with the revised figure for 1831, the 1820s would be the last decade in English agricultural history in which employment in the industry was still rising quickly. It transpires, however, that it would be very rash to accept this supposition. It is entirely possible, even likely, that stagnation in male employment had already set in by the 1820s.

In order to understand the problems involved in using occupation data relating to families, it is essential to note that at least 15 and possibly 20 per cent of all families were headed by women. Such families presented special difficulties to the overseers seeking to classify them into one of the three census categories. They could not ignore them because the total of families divided by occupation was required to equal the total number of families in the parish, and it is clear that this total included all families whether headed by men or women, since the mean family size calculated from census data corresponds so closely to mean household size derived from listings of inhabitants. It is the existence of such listings which enables the frequency of households headed by women to be established. They also show that very few female-headed households contained an adult male.[34] Many, of course, were well known to the overseers because they were in receipt of relief. Some, such as those consisting solely of an elderly widow, earned little or nothing from participation in economic activity.[35]

The decisions made by the overseers about the categorisation of families headed by women, given their large number, must make a significant difference to the way in which the 1821 census returns are interpreted. Rickman dealt with the matter summarily in his preliminary observations to the 1821 census. After describing some of the difficulties encountered in relation to miners and fishermen, and over the definition of agriculture (which he believed to have been largely overcome in correspondence

[34] Laslett published data derived from 100 English community listings over the period 1574 to 1821. In them, 20.5 per cent of all households were female headed (16.7 per cent by widows, 1.3 per cent by single women, and 2.5 per cent by women whose marital status was unclear); Laslett, 'Introduction', tab. 1.8, p. 78. Listings which detail age are rare, so that information about the proportion of female-headed households containing an adult male is much more narrowly based. As an example, however, in the Yorkshire settlement of Wetherby in 1776 there were only eight adult males (over 21) in the 39 households headed by a woman. On the excellent fit between household sizes calculated from pre-census listings and those derived from the nineteenth-century censuses, see Laslett, 'Size and structure of the household', tab. 3, p. 210.

[35] That solitaries were treated as forming households is suggested not only by continuities in mean household size, but more directly in Rickman's remark in relation to the 1821 census: 'One single person inhabiting a house cannot but be returned as a family, though the word family usually denotes more than one person.' *1821 Census*, Enumeration abstract, Preliminary observations, p. vii.

with the overseers), he continued: 'The subject of classification may be dismissed by stating, that the third or negative class appears to consist chiefly of superannuated labourers, and widows resident in small tenements; this may serve to show that scarcely any information can be drawn from the numbers which appear in the third or negative class.'[36]

Broadly speaking, Rickman's judgement is borne out by the pattern observable in the county data in table 4.9. Of the 42 percentage figures relating to the proportion of families in the 'other' category, 24 lie in the range between 10 and 17.5 per cent, a range within which it is likely that a large majority of the families were female headed. A further four were under 10 per cent. High percentages were largely confined to London (Middlesex and Surrey) and mining counties, notably Cornwall, Durham, and Northumberland. Comparatively high percentages elsewhere are almost invariably due to the presence of large urban centres with concentrations of service employment.

If, however, it is safe to suppose that all families with women as head were placed in Rickman's 'negative' class, then the distribution of male employment is clearly likely to be seriously distorted if the published totals of families in the three great divisions are used without adjustment, especially if the argument is couched in terms of the percentage distribution of employment. For example, the middle panel of table 4.10 shows how the implied proportion of the male-headed families employed in agriculture would change on the conservative assumption that 10 per cent of the overall total of families were both headed by women and placed in the third category. If we further suppose that the revised distribution of male-headed families is exactly reflected in the distribution of adult male employment, the total of males over 20 engaged in agriculture can be simply calculated. The total male population aged 20–64 was 2,608,000, and the total in agriculture 955,310 (2,608,000× 0.3663).[37] If the calculation is based on men aged 20–69, the total rises to 991,208, while if it is assumed that 15 rather than 10 per cent of the overall total of families were female headed and placed in the 'negative' class, the two comparable implied totals of male adult employment in agriculture rise to 1,011,643 and 1,049,657.

It will be recalled (table 4.3) that the total adult male employment in agriculture in 1831 was 980,750, and it is therefore clear that it would be unwise to conclude that agriculture was employing significantly more men at the end of the 1820s than at the beginning of the decade. Based on the lowest of the four figures quoted, there would be a rise of about

[36] Ibid., p. vii.
[37] For the population totals, see tab. 4.12; for the multipliers see tab. 4.10.

Table 4.9 *Percentage distribution of occupation by family for English counties 1821*

	Agriculture	Trade, manufacture, handicraft	Other
Bedfordshire	61.9	27.8	10.3
Berkshire	53.3	31.7	15.0
Buckinghamshire	57.6	28.8	13.5
Cambridgeshire	60.7	27.2	12.1
Cheshire	34.8	52.1	13.1
Cornwall	37.7	30.4	31.9
Cumberland	35.5	41.3	23.1
Derbyshire	34.4	48.4	17.3
Devonshire	40.8	37.5	21.7
Dorset	48.9	35.7	15.4
Durham	20.5	44.0	35.5
Essex	55.7	28.8	15.5
Gloucestershire	32.1	49.8	18.1
Hampshire	41.9	34.2	23.9
Herefordshire	61.9	25.7	12.4
Hertfordshire	51.5	30.3	18.2
Huntingdonshire	61.9	28.2	9.9
Kent	35.9	35.1	29.0
Lancashire	11.2	74.9	13.9
Leicestershire	35.4	55.1	9.5
Lincolnshire	59.4	27.0	13.6
Middlesex	3.6	61.6	34.8
Monmouth	42.6	43.5	13.8
Norfolk	48.8	35.2	16.0
Northamptonshire	53.4	32.9	13.7
Northumberland	26.8	47.7	25.5
Nottinghamshire	35.4	56.6	8.0
Oxfordshire	55.4	31.1	13.5
Rutland	61.2	26.3	12.5
Shropshire	44.2	42.0	13.8
Somerset	42.8	36.9	20.3
Staffordshire	26.6	61.7	11.7
Suffolk	55.9	31.6	12.4
Surrey	16.8	52.7	30.5
Sussex	50.3	35.5	14.2
Warwickshire	27.9	65.2	6.9
Westmorland	48.8	36.4	14.8
Wiltshire	52.4	35.6	12.0
Worcestershire	38.3	47.6	14.1
Yorkshire, East Riding	38.2	41.1	20.7
Yorkshire, North Riding	43.2	29.9	26.9
Yorkshire, West Riding	19.6	67.4	13.0
England	33.0	47.7	19.4

Source: 1821 Census, Enumeration abstract.

Table 4.10 *Occupational distribution of families in 1821*

	Agriculture		Trade, manufacture, handicraft		Other		Total	
	Total	Per cent	Total	Per cent	Total	Per cent	Total	Per cent
Census totals	773,732	33.0	1,118,295	47.7	454,690	19.4	2,346,717	100.0
Assuming 10 per cent of all families are female-headed and were placed in the 'Other' category								
Revised totals	773,732	36.6	1,118,295	53.0	220,018	10.4	2,112,045	100.0
Assuming 15 per cent of all families are female-headed and were placed in the 'Other' category								
Revised totals	773,732	38.8	1,118,295	56.1	102,682	5.2	1,994,710	100.0

Source: Tab. 4.7.

3 per cent. The additional complications involved in the estimation of the totals of men in the army, navy, and merchant marine and their relative importance at the two census dates suggest a preference for this supposition (see notes to table 4.12).[38]

To complete the comparison of 1821 and 1831 we may revert to the question originally posed about the changing total of families recorded as engaged in agriculture at the two censuses. It will be recalled that the published total fell from 773,732 to 761,348 but that a revised figure for 1831 is calculable, making allowance for the apparent reluctance of the overseers to include occupiers of land who employed labour on their farms in the totals of agricultural families. The revised figure was 882,669, suggesting a large increase in agricultural employment.

The problem of reconciling the evidence of family totals with that drawn from a consideration of probable totals of adult male employment, however, is more apparent than real. As in 1821, in 1831 15 per cent or more of all families were headed by women, and once again very few such families included an adult male. However, it is unlikely that the overseers were so apt to consign all such families to the third category, 'all other families not comprised in the two preceding classes', because of the influence of the new set of questions regarding the employment

---

[38] This view is reinforced by taking note of the lack of consistency in the treatment of the 'negative' class at the parish level, evident in the 1821 census. If all female-headed households, for example, had been consistently placed in that category, there would be few parishes of any size in which there were no families in the 'negative' class. But instances are easily found.

of men aged 20 or more. If they had done so it would have tended to cause the ratio shown in table 4.8 to be exceptionally low in the 'other' category since it would have greatly increased the number of families in the second column without affecting the total in the first column. But the ratio for the 'other' category was actually higher than the national average in spite of the presence of the families of the larger farmers in column 2, not offset by a corresponding boost to the total in column 1. Adjusting for this factor must, of course, increase the ratio significantly, and virtually rules out the possibility that all female-headed families were allotted to the 'other' class in 1831.

Rickman offered no comment on the placing of female-headed families in 1831, though he had done so ten years earlier. The most reasonable assumption to make is that such families were distributed between the three classes in much the same proportion as male-headed families. A further consideration which underwrites this conclusion is that the total number of men over 20 in the three categories of male adult employment that would certainly have caused their families to be placed in the 'other' category (capitalists, bankers, professional, and other educated men; labourers not employed in agricultural labour; other males over 20) represent 27.8 per cent of the total of males aged 20 or more,[39] compared with a figure of 29.2 per cent for the total of families in the 'other' category. If the larger farmers (occupiers employing labour) are included in the range of occupations to be related to families in the 'other' category, the proportion of males over 20 whose occupation would have caused their family to be placed in the 'other' category rises to 32.3 per cent. Once more, there appear to be no grounds for supposing that female-headed families were disproportionately represented in the 'other' class in 1831, though there is good reason to think that this had happened in the previous census. But, if they were distributed evenly among the three classes, then for the purpose of comparing 1821 and 1831 the revised 1831 total for agricultural families would need to be reduced by removing its share of female-headed households, which restores rough parity to the totals at the two dates.

The 'plateau' in male agricultural employment therefore probably covered the whole period from 1821 to 1851. It is conceivable that employment may have risen from, say, 900,000 to 1,000,000 over the period, but

---

[39] In the calculation of this percentage, servants were excluded from the numerator and the denominator since they were seldom married. Their number was small (70,629) in relation to either the numerator (870,322) or the denominator (3,129,355) It should be noted that military personnel and sailors were also excluded since their number is so hard to establish (see notes to tab. 4.12).

more likely that the scale of growth was much more modest, and entirely possible that there was no growth at all.

The first two censuses also contained some occupational data. What was collected in 1801 is worthless. Even the most cursory inspection and analysis reveals massive and haphazard inconsistencies in the way the questions were interpreted by the overseers.[40] In 1811, on the other hand, the questions were the same as in 1821, and there appears to be no complication affecting the comparison of these two censuses of the sort which entails such marked difficulties in comparing 1821 and 1831. As might be expected the 'other' category was an unchanging fraction of the whole, comprising, as it seems to have done, chiefly families headed by women. There was both absolute and proportional growth in trade, manufacture and handicraft, while agriculture grew in absolute numbers but declined as a fraction of the labour force (table 4.7). The total number of families in agriculture grew by just under 11 per cent.

It is tempting to interpret these data in a straightforward way, and to conclude that in the 1810s the agricultural labour force was in its last period of rapid increase, to be followed by only the most muted growth thereafter. Once again, however, first impressions may be misleading, for there is evidence that the apparent scale of expansion overstates the true position. There are two reasons for caution. First, as may be seen in table 4.11, the number of agricultural families in the most rapidly industrialising counties showed no growth. In view of the evidence that a quarter of a century later agriculture was expanding in such counties, though not elsewhere,[41] this means either that there was a striking change in the nature of agricultural growth between the 1810s and the 1830s and 1840s; or, if this was not the case, that there may have been other influences at work causing distortion in the returns for the more rural counties.

This suspicion is strengthened by detailed examination of the returns for counties in which the rise in agricultural employment appeared swiftest. Individual hundreds within the same county often show a suspiciously wide range of percentage rises. The returns for Buckinghamshire, for example, show a sharp rise in the total of families in agriculture over the decade (19.4 per cent), but this was especially marked in the hundreds of Newport and Cottesloe where the rises were 43 and 45 per cent respectively. Elsewhere in the county the overall rise was only

---

[40] Rickman was most positive on the point, writing in 1811: 'Hence the question regarding occupations may be said to have produced no result in 1801, if indeed an incorrect result be not worse than none, as giving colour to unfounded speculations.' *1811 Census*, Preliminary observations, p. x.

[41] See pp. 108–10.

Table 4.11 *Agricultural growth in the industrial counties 1811–1821*

	1811				1821			
	Agriculture	Trade, manufacture, handicraft	Other	Total	Agriculture	Trade, manufacture, handicraft	Other	Total
Derby	14,283	15,825	7,332	37,440	14,582	20,505	7,317	42,404
Durham	10,288	17,094	11,906	39,288	9,427	20,212	16,301	45,940
Lancashire	23,305	114,522	24,072	161,899	22,723	152,271	28,179	203,173
Monmouth	5,815	4,812	1,916	12,543	6,020	6,147	1,955	14,122
Northumberland	10,945	16,547	10,251	37,743	11,567	20,565	10,996	43,128
Staffordshire	18,361	34,011	10,165	62,537	18,265	42,435	8,060	68,780
Warwickshire	15,131	29,775	4,160	49,066	16,779	39,189	4,155	60,123
Yorkshire, West Riding	30,868	86,522	16,211	133,601	31,613	108,841	21,012	161,466
Industrial counties	128,996	319,108	86,013	534,117	130,996	410,165	97,975	639,136
England	697,353	923,588	391,450	2,012,391	773,732	1,118,295	454,690	2,346,717
England less industrial counties	568,357	604,480	305,437	1,478,274	642,736	708,130	356,715	1,707,581
				Percentages				
Industrial counties	24.2	59.7	16.1	100.0	20.5	64.2	15.2	100.0
England	34.7	45.9	19.5	100.0	33.0	47.7	19.4	100.0
England less industrial counties	38.4	40.9	20.7	100.0	37.6	41.5	20.9	100.0

Source: 1811 Census, Enumeration abstract, p. 427.

11 per cent. When individual parishes within the hundreds are studied in turn the large overall rise proves to be disproportionately concentrated in a few parishes, such as Ivinghoe in Cottesloe or Hanslope and North Crowley in Newport. In Ivinghoe, for example, the total of agricultural families rose from 27 to 261. Clearly increases on such a scale must be due to faulty returns. In most cases, consulting the returns for 1831, where there is much additional information about the agricultural employment of adult males, settles the question of which of the two earlier returns is the more reliable. Scattered but unsystematic checks of a number of hundreds with very rapid apparent growth in agricultural employment, such as Tendring in Essex or the Lathe of Scray in Kent, suggest that it is much more common to find a serious undercount in 1811 than exaggeration in 1821. More extensive testing would be required to substantiate this impression, but there is enough initial evidence to lend weight to the view that the number of men on the land was not rising as rapidly as the censuses appear to show at first blush.

Rickman was aware that the number of families in agriculture might be understated in 1811. He wrote of these data that they were 'a remarkable proof . . . of the difficulty of putting any question which shall be universally understood. In some places *occupiers* of land, but not *labourers* in agriculture, are supposed to belong to that class; in other places exactly the contrary'.[42] He believed such mistakes were usually evident and had been corrected, but in this he was probably too sanguine.[43]

In summary, therefore, the totals set out in table 4.12 represent reasonable estimates of the changes taking place in the male labour force actively engaged in agriculture between 1811 and 1851. After 1851 the course of change is easier to follow because the census returns, though not without inconsistencies which demand caution in constructing a time series, were collected on a broadly uniform basis. Moreover, after 1851 there is no reason to doubt that employment in the industry was beginning to ebb, though only very slowly for a further quarter-century. The table also shows the total of the male population aged 20–64 at each date to enable the adult male agricultural labour force to be expressed as a percentage of the total adult male labour force.

[42] *1811 Census*, Preliminary observations, p. x.
[43] The phrase quoted was repeated in the preliminary observations to the 1821 census, but this was very common in the compiling of the introductions to the early censuses and it may well have had less point on the second occasion. The 1811 census was not free from substantial numerical errors. For example, the population of the North Riding of Yorkshire was given as 152,445 when the 'true' figure was 165,506. The mistake arose because the total for the Liberty of Langbaugh East was given as 2,418 when it should have been 15,479. The printed total is that for the parishes of Ormsby, Skelton, Upleatham, Westerdale, and Whitby only.

Table 4.12 *The adult male labour force in agriculture in England 1811–1851*

	Males employed in agriculture (aged 20 and over) (1)	Male population (aged 20–64) (2)	Male population (aged 20–69) (3)	(1) as percentage of (2) (4)	(1) as percentage of (3) (5)
1811	910,000	2,315,000	2,407,000	39.3	37.8
1821	955,000	2,608,000	2,706,000	36.6	35.3
1831	981,000	3,025,000	3,141,000	32.4	31.2
1841	996,000	3,647,000	3,771,000	27.3	26.4
1851	1,010,000	4,099,685	4,241,827	24.6	23.8

Notes: All figures given in col. 1, except those for 1831 and 1841, were arrived at after making a series of assumptions about the changes needed to make the totals comparable with each other, and to offset various sources of distortion detected in the returns. Details will be found in the main text. The 1831 total was taken directly from the census. That for 1841 is simply an interpolation between the 1831 and 1851 figures. The census total was 962,000 (tab. 4.6) but there seems reason to fear that the number of male relatives of farmers, living and working on the farm, were undercounted relative to either 1831 or 1851 censuses (see text). The totals in cols. 2 and 3 were derived as follows:

1811: the census provides no age data. It was assumed that men aged 20–64 and 20–69 formed the same proportion of the total male population over 20 as in 1821.

1821: the census provides age data for 88 per cent of the male population. It was assumed that the male population as a whole corresponded in age structure to that part of it whose ages were known. Since the age group 60–69 was undivided, a split between those aged 60–4 and those age 65–9 was made on the assumption that their relative size was the same as was the case in 1851.

1831: the census provides a total for all males aged 20 or more. The totals for 20–64 and 20–69 were obtained on the assumption that they formed the same proportion of the male population over 20 as in 1821.

1841: as in 1821, though the number who failed to declare an age was tiny.

1851: directly from the census returns. In every census except 1851 a further adjustment was necessary because men in the armed forces and the merchant marine were reported separately without even division between English, Welsh, Scottish, or Irish men. The totals in question in the four censuses 1811 to 1841 were 640,500; 319,300; 277,017; and 188,453. Rickman drew attention to the high proportion of foreigners on British vessels when commenting on the 1811 return, suggesting that 100,000 men were involved. He implied that the figure had fallen sharply after the end of the war period. It is essential to make some allowance for these men since they formed a widely changing fraction of the adult male population. The following arbitrary adjustments were made to the raw figures. First, deduct 100,000 from the 1811 total; 25,000 from that for 1821; and 20,000 from those of 1831 and 1841. Next, reduce the resulting totals on the assumption that the English share of the total was equal to the English share of the combined populations of England, Wales, Scotland, and Ireland (at the four successive dates the factors used for multiplication were 0.539, 0.540, 0.545, and 0.562). Finally, multiply the resulting totals by 0.88. In 1851, of the total of men in the army, navy, or working in the merchant navy, 88 per cent of those under 65 years of age were in the age range 20–64. The totals yielded by this series of operations for 1811 to 1841 were 256,000; 140,000; 123,000; and 83,000 respectively. In 1851 when all such men were returned like those in any other occupation, the comparable total was 145,000.

Sources: See sources to tabs. 4.2, 4.9, and 4.11. The census totals for Ireland and earlier estimates of the Irish population totals were taken from Vaughan and Fitzpatrick, *Irish historical statistics*, pp. 1–3.

The totals given in column 1, especially for the two earlier dates, are less accurate than might be wished. It is a reasonable guess, but no more, that the figures for 1811 and 1821 are unlikely to be out by more than plus or minus 5 and 3 per cent respectively. The 1831 and 1851 totals are probably more accurate – if not in an absolute sense, then in the sense that their size relative to each other is unlikely to be seriously inaccurate. More work on the censuses themselves might narrow the margins of uncertainty further. But the estimates presented in table 4.12 permit some tentative conclusions to be drawn both about other characteristics of the male labour force, and about some wider issues.

Reflections

First, it appears that agriculture at the beginning of the nineteenth century employed a much higher proportion of the adult male labour force than of the labour force as a whole. Deane and Cole, for example, estimated that agriculture, forestry, and fishing comprised the following percentages of the total occupied population in 1811, 1821, 1831, 1841, and 1851 (table 4.12 percentages shown in brackets): 33.0 (39.3), 28.4 (36.6), 24.6 (32.4), 22.2 (27.3), 21.7 (24.6).[44] Their estimates refer to Britain rather than England and, since agriculture was probably relatively more important in Britain as a whole than in England, the true contrast is even more marked than the percentages suggest. The differences are not irreconcilable, of course, given the marked variance between male and female employment patterns. More difficult to reconcile, at first blush, is the contrast in the growth rate towards the end of the period. Deane and Cole's estimate of the total British labour force in agriculture, forestry, and fishing remains unchanged at 1.8 million from 1811 to 1831 but then rose sharply to 2.1 million in 1851.[45] Since they included women and children in their estimates and they were probably a declining fraction of the agricultural labour force, the true contrast in growth between 1831 and 1851 is understated by these totals.[46] Their estimates were explicitly rough and ready,[47] but it is highly probable that the principal reason for the discrepancy was their belief that 'up to and including 1871, persons described as "retired" from any stated occupation were classified by that occupation'.[48] As was noted earlier, this procedure was new to the 1851

[44] Deane and Cole, *British economic growth*, tab. 30, p. 142.
[45] They remarked, indeed, that 'the results are little more than guesses': ibid., tab. 31, p. 143.
[46] Snell, 'Agricultural seasonal unemployment'.
[47] Deane and Cole, *British economic growth*, note to tab. 30, p. 142.
[48] Ibid., pp. 142–3.

census. Before then some or all of the 'superannuated' were classified separately. The rise in agricultural employment in the 1840s, which is a striking feature of Deane and Cole's figures and to which they themselves drew attention, was probably therefore the spurious effect of a failure to make allowance for changes in census practice.[49] If this is taken into account, the trends in the two series are closely similar.

Second, if agricultural employment scarcely rose in the early nineteenth century, output per man must have risen substantially. This was the age of Ricardo. Both he and Malthus were concerned about the danger of declining marginal returns to factor inputs in agriculture. Both believed that it would prove very difficult if not impossible to avoid the problem in practice, just as they considered it appeared unavoidable in theory. Yet English agriculture in this period was clearly well able to overcome such pressures. It is true that the proportion of food needs covered by home agriculture declined steadily though slowly, but the physical output of agriculture must have expanded considerably. A simple calculation demonstrates the point. Between 1811 and 1851 the population rose by 77 per cent (table 4.1). Over the same period the number of adult males employed in agriculture rose by about 11 per cent (table 4.12), and total labour inputs must have risen less because of the declining extent of female participation in field work. Assuming, as an illustration of possibilities, that in 1811 the country met 90 per cent of its food needs, and in 1851 80 per cent, and that food consumption per head did not change significantly, output per man engaged in agriculture would have risen by 42 per cent.

There is room for argument about scale of growth in productivity per man, but no reason to doubt that it was considerable. Most of the improvement must reflect success in intensifying production on land already in farm use since, by the early nineteenth century, little land capable of arable or pastoral use remained to be broken in. Nor did the first half of the nineteenth century represent a new departure in this respect. The share of agriculture in total employment had been falling steadily for the preceding 200 years. Indeed a comparatively static agricultural labour force in absolute terms was a striking feature of English history from 1600 onwards. Calculations similar to that made above imply a very handsome long-term rise in output per man in agriculture over the whole period 1600–1850.

Estimates made in this way are apt to be misleading, of course, if taken in isolation. The steady, rapid growth in employment in the industries

---

[49] They had sufficient confidence in their estimates of agricultural employment to identify the 1840s as the only period in the nineteenth century in which the steady decline in the proportion of the labour force engaged in agriculture was interrupted. Ibid., p. 141.

listed in table 4.2, all of which were principally engaged in providing goods and services to the local market, is in part a reflection of the boost to local demand arising from the prosperity produced by increasing efficiency in agriculture. In part, however, it may be regarded as an element in the process by which rising productivity was achieved. To the degree that the farmer called upon carters or builders to provide goods and services which his father or grandfather might have provided for himself, a part of the proliferation of employment outside agriculture but in the countryside represents an element in the increasing specialisation of function which played a substantial role in raising output per head generally in early nineteenth-century England. Similarly, farming and labouring households created additional employment in trades such as tailoring, baking, butchering, and shopkeeping as they turned to an external market to perform what would earlier have been done at home to a greater extent. Nevertheless the productivity gains in agriculture must have been substantial. Each man at work on the land in the 1850s was capable of meeting the food needs of significantly more people engaged in other work than his predecessor in the 1800s had been able to do. Changes in techniques and organisation had more than offset the influences tending to cause declining marginal returns as land use intensified.

The third reflection is a general one. There were industries in which both productivity per head and employment were rising rapidly in the first half of the century. Cotton and iron manufacture fall into this category. There was one great industry, agriculture, in which output per head rose markedly but in which employment grew very little in absolute terms, and fell sharply as a fraction of the workforce. But there was also a host of industries, of which those represented in table 4.2 are typical, which collectively employed a very large proportion of adult men, and in which employment was fully keeping pace with the increase in the labour force, yet where it is improbable that there were any major changes in productivity per man in this period. The tools and methods of work of tailors, butchers, blacksmiths, carpenters, and bricklayers changed very little. Nor were they caught up in a process of specialisation of function akin to Adam Smith's pinmakers which might have allowed large gains in the quantity or quality of output per man. They were scattered over the country, working for the most part as isolated individuals or in tiny production units very much as in earlier generations, serving only a local market. They were beneficiaries of greatly enhanced productivity elsewhere in the economy rather than contributors to it.

Conclusion

Between 1800 and 1850 there were striking changes in the English male labour force. It grew at an unprecedented pace. Agriculture lost ground rapidly relative to other forms of employment. When the century began two men in five still worked on the land; by the mid-century fewer than one in four. The adult male labour force grew by 1.8 million between 1811 and 1851 but agriculture provided only 100,000 new jobs at most, and very possibly far fewer. It is not possible over the whole period 1811 to 1851 to quantify the relative contribution of manufacturing on the one hand and retail trade and handicraft employment on the other to the provision of work for the balance of the much enlarged labour force, but even the limited data presented in the first main section of this essay leave no doubt that the latter was much more important than the former in this regard. Retail trade and handicraft were forms of employment in which there were few changes in work practices or output per head, and where small independent masters were common and wage-paid proletarians comparatively rare; and output from such industries and service trades was principally for local markets. Thus this finding is not only significant in relation to the better appreciation of the course of economic change in the period, but needs to be taken into account when considering the history of social structure, of the development of classes, and of political allegiances. Further work on the history of English occupational structure may prove to have surprisingly far-reaching implications.

5   The occupational structure of England in the mid-nineteenth century

This essay represents an early step on what may prove a long road. That English society and economy changed greatly in the early modern period is evident, and that towards the end of the period it had become very different from its continental neighbours is also abundantly clear.[1] One aspect of change which, given suitable sources, is in principle quantifiable, was that reflected in the occupational structure of the country. The character of a country's economy at a point in time and the nature of any changes taking place over time are necessarily reflected in its occupational structure. Employment is shaped by aggregate demand. The structure of aggregate demand in turn is largely determined by the income levels of consumers. Demand for the basic necessities will always predominate where most of a population lives miserably, and it is not therefore surprising that agriculture provides employment for three-quarters or more of the labour force where poverty is deep and widespread. Food always takes priority over other requirements and among the poorer sections of society often claimed the bulk of their household budgets. But the income elasticity of demand for necessities is normally less than unity and therefore if real incomes rise there is a disproportionately rapid rise in the demand for other goods and services and a parallel rise in the percentage of the workforce which is employed in producing them. The secondary and tertiary sectors expand at the expense of primary employment, at least when expressed as percentages of the labour force rather than in absolute numbers. Reliable information about occupational structure and change, therefore, will directly reflect the structure of demand and indirectly reflect the living standards of the population.

This sketch is simplistic. In particular, occupational structure is responsive to changes in aggregate demand arising from all sources. Domestic demand may predominate but each pound of demand from overseas is

---

This essay has benefited greatly from the comments which Leigh Shaw-Taylor made on an earlier draft.

[1] See ch. 2.

as effective as a pound of demand from within the country in influencing output and therefore employment. In certain industries overseas demand bulked large or grew faster than home demand. The cotton industry, for example, was heavily dependent on export demand. It accounted for as much as half of the total of British commodity exports c.1830 (though it is interesting to note that during most of the first half of the nineteenth century the home market for cotton goods was growing faster than the export market).[2] Exports represented between a tenth and a fifth of national product at current prices during the first half of the nineteenth century. From a relatively high level of 18 per cent in the triennium centred on 1801 they fell to 11 per cent in the triennia centred on 1831 and 1841 only to rise to 14 per cent in the 1851 triennium. Since the percentage was rising towards the end of the period, exports accounted for almost 30 per cent of the *increase* in national output between 1831 and 1851.[3] To do full justice to the structure of aggregate demand, therefore, attention should not be concentrated solely on local consumers. Yet much depended on the home market and its changing character: the English economy differed greatly from that of the near continent in the early decades of the nineteenth century.

One of the most telling pieces of evidence about the scale of the differences between England and the near continent c.1800 is the fact that well over half of the English labour force was engaged in occupations other than agriculture at a time when, with the exception of the Low Countries, the comparable proportion in Europe was about a quarter, and this despite the fact that the country was still largely self-sufficient in food.[4] Crafts has emphasised the significance of this contrast between England and the continent and has linked it to another unusual feature of the English economy at that time: that productivity per head in agriculture was as high as in the rest of the economy, whereas in most of Europe productivity per head in the non-agricultural sectors of the economy was much higher than on the land.[5]

It is reasonable to assume that the distinctiveness of English occupational structure at the beginning of the nineteenth century was the effect of cumulative change over the two preceding centuries and that in, say, Elizabethan times England would not have differed greatly from her

---

[2] Deane and Cole, *British economic growth*, tab. 9, p. 31 and p. 186.
[3] Crouzet, 'Towards an export economy', tab. 6.14, p. 244; Crafts, *British economic growth*, tab. 6.6, p. 131.
[4] Jones estimated that Britain covered 90 per cent of her food needs from domestic production; Jones 'Agriculture 1700–80', tab. 4.1, p. 68. Overton reached a similar conclusion. Overton, *Agricultural revolution in England*, pp. 74–6.
[5] Crafts, *British economic growth*, pp. 49–60.

neighbours in this respect. To be in a position to confirm this supposition and, if it is justified, to plot the pace of change in occupational structure during the seventeenth and eighteenth centuries would provide a basic template for the economic history of the period into which to fit other empirical data and, more importantly, it would suggest the issues of interpretation on which attention should be focused. A substantial body of source material for the study of occupational change exists. In the later eighteenth and early nineteenth centuries, for example, both militia lists and many parish registers contain much occupational data. Both sources have been exploited in the past, but more can be achieved with them and with other sources than has so far been the case. This essay is an element in this wider enterprise. It aims to establish a *terminus ad quem* by ransacking the mid-century censuses to provide a detailed picture of the occupational structure of the country at that time.

The first three censuses, those of 1801, 1811, and 1821, provide very little information about occupation: they are, in general, valueless for the purposes of this exercise.[6] The 1831 census broke new ground by providing detailed information for counties and many towns about occupations classed as retail trade and handicraft, though only summary information for other types of employment. This census, moreover, also provided very valuable, if summary information about broad classes of occupations for every parish, and in this respect is more detailed than its successors. In 1831, as in the earlier censuses, the information about occupation was gathered by the overseers in each parish. There were no individual forms completed by the head of each household. The 1841 census was the first to be based on individual household schedules. The newly established office of the Registrar General oversaw the process by which the original returns were first collated locally in the enumerators' books and then consolidated into a very long alphabetical list of occupations for the country as a whole, for each county, and for the principal towns in each county. No attempt was made, however, to marshal individual occupations into larger groupings, and the published returns have therefore often proved ill adapted to the needs of most scholars.[7] Perhaps chiefly for this reason the census of 1851 has often been treated as the base point for the reconstruction of occupational change during the latter half of the

---

[6] See above pp. 110–25 for an account of the information about occupation contained in these censuses.

[7] This generalisation is a little too sweeping. In the preface to the 1841 census an attempt was made to quantify totals of men and women under 20 and 20 years of age and over in the major textile industries, the coal and metal mines, and the major metal manufacturing industries. *1841 Census*, Occupation abstract, Preface, pp. 15–26.

nineteenth century and thereafter.[8] In this essay I shall concentrate on the information contained in the 1841 and 1851 censuses, with occasional references only to earlier and later censuses.

Before considering the 1841 and 1851 censuses in greater detail, however, three preliminary issues must first be addressed.

Preliminary issues

First, there is a methodological aspect to this essay, running in parallel with the attempt to provide a firmer empirical base for the discussion of occupational change. Indeed, the two aspects are interdependent. The marshalling of the 'raw' returns into broader categories is a necessary part of the processing of census data into a form suitable for the description and analysis of occupational structure. The occupational descriptors used by individual household heads in filling in their census forms were numbered in thousands, and even after the census clerks had intervened to reduce the original multiplicity of occupational descriptors to a more manageable number, there still remained many hundreds of descriptors. In 1841, for example, the total for England was 853; in 1851 this figure had grown to 1,081.[9] Grouping of occupations is essential, but any scheme will inevitably reflect the assumptions made by its author about what constitutes the most appropriate criteria for this purpose. It is illuminating and, at times, sobering to compare the results obtained using the same original data but different schemes of categorisation.

A new system of occupational classification intended to facilitate the study of long-term change, and reflecting the conviction that the distinction between primary, secondary, and tertiary employment is a particularly informative basis for such an enterprise, will be employed exclusively in the main text of this essay. It is described in the next section. It provides an informative framework for considering the situation in the mid-century. But to illustrate the great variety of possible methods of marshalling the raw data, and to provide different perspectives for description and analysis, the raw data were also structured using two other schemes: that used by the Registrar General in presenting the results of the 1851 census; and that devised by Charles Booth, who was alive to the drawbacks associated with the assumptions made by the Registrar General's office in successive censuses and wished to improve both

---

[8] There are, of course, also many studies which begin with 1841, notably C. H. Lee, *British regional employment statistics*; see also Armstrong, 'The use of information about occupation', app. D.

[9] The 1851 total relates to Great Britain rather than England and therefore slightly exaggerates the contrast since a few occupations were peculiar to Scotland. The difficulty in arriving at a figure for England only will be apparent below.

clarity and comparability by imposing a uniform scheme based on different principles. These schemes are also outlined briefly in the next section
and the results obtained using the three schemes are compared in appendix 2 to this chapter.

Second, it is essential to note the implications of the fact that the totals reported in the 1841 and 1851 censuses are not directly comparable
with each other. In 1841 the question about occupation appears to have
been asked and answered naively. Those who were in employment or expected to be active in the labour force reported themselves as 'carpenter',
'butcher', 'wool dealer', and so on. Those who were neither in work nor
seeking it, for example because of advanced age, do not normally figure
as having an occupation. In 1851, however, the census authorities intervened actively to maximise the totals returned. The aged were encouraged
to record their occupation when still active, while the proportion of juveniles who were returned as having an occupation rose massively when
compared with the preceding census. As a result the overall occupational
totals rose far more than the totals of those of working age.[10] Thus, an increase of 15 per cent in, say, the total of bakers between the two censuses
is perfectly compatible with a contraction in the true level of employment
in this trade. The steps taken to minimise the distortions which would
otherwise affect comparisons of 1841 and 1851 are described below.

Third, it should be noted that all the national data presented, unless otherwise specified, refer to England only (here defined as excluding
Monmouth). The exclusion of Wales and Scotland might be thought re-
grettable, but, since much of the data for earlier periods is available only
for England, or in a much fuller and more reliable form for England, and
since it is important to preserve comparability over time as much as possible, it makes sense to focus on England alone. This decision, however, as
will become evident, gives rise to substantial problems when using 1851
census material, since much fuller detail is provided for Great Britain as
a whole than for its constituent national, county, or city elements.

The alternative schemes of classification

The scheme devised by the Registrar General for the 1851 census remained the basis for the classification of occupations in the succeeding

---

[10] Thus, for example, Armstrong's reworking of Booth's occupational totals for 1841–91
shows the total male occupational total rising from 4,334,000 in 1841 to 5,714,000 in
1851, or by almost 32 per cent, an absurd figure. The total of males aged 20 and over rose
by only 14 per cent (see tab. 5.7). Lee's tabulations display the same problem equally
clearly. Armstrong, 'The use of information about occupation', app. D, p. 280; C. H.
Lee, *British regional employment statistics*, Statistical tables, ser. A, unpag.

censuses down to 1911.[11] For this reason and since it represented what appeared to the authorities of the day a sensible method of structuring the raw returns, it seems appropriate to examine it as one of the ways of classifying occupational data for earlier periods also. In the 1851 census the population was divided into 17 main classes of which 14 were for specific groups of occupations, one contained labourers and others who could not be allocated to any of the 14 specific groups, while the two remaining classes were for 'Persons of rank or property not returned under any office or occupation' and for 'Persons supported by the community and of no specified occupation'. The main classes were divided into sub-classes,[12] each of which in turn comprised a number of individual occupations or, in the case of the two last classes, descriptors such as 'annuitant', 'almsperson', or 'vagrant'. The Registrar General, in describing the basis upon which his classification was constructed, reviewed a number of different principles which might have been used but concluded, rather grandly, that 'in conformity with the first notions of mankind of which we have record, the greatest weight has been given to the *materials* in which people work, as they generally imply important modifications not only in the tools, in the machines, in the processes, and in the products, but in the characters of the men'.[13] He appears to have believed implicitly in the validity of this last claim, remarking, for example, 'This tenth class [Persons engaged about animals] is altogether a peculiar race of men; silent, circumspective, prompt, agile, dexterous, enduring, danger-defying men, generally – but modified variously by the classes of animals which occupy them.'[14]

Charles Booth, writing in the 1880s, was conscious both of the severe difficulties in comparing returns from the successive censuses and of the objections which might be advanced to the principles upon which the census classes were based. The system of classification which he proposed to substitute for the census system was intended to re-order the data having regard 'less to occupation as such than to the industries within which people worked'[15] which he thought to be the feature of greatest general significance which could be studied using census material.

---

[11] Armstrong, 'The use of information about occupation', pp. 192–5 provides a succinct survey of the occupational classification of the 1851 census and emphasises the relatively few changes in census practice in relation to occupation thereafter down to 1911.

[12] There are four exceptions to this generalisation. Classes V, VII, X, and XVI were not subdivided (respectively 'Children, relatives, and scholars'; 'Persons who buy or sell, keep, let, or lend money, houses, or goods of various kinds'; 'Persons engaged about animals'; and 'Persons of rank or property not returned under any office or occupation').

[13] *1851 Census*, Population tables, pt II, vol. I, Report, p. lxxxiii.

[14] Ibid., p. xcii.

[15] Armstrong, 'The use of information about occupation', p. 229.

His scheme was described, reviewed, and slightly extended by Armstrong, and it is the Booth scheme as modified by Armstrong which has been used to illustrate further the range of possible classificatory schemes in appendix 2.[16]

The new scheme reflects a different approach. It represents an attempt to categorise occupations in a way which relates closely to the structure of demand rather than the process of production. Hence the initial division between primary, secondary, and tertiary occupations. In general, it is true that the income elasticity of demand for primary products is less than unity, and that for secondary products, though above unity, nevertheless lower in general than that for the products of tertiary employment. As a result, the differential rates of growth in each of these three main categories may be expected to mirror changes in the structure of aggregate demand, which in turn will reflect changes in the purchasing power of individual consumers (though the existence of export demand will complicate this over-simple picture).[17] As already noted, it is a commonplace that in conditions of acute poverty the great bulk of income is spent on the necessities of life – food, shelter, clothing, and fuel – and that of the four food is the most important by a very wide margin. It follows that the great bulk of employment will be in agriculture. With rising real incomes there is a differentially rapid rise in the demand for industrial products and a corresponding shift in occupational structure. The increased demand for pots and pans, tables and chairs, cups and saucers, sheets and blankets leads to growth in employment in the industries producing them. If the trend continues, though from small beginnings, the focus of fastest growth will eventually move from goods towards services and the number of those employed in retail and wholesale trade, transport and communication, health and education services, finance, personal services, public administration, and the like, will expand most rapidly of all. As a result, in advanced economies today tertiary employment is as dominant within the workforce as a whole as agriculture was in centuries gone by.

An emphasis on the relationship between occupational structure and aggregate demand stands in contrast to 'industrial' schemes of classification, where the aim is to determine the number of people working in a particular industry or industrial sector. There are, of course, merits to both approaches. The value of any classificatory scheme depends upon the purposes which it is intended to serve. Booth opted for the industrial principle. Other schemes are more concerned to reflect social status or class. No scheme can serve all purposes equally well: all with

[16] Ibid., app. E.
[17] See above pp. 129–30.

have drawbacks. As an example, one difficulty facing an industrial classification when using nineteenth-century English census data is plainly visible in Lee's work. He has a residual category of those 'not classified' which includes not only such groups as general labourers, apprentices, or mechanics but also all merchants, commercial clerks, commercial travellers, *et sim.* 'because of the impossibility of allocating them to industrial groups'.[18] Although such workers cannot be allocated on an industrial basis, it is normally clear whether they belong to the primary, secondary, or tertiary sectors. The scale of the problem of the 'not classified' in Lee's categorisation is considerable. In England in the successive censuses 1841 to 1881, the percentage of the total employed male population who were 'not classified' was 11.38, 7.06, 6.88, 12.43, and 12.16 respectively.[19] In three of the five censuses this was the largest single class other than agriculture.

The new PST scheme (primary, secondary, tertiary) is not without its own characteristic problems. In a great many trades it was customary both to make and to sell a product. Bakers, for example, made the bread and cakes which they subsequently sold. The boundary between secondary and tertiary employment was therefore often blurred. The problem is made more acute by the fact that the census authorities sometimes lumped together in the same occupation both those who made a given product and those who traded in it, even though the individuals concerned had identified their occupation more particularly on their census forms. This is inconvenient for a scheme which focuses on a distinction between these categories. Expedients can be devised to overcome the problem, or at least to establish the degree of uncertainty involved. For example, where the census category either explicitly includes both makers and traders or is unclear on the point, those involved can be tabulated as if all were in secondary employment and again as if all were in tertiary employment (that is, as if all were makers and again as if all were traders) or on any other convenient assumption (for example, as if 75 per cent were makers and 25 per cent traders). In this way the scale of any uncertainty can be established.[20] In this preliminary exercise no such refinement has been attempted but its value may be explored at a later date.

There may also be dispute about broader issues of allocation between the primary, secondary, and tertiary sectors. It might be argued, for example, that the digging of coal that was destined for industrial use should

[18] C. H. Lee, *British regional employment statistics*, p. 17. See also p. 24.
[19] Ibid., pt II, Statistical tables, ser. A (unpag.)
[20] See also app. 1.

be regarded as part of secondary rather than primary activity, and for the same reason that the transport of coal for industrial usage should comparably be treated as a secondary rather than a tertiary activity. Ideally, it would be instructive to explore the implications of this line of thinking for the totals in the three sectors, but the information needed to effect such alternative allocations would be very difficult, if not impossible, to muster, and customary usage suggests retaining coal mining in the primary sector. That the three categories shade into one another needs to be recognised, but the value of making the distinction remains.

The method used to marshal any body of 'raw' data into the three occupational schemes is described and illustrated in appendix 1.

Census taking

The undertaking of a national census is a challenging task; the logistics are necessarily forbidding. That in 1841 the entire operation in England, exclusive of the cost of postage and printing, cost only 1.31d per head, and in 1851 only 1.25d per head is remarkable testimony to the economy with which it was undertaken.[21] But economy was achieved at a price. The apparent authority of the printed page is delusory. It is not surprising that there are errors and inconsistencies in the returns. Indeed, some shortcomings were unavoidable whatever the level of funding of the enterprise, given the scale and complexity of the operation and the problems of data processing in a pre-electronic era. Perhaps the most troubling aspect of the present exercise is the fact that the range of problems which came to light may well represent only a fraction of the inaccuracies and inconsistencies which exist but which are impossible to specify because the process of aggregating data tends to conceal many faults. It is salutary, however, to take note of the problems which *can* be identified as a preliminary to considering the results of the tabulations. These visible defects underscore the fact that some of the findings arising from the exercise should be regarded as tentative and uncertain.

There are problems associated with every stage in the sequence of census operations. Those arising from the processing of the original household schedules by the local enumerators, the district registrars, and the census clerks have been described by Tillott.[22] They were wide-ranging and in some enumeration districts substantial. Occupational information did not escape the inaccuracies and distortions found generally in examining the successive stages between the filling in of the household

---

[21] *1851 Census*, Population tables, pt II, vol. I, Report, p. cxx, fn.
[22] Tillott, 'Sources of inaccuracy'.

schedule and the beginning of the central tabulations in the Registrar General's office. Occasional reference will be made to them in the following paragraphs, but most attention will be directed to the problems associated with the later stages of the work when the census clerks were building up regional and national portraits of the occupational structure of the country.

The 1851 census

Consider, first, the 1851 census. The main tabulation for Great Britain as a whole is very detailed. This richness of detail, however, is not paralleled for any other areal unit. The table for England and Wales, for example, repeats only some of the larger individual occupations in each sub-class, grouping all the remaining smaller occupations as 'Others engaged in defence', 'Others engaged in house construction', and so on. To secure comparable detail for England to that for Great Britain seemed desirable, and at first sight it appeared feasible to achieve this with only a limited amount of approximation. Two operations seemed to suffice. The first was straightforward. The totals for Wales and Monmouth were deducted from those for England and Wales.[23] The second was more complex, and brought to light a major problem, which might be termed the 'Others' problem.

In order to provide a full occupational breakdown, the 'Others' total in each sub-class in England was redistributed among the individual occupations which had been grouped together using the more detailed data for Great Britain. This was done on the assumption that the relative size of the occupations comprising an 'Others' group in England was the same as in Great Britain as a whole. The exercise was carried out separately for those under 20, those 20 and over, and for the total for all age groups. Since it is easier to follow what was involved by a numerical example than from prose, the process is illustrated below.

Table 5.1 shows the data relating to class I.2, local government. The totals for England on the first three lines were obtained without difficulty by subtracting those for Wales including Monmouth from the totals for England and Wales. These were occupations for which individual totals were available for all divisions of Britain as well as for the whole country. More complex action was needed to distribute the 'Other local officers' between the constituent occupations grouped under this heading, that

---

[23] No table for England only was included in the census. For Wales and Monmouth there is only a simple age division between those under 20 and those aged 20 and over, whereas for England and Wales the full breakdown by five-year age groups is maintained; this therefore limits the age breakdown for England to that possible for Wales and Monmouth.

Table 5.1 *1851 census: local government*

	Great Britain		England and Wales		Wales incl. Monmouth		England excl. Monmouth	
	20 and over	All	20 and over	All	20 and over	All	20 and over	All
Police	18,280	18,348	16,334	16,392	350	352	15,984	16,040
Union relieving officer	1,407	1,414	1,327	1,334	126	126	1,201	1,208
Officer of local board	1,756	1,794	1,309	1,336	92	92	1,217	1,244
Magistrate	2,302	2,302					(1,867)	(1,867)
Sheriff's officer and clerk	738	746					(598)	(605)
County, local officer (not otherwise distinguished)	236	239					(191)	(194)
Prison officer	1,819	1,838					(1,475)	(1,491)
Town clerk and officer	268	268					(217)	(217)
Town crier and bellman	197	197					(160)	(160)
Fireman	691	724					(560)	(587)
Other Union, District, and Parish officer	1,971	1,989					(1,598)	(1,613)
Savings bank officer	8	8					(6)	(6)
Other local officers	8,230	8,311	7,069	7,150	409	410	6,660	6,740
Total	29,741	29,867	26,039	26,212	977	980	25,062	25,232

Note: For explanation of bracketed totals see associated text.

Source: 1851 census, Population tables, II, Ages, civil condition, occupations, and birth place of the people, vol.I, tab. 54, p. cxxxviii, tab. XXV, p. ccxxii, and vol. 2, p. 846.

is to complete the two final columns, in which most of the cells were, of course, initially blank. The totals shown in brackets in these columns were obtained in the following manner. Take, for example, the category 'Sheriff's officer and clerk'. In Great Britain as a whole this group represented 0.089761 (746/8,311) of the total in the 'Other local officers' grouping. Assuming that this proportion held true for England the equivalent figure is 605 (6,740 × 0.089761). Calculating the overall England totals in each category in this way ensures that the nine occupations constituting the 'Other local officers' will total 6,740. It remains to distribute the 605 sheriff's officers between those aged under 20 and those aged 20 and above. In Great Britain 738 of the 746 men in this occupation were 20 and above. The total for England is, therefore, taken to be 605 × (738/746), or 598 (since the totals in the original calculations were carried to several places of decimals, expressing the operation in integers may lead to a different result: 605 × 738/746 produces a total which rounds to 599 rather than 598, but fuller detail would confirm 598 as the correct result). The bracketed figures in the two final columns and their equivalents for other classes and sub-classes were those on which subsequent analysis was based. Totals of those aged under 20 were calculated in the same way as those for those aged 20 and over. It should be noted that the combined totals for the two age groups for all the individual occupations in each sub-class derived in this way are constrained to match the comparable total for 'Others' in the sub-class. The same will not always be true, however, for the separate totals for the two age groups. The discrepancies arise because of the 'Others' problem described below.[24] Since the returns for Great Britain and those for England are often incompatible with each other, slight inaccuracies in deriving totals for those aged under 20 and those aged 20 may arise as a result of the fact that the individual occupational categories are of different relative sizes in the British and English data. It is for this reason that the total of the figures in brackets in the penultimate column of table 5.1 (6,672) does not equal the total for 'Other local officers' (6,660). Any differences, however, are always inconsequential.

Although some inaccuracy must arise from assuming the same occupational distribution in England as in Great Britain, it is reasonable to suppose that with few exceptions the extent of any distortion will be limited because the population of England constituted such a large fraction of the British total. In 1851 the male population of Great Britain was 10,223,558 while that of England was 8,186,432, or almost exactly 80 per cent of the former. However, although distortion arising for this

[24] See below, pp. 141–4.

reason may be limited, the exercise brought into view a much more serious problem which implies substantial uncertainty about the precision of all the published occupational data, whether for the country as a whole or for its constituent parts.

An illustration will again clarify the issue. The 'Others' total in class VII (Persons who buy or sell, keep, let, or lend money, houses, or goods of various kinds) for England is 13,714, but the Great Britain total for the occupations which comprise 'Others' is only 12,223, which is evidently illogical and should never occur. If this were an isolated instance, it might be regarded as unfortunate, but not a cause for widespread doubt. But it occurs repeatedly. In class XIII (Persons working and dealing in matters derived from the vegetable kingdom), for example, there are 13 sub-classes. In four of these sub-classes the 'Others' total for England alone is larger than that for Great Britain and in a fifth there is an opposite cause for doubt. The sub-class XIII.6 (In wood) has only 60 'Others' in England but 792 in Great Britain. The 'Others' in question can, of course, be identified from the fuller Great Britain data. They are fence and hurdle makers, and sawdust and chip merchants or dealers. It may be regarded as certain that a high proportion of men working in these trades were in England. Class XIII is not exceptional. A similar tale could be told for most occupational classes.

There are other indications of lack of consistency between the occupational totals for Great Britain and those for its constituent parts. Class VI.2 (Domestic servants, etc.), for example, in the Great Britain table consists of nine occupations (domestic servant, coachman, groom, gardener, inn servant, nurse at hospital, corn-cutter, park gate and lodge keeper, and undertaker). Of these the first five are printed in capitals, which indicates that they are categories which will be repeated individually in tabulations for England and its counties, whereas the last four are printed in lower case which indicates that they will be comprised in the 'Others' category subsequently. Yet there is no 'Others' category in this sub-class for England, implying, for example, that there were no undertakers in England in 1851.[25] Conversely in class XVI (Persons of rank or property not returned under any office or occupation) England has an 'Others' category containing a small number of individuals as well as separate totals for 'gentleman, independent', and 'annuitant'. This class in Great Britain consists simply of the latter two categories (that is, there is no apparent room for 'Others').

---

[25] *1851 Census*, Population tables, pt II, vol. I, Report, tab. 54, pp. cxxviii–cxl; and ibid., Summary tables, tab. XXV, pp. ccxxii–ccxxv.

It is abundantly clear, in other words, that the tabulations made for the whole of Great Britain are not consistent with those for England, Scotland, Wales, or any lesser divisions of the country. Extensive transfers between occupations must have been made. And it should be borne in mind that while a large number of inconsistencies can be identified many others may exist but, because of the form in which the data are presented, they remain hidden. The fact that in so many cases the 'Others' totals for England cannot be reconciled with the comparable totals for Great Britain implies, of course, that the totals for the occupations which are individually named in all tabulations must also be inconsistent between England and Great Britain. If the 'Others' total for England is larger than the comparable figure for Great Britain, then the totals for the individual occupations which are separately listed in both sets of tables must either be too small for England or too large for Great Britain since the overall total for the class as a whole will be found to be consistent between the two (in the sense that the printed total for England added to those for the other parts of Great Britain will be found to equal the printed total for Great Britain).

The 'Others' problem is not the only one to affect the comparability of the Great Britain totals with those for the other areal units reported in the 1851 census. Perhaps the most remarkable inconsistency relates to paperhangers. In the Great Britain table paperhangers are placed in the sub-class XI.15 along with occupations such as bricklayer or plasterer which relate to the building of houses (XI.15 is entitled 'Persons engaged in houses'); but in the tables for England and Wales and all the counties paperhangers are placed somewhat anomalously in sub-class XIII.13 ('Persons working and dealing in paper'). Paperhangers were not a numerous group. In Great Britain as a whole they numbered 1,876, but it is an indication of the cavalier fashion in which the census authorities treated their task that, at a relatively late stage in the processing of the occupational data, they changed their minds about the proper allocation of this group.

Inconsistency in the case of paperhangers did not arise inadvertently. A footnote in the *Report*, states that in the Great Britain table they had been transferred from sub-class XIII.13 in which they appeared in the general series of tables, though without offering any explanation for this action.[26] More generally, it is probable that the various problems which come to light on close examination of the census returns were the result less of carelessness or inadvertence than of frustration. The Registrar General dutifully recorded the economy of the census operation, but hinted at

[26] *1851 Census*, Population tables, pt II, vol. I, Report, p. xciv.

his wish to have done more than his resources allowed. 'A census', he wrote, 'in the most extended sense, and as it has been understood in some countries, embraces an enumeration of the visible property and of the annual produce; it includes, therefore, industrial and agricultural statistics.' He then noted that, by Act of Parliament, the present operation was restricted 'to an enumeration of the population, and of certain circumstances illustrative of their condition and occupations', and continued, 'No attempt could therefore be made to enumerate the number of manufactories, shops, or separate properties in the country.'[27] He had earlier described the complexity of the tabulation procedures and had suggested, albeit obliquely, that he was conscious of a difficulty with the occupations which are listed in full only for Great Britain but are elsewhere grouped together under the heading of 'Others'. He explained that the census clerks worked with analysis sheets on which the list of occupations was confined to 332 categories against each of which a series of vertical divisions made it possible to record the distribution of the individuals concerned between five-year age groups. 'To have ensured perfect accuracy in all the details, the whole of the abstracts of the occupations should have been repeated in duplicate and compared; but with the force at our disposal, this could not have been achieved in the prescribed time. The occupations which were referred to "Others" in the several sub-classes, and which appear in detail only in the large Table (54) [that is, the Great Britain tabulation], are the least satisfactory part of the abstracts.'[28] The Registrar General did not draw attention to the incompatibility between his 'large table' and all the other tables in the census in which each sub-class contained an 'Others' line, but if he had been bearded on the point, he would no doubt have laid emphasis on the degree to which straitened resources limited what he could achieve. He was, of course, conscious that inconsistencies between the Great Britain totals in the 'large table' and those printed elsewhere in the occupational returns abounded, but confined his comments to a rather tortuous and perhaps shamefaced footnote to table 54, where he wrote:

Upon a final revision of the Classified Arrangement of Occupations, the numbers in this and the preceding Table have been subjected to some alteration, owing to which they will not strictly represent a sum of the details given in the subsequent Tables. Persons not referred to definite occupations are here more numerous than in the detailed Tables, as all the persons there classed as 'Others' are not accounted for under the several sub-classes in this Table.[29]

---

[27] Ibid., p. lxxvii.
[28] Ibid., p.lxxv.
[29] Ibid., p. cxxviii, fn.

The list of defects in the 1851 census could be extended considerably. It is not reassuring, for example, to find that in many cases the totals for classes and sub-classes given for Great Britain and the Islands in the British Seas in table XXIV do not agree with the totals for the individual occupations comprised within the classes and sub-classes given in table 54 for the same unit.[30] Again, when age data are consulted minor inconsistencies are not difficult to find. For example, in sub-class III.1 in Wales and Monmouth there is one Protestant minister aged under 20, but in the parallel table for England and Wales combined there is no Protestant minister in this age group.[31] This instance came to light when subtracting totals for Wales and Monmouth from those for England and Wales in order to derive totals for England only. In the course of the same exercise comparable problems were to be found with the following occupations: bookbinder, woolstapler, slate quarrier (where 15 youngsters aged 5–9 appear in North Wales who are not present in the totals for Great Britain), tinman, whitesmith, blacksmith, and anchor smith. Once again, the form of the various tabulations means that there must be many more similar undetected inaccuracies.

All the problems which have been listed above came to light incidentally in the course of manipulations of the data needed in order to provide totals for England. Few if any would have surfaced if one of the published tabulations had happened to meet the needs of the present exercise. Many more would have been detected if a systematic search for inconsistencies had been instituted.

What conclusions should be drawn from this litany of defects? They are certainly sufficiently numerous and varied in kind to remove any aura of precision which might be associated with the printed page. Many were, no doubt, inevitable in an era when the entire operation was manual and when the Registrar General was galled by the limited resources at his disposal. Yet the census remains an immensely valuable source of information.

The 1841 census

The problems associated with the 1841 census are substantially different from those of the 1851 census. Describing them will reveal the difficulties involved in comparing data from the two censuses and will show why

---

[30] *1851 Census*, Population tables, pt II, vol. I, Summary tables, tab. XXIV, pp. ccxviii–ccxix and ibid., Report, tab. 54, pp. cxxviii–cxl.
[31] The data for Wales and Monmouth may be found in *1851 Census*, Population tables, pt II, vol. II, pp. 846–52.

direct comparison between them is bound to be misleading unless some prior processing is undertaken.

The information on the 1841 household schedules was transferred by the enumerators in each district to their enumerators' books, copies of which were in turn sent to the Registrar General's office so that the information could be consolidated into a form suitable for subsequent publication. In the preface to the census volume containing the occupational returns, Edmund Phipps and Thomas Vardon, acting on behalf of Thomas Henry Lister, the first Registrar General, who had recently died at the young age of 42, were at pains to emphasise that, in contrast with the decision taken at the previous census, when lists of occupations which were presumed to cover most of those engaged in retail trade and handicraft had been circulated to poor law officers to aid them in making their compilations, the census authorities had not sought to impose any initial structure on the description of occupations:

Upon the present occasion, instead of circulating lists to contain by anticipation every existing trade or calling, the enumerator was directed to insert each man's description of himself opposite his name, so that when the enumerators' schedules were returned to us we might arrange the whole upon such form as should be most easy of reference. The result was, that many occupations were returned that will not be found in the list of 1831, while in the instance of important manufactures minute subdivisions of labour were separately entered in the schedules, showing both the attention with which this part of their duty was performed by the enumerators, and the absolute necessity for after combination upon some uniform system.[32]

They went on to explain that the result was a plethora of initial occupational descriptors, posing difficulties for the office in deciding how to combine them in a meaningful fashion. The cotton industry in Lancashire was especially troublesome. In all 1,255 different descriptors were used by those employed in the industry 'while the whole number of distinct occupations returned for Great Britain in 1831 amounted only to 598'.[33] In the event the challenge of providing rational subdivisions of the cotton industry proved too great for the census authorities and the entire range of occupations associated with cotton manufacture was consolidated into a single entry, 'Cotton manufacture, all branches'.

The general policy of the Registrar General's office, however, was very different from that in relation to cotton, since many occupations pursued

[32] *1841 Census*, Occupation abstract, Preface, p. 7.
[33] Ibid., p. 8. It was misleading of Phipps and Vardon to make this comparison since in 1831 there were detailed returns only for retail trade and handicraft. Had the full sweep of occupations been returned in comparable detail, the number of occupations in 1831 would have been a multiple of 598.

only by a tiny number of workers were separately tabulated. No attempt at imposing an overall structure on the returns was attempted. The whole list of occupations, totalling in the case of England 853, was simply presented in alphabetical order. It included a large number of occupations with trivially small numbers of workers. In England there were 35 occupations with 3 or fewer adult male workers, including 10 with only 1 worker.[34] In the conclusion to the preface Phipps and Vardon, conscious no doubt that they might appear to have fallen short in not attempting any grouping, wrote as follows, betraying a degree of apprehension:

Our only object has been to arrange them [the published totals] in such a shape as should render them most accessible to all.

With reference to various questions, and in support of particular views, many modes of classification might be suggested which would be not the less curious and interesting because they could not be carried out with an absolute and scientific degree of accuracy; such attempts, however, would, as we feel, be here misplaced, and may be safely left to the industry and ingenuity of others who have in these pages ample materials placed within their power, and can use them without any official scruples to check their speculations.[35]

The strategy adopted by the census authorities in 1841 in presenting their returns has some advantages. In particular the same degree of detail is normally given for every tabulation, whether relating to Great Britain as a whole at one extreme, or to an individual county or major town at the other, thus avoiding the difficulties associated with the fact that a complete listing of every occupation is available in 1851 only for the whole of Great Britain.

It was therefore a comparatively straightforward exercise to marshal the 1841 returns into the three schemes used to classify occupational data in this essay. One initial modification was needed. The census provides totals for each occupation separately for England, Wales, Scotland, and isles in the British Seas, as well as for Great Britain, but because England was taken to include Monmouth, the totals for Monmouth had to be deleted from the England total to conform to the definition of England given earlier. This exercise was straightforward but it is worth noting that the county listing of occupations sometimes showed that detail was sacrificed in moving from the smaller to the larger unit. For example,

---

[34] These were: aeronaut, anti-dry-rot works, articulator (anatomical instrument maker), baby-linen dealer and maker, bee dealer, cartridge maker, ormulu maker, plaster and strapping maker, press worker, respirator maker, rice miller and merchant, shot dealer and factor. It should be noted that in the case of several of these occupations the national totals for Great Britain were larger than for England either because of employment in Scotland and Wales or because there were women engaged in them.

[35] Ibid., p. 72.

there were 67 'block layers' in Monmouth but there is no similar heading for England (the problem was resolved in this instance by deleting them from the category 'mason, pavior, and statuary'). Such examples could be multiplied even for a single, small county, and would prove far more numerous if a general comparison of the county and national data were undertaken. This is highly desirable but beyond the scope of the present exercise.

Comparing the 1841 and 1851 censuses

The major differences in census procedure between the 1841 and 1851 censuses make naive comparison perilous. The differences stem in the main from the former being, in a sense, passive while the latter was proactive. In 1851 the Registrar General, George Graham, struck something of a triumphalist note in his report. He noted that although there were penalties attaching to any refusal to fill in the census schedules or to making a false return, the 4,342,226 occupiers of houses or parts of houses had responded so zealously that: 'It was not found necessary to enforce the penalty in a single instance.'[36] He did add that one occupier had refused to supply a schedule to the enumerator, but that he was a magistrate and 'upon being privately written to' immediately complied with the provisions of the Act. And he allowed himself the luxury of referring in a footnote to a clergyman who 'refused to return the schedule to the parish clerk, who was the enumerator, and sent it direct to the Central Office, alleging that if he had done otherwise his wife's age would have become a topic of gossip in the beershops of the village', but his general message was of a mammoth task carried through with much success.[37] He also remarked that 'the number of people that have no occupation in Great Britain is surprisingly small'.[38] That this appeared to be the case, however, was largely due to the action which he had taken to ensure that it would be so, and this in turn poses problems when attempting a comparison between 1841 and 1851, since in 1841 no similar action was taken.

[36] *1851 Census*, Population tables, pt II, vol. I, Report, p. cxix.
[37] Ibid, p. cxix.
[38] Ibid., p. c. Booth was very conscious of the waywardness of the Registrar General in this regard. He wrote: 'it may be admitted that under any system of enumeration a considerable number of persons would creep into the occupied class who had no business to be there; but the fact that a return cannot be made perfect, does not seem a sufficient reason why it should not be as nearly accurate as possible, and therefore to class as workers a vast number of persons who are known to be not only outside the ranks of labour, but a dead weight and burthen upon it, appears to be inadmissible'. Booth, 'Occupations of the people', p. 317.

In 1851 individuals were to state their current occupation, but also, if not currently occupied, what occupation they had earlier followed. Thus in England and Wales the proportion of the male population in the age group 60–4 returned as having an occupation was 96.7 per cent, a very high figure but not perhaps greatly above what might have been expected on general grounds, but in the successive age groups of older men the percentages having an occupation suggest that an increasingly large fraction of each total related to the past rather than the present: for 65–9, 70–4, 75–9, 80–4, and 85 and over, the percentages were respectively 95.1, 91.4, 87.6, 82.2, and 79.0.[39] The same wish to maximise the numbers having an occupation is evident in the treatment of paupers, prisoners, lunatics, and hospital patients. In each case a determined attempt was made to discover the occupations of the individuals in question, and where this could be done they were included in the occupational totals. For example, there was a total of 20,419 male prisoners in England and Wales in 1851. Of these all but 1,079 were returned as having an occupation.[40] In 1841, in contrast, such groups were excluded from the occupational count,[41] and it is clear from the far greater size of the 'residue of the population' that many elderly men returned themselves as without occupation in this census. Another way of specifying the scale of the problem is to consider the totals of men aged 20 and over with occupations in 1841 and 1851. In England this total increased from 3,437,384 to 4,275,318, or by 24.4 per cent, while the total population in this age band increased only from 3,857,471 to 4,399,377, or by 14.0 per cent.

The 1841 census provides little information about age in its occupational tabulations. Each occupation was divided into those under 20 and those 20 and over, but no other breakdowns are given. It is not therefore possible to ensure comparability between the two censuses by, say, ignoring all those aged 65 and over. A simple, perhaps simplistic, device was chosen to enhance comparability. In 1851 97.18 per cent of all men aged 20 and over were returned as having occupations (those

---

[39] Those having an occupation were treated as all those returned in the first 15 classes (except for class V 'Persons returned only as children, or relatives, and scholars' of whom there were still a tiny number even at advanced ages), leaving only classes XVI and XVII, 'Persons of rank or property not returned under any office or occupation' and 'Persons supported by the community, and of no specified occupation'.

[40] *1851 Census*, Population tables, pt II, vol. I, Summary tables, tab. LII, pp. cccxxii–cccxxv.

[41] Information about the occupations of persons in workhouses, hospitals, gaols, and lunatic asylums was collected, however, in 1841, even though the totals were not included in the national totals for each occupation. The census authorities admitted that they were 'not actually authorized by the Act to demand such particulars', but felt that they 'might serve to show, out of a number of instances, the more prevailing causes of the poverty, the sickness, the crime, and the mental affliction to which each of these classes of public institution minister'. *1841 Census*, Occupation abstract, Preface, p. 26.

treated as not having an occupation were all those in classes V, XVI, and XVII[42]) whereas in 1841 the comparable figure was 89.11 per cent (all those returned as having a specific occupation plus those returned as 'Other persons employed in trade (branch not specified)'). The ratio between these two percentages is 0.9170. All totals for male occupations in 1851 referring to men aged 20 and over were therefore multiplied by 0.9170. The drawback of this simple solution is that the age distribution of employment differed substantially between occupations so that it is imposing a uniform solution on a complex reality. Unfortunately, although the 1851 census contains details of the age distribution of those claiming to have an occupation, it does not enable the currently active to be distinguished from those no longer active, and there is no reason to suppose that this variable was the same in all occupations. Therefore, any scheme must be arbitrary and a simple scheme has much to recommend it. As a minimum it must produce totals for 1851 which enable more meaningful comparisons with 1841 to be made than can be made without adjustment.

Problems of comparability affect those under 20 as acutely as those 20 and above, once again because of the determination of the census takers in 1851 to maximise the occupational totals. Sometimes the effect was achieved by fiat. All farmers' sons, grandsons, brothers, and nephews aged 15 or over were added to class IX.1 unless they were specified on the schedules as having a different occupation (class IX.1 covered agricultural employment in fields and pastures). But the census checkers were also prone to produce the same effect by *ad hoc* decisions. Tillott, for example, noted that the totals printed in the census for boys age 10–4 'may overstate the number actually returned by the householders and enumerators... Thus, in the Doncaster registration district the checker was much given to assigning occupations in this way, his enthusiasm so far outrunning his judgement as to make a 10-year-old boy a railway engine driver like his father. As a result there are in Tickhill (which lay in that district) in 1851 twice as many such boys given occupations by the checker as by the enumerator.'[43]

A direct comparison of the 1841 and 1851 totals for males under 20 returned as having an occupation indicates the severity of the problem. In 1841 the English total was 625,816; in 1851 1,085,074, an increase of 73.4 per cent. Over the same period the total male population under 20 grew from 3,399,440 to 3,787,055, an increase of only 11.4 per cent.

---

[42] The classes in question were: 'Persons returned only as children, or relatives, and scholars'; 'Persons of rank or property not returned under any office or occupation'; and 'Persons supported by the community, and of no specified occupation'.

[43] Tillott, 'Sources of inaccuracy', p. 124.

The massive inflation of the numbers of youths and children in employment between the two censuses, and especially the very large differential percentage increases in different occupations defeat any system of adjustment. As a result, it seemed best to exclude all those aged under 20 from the comparison between the two censuses. This decision is reinforced by the consideration that most of the earlier sources of information about occupation, such as, for example, parish baptism registers or militia lists, refer primarily or exclusively to adult males, and it will facilitate comparison over time if the mid-nineteenth century data have similar age coverage.

It may be helpful to recapitulate briefly the steps by which the occupational totals which will be used hereafter were obtained. As will be clear from the foregoing, the individual totals for particular occupations in 1841, which underlie the totals for categories and sub-categories in the tables, were secured directly from the 1841 census returns by subtracting the totals for Monmouth from the totals for England. Totals for individual occupations in 1851, however, could not be secured so straightforwardly. The first operation mirrored that just described for 1841, except that totals for Wales and Monmouth were subtracted from the totals for England and Wales combined. Next, totals for occupations which were not separately listed for England but which did appear in the main table for Great Britain as a whole were estimated by the procedure illustrated in table 5.1 above. Finally, all the totals of men aged 20 and over were reduced by multiplying them by 0.9170 to improve comparability with the 1841 totals. Returns for men under 20 were set aside because the 1851 totals are not comparable with those for 1841.

The totals for 1841 and 1851 obtained in this fashion form the base data for all the tabulations which are reported in the subsequent sections of this essay and in the appendices, whether using the PST system, the 1851 system, or Booth's system. This ensures that the individual totals for particular categories and sub-categories sum to the same overall total under each of the three schemes. Consideration of the results obtained using the latter two systems and their comparison with PST tabulations is reserved for appendix 2. The remainder of the main text is taken up with a discussion of the results produced by the PST system.

Adjustments to the published totals

Since the 1841 and 1851 censuses were conducted on such widely varying bases, it is not surprising that they remain difficult to compare, even after making the modifications to the original totals already described. However, much can be done to moderate the problems that arise, since the county-level returns often contain information which clarifies the issues involved. Some further corrective measures are now described. They are intended both to improve the comparability of data from the two censuses and at the same time to throw light on a number of substantive issues related to differential growth rates during the decade. Note that, whereas the modifications to the census totals described in the previous section will be reflected both in tabulations made using PST methods of classifications and in those made using the 1851 and Booth systems, the further changes which are about to be described affect PST tabulations only.[44]

Consider, first, agriculture. The most substantial imponderable in estimating the numbers engaged in agriculture might be thought to relate to 'labourers'. In both censuses labourers and agricultural labourers were separately distinguished, but the census authorities suspected that the former included many who should have been counted among the latter. This suspicion so far as 1841 is concerned seems to be strengthened by the fact that the number of labourers dropped steeply between the two censuses, from 269,788 in 1841 to 228,498 in 1851 when greater efforts were made to reduce the numbers in catch-all categories. Even in 1851, however, the Registrar General felt sure that the problem remained. He remarked of the category of labourers that they 'undoubtedly include many agricultural labourers, many road labourers, many bricklayers' labourers, many dock labourers; and also many who are ready to work in any of the ordinary mechanical employments'.[45] It is probable that he was mistaken so far as agriculture is concerned.

Table 5.2 shows how difficult it is to suppose that any considerable number of those described as labourers were engaged in agricultural labour. The broad pattern of the distribution of labourers between town and country is shown in the top two rows of the table. In 1841 labourers formed a substantially higher fraction of the total male labour force in towns than in the country, and this was still true ten years later, though by 1851 the difference between the two was much reduced, since the percentage figure for towns fell by one-third over the decade, but there was only a fractional fall in rural areas. At both dates labourers were less numerous in the country than in the town, though there was, of course, need for labour in the building industry and in the transport infrastructure in rural as well as in urban areas. It is particularly telling that labourers were a smaller proportion of the labour force in the most agricultural counties than in the countryside generally, whereas the opposite was to

---

[44] See appendix 2 for further discussion of this point.
[45] *1851 Census*, Population tables, pt II, vol. I, Report, p. xcix.

Table 5.2 *Labourers as an element in the labour force in 1841 and 1851 (males aged 20 and over)*

	Urban			Rural			All		
	Labourers	Total	Per cent labourers	Labourers	Total	Per cent labourers	Labourers	Total	Per cent labourers
1841	92,827	954,783	9.7	111,947	2,163,033	5.2	204,774	3,117,816	6.6
1851	60,724	940,763	6.5	129,019	2,602,981	5.0	189,743	3,543,744	5.4
1841									
'Agricultural' counties	4,776	49,362	9.7	23,289	497,711	4.7	28,065	547,073	5.1
'Industrial' counties	51,710	559,483	9.2	27,953	478,617	5.8	79,663	1,038,100	7.7
1851									
'Agricultural' counties	3,239	51,723	6.3	24,063	521,994	4.6	27,302	573,717	4.8
'Industrial' counties	33,658	527,977	6.4	38,819	768,190	5.1	72,477	1,296,167	5.6

Notes: Because London was so large and would dominate any urban calculation which included it, the totals above were derived after excluding London and the metropolitan counties of Middlesex, Kent, and Surrey from the national totals. The urban totals for each county in 1841 were derived from the cities and boroughs listed in the county returns. Those for 1851 were obtained similarly from the principal towns in each county. The rural totals were obtained by subtracting the urban totals from the overall totals for each county. The county totals under each head were then aggregated to provide the totals shown on the first two rows of the table. The 'agricultural' counties were taken as those in which in 1841 40 per cent or more of the males aged 20 and over were either farmers or agricultural labourers; the 'industrial' counties were those where the corresponding figure was less than 20 per cent. The 'agricultural' counties were: Bedfordshire, Buckinghamshire, Cambridgeshire, Essex, Hereford, Huntingdon, Lincolnshire, Northamptonshire, Rutland, Suffolk, and Wiltshire; the 'industrial' counties were: Durham, Lancashire, Staffordshire, Warwickshire, and the West Riding of Yorkshire.
Sources: 1841 and 1851 censuses.

be expected if many of those recorded as labourers had been employed in agriculture. It is also instructive that in both censuses the contrast between urban and rural areas was closely similar in both the 'agricultural' and 'industrial' counties, except that the percentage of labourers in rural areas was a little lower in the former than in the latter.

The large fall in the percentage of labourers in urban areas between 1841 and 1851 probably reflects a greater determination on the part of the census authorities in 1851 to reduce as much as possible the size of indeterminate designations. In 1851 several types of labourer were separately designated under headings which do not appear in 1841, such as road labourer, railway labourer, dock labourer, gravel labourer, and even oatkiln labourer. Nevertheless there remained many types of labourer which were not separately designated. One of the most important of these was that of labourer in the building industry. There were, for example, large numbers of bricklayers and masons who required the support of labourers in their work. The distribution of bricklayers and masons throughout the country further underlines the improbability that any considerable number of those returned as labourers in the rural areas of England were engaged in agricultural work.

Table 5.3 sets out the relative prevalence of bricklayers and masons in the male labour force in 1841 for England, for England less London, and for the 'agricultural' and 'industrial' counties as in the previous table. It makes sense to amalgamate the bricklayers and masons into a single category, since, although their relative importance varied greatly from county to county, when treated as a single category they were a relatively stable element in the occupational structure of all counties. For example, in Sussex there were 1,625 bricklayers but only 287 masons, whereas in Gloucestershire the figures were roughly reversed with 305 bricklayers but 2,818 masons, yet the combined total of bricklayers and masons represented 24.9 per 1,000 of the adult male labour force in Sussex and 28.4 per 1,000 in Gloucestershire.[46] Table 5.3 shows that in England as a whole there was almost no difference between town and country in the percentage of the male labour force in the two building crafts; that in London, perhaps surprisingly, bricklayers and masons were a smaller element in the labour force than in the country as a whole, so that removing London from the national picture increased the urban percentage; and that in the most 'agricultural' of the counties the urban areas had substantially more bricklayers and masons than the rural areas (though, since the

---

[46] In general counties where bricklayers predominated had a lower combined figure per 1,000 for bricklayers and masons combined than was the case in counties where masons were the dominant trade.

Table 5.3 *Bricklayers and masons as an element in the labour force in 1841 (males aged 20 and over)*

	Urban			Rural			All		
	Bricklayers and masons	Total	Bricklayers and masons per 1,000	Bricklayers and masons	Total	Bricklayers and masons per 1,000	Bricklayers and masons	Total	Bricklayers and masons per 1,000
England	31,619	1,465,264	21.6	51,038	2,388,619	21.4	82,657	3,853,883	21.4
England without London	24,451	1,060,964	23.0	50,607	2,358,738	21.5	75,068	3,419,702	21.9
'Agricultural' counties	1,495	49,362	30.3	8,875	497,711	17.8	10,370	547,073	19.0
'Industrial' counties	11,874	559,483	21.2	10,622	478,617	22.2	22,496	1,038,100	21.7

Notes: For definitions of 'agricultural' and 'industrial' see notes to tab. 5.2. The total of males aged 20 and over for England given above (3,853,883) is the cumulated total of the individual county figures. It differs slightly from the total given in the census for England less Monmouth (3,857,471). The reason for the discrepancy is unclear.
Sources: 1841 and 1851 censuses.

towns in the counties were few and small, the numbers involved were very modest), whereas this feature was absent from the 'industrial' counties. Assuming that the ratio of labourers to bricklayers and masons was much the same in town and country, this example suggests something which might be expected on general grounds – that labourers were needed in the countryside in industries other than agriculture and that the category of 'labourer' may well have been as large, or almost as large, a percentage of the whole labour force in rural as in urban areas. If there was any understatement of the agricultural labour force because of the large number of 'labourers' in the mid-century censuses, it was probably very slight.

In assessing the evidence for growth or decline in agricultural employment in the mid-century two other issues prove to be of much greater importance. The first concerns farm servants. In 1851 the returns specified separately 'agricultural labourer (outdoor)' and 'farm servant (indoor)'.[47] The 1841 census did not distinguish the two. There was then only a single category for 'labourer, agricultural'. There is strong reason to suppose, however, that the heading 'servant, domestic' in 1841 included a large number of agricultural workers who were living in their masters' houses. This is suggested by the information contained in table 5.4.

The pattern of change in the percentages of domestic servants in town and country between the two censuses is in sharp contrast with the comparable pattern for labourers. In the case of labourers there was a substantial fall in the urban percentage but little change in the rural percentage. In the case of domestic servants the fall was much more pronounced in rural areas than in the towns, though even in the towns the fall was marked. In 1851, with a separate category for indoor farm servants, the urban and rural percentages were almost identical, whereas ten years earlier the rural percentage was two-thirds larger than the urban percentage. The probable explanation of the earlier divergence and later similarity is that many of the servants in rural areas in 1841 were farm servants. The fact that in the rural areas of the most agricultural of the counties the pattern was much the same as in rural areas in other counties suggests a common pattern throughout England.[48] On the assumption that, but for the inclusion of indoor farm servants in the total, the servant

---

[47] The census authorities explained in a footnote to a table that: 'All labourers in agriculture (except shepherds) not living in the farmhouses are returned under the head "Agricultural labourer (outdoor)"; those living in the house of the farmer are classed under "Farm servant (indoor)", including, among others, waggoner, carter, farmer's groom, and general servant.' *1851 Census*, Population tables, pt II, vol. I, Summary tables, tab. XXV, p. ccxxiii.

[48] The lower percentage of domestic servants in the rural areas of 'industrial' counties is probably somewhat misleading. The percentage in the urban areas in these counties was exceptionally low and much of the remainder of the these counties consisted of communities which were not urban but far from agricultural, as, for example, in mining villages.

Table 5.4 *Servants as an element in the labour force in 1841 and 1851 (males aged 20 and over)*

	Urban			Rural			All		
	Servants	Total	Servants per 1,000	Servants	Total	Servants per 1,000	Servants	Total	Servants per 1,000
1841	17,561	954,783	1.8	66,010	2,163,033	3.1	83,571	3,117,816	2.7
1851	7,572	940,763	0.8	23,272	2,602,981	0.9	30,844	3,543,744	0.9
1841									
'Agricultural' counties	1,578	49,362	3.2	14,844	497,711	3.0	16,422	547,073	3.0
'Industrial' counties	7,457	559,483	1.3	10,192	478,617	2.1	17,649	1,038,100	1.7
1851									
'Agricultural' counties	854	51,723	1.7	4,644	521,994	0.9	5,518	573,717	1.0
'Industrial' counties	2,293	527,977	0.4	4,569	768,190	0.6	6,862	1,296,167	0.5

Notes: As in tab. 5.2, and for the same reason, London and the metropolitan counties were excluded from the calculations. The urban totals for each county in 1841 were derived from the cities and boroughs listed in the county returns. Those for 1851 were obtained similarly from the principal towns in each county. The rural totals were obtained by subtracting the urban totals from the overall totals for each county. The county totals under each head were then aggregated to provide the totals shown on the first two rows of the table. For definitions of 'agricultural' and 'industrial' see notes to tab. 5.2.

Sources: 1841 and 1851 censuses.

percentage in rural areas in 1841 would have been similar to the percentage in urban areas, as was the case in 1851, the 'true' servant total in rural areas would have been $2,163,033 \times 0.0184 = 39,800$ and the balance of those recorded, 26,210 (66,010–39,800), should be added to the total of agricultural labourers in 1841.

The second reason for adjusting the census returns relating to agricultural employment arises from the decision made by the Registrar General in 1851 to include all farmers' sons, grandsons, brothers, and nephews resident in a farm family and over the age of 15 as engaged in agriculture 'because they almost invariably work in some way on the farm'. This assertion is dubious. In the next two censuses the same categories were used, but whereas the total of farmers scarcely changed, the total of farmers' male relatives fell markedly, by about 19 per cent between 1851 and 1861, and by about 36 per cent between 1851 and 1871. The fall was massive in the south-east of the country, where farms were large and employed many labourers, but marginal or non-existent in the west midlands, where there were more family farms with less hired help, suggesting that the census officials exercised increasing discretion in their assumptions about the activities of male relatives in farming households.[49] Whether the Registrar General was justified in treating farmers' male relatives in this fashion is less important in this context than the fact that, because he chose to do so, some further adjustment is needed to place the two censuses as nearly as possible on the same basis. A simple correction procedure is suggested by the contrast between the number of farmers in 1841 and in 1851. In the former year the census recorded a total of 192,333 farmers in England; in the latter the comparable figure was much smaller at 174,734 (172,541 farmers plus 2,193 graziers). It is highly improbable that the true total of farmers changed appreciably during the decade. It was almost unchanged between 1851 and 1871.[50] The difference may well reflect the inclusion at the earlier date of farmers' male relatives who were actively engaged on the farm, who would be recorded in 1851 among the separate category of farmers' male relatives. Since there was probably very little change during the decade, comparison is facilitated if, instead of accepting the reported total of farmers'

---

[49] See above, pp. 98–9. It is of interest to note that when the 1831 census was taken in the four East Anglian counties of Cambridgeshire, Essex, Norfolk, and Suffolk, there were 16,737 farmers employing labour, 5,993 farmers employing no labour, and 124,438 agricultural labourers. In the five west midland counties of Cheshire, Herefordshire, Shropshire, Staffordshire, and Worcestershire, the comparable figures were 17,128; 12,786; and 76,005. The ratio of farmers not employing labour to those employing labour was more than twice as high in the west as in the east, while the ratio of labourers to farmers employing labour was two-thirds higher in the east than in the west.

[50] See tab. 4.4., p. 99.

male relatives in 1851 (55,114), they are assumed to equal the difference between the totals for farmers at the two dates (17,599), which means reducing the total of those employed in agriculture in 1851 by 55,114 − 17,599 = 37,515. Even if this procedure leads to an understatement of the 'true' numbers of farmers' male relatives working on the farm, it must improve the comparability of agricultural employment in the two censuses.

The upshot of the two adjustments is to increase the total engaged in agriculture in 1841 to 935,875 (909,665 + 26,210 (the adjustment for farm servants)) and to reduce the 1851 total to 914,503 (952,018 − 37,515 (the adjustment for male relatives)). It is therefore more likely that agricultural employment was falling during the 1840s than that it was rising. Indeed, it may have been falling for some time. It is not easy to reduce the agricultural returns in the 1831 census to the same form as in the next two censuses, but it is possible that it was no higher in 1851 than in 1831, and even unclear whether agricultural employment was still rising in the 1820s.[51]

The totals for two other major occupational groups also benefit from adjustment to counter the effects of different practice in the two censuses. Textiles and mining were two of the most dynamic industries in England in the mid-nineteenth century. It is therefore of particular interest to establish the speed of their advance. As with agriculture, however, employment trends in both are apt to be misunderstood unless the raw census totals are 'improved'. The limitations of the 1841 census appear, at first sight, to restrict any measurement of growth to the overall totals in all textile and mining activities, and for the same reason in both cases. For example, there were 57,908 coal miners in England in 1841, but there were also 11,146 'miners' who might have been engaged in the mining of coal, but equally of copper, tin, lead, or iron. Similarly, there were large numbers of men described simply as weavers rather than being linked to a particular branch of the textile industry, and a smaller number described as spinners and bleachers of whom the same was true. In 1851 this was no longer the case (though many individuals when filling in their schedules probably described themselves simply as 'miner' or 'weaver', but the local enumerators or the census checkers took it upon themselves to make a particular allocation in this more proactive exercise). Once again, the existence of county-level data makes it possible to effect plausible

---

[51] See above, pp. 110–25. It is of interest to note that Booth, though clearly very dubious about the scale of the increase in the agricultural labour force in the 1840s, nevertheless concluded that 'it is certain that a great increase (amounting according to these returns to 462,000) must have taken place in the agricultural population between 1841 and 1851'. Booth, 'Occupations of the people', p. 325.

Table 5.5 *Totals of miners in 1841 and 1851 (males aged 20 and over)*

	1841 census total	Tin and copper adjustment	Effect of reallocation of 'miners'	Revised 1841 total	1851 census total
Coal	62,760		+8,186	70,946	93,438
Lead	6,762		+592	7,354	9,616
Tin	4,586	+1,519	+108	6,213	7,886
Copper	12,179	−1,519	+270	10,930	10,691
Iron	3,918		+1,096	5,014	6,087
Miner	11,146		−10,252	894	0
Total	101,351	0	0	101,351	127,718

Note: For reasons for adjustment of totals see associated text.
Source: 1841 and 1851 censuses.

corrections to the national totals and to distribute the 'unattached' miners, weavers, and spinners to individual industries in the great majority of cases. For example, in Derbyshire there were 3,268 coal miners, 1,260 lead miners, 431 iron miners, and 209 men described simply as miners. On the assumption that the last group were distributed among coal, lead, and iron mining in the same proportions as the miners whose industry was specified, the total of coal miners is increased by 138, of lead miners by 53, and of iron miners by 18. There are minor problems with this procedure, such as that associated with the fact that the sum of the county totals of 'miners' does not equal the printed national total for England as a whole, which explains the survival of a small number of 'miners' in the revised totals, but the operation, while arbitrary, enables direct and instructive comparisons to be made. Consulting the county totals also brought to light an arbitrary action on the part of the census authorities which led to a significant distortion in the totals in tin and copper mining, and to the likelihood of misleading inferences being drawn from the comparison of 1841 with 1851. The returns for the county of Cornwall include a total of 3,038 men who are described as in 'tin and copper' mining, but there is no similar entry in the national totals, and it is clear by summing county totals that all these men were included in the total for copper miners when the county data were aggregated to form national totals.

Table 5.5 shows the outcome of the distribution of 'miners' to the several mining industries. The 3,038 Cornish men who were engaged in tin and copper mining were divided equally between tin and copper rather than being allocated exclusively to copper, on the assumption that they were working in mines producing both minerals. The picture which

Table 5.6 *Totals of textile workers in 1841 and 1851 (males aged 20 and over)*

	1841 census total	Effect of reallocation of weavers, spinners, and bleachers	Revised 1841 total	1851 census total
Cotton	75,085	+23,646	98,731	120,058
Wool	72,504	+18,371	90,875	89,721
Silk	24,776	+10,520	35,296	33,463
Linen	10,828	+1,997	12,825	13,158
Textiles, other	67,748	−54,534	13,214	11,264
	250,941	0	250,941	267,664

Note: For reasons for adjustment of totals see associated text.
Source: 1841 and 1851 censuses.

emerges after these reallocations is, of course, of slower growth in the major mining industries than would appear without redistributing the 'miners', except in the case of copper mining, where the effect is to replace a substantial fall with virtual stability.

A very similar exercise is possible for the main textile industries. There were very large numbers of 'weavers' (49,280) and smaller numbers of 'spinners' (2,311) and 'bleachers' (2,943) in the national returns. They, too, can be reallocated using the same logic as for miners by consulting the county data. The results are shown in table 5.6. The revised totals for 1841 for the major textile industries suggest that there was very little change in adult male employment except in the case of cotton where employment increased by 34 per cent during the 1840s.

Two further minor adjustments were made to the 1841 occupational totals. In the national tabulations there is a single category for 'Shop-keeper and general dealer', but in 1851 the two are separated. However, the county tabulations in 1841 always enter the two occupations separately, so that it is a simple matter, by aggregating the county totals, to provide the same information for 1841 as for 1851. The combined total for the two occupations was 13,708 of which 5,942 were general dealers and 7,766 shopkeepers. Secondly, tobacconists and manufacturers of tobacco were combined in a single category in 1841 but were separately returned in 1851. To facilitate comparison the 1841 combined total of 2,614 was divided between tobacconists (1,570) and tobacco manufacturers (1,044) in the same ratio as characterised the two in the later census.

These several changes may improve the comparability of the 1841 and 1851 censuses, but there remain difficulties which call for comment but are less straightforward. For lack of a plausible basis for adjustment, the totals in question were left unchanged.

The three most important in numerical terms concern labourers, domestic servants, and clerks. As already noted, the number of labourers fell from 269,788 in 1841 to 228,498 in 1851, while the number of domestic servants fell much more sharply from 123,923 to 45,109. Clerks also declined in number from 39,601 in 1841 to 33,920 ten years later ('clerks, commercial' in 1841; 'commercial clerks' plus 'law clerks' in 1851). In the case of the first two groups, it is improbable that there was much change in the true figure over the decade. In the case of clerks, it is more likely that the true figure was rising.

For labourers, a plausible explanation is not far to seek. A number of labouring occupations were separately itemised in 1851 but not in 1841. They were the following (totals in 1851 are given in brackets in each case): in construction, excavators (2,544) and road labourers (6,237); in the rail industry, railway labourers (22,433); in transport, dock service (13,577)[52] and dockyards (H.M.) labourers (3,976); and, again in transport, coal heavers (9,308): in all a total of 58,075 men. It would be reasonable to guess that the same occupations employed, say, 35,000–40,000 men in 1841, even allowing for the huge growth in the number of railway labourers during the 1840s. If these are, indeed, reasonable assumptions, any anomaly between the two censuses disappears.

Accounting for the apparent decline in domestic service involves greater imponderables. A part of the fall occurred because of the introduction of the new category of farm servant (indoors) in 1851, which has already been discussed. It suggests a little over 26,000 of the domestic servants in 1841 were farm servants. But this still leaves a very large difference of perhaps 50,000 men who would apparently have been treated as servants in 1841 but appear elsewhere in 1851. The bulk of this total, however, disappears readily if it is safe to assume that the servants who were recorded within the general category of servants but separately designated as coachman, groom, gardener, and inn servant in 1851 would have been included simply as servants ten years earlier. This supposition is plausible in the sense that there were also separate entries for gardener, coachman, and groom with their appropriate occupational groups in 1851 in addition to those in each category who were treated as servants. Since coachmen, grooms, gardeners, and inn servants who were counted as servants numbered in total 33,804 in 1851 (the individual totals were 6,079; 9.243; 3,757; and 14,725 respectively), the remaining difference is of the order of 15,000–20,000. Part of the remaining shortfall

---

[52] This was not a null category in 1841 but the number of men was small, only 351 workers.

may be genuine. Male domestic service declined fairly steadily, if slowly, throughout the second half of the nineteenth century.[53] It may also be the case that family members were more frequently termed servants in 1841 than in 1851 when the census takers were inclined to assume that family members were engaged in the same industry or activity as that of the head of the household. Further work on enumerators' books from the two censuses may throw light on this question.

In the case of clerks, there can be little doubt that their numbers were increasing, even if the census seems to refute this. A first point to note is that this was an occupational group which troubled the census authorities in 1841. The county totals of clerks sum to a figure of 44,066 but the national figure for England is given as 39,601. The difference is explained by the fact that, as a footnote to the main table in the preface put it:

Considerable difficulty has occurred in ascertaining the number of clergymen in England and Wales correctly, in consequence of the word 'clerk' being equally applicable to clergymen and to the large class of persons employed by bankers, merchants, and professional men. The above results have been arrived at after a careful examination and correction of the totals returned under these heads in the several counties.

The correction seems to have been carried out tolerably accurately since the total of clergymen in 1841 (13,511) bears a credible relationship to the total in 1851 (14,903), the increase of just over 10 per cent being somewhat lower than the 14 per cent increase in the total of men aged 20 or more. It is therefore unlikely to have any bearing on the anomalous fall in the totals of clerks between the two censuses. It is probable that a part of the shrinkage in the number of clerks bears some resemblance to that in labourers in that an increased proportion were allocated to particular industries rather than being classified simply as 'clerks'. For example, there were 8,185 men described in 1851 as 'railway officer, clerk, station master'. It is likely that the largest element in this group was that of railway clerk, which might otherwise have added, say, 5,000 to the total of clerks. A conclusive explanation of the puzzling failure of the total of clerks to expand is, however, lacking.

This somewhat wearisome list of 'improvements' to the information contained in the two censuses falls well short of the implicit aim of placing the data which they contain on a common footing. Comparisons must always be made with discretion and will involve many caveats. Sometimes what seems anomalous when considering a single trade or occupation, ceases to be so when a broader category is considered. For example, there

[53] Armstrong, 'The use of information about occupation', app. D, p. 279.

are no goldsmiths in the 1841 census and very few jewellers in the 1851 census, but the overall totals for the general category 'Gold, silver, jewelry' appear plausible (9,250 and 9,763 respectively). It seems clear that in the earlier census all goldsmiths were subsumed under the heading 'jeweller', whereas in the later census goldsmiths were separately identified. Other apparent anomalies are less easy to explain, though in many cases the anomalies may disappear within broader categories, even if it may be less easy to demonstrate the point than in the case of goldsmiths and jewellers. But some anomalies remain and cannot readily be accommodated. For example, the number of provision dealers jumped from 769 in 1841 to 5,399 in 1851, and the total in the wider category of trading and dealing in food and drink rose from 6,462 to 15,150. Without the provision dealers the rise in food and drink would still be substantial, but credible. With them, it suggests the need for adjustment, but no well founded basis for adjustment suggests itself.

The occupational structure in the mid-century revealed by the PST classification system

It makes the information to be considered more digestible if it is first presented in its most aggregated form, and then in greater detail. Table 5.7 deals simply with the numbers engaged in the three basic sectors, primary (agriculture, forestry, fishing, and mining); secondary (building and manufacture); and tertiary (transport and the range of service industries and activities). The first three lines of data are self-explanatory. The total labelled 'Others' concerns those in categories such as pensioners, prisoners, lunatics, vagrants, those of independent means, gentlemen, capital owners, or retired who could not conveniently be allocated as primary, secondary, or tertiary. In 1841 the combined total of the three basic sectors and 'Others' is the same as that for the entire population of men aged 20 and over but in 1851 the two are not the same because of the action, described above, by which each occupational category was multiplied by 0.917 to improve comparability between the two censuses in view of the far higher proportion of the adult male population who were returned as in employment in 1851.[54] Those with an eye to detail may notice that the combined total of 4,032,514 is not exactly the same figure as that obtained by multiplying 4,399,377 by 0.917 (4,034,299). The latter figure is 0.04 per cent larger than the former. This occurs because of the problem described above, and is related to the inconsistencies between

[54] See above pp. 147–9.

Table 5.7 *Primary, secondary, and tertiary (PST) occupational totals, England 1841 and 1851 (males aged 20 and over)*

	1841	% of PST total	1851	% of PST total	1851/1841 × 100
Primary	1,126,270	33.0	1,168,926	30.5	103.8
Secondary	1,608,423	47.2	1,762,051	46.0	109.6
Tertiary	675,288	19.8	897,672	23.4	132.9
PST total	3,409,981		3,828,649		112.3
Others	447,490		203,865		45.6
Combined total (PST and Others)	3,857,471		4,032,514		104.5
Total of males aged 20 and over	3,857,471		4,399,377		114.0

Notes: The total for 'Others' is much larger in 1841 than in 1851 primarily because there were many men in a final category termed 'Residue of the population' for which there was no equivalent in 1851. In 1841 this category included a large number who were no longer in active employment by reason of age. The combined total in 1841 is the same as the total for all males aged 20 and over. This was not the case in 1851 because, in order to offset the very different treatment of the retired population in the two censuses, the reported totals in the 1851 census were reduced by just over 8 per cent (see pp. 148–9.)
Sources: 1841 and 1851 censuses.

the Registrar General's returns for Great Britain as a whole and those for its constituent parts.[55]

The rapidity of change in the English economy in the 1840s is clearly visible in table 5.7. Primary employment grew by less than 4 per cent, secondary employment by 10 per cent, but tertiary employment ballooned by 33 per cent. The combined employment in all three categories grew by 12 per cent over the decade, so that both the first two groups were growing by less than the overall figure, and as a result their shares in the national totals both fell: in the case of primary employment sharply, in the case of secondary employment more modestly, while tertiary employment's share of total employment rose from 19.8 to 23.4 per cent, or by almost a fifth. Aggregate income was directed increasingly and differentially towards the supply of services of all kinds. In a rapidly growing economy this is not surprising; indeed, to have found anything else would be unexpected, but the extent of the contrast is notable. This is, however, a very 'broad brush' treatment of occupational change. Only more

[55] See above p. 140.

detailed tabulations can reveal the nature and consistency of the changes taking place. Other topics appeal. How close was the link between differential rates of expansion in employment and output trends? In particular, were there industries, for example in textile industries other than cotton, in which stasis in male employment[56] was a function of a rapid growth in manpower productivity rather than an indication of stagnation? A fuller discussion would also need to take account of the impact of foreign demand on differential occupational growth. These questions and others like them, however, are, in the main, topics for another day.

Table 5.8 is intended to provide the additional detail needed to interpret the brief sketch provided in the previous table. Among the primary industries, agriculture, as already noted, was probably contracting slightly.[57] The large proportionate increase in 'other agriculture' occurs because the 1851 census divided categories which had not earlier been separated. For example, in 1851 there were 9,050 shepherds: in 1841 these were counted among the agricultural labourers. There was a very marked increase in the number of gardeners. To a minor degree the increase is a matter of definition: 3,757 of the total in 1851 were recorded in the census as 'gardeners (domestic servant)'. They were included with those described simply as gardeners, but, on different assumptions, might have been allocated elsewhere. In any case, the increase is marked. It seems clear, however, that the rise was not produced by a major expansion in market gardening. If that had been the case, expansion would have been most marked in counties near to London and in Lancashire where urban demand was growing most quickly. But the counties in which growth was most marked were widely scattered and generally remote from the big urban centres (Berkshire, Buckinghamshire, Cheshire, Derby, Dorset, Gloucestershire, Herefordshire, Somerset, Hampshire, Westmorland, and Worcestershire). There was a clearer regional patterning in the absolute level of gardening employment. It was universally low in the north, whether for climatic or social reasons. In 1851 gardeners were less than 10 per 1,000 of the adult male labour force in Cumberland, Durham, Northumberland, Westmorland, Lancashire, the North and West Ridings of Yorkshire, Derbyshire, and Staffordshire; and also in Lincolnshire and Cornwall. They were most numerous at 18 per 1,000 adult males or more in Bedfordshire, Berkshire, Buckinghamshire, Essex, Gloucestershire, Hampshire, Worcestershire, and the extra-metropolitan

---

[56] See tab. 5.6.

[57] In view of the adjustment to the totals of farmers in 1851 described above (pp. 157–8), it may appear surprising that the totals in the two censuses in tab. 5.8 are not the same. The difference is explained by the presence of ten 'colonial farmers' in England in 1851.

Table 5.8 *Detailed primary, secondary and tertiary occupational totals, England 1841 and 1851 (males aged 20 and over)*

	1841	1851	1851/1841 × 100	% of 1841 column total	% of 1851 column total
PRIMARY	**1,126,270**	**1,168,926**	103.8	33.02	30.53
Agriculture	**935,875**	**914,503**	97.7	27.45	23.89
farmer	192,333	192,352	100.0	5.64	5.02
farm labourer	737,415	697,694	94.6	21.63	18.22
other agriculture	6,127	24,457	399.2	0.18	0.64
Estate work	**46,498**	**65,857**	141.6	1.36	1.72
gardener	41,011	59,350	144.7	1.20	1.55
other	5,487	6,507	118.6	0.16	0.17
Forestry	**24,910**	**29,981**	120.4	0.73	0.78
Fishing	**8,621**	**12,235**	141.9	0.25	0.32
Mining	**110,366**	**146,350**	132.6	3.24	3.82
coal	71,542	93,666	130.9	2.10	2.45
lead	7,354	9,616	130.8	0.22	0.25
tin	6,213	7,886	126.9	0.18	0.21
copper	10,930	10,691	97.8	0.32	0.28
iron	5,014	6,087	121.4	0.15	0.16
quarrying	7,408	17,426	235.2	0.22	0.46
other mining	1,905	978	51.3	0.06	0.03
SECONDARY	**1,608,423**	**1,762,051**	109.6	47.17	46.02
Food and drink	**106,913**	**132,382**	123.8	3.14	3.46
baker *et sim.*	32,292	38,484	119.2	0.95	1.01
butcher *et sim.*	37,977	43,000	113.2	1.11	1.12
other food	19,912	26,007	130.6	0.58	0.68
drink	16,732	24,891	148.8	0.49	0.65
Clothing and footwear	**277,562**	**288,375**	103.9	8.14	7.53
tailor	82,259	84,348	102.5	2.41	2.20
boot and shoe	145,855	152,311	104.4	4.28	3.98
hats and headwear	13,946	11,414	81.8	0.41	0.30
glover	2,705	3,833	141.7	0.08	0.10
hosier, stockinger, knitwear	24,259	25,855	106.6	0.71	0.68
other clothing	8,538	10,614	124.3	0.25	0.28
Building and construction	**257,986**	**307,529**	119.2	7.57	8.03
carpenter	111,837	114,672	102.5	3.28	3.00
bricklayer	35,392	52,926	149.5	1.04	1.38
mason	48,941	56,199	114.8	1.44	1.47
painter, paperhanger	37,677	44,145	117.2	1.10	1.15
other building	24,139	39,587	164.0	0.71	1.03
Boat, barge, and ship building	**17,986**	**20,670**	114.9	0.53	0.54
Textiles	**250,941**	**267,664**	106.7	7.36	6.99
cotton	98,731	120,058	121.6	2.90	3.14
wool	90,875	89,721	98.7	2.66	2.34

Table 5.8 (cont.)

	1841	1851	1851/1841 × 100	% of 1841 column total	% of 1851 column total
silk	35,296	33,463	94.8	1.04	0.87
linen	12,825	13,158	102.6	0.38	0.34
textile, other	13,214	11,264	85.2	0.39	0.29
Leather, bone, fur, hair, glue	**29,170**	**31,632**	108.4	0.86	0.83
leather, general	8,492	9,238	108.8	0.25	0.24
saddle, harness	12,267	12,127	98.9	0.36	0.32
other	8,411	10,267	122.1	0.25	0.27
Woodworking	**52,758**	**58,361**	110.6	1.55	1.52
cooper	12,368	12,156	98.3	0.36	0.32
joiner, turner, cabinet maker	24,555	27,016	110.0	0.72	0.71
other wood	15,835	19,189	121.2	0.46	0.50
Instrument making	**13,969**	**17,562**	125.7	0.41	0.46
clock, watch	11,036	12,435	112.7	0.32	0.32
other instruments	2,933	5,127	174.8	0.09	0.13
Gold, silver, jewelry	**9,250**	**9,763**	105.6	0.27	0.25
Papermaking	**7,090**	**8,466**	119.4	0.21	0.22
Printing and publishing	**25,288**	**30,979**	122.5	0.74	0.81
Cart, carriage, coach					
building	30,712	32,504	105.8	0.90	0.85
wheelwright	20,656	20,628	99.9	0.61	0.54
other	10,056	11,876	118.1	0.29	0.31
Pottery, glass, brick, lime	**34,313**	**42,648**	124.3	1.01	1.11
pottery, earthenware	13,596	15,857	116.6	0.40	0.41
glass	5,374	7,341	136.6	0.16	0.19
brick and tile, lime burning	15,343	19,450	126.8	0.45	0.51
Brass, tin, copper, lead, and zinc	**27,397**	**31,907**	116.5	0.80	0.83
brass	9,343	9,233	98.8	0.27	0.24
tin	5,569	7,740	139.0	0.16	0.20
other	12,485	14,934	119.6	0.37	0.39
Iron and steel	**109,150**	**135,116**	123.8	3.20	3.53
blacksmith	62,624	64,218	102.6	1.84	1.68
iron and steel manufacture	14,400	35,092	243.7	0.42	0.92
nails, screws	11,404	11,497	100.8	0.33	0.30
edge tools	10,180	13,387	131.5	0.30	0.35
other	10,542	10,922	103.6	0.31	0.29
Engineering	**43,208**	**53,640**	124.1	1.27	1.40
machines, implements, tools	15,312	16,804	109.7	0.45	0.44
general	27,896	36,836	132.1	0.82	0.96
Gunmaking	**4,529**	**4,896**	108.1	0.13	0.13
Chemical industries	**3,976**	**8,005**	201.3	0.12	0.21
Gas, coke, water	**2,528**	**7,618**	301.3	0.07	0.20
gas	1,902	5,457	286.9	0.06	0.14
other	626	2,161	345.2	0.02	0.06

Table 5.8 (*cont.*)

	1841	1851	1851/1841 × 100	% of 1841 column total	% of 1851 column total
Furniture and furnishing	**9,083**	**13,202**	145.4	0.27	0.34
Rope making	**7,064**	**7,136**	101.0	0.21	0.19
Straw and rush	**5,194**	**6,000**	115.5	0.15	0.16
Minor trades	**8,201**	**10,264**	125.2	0.24	0.27
Secondary, general	**274,155**	**235,732**	86.0	8.04	6.16
TERTIARY	**675,288**	**897,672**	132.9	19.80	23.45
Transport	**140,036**	**270,549**	193.2	4.11	7.07
road	54,082	78,221	144.6	1.59	2.04
rail	2,657	44,451	1673.0	0.08	1.16
sea	32,279	55,184	171.0	0.95	1.44
inland water	20,857	28,105	134.8	0.61	0.73
warehousing, storage, packing	10,874	29,743	273.5	0.32	0.78
porter, messenger *et sim.*	19,287	34,845	180.7	0.57	0.91
Trading, dealing, agency	**75,684**	**113,643**	150.2	2.22	2.97
food, drink	9,342	20,609	220.6	0.27	0.54
livestock	4,850	6,174	127.3	0.14	0.16
textiles, textile materials, clothing	22,652	31,071	137.2	0.66	0.81
minerals, mineral products	6,987	12,926	185.0	0.20	0.34
raw products and materials	4,923	8,907	180.9	0.14	0.23
other dealing, etc.	4,819	9,259	192.1	0.14	0.24
unspecific	22,111	24,697	111.7	0.65	0.65
Retail trade	**91,753**	**121,117**	132.0	2.69	3.16
shopkeeper	7,899	10,550	133.6	0.23	0.28
grocer	28,477	41,528	145.8	0.84	1.08
greengrocer, fruiterer	4,911	6,957	141.7	0.14	0.18
fishmonger, meat seller	5,111	7,350	143.8	0.15	0.19
other food	8,241	11,174	135.6	0.24	0.29
coffee, tea, tobacco	1,570	2,390	152.2	0.05	0.06
chemist *et sim.*	7,559	9,511	125.8	0.22	0.25
bookseller, stationer, newsagent	3,633	4,450	122.5	0.11	0.12
other	24,352	27,207	111.7	0.71	0.71
Food, drink, lodging	**47,700**	**67,535**	141.6	1.40	1.76
Public services	**32,528**	**49,576**	152.4	0.95	1.29
post	2,875	6,636	230.8	0.08	0.17
inland revenue, customs and excise	9,194	11,940	129.9	0.27	0.31
other central government service	2,598	6,683	257.2	0.08	0.17
local and parish government	17,861	24,317	136.2	0.52	0.64

Table 5.8 (*cont.*)

	1841	1851	1851/1841 × 100	% of 1841 column total	% of 1851 column total
Professions	**85,369**	**97,162**	113.8	2.50	2.54
law	13,590	16,417	120.8	0.40	0.43
medicine	15,668	15,865	101.3	0.46	0.41
clergy	18,675	21,691	116.2	0.55	0.57
teaching	19,303	21,883	113.4	0.57	0.57
other	18,133	21,306	117.5	0.53	0.56
Clerical, secretarial, administrative	**39,642**	**35,433**	89.4	1.16	0.93
clerk (all descriptions)	39,601	33,920	85.7	1.16	0.89
secretarial and administrative	41	1,513	3690.2	0.00	0.04
Armed forces	**36,951**	**46,265**	125.2	1.08	1.21
army	28,898	32,788	113.5	0.85	0.86
navy	8,053	13,477	167.4	0.24	0.35
Domestic service	**97,713**	**60,442**	61.9	2.87	1.58
servant, domestic	97,713	45,120	46.2	2.87	1.18
servant, other	0	15,322		0.00	0.40
Entertainment	**1,076**	**1,523**	141.5	0.03	0.04
Services	**13,962**	**20,297**	145.4	0.41	0.53
barber	7,856	8,327	106.0	0.23	0.22
chimney sweep	2,649	3,729	140.8	0.08	0.10
other	3,457	8,241	238.4	0.10	0.22
Banking, financial	**8,522**	**10,998**	129.1	0.25	0.29
banking	1,418	1,611	113.6	0.04	0.04
other financial services	7,104	9,387	132.1	0.21	0.25
Tertiary, general	**4,352**	**3,132**	72.0	0.13	0.08
TOTAL	**3,409,981**	**3,828,649**	112.3	100.00	100.00

Note: The overall totals in this table are those of men in active employment rather than the national totals of men aged 20 and over. For the latter see tab. 5.7.
Sources: 1841 and 1851 censuses.

areas of Kent and Surrey.[58] Employment in forestry and in fishing also expanded markedly, though the totals involved in the latter group were modest. The number of men in the mining industry rose by a third, and the expansion was widespread. The coal industry in the 1840s, though very much the largest among the mining groups, was not outpacing the

[58] The complexities of the growth in gardening and market gardening is discussed at greater length on pp. 100–10 above.

others, apart from copper, which was treading water. Quarrying more than doubled in size on the evidence of the census.

Secondary industry in general grew by about 10 per cent, but the fortunes of its constituent elements varied greatly. In considering the relative growth rates the marked shrinkage in the last secondary category, 'Secondary, general', should be borne in mind. Numbers in this category fell because of the large reduction in the number of 'labourers', which has already been discussed. Many of those who had been included in this category in 1841 were allocated to particular industries in 1851. The large rise in building and construction, in particular, would in all probability have been far less pronounced if labourers had been treated similarly in both censuses, and the same is likely to be true, if in a lesser degree, of some other categories, such as pottery, glass, brick, and lime; brass, tin, copper, lead, and zinc; and iron and steel. Some contrasts seem clear, however. Employment in the food and drink industries was growing much faster than the population as a whole, but the opposite was true of clothing and footwear, and particularly of the two largest elements in this category, tailors and shoemakers. It is particularly striking that, although there was a small increase in the numbers in textiles as a whole (7 per cent), the growth was confined to the cotton industry which expanded by a little over a fifth. If cotton is subtracted from the textile total, the number of men in the remainder of the industry shrank by 3 per cent. Within the cotton industry growth was concentrated in Lancashire, where the total rose from 71,132 to 101,158, or by 30,026. The national total in the cotton industry rose by substantially less than this, from 98,731 to 120,058, or by 21,327, suggesting contraction outside Lancashire.[59]

In general, what might be termed traditional industries, such as leather, woodworking, jewelry, coach building, gunmaking, and rope making were growing less rapidly than the adult male population as a whole. In contrast some of the 'new' industries were growing much faster than the general growth of population. This was true of iron and steel; engineering; printing; papermaking; chemical industries; and gas, coke, and water. Employment in these industrial groups grew by 27 per cent, from 191,240 to 243,824, but their combined total in 1851 still fell well short of the total in, for example, clothing and footwear. England remained a country in which long-established trades provided much more employment than the eye-catching newer industries. There was, for example, a combined total of 318,143 bakers, butchers, tailors, and shoemakers in that year, and their numbers had grown by almost 20,000 in the preceding decade.

[59] The 1851 figure for Lancashire is slightly understated, because it was not possible to allocate accurately to cotton its share of the catch-all category of 'Other workers, dealers in flax, cotton'.

Growth in tertiary industries was uniformly marked, even dramatic, with the sole exception of domestic service and clerks, special cases discussed above.[60] Breakneck expansion in the rail industry is to be expected in view of the huge enthusiasm for railway projects in the 1840s, but the striking growth in all the other transport categories is equally notable, though in the last two elements in the transport category, much of the apparent growth is probably due to the different treatment of labourers in the two censuses. Labourers were more frequently allocated to particular industries or activities in 1851 than in 1841, and many of these employments were in the tertiary rather than the secondary sector. Since labourers in 1841 were all treated as in the secondary sector, a change of this type tends to exaggerate tertiary growth and, symmetrically, to understate secondary growth, though even when allowance is made for this, the tertiary sector was still growing much faster than the secondary sector. Consider an extreme case. In 1841 the total of labourers was just under 270,000. If there had been no change in the census definitions, this figure might have risen to, say, 300,000 in the course of the decade. In 1851 the recorded total of labourers was just under 230,000, a difference of 70,000.[61] If one were to assume that all the 70,000 were labourers who would have been included in the secondary sector under the conventions prevailing in 1841, this would increase the decadal growth rate in the secondary sector from 10 to 14 per cent, and decrease the growth rate in the tertiary sector from 33 to 23 per cent. The difference in growth rates remains substantial, and the calculation certainly overstates the case, since many of the labourers who were 'reallocated' between the two censuses remained in the secondary sector.

Part of the exceptional apparent rate of growth in transport, therefore, was spurious, but there was also a striking expansion elsewhere in the tertiary sector where the 'labourer' issue does not arise, or was of minor significance. Both dealing and the retail trades, for example, were growing fast. Expansion was remarkably evenly spread among the subdivisions of these two categories. Many other tertiary industries, like dealing and the retail trade, grew by between 30 and 50 per cent in the 1840s. This occurred in food, drink, and lodging; public services; entertainment; and other services. Growth was less marked in the professions, the armed forces, and banking, though in all of these the rate of expansion would have been counted very rapid in a secondary industry.

Attention is conventionally focused on manufacturing expansion in this, the heyday of British economic dominance, but a balanced

---

[60] See above pp. 155–7, 161–2.
[61] For totals of labourers at the two censuses see tab. 5.A1.2, p. 184.

account of the economic history of the country should not ignore the fact that although employment in tertiary industry in 1841 was far less than half that in secondary industry, the growth in numbers in the former was almost half as great again as that in the latter in the decade which followed.[62] The tertiary total grew by 243,824, while the secondary total grew by 191,240. The scale of the differential would be reduced if accurate adjustment could be made for the 'labourer' problem, but the contrast remains notable. Growth in both the secondary and tertiary sector overshadowed that in the primary sector, which stood at 42,656. The nation of shopkeepers deserved its title.

The retail and wholesale trades

As an illustration of this last point, and also of the immense wealth of information which can be gleaned from county-level data, it is illuminating to consider the county returns for a small number of occupations in the retail and wholesale trades. The trades in question were chosen quite casually. They have it in common that all were growing rapidly during the 1840s and were of substantial size, so that county totals were meaningful. Ideally, the individual county totals should be considered, but space prohibits this. Instead, the counties were grouped into four broad categories – the metropolitan counties of Middlesex, Surrey, and Kent in which London was the dominant element; the agricultural counties; the industrial counties; and the rest of the country.[63] Ideally, too, county totals for all occupations should have been input. This would have allowed a wide range of issues to be probed much more effectively, but was beyond the scope of the present essay.

The top panel of table 5.9 shows the extent of the contrast in rates of growth between the four county groups. Whereas the adult male population of the country as a whole grew by 14 per cent during the 1840s, the industrial counties grew far faster, by 25 per cent, yet, at the other extreme, growth had almost ceased in the agricultural counties where the increase fell just short of 5 per cent. The metropolitan counties as a group grew a little faster than the national average, while the other counties enjoyed a more sedate expansion, though well above the rate found in the agricultural counties.

The rest of table 5.9 gives details of the number of men engaged in each of eight trades and shows the proportion of the adult male population

[62] The tendency to neglect tertiary occupations and to focus excessively on manufacturing when reviewing the growth of the Victorian economy is the central theme of an important article by C. H. Lee, 'The service sector'.

[63] For definitions of the agricultural and industrial counties, see notes to tab. 5.2, p. 152.

engaged in each trade in each county group. In addition two of the trades, those of grocer and shopkeeper, are treated as a single entity in a final tabulation. The table is instructive for several reasons. As might be expected on general grounds, the metropolitan counties showed the highest rates per 1,000 adult males in every trade in 1851, and in every trade except that of shopkeeper in 1841 (this was probably an accident of nomenclature; by 1851 the anomaly had disappeared). But the difference between 'London' and the rest was not pronounced in most cases, and the differences between the other county groups were, in general, minimal. The largest single trade was that of grocer. Since it was an occupation which probably overlapped with that of shopkeeper, the final tabulation shows the two combined. 'London' had the greatest concentration of grocers and shopkeepers, with a rate of 13.2 per 1,000, but it was not far ahead of the pack. All the others were very closely bunched with rates between 11 and 12 per 1,000. The opportunities for grocers and shopkeepers to make a living were as good in the slow-growing agricultural counties as they were either in the industrial counties where growth was hectic, or in the rest of the country. The homogeneity of the national picture is notable. In agricultural counties, neither the fact that a large proportion of the labour force consisted of agricultural labourers nor the fact that a much larger proportion of the population lived in villages and that the urban proportion was tiny caused divergence from the national pattern. The same was true of drapers and ironmongers. Chemists and coal dealers were less common in the agricultural counties than elsewhere, but even here differences were modest and, at least in the case of coal dealers, the gap was closing during the decade.

The two remaining occupations are those of groom and stationer. Stationer was the one occupation among the eight in the table where the metropolitan counties were truly dominant. In 1851 two-thirds of all stationers were to be found in London. All the other trades served a predominantly local market and were dependent upon the scale of demand in the immediate neighbourhood, but stationers were presumably able to trade effectively at a distance from many of their customers, essentially because the demand for their products was specialised and intermittent, rather than widespread and localised. The very vigorous growth in the number of grooms is testimony to the continued importance of the horse. The metropolis and the agricultural counties had the highest proportions of grooms, and the industrial counties much the lowest proportion, but the number of grooms was rising everywhere (the totals in 1851, incidentally, did not include grooms in domestic service). The category of groom included hostlers in 1841 and this was probably also true

Table 5.9 Totals and rates of growth in a selection of retail and wholesale trades by groups of counties in the 1840s (males aged 20 and over)

	Males aged 20 and over		
	1841	1851	Ratio[a]
'London' counties	736,037	855,633	116.2
Agricultural counties	547,073	573,717	104.9
Industrial counties	1,038,100	1,296,167	124.9
Other counties	1,532,643	1,673,860	109.2
England	3,853,883	4,399,377	114.2

	Chemist		Rate per 1,000[b]	
	1841	1851	1841	1851
'London' counties	1,966	2,517	2.7	2.9
Agricultural counties	788	888	1.4	1.5
Industrial counties	2,028	3,011	2.0	2.1
Other counties	2,691	3,345	1.8	2.0
England	7,473	9,511	1.9	2.2

	Coal dealer		Rate per 1,000	
	1841	1851	1841	1851
'London' counties	1,801	2,127	2.4	2.5
Agricultural counties	397	866	0.7	1.5
Industrial counties	1,425	2,513	1.4	1.9
Other counties	1,882	3,092	1.2	1.8
England	5,505	8,598	1.4	2.0

	Draper		Rate per 1,000	
	1841	1851	1841	1851
'London' counties	2,941	6,490	4.0	7.6
Agricultural counties	1,868	2,395	3.4	4.2
Industrial counties	3,442	5,386	3.3	4.2
Other counties	5,274	7,270	3.4	4.3
England	13,525	21,541	3.5	4.9

	Grocer		Rate per 1,000	
	1841	1851	1841	1851
'London' counties	6,121	8,620	8.3	10.0
Agricultural counties	3,903	5,187	7.1	9.0
Industrial counties	7,359	12,280	7.1	9.5
Other counties	11,094	15,441	7.2	9.2
England	28,477	41,528	7.4	9.4

	Groom		Rate per 1,000		Ironmonger		Rate per 1,000	
	1841	1851	1841	1851	1841	1851	1841	1851
'London' counties	3,818	5,947	5.2	7.0	1,242	1,565	1.7	1.8
Agricultural counties	2,042	3,637	3.7	6.3	513	607	0.9	1.1
Industrial counties	2,593	3,403	2.5	2.6	867	1,191	0.8	0.9
Other counties	5,221	7,251	3.4	4.3	1,628	1,979	1.1	1.2
England	13,674	20,238	3.5	4.6	4,250	5,342	1.1	1.2

	Shopkeeper		Rate per 1,000		Stationer		Rate per 1,000	
	1841	1851	1841	1851	1841	1851	1841	1851
'London' counties	808	2,679	1.1	3.1	1,410	1,862	1.9	2.2
Agricultural counties	827	1,298	1.5	2.3	100	85	0.2	0.1
Industrial counties	3,430	2,969	3.3	2.3	327	406	0.3	0.3
Other counties	2,701	3,351	1.8	2.0	419	450	0.3	0.3
England	7,766	10,297	2.0	2.3	2,256	2,803	0.6	0.6

	Grocer and Shopkeeper		Rate per 1,000	
	1841	1851	1841	1851
'London' counties	6,929	11,299	9.4	13.2
Agricultural counties	4,730	6,485	8.7	11.3
Industrial counties	10,789	15,249	10.4	11.8
Other counties	13,795	18,792	9.0	11.2
England	36,243	51,825	9.4	11.8

Notes: [a] 1851/1841 × 100. [b] This rate relates the total in the named trade to the population of the county group in question. The 'London' counties are Middlesex, Surrey, and Kent. For definition of the agricultural and industrial counties, see notes to tab. 5.2.
Source: 1841 and 1851 censuses, county data.

in 1851, so that it is a more inclusive description than might appear at first sight.

This excursion into the use of disaggregated data does no more than scratch the surface. It would be possible, for example, to divide the populations of each of the four county groups between urban and rural, and so to pursue further the degree of similarity between them, and the probable source of any dissimilarities. But even a cursory glance at county data shows how valuable they might be in obliging a reassessment of some elements in the received wisdom about England in the mid-century. If the pattern to be found in table 5.9 is typical of most of the tertiary occupations which were closely linked to local demand, it will be necessary to account for a scale and structure of demand for a wide range of services which did not differ greatly between areas of the country whose overall economic constitution contrasted sharply, and whose rates of growth differed widely. Much that was readily visible, both to contemporaries and to later generations, suggested a country of massive regional contrasts. In other respects, however, there may have been much greater similarities than is commonly suspected.[64]

General reflections

My original intention in embarking on a fuller exploitation of the material in the 1841 and 1851 censuses was largely confined to establishing a point of comparison for occupational data from the preceding century of English history, and testing the value of alternative methods of tabulating such data. In the event, the exercise turned out to produce substantive results which appear instructive in their own right. Taken neat, so to speak, the census returns are of limited value, since changes in the conventions imposed by successive Registrars General obscure the import of the material. This is true not only between censuses, but also, less obviously but equally damagingly, within censuses. The serious and pervasive inconsistencies between the returns for Great Britain as a whole and its constituent parts in 1851 represent an object lesson in this regard. Nevertheless, many of the problems at issue can be identified and in most cases something can be done to offset the inaccuracies which would otherwise arise. Oddly, this discovery is a mixed blessing since it underlines how much might profitably be done in addition and how incomplete is the

---

[64] Lee, in his analysis of tertiary employment in Victorian Britain, takes a different line, presenting evidence of marked regional specialisation in the level and type of service employment. The period covered in his analysis and the fact that his data refer to total employment rather than to adult males, however, make if difficult to determine how far his conclusions are at odds with the view presented here: C. H. Lee, 'The service sector'.

present state of the work. Some deficiencies in the present state of the exercise may be briefly reviewed in conclusion.

First, if it is reasonable to hope that trends in occupational change can be recovered with fair accuracy from nineteenth-century censuses despite their shortcomings, it is illogical to confine attention to the 1841 and 1851 censuses. There is no reason to doubt that similar work could be carried out on their successors. If the contrasting rates of growth between occupations so evident in the 1840s proved persistent over a longer period, this would greatly strengthen some of the claims made in this essay. Equally, a lengthier time span might enforce significant modifications of these claims. For example, it would be possible to test more extensively the belief that the agricultural labour force had reached its peak in 1831 at the latest and was thereafter in decline. Again, it would be fascinating to plot the relative growth rates of the main components of secondary and tertiary employment to see whether the differentials which characterised the 1840s were maintained thereafter.

Second, it is, of course, artificial to restrict attention to the adult male labour force. There is good reason to do this looking backwards, so to speak, since this is the sector of the labour force whose occupational structure is easiest to recover from earlier records. It is also true that census information about adult males is considerably more reliable than that for women and juniors, and probable that, in many occupations, the trends for the labour force as a whole mirrored that for adult men. Much of value could, none the less, probably be brought to light by enlarging the scope of the exercise to cover women and juveniles. The same is also true of the geographical coverage of the material presented in this essay. Wales and Scotland were excluded. Once again, their exclusion makes good sense in relation to the availability of earlier material, but seems artificial if the focus of discussion is the substantive situation in the middle of the nineteenth century.

Even within the context of the two censuses covered in this essay there are many issues which could with profit be pursued further. Two points in particular should be noted. The first is not easy to resolve. Table 5.8 contains the most detailed form in which data are presented in this essay, but it is already much compressed from its original form. The successive stages which lie between an entry on a census page and a total in table 5.8 are described in outline and illustrated in appendix 1 to this chapter, but ideally the appendix should contain details of the full set of look-up tables involved, rather than an abstract from them, since they were the instrument created to process any source of occupational information into a uniform structure. Without them the reader is unable to decide whether the decisions about the allocation of the occupations carry conviction, or not, but, since even the final table contains well over 2,000 individual entries, it is impossibly cumbersome to reproduce in full.

Secondly, it is abundantly clear that much can be learned from making use of county data and by using the additional breakdowns within the county returns to explore the contrasts between urban and rural communities. Such data have been used from time to time in this essay. They figure in several of the tables, but they have not been exploited systematically. They appear to offer the most promising way of testing the internal consistency of the census returns, of gaining a fuller insight into the workings of the official mind in processing and classifying the enumerators' returns, and of pursuing a host of issues which cannot be examined so effectively using only the national returns. Systematically exploited, it is reasonable to expect that they would add greatly to what can be learned from national data, confirming some conclusions but modifying others substantially. For example, national data show that butchers were a large occupational group in the middle of the nineteenth century. They formed about 1 per cent of the adult male labour force and were as common as masons or bricklayers. The national figure is illuminating in suggesting that meat consumption was widespread among the population and substantial in scale, but the county-level data add substantially to the interest of the finding, for butchers were remarkably evenly spread throughout the country, as numerous in slow-growing agricultural counties as elsewhere, a fact difficult to reconcile with the supposition that there were major differences in diet between impoverished agricultural areas and urban or industrial districts.[65]

'To travel hopefully is a better thing than to arrive, and the true success is to labour', Robert Louis Stevenson wrote.[66] If the second half of the sentence is true, then this essay should be judged a success, since it has involved much labour. If the first half of the sentence is also true, I can again take comfort, for it will be abundantly clear that I have not arrived, but in travelling I have found much which is intriguing and which will encourage further labour.

Appendix 1

The original entries in an occupational census consist of a large number of individual occupations against each of which a total is entered. Since they are too numerous to be readily interpreted and may be set out

---

[65] See tab. 4.2 and associated text.
[66] Stevenson, 'El Dorado' p. 141.

idiosyncratically, they must be marshalled into a standard form if they are to become readily intelligible. Similarly, if the information source is, say, a militia list or a parish register in which there may be hundreds or even thousands of individuals listed, each with an occupation, it is again imperative to reduce the entries to a structured form. In this essay three such structuring schemes were employed; that used by the Registrar General in 1851; that originally devised by Booth to provide an 'industrial' classification system as an alternative to the Registrar General's 'materials' system and to improve the comparability of material from successive censuses; and a new system, termed for convenience PST to reflect the importance of separating primary, secondary, and tertiary occupations. Each of the three structures is formed from exactly the same individual items of information,[67] but they are grouped differently, reflecting the interests and preconceptions of the authors of each system.

In order to produce the three different structures, the data were manipulated within a data base system (Access). In considering its features, it is convenient to begin by illustrating the last stage in the process, the function performed by the final look-up table. Table 5.A1.1 shows the descriptors relating to agriculture. They are sorted first by the sub-categories in the PST system, and within each sub-category alphabetically. Also shown are the allocations for each occupation within the 1851 census system and the Booth system. The identities of the various categories are listed at the head of the table. It should be noted that sorting in this fashion will have excluded from the table some occupations which would have been included in agriculture by the 1851 system or by the Booth system, just as some of the occupations which are listed in the table and treated as agricultural within PST are allocated elsewhere by the other two systems. The full list of occupations in its current form runs to about 2,400 entries and is therefore much too large to reproduce in full. It will be obvious that any occupation on the list which appears in a given source can readily be allocated to the appropriate sub-category in each of the three systems (and indeed in as many other systems as it may be convenient to employ).

The PST system was devised with the intention of using information from earlier centuries, such as the occupations of fathers recorded in Anglican baptism registers, as well as mid-nineteenth century census material. There are therefore many descriptors in the look-up table which will not be found in either the 1841 or 1851 censuses. This explains the presence of two sub-categories within the PST system, listed at the head of

---

[67] This statement is slightly misleading in that in the PST tabulations, but not in the other two, a limited number of adjustments were made to improve the accuracy of the individual totals. See pp. 150–63 above.

Table 5.A1.1 *Look-up table sample*

PST system		1851 system		Booth system	
1.1.1	farmer	VIII.4	seas and river	AG.1	agriculture
1.1.2	farm labourer	IX.1	in fields and pastures	AG.2	land service
1.1.3	husbandman	IX.3	in gardens	AG.3	breeding
1.1.4	yeoman	X.1	engaged about animals	B.1	management
1.1.5	animal husbandry	XII.1	in animal food	D.2	raw materials
1.1.6	market gardening	XIII.1	in vegetable food	D.12	general dealers
1.1.7	other agriculture	XIII.10	in cane, rush, straw	DS.1	domestic service
		XV.2	indefinite employment	PO.1	property owning

Occupation	PST classification	1851 classification	Booth classification
colonial farmer	1.1.1	IX.1	AG.1
colonial planter	1.1.1	IX.1	AG.1
farmer	1.1.1	IX.1	AG.1
farmer's son, grandson, nephew, brother	1.1.1	IX.1	AG.1
gentleman farmer	1.1.1	IX.1	AG.1
grazier	1.1.1	IX.1	AG.1
sugar planter	1.1.1	IX.1	AG.1
agricultural labourer	1.1.2	IX.1	AG.1
farm servant	1.1.2	IX.1	AG.1
farm servant (indoor)	1.1.2	IX.1	AG.1
hind	1.1.2	IX.1	AG.1
labourer in husbandry	1.1.2	IX.1	AG.1
servant in husbandry	1.1.2	IX.1	AG.1
husbandman	1.1.3	IX.1	AG.1
yeoman	1.1.4	IX.1	AG.1
animal keeper	1.1.5	X.1	AG.1
bee keeper	1.1.5	X.1	AG.3
boar keeper	1.1.5	X.1	AG.3
castrator	1.1.5	X.1	AG.3
colt breaker	1.1.5	X.1	AG.3
cowman	1.1.5	XII.1	AG.3
dairyman	1.1.5	IX.1	AG.3
herdsman	1.1.5	IX.1	AG.3
horse breaker	1.1.5	X.1	AG.3
horse breeder	1.1.5	X.1	AG.3
horse clipper	1.1.5	X.1	AG.3
horse trainer	1.1.5	X.1	AG.3
leech breeder	1.1.5	X.1	AG.3
oxman	1.1.5	X.1	AG.1
shepherd	1.1.5	IX.1	AG.1
swineherd	1.1.5	X.1	AG.3
herb grower	1.1.6	IX.3	AG.1

Table 5.A1.1 (*cont.*)

Occupation	PST classification	1851 classification	Booth classification
hop grower	1.1.6	IX.1	AG.1
market gardener	1.1.6	IX.3	AG.1
nurseryman	1.1.6	IX.3	AG.1
teazle grower	1.1.6	IX.1	AG.1
watercress gatherer	1.1.6	XIII.1	D.12
watercress grower	1.1.6	IX.3	AG.1
agricultural student	1.1.7	IX.1	AG.1
bailiff	1.1.7	IX.1	AG.1
chaff cutter	1.1.7	XIII.10	D.2
delver	1.1.7	IX.1	AG.2
drainer	1.1.7	IX.1	AG.2
farm bailiff	1.1.7	IX.1	AG.1
farmer's man	1.1.7	IX.1	AG.1
farming bailiff	1.1.7	IX.1	AG.1
grape grower	1.1.7	IX.1	AG.1
harvester	1.1.7	IX.1	AG.1
hay binder	1.1.7	IX.1	AG.1
hay keeper	1.1.7	IX.1	AG.1
hay maker	1.1.7	IX.1	AG.1
land agent	1.1.7	IX.1	AG.1
land bailiff	1.1.7	IX.1	AG.1
land surveyor	1.1.7	IX.1	B.1
landing surveyor	1.1.7	IX.1	AG.1
looker	1.1.7	XV.2	AG.1
mole catcher	1.1.7	IX.1	AG.1
overlooker, bailiff	1.1.7	XV.2	AG.1
ploughman	1.1.7	IX.1	AG.1
portioner	1.1.7	IX.1	PO.1
rabbit catcher	1.1.7	X.1	AG.3
steward	1.1.7	VIII.4	DS.1
thresher	1.1.7	IX.1	AG.1

Note: Fuller information about the categories briefly described in the top panel of this table will be found in tabs. 5.A2.1 and 5.A2.2.

the table, which are redundant as far as the 1841 and 1851 censuses are concerned. There were no husbandmen or yeomen in these censuses. In seventeenth and eighteenth centuries, however, many men who worked on the land would have identified themselves under one of these two heads. Indeed both terms were still to be found in parish registers in the early decades of the nineteenth century, though they were rapidly becoming archaic.

The full process of converting an original data source, which can often be recalcitrant, to a neat tabular form such as those printed in this essay, however, normally involves a substantial amount of earlier processing before reaching the stage illustrated in table 5.A1.1. The start and finish are self evident. There is always an archival form of the data which is ultimately reduced to the form shown in the table. The term 'archival' is perhaps ambiguous. It may refer to a source which would be described by this term in normal historical usage, as when, for example, the data are taken from an eighteenth-century militia list, but for present purposes I shall use it also in relation to the occupations listed in a census before any grouping into wider categories has taken place. It is, of course, true that it is possible to move further back up the data chain from an entry in the census to the enumerators' books, and even, in principle, if they still existed, from the enumerators' books in turn to the census forms filled in by individual householders on the night of the census. In this context, however, the archival form of any source of occupational information is that set of descriptors which represent the data *in its most disaggregated form within a particular, discrete information source.*

Several types of intermediate processing may be needed in moving from original input to a final look-up table. It must be possible to effect the translation of information taken from an archival source into an entry in the final look-up table, which in turn allows it to be allocated to a category or sub-category within an occupational system. The problems which arise may be grouped under two main heads; alternative forms and equivalents.

Under the first head provision must be made to cope with a range of minor problems such as the following. Abbreviations may occur (lbr for labourer; kpr for keeper; mfr for manufacturer; and so on). Inversions are common in some sources, of which an example is 'labourer, agricultural'. And in many sources, where the original material is in manuscript, variant spellings of the same descriptor may be common. The process of moving from an archival entry to an entry in the final look-up table is equivalent to passing through an intermediate look-up table or series of look-up tables. Sometimes the archival entry is present also in the final look-up table, as would be the case, for example, if someone were described as a shepherd since this descriptor appears in the final look-up table (see table 5.A1.1). Frequently, however, abbreviation, inversion, a variant spelling, or some other alternative form calls for an intermediate step or steps before reaching a form recognised by the final look-up table.

Dealing with equivalents may involve more taxing decisions. Again, an example will illustrate what is at issue. In early nineteenth-century material the terms 'maker' and 'manufacturer' appear, in general, to be used indifferently to describe the same occupation. 'Clog maker' and 'clog manufacturer' can normally be treated as interchangeable terms. Yet decisions about equivalents will sometimes entail fine judgement, since what is sensible in one period of time or in one area of the country may be inappropriate at another time or in another place. There are many other cases where two or more occupational descriptors occur but, arguably, refer to the same activity: for example 'well digger' and 'well sinker'; or 'chain maker' and 'chain smith'. Where this is the case, only one term survives in the final look-up table; in other words, equivalents are amalgamated. Since an element of judgement is involved, there may be disagreement about whether or not two descriptors are equivalent. Reference back from the final look-up table to an intermediate form or to the archival entry, however, is always possible and ensures that no information is definitively lost. An alternative treatment for a different purpose can always be undertaken. Decisions about alternatives and equivalents could, of course, be made in the course of inputting the data, thus reaching the situation shown in table 5.A1.1 without intervening steps, but to ensure maximum rigour and consistency it is prudent to accept entries in their archival form and to move to the final look-up table form by processing within the data-base system via intermediate look-up tables.

There are, of course, limits to the precision and authority of any system of marshalling occupational data. For example, it is well to be alert to the different ways in which an occupation can be attributed to an individual. The designation which an individual might give himself, for example, may differ from that attributed to him by a minister or a census enumerator, so that the occupational structure of a given community may differ somewhat according to whether the information was derived directly by self-designation or was the responsibility of a particular official. Again, some occupational terms are ambiguous so that allocation to a particular category is necessarily uncertain. 'Waterman', for example, was often used interchangeably with 'boatman', but could also refer to a man at a cabstand with responsibility for watering horses (and indeed had other less common usages). Regional usage may cause confusion when national groupings are formed. In the case of nineteenth-century censuses the grouping of original descriptors into more inclusive categories by the enumerators and census checkers was often arbitrary and ill judged, at least from the point of view of later users. Arithmetic, copying, and printing errors may abound in some sources; and so on.

Table 5.A1.1, as it happens, does not contain an illustration of one further feature of the final look-up table. Where an occupational descriptor is phrased in a way which implies that the occupation might be allocated to two different categories, as, for example, with 'blacking maker, dealer' a dual allocation is made in the final look-up table, so that it will be possible to derive alternative totals for the categories concerned. This can

Table 5.A1.2 Individual occupations numbering 10,000 or more, England 1841 and 1851 (males aged 20 and over)

1841		1851	
Occupation	Total	Occupation	Total
labourer, agricultural	711,205	agricultural labourer (outdoor)	632,015
labourer	269,788	labourer (branch undefined)	228,498
farmer and grazier	192,333	farmer	172,541
boot and shoe maker	143,292	shoe and boot maker	149,727
servant, domestic	123,923	carpenter, joiner	114,672
carpenter and joiner	111,837	cotton manufacture	106,082
tailor and breeches maker	80,962	coal miner	93,438
cotton manufacture (all branches)	63,734	tailor	83,239
blacksmith	62,624	farm servant (indoor)	65,679
miner, coal	57,908	blacksmith	64,218
woollen and cloth manufacture (all branches)	52,605	gardener	55,593
weaver (branch not specified)	49,280	farmer's son, grandson, brother, nephew	55,114
mason, pavior, and statuary	48,462	mason, pavior	53,265
gardener	41,011	bricklayer	52,926
clerk (commercial)	39,601	seaman	51,980
butcher	37,306	woollen cloth manufacture	48,797
painter, plumber, and glazier	36,680	servant, domestic (general)	45,109
bricklayer	35,392	butcher, meat salesman	42,969
seaman (on shore)	30,510	painter, plumber, glazier	42,197
publican and victualler	28,951	grocer	41,528
baker	28,639	iron manufacture, moulder, founder	33,957
grocer and tea dealer	28,477	carman, carrier, carter, drayman	33,557
army (at home)	27,953	baker	32,989

Occupation	Number	Occupation	Number
hose (stocking) manufacture (all branches)	23,815	engine and machine maker	31,146
carrier, carter, and waggoner	23,019	licenced victualler, beershop keeper	30,041
sawyer	21,679	worsted manufacture	29,792
wheelwright	20,630	silk manufacture	28,459
boat and barge man	20,239	soldier	28,035
cabinet maker and upholsterer	19,635	clerk (commercial)	25,329
porter, messenger, and errand boy	19,176	messenger, porter (not government), and errand boy	25,081
miller	18,615	boat and barge man	24,899
silk manufacture (all branches)	17,842	sawyer	23,612
engineer and engine worker	17,229	hose (stocking) manufacture	23,483
schoolmaster and assistant, tutor	16,075	railway labourer	22,433
iron manufacture (all branches)	14,303	miller	22,398
surgeon, apothecary, and medical student	14,011	cabinet maker, upholsterer	22,105
brick and tile maker	13,866	draper	21,541
shop keeper and general dealer	13,708	wheelwright	20,489
groom and hostler	13,674	groom (not domestic servant), horsekeeper, jockey	20,238
draper	13,527	brick: maker, dealer	19,450
clergyman	13,511	innkeeper	17,712
police officer, constable, and watchman	13,008	Chelsea pensioner	16,525
hatter and hat manufacture (all branches)	12,886	schoolmaster	15,091
ship builder, carpenter, and wright	12,528	clergyman of established church	14,903
coachman, coach guard, and postboy	12,474	inn servant	14,725
printer	12,029	police	14,657
cooper	11,793	land proprietor	14,637
pottery, china, and earthenware manufacture (all branches)	11,640	brewer	14,428
merchant	11,249	printer	14,389
hotel and innkeeper	11,247	shipbuilder, shipwright	14,039
miner (branch not specified)	11,146	harbour, dock service, dock labourer	13,577

Table 5.A1.2 (*cont.*)

1841		1851	
Occupation	Total	Occupation	Total
nail manufacture (all branches)	11,084	earthenware manufacture	13,438
saddler, and harness, and collar maker	11,053	stone quarrier	12,914
clock and watch maker	11,036	coachman (not domestic servant), guard, postboy	12,733
attorney, solicitor, writer, and law student	10,854	watch and clock maker	12,435
		hawker, pedlar	12,244
		fisherman	12,229
		surgeon, apothecary	11,828
		cooper	11,656
		coach maker	11,655
		plasterer	11,309
		saddler, harness maker	11,043
		nail manufacture	11,019
		copper miner	10,691
		shopkeeper (branch undefined)	10,297
		hatter and hat manufacture	10,045
		solicitor, attorney, writer to the signet	10,023

Note: The 1851 totals have been reduced by approximately 8 per cent from those recorded in the census to facilitate comparison with 1841. See pp. 148–9 for details of the procedure and the reasons for undertaking it.
Sources: 1841 and 1851 censuses.

either be done by allocating all those in the occupation in question to one category in an initial tabulation and then to the other in a subsequent run, or by assigning, say, one half of the total to each category, or by making any other plausible division between them. The same can be done where the ambiguity is less obvious.

Both for its intrinsic interest and also to illustrate the way in which the creation of occupational categories makes the original entries invisible by grouping them into larger units (so that, for example, few of the totals shown in table 5.A1.2 match the related sub-category totals in table 5.8), table 5.A1.2 lists for both censuses all separately distinguished occupations totalling 10,000 or more men aged 20 and over. In most cases it will be obvious to which sub-category an occupation was allocated by each of the three systems, but only the complete version of the look-up table of which an illustrative section is shown in table 5.A1.1 would enable all allocations to be traced with certainty in the three systems used in this essay.

Appendix 2

This appendix compares the picture of occupational structure and change provided by the PST system with those which appear when the 1851 and the Booth schemes are used to structure the individual occupational totals. Its purpose is not to point to substantive findings but to illustrate the way in which different schemes for structuring identical original data inevitably produce contrasting impressions of the economy which they portray. It is convenient to discuss the nature of the 1851 and Booth systems briefly, and to take note of the picture of occupational change which they provide, before considering the three comparatively. In considering the comparison, it should be borne in mind that the PST tabulations reflect adjustments to a few original totals, but the other two systems do not. This was a deliberate choice. It is instructive to examine the implications of the allocation decisions made by the Registrar General and by Booth without introducing changes which they did not see fit to make themselves, and comparison with PST totals is affected only in a few occupations, principally in mining and textiles.[68]

The Registrar General's 1851 classification system

The multiplicity and disaggregated nature of individual occupational totals make them highly indigestible. Grouping individual totals into categories and sub-categories is undertaken to overcome this inconvenience.

---

[68] See pp. 158–60 above for details of the changes made.

It should ensure that closely similar occupations are kept together in the same grouping. While it is true that what constitutes similarity may be viewed differently for different purposes, some of the decisions made by the 1851 census authorities still seem bizarre in retrospect, even when their professed wish to use the materials on which people worked as the key criterion in making allocation decisions is taken into account.

To attempt a complete list of odd allocations in 1851 is beyond the scope of this exercise, but a few illustrations will reveal their character. Thatchers were placed in sub-class XIII.10 which contains those 'In cane, rush, and straw'. Class XIII as a whole was devoted to 'Persons working and dealing in matters derived from the vegetable kingdom', which presumably explains why it was chosen for thatchers. Yet sub-class XI.15 'In houses', which seems a more appropriate choice, contains not only trades closely akin to thatchers, such as slaters, but also carpenters who, no less than thatchers, were working with 'matters derived from the vegetable kingdom'. Within class XI 'Persons engaged in art and mechanic productions', the sub-class XI.16 consists of those 'In implements'. The largest single occupation in this sub-class is that of wheelwrights even though sub-class XI.12 'In carriages', which includes, for example, axle-tree makers, seems a more appropriate choice. Comparable oddities could be multiplied. In sub-class XIV.1 'In coal', there are to be found charcoal burners and chimney sweeps, while in sub-class XIV.2 'In stone, clay' there are platelayers, crossing sweepers, dust collectors, scavengers, and nightmen, among others. The cumulative effect of decisions of this kind upon class and sub-class totals was often slight (though, for example, thatchers accounted for almost half the total in sub-class XIII.10), but in considering the census totals in 1841 and 1851 when tabulated to conform with the principles used by the Registrar General in 1851, not only should the effect of the decision to use the 'materials' criterion in grouping be borne in mind, but also the idiosyncratic application of the criterion in individual cases. Table 5.A2.1 shows how the totals in 1841 and 1851 compare when using the 1851 census system.

Class totals are shown in bold. Under each class total the subtotals relate to individual sub-classes of occupation which jointly constitute the class. Sometimes the subtotals throw light on changes in the class totals which might otherwise appear inexplicable. For example, the decline of 4.6 per cent in class VI, which might be thought surprising on general grounds, is due to the very marked decline in the total of men in domestic service, which has already been discussed.[69] Without this element numbers in the class would have grown by 11 per cent.   Some other

[69] See pp. 161–2.

Table 5.A2.1 *1841 and 1851 occupational totals using the Registrar General's system (males aged 20 and over)*

	R.-G.'s notation	1841 Total	1851 Total
Class I			
General or local government		**32,518**	**55,493**
national government	I.1	14,636	29,529
local government	I.2	17,537	22,996
East India service	I.3	345	2,968
Class II			
Defence		**36,997**	**69,713**
army	II.1	28,921	49,356
navy	II.2	8,076	20,357
Class III			
Learned professions		**55,990**	**74,705**
clergymen and ministers	III.1	18,675	21,771
lawyers	III.2	12,970	13,545
physicians and surgeons	III.3	15,527	15,394
church officers	III.4	—	3,452
law clerks, court officers, and stationers	III.5	963	10,411
chemists and surgical instrument makers	III.6	7,855	10,132
Class IV			
Literature, the fine arts, and the sciences		**25,037**	**30,624**
authors	IV.1	581	2,191
artists	IV.2	4,987	6,288
scientific persons	IV.3	166	359
teachers	IV.4	19,303	21,786
Class V			
Children, relatives, and scholars		—	**15,361**
children, relatives, and scholars	V.1	—	15,361
Class VI			
Entertaining, clothing, and personal offices		**416,202**	**397,172**
boarding and lodging	VI.1	2,758	23,500
domestic servants	VI.2	130,296	79,908
providing dress	VI.3	283,148	293,764
Class VII			
Buying, selling, etc., money, houses or goods		**96,545**	**101,337**
buying, selling, etc., money, houses or goods	VII.1	96,545	101,337

Table 5.A2.1 (*cont.*)

	R.-G.'s notation	1841 Total	1851 Total
Class VIII			
Conveyance of men, animals, goods, and messages		**126,400**	**213,263**
railways	VIII.1	2,032	20,270
roads	VIII.2	39,988	57,867
canals	VIII.3	21,042	28,271
seas and rivers	VIII.4	34,554	71,230
warehousemen and storekeepers	VIII.5	9,517	10,276
messengers and porters	VIII.6	19,267	25,349
Class IX			
Possessing or working the land		**953,292**	**1,026,381**
in fields and pastures	IX.1	908,092	963,045
in woods	IX.2	3,058	5,871
in gardens	IX.3	42,142	57,465
Class X			
Persons engaged about animals		**34,314**	**55,188**
persons engaged about animals	X.1	34,314	55,188
Class XI			
Art and mechanic productions		**416,976**	**476,383**
in books	XI.1	20,147	23,981
in plays (actors)	XI.2	887	1,092
in music	XI.3	5,012	7,422
in pictures and engravings	XI.4	4,898	6,283
in carving and figures	XI.5	951	2,049
in shows and games	XI.6	1,593	1,946
in plans and designs	XI.7	1,770	3,529
in medals and dies	XI.8	367	312
in watches and philosophical instruments	XI.9	13,084	14,615
in arms	XI.10	4,452	5,307
in machines	XI.11	28,084	35,634
in carriages	XI.12	9,978	11,817
in harness	XI.13	12,125	11,750
in ships	XI.14	16,872	18,656
in houses	XI.15	257,093	291,135
in implements	XI.16	27,673	26,962
in chemicals	XI.17	11,990	13,893
Class XII			
Working and dealing in animal matters		**184,029**	**239,488**
in animal food	XII.1	49,031	68,463
in grease, bones, horn, etc.	XII.2	6,835	8,395
in skins	XII.3	16,435	18,569

Table 5.A2.1 (*cont.*)

	R.-G.'s notation	1841 Total	1851 Total
in feathers and quills	XII.4	407	478
in hair and fur	XII.5	4,896	6,134
in wool	XII.6	79,408	100,799
in silk	XII.7	27,017	36,650
Class XIII			
Working and dealing in matter derived			
from the vegetable kingdom		**426,151**	**472,646**
in vegetable food	XIII.1	61,194	77,634
in drinks and stimulants	XIII.2	97,757	109,899
in gums and resins	XIII.3	2,962	5,521
in timber	XIII.4	1,824	5,037
in bark	XIII.5	1,247	1,312
in wood	XIII.6	22,965	24,860
in wood furniture	XIII.7	31,443	35,922
in wood utensils	XIII.8	12,943	12,762
in wood tools	XIII.9	4,147	5,004
in cane, rush, and straw	XIII.10	9,591	12,418
in hemp	XIII.11	11,450	12,846
in flax, cotton	XIII.12	161,246	159,618
in paper	XIII.13	7,382	9,813
Class XIV			
Working and dealing in minerals		**333,674**	**470,067**
in coal	XIV.1	74,131	123,521
in stone, clay	XIV.2	26,025	78,101
in earthenware	XIV.3	15,332	18,314
in glass	XIV.4	5,587	7,420
in salt	XIV.5	920	1,435
in water	XIV.6	453	1,365
in precious stones	XIV.7	7,390	519
in gold and silver	XIV.8	5,310	12,487
in copper	XIV.9	13,214	12,250
in tin	XIV.10	10,455	16,003
in zinc	XIV.11	162	317
in lead	XIV.12	8,588	12,118
in brass and other mixed metals	XIV.13	36,388	23,821
in iron and steel	XIV.14	129,719	162,396
Class XV			
Labourers and others		**274,654**	**236,368**
labourers	XV.1	269,788	228,498
other persons of indefinite employment	XV.2	4,866	7,870
Total of classes I–XV		**3,412,779**	**3,934,189**

Table 5.A2.1 (*cont.*)

	R.-G.'s notation	1841 Total	1851 Total
Class XVI			
Persons of rank and property not returned			
under any office		**113,060**	**27,007**
persons of rank, etc. not returned elsewhere	XVI.1	113,060	27,007
Class XVII			
Persons supported by the community		**44,864**	**29,736**
living on income from voluntary sources and rates	XVII.1	44,864	22,076
prisoners	XVII.2	—	712
vagrants	XVII.3	—	6,948
Class XVIII			
Other		**286,768**	**41,582**
no stated occupation or condition	XVIII.1	286,768	41,582
Total of classes I–XVIII		**3,857,471**	**4,032,514**

Note: The combined total in 1841 is the same as the total for all males aged 20 and over. This was not the case in 1851 because, in order to offset the very different treatment of the retired population in the two censuses, the reported totals in the 1851 census were reduced by just over 8 per cent (see pp. 148–9 and tab. 5.7).
Sources: 1841 and 1851 censuses.

anomalies also yield readily to further investigation. The numbers in class III, the learned professions, for instance, rose by a third between the two censuses, which is intrinsically improbable. The explanation lies in the inclusion of law clerks in class III.5, a group not separately distinguished in the previous census. If they are excluded the increase for class III as a whole falls to 18.1 per cent, only a little above the general growth in the male population over 20, and a credible figure. In general, very marked apparent changes must be regarded with suspicion given that the censuses were only ten years apart. Class II provides another example. Taken at face value, it would appear that there was a very rapid expansion both in the army and the navy during the 1840s. But this is due to the inclusion of Chelsea pensioners and Greenwich pensioners in the army and navy totals. In 1841 they were probably included in the general category of pensioners and treated as outside the occupied population. The same problem causes a parallel anomaly using the Booth system. Because the reasons for many of the anomalies which are visible in any detailed comparison of 1841 and 1851 were discussed above in connection with tables 5.7 and 5.8, it would be otiose to repeat them here, but they should be borne in mind in reviewing the table.

Booth's classification system

Booth's system was 'industrial' in nature. Once again, some of the groupings may be thought surprising. For example, it might seem more appropriate to include the sub-class for brickmaking, and indeed also those for salt and waterworks, under manufacture rather than under mining; and it seems astonishing to place those engaged in banking, insurance, and accountancy in a class whose only other member consists of general labourers. In general, however, the sub-classes in Booth's system make good sense, even if their grouping into classes is sometimes questionable. Table 5.A2.2 shows the results of his categorisation of occupations for 1841 and 1851.

While Booth's scheme results in a readily intelligible picture of occupational structure, some of his decisions about the allocation of individual occupations produce misleading results. For example, there is a fall between the two censuses in the number of men working in cotton and silk (MF.19). This arises because Booth allocated weavers (undefined) to this sub-class. In 1841 there was a very large number of weavers: in 1851 almost all those engaged in textiles were placed under one or other of the major textile heads – wool, cotton, silk, linen. As a result employment in woollens is seen to expand over the decade while cotton marks time. As we have seen, this is a reversal of the true situation.[70] It may be that Booth himself was willing on occasion to ignore his own rules. Armstrong reproduced Booth's reworking of the censuses from 1841 to 1881 as an appendix table. It shows an increase of 78 per cent in the number of men in cotton manufacture between 1841 and 1851, yet his allocation rules, as reproduced by Armstrong, suggest a very different picture as is clear from table 5.A2.2. Direct comparison between the two sets of cotton industry occupational totals is not possible since Booth's totals refer to Great Britain and he did not exclude youths under 20, but the difference is massive and puzzling. It would warrant further investigation.[71] Even odder was his treatment of some types of dealers. Booth created a whole class exclusively for dealing, and yet sometimes allocated dealers to manufacturing sub-classes. For example, straw plait dealers no less than straw plait manufacturers were allocated to MF.23. Those dealing in tools or machines were allocated to MF.2, while animal dealers

[70] See tab. 5.6 and associated text.
[71] Armstrong, 'The use of information about occupation', p. 264.

Table 5.A2.2 *1841 and 1851 occupational totals using Booth's system (males aged 20 and over)*

	Booth's notation	1841 total	1851 total
Agriculture and breeding		**987,776**	**1,059,958**
farming	AG.1	953,443	1,010,973
land service	AG.2	—	60
breeding	AG.3	25,671	36,690
fishing	AG.4	8,662	12,235
Mining		**127,264**	**176,118**
mining	M.1	97,980	128,573
quarrying	M.2	9,131	24,459
brickmaking	M.3	19,151	20,882
salt and waterworks	M.4	1,002	2,204
Building		**264,739**	**338,141**
management	B.1	13,227	18,539
operative	B.2	250,887	286,640
roadmaking	B.3	625	32,962
Manufacture		**1,035,406**	**1,167,074**
machinery	MF.1	38,682	49,747
tools	MF.2	25,350	29,213
shipbuilding	MF.3	16,872	19,227
iron and steel	MF.4	96,312	118,262
copper, tin, lead, etc.	MF.5	28,869	33,328
gold and silver	MF.6	1,028	1,393
earthenware	MF.7	17,304	21,300
coals and gas	MF.8	2,025	5,634
chemicals	MF.9	4,240	8,084
furs and leather	MF.10	27,855	29,750
glue, tallow, etc.	MF.11	3,904	5,176
hair, etc.	MF.12	6,398	7,891
woodworkers	MF.13	52,959	53,967
furniture	MF.14	26,704	34,139
carriages and harness	MF.15	31,689	33,096
paper	MF.16	6,744	7,879
floorcloth, waterproofs, etc.	MF.17	1,234	1,606
woollens	MF.18	64,721	89,038
cotton and silk	MF.19	147,630	145,603
flax, hemp, etc.	MF.20	18,354	20,823
lace	MF.21	6,872	6,966
dyeing	MF.22	22,740	20,153
dress	MF.23	278,652	280,962
sundries	MF.24	3,495	4,354
food preparation	MF.25	20,130	25,419
baking	MF.26	32,292	38,484
drink preparation	MF.27	16,685	24,651
smoking	MF.28	1,951	3,978

Table 5.A2.2 (*cont.*)

	Booth's notation	1841 total	1851 total
watches, instruments, toys	MF.29	20,419	19,330
printing	MF.30	13,296	20,387
unspecified	MF.31	—	7,234
Transport		**125,571**	**211,931**
warehouses and docks	T.1	30,299	51,012
ocean navigation	T.2	32,101	54,644
inland navigation	T.3	21,042	28,105
railways	T.4	2,032	20,322
roads	T.5	40,097	57,848
Dealing		**256,540**	**337,312**
coals	D.1	10,357	17,906
raw materials	D.2	7,293	15,767
clothing materials	D.3	4,476	4,968
dress	D.4	20,927	27,828
food	D.5	83,207	118,866
tobacco	D.6	2,614	2,396
wines, spirits, hotels	D.7	47,928	54,054
lodging and coffee houses	D.8	2,326	4,138
furniture	D.9	2,215	3,822
stationery and publications	D.10	11,262	10,370
household utensils, ornaments	D.11	13,578	16,985
general dealers	D.12	24,940	32,939
unspecified	D.13	25,417	27,273
Industrial service		**315,015**	**263,300**
banking, insurance, accountancy	IS.1	45,227	34,802
labour	IS.2	269,788	228,498
Public service and professional		**158,370**	**237,119**
central administration	PP.1	15,012	32,203
local administration	PP.2	4,853	5,821
sanitary administration	PP.3	1,188	1,118
army	PP.4	28,921	49,356
navy	PP.5	8,076	20,357
police and prisons	PP.6	13,008	16,010
law	PP.7	13,500	23,367
medicine	PP.8	23,166	25,190
art and amusement (painting)	PP.9	8,158	8,646
art and amusement (music)	PP.10	3,823	5,486
literature	PP.11	581	1,529
science	PP.12	106	446
education	PP.13	19,303	22,367
religion	PP.14	18,675	25,223
Domestic service		**140,881**	**98,984**
indoor	DS.1	124,303	60,381
outdoor	DS.2	5,487	25,381
extra service	DS.3	11,091	13,222
Total of above		**3,411,562**	**3,889,937**

Table 5.A2.2 (*cont.*)

	Booth's notation	1841 total	1851 total
Property owning and			
independent, and other		**445,909**	**127,216**
property owning and			
independent	PO.1	114,276	37,382
other	PO.2	331,633	89,834
Total		**3,857,471**	**4,017,153**

Notes: The combined total in 1841 is the same as the total for all males aged 20 and over. This was not the case in 1851 because, in order to offset the very different treatment of the retired population in the two censuses, the reported totals in the 1851 census were reduced by just over 8 per cent (see pp. 148–9 and tab. 5.7). The total for 1851 is lower than the comparable total in tab. 5.A2.2 by 15,361. This was the number in class V of the Registrar General's scheme, 'son, grandson, brother, nephew (not otherwise returned)'.
Sources: 1841 and 1851 censuses.

went to AG.3; and so on.[72] It is true that in both censuses makers and dealers in some occupations were sometimes grouped together under a single heading by the census authorities, thereby obliging an arbitrary allocation to be made either to a manufacturing or dealing class, but this was by no means always a problem, and as a result it appears likely that Booth's allocations tended to overstate the numbers in manufacturing and, to a lesser extent, in agriculture while depleting numbers in dealing. It is, however, difficult to trace his actions in dealing with the problem of distinguishing dealing from manufacturing. He made it clear that, in order to give uniformity to his tables and to make comparison between successive censuses feasible, he had divided some published census totals as seemed most appropriate. He listed a few occupational categories to illustrate the dilemma which they occasioned, but stopped well short of a full description of his actions. It is therefore unclear how extensive his revisions were.[73] An extended critique is out of place here, however, given that many causes of confusion have already been dealt with when discussing the PST system in the main text of this essay.

[72] In describing these allocations as Booth's decisions, it should be made clear that I have relied exclusively on the list of his allocations of the occupations which occur in the 1861 census reproduced in ibid., app. E. The appendix includes both allocations reproduced directly from Booth's manuscript list and also, since not all occupations were included in this list, some allocations made by Armstrong in conformity with Booth's principles.
[73] Booth, 'Occupations of the people', p. 349.

Comparing the three systems

In order to make a general comparison of the three systems, it is necessary to provide a PST table comparable to those for the 1851 and Booth systems. Table 5.A2.3 is a reduced form of table 5.8. It should be noted that, whereas the subtotals in the two previous tables always add up to the totals shown in bold, in this table the subtotals refer only to the more important elements within each category.

The first comment which springs to mind in comparing the three tables is that direct comparison is often difficult or impossible at the level of aggregation shown in the tables. As an example, although coal mining was a major industry and a big employer, the individual total of coal miners is not distinguished as a separate sub-class but is englobed within the class M.1 'Mining' in the Booth system, while in the 1851 system coal miners fall within sub-class XIV.1 which covers both those working and dealing in coal as well as a host of others from peat cutters to chimney sweeps. Where there are apparent discrepancies between the three systems, therefore, they are seldom capable of being resolved fully without reference back to the original data in conjunction with a table specifying allocations in detail, such as that illustrated in table 5.A1.1.

One crude but illuminating way of bringing home the different impressions of occupational change produced by the three systems is to revert once more to the distinction between primary, secondary, and tertiary employment. The new PST system is, of course, explicitly constructed to focus on this method categorising occupational structure. The other two systems were not designed with this end in view, but in the case of Booth it is not difficult to reorganise his system to fit a threefold division of this kind. Of his principal classes, agriculture and mining clearly belong to the primary sector; building and manufacture to the secondary sector; and transport, dealing, public service and professional, and domestic service to the tertiary sector. This leaves only the curiously titled 'Industrial service' class. It seems reasonable to treat IS.1 as tertiary, and IS.2 as secondary.

The 1851 system presents far greater difficulties in allocating its classes and sub-classes in a reasonable fashion between the primary, secondary, and tertiary sectors. I have made allocations as follows: classes IX, X, XIV.1, and XIV.2 as primary; classes VI.3, XI.4–5 and 8–17, XII.3–7, XIII.3–13, XIV.3–14, and XV.1 as secondary; classes I, II, III, IV, VI.1–2, VII, VIII, XI.1–3, 6–7, XII.1–2, XIII.1–2 as tertiary. Many of these allocations, especially where classes are split are highly arbitrary, unavoidably so given the Registrar General's belief that class boundaries

Table 5.A2.3 *1841 and 1851 occupational totals using the PST system (males aged 20 and over)*

	1841	1851	1851/1841 × 100	% of 1841 column total	% of 1851 column total
PRIMARY	**1,126,270**	**1,168,926**	103.8	33.02	30.53
Agriculture	**935,875**	**914,503**	97.7	27.45	23.89
farmer	192,333	192,352	100.0	5.64	5.02
farm labourer	737,415	697,694	94.6	21.63	18.22
Estate work	**46,498**	**65,857**	141.6	1.36	1.72
gardener	41,011	59,350	144.7	1.20	1.55
Forestry	**24,910**	**29,981**	120.4	0.73	0.78
Fishing	**8,621**	**12,235**	141.9	0.25	0.32
Mining	**110,366**	**146,350**	132.6	3.24	3.82
coal	71,542	93,666	130.9	2.10	2.45
quarrying	7,408	17,426	235.2	0.22	0.46
SECONDARY	**1,608,423**	**1,762,051**	109.6	47.17	46.02
Food and drink	**106,913**	**132,382**	123.8	3.14	3.46
baker *et sim.*	32,292	38,484	119.2	0.95	1.01
butcher *et sim.*	37,977	43,000	113.2	1.11	1.12
drink	16,732	24,891	148.8	0.49	0.65
Clothing and footwear	**277,562**	**288,375**	103.9	8.14	7.53
tailor	82,259	84,348	102.5	2.41	2.20
boot and shoe	145,855	152,311	104.4	4.28	3.98
hosier, stockinger, knitwear	24,259	25,855	106.6	0.71	0.68
Building and construction	**257,986**	**307,529**	119.2	7.57	8.03
carpenter	111,837	114,672	102.5	3.28	3.00
bricklayer	35,392	52,926	149.5	1.04	1.38
mason	48,941	56,199	114.8	1.44	1.47
painter, paperhanger	37,677	44,145	117.2	1.10	1.15
Boat, barge and ship building	**17,986**	**20,670**	114.9	0.53	0.54
Textiles	**250,941**	**267,664**	106.7	7.36	6.99
cotton	98,731	120,058	121.6	2.90	3.14
wool	90,875	89,721	98.7	2.66	2.34
silk	35,296	33,463	94.8	1.04	0.87
linen	12,825	13,158	102.6	0.38	0.34
Leather, bone, fur, hair, glue	**29,170**	**31,632**	108.4	0.86	0.83
Woodworking	**52,758**	**58,361**	110.6	1.55	1.52
joiner, turner, cabinet maker	24,555	27,016	110.0	0.72	0.71

Table 5.A2.3 (*cont.*)

	1841	1851	1851/1841 × 100	% of 1841 column total	% of 1851 column total
Instrument making	13,969	17,562	125.7	0.41	0.46
clock, watch	11,036	12,435	112.7	0.32	0.32
Gold, silver, jewelry	9,250	9,763	105.6	0.27	0.25
Papermaking	7,090	8,466	119.4	0.21	0.22
Printing and publishing	25,288	30,979	122.5	0.74	0.81
Cart, carriage, coach building	30,712	32,504	105.8	0.90	0.85
wheelwright	20,656	20,628	99.9	0.61	0.54
Pottery, glass, brick, lime	34,313	42,648	124.3	1.01	1.11
pottery, earthenware	13,596	15,857	116.6	0.40	0.41
glass	5,374	7,341	136.6	0.16	0.19
brick and tile, lime burning	15,343	19,450	126.8	0.45	0.51
Brass, tin, copper, lead and zinc	27,397	31,907	116.5	0.80	0.83
Iron and steel	109,150	135,116	123.8	3.20	3.53
blacksmith	62,624	64,218	102.6	1.84	1.68
iron and steel manufacture	14,400	35,092	243.7	0.42	0.92
nails, screws	11,404	11,497	100.8	0.33	0.30
Engineering	43,208	53,640	124.1	1.27	1.40
Gunmaking	4,529	4,896	108.1	0.13	0.13
Chemical industries	3,976	8,005	201.3	0.12	0.21
Gas, coke, water	2,528	7,618	301.3	0.07	0.20
Furniture and furnishing	9,083	13,202	145.4	0.27	0.34
Rope making	7,064	7,136	101.0	0.21	0.19
Straw and rush	5,194	6,000	115.5	0.15	0.16
Minor trades	8,201	10,264	125.2	0.24	0.27
Secondary, general	274,155	235,732	86.0	8.04	6.16
TERTIARY	675,288	897,672	132.9	19.80	23.45
Transport	140,036	270,549	193.2	4.11	7.07
road	54,082	78,221	144.6	1.59	2.04
rail	2,657	44,451	1673.0	0.08	1.16
sea	32,279	55,184	171.0	0.95	1.44
inland water	20,857	28,105	134.8	0.61	0.73
Trading, dealing, agency	75,684	113,643	150.2	2.22	2.97
food, drink	9,342	20,609	220.6	0.27	0.54
textiles, textile materials, clothing	22,652	31,071	137.2	0.66	0.81
Retail trade	91,753	121,117	132.0	2.69	3.16
shopkeeper	7,899	10,550	133.6	0.23	0.28
grocer	28,477	41,528	145.8	0.84	1.08
Food, drink, lodging	47,700	67,535	141.6	1.40	1.76

Table 5.A2.3 (*cont.*)

	1841	1851	1851/1841 × 100	% of 1841 column total	% of 1851 column total
Public services	**32,528**	**49,576**	152.4	0.95	1.29
inland revenue, customs and excise	9,194	11,940	129.9	0.27	0.31
local and parish government	17,861	24,317	136.2	0.52	0.64
Professions	**85,369**	**97,162**	113.8	2.50	2.54
law	13,590	16,417	120.8	0.40	0.43
medicine	15,668	15,865	101.3	0.46	0.41
clergy	18,675	21,691	116.2	0.55	0.57
teaching	19,303	21,883	113.4	0.57	0.57
Clerical, secretarial, administrative	**39,642**	**35,433**	89.4	1.16	0.93
clerk (all descriptions)	39,601	33,920	85.7	1.16	0.89
Armed forces	**36,951**	**46,265**	125.2	1.08	1.21
army	28,898	32,788	113.5	0.85	0.86
navy	8,053	13,477	167.4	0.24	0.35
Domestic service	**97,713**	**60,442**	61.9	2.87	1.58
servant, domestic servant	97,713	45,120	46.2	2.87	1.18
Entertainment	**1,076**	**1,523**	141.5	0.03	0.04
Services	**13,962**	**20,297**	145.4	0.41	0.53
barber	7,856	8,327	106.0	0.23	0.22
Banking, financial	**8,522**	**10,998**	129.1	0.25	0.29
Tertiary, general	**4,352**	**3,132**	72.0	0.13	0.08
TOTAL	**3,409,981**	**3,828,649**	112.3	100.00	100.00

Note: The overall totals in this table are those of men in active employment rather than the national totals of men aged 20 and over. For the latter see tab. 5.7.
Sources: 1841 and 1851 censuses.

should reflect the materials in use, whether in making or dealing. The upshot is set out in table 5.A2.4.

For each of the three systems the table shows the totals in each of the three sectors in 1841 and 1851, the percentage distribution of employment between them at each date, and the ratio of the totals in the primary, secondary, and tertiary sectors in 1851 to their totals in 1841. The contrast between the three pictures is sufficiently marked to leave differing impressions of change during the decade. Under the PST system the primary sector barely expanded in absolute number and contracted sharply as a percentage of the total active population; under the Booth system there was a substantial rise in numbers but a modest fall in percentage share; while under the 1851 system, not only was there a far larger growth in numbers, but the share of the primary sector in overall employment rose as substantially as it had fallen in the Booth system. In part the differences between the three relate to agriculture. The adjustments made in arriving at the totals for agricultural occupations shown in table 5.8 caused the overall figure for agriculture in the PST system to fall, whereas making allocations in conformity with the 1851 and Booth systems resulted in a rise in the agricultural total. But the contrast was further heightened in the case of the 1851 system by the inclusion of XIV.1 and XIV.2, 'In coal' and 'In stone, clay' in the primary sector. Since some of the biggest individual occupations in these sub-classes were coal miners and stone quarriers, it is difficult to place them elsewhere, but they also contained such occupations as those employed in gasworks and railway labourers, both of which were growing very rapidly indeed in the 1840s. The result was that the primary sector, if its growth were inferred from the sub-class totals within the 1851 system, might be taken to be growing faster than overall employment (by 18.0 per cent compared with 14.8 per cent).

The secondary sector declined in relative importance over the decade under all three systems, but much more markedly in the 1851 system than in the other two. The PST system at each date allotted a larger percentage share of total employment to the secondary sector than the other two systems and the decline in its percentage share was the smallest. The 1851 system showed the largest relative fall. The rise in absolute numbers in the secondary sector was muted in the 1851 system, at little more than 100,000, where the other two systems both showed much larger rises, a little over 150,000 in the case of PST, and in the Booth system a still higher figure in excess of 160,000.

The patterns in the tertiary sector were in sharp contrast to those in the secondary sector. In all three schemes this was the fastest growing sector, and fastest of all in the PST scheme. But the absolute numbers involved were smallest under the PST scheme at both dates, in sharp contrast with secondary totals, though the difference with Booth was no longer large by 1851. The differences between the PST totals and those produced by the Booth and 1851 schemes spring from the more focused attempt to minimise confusion between making and trading which informs the PST scheme. Under all three schemes, however, the much more rapid growth of employment in tertiary occupations than in either of the other two sectors is clear. The contrast is most striking with PST allocations, but is also very clear with Booth.

Table 5.A2.4 A comparison of the three systems

	PST system					1851 system					Booth system			
	1841	% of total	1851	% of total		1841	% of total	1851	% of total		1841	% of total	1851	% of total
Primary	1,126,270	33.0	1,168,926	30.5		1,087,762	31.9	1,283,191	32.8		1,115,040	32.7	1,236,076	31.8
Secondary	1,608,423	47.2	1,762,051	46.0		1,569,384	46.1	1,676,863	42.9		1,569,933	46.0	1,733,713	44.6
Tertiary	675,288	19.8	897,672	23.4		750,767	22.0	950,904	24.3		726,589	21.3	920,148	23.7
All	3,409,981	100.0	3,828,649	100.0		3,407,913	100.0	3,910,958	100.0		3,411,562	100.0	3,889,937	100.0
			1851/1841 × 100					1851/1841 × 100					1851/1841 × 100	
Primary			103.8					118.0					110.9	
Secondary			109.6					106.9					110.4	
Tertiary			132.9					126.7					126.6	
All			112.3					114.8					114.0	

Sources: Tabs. 5.A2.1, 5.A2.2, and 5.A2.3.

Comparing the occupational structures produced by three different schemes is bound to be somewhat frustrating since, by design, like is seldom compared with like. It is therefore worth stressing that if each of the three tables in this appendix were expanded from the sub-class or its equivalent down to the individual occupations comprised within it, it would be possible to identify the reasons for every apparent difference with precision. The original input is identical in all three cases (except in the limited number of occupations in which the PST totals were adjusted to offset anomalies in the published totals),[74] but the individual occupational totals, directed by the provisions of the final look-up table, are filtered through to different resting places within each of the three systems. Because there is a constant tension between comprehensiveness and intelligibility, the former providing detailed but inconveniently disparate information, the latter providing clarity at the cost of concealing the original data, it is never a simple matter to make inferences from occupational data. Since for most purposes it is essential to refashion the welter of archival information into an ordered scheme, contact with the original data is inevitably lost at some stage. Marshalling the data in more than one way, however, has the merit of demonstrating how important it is to be wary of drawing conclusions about occupational structure and change from a single source. Hence this appendix.

---

[74] See pp. 150–63 above.

6   Corn and crisis: Malthus on the high price of provisions

The OED gives the following base definition of the word dearth: 'dearness, costliness, high price', though cautiously noting 'This sense, though etymologically the source of those that follow, is not exemplified very early, and not frequent.' It goes on to offer other usages: 'A condition in which food is scarce and dear; often, in earlier use, a time of scarcity with its accompanying privations, a famine' and 'scarcity of anything, material or immaterial'. That there should be a link between high prices and food shortage is entirely natural given the nature of all pre-industrial economies, and therefore that the same word should have come to assume the range of meanings defined in the OED is not surprising. Yet achieving an effective understanding of some aspects of the nature of the relationship between the two has proved surprisingly elusive, given the central importance of the harvest in all economies until the recent past.

Of the four necessities of life recognised by the classical economists, food, shelter, clothing, and fuel, the first was by far the most important. Amongst the poor three-quarters or more of all income might have to be devoted to food even in normal times, and in most European economies the great bulk of this expenditure went on bread grain. Little wonder, therefore, that the bounty or otherwise of the last harvest, which, together with the scale of any carryover from earlier years, determined current supply, and the prospects for the next harvest, which began to affect the price of grain many months before any corn was cut, were matters of such pressing concern to individuals, to communities, and to governments. The petition, 'give us this day our daily bread' is the only material concern mentioned in the Lord's Prayer. It symbolises the central importance of the grain harvest to all those living in organic economies, economies, that is, in which animal and vegetable products were not only the sole source of food but were also the basis of almost all forms of material production.

Because the demand for bread grain was inelastic, relatively small variations in its supply had a very marked impact on its price. Hence the superficially paradoxical fact that years of bad harvest were years of prosperity for any farmer with a substantial surplus to sell after meeting his domestic needs. The relationship between the supply and price of grain was an issue that attracted the attention of the pioneers of political arithmetic. Davenant, who was substantially indebted to Gregory King in this regard, published a formula intended to capture this relationship which showed, for example, that when supply fell below the normal level by 30 per cent the price of grain might be expected to be about 160 per cent above its long-run average, while in the disastrous circumstance of a 50 per cent fall in supply the price would be 450 per cent above normal. More than a century and a half later Jevons devoted attention to the question and suggested an algebraic formulation of the relationship which produces results closely similar to those suggested by Davenant. Others, notably Bouniatian, studying the same relationship also confirmed the broad accuracy of Davenant's pioneering initiative.[1]

But although the formulation of the relationship which was first suggested by Davenant in the 1690s has proved able to capture fairly robustly the *average* behaviour of price in response to supply changes, it may prove a very poor guide to the relationship in particular instances. For the model to 'save the phenomena', a number of assumptions about the state of the market, and particularly about the nature of effective demand, must hold true. This is an issue to which Amartya Sen devoted much attention about twenty years ago. His exposition of the influences which can both give rise to starvation even when the local harvest is of a normal size and yet can also leave prices largely unaffected, even in conditions of food shortage so acute that there are many famine deaths, gave a very different shape both to academic analysis of the topic and to the politics of food shortage and public action.[2]

It is a singular tribute to the breadth of Malthus's interests and to his acuteness of mind that he considered the same issue and arrived at a fundamentally similar understanding of the nature of the question in his second work, which, like the first, was published anonymously. It was entitled *An investigation of the cause of the present high price of provisions, containing an illustration of the nature and limits of fair price in time of scarcity, and its application to the particular circumstances of this country.* This

---

[1] Establishing a general relationship of this kind is, of course, at best only a first step. Many factors have a bearing on the quantity of corn effectively available in the market place and therefore able to influence its price. It is important, for example, to take into account the necessity of ensuring that sufficient grain is reserved from the current crop to meet the seed needs of the next year. When yields are low, as, say, in medieval England, seed grain may well account for a quarter of the crop in an average year: Wrigley, 'Some reflections on corn yields'.

[2] Sen, *Poverty and famines.*

pamphlet, only twenty-eight pages long, was published in 1800, when Malthus was still only 34 years old, immediately after his return from a lengthy tour of Scandinavia which occupied the second half of 1799. He had discovered that the high price of bread in England had become a burning issue during his absence and the essay, published within a few months of his return, represents his analysis of its cause.

The price of wheat per quarter in England in the 1780s and early 1790s had fluctuated between 40 s. and 55 s., but rose steeply during the war years of the 1790s, and in 1800 and 1801 reached 113s. and 119s. respectively. These figures are annual averages and at times during the crisis years prices were significantly higher. Wheat was never again so costly throughout the Napoleonic war period, except for 1812, and once the wars were over wheat prices dropped back to the range between 50s. and 70s. a quarter. The price of wheaten bread in London rose roughly in step with the price of the grain. The 4 lb loaf cost between 5 1/2 d. and 7 d. in the 1780s and early 1790s but was over 15 d. in both 1800 and 1801.[3] Its price had roughly doubled during Malthus's absence in Scandinavia.

Malthus's view of the cause of the rise in bread prices was heavily conditioned by his experiences while in Sweden. The nature of the question he set out as follows: 'It cannot admit of a doubt – that, during the last year, there was a scarcity, to a certain extent, of all sorts of grain; but it must be at the same time acknowledged, that the price was higher than the degree of that scarcity would at first sight appear to warrant.'[4] He then went on to describe what he had recently seen when abroad:

In the summer of 1799, in the course of a northern tour, I passed through Sweden. There was at that time a general dearth of corn throughout the country, owing to a long drought the preceding year. In the province of Värmland, adjoining to Norway, it approached almost to a famine, and the lower classes of people suffered most severe distress. At the time we were passing through that part of the country, which was in July, they were reduced to two most miserable substitutes for bread; one, made of the inner bark of the fir, and the other, of the common sorrel dried, and powdered. These substances, though made into the usual shape of their rye bread, had no affinity to it whatever in taste, and but very little, I believe, in nourishment, as the effects of this miserable food were but too visible in their pallid and unhealthy countenances.[5]

Malthus went on to remark that there could be little doubt that the degree of scarcity then prevailing in Värmland was 'considerably greater'

[3] Mitchell, *British historical statistics*, ch. 14, tabs. 17 and 22.
[4] Malthus, *High price of provisions*, p. 5.
[5] Ibid., p. 5.

than that found in England at the same time, but, he added, 'yet, as far as we could learn, the price of rye, which is the grain principally used for bread, had not risen above double its usual average; whereas in this country last year, in a scarcity that must be acknowledged to be greatly inferior in degree, wheat rose to above three times its former price'.[6]

Malthus then addressed the question of whether any individuals or groups were to blame for the situation in England, an issue which had been the occasion for much heated debate in 1800 as in similar situations time out of mind. He criticised the Lord Chief Justice, amongst others, for pandering to the wish to find scapegoats in the guise of corn merchants and big farmers who were accused of withholding supplies in order to maximise their profits. He repeated the orthodox riposte of the classical economists that the workings of the market through the decisions of interested individuals were beneficial in this respect and elaborated on this theme at intervals throughout the essay. The essence of his case is captured in a later passage in the following terms:

A reflecting mind, far from being astonished that there are now and then errors in speculation, must feel much greater astonishment that there are so few; and that the supplies of a large nation, whether plentiful or scanty, should be distributed so equally throughout the year. Most happily for society, individual interest is, in these cases, so closely and intimately interwoven with the public interest, that one cannot gain or lose without a gain or loss to the other. The man who refuses to send his corn to market when it is at £20 a load, because he thinks that in two months time it will be at £30, if he be right in his judgement, and succeed in his speculation, is a positive and decided benefactor to the state; because he keeps his supply to that period when the state is much more in want of it; and if he and some others did not keep it back in that manner, instead of its being £30 in two months, it would be £40 or £50.[7]

Though Malthus was concerned to dismiss what he regarded as outdated and ignorant explanations of the high prices then current, the prime purpose of the essay was to offer an alternative explanation, which he first expressed in these terms:

To proceed to the point: I am most strongly inclined to suspect, that the attempt in most parts of the kingdom to increase the parish allowances in proportion to

[6] Ibid., p. 6. It should be noted that Malthus kept travel diaries during his tour of Scandinavia. Most unfortunately those that have survived cover only his account of events and his reflections on them up to the point at which he crossed the border between Norway and Sweden, so that his observations on the situation in Värmland and the suffering of its inhabitants can no longer be consulted. James, *Travel diaries*, p. xv.

[7] Malthus, *High price of provisions*, pp. 10–1.

the price of corn, combined with the riches of the country, which have enabled it to proceed as far as it has done in this attempt, is, comparatively speaking, the sole cause, which has occasioned the price of provisions in this country to rise so much higher than the degree of scarcity would seem to warrant, so much higher than it would do in any other country where this cause did not operate.[8]

He went on to suggest that a combination of humane feelings on the part of the more affluent classes of society and the complaints of the poor to the justices had led to increases in the scale of poor relief which transferred purchasing power into the hands of those most in need, thereby encouraging speculators to withhold supplies in anticipation of further price increases, and thus ensuring a further cycle of similar increases in poor relief and hence in prices.

Malthus was, of course, an opponent of the poor law system of relief, trenchantly so in his early days, but throughout his life was notably willing to act in accordance with the principle that circumstances alter cases.[9] In 1800 he was in no doubt that the existence of the poor laws was a saving grace in the face of severe shortages because they ensured a substantial transfer of purchasing power to those who might otherwise have faced the same sort of terrible alternatives to normal foodstuffs of which he had been a witness a few months previously in Sweden. He concluded this section of his essay by making clear both his general prejudice against the poor law system and his relief that it had mitigated the effects of the shortage of bread grain so effectively. The same passage demonstrates that he had achieved an understanding of the nature of the interaction of supply and demand in conditions of dearth strongly reminiscent of Sen's later discussion:

I do not, however, by any means, intend to infer, from what I have said, that the parish allowances have been prejudicial to the state; or that, as far as the system has been hitherto pursued, or is likely to be pursued, in this country, that it is not one of the best modes of relief that the circumstances of the case will admit. The system of the poor laws, in general, I certainly do most heartily condemn, as I have expressed in another place, but I am inclined to think that their operation in the present scarcity has been advantageous to the country. The principal benefit which they have produced, is exactly that which is most bitterly complained of – the high price of all the necessities of life. The poor cry out loudly at this price; but, in so doing, they are very little aware of what they are about; for it has undoubtedly been owing to this price that a much greater number of them has not been starved.

[8] Ibid., pp. 6–7.
[9] Malthus's unwillingness to succumb to the temptation of ignoring exceptions to simplifying generalisations is forcefully set out in the introduction to *Principles of political economy*, pp. 11–8.

It was calculated that there were only two thirds of an average crop last year. Probably, even with the aid of all that we imported, the deficiency still remained a fifth or a sixth. Supposing ten millions of people in the island; the whole of this deficiency, had things been left to their natural course, would have fallen almost exclusively on two, or perhaps three millions of the poorest inhabitants, a very considerable number of whom must in consequence have starved. The operation of the parish allowances, by raising the price of provisions so high, caused the distress to be divided among five or six millions, perhaps, instead of two or three, and to be by no means unfelt even by the remainder of the population.[10]

Sen defined his form of analysis of poverty and famine as the entitlement approach. 'The entitlement approach to starvation and famines concentrates on the ability of people to command food through the legal means available in the society, including the use of production possibilities, trade opportunities, entitlements *vis-à-vis* the state, and other methods of acquiring food.'[11] The scale of personal entitlement was a function of two parameters, the 'ownership bundle' belonging to a person, which Sen termed his or her endowment, and the exchange entitlement mapping of the person in question, or 'the function that specifies the set of alternative commodity bundles that the person can command respectively for each endowment bundle'.[12] Starvation can occur either because of a fall in endowment or because of an unfavourable shift in exchange entitlement mapping. Bengali fishermen in 1943, Sen noted, might still be able to catch fish but this was of little benefit to them in meeting their need for food other than fish if the demand for fish declined sharply relative to that of rice; and fish was, comparatively, a luxury food.[13] Or to take an historical example from a period not long before Malthus's lifetime, in the aftermath of harvest failure in the Beauvaisis in 1693–4, the rural community which suffered perhaps the most severely of all, of those which were analysed in detail by Goubert, was Mouy. Mortality there was especially heavy because Mouy was dependent primarily on woollen manufacture for its income. Weavers were still able to produce cloth, but could no longer find a market for their wares since under pressure of necessity purchasing power in the Beauvaisis was directed more and more exclusively to food. Mouy's inhabitants, therefore, suffered both because they did not produce food directly themselves and because what they did produce was no longer able to command a price which would

[10] Ibid., pp. 13–4.
[11] Sen, *Poverty and famines*, p. 45.
[12] Ibid., p. 46.
[13] Ibid., p. 51.

enable them to buy sufficient food to keep them alive.[14] Their exchange entitlement map had deformed greatly to their disadvantage.

In his essay on the high price of provisions Malthus was making use of the same insight into the determinants of life and death when food is short or dear. His was a much less comprehensive analysis than that of Sen, but when he claimed that 'Among the many causes that have been assigned of the present high price of provisions, I am much inclined to suspect, that the principal one has hitherto escaped detection',[15] he was probably making a fair assertion, and his explanation consisted in noting that starving or avoiding starvation was as much a matter of the way in which the cake was divided up as it was about the size of the cake. The operation of the allowance system under the poor law was transferring purchasing power into the pockets of those most in need and was spreading more uniformly through an increased proportion of the population the deficit which would otherwise have been visited almost exclusively on those who were most vulnerable. In contrast, in Värmland the very fact that prices had risen more modestly, though the degree of harvest failure and the consequent shortage of supply were more acute, was testimony to the inability of the poor to make any effective claim upon the stocks available. A desperate need for food would only produce a matching surge in price where those most exposed could translate their plight into *effective* demand.

The situation in Värmland was not unlike that which Sen described in Wollo province in Ethiopia in the famine year of 1973. 'People starved to death', he wrote, 'without there being a substantial rise in food prices. In terms of the entitlement approach, there is, of course, no puzzle in this. Since the farmers' food entitlement is a direct entitlement (without going through the market), a collapse of it can operate without a rise in market prices.'[16] Whether the peasants in Värmland were in a similar state, or whether those who were dying were in the market sector of the economy, is unclear. Perhaps it was a combination of these two possibilities. In any case Malthus had pointed to an element which is essential to any adequate analysis of food shortage and starvation and had done so in a manner which was both innovative and ingenious.

---

[14] After describing the linkage between harvest failure and the demographic crisis in the rural Beauvaisis in 1693–4, Goubert added, 'Mouy présente une variante sociale: ce gros bourg manufacturier fut atteint plus rapidement, plus tôt, et plus fortement que les bourgs agricoles. Les ouvriers du textile qui le peuplaient voyaient disparaître, en temps de cherté céréalière, à la fois le travail et le salaire.' Goubert, *Beauvais et le Beauvaisis*, I, pp. 52–3.

[15] Malthus, *High price of provisions*, p. 5.

[16] Sen, *Poverty and famines*, p. 96.

When considering Malthus's place in intellectual history, therefore, and in honouring his better-known achievements, such as the development of a model which has proved remarkably fruitful for the analysis of the relations between the population and economy of any pre-industrial society, or the description of the relationship between resources and reproduction which was later to provide for Darwin an engine to drive the process of natural selection, we should not lose sight of his less well-known achievements. I have described one of them in these remarks. But there were others. For example, he was aware of a point which has concerned some development economists in recent years. One of the disadvantages of a peasant economy and of the predominance of peasant values is sometimes held to be that the marginal member of a family on a peasant holding will only leave the land when the *average* income of the family falls below subsistence level and not when the *marginal* income falls to that point. This in turn, inasmuch as the model is correct, implies that there may be a substantial proportion of the rural workforce producing less than it consumes. In pointing out that, in a capitalist economy, it can never pay the landlord or the farmer to retain in his employment any worker whose output is worth less than the value of a wage sufficient to provide him and his family with some minimum command of the necessities of life, Malthus was making the same point. Such a system put a floor to living standards beneath which they could not fall.[17] He pointed out, however, that under other systems such a floor might be lacking and that exceptional misery might thereby result.[18]

Malthus's habit of qualifying most of his assertions and his respect for the complexity of reality tend to make his work both less accessible and less immediately striking than that of those who prefer clarity to comprehensiveness. The first edition of the *Essay on population* remains his most widely read work in part because it is the least typical of his works in this regard. But his other writings also repay study. It is no accident that in 1998 no less than in 1798 he remains a vital and protean influence on thinking about many social, economic, and demographic topics, and especially about the constitution of all those societies which were essentially dependent on the productivity of the soil, those commonly termed pre-industrial, which were, of course, the only societies with which he was familiar.[19]

---

[17] Provided, that is, that those who are dismissed from employment on the land can find alternative employment which rewards them equally well or better. Broadly, this was the case in early modern England.

[18] Malthus, *Essay on population* [1826], pp. 405–6.

[19] I have discussed some aspects of this issue at greater length in Wrigley, 'Elegance and experience'.

7   Why poverty was inevitable in traditional societies

That poverty was the lot of the large majority of people in all or almost all societies before the industrial revolution is widely recognised. Poverty is a general and rather abstract concept. Its reality was bitter and particular: a hungry child, apathetic from lack of food; a shivering family unable to buy fuel in a harsh winter; the irritation of parasites in dirty clothing and the accompanying sores and stench. The extent and severity of poverty in the past is difficult to express in quantitative terms for lack of relevant data in most cases, but that the poor were very numerous and that they suffered greatly at times in most societies is an assertion unlikely to be widely challenged. When St Matthew reports Jesus as saying, 'ye have the poor always with you', the context suggests that the remark was not controversial.[1]

In industrialised countries today poor people may still be found. Their poverty is, however, now taken to be problematic in a way that used not to be the case, because it is widely believed that the continued existence of poverty reflects not the intrinsic nature of the human condition but the failure of the social system or the political regime. The capacity to produce on a scale to provide acceptable minimum conditions for all patently exists, and it is therefore natural to argue that poverty can be overcome by an act of will, by a suitable piece of social engineering. Looking back from a vantage point in the late twentieth century, it may be tempting to suppose that the same was true of earlier times, that the misery of the masses could have been alleviated by deliberate policy or institutional change. The purpose of this essay is to examine the constraints common to all traditional societies which meant that the ambition to achieve a general escape from poverty belonged to the realm of pipedreams rather than policy. My argument is general and simplistic. It should not be taken as an assertion that social structure and political forms had no bearing on the incidence of poverty in traditional societies, but rather as reflecting

[1] St Matthew, 26:11.

the conviction that any room for manoeuvre was greatly circumscribed by certain features common to the economies of all such societies.

The hierarchy of human wants and individual productivity

The hierarchy of human wants is well reflected in the employment structure and the allocation of hours of work in traditional societies. Food, clothing, shelter, and fuel were the basic necessities of life, the three last increasing in relative importance with increasing distance from the equator. Everywhere food was the dominant concern, whether in the lives of individuals or in the preoccupations of governments. The dominance of the demand for food is clear from the fact that it was common for 70–90 per cent of the total labour force to be engaged in agriculture. Probably the proportion of all the hours devoted to productive labour that was spent in farm work was broadly similar.[2] In most traditional societies the bulk of food output did not go through the market but was consumed on the holding which produced it. Therefore little can be learnt from estimates of the proportion of total market demand spent on food, but the structure of the labour force is a good proxy measure of the point at issue – how much of the total productive effort of a society went into satisfying the demand for the most basic of all necessities.

The three lesser necessities were also satisfied by the flow of produce from the land. A productive agriculture meant comparatively abundant supplies of wool, cotton, flax, and silk, while the size of cattle herds determined whether leather for footwear was scarce or readily available. The relative abundance or scarcity of such materials determined the cost of the raw materials of clothing and thus standards of attire. Wood was normally the prime fuel and often also the most important material used in construction. Thus the degree of success achieved in maximising the flow of produce from the land governed how far man was able to meet not only his need for food, but also his need for clothing, shelter, and fuel.

Until basic needs are met, the demand for other material goods or for services will remain minimal in the bulk of the population; or to express the same idea in different language, the income elasticity of demand for the necessities will remain close to unity as long as basic wants are only

---

[2] In other words, although many craftsmen laboured in the fields at times of greatest activity on the land, such as harvest time, it is also true that yeomen, husbandmen, and labourers devoted a part of their time to building work, crude carpentry, and rough handicrafts.

met inadequately.[3] If a half-starved family experiences a sudden rise in income, all the additional spending power may go towards alleviating the hunger from which its members suffer. If, therefore, a large proportion of the population lived in poverty, a modest improvement in their circumstances might cause very little change in the structure of employment or in the pattern of economic activity. Only a substantial rise in income could have produced significant structural change, and that in turn could only have arisen from a major change in output per head.

When the great majority of the workforce labours on the land, a big rise in overall productivity must involve a major increase in individual output amongst those living and working on the land. An escape from poverty, therefore, must begin in this way. Without it there will be no significant demand for products other than the four main necessities, and no major surge in employment off the land. An escape from poverty hinged upon the possibility of securing a major improvement in output per head in agriculture. This was the key. Why was it so hard to achieve?

One answer to this question which has influenced subsequent thinking powerfully was given by Adam Smith. At the very beginning of the *Wealth of nations* he suggested a paradigm for productivity growth in the parable of the pinmakers. Smith was anxious to illustrate the sensational increases in output per head that might be obtained even without major changes in production techniques if there were division of function. Specialisation could bring immense benefits. Ten pinmakers acting collaboratively could produce at least 240 times as many pins each as could have been made by one man working on his own.[4] Moreover there would be an improvement in quality as well as in quantity since a worker, relieved of the necessity of being a jack of all trades, could succeed in becoming the master of his particular specialism. An increase of productivity on this scale, even an increase one tenth as large, is so vast that it might seem that poverty must be easy to vanquish. Smith drew no such conclusion: indeed he was in general pessimistic about the future prospects for real incomes.[5] His pessimism sprang from several considerations, but one he mentioned almost immediately after telling the pinmaker parable. Having described the pin manufactory, Smith initially emphasised the general relevance of his example:

In every other art and manufacture, the effects of the division of labour are similar to what they are in this very trifling one; though, in many of them, the labour can

---

[3] There is some fascinating material bearing on this issue, derived from Gregory King's estimates of the consumption patterns in social groups with differing income levels in Stone, 'Some seventeenth century econometrics'.

[4] A. Smith, *Wealth of nations*, I, p. 9.

[5] Wrigley, *People, cities and wealth*, pp. 30–4.

neither be so much subdivided, nor reduced to so great a simplicity of operation. The division of labour, however, so far as it can be introduced, occasions, in every art, a proportionable increase of the productive powers of labour.

The prospect seemed fair, but Smith then noted that farming formed an exception:

The nature of agriculture, indeed, does not admit of so many subdivisions of labour, nor of so complete a separation of one business from another, as manufactures . . . The spinner is almost always a distinct person from the weaver; but the ploughman, the harrower, the sower of seed, and the reaper of the corn, are often the same.[6]

The most important means by which manpower productivity could be increased only applied to a limited extent to agriculture, by far the largest industry.

A first obstacle to the radical improvement in living standards in traditional societies, therefore, stemmed from the fact that advances that might be available in much of the rest of the economy through specialisation were much harder to secure on the land. Had this been the only problem, however, poverty might still have proved a tractable issue, but other dragons lay in the path.

The most fearsome dragon in the eyes of the classical economists who followed Adam Smith, such as Ricardo and Malthus, was the spectre of diminishing marginal returns.[7] Since nothing could be done to expand the land surface available for cultivation, it seemed inevitable that a growing demand for the products of the land, whether arising from an increasing population or from industrial growth with an associated increase in the demand for raw materials, must at some stage lead to the use of more marginal land, or to the more intensive cultivation of existing agricultural land, or to both. Even though some technical progress was to be expected, the difficulty could only be postponed and not circumvented. To squeeze increased production from the intensive or extensive margins must involve the use of more labour or capital, or more probably of both, to secure a unit increase in output. Declining returns to labour (and also, of course, to capital) must ensue.

This constituted a problem central to the entire economy and not just to the supply of food, for traditional societies were organic economies, economies in which animal and vegetable raw materials were used exclusively in almost all branches of material production. Spinners, weavers,

---

[6] A. Smith, *Wealth of nations*, I, pp. 9, 10.
[7] The classical statement of the principle may be found in Ricardo, *Principles of political economy*, I, pp. 120–7. Similar ideas, however, may be found in Malthus, *The nature and progress of rent*.

tailors, shoemakers, millers, brewers, glovers, hatters, carpenters, coopers, bakers, butchers; these were the occupations in which most of those engaged in material production worked, apart from agriculture. In all of them the raw materials used were animal or vegetable in origin. Furthermore, even those industries which used mineral raw materials, such as metal-working, brickmaking, or glassmaking, needed much energy in the form of heat to transform their raw materials, and this came largely from wood, leaving them also closely dependent on the productivity of the land and exposed to the risks associated with declining marginal returns.

This sketch of the reasons why the parable of the pinmakers did not serve to sustain hope of an escape from poverty in a traditional society is too stark. Even within the context of a Ricardian world there were important sources of improved agricultural productivity available in favourable circumstances. For example, while opportunities for specialisation of function among workers on a particular farm were limited, specialisation by farming region was capable of increasing productivity significantly by allowing each region to concentrate its production on the crops or pastoral products to which it was suited by geographical circumstances or by distance to market. There might also be gains from specialisation among workers on individual farms where the farm ceased to be a self-sufficient unit and was devoted instead to raising a more limited range of crops or animals. That large gains in output per head were possible even in a long-settled land and despite the problem of declining marginal returns is shown by English agricultural history, since in round terms output per head on English farms probably doubled between 1600 and 1800.[8]

Further constraints on the growth of individual productivity

The problem of endemic and ineluctable poverty in traditional societies, though heavily conditioned by the difficulty of increasing agricultural productivity, embraced a much wider range of issues. A second such issue will always be associated with the name of Robert Malthus.[9] The argument associated with his name, expressed in its crudest form, is that adventitious improvements in living standards among the labouring poor will always prove short-lived because they will tend to cause mortality to fall and fertility to rise, thus increasing the rate of population growth,

[8] Wrigley, 'Urban growth', esp. pp. 164–74.
[9] Although Thomas Robert Malthus is usually referred to by his first given name, it seems plain that this is mistaken. He was always known to his contemporaries as Robert. James, *Population Malthus*, p. 1.

and the resultant additional supply of labour will soon force wages back towards some conventional minimum. The argument was not original to Malthus; for example, it can be found succinctly and starkly stated in the *Wealth of nations*.[10]

The argument attributed to Malthus usually fails to do justice to the nature and subtlety of his thinking. He asked to be granted two *postulata* – that food is necessary to support existence and that 'the passion between the sexes' is a constant.[11] He believed it to be safe to deduce from the former that population could not grow faster than the supply of food, and from the latter that the rate of growth of population, unless checked by an exterior, intervening force, was constant. Further, he considered that the rate at which the supply of food could be increased always tended to be lower than the rate at which population would grow if unhindered.[12] It followed, of course, that, except where there was a large stock of unsettled land, when for a time the output of food could keep pace with the rise in population, some checks must constantly be at work constraining the growth of population to keep it in step with the rise in food output. Interpreted in an extreme and mechanical way, this schema can lead to the assertion that populations are kept constantly close to a precipice over which some fraction will plunge from time to time because of a chance event, such as a run of poor harvests.

Malthus himself was not a Malthusian in this sense. Even in the first version of his *Essay*, published in 1798, he recognised and enumerated the complexity of the factors affecting the reactions between production and reproduction. Later, with the benefit of much wider reading, foreign travel, and more reflection, he moved towards a position that was, perhaps paradoxically in view of the later use of the adjective 'Malthusian', more shaded and flexible than that of either Adam Smith or Ricardo. He distinguished between a 'European' case, representing one extreme, and the 'Chinese' case at the other. Everywhere there was tension between production and reproduction, but in much of western Europe the accommodation between the two was secured chiefly by moderating fertility to avoid too rapid a rise in numbers, whereas in the 'Chinese' case savage bursts of mortality operated as the prime regulator.

The difference between the two was associated with the differences in marriage practice in Malthus's view. Where marriage was early and universal, as in China, and fertility was therefore not responsive to economic circumstances, the potential rate of growth was high, and, since

[10] A. Smith, *Wealth of nations*, I, pp. 88–90.
[11] Malthus, *Essay on population* [1798], p. 8.
[12] Malthus, *Essay on population* [1798], pp. 8–10.

high population growth rates were unsustainable, mortality must also be high to offset the high fertility. It should, perhaps, be noted that his knowledge of China was limited. His depiction of the 'Chinese' situation should be regarded rather as an illustration of a limiting extreme rather than of empirical reality. Marital fertility, for example, was much lower in China than in Europe, compensating, in a sense, for earlier and more universal marriage.[13] In contrast with the 'Chinese' case, where celibacy was comparatively common, and marriage came later in life and was a moveable feast responsive to economic pressures, as in much of western Europe, the potential population growth rate was lower and, even though the economy might be slow growing, the prevailing mortality level could be comparatively modest. Living standards could be substantially higher in such circumstances.[14] The standard of living prevailing in a traditional society might therefore vary substantially from a 'worst case' in which many people lived on the margin of bare subsistence to a situation in which even the labouring poor were reasonably well-buffered against outright starvation and most families could secure the four main necessities of life and even aspire to modest comforts. Malthus's bitter opposition to the poor law of his day sprang from his belief that it was undermining some of the most important institutional constraints upon fertility, thereby provoking faster population growth, and so tending to ensure that the lot of the poor would deteriorate.[15] More generally, however, Malthus regarded the capitalist system as possessing features that were likely to inhibit poverty, while he believed the reverse to be true of

[13] See, for example, Lee and Feng, *One quarter of humanity*, esp. chs. 5 and 6. The power and pervasiveness of Malthusian thinking is, however, clear from the design of *One quarter of humanity*, which is explicitly intended as a refutation of Malthus's 'Chinese' model.

[14] For a simple graphical exposition of this point see Wrigley, *Continuity, chance and change*, fig. 1.1, p. 21.

[15] 'The poor laws of England tend to depress the general condition of the poor in these two ways. Their first obvious tendency is to increase population without increasing the food for its support. A poor man may marry with little or no prospect of being able to support a family without parish assistance. They may be said therefore in some measure to create the poor which they maintain.' (His second point is to do with workhouses.) Malthus, *Essay on population* [1798], p. 33. It should be noted that Malthus was not at all opposed in principle to the transfer of income between rich and poor, rather the reverse; but he feared that it must prove futile. 'I should indeed think that the whole, or a much greater sum [than currently levied under the poor law], was well applied, if it merely relieved the comparatively few that would be in want, if there were no public provision for them, without the fatal and unavoidable consequence of continually increasing their number, and depressing the condition of those who were struggling to maintain themselves in independence. Were it possible to fix the number of the poor and to avoid the further depression of the independent labourer, I should be the first to propose that those who were actually in want should be most liberally relieved, and that they should receive it as a right, and not as a bounty.' Malthus, *Amendment of the poor laws*, p. 9.

the political systems prevailing in some extra-European areas, such as the Turkish Empire.[16]

Malthus's analysis, therefore, created a wide spectrum of possibilities. Nevertheless, the tension between production and reproduction was inescapable except in countries of recent settlement with large areas of unsettled land available. The rate at which production could be expanded was less than the rate at which population growth would occur if unchecked. The history of settlement in North America appeared to provide an excellent illustration of the truth of the belief that populations would grow rapidly when unchecked by land shortage. There a European stock, drawn largely from the British Isles, and closely similar in social, cultural, and political character to the communities which the settlers had left behind, had doubled in number by natural increase alone in every quarter-century since the beginning of settlement, though their communities of origin on the eastern side of the Atlantic had grown far more slowly.

Malthus was less pessimistic than either Adam Smith or Ricardo about the necessary implications for living standards of the interplay between economic and demographic forces.[17] But even in his analysis the pressure of population was a prime reason for widespread poverty. He used an intriguing metaphor to make his view clear:

In an endeavour to raise the proportion of the quantity of provisions to the number of consumers in any country, our attention would naturally be first directed to the increasing of the absolute quantity of provisions; but finding that, as fast as we did this, the number of consumers more than kept pace with it, and that with all our exertions we were still as far as ever behind, we should be convinced, that our

---

[16] Malthus argued that in capitalist agriculture the interest of the farmer ensured that the product of the marginal worker could never be less than the conventional minimum wage, whereas in other systems this restriction did not apply (in an extreme case, the product of the *average* worker might fall to this level). Malthus, *Essay on population* [1826], II, p. 405. Comments on the disadvantages of Turkish political institutions may be found in ibid., I, pp. 110–3.

[17] Malthus held that there were what he termed 'oscillations' in the relationship between output and population which meant that living standards did not continue at an invariant level but moved up and down in sympathy. Whether or not any period of improved living standards was consolidated or was succeeded by starker times depended on the particular circumstances of the society in question. 'From high real wages, or the power of commanding a large portion of the necessaries of life, two very different results may follow; one, that of a rapid increase of population, in which case the high wages are chiefly spent in the maintenance of large and frequent families; and the other, that of a decided improvement in the modes of subsistence, and the conveniences and comforts enjoyed, without a proportionate acceleration in the rate of increase.' Malthus, *Principles of political economy*, p. 183. The bluntness of Adam Smith's view that the long-term prospect for real wages was poor may be found, for example, in Smith, *Wealth of nations*, I, pp. 88–91. Ricardo's judgement was closely similar.

efforts directed in this way would never succeed. It would be setting the tortoise to catch the hare. Finding, therefore, that from the laws of nature we could not proportion the food to the population, our next attempt should naturally be, to proportion the population to the food. If we can persuade the hare to go to sleep, the tortoise may have some chance of overtaking her.[18]

All traditional societies faced the problem confronting the tortoise. Prudence and foresight might alleviate poverty; nothing could be found to justify the hope that it might be banished.

To the difficulties associated with declining marginal returns on the land, the elusiveness of gains from specialisation, and the tensions arising from the expansive power of population, must be added a further reason why poverty was built into the nature of traditional societies. Even if none of the difficulties just enumerated were of serious consequence in a given traditional society, it would not follow that living standards would be high, or capable of being raised significantly. To secure a high level of output per head it was essential to command energy on a large scale. Producing a finished product fit for use or consumption always entailed the expenditure of energy. This was true of each stage in the process, from the primary stage of production onwards. Many of the most important operations of the agricultural year were heavily energy-intensive. Ploughing, manuring, scything, stooking, carting, and winnowing all required the expenditure of much mechanical energy, as did almost all aspects of production from mines. Later in the production sequence the same held true in varying degrees. Either heat or mechanical energy was needed wherever a material was cut, twisted, bent, hammered, shaped, woven, smelted, boiled, or baked; in short, when it was subjected to some form of physical or chemical change. And if the consumer was finally to benefit from the production process, the finished product had to be transported from the site at which it was produced to the market in which it was sold. This, too, meant the expenditure of energy.

Traditional economies, however, were grievously short of energy. This was true in a general and absolute sense. It is estimated, for example, that, although energy sweeps in from the sun in vast abundance even to a small northern land such as Britain, the proportion that could be tapped in traditional societies was tiny because photosynthesis only captures at best perhaps 0.4 per cent of the inflow of solar energy. Commonly its efficiency is much lower, only about 0.1 per cent. Yet photosynthesis forms the base of the pyramid of vegetable and, further up the food chain, of animal life from which all useful mechanical and heat energy had to be derived in organic economies, while at the same time providing almost

[18] Malthus, *Essay on population* [1826], II, p. 486.

all raw materials and food. Photosynthesis might notionally capture the energy equivalent of about 20 million tons of coal over the land surface of Britain each year and convert it into vegetable matter. Of this relatively modest theoretical total (less than a fifteenth of the consumption of energy in Britain in the 1980s), in practice only a limited amount could be harnessed to productive ends.[19]

Extending the analysis from the general to the particular underlines the seriousness of the limitations on productivity imposed by energy constraints. Heat energy, for example, came principally from the burning of wood. Even if the whole of Britain had been forested wherever physically possible and the whole of the annual cut of timber had been devoted to combustion, the resulting quantity of heat energy would have fallen well short of the theoretically possible figure just quoted. But, since the same land had also to provide all the mechanical energy used by man, the operative maximum figure was far lower. The mechanical energy used in the productive process came chiefly from human muscle, supplemented in some contexts by animal muscle. The wheat, barley, and rye from which bread was made not only served to sustain life but also represented the fuel needed to 'drive' tools, instruments, and machines.[20] Looms and saws were not driven by steam generated from coal or by electricity derived ultimately from nuclear fission, but by muscles fuelled by bread. Similarly, the grass grazed by livestock was not simply being turned into beef, pork, or mutton, but was charging the muscles of oxen and horses to pull the plough or pump water from a mine. The many disparate material needs of traditional societies all entailed the exploitation of the land and therefore only a fraction of the land could be devoted to the production of heat or mechanical energy.

Empirical studies suggest that there is a close connection between productivity per head and the amount of energy per head consumed, at least when the great bulk of employment is in primary or secondary industry.[21] The implication of this relationship was gloomy so far as living standards in traditional economies were concerned. Many types of production are inescapably energy-intensive, and productivity must be low if energy is in

---

[19] Wrigley, *Continuity, chance and change*, p. 52, n. 46.

[20] In round terms an intake of 1,500 calories a day is needed to maintain vital bodily functions even when no exertions are undertaken. Above this level there is a linear relationship between food intake and ability to produce useful work up to an intake level of about 4,000 calories a day, such that an intake of 3,000 calories permits twice as much work to be performed as a intake of 2,250 calories. At a normal level of nutrition, therefore, about half of the consumption of food was needed to keep the 'machine' viable, while the balance was available to carry out work. See, for example, Cottrell, *Energy and society*, p. viii; or Cook, *Man, energy and society*, pp. 27–8.

[21] Kindleberger, *Economic development*, fig. 4.4, p. 70.

short supply. For example, to cultivate the soil the sod must be turned, but it is heavy and often difficult to work. Where this task is performed by a man with a spade or some other digging tool, the total area that he and his family can cultivate may be so limited that it is a struggle to produce enough food and other raw materials to meet their needs, and there is little possibility of growing enough to maintain other families as well. This remains true even where there is no shortage of land, no evidence of population pressure, where no Ricardian or Malthusian devils lurk. But if this is the case, there is also by the same token little possibility of large-scale employment in manufacturing or of urban growth, since a man cannot be a specialist weaver unless he can obtain food from others, nor can town dwellers meet their own food needs. A more generous production horizon opens up where animal muscle can be used to supplement human effort. A ploughman with a horse can dwarf the achievement of a peasant with a spade. There is thus a sense in which the domestication of draught animals was a precondition for the existence of any considerable proportion of the population engaged in non-agricultural work.

The seriousness of any constraints associated with limited energy supplies varied with context. It was pronounced in many aspects of arable cultivation but less significant in pastoral activities. It was acute in, say, metal manufacture, but minimal in clockmaking. Its overall impact is hard to quantify. It is likely, however, that it was one of the most significant of all the influences that made an escape from poverty out of the question in traditional society. Equally, access to abundant and cheap supplies of energy was one of the key changes associated with the industrial revolution, arguably constituting the most important single factor enabling output per head to be raised steadily and substantially.[22]

Faced with the combined pressures exerted by all the constraints that have now been briefly surveyed, any tendency towards increased output per head that might in time have rescued a population from poverty was foredoomed to lose momentum. Attempts to measure the standard of living are fraught with both empirical and theoretical problems even in modern economies. The same is true *a fortiori* for societies in the past. Reliable price and wage series seldom exist, and any study that attempts to cover centuries must run into difficulties from which studies of shorter periods are largely free. It would be quixotic to ignore the data that are available, however, on the grounds that they are less reliable than one might wish. The study with the longest time span is that carried out

---

[22] Wrigley, *Continuity, chance and change*, esp. chs. 2 and 3.

by Phelps Brown and Hopkins (PBH).[23] It strongly suggests that while real wages in England varied substantially between the thirteenth and eighteenth centuries, displaying wide secular fluctuations,[24] there was no long-term tendency for real wages to rise, no evidence that poverty was declining.

There may be technical reasons for wishing to question this conclusion,[25] but, such as it is, the PBH series provides no ammunition for those who might hope to discern an approaching end to poverty in the early modern period. Since in this period there were substantial changes in material technology; in the geographical scope of the trading economy focused on western Europe; in the institutions through which economic activity was carried on; and, in England, in the scale of urbanisation,[26] the apparent near-constancy in the real wage over the long run cannot be lightly ignored. It may be very difficult to pinpoint the particular constraints that were most powerful but their collective impact seems to have been as weighty even in the last decades of the traditional economy as they had been half a millennium earlier.

The classical economists, who were surveying the last decades of the traditional, organic economy in England, and who had, of course, no expectation that the basic structure of the economy would change, were united in their expectation that the period of growth that was visible

---

[23] Phelps Brown and Hopkins, 'Seven centuries of the prices of consumables'.

[24] Fluctuations in the PBH series reflect the volatile behaviour of wholesale prices. Retail prices tended to be far less volatile, and therefore the 'true' standard of living of that part of the population chiefly dependent on wages probably moved up and down less violently, especially in the long term, than the PBH series suggests. See Rappaport, *Worlds within worlds*, ch. 5, 'The standard of living'.

[25] The fallibility of the index of Phelps Brown and Hopkins is widely recognised, not least by its authors. It is unrealistic to assume that the proportionate share of items within the 'shopping basket' will remain the same over such a long period of time. The prices are wholesale prices but for the family budget retail prices were the relevant statistic, and retail prices were much less volatile than wholesale prices. The wage data were drawn largely from the south of England for very long periods and relate only to craftsmen and labourers in the building trade. Some important elements in the budget of every family, notably the cost of accommodation, could not be included in the index for lack of relevant data. And so on. It is tempting to suppose that the series may fail to capture an improvement in the real wage in the early modern period, if only because the marked change in employment structure away from agriculture in the seventeenth and eighteenth centuries suggests that an increasing proportion of income was available for the purchase of comforts and even luxuries after meeting the continued requirement for necessities.

[26] On the extent of the contrast between England and the continent in the degree to which urbanisation increased in the seventeenth and eighteenth centuries, see Wrigley, 'Urban growth', esp. tab. 7.7, p. 179. On the continent there appears to have been remarkably little change in the extent of urbanisation over almost half a millennium between 1400 and 1800; at both dates the proportion of the population living in towns with 5,000 or more inhabitants was about 13 per cent. Bairoch, Batou, and Chèvre, *La population des villes*, tab. B2, p. 255.

over the two preceding centuries would prove difficult to sustain and that the stationary state would supervene. Adam Smith set the tone both in expecting that this would occur and in supposing that the stationary state, though incorporating the most advanced commercial practices and technology, would be a bleak place both for labour and for capital:

In a country which had acquired that full complement of riches which the nature of its soil and climate, and its situation with respect to other countries, allowed it to acquire; which could, therefore, advance no further, and which was not going backwards, both the wages of labour and the profits of stock would probably be very low.[27]

Both the expectations of well-informed contemporaries and the fruits of modern empirical research, therefore, suggest that poverty had been an unchanging feature of the human condition. Mercifully, subsequent events have shown that the expectations of the classical economists were ill-founded. To the degree that poverty is still to be found in industrialised countries, this may more properly be regarded as evidence of the deficiencies of particular social and political arrangements, assumptions, and institutions than as an affliction arising directly from the limited productive powers of society. There is now ample evidence that output can be induced to rise exponentially decade after decade at a greater pace than population growth, thus opening up the possibility of steadily rising real incomes. And, in any case, the inference that Malthus drew from one of his two postulates has proved wrong. The passion between the sexes may be as strong as ever, but that does not imply that population growth will continue, even though mortality before the end of the child-bearing period is now negligible. Few women now die before their fiftieth birthday, but, equally, few choose to bear many children. Prosperity is regarded as more likely to reduce than to increase fertility, a development that would greatly have surprised social commentators in earlier years. A society may still wilfully or inadvertently fail to match resources to need but there is no longer any difficulty in the right institutional environment in matching the sum total of production to the sum total of needs, or even to the total of needs plus comforts and many luxuries. Problems of the distribution of wealth may remain; problems of its production are much less oppressive.

---

[27] A. Smith, *Wealth of nations*, I, p. 106.

Why growth might aggravate rather than alleviate difficulties

One characteristic of economic growth in traditional societies deserves special emphasis when considering the prevalence of poverty. The process of growth itself tended to aggravate the underlying difficulties. If the statics of poverty were discouraging, its dynamics were even more so. Negative feedback tended to prevail both sectorally and within the economy as a whole. Economic models that assume linear relationships between the variables incorporated in the model fail to do justice to the reality of economic life in the past.

The basic problem was straightforward. In an organic economy growth necessarily entailed finding ways of making the land yield more abundantly than previously. This necessity followed directly from the fact that all food and almost all the raw materials of industry were of vegetable or animal origin. A process of growth that did not increase the demand for food and raw materials is not easy to conceive. Even with a stationary population this was likely to be true. But normally economic growth was associated with a rise in population as well. It was almost unanimously expected by contemporaries that if individual prosperity improved there would be a fall in mortality, or a rise in fertility (whether as a result of earlier and more universal marriage or for other reasons), or both. If this happened the intrinsic growth rate must rise. If population was increasing, and *a fortiori* if real income per head was also rising, the demand for food and raw materials was bound to grow. Either output from agriculture and forestry rose in step with the increased demand, or, if not, growth would decelerate, output per head and real incomes would be likely to fall, and the growth process would grind to a halt. Securing the required increase in output, without at the same time suffering Ricardian penalties, must prove inordinately difficult.

Some relief from the problems of expansion was attainable. The classical economists depicted growth as, in effect, a constant struggle between those elements in the economic system where there could be increasing returns to scale, as in the case of the pinmakers, and those where increasing returns were always hard to secure and must eventually be replaced by their opposite, as in the case of agriculture. Their understanding of the process seems just. The extent and duration of any reprieve from decreasing returns depended principally on the pace of innovation, broadly understood to include changes of an organisational nature as well as changes in material technology.

In agriculture, for example, not only might the introduction of new crops, of better breeds of cattle, of improved drainage, or of more appropriate and sophisticated implements, increase both total output and output per head, but so also might better labour discipline, more effective cultivational techniques, more complex crop rotations, specialisation of land use as a result of creating a larger integrated market area, or more efficient transport and marketing facilities. For decades, generations, even centuries, such developments might preserve or even enhance living standards in spite of more intensive use of land and the steady growth in aggregate output, but eventually further growth would entail a reduction in output per head and therefore in living standards as more and more effort was needed to secure a unit increase in production.

The malign effects of the presence of negative feedback in the economy might be postponed but could not finally be denied. Further aggregate growth was always possible but at some stage could only occur at the expense of output per head. The dynamics of growth in an organic economy were such that at some point further growth, in the sense of an increase in the aggregate output of the economy, might be expected to increase the prevalence and severity of poverty in the population.

Conclusion

The line of argument that I have pursued in this essay implies that poverty in traditional society could not have been overcome whatever the institutional forms of social and political life prevailing; that societies dependent upon the land, organic societies, were subject to physical restrictions that ensured this outcome. Not all traditional societies, however, were equally poor, nor was poverty equally widespread and acute in all of them. Social and political structures played a considerable part in determining how many were poor and how poor they were.

In some societies responsibility for the poor lay principally with their family and kin. In others the church played a prominent part in trying to help the victims of poverty. In yet others the secular authorities created an institutional structure designed to alleviate poverty, as in the case of the Tudor poor law and its subsequent modifications. Custom or the law in varying combinations provided rules by which the poor were judged. Some forms of poverty were taken to be less culpable than others. The poverty of a widow and her dependent children might evoke pity and be recognised as constituting a decisive claim upon the resources of others. The poverty of an able-bodied man who was out of work was much less certain to be seen as worthy of relief. His destitution might be no less real but he was much more likely to be seen as at fault and so disqualified from help.

Sometimes both the proportion of the population which enjoyed relief and the scale of the transfer payments involved were substantial. Under the English poor law, for example, help might be forthcoming both to cope with an abrupt, unpredictable crisis, such as the failure of a harvest, and to counter long-term difficulties, such as those associated with chronic sickness or increasing age. The cumulative weight of such provision might involve a significant tax burden.[28] Where the community was both tolerably prosperous and generous, starvation might be rare or non-existent, few would need to go barefoot, and fuel to heat the cooking pot might seldom be lacking. But the fact that careful provision could hold the worst ravages of poverty at arm's length should not be taken to imply that greater generosity would have put comforts as well as necessities within reach of the poor (that is, that the problem of poverty was a problem of maldistribution).

Marx excoriated capitalism because it exploited the bulk of the population who depended for their livelihood upon the sale of their labour for the exclusive benefit of the small and shrinking minority who owned capital. Huge new income flows and vast wealth were coming into being but only to enlarge the gulf between the fortunate few and the deprived multitude. Marx's appreciation of the trends in income distribution was at fault, though it may have been hard to detect this at the time when he was writing *Capital*. But his analysis is not only a tribute to his sense of justice but also to his understanding of the depth of the transformation wrought by man's new ability to expand the productive powers of society in a manner without previous parallel. He was mistaken in thinking that the poor were not to share in the rising tide of income, but he was fully justified in believing that the means to overcome poverty were rapidly coming into being. He lived in the first age in which poverty had become problematic. If the capitalists had monopolised all income gain, no doubt the proletariat would have risen in revolt. Certainly it would have been hard to deny them any right to aspire to do so, since the gap between their poverty and the wealth of the few would have grown steadily greater. The scale of new wealth was becoming so great that its redistribution could solve the worst material ills of the poor. It was reasonable to suppose that an act of political will combined with some appropriate social engineering could abolish poverty, and could give to man whatever dignity can be conveyed by adequate food, fuel, housing, clothing, and the like.

---

[28] Putting some of Gregory King's data into a modern national income accounting framework, for example, Stone has estimated that social welfare provision through the poor law represented more than a fifth of the combined total of central and local government expenditure in England in the late seventeenth century. Stone, *Some British empiricists in the social sciences*, tab. 3.7, p. 98.

The mid-nineteenth century, however, was the first age in which such a view was tenable. Before then there had been insufficient headroom for mankind to stand up free from poverty, whatever the political regime or institutional framework. It was not merely that existing income flows or accumulations of wealth however dispersed could not have matched the basic needs of the multitude, but that the obstacles that stood in the way of increasing income and wealth were first and foremost physical and bio-logical, and not primarily social, political, or economic. The doubts about the possibility of sustained growth and individual well-being reflected in the writings of the classical economists, and the further doubts associated with the limited availability of both heat and mechanical energy, were well founded in the world that existed before the industrial revolution. Between them they set bounds to the growth that could occur, and all had the frustrating characteristic that the very process of growth tended to make them act with steadily increasing severity. Success now meant failure later.

8   Malthus on the prospects for the labouring poor

In the penultimate chapter of St Matthew's gospel, immediately before the account of the betrayal by Judas, the story is told of a visit which Jesus paid to the house of Simon the leper. As he sat eating a woman came and poured a precious ointment over his head. The disciples were indignant, saying, in the words of King James's Bible, 'To what purpose is this waste? For this ointment might have been sold for much, and given to the poor. When Jesus understood it, he said unto them, why trouble ye the woman for she hath wrought a good work upon me? For ye have the poor always with you; but me ye have not always.'[1]

St Matthew appears to have regarded Jesus's remark as a conclusive dismissal of the disciples' complaint. The problem of poverty was permanent; it was to be regarded as a sad but inevitable feature of life in society, incapable of cure by human agency.

It is a measure of the extent of the gulf separating us from the pre-industrial world that the remark may strike some hearers today as insensitive. We are familiar enough with the notion of *relative* deprivation but it is now several generations since *absolute* deprivation was common in industrialised western countries, and poverty is no longer regarded as incapable of cure. Even those at the bottom of the social pyramid are unlikely to starve or to be clad in rags. The industrial revolution has endowed society with productive powers sufficient to secure a far better standard of living for all, though it does not follow that relative differences have also been reduced.

Perhaps no other social analyst belonging still to the period in which Jesus's remark would have seemed unobjectionable, at least as a statement of fact, made as great a contribution to the understanding of the reasons for poverty and of the possibility of alleviating it in a pre-industrial setting as did Robert Malthus. Since there was much common ground between

---

This chapter was delivered as a James Ford Special Lecture in Oxford on 3 December 1986.
[1] St Matthew, 26:8–11.

him and the other great classical economists on the question of poverty, and yet his analysis was distinctive, it is convenient to consider first the extent of the common ground.

The view of the classical economists

The classical economists in general regarded the prospects for the labouring poor as bleak. It was their view that the secular tendency of real wages was likely to be flat, if not tending downwards, because any increase in the funds available to pay the wages of the labouring poor would be matched by a corresponding rise in their aggregate number. There was likely to be some timelag before the demographic adjustment could fully compensate for the economic change, and in the meantime fuller employment as well as a higher daily wage might improve the living standards of the average family, but eventually the balance would be restored. This did not necessarily imply that the real wage of the labouring poor must be at or near the level of bare subsistence even when labour was in abundant supply. There could be a conventional minimum, which in the case of western Europe might be well above bare subsistence, which would constitute an effectual floor to living standards.

Adam Smith, for example, insisted that there was a wide gulf between the living standards of the poor in Europe generally and those to be found in China. He used strong language to drive home the truth of his view that, 'The poverty of the lower ranks of people in China far surpasses that of the most beggarly nations in Europe.' Of the boat people of Canton he remarked that, 'The subsistence which they find there is so scanty that they are eager to fish up the nastiest garbage thrown overboard from any European ship. Any carrion, the carcase of a dead dog or cat, for example, though half putrid and stinking, is as welcome to them as the most wholesome food to the people of other countries.'[2]

Although Adam Smith believed that real wages in England had risen in the course of the eighteenth century,[3] he was not sanguine about the future prospects for the labouring poor in England or elsewhere, essentially because 'the demand for men, like that for any other commodity, necessarily regulates the production of men; quickens it when it goes too slowly and stops it when it advances too fast'. Periods of rising real wages occurred only when the stock of capital was rising so fast that the demand for labour tended to outstrip its supply. But the increase of stock reduced the return to be had from its employment as opportunities for profitable

[2] A. Smith, *Wealth of nations*, I, pp. 80–1.
[3] Ibid., I, p. 100.

investment were exhausted.[4] The gradation in interest rates from high to very low was an indication of the distance between the present state of a country and its final state. This last Adam Smith characterised in the following terms: 'In a country which had acquired that full complement of riches which the nature of its soil and climate, and its situation with respect to other countries, allowed it to acquire; which could, therefore, advance no further and which was not going backwards, both the wages of labour and the profits of stock would probably be very low.'[5] Although he did not think that any country had reached the final position indicated by the logic of his analysis, he suggested that China and Holland both displayed some of the characteristics associated with it, while at the same time illustrating the widely different forms which it could take.[6]

Adam Smith took a harsh view of the mechanism by which the demand for labour and its supply were to be kept in balance. 'Every species of animals naturally multiplies in proportion to the means of their subsistence, and no species can ever multiply beyond it.'[7] In civilised society the necessary adjustment took place at the margin rather than threatening the whole community. The inferior ranks alone suffered. Amongst them the scantiness of subsistence set limits to their number 'by destroying a great part of the children which their fruitful marriages produce'.[8]

Malthus's initial views were not greatly dissimilar from those expressed by Adam Smith. In the first edition of the *Essay on population* he emphasised the stunted growth of the labourers in husbandry, brought on by inadequate nutrition, and suggested that the necessary tailoring of numbers to resources would probably take place chiefly through periodic mortality surges.[9] At the same time the first *Essay* (1798) added a new

---

[4] Ibid., I, pp. 99–102.

[5] Ibid., I, p. 106.

[6] Ibid., I, pp. 106–7, 108.

[7] Ibid., I, p. 89.

[8] Ibid., I, 89.

[9] 'The sons and daughters of peasants will not be found such rosy cherubs in real life as they are described to be in romances. It cannot fail to be remarked by those who live much in the country, that the sons of labourers are very apt to be stunted in their growth, and are a long while arriving at maturity. Boys that you would guess to be fourteen or fifteen, are upon inquiry, frequently found to be eighteen or nineteen. And the lads who drive plough, which must certainly be a healthy exercise, are very rarely seen with any appearance of calves to their legs; a circumstance, which can only be attributed to a want either of proper or of sufficient nourishment.'

And, in an apocalyptic mood, 'The power of population is so superior to the power in the earth to produce subsistence for man, that premature death must in some shape or other visit the human race. The vices of mankind are active and able ministers of depopulation. They are the precursors in the great army of destruction; and often finish the dreadful work themselves. But should they fail in the war of extermination, sickly seasons, epidemics, pestilence, and plague, advance in terrific array, and sweep off their thousands and ten

dimension to the discussion of poverty by defining a new framework for its analysis, a framework which has sometimes been seen as quintessentially pessimistic, but which ultimately enabled Malthus to attain a new insight into the determinants of poverty, and led him in later life to take a much less jaundiced view of the possibilities for ameliorating the lot of the poor.

The new framework arose by deduction from the two postulates with which Malthus began his famous pamphlet: that food was necessary to the existence of man, and that the passion between the sexes could be regarded as a constant. In conformity with these postulates, Malthus regarded it as safe to assume that any rise in population would have to be matched by an equal proportional rise in the supply of food, and that populations would tend to rise at a constant rate unless checked. He was much strengthened in his conviction that the second of these two supplementary assumptions was correct by the evidence that the populations of the English colonies in North America, where land was readily available in what seemed limitless profusion, doubled regularly by natural increase alone every quarter century. He held that because the supply of land was fixed and yet populations displayed an inherent tendency to grow exponentially, there must be a constant tension between man's limited powers of production and his formidable powers of reproduction. Malthus chose to draw attention to the issue by his famous contrast between arithmetic and geometric growth series, a formulation that both secured immediate attention and attracted much adverse comment, but the underlying point is quite general. It only requires that population should tend towards a growth rate in excess of the attainable rate of growth of production to retain its validity.

Furthermore, as Malthus initially viewed the matter, except in areas of new settlement, the tension between production and reproduction was endemic and systemic. It was present whether or not population was growing: indeed it would be present even if population was declining. Like death and taxes, it was an inescapable concomitant of life.

At first blush, this line of argument is deeply pessimistic. An ineluctable pressure, linked to basic biological features of human condition, is constantly at work denying to man the possibility of a general improvement in his lot. Save to the degree that certain criteria for minimum acceptable living standards were recognised and observed, the existence of the pressure would force the labouring masses to put up with a life close to bare

thousands. Should success still be incomplete, gigantic inevitable famine stalks in the rear, and with one mighty blow, levels the population with the food of the world.' Malthus, *Essay on population* [1798], pp. 29–30, 51–2.

subsistence. Malthus's analysis has often been interpreted in this sense, but he himself came to adopt a different attitude.

Malthus refines his initial stance

In the five years separating the first from the second edition of the *Essay on population*, Malthus collected much empirical data both by combing the available literature and by travel. Although he had first formulated his analysis in a deductive form, he was deeply averse to arguments couched exclusively in this way. A passage from the introduction to the *Principles of political economy* captures his bent of mind very well:

The tendency to premature generalisation occasions also, in some of the principal writers on political economy, an unwillingness to bring their theories to the test of experience. I should be the last person to lay an undue stress upon isolated facts, or to think that a consistent theory, which would account for the great mass of phenomena observable, was immediately invalidated by a few discordant appearances, the reality and the bearings of which there might not have been an opportunity of fully examining. But certainly no theory can have any pretension to be accepted as correct, which is inconsistent with general experience.[10]

Putting his own precepts into practice led Malthus to alter the emphasis of his analysis in the first *Essay*. He learnt, for example, that although his views about the behaviour of colonial populations in North America were borne out by the empirical evidence, his assumption about the course of English population history was not. He had argued *a priori* that the population of England must be increasing only very slowly since England was a long-settled country and should be subject to the problems whose nature he had identified. He discovered, having the evidence of the first census before him, that the English population was growing rapidly, and indeed subsequently learnt, when later censuses were to hand, that the rate of growth was not only high but rising. Still more striking, he came across evidence that showed beyond reasonable doubt that in some European countries, notably in Switzerland, both fertility and mortality had fallen considerably from the levels prevailing in earlier periods.[11]

Evidence of this sort both demonstrated that population behaviour in relation to economic opportunity was a more complex phenomenon than he had at first been inclined to allow, and also that the relative importance of the prudential as opposed to the positive check might be greater than

---

[10] Malthus, *Principles of political economy*, p. 10.
[11] See, for example, Malthus, *Population*, pp. 210–2. Malthus believed the fall in mortality was general in Europe; Malthus, *Essay on population* [1826], p. 231.

he had supposed. As a result he began to lay greater emphasis on the difference between European patterns of relationship between production and reproduction and those to be found elsewhere in the world. His mature position might be described in the following terms. The material technology at the disposal of a given community sets limits to what it can produce and therefore imposes a ceiling to its possible output, though improvements in technology, investment, and change in the institutional structure of the polity may all enable a growth in output to occur, so that the ceiling, rather than being fixed, might be regarded as rising gradually in favourable circumstances. It still represented a constraint upon population growth, however, since population, if left unhindered, was capable of outpacing economic growth. What mattered was *how* the constraint on numbers operated. If it operated solely through mortality rising to match a prevailing level of fertility the result would tend to be misery and deprivation. If it operated rather through reduced fertility and occurred before mortality had risen, a much higher equilibrium level of real wages was attainable and might be sustained indefinitely. Fertility within marriage might be high and invariant, but delay in marriage could reduce family size substantially. Malthus became increasingly convinced that nuptiality in western Europe responded to economic circumstances with sufficient sensitivity to dampen growth rates effectively and so secure a relatively favourable outcome even for those at the base of the economic pyramid.

Recent work has shown that there were two aspects of west European nuptiality which were of importance in this connection. The first may be described as a structural characteristic. In many other societies marriage for women was early and almost universal. It was thought shameful for a woman to be sexually mature but unmarried. In India, for example, the average age at marriage was in the early or mid-teens until the very recent past and only those suffering from severe physical and mental handicap were likely to remain unmarried. In much of western Europe, in contrast, the average age at first marriage was in the mid-twenties and between 5 and 20 per cent of each cohort of women who survived to the end of their child-bearing period remained unmarried. This structural feature meant that women spent much of their adult life single, and *ceteris paribus* could have resulted in levels of fertility little more than half those found in other traditional societies, though, since fertility within marriage was often relatively high in western Europe, the difference in general fertility levels between western Europe and elsewhere was normally less marked than might have been expected.

The mere fact of a generally lower level of fertility may be expected to lead to a lower equilibrium level of population in relation to productive resources and to a higher prevailing level of real wages.[12] But a second aspect of the west European marriage system was capable of enhancing this advantage significantly, for marriage not only came later in life but was a movable feast. In other societies marriage was governed by a biological trigger. For women the onset of menarche meant the transition from the single to the married state. In western Europe marriage was, in part at least, determined by economic pressures. In the main it was embarked upon only when the two principals and their families, guided by the norms of their community, considered that it was reasonably prudent to do so. Many couples threw caution to the winds, of course, but the reality of an economic discipline is clearly visible in several aspects of nuptiality in the past. It has long been known that in prosperous years following a good harvest many marriages were contracted but that in harsher times in the wake of a poor harvest, marriages were postponed.[13] It is now clear not only that short-term pressures influenced marriage behaviour, but also that nuptiality could be responsive to secular economic changes. When a long-term decline in real wages occurred in early modern England, there was a corresponding rise in the proportion never marrying, or in age at marriage, or both. And there were symmetrical changes in the opposite sense when living standards were rising in the long term.[14] The European marriage system, in short, was not only capable of creating a favourable economic context, but of adjusting to deteriorating economic circumstances so as to avoid or limit any impact on living standards.

Malthus understood the significance of both aspects of the west European marriage system and pointed to a further feature of the dynamics of the system. Already in the second chapter of the first *Essay* he had directed attention to what he termed 'oscillation' in the balance between population and production which produced long, slow variations in the living standards of labourers and in their employment opportunities. 'This sort of oscillation', he remarked, 'will not be remarked by superficial observers; and it may be difficult even for the most penetrating mind to calculate its periods.'[15] Later, when he had gained a better appreciation of the nature and significance of the west European marriage system, he returned to the question of oscillations. As he had originally envisaged their nature, they arose and were repeated because the several elements in the economic and demographic system responded to one another

---

[12] For a graphical illustration of this point, see Wrigley, *Continuity, chance and change*, fig. 1.1, p. 21.

[13] See, for example, Thomas's testing of Sundbärg's views on this issue. D. S. Thomas, *Swedish population movements*, pp. 80–8.

[14] Wrigley and Schofield, *Population history of England*, ch. 10.

[15] Malthus, *Essay on population* [1798], p. 15.

sluggishly. The system as a whole was homeostatic but none the less subject to considerable fluctuation even though the secular trend was neither up nor down. Two decades later he refined his earlier stance, pointing to the opportunity for secular change implied by the oscillations. At the point in the cycle where real incomes were at a peak the favourable ratio of productive resources to population might be preserved wholly or in part if the population exercised sufficient restraint through delayed marriage to avoid an increase in the rate of population growth. If the population as a whole were content with a low and static standard of living, it would respond to prosperity by relaxing constraints on marriage, thereby increasing the growth rate. If, on the other hand, it had acquired a taste for better living standards, it possessed the means to preserve what it had gained through refraining from imprudent marriage; and presumably, given the oscillatory nature of the balance between production and population, other similar opportunities might arise and be seized in the future, thus offering a ratchet-like possibility of upward motion in the standard of living.

Malthus expressed the possibility in the following terms:

> From high real wages, or the power of commanding a large portion of the necessaries of life, two very different results may follow; one, that of a rapid increase of population, in which case the high wages are chiefly spent in the maintenance of large and frequent families; and the other, that of a decided improvement in the modes of subsistence, and the comforts and conveniences enjoyed, without a proportionate acceleration in the rate of increase.

The choice depended on the prevailing habits of the lower classes which either led them to put present gratification first, or else might induce them to 'act as beings who "look before and after"'. And prevailing habits in turn were much influenced by the prevailing political regime. Despotism, oppression, and ignorance meant irresponsibility; prudence was associated with civil and political liberty and education.[16]

Malthus did not, of course, expect that populations would often rise to the opportunity periodically offered to them. Whether or not they did so was dependent upon many conditional factors – the nature of the government and constitution; the functioning of the legal system; the weight and nature of taxation; the educational system; the prevailing beliefs and aspirations of the people; and a host of other factors. In Malthus's view it was in this context that the malign influence of the English poor law system was most evident, but before considering his long polemic against the poor laws, it is convenient to refer to another feature

---

[16] Malthus, *Principles of political economy*, pp. 183–4.

of English society and economy which Malthus thought to be conducive to a relatively high level of real wages among the labouring mass of the population.

His argument was closely similar to that used by development economists today when deploring the effect of the ordering of priorities observed by families in many peasant societies. If a peasant father has several sons, so it is argued, the labour requirements of his holding may be such that each son after, say, the second is adding less to the output of the holding than he is consuming, but all his sons will remain on the holding until the average product, rather than the marginal product, drops below the level of subsistence. This results in maldistribution of labour and a lower standard of living than might otherwise be attained, but it is in accord with the wishes of the families in question because their scale of values is not that of a western, capitalist system. They are maximising something other than economic utility.

A similar line of thought led Malthus to conclude that the nature of the farming system in England provided a floor to living standards which was absent, or might be less effective elsewhere. It was one of the benefits flowing from the establishment of the capitalist system in agriculture.[17] No farmer, he remarked, would consider employing a man unless he was confident that he would produce more than he cost in wages. There could never arise a situation in which the marginal product fell lower than the conventional minimum wage, although under different regimes this could happen. As Malthus put it:

Upon the principle of private property, which it may be fairly presumed will always prevail in society, it could never happen. With a view to the individual interest, either of a landlord or farmer, no labourer can ever be employed on the soil, who does not produce more than the value of his wages; and if these wages be not on an average sufficient to maintain a wife, and rear two children to the age of marriage, it is evident that both population and produce must come to a stand. Consequently at the most extreme practical limit of population, the state of the land must be such as to enable the last employed labourers to produce the maintenance of as many, probably, as four persons.

But under a different political system, for example 'by the forced direction of the national industry into one channel by public authority', a less favourable situation might arise. Although he did not specifically refer to peasant farming as one of the systems which might also produce

---

[17] Malthus himself often used the term capitalist but did not habitually refer to the capitalist system.

more severe poverty, the logic of his argument is consistent with such a conclusion.[18]

Malthus and the poor law

I have spent time in describing features of English society which Malthus regarded as grounds for a degree of optimism because he is sometimes regarded as a profound pessimist. In fact he was well aware that, compared with the great majority of other countries of his own day or of earlier times, England was unusually fortunately situated. Like Adam Smith he was confident that there had been a marked advance in the English economy since Elizabethan times, and, although the command of food enjoyed by wage-paid labourers in his day was not greater than at times in the past, their command of other goods and services was substantially greater.[19]

Nevertheless Malthus regarded the labouring poor as seriously handicapped by the poor law and wished to see the poor law system abolished. He did not base his objection to the poor law upon the view that such transfer payments were impermissible in principle, or that they implied a burden of taxation which the wealthy or the country as a whole could not support. On the contrary he was most explicit in stating that if they served efficiently the end to which they were overtly directed – that of supporting those in greatest need or who were for various reasons unable to provide for themselves – it was entirely proper that the relief system should be adequately funded. He wrote:

With regard to the large sum which is collected from the higher classes of society for the support of the poor, I can safely say, that in the discussion of the question it has always been with me a most subordinate consideration.

I should indeed think that the whole, or a much greater sum, was well applied, if it merely relieved the comparatively few that would be in want, if there were no public provision for them, without the fatal and unavoidable consequence of continually increasing their number, and depressing the condition of those who were struggling to maintain themselves in independence. Were it possible to fix the number of the poor and to avoid the further depression of the independent labourer, I should be the first to propose that those who were actually in want

---

[18] Malthus, *Essay on population* [1826], p. 405.

[19] See, for example, ibid., pp. 440 and 446, where Malthus argues that although population had doubled since Elizabethan times 'the mass of wealth or the stock and revenue' must have increased more than fourfold and goes on to remark that, 'Although, therefore, the labourer may earn less corn than before, the superior value of every portion which he does not consume in kind will have in the purchase of conveniences, may more than counterbalance this diminution. He will not indeed have the same power of maintaining a large family; but with a small family he may be better lodged and clothed, and better able to command the decencies and comforts of life.'

should be most liberally relieved, and that they should receive it as a right and not as a bounty.[20]

In Malthus's view, however, the poor were injured by the English poor law system more materially than the rich. Given the difficulties associated with securing a steady expansion in almost all forms of output, it was especially rash to bring into being additional population whose continued existence would be dependent upon growth achievable only with severe penalties. Nothing therefore was more certain to prejudice the well-being of that part of the population largely or solely dependent for a living upon the sale of its labour than to increase their number improvidently. The poor laws represented a constant temptation to do this; they were a standing invitation to sacrifice long-term interests to short-term relief.

Malthus's central point was simple but strongly at variance with much prevailing opinion and indeed his views were sometimes thought shocking. It was widely held both that rising numbers were an index of national well-being, and that the future of a nation lay in the abundance of its offspring, a view embraced both by those who directly equated larger numbers with greater strength and prosperity and also by many others on less specific grounds.[21] Such a belief implies a special debt to parents of large families who undertake a burden which benefits the community as a whole, but may involve them in hardship. Both considerations of equity and a concern for the interest of the nation, therefore, suggested that those burdened by large families and unable to work should receive relief proportioned in some way to their responsibilities rather than being given a simple transfer payment which took no account of family circumstances.

For Malthus this was folly. Given that real income per head is a ratio measure with national income as the numerator and population as the denominator, and given further that the numerator could not be expected to expand *pari passu* with each rise in numbers, to provide an incentive to enlarge the denominator was the height of irresponsibility, above all because it meant creating an inexorable downward pressure on the living

---

[20] Malthus, *Amendment of the poor laws*, p. 9. Elsewhere he wrote, 'If all could be completely relieved, and poverty banished from the country, even at the expense of three-fourths of the fortunes of the rich, I would be the last person to say a single syllable against relieving all, and making the degree of distress alone the measure of our bounty. But as experience has proved, I believe, without a single exception, that poverty and misery have always increased in proportion to the quantity of indiscriminate charity, are we not bound to infer, reasoning as we usually do from the laws of nature, that it is an intimation that such a mode of distribution is not the proper office of benevolence?', Malthus, *Essay on population* [1826], p. 535.
[21] Adam Smith had written that 'The most decisive mark of the prosperity of any country is the increase in the number of its inhabitants.' Smith, *Wealth of nations*, I, p. 79.

standards of the labouring poor.[22] The fact that with each mouth there came a pair of hands was of no comfort once the implication of the law of declining marginal returns had been grasped.

Nor was this all. Malthus's comparative survey of the economic demography of the world as a whole, undertaken between the writing of the first and second editions of the *Essay*, had brought home to him very forcibly how frequently populations lived in the most grinding and hopeless poverty in areas possessing great natural wealth. In South America or in the Turkish empire, for example, it was the institutional deficiencies of the regimes which were the cause of poverty. Arbitrary government, irrational and excessive taxation, ignorance and superstition, could easily induce apathy, indifference, and fatalism and thus breed poverty no matter how fertile the soil or how favourable the ratio of land to man. Sparse population in areas of high potential agricultural productivity was not an occasion for surprise, but a confirmation of the rarity of an institutional structure capable of channelling the energy and ingenuity of man into fruitful labour. Since Malthus was convinced that mankind was apt to find indolence more attractive than labour it was important both that indolence should not be made easy and that labour should be well rewarded.[23] No institutional forms should be tolerated which must aggravate problems that could never be less than serious. The English poor laws, in his judgement, tended to promote the undesirable and to hinder the desirable. It was essential that a couple on marrying should have the liveliest possible conviction that their future and that of their children depended on their own efforts exclusively and that in justice to themselves and still more to their children they should pay heed to the injunction in the Prayer Book that marriage was, 'not to be enterprised, nor taken in hand unadvisedly, lightly, or wantonly, to satisfy men's carnal lusts and

---

[22] 'The poor laws of England tend to depress the general condition of the poor in these two ways. Their first obvious tendency is to increase population without increasing the food for its support. A poor man may marry with little or no prospect of being able to support a family without parish assistance. They may be said, therefore, to create the poor which they maintain; and as the provisions of the country must in consequence of the increased population, be distributed to every man in smaller proportions, it is evident that the labour of those who are not supported by parish assistance, will purchase a smaller quantity of provisions than before, and consequently more of them must be driven to apply for assistance.' (His second point is to do with workhouses), Malthus *Essay on population* [1826], p. 365.

[23] It is a theme, for example, which emerges in a passage containing the memorable assertion that, 'It is unquestionably true that wealth produces wants; but it is a still more important truth, that wants produce wealth', and in which Malthus goes on to remark that, 'The greatest of all difficulties in converting uncivilized and thinly peopled countries into civilized and populous ones, is to inspire them with the wants best calculated to excite their exertions in the production of wealth', Malthus, *Principles of political economy*, p. 321.

appetites, like brute beasts that have no understanding: but reverently, discreetly, advisedly, soberly, and in the fear of God'.[24]

The grounds for a limited optimism

From Adam Smith to John Stuart Mill the great figures in classical economics concerned themselves with a prospective stationary state, a state to which every economy must tend because of the logic of the principle of declining marginal returns, or some equivalent pressure. Their fears about both its inevitability and its nature have turned out to be groundless because the changes brought about by the industrial revolution have either removed or radically altered the constraints upon growth that they saw as ineluctable.[25] As long, however, as the supervention of the stationary state seemed probable, the long-term prospects for the health and prosperity of the mass of mankind were greatly coloured by its supposed nature. Adam Smith, as we have seen, was inclined to pessimism on the point. Ricardo was blunt and depressing about what lay in store for those dependent on wages for a livelihood. Like all other commodities labour had a natural price, 'that price which is necessary to enable the labourers, one with another, to subsist and to perpetuate their race, without either increase or diminution'.[26] For a time, even for an extended period, the market price for labour might exceed its natural price because capital might grow even faster than the supply of labour, but eventually the same forces which increased rent both in nominal and real terms would, by raising the price of food, increase nominal but depress real wages.[27] 'The fate of the labourer will be less happy; he will receive more money

---

[24] *First and second prayer books of Edward VI*, p. 252. Malthus made some harsh remarks about the evils and inequities which resulted from social customs disfavouring single women. In the second edition of the *Essay on population* [1803], for example, he included a passage containing some very strong language which he later deleted. 'The matron who has reared a family of ten or twelve children, and whose sons, perhaps, may be fighting the battles of their country, is apt to think that society owes her much; and this imaginary debt, society is, in general, fully inclined to acknowledge. But if the subject be fairly considered, and the respected matron weighed in the scales of justice against the neglected old maid, it is possible that the matron might kick the beam. She will appear rather in the character of a monopolist than of a great benefactor to the state. If she had not married and had so many children, other members of society might have enjoyed this satisfaction; and there is no particular reason for supposing that her sons would fight better for their country than the sons of other women. She has therefore rather subtracted from, than added to, the happiness of other parts of society. The old maid, on the contrary, has exalted others by depressing herself.' Malthus, *Essay on population* [1826], p. 698.

[25] See Wrigley, 'The classical economists'.

[26] Ricardo, *Principles of political economy*, p. 93.

[27] Ibid., pp. 94–5.

wages, it is true, but his corn wages will be reduced; and not only his command of corn, but his general condition will be deteriorated, by his finding it more difficult to maintain the market rate of wages above their natural rate.'[28] Even John Stuart Mill, though writing at a late enough date to have had an opportunity to see the astonishing capabilities of the new material technology, took a cautious line.[29] Paradoxically perhaps, in view of his reputation, Malthus offered a more shaded, even a guardedly optimistic view of what was possible for the labouring poor.

More than is the case with many writers, much more than with Ricardo for example, Malthus's works will sustain many interpretations. Both because his own views changed somewhat, and also because he was so determined not to be trapped into a deductive exposition of any topic at the cost of suppressing its richness and complexity, it is possible by selective quotation to portray him as deeply pessimistic about the prospects for the labouring poor.[30] In my view to admit this interpretation would misrepresent Malthus's view in his maturity. He did not discount the risk of the worst case entirely, but he emphasised the extent of the range of contingent possibilities and was inclined to hope that the future might turn out favourably when compared with the present or the past. Once he had thought differently. In 1798 he had written that the principle of population appeared not only to offer an invincible argument against the perfectibility of man, 'but against any very marked and striking change for the better in the form and structure of general society, by which I mean, any great and decided amelioration of the condition of the lower classes of mankind, the most numerous, and, consequently, in a general view of the subject, the most important of the human race'.[31] Even his 1798 position was couched in less absolute terms than Ricardo was apt to employ, but his later views reveal a move away from such a relatively strong position. He clung to the principle of population as firmly as ever. The tension between production and reproduction was universal

---

[28] Ibid., p. 102.

[29] In his chapter, 'Of the stationary state', it is of interest to note that Mill wrote, 'Adam Smith always assumes that the condition of the mass of the people, though it may not be positively distressed, must be pinched and stinted in a stationary condition of wealth, and can only be satisfactory in a progressive state. The doctrine that, to however distant a time incessant struggling may put off our doom, the progress of society must "end in shallows and in miseries", far from being, as many people still believe, a wicked invention of Mr Malthus, was either expressly or tacitly affirmed by his most distinguished predecessors, and can only be successfully combatted by his principles.' Mill, *Principles of political economy*, II, p. 753.

[30] As, for example, when he wrote, 'In the natural and regular progress of a country towards its full complement of capital and population, the rate of profits and the corn wages of labour permanently fall together.' Malthus, *Principles of political economy*, p. 128.

[31] Malthus, *Essay on population* [1798], p. 98.

and inevitable, but its implications were so profoundly modified by social arrangements, political systems, legal structures, educational provision, and nuptiality conventions that the gap between 'worst case' and 'best case' outcomes was very wide.

A future radically different from the past

There is now a substantial body of evidence supporting Malthus's view of the relationship between rates of population growth, real wage changes, and the operation of the preventive check during the centuries immediately before his birth. In England in the early modern period it is demonstrable that prolonged periods of rapid population growth led to even sharper rises in the cost of basic foodstuffs, and thus to falls in real wages, with symmetric changes of opposite sign in periods when population growth was slight or absent. Furthermore, since secular trends in nuptiality paralleled real wage fluctuations, a negative feedback pattern existed capable of sustaining the 'oscillations' to which Malthus had referred in the first *Essay*.[32] The factors which he had supposed capable of securing a relatively high platform standard of living existed and functioned in such a way as to offer the possibility of raising the platform from time to time in the fashion that he had envisaged. It may therefore be said that he provided an effective framework for the analysis of the vicissitudes of the labouring poor in past centuries. Nor is it open to doubt that his treatment of the problem of poverty was highly influential during his lifetime and for some decades thereafter. It has recently been described by Himmelfarb in the following terms: 'This was the extraordinary achievement of Malthus: to have formulated the terms of discourse on the subject of poverty for half a century – and not only in respect to social policy (the debate over the poor laws, most notably), but in the very conception of the problem. It was Malthus who defined that problem, gave it a centrality it had not had before, made it dramatically, urgently, insistently problematic.'[33] Yet, though his understanding of the past has been verified, and his influence on contemporary debates was so profound, his view of the future prospects for the labouring poor, though less bleak than often supposed, proved far from correct.

To understand the reasons for the inadequacy of his analysis, it is necessary to turn once more to the body of assumptions that were shared by all the classical economists. It is a topic which also brings us back to

---

[32] Wrigley and Schofield, *Population history of England*, figs. 10.2 and 10.9, pp. 405 and 425, and accompanying text.
[33] Himmelfarb, *The idea of poverty*, p. 126.

St Matthew's account of the exchanges that took place in the house of Simon the leper, emphasising the width of the gulf that separates the modern world from pre-industrial societies. The crux of the matter emerges neatly in Himmelfarb's discussion of poverty in England at this period. Himmelfarb regards Adam Smith as the prophet of the industrial revolution. In her view the industrial revolution was 'presumably reflected'[34] in the *Wealth of nations,* which may account for her markedly 'upbeat' picture of the analysis contained in Smith's great book. Its effect, she writes, 'was to give technology and industry a new and decisive role not only in the economy but in society. The division of labour . . . became the harbinger of a social revolution as momentous as anything dreamed of by political reformers and revolutionaries.' It created 'a political economy that made the wealth and welfare of the people dependent on a highly developed, expanding, industrial economy and on a self-regulating "system of natural liberty"'.[35] Twenty years later, however, the *Essay on population* was published. Its effect in Himmelfarb's account is reminiscent of the well-known jingle about Newton and Einstein. In this case, one might say, 'The devil howling "Ho, let Malthus be" restored the status quo.' 'The "principle of population"', she writes, 'subverted the whole of Smith's theory, starting with his views on industrial productivity and high wages and culminating with his predictions of economic and social progress. It is hard to imagine a more thorough reversal of thought, short of a return to mercantilism.'[36]

In my view to make such a contrast between the views of the two men is to misunderstand their fundamental unity on matters relating to the limits of growth. Their common mind on these matters reflected common assumptions about the overall constraints affecting all societies and necessarily involved broadly similar conclusions about the prospects for the labouring poor. Neither need have demurred from the view of poverty that underlies the remark attributed to Jesus.

The key point is simple. Land was a necessary factor in all forms of material production to a degree not easily recognised in a post-industrial revolution setting. Almost all raw materials were either vegetable or animal: even where mineral raw materials were employed, they were capable of conversion into a useful form only by burning a vegetable fuel. Much the same was also true of the sources of mechanical and heat energy: human and animal muscle and wood fuel were the preponderant means by which raw materials were converted into useful products and transported to places convenient for their subsequent use or consumption.

[34] Ibid., p. 44.
[35] Ibid., p. 44.
[36] Ibid., p. 100.

Therefore, the productivity of the land set limits to the scale of industrial activity no less than to the level of food consumption. Each of these two great consumers of the products of the land was necessarily in competition with the other for the use of a factor of production whose supply could not be expanded.[37] Moreover, output from the land was subject to declining marginal returns. Ingenuity and technological change might postpone the day when returns began to decline, might even for a while allow a period of increasing returns, but in the course of a few centuries, if not of a few decades, the final upshot must be declining returns to unit increments of labour and capital both at the extensive and intensive margins of cultivation.

Malthus and Ricardo phrased their concern very similarly: both defined and made use of the concept of declining marginal returns on the land. Adam Smith, though he did not explicitly formulate this concept, developed arguments with similar implications.[38] It was a comparable train of thought which led him both to assert that investment in the land must always prove to be the most productive form of investment and to worry about the likelihood that opportunities for the profitable use of capital would slowly dry up.[39] The parable of the pinmakers might illustrate the possibility of increasing returns, available in many manufacturing contexts, but in a wider framework there were far stronger grounds for concern than for optimism.

---

[37] Malthus wrote, 'And it should also be recollected, that land does not produce one commodity alone, but in addition to that most indispensable of all articles – food – it produces the materials for clothing, lodging, and firing'. Malthus, *Principles of political economy*, pp. 114–5. Much later Mill still clung to the same view of the centrality of the land, 'The materials of manufacture being all drawn from the land, and many of them from agriculture, which supplies in particular the entire material of clothing; the general law of production from the land, the law of diminishing return, must in the last resort be applicable to manufacturing as well as to agricultural history.' Mill, *Principles of political economy*, I, p. 182. Mill went on to stress, however, the wide scope of increasing returns in manufacture, leaving open the question of the final implications of the two conflicting tendencies for real incomes.

[38] See above pp. 53–5.

[39] 'The capital employed in agriculture, therefore, not only puts in motion a greater quantity of productive labour than any equal capital employed in manufactures, but in proportion too to the quantity of productive labour which it employs, it adds a much greater value to the annual produce of the land and labour of the country, to the real wealth and revenue of its inhabitants. Of all the ways in which a capital can be employed, it is by far the most advantageous to the society.' See also the train of argument which led him to associate successful agriculture with cheap food and so with success in manufactures: 'The corn, which could with difficulty have been carried abroad in its own shape, is in this manner virtually exported in that of the complete manufacture.' He ends by asserting that the manufactures of Leeds, Halifax, Sheffield, Birmingham and Wolverhampton are 'the offspring of agriculture'. A. Smith, *Wealth of nations*, I, pp. 385, 430–1.

Traditional societies were organic societies in quite a different sense from that often attached to the adjective. They were almost solely organically based whereas industrialised societies are largely inorganically based, deriving almost all their useful energy from mineral sources and sustaining large sectors of their economies with mineral raw materials. Even modern agriculture owes its very high levels of productivity to the direct and indirect input of energy derived from mineral sources on a scale which dwarfs the subsequent output of food and other organic products, measured in energy terms.

Malthus, in common with the other classical economists, failed to foresee the extravagant possibilities for growth represented by a world in which the fact that land was in fixed supply would cease to have any serious relevance to the possibilities of expanding output. It is no accident that land should have become the sleeping partner in the trinity of production factors whose definition had permitted the development of the first substantial body of economic theory.[40] But, though with the benefit of hindsight we can detect evidence of the slow conversion of the English economy to a new mode of operation in the later eighteenth and nineteenth centuries, later christened the industrial revolution, Malthus remained unaware of the sea change in progress about him, even at the end of his life in the early 1830s.

The universality and severity of the limitations to growth imposed on pre-industrial societies by their almost exclusive dependence on animal and vegetable raw materials can only be appreciated today by a great imaginative effort, though accepted without question still by the classical economists. Once it has become normal to expect both that a society can expand its output of goods and services per head by, say, 2 per cent per annum decade after decade and that the bulk of the population will regulate their fertility *within* marriage effectively, and not be dependent solely on fertility regulation *by* marriage, it is easy to lose sight of the shape which the problem of poverty must assume before either assumption could be made by any man of sense.

Conclusion

Given an organic economy subject to the law of diminishing returns and the assumption that the constancy of the 'passion between the sexes'

---

[40] The change is symbolised in the frequency with which economists today make use of Cobb–Douglas production functions to characterise major analytic problems, directing attention to capital, labour, and their exponents but excluding land, a proceeding which would not have recommended itself to the classical school.

would result in a high and stable level of marital fertility, room for manoeuvre was necessarily limited. In what might be termed a 'mechanical'
analysis of the issue, the prospects for the poor were indeed depressing.
Ricardo confined himself to this analysis, which is also visible in the early
Malthus, and is reflected at times in Adam Smith's discussion of probable real wage trends. Whether because of the tension resulting from a
population constantly attempting to increase at a 'natural' or exponential growth rate and a productive capacity constrained by the principle of
diminishing returns, or because the supply of labour expanded *pari passu*
with the demand for labour, there was no credible basis for predicting a
secular rise in real wages for the labouring poor. The question was rather
whether the institutional framework of society was such as to enable a
substantial or only a tiny fraction of society to secure a higher income
and find thereby the opportunity to cultivate the arts and sciences and
to enjoy the pleasures of a more leisured life. In any case the base of the
pyramid must be wide and those at the base unable to aspire to such
delights.

Greater knowledge and further reflection caused Malthus to aban-
don any such 'mechanical' analysis and to substitute a 'dynamic' for
a 'static' view of the issues involved. The present circumstances and future prospects of the poor were contingent upon a wide range of circumstances. The poor could have no prospect of leisured ease; most men must
continue to live by the sweat of their brow. The basic limitations of an
organically based economy remained. But Malthus no longer supposed
that the wage minima need be related to physiological necessity, or that
malnutrition must be a constant threat. Adequate food, shelter, clothing,
and heating were attainable, with something to spare for the 'decencies'
of life, perhaps even an occasional 'luxury'. All depended upon labourers
being willing to look 'before and after' with circumspection and to exercise an appropriate restraint when contemplating marriage. If this were
done, and because the remuneration of labour was a function of the ratio
between the funds available for the employment of labour and the size of
the labour force, a muted and conditional optimism on the prospects for
the labouring poor was justified. He noted that it was natural initially to
try to raise output to match population growth but that this must always
tend to prove a hopeless quest:

It would appear to be setting the tortoise to catch the hare. Finding, therefore, that
from the laws of our nature we could not proportion the food to the population,
our next attempt should naturally be, to proportion the population to the food.
If we can persuade the hare to go to sleep, the tortoise may have some chance of
overtaking her. We are not however to relax our efforts in increasing the quantity of
provisions but to combine another effort with it; that of keeping the population,

when once it has been overtaken, at such a distance behind, as to effect the relative proportion which we desire; and thus to unite the two grand desiderata, a great actual population, and a state of society, in which abject poverty and dependence are comparatively but little known; two objects which are far from being incompatible.[41]

[41] Malthus, *Essay on population* [1826], p. 486.

Part II

Town and country

9   City and country in the past: a sharp divide or a continuum?

War, politics, and personality were the topics with which Plutarch was most at ease as a historian: he selected and embellished whichever account of past events best enabled him to exemplify some moral or political principle, but seldom departed from these basic themes. In his *Parallel lives*, however, when relating the deeds of Theseus, he permitted himself a brief digression about the creation of a city-state. Having described Theseus's return from Crete after overcoming the minotaur and the tragic suicide of his father Aegeus, deceived by his son's carelessness into thinking that Theseus was dead, Plutarch continues:

After Aegeus's death Theseus conceived a wonderful and far-reaching plan, which was nothing less than to concentrate the inhabitants of Attica into a capital. In this way he transformed them into one people belonging to one city, whereas until then they had lived in widely scattered communities, so that it was difficult to bring them together for the common interest, and indeed at times they had even quarrelled and fought one another.

We learn that:

He then proceeded to abolish the town halls, council chambers, and magistracies in the various districts. To replace them he built a single town hall and senate house for the whole community on the site of the present Acropolis, and he named the city Athens.[1]

Plutarch's vignette was penned long ago but has a familiar ring. Both the constraints of language and customary usage and much of the historiography of the past have conspired within the European tradition to create an expectation of contrast between city and country and an association between city life and progress, wealth, power, and high attainment in all aspects of art and culture. The special significance of great cities is fixed in our minds by the resonance of phrases familiar to everyone:

This chapter was originally given as a paper to the Thirteenth Plenary Conference of the Anglo-American Conference of Historians at the Institute of Historical Research, 3–6 July 1990.
[1] Plutarch, *The rise and fall of Athens*, pp. 29–30.

251

'All roads lead to Rome'; 'Paris vaut une messe'; 'When a man is tired of London he is tired of life; for there is in London all that life can afford.' Even today normal usage still continues to encapsulate assumptions such as that capital cities stand for the nation as a whole. Thus, if we learn that Washington has sent a firm message to Moscow, we assume that it is President Bush rather than Mayor Barry who has been active, and that he spoke for the United States and not the District of Columbia.

There is much in the history both of institutions and events to suggest how this image of the city arose and to reinforce the impression created by customary usage. The Christian church, for example, perpetuated many of the attitudes of the classical world in which it came into being. The etymology of the word 'pagan' exemplifies the point, as does the fact that the episcopal hierarchy from the bishop of Rome to the humblest see was named after the city in which the prelate had his seat. The same image is conveyed by much secular nomenclature. Of the forty ancient counties of England, twenty-three are named after the principal towns within them, as if, say, Yorkshire was in some sense a terrain subject to, or reaching its highest form, in York. Visual imagery reinforces the point. The walls of ancient cities were a visible embodiment both of the separateness of town and country and of the ability of the city to ensure that its interests were protected. The city had its liberties and privileges to defend and its rights to enforce. To it were drawn the most talented, the wealthiest, the most enterprising, the most independent of mind. If the city was where the action was, to use a modern colloquialism, the countryside was where the action was not. Literature is replete with country bumpkins. 'When I am in the country', Hazlitt remarked, 'I wish to vegetate like the country.'[2]

Shortly before his tragically premature death Philip Abrams wrote a splendid essay on 'Towns and economic growth: some theories and problems' in which he attacked the way 'the material and especially the visual presence of towns seem to have impelled a reification in which town as a physical object is turned into a taken-for-granted social object and a captivating focus of analysis in its own right'. He advocated instead studying the 'historical functions of towns – in relation to a larger social context which, following Weber, we might call the complex of domination'. In describing how Weber wished to draw away from the conventional treatment of the city 'towards the activity of the social construction, maintenance and usurpation of power', Abrams suggested that to study this process, 'we need many studies of towns – because that is where the

---

[2] Hazlitt, *The complete works of William Hazlitt*, VIII, 'On going a journey', p. 181.

process in its many varieties occurs. But we can do without studies of the town.'[3]

Although the focus of my interest in this essay is very different from the topic pursued so vigorously by Abrams, I share some of his doubts about the effects of reifying the town as a concept to be set in contrast to the rest of society or to the countryside. My approach to this question is, however, almost the polar opposite to his. Abrams attempted to show how many influential writers, Dobb, Finley, Marx, Wallerstein, Sjoberg, Redfield, Reissman, Braudel, Hoselitz, had confused themselves and others by their wish to treat the city or some class of cities as categories which could advance understanding and analysis. In attacking them, Abrams had little recourse to empirical considerations. I intend to make use of some recent empirical findings that also raise questions about the validity of making exclusive divisions between the city and the countryside or between different classes of urban settlement, and to suggest that, with such data to provide a different perspective, some issues that have traditionally been given much attention appear in a different light.

The urban hierarchy

When the city is contrasted with the countryside, the term city is normally used generically to denote all cities, just as the term countryside covers all rural areas. The two terms between them are assumed to exhaust all human settlements. But it is not always recognised that when the city is referred to with this connotation, it would be more accurate to describe the phenomenon as the urban hierarchy. Since the days of Christaller and Lösch the underlying logic that leads to the articulation of a modern urban system has been known, but how far their models 'saved the phenomena' in the past has been unclear.[4] The work of de Vries and Bairoch has recently provided a wealth of information about the populations of all European towns from the high middle ages to the present day.[5] Though scepticism about the accuracy of the estimates of the size of many urban populations, especially those for the more distant past, is no doubt well founded, there can be no reasonable doubt that de Vries has demonstrated that from 1500 onwards, and very probably from a considerably earlier date, the frequency distribution of the population size of towns in Europe conformed reasonably closely to the rank-size rule.[6]

[3] Abrams, 'Towns and economic growth', pp. 9, 31, 30.
[4] Christaller, *Die zentralen Orte*; Lösch, *Die räumliche Ordnung*. For a summary of Löschian theory, see Berry, *Geography of market centers* or Haggett, *Locational analysis*, ch. 5.
[5] De Vries, *European urbanization*; Bairoch, Batou, and Chèvre, *La population des villes*.
[6] De Vries, *European urbanization*, ch. 6.

This rule expresses the relationship between the number and size of cities. The larger the size category, the smaller the number of cities within it. The form of the relationship is such that in the simplest case the second largest city within an urban system will be one-half as big as the largest; the tenth city one tenth as large; and so on. More generally, if, when the populations of towns and cities are plotted in size order on logarithmic paper, the points fall on or close to a straight line, they are said to display a lognormal distribution, and to exemplify the rank-size rule. Except at the top of the pyramid, the relationship between the size and number of cities within an urban system is normally surprisingly stable, so stable indeed that a knowledge of the number of towns in a few adjacent size categories suffices to enable the number in other size categories to be predicted with tolerable accuracy. The tip of the pyramid, consisting of the major centres of trade, the chief seats of government, the great centres of industry, is supported by a much larger mass of smaller urban centres in a notably regular fashion.

The key point about the urban sector in early modern Europe was not its absolute size, nor the proportion of the total urban population living in cities above a given population size. It was rather its striking regular shape. The urban settlement pyramid, resting upon its rural base, progressed with great regularity through each successive size category up to a metropolis at its apex. The apex has always caught the eye. Apex cities were often symbols of wealth, power, and culture in their day: Venice, Florence, Paris, Antwerp, Amsterdam, London. What lay beneath them, however, formed a pyramid, rather than a mound of variable and indeterminate shape. From villages that could boast no more than a small, occasional market, through market towns, provincial centres, and nationally important towns, to the great metropolises, the extraordinary complexity and heterogeneity of urban activities, urban forms, and urban populations, so striking to the eye of the casual traveller, resolves itself into a stable hierarchy of number and size of settlement.

The observed regularity is unsurprising but important. It is unsurprising in that it conforms to the expectations engendered by central place theory. Needs that arose frequently had to be satisfied locally; those that arose at longer intervals could be met without inconvenience from a greater distance. Each village might need a tailor, a shoemaker, a baker, and a priest, but would have only intermittent need for a cabinet maker, a clockmaker, a lawyer, or an apothecary. The stability of the urban hierarchy reflected the stability of human need, translated through market mechanisms into patterns of demand. In general and on average, each successive category of more and more populous settlements contained all the occupations, trades, and professions to be found in smaller places plus some not normally found in any smaller size category, culminating in a metropolis where alone the highest echelons within government, the church, the professions, and the merchant community were to be found, but which possessed also representatives of all the activities present in the tributary cities, towns, and smaller settlements lower down the hierarchy.

Great cities did not and could not exist in isolation surrounded only by what the Dutch call the *platteland*, the rural hinterland. True, this might be the visual impression from the city walls of, say, Florence or Paris, but the appearance was deceptive. Every great city owed its position to the support and exchange afforded by a graduated network of large and small towns, a network which displayed predictable characteristics. No other town might lie within sight of the walls of the great city, but the functional connections to other towns were close, even if maintained at a distance. There was a continuum running between the myriad of small market centres and the great central places. It was of the essence of an urban system that there should be constant interchange throughout the settlement hierarchy, a constant flow of products, services, and people between settlements in different size categories. Leicester, say, was an important regional centre precisely because merchants and craftsmen from Leicester were in frequent contact with smaller settlements within the country, and vice versa, and because Leicester was the focus through which much of the contact between the county and the metropolis was channelled.

The increasing occupational complexity associated with growing settlement size was paralleled by more and more intensive and extensive links between central places and the smaller centres within their economic hinterlands. And the nature of the inter-urban linkage was such as to impart a remarkably regular shape to the pyramid of urban centres that supported every metropolis. This regularity was important because it suggests that if there was a sharp divide between city and country we must expect to find it between the urban system as a whole and the countryside rather than between prominent cities and the rest of society.

It may be objected that this depiction of an urban hierarchy is a stereotype which represents only the average case, or one that was typical only of early modern western Europe as it became suffused by an increasingly commercialised market economy. It is too early to be sure how much weight should be attached to objections of this sort, but it should be remembered that the value of a stereotype lies as much in its ability to create a set of expectations about the norm as in the completeness with which it succeeds in 'saving the phenomena'. Thus, provided that empirical investigation shows the predominance of a particular pattern in statistical terms, any departure from the pattern will hold a special interest.

For example, the fact that London has been for almost a millennium far too 'big' for the rest of the English urban hierarchy, though a persistent anomaly to the symmetry of urban systems if judged solely within the national framework, does not constitute a reason for abandoning the model. Rather the model allows the size and nature of the anomaly to be identified, and may indirectly suggest how the riddle should be solved – for example, by treating London as part of a larger system embracing parts of the near continent and, at a later date, much of the north Atlantic basin. Or again, the advent of a technological change that transforms the economics of the location of production, such as the change brought about by the immense pulling power exerted by the coalfields upon industry in the era of steam power, may create some striking anomalies within the urban system, whose structure is normally more closely dependent upon the locational patterns arising from trade, exchange, communication, and the provision of services. Yet experience suggests that, in general, after a period of adjustment, the system seems to absorb such anomalies and again displays the same characteristic features: its inner logic prevails.[7]

Since the existence of urban hierarchies with marked similarities appears to be so widespread,[8] it follows that it is compatible with a wide range of different political, social, economic, and other characteristics, and this has important implications for some long-running debates about its functions and characteristics. Take, for example, the vigorous debate of the early postwar period about generative and parasitic cities.[9] The archetypal parasitic city was said to be one in which a ruling elite consumed the surplus levied from country dwellers by the exercise of power. The tribute thus realised, whether in money or kind, was used by the elite to surround themselves with specialist craftsmen and to maintain numerous servants. These jointly ministered to the comforts of the elite, without there being a return flow of goods and services to the countryside. The urban residence of the elite in gracious and imposing mansions, close to the highest offices of law, religion, and government, and intimately associated with the great symbolic occasions of church and state, at once exemplified, symbolised, and legitimated their dominant position. The notion of the city as a parasite was widely employed. Sjoberg, indeed, used it as a model in writing about the pre-industrial city generally.[10]

---

[7] How far the stereotype is applicable indifferently to all urban systems is a matter for further examination: so far as I am aware, however, available data for Japan and China suggest that the same pattern obtained as may be seen in western Europe.

[8] See, for example, Rozman, 'Urban networks'.

[9] See, for example, Hoselitz, 'Generative and parasitic cities'.

[10] Sjoberg, *The pre-industrial city*. One should, perhaps, note that Hoselitz, whose writings helped to give wide currency to the terms generative and parasitic, remarked that, 'It is

If it is reasonable to assume that the urban hierarchy in a society whose urban structure might be classed as parasitic shows the same structural pattern as that found in societies where the urban sector could be termed generative, then it is probably also fair to suppose that the nature, perhaps also the value, of the distinction needs to be reconsidered. If the ruthless tapping of a rural surplus for the benefit of the privileged few living amid the splendours of the capital city none the less brought into being subordinate settlements that conformed to the same rank-size rule that may be found elsewhere, the concept of a parasitic city may need to be modified. It may be that empirical data that would allow the point to be tested are currently lacking. And it seems likely *a priori* that inasmuch as the concept of parasitic and generative cities is useful it should be held to define the opposite ends of a spectrum in which many cities lay towards the middle, rather than as defining mutually exclusive alternatives. But the value of testing how far empirical patterns conform to a stereotype is confirmed if an investigation of this sort were to reveal the *absence* of a difference that might have been expected.

Urban growth and stagnation

The same studies that have thrown light on the regularity of the structure of the urban sector in the past have also provided much more authoritative evidence about its size than used to exist. Bairoch's compilation of estimates of the size of cities throughout Europe from 1300 onwards suggests that, if 'urban' is taken to mean settlements with 5,000 inhabitants or more, there was remarkably little change over the half millennium between 1300 and 1800: over these five centuries the urban proportion fluctuated between 11 and 14 per cent without decided trend. The lowest figure, 11 per cent, is for the earliest year, 1300, but the percentages for 1400 and 1800 were virtually the same. The absolute urban population totals rose a great deal over the period, of course, from 8 to 21 millions, but very little faster than the population of Europe as a whole.[11]

Using the same definition of what constituted a town, but a somewhat different definition of what constituted Europe, de Vries's independent estimates for the period from 1500 to 1800 show a slightly different pattern. They suggest that the urban proportion rose from 10 per cent in 1500 to 13 per cent in 1800 and that the growth, though very modest,

---

not easy to discover actual instances in which the city exerted long-run parasitic influence on the economic development of the region which it dominated'; Hoselitz, 'Generative and parasitic cities', p. 282.

[11] Bairoch, Batou, and Chèvre, *La population des villes*, tab. B1, p. 254.

was continuous.[12] Both sets of estimates support the view that urban growth, defined as a percentage of the total population rather than in absolute numbers, was slight and hesitant between the high middle ages and the beginning of the nineteenth century. It is especially striking that this should be the case given that the last two centuries of the period are so often regarded as the heyday of commercial capitalism, a development that might be thought likely to have led to vigorous urban growth.

That it did not do so is sometimes attributed to the limitations imposed on urban growth by agricultural productivity. If, in the course of the working year, the average family living and working on the land can barely satisfy its own food needs, the scope for urban growth is severely restricted. This is equally true of feudal and of capitalist economies, of course, and the fact that urban growth was so slight even after the decay of feudal economic and social structures in favour of a regime that might have been expected to be more congenial to urban growth seems testimony to the existence of some effective curb.

The same point can be made differently. Every time a man puts his hand into his pocket, or a woman her hand into her purse, he or she is helping to determine both how people make a living and where they live. If the composition of aggregate demand is dominated by food, the great bulk of the labour force will be engaged in agriculture and will live in a rural setting. Consumer preferences follow a strict hierarchy with food always accorded first priority over other claims, and the other necessities, shelter, clothing, and fuel, having the next strongest claims. If real incomes are low, most spending power will be directed to the purchase of food and this will ensure that most of the labour force will remain on the land. It might be argued, therefore, that the fact that the urban percentage changed little between 1300 and 1800 should be associated with the evidence from price and wage data that real wages showed no decisive trend over this long period, though they fluctuated quite widely in long, slow waves.[13] It is persuasive in this regard that in England, the one country in western Europe, other than the Netherlands, in which there is clear evidence of a substantial rise in productivity per head in the agricultural sector in the early modern period, there was also a rapid increase in the urban percentage. In 1600 England was less urbanised than the average for Europe as a whole. In 1800 she was more urbanised than anywhere else except for the Netherlands, where, however, urban decline had set in early in the eighteenth century. In the second half of

---

[12] De Vries, *European urbanization*, tab. 4.14, p. 76.
[13] See, for example, Phelps Brown and Hopkins, *A perspective of wages and prices*, fig. 3, p. 19 and fig. 1, p. 62.

the eighteenth century, indeed, 70 per cent of the total of urban growth in Europe as a whole was taking place in England alone.[14]

The connection between the size of the agricultural surplus above subsistence needs and the growth of towns was apparent to writers in the past. This is vividly clear in a trenchant passage of Adam Smith, even though he directed his analysis to the reasons for the development of manufacture, rather than urban growth *per se*. He depicted a tract of land well away from cheap water communication but blessed with abundant, fertile land where, in consequence, provisions were plentiful and living costs low. Raw materials would similarly be abundant and cheap. Workmen would therefore flock to the area. They would 'give a new value to the surplus part of the rude produce' and by producing manufactured goods which could bear the cost of inland transport and still be competitive in remote markets, they would overcome the disadvantage of poor communications which would have inhibited growth. Thus:

The corn, which could with difficulty have been carried abroad in its own shape, is in this manner virtually exported in that of the complete manufacture, and may easily be sent to the remotest corners of the world. In this manner have grown up naturally, and as it were of their own accord, the manufactures of Leeds, Halifax, Sheffield, Birmingham and Wolverhampton. Such manufactures are the offspring of agriculture.[15]

We may envisage the urban sector, therefore, as roughly reflecting the division of expenditure between food on the one hand and manufactured goods and services on the other. Where three-quarters or more of all income was spent on food, a broadly comparable fraction of the labour force was employed in its production, and the urban sector could not exceed in proportionate size the residue of income left over after meeting food needs. To the degree that non-food needs were met by rural craftsmen rather than by town dwellers, of course, the urban sector would fall short even of that share of the total population that might appear its due from the consideration of consumer expenditure.

The assertion that the productivity of agriculture, both per worker and in a more general sense, was the fundamental regulator of growth in all pre-industrial economies is not a contentious statement. All pre-industrial economies were organic economies, economies in which the great bulk of the raw materials used to manufacture goods of use to man were either vegetable or animal. Industry depended upon wood, wool, wheat, barley, leather, flax, bark, straw, reeds, hair, and bone. Even the production of metal from ore was possible only by turning very large

---

[14] Wrigley, 'Urban growth', tab. 7.7, p. 179.
[15] A. Smith, *Wealth of nations*, I, pp. 430–1.

quantities of wood into charcoal. The land, therefore, not only provided almost all the food consumed but most of the input to manufacturing production. The constraints inherent in an organic economy were multiple and severe. There is good reason to suppose, for example, that difficulty in obtaining firewood was often a more important problem in the provisioning of large cities than any difficulty over food supply.[16]

The stability of the urban proportion over time makes it attractive to hypothesise that low and static agricultural productivity was at the root of the phenomenon, and that the low productivity in turn was a function of a comparatively primitive agricultural technology. It is doubtful, however, whether the problem of raising agricultural productivity was peculiarly associated with technical limitations that kept the output of the average agricultural worker at a low level.[17]

Between the early seventeenth and the early nineteenth centuries when output per head in English agriculture doubled, most of the changes in crops and cultivational practices that occurred represented the adoption of best practice that had long been known in the Low Countries. There were also important changes in farming organisation and in the proportion of energy inputs into agriculture derived from animal rather than human muscle, but the crucial change was probably in the strength of market demand and the consequent improvement in the incentives to enterprising farmers. Much of the growth in demand and of the reduction in its variability from year to year[18] was associated with the rapid growth of London, whose food needs by the time its population had risen to half a million were so large as to affect the market for produce throughout the kingdom. The scale of urban demand for food and also for industrial raw materials constituted an incentive to farmers to increase their output and to invest in improving their productive capacity, provided always that the non-agricultural sectors of the economy were producing goods and services that those on the land were anxious to acquire. This proviso may well have been of greater significance than has normally been allowed. At first blush the issue does not appear doubtful. The process of exchange between town and country seems natural. To quote Adam Smith once more:

---

[16] Van der Woude, Hayami, and de Vries, *Urbanization in history*, pp. 8–14.
[17] Grantham, 'Divisions of labour'.
[18] Since urban dwellers themselves grew little if any food, their need for food delivered via the market changed little from one year to the next, but in a peasant community, where most families were broadly self-sufficient in food in an average year, there might be only a modest demand for food via the market in most years but demand might grow massively in the wake of a bad harvest. The larger the urban sector, therefore, the less volatile market demand for food tended to be.

The great commerce of every civilized society, is that carried on between the inhabitants of the town and those of the country. It consists in the exchange of rude for manufactured produce . . . The country supplies the town with the means of subsistence, and the materials of manufacture. The town repays this supply by sending back a part of the manufactured produce to the inhabitants of the country. The town, in which there neither is nor can be any reproduction of substances, may very properly be said to gain its whole wealth and subsistence from the country.[19]

In this 'great commerce' there was clearly the possibility of what a later generation has learned to call positive feedback: a process that would promote greater specialisation and higher productivity in both town and country; a process, to use a different jargon, that would convert satisficers into optimisers; that would turn peasants into farmers. A benign circle of growth of this sort did not, of course, offer unlimited possibilities for growth. On the land Ricardian problems centring on declining marginal returns to additional inputs of labour and capital might obtrude. In the towns demographic difficulties, associated with the high level of urban mortality and the tendency for death rates to rise in parallel with city size, might result in overall deficits of births in the urban sector so large as to make further urban growth impossible since urban deficits were matching rural surpluses.[20] But the English experience of the seventeenth and eighteenth centuries showed the potential for simultaneous urban growth and agricultural advance, a potential that might seem *prima facie* to have been available much more widely.

Explaining the failure to realise this potential more fully would involve considering almost every aspect of the early modern European society and polity, but even within the sphere of economic behaviour it seems clear that although poor agricultural productivity may have been a major proximate reason for the low level of urbanisation, it would be misleading to concentrate exclusively upon it. A peasant farming sector chiefly concerned with sustaining local self-sufficiency, whose requirements for clothing and housing were largely fixed by local custom and met by local craftsmen, may wish to acquire little from outside its own autarkic entity. Indeed, where such traits were sufficiently strongly developed, the price movements of such goods as are purchased from outside may have a seemingly perverse effect on local effort and enterprise.

To take a rather extreme and partially fictitious case, consider the movements in the price of beaver fur in Paris and London in the seventeenth century. Although the beaver furs were acquired by the *coureurs du bois* in

---

[19] A. Smith, *Wealth of nations*, I, p. 401.
[20] See, for example, de Vries, *The Dutch rural economy*, ch. 3, esp. pp. 113–8.

their peregrinations through the Canadian forests, and traded at factories on the St Lawrence, the trapping itself was largely done by Indians. It is said that for the Indians the incentive to trap was their wish to acquire a gun, a knife, and a blanket. They had not learnt to suppose that they needed more. Therefore, when the price of beaver pelts rose, and they were able to satisfy their needs by trapping fewer animals, the supply of pelts perversely declined, while, symmetrically, if beaver went out of fashion, the fall in price provoked an increase in the supply of furs.[21] To the degree that the peasant sector of an economy might display similar characteristics, though in a muted form, it might not play its full part in that great commerce to which Adam Smith referred.

The interface between city and country: synergy or rural self-sufficiency

The town could not fail to depend upon the country: the lack of a flow of food and raw materials from the countryside was instantly fatal to it. But the reverse was not equally true. The countryside was dependent on the town, if the term dependent is used rather loosely, for some necessary services, religious, legal, and administrative, the last increasing in importance as a central and centralising bureaucracy developed. The upper echelons of church and state were urban in location and served the whole society. But what was true of services was not always true of goods. The countryside was not obliged to be dependent on the town for any of the economic necessities of life.

If one views the annual yield of vegetable and animal products secured by agriculture as the basis for all aspects of material production, and concentrates upon necessities (few people, whether rural or urban, possessed the means to spend any significant sum on comforts or luxuries), it is clear that any rural dependence upon the urban sector was optional. Such processing of food as was necessary to make it edible – milling grain, baking flour, brewing beer, butchering animals, making butter and cheese – could all be done in the farmhouse or at the local mill. If local tastes matched what was locally available, therefore, the town would play little part in provisioning for the country. In the days before the ubiquity

---

[21] This description of the trade in beaver fur is, alas, as much fable as fact. Certainly the price of beaver moved erratically, and supply and demand failed to accommodate to each other smoothly, sometimes resulting in vast gluts of rotting pelts, but price behaviour was more chaotic than perverse, and the native population was very quick to acquire a taste for wide range of European goods, not least strong drink; Innis, *The fur trade in Canada*, pp. 13–9, 68–84; Rich, *Montreal and the fur trade*, esp. ch. 1; and Rich, *Hudson's Bay Company*, I, esp. ch. 5.

of brick and the use of glass, houses were constructed of locally available materials, often to distinctive local architectural styles. Fuel was almost invariably locally produced. Only clothing of the necessities of life was more commonly acquired from a distance, and might have an urban origin. Hence the prominence of textile industries in towns. The constancy of the urban proportion over so many centuries was as much to do, one might speculate, with the constancy of the proportionate expenditure on textile products as with problems over agricultural productivity. Even textiles were not a sure stay of urban prosperity since wool could be spun and cloth woven as by-employments in country households, and even if cloth was produced by a more specialist workforce, it was sometimes located in the countryside, rather than in the towns.

In a closed economy, the secret of urban growth lay in the wakening of rural interest in urban products. Where external trade was important, the position was more complex, but, in general, given the dependence of the town on the products of rural economic activity, the importance of creating a reverse demand to match the urban need for the products of agriculture needs no stressing. If the towns, by deliberate policy or otherwise, sought to drain resources from the countryside by the exercise of political power, rather than by exchange, they were apt to ensure that the urban sector would remain small because the absence of any incentive to invest, innovate, or exert themselves tended to confirm peasants in practices that kept their productivity low. To overcome this meant suffusing the countryside with much the same consumption goals as might be found in an urban setting. Once the appetite for the finer quality of specialist manufactures and a range of services had been whetted, the possibility of a positive feedback between rising agricultural productivity and a growth in the urban proportion existed.

The more distinctive the urban sector, the less successful it was likely to be, if success is measured by proportionate size. A large expansion in the urban sector was dependent upon a steady reduction in any earlier differences in tastes and consumption patterns between town and country. The division of labour, the specialisation of function, which Adam Smith rightly saw as the key to economic growth and enhanced productivity in the economic circumstances with which he was familiar, could make effective progress only if the urban and rural sectors were well integrated, and this in turn was feasible only if economic actors in both contexts were responsive to the same signals. In one superficial sense, of course, this might increase the distinctiveness of town and country, since specialisation of function might well strip the countryside of many non-agricultural activities that could be more efficiently performed in the town, but in a deeper sense specialisation of this sort was prime evidence for a convergence of town and country in their responses to economic signals and opportunities, and such specialisation was a precondition for an extensive urban sector.

Whether or not there was a continuum between the urban sector and the countryside therefore emerges as a matter of great analytic importance to the understanding of the size of the urban sector in the past. A continuum within the urban hierarchy, involving imperceptible gradations of function between the simple market town and the metropolis, does not necessarily imply the absence of a sharp distinction between the small towns at the base of the urban pyramid and the surrounding expanse of tiny agricultural settlements: villages, hamlets, and isolated farmsteads. Within the urban hierarchy, for example, the occupational structure grows steadily more complex with every step in the size hierarchy but each stage largely mimics the one below, though adding some new features. But the move from the country to the small town is different in this respect. The dominant occupation of every rural area is visible only at the lowest rung of the urban ladder, and then usually only as the source of livelihood for a small minority of the population. As the size of settlement increases agricultural employment rapidly becomes vestigial.

Occupational structure and migration opportunities were closely linked. Within the urban hierarchy the comparative similarity of occupational structure underwrote ease of migration, just as frequency of trading contact made for knowledge of opportunity. The unusually gifted, ambitious, or fortunate could move within the urban system to the place where talent found its best reward. A young man from Stratford could find an opening for his genius on the London stage. Nor was Shakespeare's an unusual case; and although more young men and women took the road to London than moved the other way, interchange was common.

In spite of the existence of suggestive evidence in parish registers, in ecclesiastical court depositions, and, in the case of London, in the records of the livery companies, it is a taxing problem to secure good measures of net migration between towns, and still more to identify the scale of gross migration, which would be the more telling statistic. But all such evidence is precious in revealing the degree of integration within the urban hierarchy, and would be even more telling if it were possible to compare movement within the urban sector with movement between the urban sector and the countryside. Evidence of extensive movement in both directions between the two would constitute a persuasive reason to think that there was a convergence of expenditure and consumption patterns throughout the whole society, while evidence that such exchange was far rarer than movement *within* either sector would make it easier to understand how development of the urban sector might stall because of the lack of a sufficiently strong demand from the countryside for the products that the urban sector had to offer.

Since the possession of a skill in demand makes for ease of migration, and the lack of such a skill makes migration difficult, it might seem likely *a priori* that movement between the countryside and the urban system as a whole would be more difficult than movement within and between towns. The types of occupation practised in any one town normally had a large overlap with those practised in any other. But there were no fields to plough or crops to sickle in towns, and on the farm little call for chandlers, dyers, barbers, or plumbers. The latter could move from town to city or the reverse with fair confidence that their skills would find a market, but not from town to country. The empirical question of the scale, nature, and direction of movement between the countryside and the urban sector, and especially between that part of the rural population that practised agriculture and the urban sector, is therefore a matter of great significance. Where such movement was extensive people in both town and country would be likely to have much in common. Where, on the other hand, there was little migration between the two, it is easier to accept the reality of a sharp divide, and the concomitant expectation that urban development might be limited. It would be particularly illuminating to have comparative data from different countries. Migration appears to have been unusually common in England in the early modern period when compared to most continental areas, and perhaps especially so in the countryside, but where so little is known with precision, it would be premature to go further than to point to the possibility that a footloose population and increasing uniformity of consumption goals were closely connected to the extraordinary surge in urban growth that occurred in England but not elsewhere in the seventeenth and eighteenth centuries.[22]

Reconstitution studies have repeatedly shown that only a minority of English villagers died in the same parish in which they were born. Much of the migration was local and did not involve abandoning a rural setting, but there was also a substantial flow from country to town, from the husbandman's household to the mercer's shop, and much of this in turn took place over long distances. Even in the sixteenth century there was a very high level of migration from the northern and western counties to London. The registers of freemen on the rolls of the London livery companies leave no doubt either about the scale of the movement or about its remarkable geographical scope.[23] To take a particular example,

---

[22] P. Clark and Souden, *Migration and society* provides much information about the mobility of English men and women in the early modern period.

[23] Rappaport, *Worlds within worlds*, esp. pp. 76–86.

the intimacy of contact between the parish of Myddle, a few miles north of Shrewsbury, and the city of London, about 160 miles away, in the later seventeenth century, is abundantly clear from the remarkable notes made by Richard Gough about his fellow parishioners.[24] There is also suggestive evidence for much of the continent that rural communities were more nearly 'closed' than was the case in England, and that those who left a village community to find a livelihood elsewhere did so with the intention of returning to their birthplace either seasonally or at the end of their working lives.[25] Entitlement to support was available in one's native village but not elsewhere, whereas in England under the poor law a man or woman might qualify for support anywhere in the country after acquiring settlement.

Conclusion

Alongside discussions of the contrasts between town and country in terms of jurisdiction, legal privilege, and exemption, the concomitants of borough status, class and sectional divisions and tensions, and the interests and activities of urban power-brokers, there is a place for a different perspective on urban and rural contrasts and similarities. Though less easy to document, study of the nature, frequency, and intimacy of contacts between towns at different levels in the urban hierarchy and between the urban hierarchy as a whole and the rural, agricultural base of society, may suggest some reassessment of that image of city and country in the past which tends to be forced upon us by the nature of the descriptive language we use and the earlier historiography of the subject.

Study of these matters is not only valuable in that it would make good deficiencies in our present knowledge. It has the further attraction that

---

[24] Hey remarks in his introduction to an edition of Gough that, 'He frequently mentions London in passing as if it were commonplace that his neighbours should have been there. Men and women from all sections of his community went to the capital in search of fortune or excitement or to escape from trouble at home. Most of them kept in contact with their families, and further information about events in London and other parts of the country filtered back to Myddle through "the Gazet" and "our News letters"'; Gough, *The history of Myddle*, p. 18. As Hey implies in this passage, the extent of the contact between Myddle and other parts of the country was also striking.

[25] An interesting example of a community which conforms to this pattern even though 'objectively' its circumstances might seem to favour heavy and continuous out-migration is the village of Törbel in the Swiss Alps; Netting, *Balancing on an Alp*. Netting gives some details of the extent of the contrast between a 'closed corporate community' and the more open type of English village in ch. 5. There is scope for a much fuller and more systematic comparison of results of family reconstitution studies from all over western Europe than has so far been undertaken. Reconstitution studies permit the estimation of the extent of migration over several stages of the life-cycle in the manner pioneered by Souden, 'Pre-industrial English local migration fields'.

if we understood better the extent and nature of the integration of the urban sector and the countryside, we should probably also gain an insight into the factors determining the relative size of the urban sector. Only in a fully developed market economy with country dwellers strongly conscious of a desire to acquire urban goods and services were there the kinds of incentives to improve agricultural practice that could underwrite urban growth by providing the necessary flow of food for people and organic raw materials for industry. Whether or not there was a continuum between city and country, in short, helped to determine the relative size of the two sectors. The less marked any social or cultural gap, the more likely that urban populations would grow.

The city has always had a mixed press. To counterbalance the view that it was the focus of all that was enterprising and enlightened has been the tradition of the city as the prime source of iniquity, corruption, and moral decay. 'God the first garden made,' wrote Abraham Cowley, 'and the first city, Cain.'[26] However these balance sheets are cast up, certain features of the relationship between town and country in the past are growing increasingly clear. In spite of Abrams's doubts, there is a place for the study of the town, if by that is meant not an individual settlement but an urban system. It repays study both because urban systems possessed remarkable regularities whose functioning throws much light upon pre-industrial society generally, and because it is in relation to the urban system as a whole that the question of the sharpness or otherwise of any division between city and country can best be studied. In so doing, moreover, the intractable but deeply interesting issue of the relative size of urban and rural populations in the past is brought into focus. If it is fair to say that the most intriguing phase in the study of any subject occurs in the period when all seems fresh and fascinating, then, in spite of the considerable elapse of time since urban history first became a separate area of investigation, urban history at the start of the 1990s may be said to be in the very bloom of youth.

---

[26] Cowley, *The complete works of Abraham Cowley*, II, p. 327 in a poem called 'The garden'.

10 'The great commerce of every civilized society': urban growth in early modern Europe

Book III of the *Wealth of nations* is entitled 'Of the different progress of opulence in different nations'. It is very brief, occupying less than 5 per cent of the text of the book. It opens with a ringing declaration about the significance of urban growth to the achievement of higher levels of productivity and increasing wealth which deserves to be read in parallel with the still more celebrated argument of the opening chapters of the first book in which the relationship between the division of labour and the size of the market is examined, and with the early chapters of the second book where the intimate and necessary connection between the division of labour and the growth of the stock of capital is described.

The opening sentences of book III run as follows:

The great commerce of every civilized society, is that carried on between the inhabitants of the town and those of the country. It consists in the exchange of rude for manufactured produce, either immediately, or by the intervention of money, or of some sort of paper which represents money. The country supplies the town with the means of subsistence, and the materials of manufacture. The town repays this supply by sending back a part of the manufactured produce to the inhabitants of the country. The town, in which there neither is nor can be any reproduction of substances, may very properly be said to gain its whole wealth and subsistence from the country. We must not, however, upon this account, imagine that the gain of the town is the loss of the country. The gains of both are mutual and reciprocal, and the division of labour is in this, as in all other cases, advantageous to all the different persons employed in the various occupations into which it is subdivided. The inhabitants of the country purchase of the town a greater quantity of manufactured goods, with the produce of a smaller quantity of their own labour, than they must have employed had they attempted to prepare them themselves. The town affords a market for the surplus produce of the country, or what is over and above the maintenance of the cultivators, and it is there that the inhabitants of the country exchange it for something else which is in demand among them. The greater the number and revenue of the inhabitants of the town,

This chapter was originally given as the first Checkland Memorial Lecture, delivered at a conference held by the Economic and Social History Society of Scotland at the University of Glasgow on 27 April 1991.

the more extensive is the market which it affords to those of the country; and the more extensive that market, it is always the more advantageous to a great number.[1]

What was described in general terms in the early parts of book I and II is given a more concrete historical form in book III. Urban growth represented, in Adam Smith's mind, the mechanism by which the potential developments described earlier in his work were realised. Earlier particular illustrations, such as the famous parable about pinmaking, could now be subsumed into an intelligible, general pattern that provided a plausible dynamic of growth over time. Book III, therefore, should hold a special interest for historians. Smith frequently embarked on substantial historical asides in developing his main arguments, but in book III he offered a more ambitious exercise, reviewing briefly the whole sweep of European history from the fall of the Roman Empire until his own day. His central theme was the nature and scale of urban growth which was to him not only the core of the economic history of more than a millennium but also a phenomenon that exercised a decisive influence on the history of political and legal institutions.[2]

Adam Smith's analysis of the significance of urban growth forms an interesting background to recent work on European urbanisation in the later medieval and early modern periods. There are some instructive parallels between his vision and the picture implied by the fuller empirical data now available, but also some notable apparent disjunctions between the two. In particular, his model seems much more in accord with developments in Britain than with events in continental Europe. Exploring both aspects of the comparison provides a way of identifying some issues that appear both intriguing and important, but first the nature of Smith's model must be more fully set out.

Smith's model of urban development

We may begin by noting that Smith expounded with great clarity the marked spatial patterning associated with the stimulus that could be provided by urban growth. In the very long opening paragraph of book III, of which the passage already quoted forms the first part, he continued:

---

[1] A. Smith, *Wealth of nations*, I, p. 401. It is pleasing to be able to record that Sydney Checkland contributed to the early work on the Glasgow edition of the *Wealth of nations*, later published under the general editorship of R. H. Campbell and A. S. Skinner in two volumes in 1976, and that Professor Skinner recalls that Checkland was especially interested in bk III.

[2] These topics were covered principally in chapters 2 and 3 of bk III.

The corn which grows within a mile of the town, sells for the same price with that which comes from twenty miles distance. But the price of the latter must generally, not only pay the expence of raising and bringing it to market, but afford too the ordinary profits of agriculture to the farmer. The proprietors and cultivators of the country, therefore, which lies in the neighbourhood of the town, over and above the ordinary profits of agriculture, gain, in the price of what they sell, the whole value of the carriage of the like produce that is brought from more distant parts, and they save, besides, the whole value of this carriage in the price of what they buy. Compare the cultivation of the lands in the neighbourhood of any considerable town, with that of those which lie at some distance from it, and you will easily satisfy yourself how much the country is benefited by the commerce of the town.[3]

Here in four sentences is the kernel of an idea which, as developed half a century later by von Thünen (who acknowledged the extent of his debt to Adam Smith),[4] became the foundation of the understanding of the location and intensity of different types of agricultural activity.[5] The principle of the spatial patterning of market influences has proved capable of application at all spatial levels, from the individual farm to the world agricultural system as a whole.[6] Indeed von Thünen's work had much to do with the later creation of locational economics as a distinct sub-discipline. And, in the context of a pre-industrial economy, this effect of urban growth could represent a most important mechanism tending to expand food production in step with urban demand.

Smith's model of economic growth was one in which the gains of the town and country were 'mutual and reciprocal', or, in today's jargon, there was positive feedback between the two. An increasingly productive agriculture was a *sine qua non* of urban growth, but the benefits conferred by urban growth might serve to ensure that agriculture grew to match urban need. His emphasis changed, however, as he developed his argument. He insisted that because subsistence must precede convenience and luxury, improved cultivation was the basis of all growth. Moreover, this paralleled a natural preference for the country life, both because of its aesthetic pleasures and because capital was less at risk when employed

---

[3] A. Smith, *Wealth of nations*, I, pp. 401–2.

[4] He wrote that 'Adam Smith taught me political economy.' His chapter on the concept of rent is built round Smith's discussion of the topic, although von Thünen did not accept Smith's view of the subject. In the course of the chapter he referred to Smith as 'an inexhaustible source of knowledge and enlightenment'; von Thünen, *The isolated state*, pp. 21–2, 225.

[5] Smith was careful to emphasise that the town did not necessarily derive all its food and raw materials from local sources, so that even distant countries might play a part in its provisioning, which helped to explain 'the considerable variations in the progress of opulence in different ages and nations'. A. Smith, *Wealth of nations*, I, p. 402.

[6] There is a succinct review of these issues in Chisholm, *Rural settlement*.

in agriculture than when engaged in manufacture or trade. This line of argument suggested that urban growth would only come late to the scene after the prime opportunities for agricultural development in rural areas had been exhausted, and that therefore the positive economic feedback between town and country might be relatively feeble and limited for long periods. He asserted, for example, that 'According to the natural course of things, therefore, the greater part of the capital of every growing society is, first, directed to agriculture, afterwards to manufactures, and last of all to foreign commerce.'[7] This 'natural order of things' had, however, he conceded, often not been followed by the modern states of Europe.[8] In its simplest form, therefore, Smith's model led to the expectation of urban growth in step with economic advance generally, but he added elaborations which suggested that urban growth might be absent or muted over long periods even though growth was taking place.

Smith's description of urban growth in Europe

When Smith turned from general considerations to discuss the course of European history over the two previous millennia, however, any inconsistency in his treatment of the relationship between town and country faded into the background. He strove to show not only that economic development and city growth were intimately linked but also that there was a strong connection between the growth of towns, the decay of feudalism, the development of liberty, and the evolution of the modern state. He argued, for example, that the sovereign's desire for revenue led him to farm out responsibility for the levying of taxes to the burghers jointly rather than to the county sheriff, at first for a term of years but later in perpetuity. In return the burghers were able to secure freedoms in perpetuity, both personal and collective, which delivered them from feudal servility and endowed towns with extensive powers of self-government, wide-ranging privileges, and independent legal institutions. It suited the sovereign to act in this fashion because the increasing wealth of the towns provided him with a counterweight to the great feudal lords who were for long his rivals.

In the course of time, as cities grew prosperous and powerful, their interests and attitudes became increasingly pervasive, so that the countryside as well as the town came to reflect new attitudes and to learn to adhere to new values. At the beginning of the fourth chapter of book III,

[7] A. Smith, *Wealth of nations*, I, p. 405.
[8] Though his knowledge of the high prosperity but restricted urban development in the recent colonies of settlement in North America may well have helped to confirm Smith in his view of the 'natural order of things'.

Smith summarised the ways in which the growth of towns had come to benefit the societies in which they were situated. His first two points, which related to the stimulus to agriculture provided by urban markets and the greater effectiveness of merchants as improvers of the land compared with 'mere country gentlemen', were elaborations of the thesis he had already advanced.

His final point is worth quoting in full:

> Thirdly, and lastly, commerce and manufactures gradually introduced order and good government, and with them, the liberty and security of individuals, among the inhabitants of the country, who had before lived almost in a continual state of war with their neighbours, and of servile dependency upon their superiors. This, though it has been the least observed, is by far the most important of all their effects.[9]

Urban growth, in other words, was the cause of changes which made possible the development of a capitalist economic system with the establishment of such features as individual freedom, security of the person and of property, and the replacement of custom by contract in the conduct of affairs.

The balance of the fourth chapter is full of intriguing and persuasive illustration and analysis of the ways in which the increase of commerce and manufactures associated with the growth of towns brought benefits to many areas of social, political, legal, and economic activity and either transformed old institutions or led to the creation of new ones. But my purpose in referring to the *Wealth of nations* has not been to expound Adam Smith's thinking at length or to attempt an assessment of his reading of history, except in one respect. In attributing so decisive and extensive a role to the growth of towns, Smith appears to have assumed that urban growth was both considerable and progressive over much of the period from the early middle ages to his own day towards the end of the eighteenth century. Both the economic and political transformations engendered by commerce and manufacturing, changes so profound that Smith himself referred to them as 'that great revolution', were possible only because of that urban growth which was their most prominent result.

Smith himself has little to say directly about the scale of urban growth. The later stages of chapter 4, the last in book III, read oddly to the modern eye. In them he reverted to the question of the natural priority that agriculture should assume over other forms of economic activity. Commerce and manufacture, he had argued, should be the offspring of an

---

[9] Ibid., I, p. 433.

increasingly productive agriculture rather than the reverse, but he concluded that the recent history of Europe showed that priority lay with the former rather than the latter. The vanity of the great proprietors, confronted with a new range of baubles with which to gratify their thirst for display, caused them to dismiss the bulk of their retainers in order to secure with cash what had once been taken in kind. And their tenants, reduced in numbers by the same pressures, were able to obtain in exchange long leases, the basis for later improvement. He concluded this phase in his discussion with a much-quoted passage:

A revolution of the greatest importance to the public happiness, was in this manner brought about by two different orders of people, who had not the least intention to serve the public. To gratify the most childish vanity was the sole motive of the great proprietors. The merchants and artificers, much less ridiculous, acted merely from a view to turning a penny wherever a penny was to be got.[10]

The chapter ends with a rather curious contrast between the extremely rapid progress in wealth and population occurring in the North American colonies, which Smith attributed to their concentration upon agriculture, and the far slower, advance in England, and *a fortiori* elsewhere in Europe, which he believed to be due to obstacles hindering agricultural investment and improvement arising from the law of primogeniture and other institutional and legal provisions, and not to the absence of opportunity for a rapid increase in output from the land. 'It is thus that through the greater part of Europe the commerce and manufactures of cities, instead of being the effect, have been the cause and occasion of the improvement and cultivation of the country. This order, however, being contrary to the natural course of things, is necessarily both slow and uncertain.'[11] In Europe, in other words, because urban growth was not normally soundly based, its scale and duration were unpredictable.

Since commerce and manufactures were, incongruously in Adam Smith's view, the cause of such agricultural progress as was occurring, rather than vice-versa, and since they were more flourishing in England than in France, agricultural advance was less visible south of the Channel than north of it. Spain and Portugal languished still further behind, and, therefore, 'the greater part of both still remains uncultivated'.

It is uncertain, therefore, what Smith believed about the extent of urban growth in different countries in the early modern period as a matter of empirical fact. His argument is not inconsistent with the view that it was everywhere slight apart from Britain. Indeed, one might argue that there is an inconsistency between his emphasis on the one hand on the

[10] Ibid., I, p. 440.
[11] Ibid., I, pp. 440–1.

way in which urban growth was instrumental in transforming the political structure, legal institutions, personal freedoms, and living standards of society, and on the other hand on the 'unnatural' precedence taken by commerce and manufacture over agriculture in Europe. The fact that he considered the former change to be widely evident might be thought to imply that he believed urban growth to have been widespread. But his emphasis on the strength of the perverse failure of urban growth to have taken place downstream from agricultural progress suggests the opposite. The low level of agricultural advance in many continental countries suggests, on the latter view, that urban growth was likely to have been minimal.

The limited nature of urban growth in early modern Europe

The conventional thrust of historical writing has tended to favour an optimistic view of the scale of urban growth in early modern Europe. General considerations seem to point so strongly in this direction. This was an age in which the triumphs of European navigation and discovery opened up the whole world to commerce and when colonies of conquest and settlement were established; an age, too, when capitalist forms of enterprise became established more and more widely and modern forms of state organisation evolved, both developments held to favour urban growth. There was invention and innovation in industry and transport, initially modest in nature but becoming increasingly impressive in scale and scope during the course of the eighteenth century. Urban growth is so closely associated with general advance, and general advance is held to be so prominent a feature of early modern Europe, that it might seem perverse to find anything other than urban growth. Western Europe in the sixteenth century was still intermittently fearful of Turkish power to the east. In wealth, population, even perhaps in technical knowledge, Europe was still not a credible rival to China. Nor was China politically fragmented as Europe was. Yet by 1800 European military power was unassailable and nobody doubted that the economy of western Europe was more advanced than that of the great civilisations of the east. Surely, European urbanisation must have advanced.

It is one of the most striking and salutary features of recent historical scholarship that it is now clear that continental Europe was little if any more urbanised in 1800 than in 1600, and indeed that it is possible that there was no significant change between 1400 and 1800. A phenomenon that runs counter to such a widely held and plausible belief merits close attention, and it is natural to begin with a brief review of the new evidence.

There is an initial problem of definition. In order to make any assertion about trends in urbanisation, it is clearly necessary to decide what measure is most appropriate. I shall assume that the key variable is the percentage of the population living in towns rather than the absolute numbers involved. Thus, if the population of a country doubles while its urban population also doubles, the absolute number of people living in towns will have risen substantially, but it will not be more urbanised on this definition. This is scarcely controversial. But the question of what size of settlement should be taken to define a town can arouse strong passions.

To use a population of 5,000 as the dividing line, as I shall do, will mean that many smaller centres which were largely or entirely dependent on trade and manufacture for a living are excluded, though it minimises the risk that places that were largely agricultural in their employment structure will be included. For different purposes, and also in different countries, a larger or smaller settlement size might be more appropriate. Fortunately, however, it is unnecessary to argue the pros and cons of any particular figure at length because de Vries's work has shown that the rank-size rule applies quite accurately to the relative number of towns in each successive size range.[12] This implies that although using a higher limit, say 10,000, or a lower limit, say 2,000, would produce a different estimate of the proportion of the total population that was urban at a given date, it would make little or no difference to the *relative* change in urban proportions over time, the point of most relevance in this context.

Strictly speaking, neither of the two scholars whose work suggests that older stereotypes of urbanisation must be abandoned, produced new evidence. Rather, Bairoch and de Vries have made systematic use of existing censuses, quasi-censuses, partial censuses, tax materials, *et sim.*, together with estimates which involved an element of judgement on the part of the compiler or historian. This enabled them to offer informed guesses about population totals for all substantial towns at intervals of 50 or 100 years. The two studies were carried out independently of each other. They differ in some respects, reflecting different assumptions and critical judgement. They cover different time periods, and their definitions of Europe differed. Nevertheless the extent of their agreement is reassuring.

Using 5,000 as the threshold definition of a town, and ignoring the complications arising from the fact that their definitions of Europe differ

---

[12] De Vries, *European urbanization*, ch. 4.

somewhat (and indeed that their estimates of national population totals may vary), Bairoch and de Vries are agreed that about 13.5 per cent of the population of Europe in 1800 was urban (Bairoch 13.8 per cent: de Vries 13.0 per cent). For 1600 their estimates vary more widely, at 12.9 per cent (Bairoch) and 10.8 per cent (de Vries). In Bairoch's case the increase between the two dates is 0.9 per cent: in de Vries's case 2.2 per cent. In both cases, however, the change is modest.[13] Moreover, it substantially overstates the extent of change for continental Europe alone since in these two centuries there was a notable increase in urbanisation in England (and more generally in Britain), not paralleled on the continent.

If, for example, England is subtracted from the totals in both 1600 and 1800, the level of urbanisation rises marginally at the earlier date since England was less urbanised than the continental average at that time, but falls substantially in 1800 because towns were growing so rapidly in England in the seventeenth and eighteenth centuries. The overall increase in the level of urbanisation for continental Europe is only 1.0 per cent (from 10.9 to 11.9 per cent), using de Vries's estimates, compared with 2.2 per cent when England is included in the larger whole. If Bairoch's estimates are preferred the comparable adjustments imply a slight *fall* in urbanisation over the two centuries in continental Europe (from 13.1 to 13.0 per cent).[14] Given the greater uncertainty about population estimates for 1600, it seems prudent to conclude that there is no firm evidence that there was any increase in urbanisation on the continent between 1600 and 1800 (indeed Bairoch's estimates suggest no increase between 1400 and 1800).[15]

Equally, there can be no doubt that towns grew rapidly in England during the early modern period. In the seventeenth century the bulk of the growth was confined to London, and it was in this century that London became the largest city in Europe, having risen from about tenth place in 1500.[16] In the eighteenth century, however, urban growth became much more widespread: London grew no quicker than the country as a whole, but some of the new manufacturing and commercial centres advanced with such remarkable speed that in the second half of the century about 70 per cent of all the urban growth in Europe as a whole was taking place

[13] Ibid., tab. 3.6, pp. 36–7 and tab. 4.13, p. 72; Bairoch, Batou, and Chèvre, *La population des villes*, tab. B2, p. 255.

[14] Estimates of English urban population at the two dates were taken from Wrigley, 'Urban growth', tab. 7.4, p. 170.

[15] His percentages for Europe as a whole are 13.6 in 1400 and 13.8 in 1800; Bairoch, Batou, and Chèvre, *La population des villes*, tab. B2, p. 255.

[16] De Vries, *European urbanization*, app. 1.

in England alone.[17] What then may best serve to explain the striking absence of growth in continental Europe and the notable surge of growth across the Channel?

Discussion of the factors which set limits to the growth of towns in the pre-industrial past has highlighted a number of constraints which must always have been present, though often only as a potential rather than an immediate threat. If each is none the less capable of acting as an effective barrier to further growth, and if in different settings any one of them may prove to be the tightest constraint, they may be regarded as a series of ceilings, the lowest of which is the operative one in that time and place.

The constraints on urban growth

The most obvious constraint relates to food supply. Since towns provide little of the food they need, their continued growth depends upon the agricultural surplus growing *pari passu*. If, say, one peasant in the countryside can on average provide only for the needs of his own family and a quarter of the needs of another family, then 80 per cent of the population must labour on the land if 20 per cent are to be free to devote their energies to the provision of secondary and tertiary goods and services, and in no circumstances can the urban proportion rise beyond this level. If towns were to continue to expand, town dwellers would first go hungry and would later starve (or, by exacting more from rural areas, cause starvation elsewhere). In practice, since agriculture also needs rural craftsmen, the urban proportion will be substantially lower than the possible maximum.

The possibility of extensive and continued urban growth in Adam Smith's model depended on the positive feedback between town and country. The greater attractiveness and utility of urban products served to stimulate farmers to greater effort and to encourage them to invest more heavily, and this in turn, by expanding the scale of agricultural output, increased the market for urban goods and services, allowed towns to become larger, and increased still further the economies of scale of manufacture and the refinement of its products. However, Adam Smith implicitly, and Malthus and Ricardo explicitly, recognised the existence of the problem of diminishing returns in agriculture, which in turn implies the existence of a barrier to urban growth at some point, however successfully the problem of food supply may be met in an intervening period.

---

[17] A calculation of this type involves making certain assumptions about the definition of urban growth. For details of these assumptions and the calculation itself, see Wrigley, 'Urban growth', tab. 7.7, p. 179 and associated text.

Certainly the problem of urban food supply has been a chief concern of governments from the inception of settled agriculture in the Neolithic period to the present day. Roman emperors spent much time on the problem and it continued to figure prominently in Yeltsin's Russia.

A second constraint upon urban growth was the supply of fuel. If wheat, barley, oats, and rye were the fuels that kept men and women in health and capable of labour, fuel wood or its equivalent was essential to all forms of industry that needed a source of heat, and was equally necessary for the preparation of food and, in northern climates, for domestic heating. Wood was needed in far larger quantities than grain and was therefore likely to be the key element in any transport-related constraint upon urban growth. In round terms about five times as many carts laden with wood came through a city's gates as carts laden with grain. The average inhabitant of the town needed about 1.5 lb. of wheat or other grain each day for his bread, but 10 lb. or more of firewood to bake it, to brew his beer, roast his meat, boil his water, heat his living room, and to cover his industrial needs, heating a dye vat or working metal, for example.[18] Covering such large transport needs provoked many problems. Providing the fodder needed for the horses drawing the carts of firewood, for example, meant a reduction in the area of land that could be used to grow grain for human consumption.

The severity of the strain that this implied is revealed by the disposition of land use round the imaginary town in the centre of a featureless plain which was used by von Thünen as a model with which to analyse the prime locational features of agricultural activity. It is another aspect of the effect on land use of the presence of a town to be set alongside the beneficial effects identified by Adam Smith. In von Thünen's model of the pre-industrial economy, the innermost zone, immediately surrounding the town, was taken up with market gardening and dairying, a reflection of the perishable nature of the products of such activity. But the next zone was given over to woodland because the cost of moving large quantities of wood was prohibitive unless the distance involved was short.[19] The problem of wood supply was overcome more easily, of course, if a town was on navigable water since the cheapness of water transport greatly magnified the area that was economically accessible. The fuel supply constraint, nevertheless, may have been a serious curb at times in the past. The pause in the expansion of towns in Japan in the eighteenth century, for example, which was once attributed to the difficulty of raising the

---

[18] It has been suggested that a typical figure for wood consumption for city-dwellers in pre-industrial Europe was 1.0 to 1.6 tons of fire wood per annum and 1 kg. of grain per day: van der Woude, Hayami, and Vries, *Urbanization in history*, pp. 8–12.

[19] Von Thünen, *The isolated state*, ch. 19.

output of rice, is now often related to the severity of the fuel shortage at the time, a shortage that produced acute political tension.[20]

A third major potential constraint was demographic. Many cities before the industrial revolution experienced high mortality. Deaths often exceeded births. They were as dependent upon a flow of young men and women from the healthier countryside as they were upon a flow of food and fuel wood. Even to maintain a given population required substantial net inward migration. Growth made the problem still more severe. In the main, moreover, the level of mortality was higher the larger the city, so that success in fostering a rise in a city's population increased the relative difficulty of ensuring that numbers were maintained. If the normal surplus of births over deaths in the countryside and the corresponding deficit in towns are known, it is a simple matter to calculate the percentage of the total population that can live in towns without provoking a decline in the overall population total. De Vries has suggested, for example, that, given the demographic characteristics prevailing in the northern Netherlands at the end of the eighteenth century, the maximum proportion of the population that could live in cities of 10,000 or more inhabitants while the population of the region as a whole held its own was probably under 40 per cent.[21] A similar calculation suggests that in the later seventeenth century, when about a tenth of the population of England was living in London, migration to London from the rest of the country absorbed about one half of the total birth surplus outside the capital.[22]

That all these three constraints were capable of exerting pressures which restricted urban growth in the past is clear, not least from the unusual briskness of growth when for some special reason one or other of them was inoperative. For example, though coal was initially regarded as an inferior substitute for wood, the Newcastle coal trade was of great importance to the growth of London. From modest beginnings in the sixteenth century, it became a massive flow in the course of the next two hundred years. By the end of the seventeenth century the annual movement of coal down the east coast had reached a level of about half a million tons.[23] Nef estimated that servicing the coal trade accounted for about half of the total tonnage of the English merchant marine by the

---

[20] Van der Woude, de Vries, and Hayami, *Urbanization in history*, pp. 9–10.
[21] De Vries's argument is complicated since he divided the population into three categories and assumed an inflow of population from outside the region. Moreover, he was unable to estimate with precision the scale of rural natural increase, but this seems a fair inference from the data he presented; de Vries, *The Dutch rural economy*, p. 116.
[22] Wrigley, 'A simple model', pp. 45–7.
[23] The average annual shipment of coal from Newcastle to London in the years 1695–1704 was over 190,000 chaldrons (a chaldron was reckoned to be about 53 cwt). Mitchell,

time of the Restoration.[24] Since a ton of coal supplies the same output of heat as about two tons of dry wood, it needs no emphasis that access to cheap coal was of great value in facilitating the rapid growth of London in the seventeenth and eighteenth centuries.[25]

Though these constraints were real, it is doubtful whether, singly or in combination, they provide a persuasive reason for the absence of urban growth in continental Europe in the early modern period. It is true that securing an expansion of agricultural production always presented problems when farms were ecologically self-dependent, unable, for example, to overcome nutrient deficiencies in the soil by the application of fertilisers produced in the factory. And at some point the remorseless logic of declining marginal returns to both labour and capital must no doubt have taken hold. But the room for manoeuvre was considerable. For example, even given the limitations imposed by contemporary transport facilities and the prevailing agricultural technology, it is probable that the growth of Paris, a giant city of roughly half a million inhabitants by the eighteenth century, was not constrained by food supply problems.[26] It is also worthy of note that across a broad swathe of Europe agricultural output rose rapidly in the early decades of the nineteenth century to meet the needs of growing urban markets and the rapid rise in employment outside agriculture, and did so even in areas where neither the size of the farming units nor the methods of cultivation changed greatly (though institutional and legal structures may have done so).[27]

In the right circumstances European agriculture was probably well able to meet the food needs of the towns up to levels of urbanisation substantially higher than those found in the seventeenth and eighteenth centuries. The percentage of the population of England living in towns with 5,000 or more inhabitants, for example, rose from 8.3 to 27.5 between 1600 and 1800 yet the country remained broadly self-sufficient

---

British historical statistics, pp. 240–1. This understates the total volume of the east coast coal trade since it covers coal movement from the Tyne but not from Wearside.

[24] Nef, Rise of the British coal industry, I, p. 239.

[25] It may be of interest to note that by the late seventeenth century Londoners were consuming at least a ton of coal each in the course of a year, the equivalent of about 12lb. of dry wood each day.

[26] Grantham, 'Divisions of labour'.

[27] For example, Hoffman estimated that between 1815 and 1865 German agricultural production rose by 135 per cent compared with a population rise of 59 per cent, and suggested that, over almost exactly the same period, employment in agriculture rose by only 22 per cent, which implies a rise in output per head of 93 per cent (Hoffman himself gave a slightly different figure of 78 per cent). Hoffman, 'The take-off in Germany', p. 103.

in food, an achievement made the more remarkable by the fact that the overall population of England rose from 4.1 to 8.6 millions.[28]

Similar arguments could be advanced tending to throw doubt on the seriousness of the fuel and demographic constraints on urban growth at the levels of urbanisation obtaining in early modern Europe. Such factors must have inhibited urbanisation eventually but hardly when the overall urban proportion was well short of 15 per cent. Moreover, it is difficult to believe that the relevant constraint, the lowest ceiling, was at a constant level between the late sixteenth and the early nineteenth century, the period during which urbanisation scarcely advanced. It is more probable that it rose. A different explanation is needed.

The rural demand for urban products

In looking for an explanation, it is well to remember that all three constraints might be described as supply side factors. Resorting to them reflects a conviction that if such obstacles had not existed urban growth would have been brisker. But, in principle, the failure of cities to grow might as easily have been due to demand side constraints. Adam Smith explained very clearly how the 'great commerce' depended upon the mutual advantage that each side drew from the exchange. For it to occur, there must be as keen a wish on the part of the countryside to obtain manufactures and services from the town as to secure food and raw materials from the countryside on the part of town dwellers. For the advantage to be mutual, the appreciation of the benefit of exchange must equally be mutual.

That the town must have need of the products of the land is certain. Only from the countryside could food and the raw materials of manufacture be drawn. With increasing size, any town would need a proportionate increase in food, fuel, wood and stone for building, and materials such as wool, hides, metals, and wood in order to sustain craft industries. But the relationship was not symmetrical. The countryside was obliged to turn to the town only for a limited range of goods and services. Throughout western Europe there was a significant rural demand for religious, legal, medical, educational, and administrative services of a type that it was beyond the power of the locality to provide. The bishop's seat was always urban. Legal disputes, though begun locally, might ultimately require the attention of regional or national courts. Universities were urban

---

[28] Wrigley, 'Urban growth', tab. 7.2, p. 162; Wrigley and Schofield, *Population history of England*, tab. A3.3, pp. 531–5.

institutions and leading physicians lived in cities, though some students and patients came from the country. It may be that to describe rural resort to such services as reflecting rural 'demand' involves taking some liberty with the normal meaning of the term, since their take-up might at times represent less the free choice of the periphery than the imposition of a central will. Yet payment for the provision of services of this type supplied to the countryside by the town, whether in money or in kind, made resources available to help town dwellers to obtain what they needed from the country. In some countries and periods a large part of this flow of income into towns was a forced levy upon the countryside exacted either by landlords or by central authority, and reflecting a preference for urban life over rural residence on the part of those whose status and power enabled them to command a part of the rural economic surplus. But the flow of resources was real enough.

For rural demand to extend beyond the provision of such services, however, two conditions had to be met: that rural consumers were attracted by the goods and services on offer by the town, and that rural incomes could support the necessary payments. Neither condition could be taken for granted in a pre-industrial society. In such societies, the relationship between the urban demand for rural products and the rural demand for urban products was apt to be asymmetric, as will be clear from the following considerations.

The classical economists were accustomed to distinguish between necessities, conveniences, and luxuries. The labouring poor, always forming the bulk of the population, and in aggregate providing the lion's share of total demand, could expect to spend little outside the first category which consisted of food, shelter, fuel, and clothing. Consider the implication of this for the rural demand for urban products. Food, which might of itself represent between two-thirds and three-quarters of the total expenditure of most rural inhabitants, was almost exclusively supplied from local rural sources. Houses were built from local raw materials, wood, stone, and clay; and by local craftsmen. Fuel came from neighbouring woodland, heath, or peat bogs. These three basic categories of expenditure represented the overwhelming bulk of total demand from the mass of the population. For those who lived in the country such expenditure remained rural. Little if any of this demand benefited urban suppliers. The same items figured just as prominently in the budgets of the urban poor but, since necessities all came from rural areas, this involved purchase from the country. Moreover, although urban craftsmen might add greatly to the value of the raw materials they used, the raw materials themselves had to be bought from the rural sector. Bakers, masons, carpenters, and shoemakers might live in the town but their ability to carry on their trades depended upon purchases of flour, stone, wood, and leather from the countryside.

The fourth type of necessity was different. Whereas the rural demand for food, shelter, and fuel could not readily be met except from a rural supplier (the consumer and producer being in many cases one and the same person or family), the rural demand for clothing *might* be met by purchase from the town. It is no coincidence that textile and clothing employment was so often the largest single employment category in towns before the industrial revolution. As with other products, the raw materials of the textile industry came from the country, but urban clothmakers and tailors could produce a better product, and might even produce a cheaper product, than was commonly available from village weavers and tailors. Textiles and clothing offered the best opportunity for the urban sector to solve its balance of payments problem with the countryside. The proportion of total income spent on clothing and the proportion of total population living in the town, therefore, often bore a fairly close relation to one another.[29] Equally, however, if local custom dictated that people should be clothed only in traditional dress made locally in a traditional manner, it might be difficult for urban producers to satisfy rural clothing needs and thereby derive an income flow, even if they were efficient manufacturers.

In general, therefore, only if rural areas were both tolerably prosperous, with the resources to acquire the conveniences and even occasionally to indulge in the luxuries of life, and were also happy to seek to satisfy such aspirations from sources outside the local community, was there any prospect of the 'great commerce' flourishing. Income levels had a wide relevance. A persistent low average level of real income would result in a structure of demand unfavourable to urban growth since the great bulk of demand would be concentrated on goods and services that could only be obtained from the country. A scattering of wealthy families living in the countryside might be able to indulge themselves in the purchase of a very wide range of goods and services, and in doing so often would often make use of urban markets at a great distance from their dwelling places.[30] But if the incomes of the bulk of the population were both low and showed no secular tendency to rise, it must be expected that

---

[29] On the scale of expenditure on clothing and its implications for clothing's share of total aggregate demand, see Harte, 'The economics of clothing'; also Spufford, 'The cost of apparel'. Both authors provide evidence of the validity of Gregory King's estimates of the importance of expenditure on clothing (including footwear) within the national consumer budget of the late seventeenth century.

[30] See, for example, Dyer, 'The consumer and the market'.

the same would prove true of the percentage of the population living in towns.

Demand side considerations may help to explain why urban growth should have stalled for so long in medieval and early modern Europe. Can they also throw light on the striking difference between the English experience and that of continental Europe in the seventeenth and eighteenth centuries?

The contrast between England and the continent

It should be noted, first, that although the overall level of urbanisation in continental Europe lay within the range 10–15 per cent for half a millennium, there were several areas, notably in northern Italy and in the Low Countries where the percentage was far higher. In general, however, where the level of urbanisation was high, it had been high from medieval times onwards. Only in the Netherlands was there a large rise in the percentage of the population living in towns in the early modern period, and there the surge in urbanisation ended in the late seventeenth century, to be succeeded by a fall in the eighteenth century.[31] Britain was alone in experiencing a major and progressive increase in urbanisation. In England the urban percentage had been below the European average in 1600 but had become the second highest, after the Netherlands, by 1800.

Adam Smith had the experience of England and Scotland in the forefront of his mind when writing book III of the *Wealth of nations*. In Britain urban growth had progressed without interruption for several generations and the model of mutual advantage which he depicted seems to explain the phenomena well. The growth of London, for example, exercised a powerfully beneficial influence upon the agriculture of the whole kingdom, while, looking upon the same phenomenon from the point of view of the countryside, the habit of ready and frequent access to London steadily transformed the expectations and expenditure patterns of families across a wide range of income bands.[32] What made England different from, say, France where Paris, though a very large city, grew only roughly in step with the growth of national population throughout the early modern period?

[31] De Vries's urban data base was intended to include estimates of the population at 50-year intervals for every city which exceeded 10,000 inhabitants at some point during the period 1500–1800. There were 21 such Dutch cities. Their combined population in 1700 was 645,000 and in 1800 was 619,000 representing 34 and 29 per cent respectively of the total population of the country at the two dates. De Vries, *European urbanization*, tab. 3.7, p. 39 and app. 1, p. 271.

[32] See, for example, Kussmaul, *Rural economy of England*, ch. 5; or, from a very different perspective, McKendrick, 'The consumer revolution'.

One possible explanation lies not so much in economics as in anthropology, in attitudes rather than income. In a peasant society that was true to its stereotype local self-sufficiency would have high priority. The peasant holding is managed with an eye above all to ensuring that the food needs of the family are met from their own resources. Fuel is obtained from local woodland, hedgerow, or common. The farmstead is built by local craftsmen from local wood and stone. Thread is spun and cloth woven within the household or at most within the village. Not only are 'foreigners' viewed with suspicion, the products of 'foreigners' are unwelcome. Some things, such as salt, may only be obtainable from a distance, but what can be produced locally is preferred if a choice is feasible. This stereotype is helpful in defining one end of a spectrum of possibilities, even though it may seldom have been matched in full by particular communities.

At the other extreme lies an opposite stereotype. The market-orientated farmer sets no store on self-sufficiency. If a market exists for a product in whose production he enjoys a comparative advantage, he is content to concentrate upon, say, raising beef cattle, and will buy his bread, cheese, and bacon elsewhere. If clothes of a given quality can be had more cheaply from a distant market, he will buy them. If they fail to conform to the local notion of what constitutes a proper form of clothing, he and his wife may either be indifferent to local custom, or may view it as an advantage that by wearing clothes that reflect a national fashion, they are making a statement about their status and aspirations that gratifies them. And so also with other forms of expenditure.

While France may not have lain at one end of this spectrum of possibilities, nor England at the other, there can be little doubt about the relative positioning of the two. Nor can there be much doubt that between Tudor and Regency times England moved a long way across the spectrum, while change in France was more muted. Over the same period towns grew rapidly in England, far outstripping the general growth of population, whereas in France urban growth went broadly in step with the rise in population.[33] These contrasts were not accidental. Because the demand for urban goods and services depended so heavily on the attitudes of rural consumers; because the town dweller had to buy from the country to survive, but the country dweller enjoyed a wider discretion in making his purchases, the scale of the urban sector and the pace of its growth was strongly conditioned by the mind set and life-style of

---

[33] The percentage of the French population living in towns with 5,000 or more inhabitants rose only from about 9 per cent to 11 per cent of the total population between 1500 and 1800: Wrigley, 'Urban growth', tab. 7.9, pp. 184–5.

those living in the countryside. For the town to grow, one might say, the country had to become urbanised.

Conclusion

When Adam Smith's phrase 'the great commerce of every civilized society' is used in relation to urban–rural exchange, perhaps the adjective 'civilized' should receive most stress. An earlier generation of sociologists used habitually to distinguish 'parasitic' from 'generative' cities.[34] The former existed because income, whether in cash or kind, was drawn into the city from the countryside through the exercise of political power. Such cities were based on taxes and tribute. The latter depended upon the kind of exchange which constituted Smith's 'great commerce'. If 'civilized' is intended to connote, among other things, open to market forces, his assertion has an added cogency. Since he went on immediately to define the 'great commerce' as 'the exchange of rude for manufactured produce', and since the development of such an exchange may well have depended upon the openness of the countryside to market forces, it is not fanciful to suppose that 'civilized' should be construed in this way.

At the end of chapter 3 of book III Smith placed a long and complex paragraph which is worth quoting in full despite its length since it is redolent with assumptions about the degree to which the market suffused the everyday life of the whole population in a manner which may accurately reflect the state of affairs in eighteenth-century England, but which scarcely seems to fit the patterns of economic and social life found in most pre-industrial societies. It is complex partly because Smith was concerned to exemplify his conviction that it was more natural for manufacturing to grow out of a flourishing local agricultural base than for it to arise from commercial contacts. The passage follows a discussion of manufactures, like that of silk in Spitalfields, which were established to imitate a foreign commodity in great demand and which were based on foreign raw materials rather than a productive local agriculture, a form of growth that Smith's approach to economic development obliged him to regard as, in a sense, artificial. Having dealt with the artificial, he turned to the natural type of manufacturing development.

At other times manufactures for distant sale grow up naturally, and as it were of their own accord, by the gradual refinement of those household and coarser manufactures which must at all times be carried on even in the poorest and rudest countries. Such manufactures are generally employed upon the materials which the country produces, and they seem frequently to have been first refined and

---

[34] Hoselitz, 'Generative and parasitic cities'.

improved in such inland countries as were, not indeed at a very great, but at a considerable distance from the sea coast, and sometimes even from all water carriage. An inland country naturally fertile and easily cultivated, produces a great surplus of provisions beyond what is necessary for maintaining the cultivators, and on account of the expence of land carriage, and inconveniency of river navigation, it may frequently be difficult to send this surplus abroad. Abundance, therefore, renders provisions cheap, and encourages a great number of workmen to settle in the neighbourhood, who find that their industry can there procure them more of the necessaries and conveniences of life than in other places. They work up the materials of manufacture which the land produces, and exchange their finished work, or what is the same thing the price of it, for more materials and provisions. They give a new value to the surplus part of the rude produce, by saving the expence of carrying it to the water side, or to some distant market; and they furnish the cultivators with something in exchange for it that is either useful or agreeable to them, upon easier terms than they could have obtained it before. The cultivators get a better price for their surplus produce, and can purchase cheaper other conveniences which they have occasion for. They are thus both encouraged and enabled to increase this surplus produce by a further improvement and better cultivation of the land; and as the fertility of the land had given birth to the manufacture, so the progress of the manufacture re-acts upon the land, and increases still further its fertility. The manufacturers first supply the neighbourhood, and afterwards, as their work improves and refines, more distant markets. For though neither the rude produce, nor even the coarse manufacture, could, without the greatest difficulty, support the expence of a considerable land carriage, the refined and improved manufacture easily may. In a small bulk it frequently contains the price of a great quantity of rude produce. A piece of fine cloth, for example, which weighs only eighty pounds, contains in it, the price, not only of eighty pound weight of wool, but sometimes of several thousand weight of corn, the maintenance of the different working people, and of their immediate employers. The corn, which could with difficulty have been carried abroad in its own shape, is in this manner virtually exported in that of the complete manufacture, and may easily be sent to the remotest corners of the world. In this manner have grown up naturally, and as it were of their own accord, the manufactures of Leeds, Halifax, Sheffield, Birmingham, and Wolverhampton. Such manufactures are the offspring of agriculture. In the modern history of Europe, their extension and improvement have generally been posterior to those which were the offspring of foreign commerce.[35]

This picture, intended as a paradigm of a healthy form of manufacturing growth, was drawn from recent English experience as understood by Adam Smith, and was meant to stand in contrast to what had happened more commonly where manufactures had developed on the continent, as the final sentence makes clear. But while his intention may have been primarily to define the most desirable form of manufacturing growth, the detailed description reflects a society in which all those engaged in

[35] A. Smith, *Wealth of nations*, I, pp. 430–1.

economic activity, rural and urban, manufacturing and agricultural, were fully and unquestioningly committed to a market economy. To the degree that the picture is accurate, it underlines the completeness of the abandonment by the English population of habits of mind and customary practices so deepset in many peasant societies.

It is mistaken to suppose that it was the industrial revolution which set England apart for a time from the continent of Europe. Almost the reverse was the case. Once the industrial revolution had started to transform English society and economy, the days of its distinctiveness were numbered and its economic dominance was doomed. Others found it easy to follow and in time to surpass. But for about two centuries before this transition took place, England had been growing steadily apart from the continent, acquiring in the process increasing economic and political power.[36] Between 1600 and 1800 the population of England was growing faster than that of any major continental country, but the growth was confined entirely to the towns and to that part of the rural population which did not make its living from agriculture. While precision will always remain out of reach, it is probable that the rural agricultural population was roughly stationary in number.[37]

Understanding 'the great commerce of every civilized society', therefore, is of singular importance to the wider issue of the distinctiveness of English history in the period. Urban growth and economic development were intimately connected and the relationship between the two was not the same in England as on the continent. With his customary perspicacity, Adam Smith suggested the nature of the link in a market-orientated, capitalist society. His is a model to which the island experience conformed quite closely, though his discussion is clouded to the modern eye by his determination to incorporate into it an insistence upon the natural priority of agriculture over manufacture, and of the latter over commerce. But just as striking as the increasing momentum of urban growth in Britain was its absence on the continent, and Adam Smith can be useful here too, though he did not address the issue himself, since a consideration of the conditions that must be met for 'the great commerce' to flow freely suggests what it was that handicapped the continent for so long.

To be platitudinous, a market economy presupposes a market, and a successful market economy cannot develop where the assumptions that underlie classical economics do not obtain. In every economy there are classes of transaction that do not conform to such expectations, notably those within the family, but in some a wide swathe of transactions may

[36] Wrigley, 'Society and the economy'.
[37] Wrigley, 'Urban growth', tab. 7.4, p. 170.

conform fairly closely to the market model. It may have been critical to the growth of towns in the past that the market model should apply tolerably well to the behaviour of country dwellers. Where this was not the case urban growth was liable to falter in the face of an insufficient demand for urban goods and services on the part of rural society. The 'great commerce of every civilized society' had to attract equally *both* participants in the exchange. If one was half-hearted or hostile, the growth of the other was crippled. If the feedback was partial and feeble, the conditions of growth would be absent.

11   Country and town: the primary, secondary, and tertiary peopling of England in the early modern period

There are many ways of depicting the constitution of a given society and of defining and measuring the changes taking place within it. They will reflect the interests and purposes of the scholars concerned, tempered by the source materials available to them. This essay reflects the conviction that the occupational structure of a society and the changes therein offer the opportunity to gain an insight into much else about that society and its development. The way in which men and women earned a living reveals much about them and their communities. Though true of all societies, this was perhaps especially true of societies before the industrial revolution.

It is instructive to consider why this should be so. At bottom it follows from the fact that occupational structure in pre-industrial societies reflected the hierarchical nature of human needs, which produced some notable and readily observable regularities. The thinking and terminology of the classical economists reflected their appreciation of this point. They frequently referred to what they termed the necessities of life, of which there were four: food, shelter, clothing, and fuel.[1] These they distinguished both from what they characterised as comforts or conveniences, other material products which were less central to life than the necessities but eagerly sought after when circumstances permitted; and from luxuries, goods, or services to which only the affluent could aspire. If circumstances are sufficiently bleak people will favour spending on necessities above all other forms of expenditure, so that a very high proportion of the total spending of the poor will be devoted solely to necessities and above all to food. It was not uncommon for an impoverished household in early modern England to spend as much as three-quarters of its income on food alone and a still higher proportion, of course, on the four necessities taken together. But when income rises the proportion spent on necessities

---

This chapter was originally given as one of the Linacre Lecture series on 'The peopling of Britain: the shaping of a human landscape' in 1999.

[1] The term used by the classical economists was normally 'necessaries' but it avoids confusion to use the modern equivalent.

declines. If a poor man's income suddenly doubles, he and his family will spend more thereafter on food but their expenditure on food will not double. Or, to express the matter more formally, the income elasticity of demand for the necessities of life is less than unity. Conversely, of course, spending on comforts and, if resources permit, on luxuries, will more than double in the same circumstances. In an era of rising real incomes expenditure on comforts and luxuries will increase disproportionately rapidly. In an era of contracting real incomes, in contrast, the percentage share of spending on necessities will rise.

Types of employment

The eminent economist Colin Clark interested himself in these and cognate issues.[2] He distinguished between primary, secondary, and tertiary forms of employment. These were not, of course, the same categories as necessities, conveniences, and luxuries, but his three categories can be used for broadly comparable analytic purposes. Primary employment comprises agriculture, forestry, fishing, and mining, those forms of production which supply the raw materials from which finished products are made. Secondary employment refers to productive activities which convert raw materials into forms which can be consumed or otherwise made use of by their final purchasers. Tertiary employment relates to the production of services rather than material products: the professions; government service; the arts and entertainment; the provision of food, drink, and lodging; and transport, for example.[3]

Because of the way in which the marginal unit of income is spent as personal income rises, in the transition from a traditional society where income levels are low to a modern economy with high average incomes, such as may be found in contemporary western Europe or North America, the structure of aggregate demand will change steadily. The absolute level of demand will rise for the products of all the three main employment categories, but the rate of growth will be least in the primary sector and greatest in the tertiary sector. Occupational structure must change in sympathy, since one man's expenditure is another man's source of employment. As a result, the percentage of the labour force engaged in primary production will fall slowly but inexorably from, say, 75 per cent to 5 per or less, while the percentage in the tertiary sector will rise from a

---

[2] C. Clark, *The conditions of economic progress*. Ch. 8 of this work provides much empirical information about income elasticities of demand for a wide variety of products principally drawn from the first half of the twentieth century.

[3] There is room for argument about the placing of certain economic activities within the three chief categories of employment, but this is not an issue that requires exhaustive treatment in this context.

very modest level initially to 75 per cent or more in wealthy countries. In the interim period, reflecting the differing income elasticities of demand for the products of the three categories of employment, the percentage employed in secondary industry will rise rapidly at first, attaining at its peak perhaps 35 to 50 per cent of the labour force, but will subsequently fall back substantially as the tertiary sector comes to dominate the economy. Expressed in the language of the classical economists, if real incomes rise there will be a fall in the proportion of the labour force engaged in the production of necessities and a matching rise in the proportion engaged in the making of conveniences and the provision of luxuries.

Since the form which economic growth has taken in the past two centuries, the form brought about by the industrial revolution, was first apparent in England, there is a special interest in any source of information or technique of analysis which can throw light on what was distinctive about England in the centuries preceding the industrial revolution. One should perhaps pause to note that making use of the term industrial revolution has become a possible source of confusion. What was largely unproblematic thirty years ago has ceased to be so. Neither the dating of the event to the last decades of the eighteenth and the early decades of the nineteenth century, nor the view that the rate of growth increased abruptly when the industrial revolution began, nor the conviction that England served as a paradigm for other countries has survived unscathed.[4] Despite this, it remains instructive to identify the respects in which England had become demonstrably different from continental Europe by the early nineteenth century. Among the more striking of these were the distinctive changes in its occupational structure, and the growing urbanisation taking place during the seventeenth and eighteenth centuries. These two developments were closely interrelated. They jointly constitute the core of this essay because they afford an opportunity to explore several aspects of the peopling of England during the centuries preceding the industrial revolution.

Types of peopling

This general theme can be explored by extending the distinction between primary, secondary, and tertiary employment to serve an unfamiliar

---

[4] On these issues see Crafts, 'Patterns of development' and *British economic growth*. The very validity of the concept of the industrial revolution has been contested by Cameron, 'The industrial revolution: a misnomer'. There is a stimulating review of the historiography of the industrial revolution in Cannadine, 'The present and the past in the English industrial revolution'. A critical survey of studies of the industrial revolution may be found in Hoppit and Wrigley, 'Introduction'. See also Hoppit, 'Counting the industrial revolution' and Berg and Hudson, 'Rehabilitating the industrial revolution'.

purpose. I shall use the term primary population to refer to those engaged
in primary production; and define secondary and tertiary population using the same principle. The primary peopling of England therefore, for
example, does not refer to that which occurred first chronologically, but
to that part of the population at a given point in time which earned its
living from farming, forestry, and fishing.[5] The primary population includes, of course, not only those who were actually labouring on the land
or putting to sea in fishing boats but all those directly dependent upon
them. *Mutatis mutandis*, the same applies to secondary and tertiary population so that every individual in a given area must always fall into one
of the three categories. The three types of peopling may be thought of
as successive layers superimposed upon the surface of the country. The
population distribution as a whole is the joint product of these layers.

The distributional characteristics of the three population categories differed markedly. Before considering the particular circumstances of early
modern England, the general nature of the three distributions requires
brief discussion. The primary population characteristically formed a shallow covering over the whole country. Its depth was closely proportional
to the fertility of the soil, shallowest where the land was high, or steeply
sloping, or where the soil was thin, acidic, or waterlogged; deepest where
the soil was a productive loam. The covering was very shallow on, say,
high moorland, but even on fertile soils it was nowhere very thick. Even
in early fourteenth-century East Anglia, for example, the most densely
peopled part of the country in the period when the medieval population of England was at its peak, the primary peopling was probably no
greater than 150 persons per square mile, or 4 acres per person, over the
region as a whole, though locally densities might be two or three times
greater.[6] This is a high density for primary population, but very sparse
when compared with the densities which were supported by some types
of secondary and tertiary employment.

Because the primary population was always widely and thinly spread,
if its density were plotted using contour lines, the resulting map would
reflect a landscape without prominent relief. The highest ground, the

---

[5] Primary employment is normally taken to include mining. I have excluded it in this case
because the distributional characteristics of mining employment are more akin to certain
types of industrial employment than to farming, forestry, and fishing.

[6] The 1377 poll tax data reveal taxpayer densities of 20 per square kilometre, or 50 per
square mile, over East Anglia as a whole. On the assumption that taxpayers were roughly
one half of the total population and that population had halved between its early century
peak and 1377, this suggests the figure of 200 per square mile for the total population in
1300. However, since East Anglia had many towns and an important woollen industry,
it is unlikely that the primary population density was higher than 150 per square mile.
R. M. Smith, 'Human resources', pp. 190, 196–202.

areas with the densest primary population, did not rise dramatically. Secondary and tertiary populations, in contrast, were often highly localised and sometimes large in number. To extend the contouring analogy, these populations might at times produce Himalayan heights in sharp contrast with the Ganges plain-like pattern of primary population. The tendency to cluster was not by any means universal in secondary and tertiary peopling. The use of such inclusive general categories tends to obliterate the different characteristics of their constituent occupations. Some secondary and tertiary occupations, bakers or barbers, for example, were necessarily found distributed about the country in broad sympathy with the overall distribution of the population. The perishability of bread and the unwillingness of the purchasers of a cheap service to move far to obtain it left those employed in such occupations no option but to mirror the geographical distribution of the purchasers of their products.

But there were also elements within the secondary and tertiary peopling of the country which were subject to very different economic imperatives. Consider, to take an example which illustrates the opposite extreme, Adam Smith's pinmakers. The product of the pin manufacture is almost weightless, so that, as with spices, the cost of transporting the finished product to market can only be a tiny fraction of the cost of manufacture. If, therefore, the division of labour were capable of being carried even further than Adam Smith suggested, so that unit costs of production would continue to fall appreciably in consequence of achieving higher and higher levels of output through increased specialisation, then production would become concentrated on fewer and fewer sites, and, ultimately, in the paradigm case, on a single site. If employment in a given industry is highly concentrated, those who make their living from it will be equally concentrated.

In both secondary and tertiary industries a pattern that lies partway between these two extremes is more commonly found. In tertiary industry the professions illustrate the point well. An increasingly prosperous country, for example, can afford more lawyers and demand for their services will rise. Those lawyers who are least specialised in their skills will be found relatively widespread throughout the country, though more commonly in the larger than in the smaller towns and rarely in mere villages. In contrast, barristers will be found disproportionately in the largest centres. To illustrate the point, in 1841 69.2 per cent of all men aged 20 and over in the occupational category 'barrister, advocate, and conveyancer' in England were in the metropolis. In the category 'attorney, solicitor, writer and law student', in contrast, only 31.5 per cent were in London. Similarly, the country's carpenters and joiners were widely scattered. Only 15.0 per cent were in London, but 32.9 per cent of the more specialist occupational category of cabinet makers and upholsterers were in the capital[7] (in 1841 Greater London contained 2,239,000 people or 14.9 per cent of the total English population of 15,929,000).[8]

Most pre-industrial societies were poor and in consequence primary population dominated. A three-dimensional map of a typical pre-industrial society, displaying primary, secondary, and tertiary population as successive layers upon the land surface, would show that the bulk of the total population portrayed was contributed by the primary layer even though there might be prominent local peaks of secondary and tertiary peopling. What set England apart from the major countries of continental Europe in the seventeenth and eighteenth centuries was that the primary layer gradually ceased to dominate the scene during these two centuries, whereas on the continent the early modern period saw only relatively slight changes in this regard. Early modern England experienced a remarkable surge in its secondary and tertiary peopling.

England and the continent

The scale of England's exceptionalism is reflected in table 11.1 which reproduces some data collected by Crafts for a somewhat different purpose. He wished to illustrate how different Britain was from continental countries at the *same point of general economic advance* (when average real incomes had reached the equivalent of $550 (1970 US dollars)). A far smaller proportion of the British workforce was to be found in agriculture at this 'standard' stage of development than was the case in Germany, France, or Italy and, most unusually, output per head in agriculture was little different from output per head in the rest of the economy, as may be seen from a comparison of the percentages of the labour force in the primary sector and the percentages of national income generated in that sector. Elsewhere agriculture dominated the employment scene to a far greater extent, but output per head in agriculture was modest compared with that in secondary industry. The dates at which each country reached the 'standard' stage varied substantially, of course, with England well before the others. If it were feasible to make a similar comparison at the *same date* for each country and at a relatively early point in time, the contrasts

---

[7] The relevant totals of barristers, solicitors, carpenters, and cabinet makers were respectively (total for London in brackets): 2,076 (1,437); 10,919 (3,437); 112,872 (16,965); and 19,752 (6,497). *1841 Census*, Occupation abstract. Preface. 'Occupations of persons enumerated in Great Britain, distinguishing England and Wales, Scotland, and isles in the British seas in the year 1841', pp. 31–44; and 'Occupations of persons enumerated in the metropolis in the year 1841', pp. 48–51.

[8] Mitchell, *British historical statistics*, tab. I.3, p. 11 and tab. I.6, p. 25.

Table 11.1 *Contrasting levels of agricultural employment and of urbanisation in Britain and the continent (percentages)*

	Great Britain 1840	Germany 1870	France 1870	Italy 1910
Urbanisation	48.3	36.1	31.1	n.a
Labour force in primary sector	25.0	50.0	49.3	55.4
Income generated in primary sector	24.9	39.9	33.5	38.2
Male labour force in industry	47.3	n.a	28.7	26.5
Income generated in industry	31.5	29.7	36.0	23.9

Note: The dates shown at the head of each column indicate the approximate date at which each country reached an average income level equal to $550 (1970 US dollars).
Source: Crafts, *British economic growth*, tab. 3.4, pp. 57–8.

in occupational structure between a 'peasant' Europe and a relatively non-agricultural England would be even more pronounced.

Such a comparison is not readily possible because national occupational census data are rarely available before the middle of the nineteenth century. By then countries such as Belgium, France, or Germany were already in the course of rapid economic change and urbanisation. Extensive tracts of Europe, however, were still at a much earlier stage of development in the mid-century. The data in table 11.2 refer to male occupational patterns. The information for Italy, Ireland, and Sweden is taken from the earliest readily available source, which was in each case in the middle decades of the century. Exceptionally, there is information for a much earlier date for Finland. Broadly speaking, in Italy, Ireland, and Sweden about two-thirds of the male labour force were working on the land. In Finland at the beginning of the century the comparable proportion was four-fifths. If returns existed for the other three countries for *c.*1800, it is highly probable that about three men in four would have been engaged in primary occupations. Yet in England in 1811 only 39 per cent of adult males aged 20–64 were employed in agriculture.[9] Although the different ways in which occupational data were collected and tabulated in different countries should discourage the belief that precise comparisons can be made, the scale of the contrast in inescapable. Nor can the much lower English figure be attributed to dependence on imported food. At that time, England, though a net food importer, was still very largely self-supporting.[10]

[9] Tab. 4.12, p. 124.
[10] Jones has suggested that 90 per cent of the population of Great Britain was fed from domestic agricultural production in 1800, while Thomas estimated that in 1814–6 the

Table 11.2 *Sectoral structure of the male labour force (percentages)*

	Italy 1871	Ireland 1841	Sweden 1860	Finland[a] 1805
Agriculture, forestry, and fishing	61.2	68.5	64.6	82.1
Manufacturing	13.2[b]	12.2	20.8	3.6
Other	25.6	19.3	14.6	14.3
	100.0	100.0	100.0	100.0

Notes: [a]Male and female combined.
[b]Assumes manufacturing and construction split in 1871 in the same ratio as in 1881.
Source: Mitchell, *European statistics*, tab. C1, pp. 61–73.

It appears to be a fair inference from tables 11.1 and 11.2 that during the quarter-millennium before the nineteenth century the course of economic change in England must have been very different from that of her near neighbours. On the assumption that her occupational structure in the early sixteenth century did not set England apart from, say, France, much must have changed in the interim to have produced such wide differences by the beginning of the nineteenth century. This assumption is difficult to substantiate by direct quantitative evidence about occupational structure, but it is much strengthened by considering the course of urban growth in England and elsewhere over this period. Here the empirical evidence, while not without its problems, is much more abundant and tolerably reliable. In the early sixteenth century England was less urbanised than most continental countries. In 1800 it was the most highly urbanised country in Europe with the exception of the Netherlands. The difference between England and the larger continental states was marked. About 28 per cent of the population of England lived in towns and cities of 5,000 or more inhabitants in 1800, for example, compared with a figure of 11 per cent for France at the same date.[11] In contrast, in the early sixteenth century, the comparable proportion in England was only

value of imports of grain, meat, and butter was equal to 6.4 per cent of the total income of British agriculture: Jones, 'Agriculture 1700–80', p. 68; B. Thomas, 'Escaping from constraints', tab. 2, p. 743.

[11] Wrigley, 'Urban growth', tab. 7.2, p. 162; tab. 7.9, pp. 184–5; the comparable figure for the Netherlands was 33 per cent: ibid., tab. 7.8, p. 182. Choosing 5,000 inhabitants as the criterion for inclusion in the category 'urban' is arbitrary. Many market centres with 'urban' characteristics had fewer than 5,000 inhabitants but, equally, there were many small towns in which a substantial proportion of the workforce was engaged in agriculture. Using 5,000 inhabitants as a lower bound for urban population ensures that only a tiny fraction of the urban workforce was agriculturally employed.

5 per cent, though in France it was already 9 per cent.[12] The pattern of change in Germany or Spain was similar to that in France, nor was Italy greatly different despite the vivid and vigorous history of urban achievement there.[13] The striking contrast in the extent of urban growth between England and her neighbours, especially in the course of the eighteenth century, is reflected in the fact that during the second half of the eighteenth century approximately 70 per cent of all the urban growth taking place in Europe as a whole was occurring in England alone, even though the English population constituted less than 8 per cent of the European total.[14]

The course of change in England

Rapid urban growth connotes rapid change in occupational structure. A major increase in the urban percentage necessarily means a substantial fall in the proportion of the population engaged in agriculture. It also implies a proliferation of occupational categories since the greater the size of the settlement, the wider the range of specialised individual occupations. And in parallel with any relative decline in the primary population, there must be, of course, a commensurate relative rise in secondary and tertiary employment.

Although direct evidence of occupational change in England is limited, there is support for the belief that rapid change was taking place in the seventeenth and eighteenth centuries from the investigations carried out by Gregory King at the end of the seventeenth century and by Joseph Massie in the middle of the eighteenth. Both men produced tables from which national occupational structure can be approximately estimated.[15] King's work is particularly interesting in this context. He was in a position to make use of such information as was at the disposal of the government of the day, and he found a compulsive fascination in the assemblage and

[12] Wrigley, 'Urban growth', tab. 7.2, p. 162; tab. 7.9, pp. 184–5.

[13] In Italy 18 per cent of the population was living in towns with 5,000 or more inhabitants in 1800. This estimate of Italian urban population was obtained by inflating the total population of individual towns with 10,000 or more inhabitants in 1800 by a factor which represents the ratio of the population of towns of between 5,000 and 10,000 inhabitants to towns of 10,000 and above derived from a table showing the relative size of towns in different size groups in Mediterranean Europe as a whole at that date, and then relating the resulting total to the national population total to obtain a percentage figure. The data were taken from de Vries, *European urbanization*, tab. 3.7, p. 39; tab. 4.13, p. 72, and app. 1, pp. 269–78.

[14] Ibid., tab. 7.7, pp. 179. Europe in this calculation comprised the British Isles, Scandinavia, Spain, Portugal, the Low Countries, Germany, France, Italy, and Switzerland.

[15] Mathias, 'The social structure in the eighteenth century', provides an interesting discussion of the work of Massie and its relation to that of King.

interpretation of these data and other sources of economic, social, and demographic information.[16] King was not attempting to produce an occupational census as the term is understood today.[17] The descriptors he used sometimes represented status rather than occupation. Nevertheless, his estimates can be recast in such a way as to allow the extent of the reduction in the dominance of primary employment during the eighteenth century to be gauged, and the same is possible with Massie's estimates. King's investigations suggest that about 60 per cent of families were making a living from agriculture in 1688. Massie's work suggests a figure of about 50 per cent c.1760.[18] Their estimates, therefore, support the common-sense view that England had once been similar in occupational structure to the continent, just as it had once been in the extent of its urbanisation. The change in the share of agriculture in total employment implied by the estimates of Massie and King, if extrapolated backwards, would suggest a 'continental' occupational structure in Tudor times.[19] If

[16] Stone, 'Gregory King', offers a penetrating review of King's aims and methods, and of the validity of his findings.

[17] He was probably moved chiefly by a wish to improve his knowledge of data bearing on the relative strengths of England and her rivals, and especially to arrive at a better assessment of the tax potential of the country at a time of expensive war.

[18] The assumptions made in deriving these percentage estimates from the original tables are set out in Wrigley, 'Urban growth', pp. 171–2, n.19.

[19] There is scope for much further work on this point. One of the few tolerably confident comparisons which can be made between the early seventeenth and the early nineteenth centuries, and which covers a significant area, is possible because of the work of the Tawneys on the Gloucestershire muster roll of 1608. This affords occupational data relating to men aged between 20 and 60 years of age for the whole county excluding Bristol. The Tawneys discuss at length the possible defects and sources of bias in the source but conclude that it will yield trustworthy estimates of such matters as the proportion of the male population engaged in each named occupation. Their tabulations show that 46.2 per cent of the men for whom occupational information is given were engaged in agriculture: Tawney and Tawney, 'An occupational census of the seventeenth century', tab. 1, p. 36. The 1831 census provides the data necessary to calculate the comparable percentage for the same area. In 1831 there were 25,866 men aged 20 and over engaged in agriculture in Gloucestershire excluding Bristol out of a total population of men of 69,502 in the same age range: 37.2 per cent of adult males were therefore farmers or agricultural labourers: *1831 Census*, Enumeration abstract, I, pp. 226–7. The fall in the percentage engaged in agriculture is modest, and if this pattern were typical of the country as a whole, it would suggest that the key issue is to account for an exceptionally high percentage of the workforce outside agriculture in the sixteenth century rather than to explain the rise in secondary and tertiary employment subsequently. However, it is improbable that Gloucestershire was typical of England as a whole. It was early a centre of the wool textile industry which subsequently declined substantially in importance. Textiles employed 15.5 per cent of the male labour force in 1608, but only about 6.5 per cent in 1831 (the 1831 census provides sufficient information to make a calculation possible but not sufficient to remove some doubt as to its accuracy). If textile employment is excluded at both dates the decline in the agricultural percentage is more pronounced: from 54.7 to 39.8. The presence of a large textile industry in 1608 also created related employment dealing and retailing, so that the true impact of its presence on the

this assumption is justified, the distinctive character of this aspect of the population history of England in the early modern period is plain.

An earlier exercise suggested that in England the absolute number of men directly employed on the land at the end of the sixteenth century did not differ materially from the number similarly engaged at the beginning of the nineteenth century. The fall in the percentage of the labour force employed in agriculture offset the rise in total population. On the continent, in contrast, even though there was probably a modest decline in the *percentage* of the primary population, the rise in overall numbers was sufficient to ensure a considerable growth in its *absolute size*. The rural agricultural proportion of the total population of France may have fallen from *c*.76 per cent to *c*.66 per cent between 1600 and 1800, but this would still imply an increase in the absolute size of the rural agricultural population of about 30 per cent.[20]

To underline the exceptional character of the history of the primary peopling of England, it is illuminating to glance still further back in time. It is virtually certain that the primary population of the country reached a level early in the fourteenth century which was never again to be matched. It is now widely supposed that at its medieval peak, which was reached about that time, the total population of the country exceeded 6 million.[21] The comparable total in 1600 was only about two-thirds as great, at 4.2 million.[22] Since the proportion of the total population engaged in agriculture was probably as high in 1300 as in 1600, if not higher, and on the assumption that there was little growth in the agricultural population in the two-and-a-half centuries after 1600, it follows that there were more, and probably substantially more, men and women working in English fields and meadows in the early fourteenth century than at any subsequent time. Agricultural employment may have risen somewhat in the early decades of the nineteenth century before declining after the mid-century, but even in 1851 it was probably less than in *c*.1300. It is extremely improbable that such a statement would hold true for any substantial tract of the European mainland.

---

agricultural percentage is probably understated by removing textile employment alone from the calculation. Nevertheless, Gloucestershire data suggest caution in attempting to estimate the scale of the decline in primary employment and underlines the urgency of making fuller use of all available evidence on this point.

[20] Wrigley, 'Urban growth', tab. 7.9, pp. 184–5.

[21] In a recent review of many aspects of the demography of medieval England, Smith suggests that in 1348 the national total probably lay in the range between five and six millions but also that it was probably significantly higher at the beginning of the fourteenth century. Smith, 'Human resources', p. 191.

[22] Wrigley *et al.*, *English population history*, tab. A9.1, pp. 614–5.

By 1800 about 64 per cent of the population of England was making a living outside agriculture, and therefore formed part of the secondary or tertiary population of the country.[23] The number of people dependent on non-agricultural income may be estimated to have increased from about 1.24 million in 1600 to about 5.52 million in 1800, a rise of almost 350 per cent.[24] The contour map of overall population, produced by the superimposition of secondary and tertiary peopling on top of the primary surface was beginning to acquire the vertiginous peaks which are the distinguishing mark of a modern society. London became the largest city in Europe, and one of the largest in the world, before the end of the seventeenth century and at the end of the eighteenth was nearing the million mark. During the eighteenth century, several English towns approached a total of 100,000 inhabitants, at a time when such a size was still most unusual.[25] Moreover, several of the largest cities at the end of the eighteenth century had only arrived very recently in the upper echelons of city size. Before the mid-nineteenth century there were no parallels on the continent to Liverpool, Birmingham, and Manchester in their combination of large size and rapid growth without the stimulus of being a seat of government. Such urban growth as there was elsewhere in Europe usually failed to disturb the existing city rank order. In France, for example, the eight cities which were largest in 1600 were still the eight largest in 1800 with only minor changes in their rank ordering. In England, London was always by far the largest city, but only two other of the eight largest towns in 1600 were still in the top eight in 1800. After London, five of the next six were newcomers (Manchester, Liverpool, Birmingham, Leeds, and Sheffield).[26] Plainly, exceptional changes were afoot in England which were transforming its economy and its peopling at a time when on the continent such change was, by comparison, in a very minor key.

It should not be supposed, however, that a move away from agriculture as a means of livelihood necessarily meant a move away from the land. Much of the growth in secondary and tertiary peopling took place in the

---

[23] Wrigley, 'Urban growth', tab. 7.4, p. 170. An estimate made on a different basis and relating only to male adults suggests that non-agricultural employment formed between 60 and 62 per cent of the total; tab. 4.12, p. 124.

[24] Ibid., tab. 7.4, p. 170.

[25] In the whole of Europe in 1800 there were 17 towns with a population of 100,000 or more. Only 8 at most were not capital cities: Hamburg (100,000); Lyon (100,000); Milan (135,000); Venice (138,000); Palermo (139,000); Barcelona (115,000); Naples (427,000); and Dublin (168,000): de Vries, *European urbanization*, app. 1, pp. 269–78. Several of these might reasonably be treated as capitals or quasi-capitals.

[26] Wrigley, 'Urban growth', tab. 7.1, pp. 160–1; de Vries, *European urbanization*, app. 1, pp. 269–78.

countryside rather than in the town.[27] To clarify this development, a brief digression into the complex issues to do with occupational descriptors may not be out of place.

Measurement issues

In an advanced economy in the late twentieth century if a man describes himself as a solicitor's clerk or as a garage mechanic, it is likely that his income is derived exclusively, or at least predominantly, from the occupation which he has named. His contribution to the total output of goods and services in the community may well comprise things not produced in the solicitor's office or the on the floor of the garage. The clerk may make violins in his spare time; the mechanic may be an amateur carpenter. But normally a single occupational descriptor will capture most of the contribution made by the individual in question to the total output of goods and services in the community. This was less true in the past, and this has sometimes been seen as presenting a serious obstacle to the use of occupational data for historical purposes.

The implicit assumption which justifies using occupational information for the analysis of economic activity in the past is that if, say, 5 per cent of the labour force described themselves as framework knitters, then in round terms about 5 per cent of the hours worked by the labour force were devoted to framework knitting. There are several persuasive reasons for doubting that this is a legitimate inference. One of the most important stems from the nature of the seasonal pattern of activity in most agrarian societies. In general, the cereal harvest was the centrepiece of the agricultural year. In the great majority of communities it was vital to the well-being of the population that the harvest should be brought in as rapidly as possible in order to limit the loss to pests, sprouting, and foul weather. But the scale of the labour force needed to minimise harvest-time loss was much larger than that needed during the rest of the year. The 'normal' agricultural labour force was insufficient, yet to have retained in agriculture a workforce large enough to cope with the peak demand of harvest would have involved many men and women being idle for much of the year. Equally, to have failed to provide enough hands to bring in the harvest would have meant running the risk of communal disaster. It was therefore frequently beneficial that there should develop other types of local employment, such as framework knitting, to provide profitable

---

[27] For a convincing demonstration of the nature of this process, see Patten, 'Changing occupational structures'.

occupations during the bulk of the year for the additional hands needed at harvest. Occupational symbiosis as well as specialisation was essential.

The same basic point can be expressed slightly differently. If it were possible, it would be preferable to measure hours worked on primary, secondary, and tertiary tasks, or in particular occupations in each category, rather than counting occupational designations. This would serve not only to overcome the problems associated with the harvest peak problem but also many comparable difficulties. The more prominent include the following. Some men changed their jobs seasonally. A seventeenth-century London coal heaver, who could find employment in the summer when colliers brought coal south from Tyneside to the Thames, would need to find other employment in the winter since the ships were then laid up. Or again, many men habitually and routinely had two jobs simultaneously, or more accurately, found that two different forms of employment dovetailed neatly. Occasionally this may be stated explicitly. For example, under the provisions of Rose's Act,[28] the occupation of fathers was set down in Anglican baptism registers. A man might there be described as, say, 'grazier and butcher', but when in this or any other source a man is described only as a 'butcher', this should not necessarily be taken to mean that he pursued no other trade. A comparable problem arises because specialisation of function was much less far advanced in the past than in the present. As a result, for example, many farmers carried their produce to market and therefore might spend several hours a month, in effect, as transport workers. Or again, a large fraction of all those engaged in domestic manufacture or in mining covered a variable, but often significant, part of their food needs by what they grew in their closes, gardens, or allotments.

Another important difference between the past and the present was the very extensive amount of work which would today appear as a form of economic activity giving rise to a marketable product but which was then performed at home, chiefly by women, and largely consumed by the household in question. The conversion of milk into butter, the baking of bread, the repair and often the making of clothes, the nursing of the sick, even such mundane tasks as the washing of potatoes or the shelling of peas, which are now done outside the home by a paid labour force, were in the past performed unpaid within the home. All such tasks were part of the production process and involved a substantial opportunity cost, and it is a defect of occupational data, which, with rare exceptions, relate principally to men, that information about a substantial part of the work which turned raw materials into finished products escapes the net when

[28] 52 Geo. III, cap. 146.

using occupational data. They almost always refer to work performed in the market sector of the economy but, in the past, a much larger fraction of productive activity was performed outside the market economy than is the case today.

It follows from the above that occupational data must be interpreted with discretion. If there were detailed information about the hours of work devoted to productive tasks by individuals in particular occupational groups, it would be clear, for example, how much of the time spent by those who described themselves as framework knitters was spent in work on the land. The crude data about occupational structure could then be weighted to reflect the realities of economic life in the past. Such information, however, except in the rarest instances, is not attainable. Yet it does not therefore follow that occupational data are such a fallible guide to the structure of the economy in the past as to be of little value. Notwithstanding their limitations as a surrogate measure of the relative amounts of time spent on different productive activities, there is much to be learnt from them.

First, a distinction should be drawn between the absolute and the relative. It may be impossible to discover with precision from occupational data what proportion of total labour time was devoted to agricultural tasks in 1600 or 1800. But if at one point in time 60 per cent of the labour force in a given area were agriculturally employed and at a later date only 35 per cent, this may be taken as clear evidence that agriculture had declined substantially in *relative* importance, even though it may be unsafe to assume that at the earlier date 60 per cent of hours worked were spent on agricultural pursuits and only 35 per cent at the later date. And what is true of change over time is true *a fortiori* of assessing regional or local differences at the same point in time. Occupational data may be a less than perfect guide to *absolute* quantities and yet a safe indication of *relative* differences.

Second, many of the difficulties in using occupational data to which reference has been made are, so to speak, partially self-correcting. The farmer who spends part of his time in carting produce to market is offset to some extent by the carter who grows vegetables on his croft. The carpenter who joins in harvest work is matched by the agricultural labourer who mends his own floor boards. And, in any case, the scale of alternative and supplementary activities outside a man's main occupation is easy to exaggerate. The craft or trade referred to by a man's stated occupation frequently represented the overwhelming bulk of his productive activity.

Third, the complexity of the occupational mix present in a particular community is instructive. A community which has reached a relatively high level of economic development will have a more diverse occupational structure than a community of the same size but more

impoverished. Some sources which do not permit even a primitive quantification of occupational structure but which do provide an insight into
its occupational complexity may therefore prove instructive, just as data
on nominal or ordinal scales can have great value even in the absence of
interval data. Local trade directories are a case in point. They do not provide a full coverage of local occupations since their principal purpose was
to put buyers in touch with sellers. Nevertheless to be able to enumerate
the range of specialist occupations locally present gives a valuable insight
into the degree of development of the local economy and provides clear
evidence of the existence of a market for the products in question. At
one extreme, the metropolis supported a bewildering range of specialised
occupations. In the parish of St Margaret's Westminster, for example,
well over 400 occupations appear in the baptism register in the period
1813–20 including the following highly specialised trades: optician, math-
ematical instrument maker, fiddle string maker, livery lace weaver, paper
stainer, and even a comedian.[29] But lesser urban centres and even many
rural parishes also provide evidence of a notable degree of specialisation
of function.

One further comment may be made about the use of occupational data,
a point which leads us back to the issue of the distinctiveness of early
modern England. Occupational terminology itself sometimes changed
as time went by. This is both instructive in itself and a reason to be
cautious in interpreting change. For example, the descriptors used for
those working in agriculture changed radically between the sixteenth and
nineteenth centuries. Husbandman and yeoman were largely displaced as
occupational terms by labourer and farmer. That there should have been
a wholesale change of this kind in the most important single industry in
the country is itself highly suggestive about the fundamental nature of
change in English agriculture, but it would be an error to suppose that
agricultural tasks had necessarily changed radically or that the changes
which did occur kept step with the changes in terminology.[30]

---

[29] The list of unusual occupations could be extended enormously. It should be noted that
in arriving at a total in excess of 400 occupations in St Margaret's subdivisions within
certain common occupational categories were ignored: there were, for example, scores
of different types of clerk, labourer, messenger, porter, soldier, and servant, but these
were largely ignored in arriving at a total of occupations in the years 1813–20.

[30] One man's husbandman was another man's labourer, as is very clear from some parish
registers in the early nineteenth century. The same man might appear as a husbandman
in one year and a couple of years later when his next child was baptised be described
as a labourer. The parish of Blackawton in Devon provides a striking example of the
waywardness of usage, since, having earlier adopted the modern term 'labourer', 'husbandman' returned to favour in 1814, only to be superseded once more by 'labourer'
in 1819. The occupation which was variously designated in this fashion did not alter,
however.

The expansion of secondary and tertiary peopling

Having described the uncertainties attaching to the use of occupational data, we may revert to a discussion of the great expansion in the secondary and tertiary peopling of the country which took place during the early modern period. This did not consist, for the most part, of employment in 'new' industries making use of major advances in productive technique. Even as late as the 1831 census, the first which allows analysis of the point, only one man in ten in the adult male labour force was engaged in 'manufacture', which comprised both factory-based production and those types of domestic manufacture which were tied to distant markets, the range of employments, that is, which is sometimes termed proto-industrial.[31] Well over half of the men aged 20 and over engaged in 'manufacture' were living either in Lancashire or the West Riding of Yorkshire. Out of a national English total of 314,106, Lancashire and the West Riding accounted for 172,186.[32] Elsewhere manufacture afforded little employment; less than 6 per cent of adult males in the other 40 counties of the country were engaged in 'manufacture'.[33] 'Retail trade and handicraft' was a much larger category than 'manufacture', by a factor of three nationally, and by a factor of six in the country excluding Lancashire and the West Riding.[34] The occupations under this head were all or almost all long-established forms of employment using traditional techniques of production in the main. The great bulk of the rapidly growing secondary and tertiary population, in other words, drew its livelihood from occupations which were already familiar in Tudor England. The ten largest sources of adult male employment in retail trade or handicraft in

---

[31] The collection of the occupational information for the 1831 census was carried out by the parish overseers. The definitions of the occupational categories in their instructions which were intended to determine the allocations which they made were quite brief. In the case of manufacture those to be included were 'males upwards of twenty years old – employed in manufacture or in making manufacturing machinery; but not including labourers, porters, messengers, etc.' while the comparable definition for retail trade and handicraft referred to those employed in 'retail trade or in handicrafts as masters, shopmen, journeymen, apprentices, or in any capacity requiring skill in the business' with the same exclusion of labourers, etc. *1831 Census*, Enumeration abstract, I, Preface, p. vi. However, what was intended to be included in retail trade and handicraft was made much clearer by appending a list of the 100 individual occupations which were supposed to occur most commonly, while the main manufacturing occupations in each county were listed at the end of the county statement. This further information sustains the interpretation of the difference between the two categories given in the main text.

[32] *1831 Census*. Enumeration abstract, II, Summary of England, pp. 832–3.

[33] See p. 89 above.

[34] There were 964,177 men aged 20 and over engaged in retail trade and handicraft compared with 314,106 in manufacture. Excluding Lancashire and the West Riding the totals were 817,989 and 141,920. Ibid.

descending order of size in 1831 were shoemakers, carpenters, tailors, publicans, shopkeepers, blacksmiths, masons, butchers, bricklayers, and bakers. These ten occupations jointly employed just over half a million men aged 20 and over (516,979) and between them they alone supported five men and their families for every three supported by 'manufacture' (i.e. those working in factories or engaged in proto-industrial activities). The total male labour force employed outside agriculture was 2,219,234: therefore almost a quarter of adult male non-agricultural employment was in the 10 occupations listed.[35] Of these occupations, all except that of shopkeeper and possibly bricklayer would have been widely found two centuries earlier.

The dominance of trades such as the ten quoted in providing employment outside agriculture; the fact that they represented forms of economic activity tied exclusively or dominantly to local demand; and their ubiquity, all suggest that increased purchasing power was a pervasive phenomenon. It is a pattern which, when combined with the knowledge that a roughly stationary agricultural labour force coped effectively with the food needs of a rapidly growing population, sits easily with the supposition that the striking divergence of England from the continental norm during the seventeenth and eighteenth centuries was largely a function of a distinctive surge in agricultural productivity. It is instructive in this regard that the ten occupations formed almost exactly the same fraction of total male employment in the rural counties as in the rest of the country, suggesting that the rise in the demand for the goods and services provided by retail trade and handicraft was very evenly spread.[36]

The altered balance between the primary population on the one hand and secondary and tertiary population on the other hand was to be found throughout the length and breadth of the country. The effect was to raise the population totals of settlements of all sizes, but rates of growth were not uniform in the several size categories. In small rural parishes growth was relatively modest and was largely confined to the trades which figured so prominently in the 1831 census returns. Even very small villages commonly had a resident carpenter, shoemaker, and tailor, and many had a variety of other basic trades and services, able to secure sufficient custom from the farming community, from one another, from the local parson, and, in some instances, from the households of any resident gentry, to make an adequate living. Occupations frequently found in predominantly rural parishes in addition to the ten listed above included miller, sawyer,

[35] *1831 Census*. Enumeration abstract, II, pp. 832–3, 1044–51.
[36] Tab. 4.2, pp. 92–3.

gardener, coachman, gamekeeper, painter, plumber and glazier, barber or hairdresser, and wheelwright.[37]

Moving further up the settlement hierarchy, rates of growth increase, though some long-established centres did not outpace the general rise in numbers in the early modern period.[38] But urban England as a whole was, of course, expanding very rapidly indeed. Port cities, such as Liverpool, Bristol, or Sunderland; new industrial centres, of which the two most outstanding examples were Manchester and Birmingham, but which included a large clutch of other towns, such as Leeds, Sheffield, Bolton, Stockport, Stoke, and Wolverhampton; and leisure centres, notably Bath and Brighton: these towns enjoyed strikingly high rates of increase. The combined population of Manchester, Birmingham, Leeds, and Sheffield, for example, was 70,000 in 1750 and 262,000 in 1801, a rate of growth of 2.6 per cent per annum.[39] London, however, which in the seventeenth century had grown far more quickly than other urban centres, settled back to a more sedate growth rate in the eighteenth century. It remained by far the largest city in the country, enjoying the full range of stimuli to further growth experienced elsewhere and in addition those of an imperial capital, but it ceased to display the disproportionately high growth rates of the previous century, expanding in step with national growth rather than well ahead of it. At all levels of the urban hierarchy the same rule normally held true: the bigger the settlement, the greater the variety of occupations to be found.

Explaining the changes which occurred

The basic assumption underlying much of the description and analysis embodied in this essay was set out in its opening paragraphs. Given that people will always ensure that they have an adequate supply of the

---

[37] This information is drawn from a study which is in progress based on the occupational information routinely recorded in Anglican baptism registers over the eight-year period 1813–20. Rose's Act of 1812 required this information to be recorded in the new printed registers which came into use under the provisions of the Act from the beginning of 1813. The data are drawn from a random sample of 300 registers used for this purpose. The county details in the 1831 census are also informative in this regard.

[38] For example, Exeter, King's Lynn, Chester, Cambridge, Worcester, Oxford, Colchester, and Ipswich, all in the upper echelons of urban England in the sixteenth century, grew collectively by 115 per cent between 1600 and 1800. At the former date their combined total population was 46,000; at the latter date 99,000. This increase was almost exactly in step with the national population total which rose from 4.16 to 8.67 million, or by 108 per cent: Wrigley, 'Urban growth', tab. 7.1, pp. 160–1; Mitchell, *British historical statistics*, ch. 1, tab. 7, pp. 26–9.

[39] Wrigley, 'Urban growth', tab. 7.1, pp. 160–1.

necessities of life before indulging in other expenditures, it seems safe to argue that a major proportional shift in the structure of the labour force, favouring secondary and tertiary employment at the expense of primary employment, must reflect a large improvement in the lot of the average consumer. This in turn can only be secured if the consumer, wearing a different hat as a producer, increases his productivity commensurately. In some industries the strength of the evidence of major gains in productivity per head during the quarter-millennium before about 1800 is plain. In agriculture, for example, the fact that a largely static workforce coped with the food needs of a greatly increased population leaves no room for doubt on this score.

The balance of evidence favours the view that access to the comforts of life and to some of its luxuries was widespread in the population as a whole, but this view is not shared universally, and there are a number of grounds on which it can be challenged. Since the direct evidence is not conclusive, it may be of interest to close by reviewing some of the difficulties which attend the argument advanced.

The first difficulty is well known and has attracted much attention. Almost half a century ago Phelps Brown and Hopkins, in a remarkable pioneering study, produced a real wage series which, while displaying striking secular fluctuations between the mid-sixteenth and early nineteenth centuries, showed no decided upward trend.[40] Their work does not suggest that there was a large enough rise purchasing power to have underwritten the sweeping changes in occupational structure which occurred. Having been at a very high level in the later fifteenth century, the index declined in the early decades of the sixteenth century and plunged thereafter. Using decadal averages, if the 1530s are taken as 100, the index falls to a nadir of 57 in the 1610s before rising to a high point in the 1730s at 107, but thereafter falling back again to no more than an average of 72 in the 1800s, largely because the impact of poor harvests could not readily be offset by increased imports during wartime and therefore food was costly. Only in the 1840s did the series exceed its 1730s level, reaching 108 in that decade.[41]

The violence of the secular fluctuations in the series is partly spurious so far as the experience of individual families was concerned. The price series used consisted of wholesale prices and Rappaport's work has

---

[40] Phelps Brown and Hopkins, 'Seven centuries of building wages' and 'Seven centuries of the prices of consumables'.

[41] Wrigley and Schofield, *Population history of England*, tab. A9.2, pp. 642–4. The accompanying text makes clear the assumptions which were used in deriving estimates of values in the PBH series for years which were missing in the original.

shown convincingly how strongly the swings in the series are damped if retail prices are used. The purchasing power of individual consumers did not fall by one half between the early sixteenth and the early seventeenth century, as the PBH series suggests. The fall was probably closer to a quarter than to a half.[42] The issue of long-term trend is more complex and has been the focus of much discussion. Those who find difficulty in accepting an absence of significant gain in household purchasing power during the early modern period can advance the following arguments. First, the PBH series, as its authors well knew, probably understates the rise in wages during the eighteenth century because its data are drawn from the agricultural south of England and therefore both the effect of rising wages in the northern industrial areas and the impact of their rapidly rising share in the national population are ignored.[43] Second, the index assumes, in effect, that adult male daily wages are a dependable guide to average earnings. If, however, the average number of days worked each year changed, or if the balance of earning power between men, women, and children altered, or if what was given in kind rather than in cash rose or fell, the match between the PBH series and the 'real' world would be affected.[44] The exploration in recent literature of the idea of an 'industrious' revolution as a prelude to the industrial revolution shows how it is possible to reconcile an absence of secular increase in male daily wages with a substantial rise in household purchasing power.[45]

The PBH series is therefore a fallible guide to trends in adult male annual earnings, and a still more fallible guide to the purchasing power of families. Moreover, if the focus of attention is switched from trends within England to a comparison between England and other countries, it is difficult to resist the conclusion that English consumers were unusually

---

[42] See the discussion and evidence presented in Rappaport, *Worlds within worlds*, pp. 144–53.

[43] The effect of taking into account the very different wage trends in the north of England in the eighteenth century is illustrated by the discussion in Wrigley and Schofield, *English population* history, pp. xx–xxii.

[44] There are also further grounds for disputing the authority of the PBH series as a guide to secular real wage trends. In addition to the problems created by the advent from time to time of new and ultimately important elements into the consumer price index, such as the potato, some major items of consumer expenditure which must be important at all times were not included for lack of an available data series. The most notable example under this head is the absence of a measure of the cost of accommodation. In addition, many of the price series which were employed were subject to lengthy gaps. All these problems were, of course, well known to Phelps Brown and Hopkins who were admirably candid about the deficiencies of their index.

[45] De Vries, 'The industrial revolution and the industrious revolution'; Voth, 'Time use in eighteenth-century London'.

favourably placed to acquire necessities and to purchase comforts by the end of the early modern period.[46]

No other scholar has been more active than Maddison in assembling comparative national economic data over long periods of time. He has taken a particular interest in deriving estimates of output per head for this purpose. Output per head and income per head are necessarily closely correlated. At first sight his work does not suggest large differences between England and advanced continental countries at the beginning of the nineteenth century. For example, his estimates of gross domestic product (GDP) per head in 1820 for France, the Netherlands, and the United Kingdom fall within quite a narrow range: that for France is $377, for the Netherlands $400, and for the United Kingdom $454 (all expressed in 1970 US dollars). But the UK figure includes Ireland and Maddison estimated Irish output per head at only half the British figure. Since Irish population was 32.6 per cent of the UK total in 1821, this implies that the British figure for GDP per head would be $542 rather than $454, or 36 per cent higher than the Dutch and 44 per cent higher than the French, rather than 14 and 20 per cent as suggested by a comparison using UK GDP estimates. Since Scottish output per head was lower than the English, a figure for England only would be still higher and the advantage over France and the Netherlands therefore still more pronounced.[47] Unless Maddison's work can be shown to be deeply flawed, therefore, the scale of the contrast between England and other European countries at the end of the early modern period suggests a substantially different structure of aggregate demand in England, and reinforces the likelihood of a distinctive prior history. If data for other European countries were available, the contrast would, in general, be still more pronounced.[48]

---

[46] It is worth noting that both Adam Smith and Malthus were convinced that the living standards of labourers had improved substantially since Elizabethan times: see, for example, A. Smith, *Wealth of nations*, I, p. 100; Malthus, *Principles of political economy*, pp. 181–8.

[47] Maddison, *Phases of capitalist development*, tab. 1.4, p. 8 and p. 167; Mitchell, *British historical statistics*, tab. 1.2, pp. 9–10.

[48] It should be noted that Maddison has produced a number of revised estimates since the early 1980s. In a more extended study these should be considered. In the main they imply a more marked difference between England and other countries in 1820 than that described in the main text since Maddison has accepted the arguments of Crafts that growth in England was slower in the later eighteenth and early nineteenth centuries than had earlier been supposed, which implies a higher level of output in, say, 1820 than in earlier estimates, since the mid nineteenth-century estimates are little changed. To balance this point it should also be noted, however, that it is probable that a higher proportion of the total output of goods and services in England went through the market and was therefore more readily mensurable than was the case in France or much of the rest of continental Europe in the early nineteenth century.

There are further grounds on which the argument of this essay can be challenged. For example, one might concede that there must have been a major increase in purchasing power to have provoked such a massive shift in occupational structure as took place in England, but put a different gloss on the change by arguing that the bulk of the population was no better provided for in Georgian than in Tudor times. Such a pattern was not unknown. In the countryside of southern England, for example, agricultural labourers derived little benefit from rising agricultural productivity, though it should not be overlooked that agriculture employed a declining share of the total population even in rural areas. Economic growth might have benefited only a relatively small minority. Even if the increase in purchasing power was chiefly enjoyed only by a small minority of the population, there might still conceivably have been a sufficient increase in the total demand for the products of secondary and tertiary industry to have caused a surge of employment in these industries. Put so starkly the argument is hardly persuasive but a less extreme version, focusing on the greatly increased prosperity of the middling groups in the population, has a respectable ancestry.[49]

Or again, England might have been experiencing at a later date a reorientation of her economy comparable to that which occurred in the Netherlands in the sixteenth and early seventeenth centuries. In this period the Netherlands became a major importer of some basic foodstuffs, grew heavily dependent upon international trade, and became the most urbanised country in Europe. Although developments in England did not in all respects parallel those in Holland since, for example, England remained largely self-sufficient in basic foodstuffs, and indeed was for a time a major exporter of grain,[50] nevertheless the rapid expansion in her trading links with the rest of the world might be held to account for a substantial part of the growth in employment outside agriculture. In principle, it might have been international rather than local demand which occasioned the rise in secondary and tertiary employment, though attempts to quantify the relative importance of home and foreign demand lend little support to this possibility.[51] And, of course, both of these reasons for doubting the thesis advanced earlier might have been operative simultaneously, reinforcing one another. A reorientation of the economy towards international markets and a marked shift in the distribution

---

[49] Eversley, 'The home market and economic growth'.

[50] See n.10 above on the first point; on the second, Deane and Cole, *British economic growth*, tab. 17, p. 65; also Ormrod, 'Dutch commercial and industrial decline'.

[51] See Cole, 'Factors in demand' and McCloskey, '1780–1860: a survey', pp. 253–8; also O'Brien 'European economic development', who reviews a wider but related issue.

of income towards elite groups, for example, might easily have run in parallel.

There are, therefore, grounds for hesitation about accepting the argument for a significant rise in the purchasing power of the average household in the early modern period. None should be dismissed out of hand. They may prove to require some shading of an explanation of the changing occupational structure of the country which depends principally on a substantial rise in real incomes spread widely through the population. But the evidence of the divergence of England from the continent in the seventeenth and eighteenth centuries seems incontrovertible and is most easily explained by the occurrence of major changes in the pattern of aggregate demand for goods and services arising from a widely based increase in purchasing power to match the occupational diversification and the changes in local and regional occupational characteristics which took place. There is much support for this interpretation from the evidence of developments other than those described in this essay, though space prevents their recounting at length here. The penetration of new products into more and more households; the increased sophistication of articles of attire and fabrics of all kinds; the proliferation of retail outlets for a widening range of products; a burgeoning network of credit; as well as evidence of extensive new domestic construction to much higher standards, all offer support in this connection.[52]

New and better empirical evidence would nevertheless be of great help in resolving some of the remaining paradoxes. It is important to make progress in this regard since the transition from an agrarian world of limited productive potential to a world of exponential economic growth at a relatively high annual rate has revolutionised so many aspects of individual and social life in the last two hundred years. There is therefore a compelling interest in achieving a better understanding of how this came about. The striking changes in the peopling of England which took place in this period were, of course, a reflection of the contemporary economic changes which were in train. Effecting a complete account of the history of the primary, secondary, and tertiary peopling of England in the seventeenth and eighteenth centuries would go far towards achieving a definitive economic and social history of the period. This is not an ambition likely to be fulfilled even over an extended timescale, but making fuller

---

[52] There is a large and varied literature to support these claims as, for example, Hoskins, 'The rebuilding of rural England'; Machin, 'The great rebuilding'; Weatherill, *Consumer behaviour and material culture*; Shammas, *The pre-industrial consumer*; Muldrew, *The economy of obligation*; Falkus and Jones, 'Urban improvement'; Spufford, *The great reclothing of rural England*; Harte, 'The economics of clothing'; Thirsk, *Economic policy and projects*; McKendrick, Brewer, and Plumb, eds., *The birth of a consumer society*.

use of the substantial, if scattered evidence about occupational structure and change, and further reflection on its best use, bids fair to inform and improve future discussion of the divergence of England, of that period in English history which was not only the herald of radical change in this country, but also a portent of the changes which have transformed the face of the globe as they fanned out from their point of origin.

Part III

The numbers game

12 Explaining the rise in marital fertility in England in the 'long' eighteenth century

The two most effective ways of converting parish register data into estimates of fertility, mortality, and nuptiality in the past are generalised inverse projection and family reconstitution. In general, they produce reassuringly similar results for England in the early modern period.[1] An earlier version of inverse projection, using aggregative tabulations from 404 parishes, was employed to generate the demographic estimates presented in the *Population history of England*, while, 16 years later, data from 26 parish reconstitutions formed the basis for the findings published in *English population history from family reconstitution*.[2] The more refined measures produced by family reconstitution have enabled some of the input parameters used in inverse projection to be specified more accurately, and this in turn has led to minor modifications in the results obtained from the aggregative data, but, whether the original or the modified parameters are used, comparison of the output from the two methods suggests that both yield the same 'big picture'.[3]

Nevertheless, reconstitution has brought to light many previously unknown or obscure features of English population history, some of which are simultaneously illuminating and puzzling: illuminating because they enforce a revision of the received wisdom; puzzling because, although the existence of an unexpected pattern can be demonstrated, its explanation

I am indebted to an anonymous referee acting on behalf of the *Economic History Review* for a number of acute and helpful suggestions, almost all of which I have taken on board.

[1] Wrigley *et al.*, *English population history*, ch. 8.
[2] Ibid., ch. 2.
[3] The most significant alteration to the input data used in the *Population history of England* was a reduction in the estimated totals of births and deaths in the late eighteenth and early nineteenth centuries. This change was made in view of the new reconstitution-based evidence about mortality trends in the early decades of the nineteenth century which suggested that mortality was worsening during this period rather than remaining broadly unchanged as had previously been supposed. This in turn implied that the birth cohorts of the period calculated by reverse surviving certain age group totals of the 1821 and 1841 censuses were to be reduced from the totals estimated in the *Population history of England*, and fewer births also implied fewer deaths given unchanging totals of intercensal increase.

is unclear. The bulk of this essay is devoted to a possible explanation of one of the new findings of reconstitution, the rise in marital fertility which took place during the eighteenth century, for which no satisfactory explanation was offered in *English population history*. In a concluding section, the possible links between economic circumstances and population growth are discussed.

The rise in marital fertility

The age-specific marital fertility rate is widely regarded as the most convenient measure for the study of fertility within marriage, and is readily calculable from reconstitution data. However, the most authoritative, if cruder guide to fertility trends in early modern England is the mean birth interval rather than the age-specific marital fertility rate because it enables a far larger data base to be employed. Family reconstitution forms which lack both the date of birth of the wife and the date of the marriage can still yield useful data on birth intervals, whereas both classes of information are a *sine qua non* for deriving age-specific fertility rates.[4] Used with discretion, birth interval data can prove a reliable indication of fertility trends.

Table 12.1 sets out mean birth intervals for 30-year periods, while figure 12.1 plots decennial data. Between the 30-year period 1640–69, when birth intervals were at their longest during the parish register era, and the period 1790–1819, when they were at their shortest, the mean birth interval in England fell by more than 8 per cent from 33.3 to 30.5 months. The more volatile decennial series fell from a maximum of 33.6 months in 1660–9 to 29.9 months in 1810–9, or by about 11 per cent.[5]

In table 12.1 parity 0 birth intervals were excluded because the interval from marriage to first birth is much shorter than later intervals.[6] Also excluded were birth intervals following an infant death. Such intervals were about 8 months shorter on average than was the case when the earlier child of the pair survived the first year.[7] There were changes in the relative frequency of both these types of birth interval, which would have distorted the measurement of fertility change over time if they had not been excluded. Several other types of birth interval, which have not

---

[4] For a discussion of the use of birth interval data in measuring fertility trends and their relationship to conventional age-specific fertility rates, Wrigley *et al.*, *English population history*, pp. 430–57.

[5] Ibid., tab. 7.36, p. 447

[6] Indeed, strictly speaking, the parity 0 interval should perhaps not be regarded as a birth interval at all.

[7] Wrigley *et al.*, *English population history*, tab.7.35, pp. 438–9.

Table 12.1 *Mean birth intervals (months), 1580–1837: all parities except 0;*
earlier child of pair survives infancy

Date	Interval	Date	Interval	Date	Interval
1580–1609	32.58	1660–89	32.51	1740–69	31.33
1590–1619	32.79	1670–99	32.11	1750–79	30.85
1600–29	32.36	1680–1709	31.84	1760–89	30.72
1610–39	32.58	1690–1719	31.61	1770–99	30.62
1620–49	32.72	1700–29	31.69	1780–1809	30.85
1630–59	32.90	1710–39	31.65	1790–1819	30.54
1640–69	33.27	1720–49	31.93	1800–37	30.57
1650–79	32.92	1730–59	31.44		

Source: Wrigley *et al.*, *English population history*, tab. 7.36, p. 447.

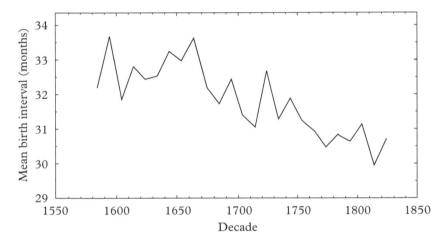

Figure 12.1. *Decennial mean birth intervals, England 1580–9 to 1820–37*
Source: Wrigley *et al.*, *English population history*, tab. 7.36, p. 447.

been excluded, might also in principle have introduced distortions into
the measurement of fertility change. Extensive testing of other possible
sources of distortion, however, suggested that it was unnecessary to introduce any other exclusions.[8]

A change in fertility on the scale suggested by table 12.1 and figure
12.1 will have a significant impact on the rate of population growth. In a
community in which the crude birth rate was 30 per 1,000 and the crude
death rate 25 per 1,000, for example, the resulting growth rate of 0.5 per

[8] Ibid., pp. 430–43.

cent per annum would cause an increase in population of 65 per cent over a period of a century. *Ceteris paribus*, if the birth interval were then to fall by 10 per cent, the crude birth rate would rise to 33 per 1,000, causing the growth rate to rise to 0.8 per cent per annum, which would give rise to an increase of 122 per cent in a century, almost twice the previous figure. Since the change in marital fertility was substantial, it is tempting to try to identify its cause.

So many examples of the importance of the average length of breast-feeding in influencing the birth interval have accumulated in recent decades that it is understandable that a change in breastfeeding prac-tice should attract initial attention as an explanation.[9] Relatively minor changes in the length or intensity of breastfeeding might account for a reduction of 3 months in the mean birth interval, where only dramatic changes in other components of the birth interval could have a compara-ble effect. For example, a reduction in the average length of breastfeeding from, say, 18 months to 12 months would probably more than suffice to reduce birth intervals by the required amount.[10] To produce the same effect very marked changes in, say, the frequency of coitus would be re-quired.[11]

It appears probable, however, that it is unnecessary to suppose that there was any significant change in breastfeeding practice or in such vari-ables as the frequency of coitus. A satisfactory explanation is to be found in the changing incidence of stillbirth between the later seventeenth and the early nineteenth century.[12] To substantiate this claim, however, in-volves the use of indirect if persuasive evidence, since stillbirths were very rarely recorded in a consistent and systematic fashion during the three centuries in which the Anglican parish registers are the prime source of information about fertility, mortality, and nuptiality.[13] The argument depends upon the plausibility of regarding mortality early in the first year of life as a reliable indicator of late foetal mortality. In particular, it presupposes that much can be learnt from trends in endogenous infant

---

[9] For a brief, general discussion of this question, see Knodel, 'Breast feeding and pop-ulation growth'. See also fuller discussions of the same issue in Knodel, *Demographic behavior in the past*, app. F; and in Knodel and van de Walle, 'Breastfeeding, fertility, and infant mortality'.

[10] There is a discussion of possible changes in breastfeeding practice and their impact on birth intervals in Wrigley *et al.*, *English population history*, pp. 445–6.

[11] Leridon, *Human fertility*, tab. 5.4, p. 89 and pp. 41–5.

[12] I am greatly indebted to Nicky Hart when focusing on the importance of stillbirth as a potential explanation of changes in the level of observed fertility. See, for example, Hart, 'Famine, maternal nutrition and infant mortality'.

[13] Thomas Cromwell instituted parochial registration of weddings, christenings, and burials in 1538 by means of royal injunctions. The Registrar General began to collect and publish national returns of births, deaths, and marriages from 1837 onwards.

Table 12.2 *Infant mortality of legitimate children,*
England 1580–1837 (rates per 1,000 live-born)

Date	Endogenous	Exogenous	Total
1580–99	77.6	93.1	170.7
1600–24	88.5	76.7	165.2
1625–49	80.0	73.3	153.3
1650–74	87.3	79.4	166.7
1675–99	88.3	97.1	185.4
1700–24	84.0	106.7	190.7
1725–49	80.5	110.3	190.8
1750–74	61.3	101.5	162.8
1775–99	52.6	104.1	156.7
1800–24	41.0	95.0	136.0
1825–37	33.3	110.8	144.1

Source: Wrigley *et al.*, *English population history*, tabs. 6.1 and
6.4, pp. 215 and 226.

mortality. All endogenous mortality takes place soon after birth and there
are good reasons to suppose that trends in endogenous infant mortality
and in the stillbirth rate were similar.

Endogenous and exogenous infant mortality in England in the early modern period

Table 12.2 shows that infant mortality in England reached a peak in the
first half of the eighteenth century. Legitimate infant mortality was then
191 per 1,000, well above the level prevailing in the early seventeenth
century and much higher also than in the early nineteenth century, when
it averaged about 140 per 1,000.[14] However, when infant mortality is
divided into its two components, endogenous and exogenous mortality,
the trends in the two rates do not mirror that of the combined rate.

Exogenous mortality, as the adjective suggests, includes all deaths attributable to infection or to such causes as accident or maltreatment,
while endogenous mortality refers to deaths brought about by the trauma
of birth, inherited genetic defects, or lack of independent viability caused,

[14] Overall infant mortality, including both legitimate and illegitimate births, was at a somewhat higher level than the rate for legitimate mortality alone. For example, in 1725–49
the overall rate was 196.4 per 1,000 compared to the legitimate rate of 190.8, while
in 1825–37 the two rates were 151.7 and 144.1 per 1,000 respectively. Wrigley *et al.*,
English population history, tab. 6.2, p. 219.

for example, by prematurity. The two types of cause can be roughly distinguished, where suitable age at death information is available, by a method pioneered by Bourgeois-Pichat.[15] The chief attraction of the technique is that it enables some inferences about causes of death to be made, even in the absence of any direct information under this head.

The technique depends upon the fact that, using a suitable logarithmic transform, the cumulative total of deaths within the first year of life, plotted at, say, monthly intervals, often conforms closely to a straight line, though this is not invariably the case.[16] A best fit regression line, based on the plotted points, when projected to the vertical axis, yields an estimate of the level of endogenous infant mortality. The logic underlying this procedure is that all mortality after the end of the first month of life is exogenous. If the regression line captures the cumulative impact of exogenous mortality from the first month onwards, then its extension back to the vertical axis should enable exogenous mortality to be distinguished from endogenous mortality within the first month.

Since endogenous infant mortality is normally a high proportion of all first month mortality, trends in endogenous infant mortality and neonatal mortality (mortality in the first month of life) are normally very similar. Endogenous infant mortality has been widely used as a measure by historical demographers, but less frequently by others. Therefore, neonatal mortality will often be used as an alternative measure to endogenous mortality in subsequent discussion when modern data are invoked.

Table 12.2 shows that a substantial rise in exogenous mortality was the reason for the increase in infant mortality in the seventeenth century, but that after 1700 there was no further significant change in this component of infant mortality during the remainder of the parish register period. Endogenous mortality shows a radically different pattern of change over time. Throughout the whole period 1580 to 1750 it stood at a very high level, averaging 84 per 1,000 live births, with only minor changes over time. After 1750 it fell steeply to well under half the level of the seventeenth century plateau until in 1825–37 it was only 33 per 1,000. The Registrar General did not publish a sufficiently detailed breakdown of infant mortality in the early decades of civil registration to enable the endogenous rate to be calculated routinely in the period immediately after the end of the parish register era, though the relevant information was published for a few years in the 1840s. However, in the supplement to his twenty-fifth *Annual report*, he published a breakdown of mortality within the first year of life for England and Wales for the period covered by the

[15] Bourgeois-Pichat, 'La mesure de la mortalité infantile'.
[16] See, for example, Wrigley *et al.*, *English population history*, figs. 6.3, 6.5, and 6.6, pp. 227, 232, and 235 and the associated discussion.

third English life table, 1838–54, after correcting for deficiencies in the recording of births and deaths in the period. This yields an estimated endogenous infant mortality rate of 28 per 1,000, agreeing closely with the estimates for the individual years in the 1840s for which the endogenous rate can be calculated.[17] Thus the estimates derived from ecclesiastical sources and those from civil registration provide very similar results over the period when they can best be compared.

Although exogenous and endogenous infant mortality displayed such a striking contrast in their trends over time, there is nothing intrinsically anomalous about this, since the causes underlying the two types of infant death were very different. In the case of the former, sanitary conditions, the treatment of sewage and household waste, domestic heating, the season of the year in which the birth occurred, the type and quality of nutrition, and the nature and virulence of locally prevalent diseases all influenced the level and trend of mortality. In the case of the latter, the health and nutritional status of the mother were of crucial importance, though circumstances such as delivery skills and childbed practices may also have been important.

Susceptibility to death very early in life is powerfully influenced by birth weight, and this in turn is chiefly a function of maternal nutrition both during pregnancy itself and, more generally, over the whole of the mother's life-span. Indeed, a mother's own birth weight will have been affected by *her* mother's health, and this may affect her subsequent vitality, so that the life chances of a new-born infant will be influenced by the prior nutritional history of the maternal line over several decades.[18] Levels of endogenous infant mortality are therefore likely to be sensitive to the nutritional circumstances of the community cumulatively over a long period of time.

In some populations breastfeeding practice may complicate the attempt to distinguish between exogenous and endogenous deaths, since the mortality associated with weaning may come to be included in either category, when using the method of Bourgeois-Pichat. In principle such mortality is exogenous, since infectious ailments, taking advantage of the increased exposure to disease caused by weaning, are the principal reason for the increase in mortality which weaning provokes. In a population where weaning occurs at birth, as, for example, in parts of Bavaria in the nineteenth century, a proportion of first month mortality will be due to this custom but will serve to boost the level of endogenous mortality, given

[17] Fig. 12.3 below.
[18] See, for example, Rosso and Cramoy, 'Nutrition and pregnancy'.

the method by which it is calculated as a residual.[19] Where breastfeeding was widely practised and prolonged, which was the case in early modern England,[20] no problem arises since any mortality associated with the cessation of breastfeeding will occur long after the end of the first month of life.

It is clear from table 12.2 that, but for the fall in its endogenous component, infant mortality in England would not have fallen from the relatively high level which prevailed in the first half of the eighteenth century. In the absence of such a fall, population growth would have been appreciably slower.[21] The fall in endogenous infant mortality, though it increased the rate of population growth, did not, of course, directly affect the birth rate. But it was almost certainly accompanied by a comparable fall in another type of mortality occurring close to birth which did raise fertility. Unlike a fall in endogenous infant mortality, a fall in the stillbirth rate causes a change in the conventional (live) birth rate, since if fewer children die in the last weeks before birth, the average interval between births will fall, causing a rise in the birth rate.

Stillbirths and early infant deaths

Stillbirths, also sometimes termed late foetal mortality, consist, by modern convention, of foetal deaths occurring later than the 28th completed week of pregnancy. The expectation of a close tie between stillbirths and endogenous infant mortality is reflected in the widespread use of the concept of perinatal mortality in measuring the loss of life close to birth. The perinatal mortality rate is obtained by combining all stillbirths with first week infant mortality, and expressing the combined total of all such deaths as a rate per 1,000 total births (that is, live births plus stillbirths).

Stillbirths were recorded only sporadically in Anglican parish registers, and were not recorded by the Registrar General until 1927. In England, therefore, until the recent past, late foetal mortality was an aspect of the demographic life of the country which largely escaped direct measurement, and which has excited little comment. But its importance should

---

[19] For information about weaning at birth in Bavaria see Knodel, *Demographic behavior in the past*, app. F; and Knodel and van de Walle, 'Breastfeeding, fertility, and infant mortality'.

[20] The evidence for this is to be found in Wrigley *et al.*, *English population history*, pp. 489–92.

[21] A fall of about 50 per 1,000 in early infant mortality, such as took place in England between the early eighteenth and the early nineteenth century, is equivalent to a rise of 5 per cent in the crude birth rate. Assuming a crude birth rate of 30 per 1,000, for example, a fall in infant mortality on this scale is equivalent to a rise in the birth rate, and therefore in the rate of population increase of 1.5 per 1,000 p.a.

not be overlooked for this reason. When the Registrar General began to record stillbirths in the late 1920s, they constituted about 4 per cent of the total of all births both live and still, and remained close to this level throughout the balance of the interwar period. Evidently, if 1 in 25 of all foetuses living at the end of the 28th week of pregnancy die before birth, any major change in the stillbirth rate will have a significant impact on the live birth rate. The higher the stillbirth rate, the greater the 'leverage' upon the live birth rate associated with a given percentage change in the stillbirth rate.

Both general considerations and such empirical information as can be marshalled suggest strongly that the late foetal death rate and mortality very early in life normally moved in sympathy with one another in the past. It is widely accepted that the same nutritional factors which cause a high proportion of babies to be born under weight, and therefore subject to a much increased danger of early death, will also cause stillbirths to be common, and therefore that improvements in nutrition which induce a fall in one rate may confidently be expected to reduce the other also, while a deterioration in nutrition may be expected to have an opposite effect.[22] There is much empirical evidence from developing societies in the twentieth century that stillbirth rates and neonatal mortality are closely linked.[23]

Perinatal mortality increases exponentially as a function of birthweight moving downwards from the lower end of the optimum birthweight range of 3,500–3,900 grams. The extent of the contrast in perinatal mortality between optimal birthweight and low birthweight babies is massive. For example, the stillbirth rate at an average birthweight of 2,500 grams, conventionally regarded as marking 'low birthweight', may be between 10 and 30 times higher than at an average birthweight of 3,500 grams, yet birthweights even lower than 2,500 grams may be common in communities in which serious malnutrition is rife.[24] But the proportion of all babies

[22] Kline, Stein, and Susser, for example, in summarising a large body of empirical studies, remark, 'Low birth weight certainly contributes in an important way to stillbirth rates and to neonatal rates all over the world. In less developed countries... birth weight predicts perinatal mortality as it does in developed countries. Therefore we have reason to think that low birth weight, as a final common pathway to perinatal mortality, would account for better than 90 per cent of the variance in less developed countries, as it does in New York.' Kline, Stein, and Susser, *Conception to birth*, p. 253. See also Tafari, 'Low birthweight'; and Ward, *Birth weight and economic growth*.

[23] Indeed, the reason for employing the concept of perinatal mortality is the close presumptive connection between foetal mortality after the end of the twenty-eighth week of pregnancy and deaths in the first postnatal week which in combination connote perinatal mortality.

[24] Rosso and Cramoy consider that within the weight range between 2,500 and 3,500 grams a difference of 200 grams equates with a doubling of perinatal mortality, suggesting that

born weighing less than 2,500 grams is very variable. In rich, healthy countries in the later twentieth century the proportion may be less than 5 per cent but in poor communities where deprivation is widespread, such as Guatemala or Bombay, it may exceed 40 per cent. Moreover, low birthweight babies who are carried to term are far commoner in impoverished countries, where the proportion may exceed four-fifths of all low birthweight babies, than in wealthy countries, where it is normally less than one half.[25] This is a further unfavourable circumstance tending differentially to increase perinatal mortality where nutrition is poor. Historical data about birthweight are lacking, in general, before the nineteenth century, but it is highly probable that birthweight distributions would have resembled those in Third World countries in the recent past in many instances.

Because of its nature, which in principle excludes deaths from infection and similar 'external' causes, endogenous infant mortality, like neonatal mortality, may be expected to be closely linked to the stillbirth rate. Assuming that the stillbirth rate tended to fluctuate in sympathy with the endogenous mortality rate, this has important implications for the explanation of fertility trends in the past. The spectacular fall in endogenous infant mortality in eighteenth-century England would imply a parallel fall in stillbirths, and a matching rise in the number of live births.

Before considering this suggestion further, it is appropriate to consider some of the historical evidence available to test the assertion that trends in stillbirths and early infant mortality tended to move in parallel with one another. It was common practice in Scandinavian countries to record stillbirths as well as live births in parish registers, and from varying dates this information formed part of the consolidated returns tabulated and published by the state. For example, in Sweden a national stillbirth series is available from 1751.[26] In due course, infant mortality was made the subject of separate annual tabulations when interest moved beyond

a baby born at the low end of the range might experience 30 times as high a risk of death in the perinatal period as one weighing 3,500 grams; Rosso and Cramoy, 'Nutrition and pregnancy', pp. 184–5. Alternatively, Ward suggests that each reduction of 100 grams in average birthweight below the optimum level is associated with a rise of 25 per cent in the stillbirth rate, which implies a rate at 2,500 grams about 10 times greater than at 3,500 grams: Ward, *Birth weight and economic growth*, p. 10. On either rule of thumb the very marked potential significance of apparently minor changes in mean birthweight needs no emphasis.

[25] Kline, Stein, and Susser, *Conception to birth*, pp. 246–7. The very much higher perinatal mortality rate of twins appears to be essentially a function of their birthweight. Indeed, controlling for birthweight, the singleton rate is the higher of the two, probably because at equal weights twins have a higher gestational age: D. M. Campbell and MacGillivray, 'Outcome of twin pregnancies', tab. 10.10, p. 192.

[26] Basic demographic statistics were collected by the Swedish state from 1749 onwards. The stillbirth data from 1751 onwards are conveniently reproduced in *Historisk statistik för*

the simple totals of deaths, though the subdivision of infant mortality came much later, so that first week or first month mortality cannot be separately identified until long after overall infant rates were published. Data for stillbirths and early infant mortality are, however, available for Norway from a relatively early date and are set out in table 12.3 and figure 12.2. During the period 1876 to 1965 there was a close correspondence in both level and trend between first month mortality and the stillbirth rate, even though the absolute rate in both cases fell steeply to only one-third of its initial level.

In spite of this close parallelism, it would be incautious to assume that the two rates were necessarily closely related. Table 12.3 also shows very clearly that mortality rates *within* the first month did not move uniformly. First day mortality showed no decisive trend until the last 15 years of the period covered in the table, nor did the first week rate fall much before 1940, but the rate for the balance of the first month, between the beginning of the second week and the end of the fourth week, compensated for the sluggish movement in the first week, falling by 90 per cent over the period as a whole, and beginning its fall much earlier, about 1880. Such diversity of behaviour suggests that any link between the overall first month mortality and the stillbirth rate may not arise from a common cause. It is not even the case that a close agreement in trend between the stillbirth and first week neonatal rates, which together make up perinatal mortality, is invariably to be found, though Vallgårda demonstrates a similarity in the movements of the two rates in Sweden and Denmark from 1920 onwards, and indeed this was true of Norway if the decades before 1930 are ignored. The Norwegian data, however, suggest caution in assuming that the same held true in earlier periods.[27]

Furthermore, although an exact definition of what is meant by a stillbirth has been generally agreed for much of the twentieth century, the term had a less precise meaning in earlier times. This inevitably means both that stillbirth rates from different sources may not be comparable with one another and that the interpretation of rates calculated from the same source for different periods may also present problems.

The reality of this difficulty can be illustrated from the *Statistical review of England and Wales for 1927*. This was the first occasion on which the

Sverige, del. I, Befolking 1720–1967, tabs. 37 and 38, pp. 108–9. Stillbirths were recorded in the parish registers from an earlier date but such information was not collated and published centrally until 1749. The history of the recording of demographic information in Sweden and of the action of the state in collecting, tabulating, and publishing such data are summarised in Hofsten and Lundström, *Swedish population history*, app. 1, esp. pp. 150–9.

[27] Vallgårda, 'Trends in perinatal death rates', fig. 2, p. 204; for Norway see tab. 12.3.

Table 12.3 Stillbirth and infant mortality rates, Norway 1876–1965 (rates per 1,000 live births)

Date	(1) Stillbirths	Infant mortality				1881–90 = 100	
		(2) 0–27 days	(3) 0 days	(4) 0–6 days	(5) 7–27 days	(6) Stillbirths	(7) Infant mortality 0–27 days
1876–80	35.7	35.2	7.9	16.7	18.5	121	104
1881–90	29.4	33.7	8.4	16.9	16.8	100	100
1891–1900	26.5	34.3	8.8	17.3	17.0	90	102
1901–10	23.8	27.2	7.8	15.0	12.2	81	81
1911–20	22.7	25.6	7.4	15.3	10.3	77	76
1921–30	23.6	23.3	7.5	15.6	7.7	80	69
1931–40	24.3	21.9	8.3	16.2	5.8	83	65
1941–50	19.2	17.2	7.2	12.7	4.6	65	51
1951–60	15.0	12.8	5.9	10.7	2.1	51	38
1961–5	12.5	12.0	5.7	10.2	1.8	43	36

Source: Norges offisielle statistikk, XII, tabs. 20 and 30, pp. 44–7 and 54.

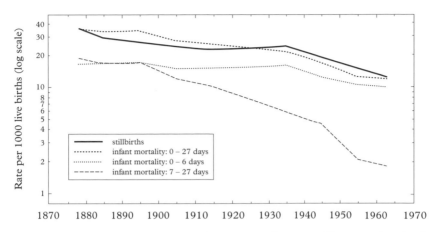

Figure 12.2. *Stillbirth and infant mortality rates, Norway 1876–1965*
Source: *Norges offisielle statistikk*, XII, tabs. 20 and 30, pp. 44–7 and54.

Registrar General published a return of stillbirths. In the second half of 1927, the first period covered by the new return, the rate was 40 per 1,000, a level which was maintained with only insignificant variation for the next decade. In introducing the new series, however, the Registrar General noted that under the Notification of Births (Extension) Act of 1915 it had become compulsory to notify both live and stillbirths to the local Medical Officer of Health, and that the Chief Medical Officer of Health had made annual returns for each year from 1918 to 1926, which recorded national rates in the range 30 to 33 per 1,000, a rate about a quarter lower than the rate reported under the provisions of the Births and Deaths Registration Act of 1926, even though in principle the two exercises should have yielded similar rates.

Defining the end of the period during which a dead foetus was treated as a stillbirth might involve as much imprecision as defining its beginning. In Catholic countries, for example, the boundary between a stillbirth and an early infant death was blurred in the period before civil registration by the ecclesiastical practice of baptising a limb of a child as it first appeared if the delivery was difficult. This inflated the apparent level of infant mortality by causing children, many of whom proved to be stillborn, to be recorded indistinguishably from live-born children who died very soon after birth.[28] At the other extreme, after the beginning of civil registration,

---

[28] Blayo has provided estimates of the proportion of all deaths within the first month of life which were 'ondoyés decédés' for each decade from 1740–9 to 1820–9; Blayo, 'La mortalité en France', tab. 5, p. 130.

for many years any child dying before the registration of the birth was designated as a stillbirth in Belgium and France, while in Spain all live-born
children dying within twenty-four hours of birth were registered as stillbirths.[29] Published statistics concerning the stillbirth rate are therefore
subject to significant margins of error in many cases. It is probable, for
example, that the rise in the Swedish stillbirth rate from 24.7 per 1,000
in 1811–20 to 32.7 per 1,000 in 1861–70, a rise of almost one-third, was
due to better registration rather than to an increase in the true incidence
of stillbirths, especially as infant mortality fell markedly over the same
period from 183 per 1,000 to 139 per 1,000, a fall of almost a quarter.[30]
A rise in the stillbirth rate during the early middle decades of the nineteenth century has also been observed in Germany and France, and in
both cases there is persuasive evidence that the rise was not genuine.[31]

To support evidence of similarity in trend between early infant mortality and stillbirth rates drawn from time series data, there are many
examples of cross-sectional data which encourage the belief that the two
rates were normally closely linked, thus further underwriting the view that
it would be surprising, in the circumstances of pre-industrial societies, if
a rise or fall in one rate were not matched by a similar change in the other.
For example, table 12.4 shows the stillbirth and neonatal death rates in
county Durham in 1930. In that year the endogenous infant death rate in
England was still at much the same level as it had been a century earlier,[32]
and it is therefore likely that the patterns visible in 1930 were similar to
those in the mid-nineteenth century. The table shows the two rates by
birth order. The neonatal rate is always higher for first children (parity 0)
than for other low parity births. It is usually lowest for second children
(parity 1), and thereafter rises with parity. In this table, surprisingly, the
lowest neonatal rate is found among parity 2, rather than among parity
1, children. The stillbirth rate displays the expected pattern. In general,
there is an impressive similarity in the behaviour of the two rates by parity,
both in level and trend. With larger numbers the symmetry would, in all
probability, be even clearer.[33]

---

[29] United Nations, *Foetal, infant and early childhood mortality*, p. 6. In each country, however,
the situation was complex and apt to change over time. For example, for France and
Belgium, see van de Walle, *Female population of France*, pp. 47–9.

[30] *Historisk statistik för Sverige*, I, tabs. 38 and 41, pp. 109 and 115–6.

[31] Knodel, *The decline of fertility in Germany*, tab. 1.6, p. 26 and accompanying text; van de
Walle, *Female population of France*, tab. 2.5, p. 50 and accompanying text.

[32] See below fig. 12.3.

[33] The relationship between parity and infant mortality is a notoriously complex one in
which, among other factors, maternal age and sibship size must be taken into account,
and endogenous and exogenous mortality distinguished. See, for example, Knodel and
Hermalin, 'Effects of birth rank'.

Table 12.4 *Stillbirth and neonatal mortality rates by parity, Co. Durham 1930 (rates per 1,000 total births)*

Parity	Number of births	Stillbirth rate	Neonatal mortality rate
0	4,866	43.2	39.5
1	3,305	25.7	33.9
2	2,359	31.8	28.4
3	1,733	34.6	35.2
4	1,243	40.2	34.6
5	927	48.5	58.3
6	684	68.7	67.2
7	470	70.2	74.5
8	332	39.1	69.3
9	230	56.5	69.5
10	139	64.8	79.2
11	91	77.0	66.0
12	60	50.0	100.0
13 and over	61	98.3	115.0

Source: Burns, *Infant and maternal mortality*, tab. 4, p. 76.

Trends in the stillbirth rate over time

Fortified by the evidence that neonatal infant mortality (and its close equivalent, endogenous infant mortality) on the one hand, and the stillbirth rate on the other, normally moved together, we may now turn to the estimation of stillbirth rates from the mid-seventeenth century onwards, and therefore also to the estimation of the impact of these changes on live birth rates.

English civil registration data for the twentieth century provide a background to the estimation of stillbirth rates in earlier periods. Table 12.5 shows rates within the first year of life from 1906 onwards, and also the endogenous and exogenous rates which these data imply. The endogenous rates were obtained by using best fit quadratic regressions derived from the cumulative rates at intervals during the first year of life, as may be seen in figure 12.3, where endogenous rates for the twentieth century are displayed, together with those for 1838–54, and for a variety of earlier periods using reconstitution data. The endogenous rate is measured as the point at which the regression line cuts the vertical axis.

During the brief period for which there are national stillbirth rates as well as endogenous infant mortality rates for England and Wales, they follow a very similar course. The ratio of the former to the latter for the five decades for which both exist was 1.65, 1.75, 1.66, 1.56, and

Table 12.5 *Mortality rates within the first year of life, endogenous and exogenous infant mortality, and stillbirth rates; England and Wales 1906–1970 (rates per 1,000 live births, but stillbirth rates per 1,000 total births)*

| Date | Months | | | | | Endogenous | Exogenous | Stillbirths |
	0	1–2	3–5	6–11	0–11			
1906–10	40.2	22.8	22.0	32.1	117.1	23.4	93.7	
1911–20	38.0	18.3	17.1	26.4	99.8	25.1	74.7	
1921–30	32.6	11.8	10.4	16.5	71.3	24.4	46.9	40.3[a]
1931–40	30.3	9.4	8.1	10.8	58.6	22.8	35.8	39.8
1941–50	23.5	7.4	6.4	5.8	43.1	16.4	26.7	27.3
1951–60	17.1	3.0	2.5	2.2	24.8	14.2	10.6	22.2
1961–70	13.3	2.5	2.1	1.6	19.5	10.8	8.7	15.8

Note: [a] 1928–30.
Sources: Registrar General's statistical review of England and Wales 1960, III, Commentary, tab. LII, p. 113; *Registrar General's statistical review of England and Wales 1971*, I, Medical, tab. 24, supp., p. 396.

1.46 respectively, while the comparable ratio to the neonatal rate was 1.24, 1.31, 1.16, 1.30, and 1.19 respectively (table 12.5). Comparison of England and Wales with Norway (table 12.3) reveals marked similarities. Norwegian rates were always lower than English rates but the change over time in the two countries was similar, as was the ratio of the stillbirth rate to the neonatal rate. For the five time periods from 1921 onwards, shown in table 12.3, the Norwegian ratios were 1.01, 1.11, 1.12, 1.17, and 1.04 respectively. Earlier, however, the Norwegian ratio had normally been below unity, a point to be borne in mind when considering England in the nineteenth century or earlier.

The endogenous infant mortality rate declined only slightly over the century before the 1930s. In 1825–37, at the end of the period during which the parish registers are the sole source of information, it was 33 per 1,000. In 1838–54 it was 28 per 1,000; and from 1906–10 until the decade 1931–40 it averaged 24 per 1,000. Only thereafter was there a sharp and sustained fall. The comparative constancy of the endogenous infant mortality rate for at least a century until the 1930s is striking in view of the marked fall in the exogenous infant mortality which was taking place. Between 1906–10 and 1931–40, for example, infant mortality as a whole fell by one half and exogenous infant mortality much more sharply, from 93.7 to 35.8 per 1,000, a fall of 62 per cent, but the endogenous rate showed no clear change.

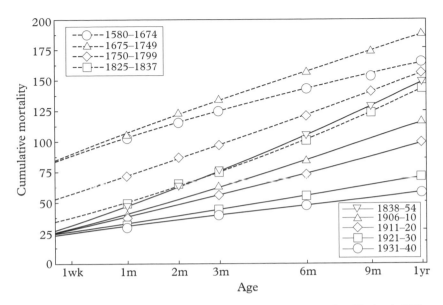

Figure 12.3. *Endogenous and exogenous infant mortality, England 1580–1940* (per 1,000 live-born)
Note: The infant mortality data for the parish register period (1580–1837) refer to legitimate births only. The rates would be somewhat higher for all births.
Sources: Wrigley et al., English population history, tab. 6.4, p. 226; 1838–54; *Supplement to the twenty-fifth annual report of Registrar General*, p. vii; 1906–40:*Registrar General's statistical review of England and Wales 1960*, III, Commentary, tab. LII, p. 113; *Registrar General's statistical review of England and Wales 1971*, I, Medical, tab. 24, supp., p. 396

During the first dozen years of stillbirth registration the stillbirth rate was always close to 40 per 1,000. Assuming a constant relationship between endogenous infant mortality and stillbirths, this would suggest that the stillbirth rate in England in the mid-nineteenth century was also approximately 40 per 1,000, or a little higher, since endogenous infant mortality was broadly stable, if with a slight and uncertain tendency to decline over time. The belief that this is a plausible assumption is strengthened by such estimates of English stillbirth rates as are available for the century before the inception of national stillbirth registration in 1927. For example, the stillbirth data from 1890 compiled by a Scottish physician, Robert Rentoul, which were subsequently printed in a Parliamentary Paper have recently been reworked by Mooney who arrives at an estimated national stillbirth rate of 41.8 per 1,000 total births. Using the same source Glass had earlier inferred a rate of 44.8 per 1,000.[34] Another fragment of evidence which also tends to confirm a rate of this order of magnitude may be found in the remarkable compilation of data derived from letters from working-class women published in 1915 by Margaret Llewelyn Davies. The letters were written by married women all of whom were or had been officials of the Women's Co-operative Guild and referred to their experience over the past quarter century. A total of 348 women replied in full to the questionnaire which they had been invited to complete. Between them they had borne 1,348 live-born children, with 83 stillbirths and 218 miscarriages.[35] In all 59 women had suffered one or more stillbirths. The stillbirths represent a rate of 58 per 1,000 total births. This is a higher rate than the supposed national rate at the time, but, although Davies is careful to stress that her respondents were wives of men with incomes larger than the working-class average and must, from the nature of their offices in the Guild, have possessed greater initiative than the average, she also leaves no doubt that the condition of life of the women concerned, both economically and in other respects, was often very poor. The material that Davies had assembled she summarised as giving 'on the whole an impression of perpetual overwork, illness, and suffering'.[36] It is particularly significant that William Farr, better placed than anyone in the mid-nineteenth century to give an informed estimate, believed that the stillbirth rate was about 40 per 1,000 total births at that time.[37]

An estimated rate of 40 per 1,000 may appear to represent a conservative estimate of the level of the stillbirth rate in the mid-nineteenth century, given that endogenous infant mortality probably declined slightly between the mid-nineteenth and early twentieth centuries, but it allows for the possibility that the ratio of stillbirths to endogenous infant mortality may have been lower in the earlier than in the later period, as suggested, somewhat ambiguously, by Norwegian experience.[38] Alternatively, if the relationship of the English stillbirth rate to Scandinavian rates was constant over the period, then the rate in the early middle decades of the nineteenth century would be approximately 50 per 1,000 since Scandinavian rates were 27 per cent higher at the beginning of the period than at its end (the average of the Norwegian and Swedish rates in 1821–40,

[34] Mooney, 'Stillbirths', tab. 3, p. 48; Glass, *Numbering the people*, p. 195.

[35] Davies, *Maternity*, p. 194.

[36] Ibid., p. 3.

[37] Farr, *Vital statistics*, p. 107. It is of interest to note that Glass quotes data compiled by James Cleland, Superintendent of Public Works for Glasgow, revealing a stillbirth rate for that city of 47 per 1,000 in 1821, and of 69 per 1,000 in 1830: Glass, *Numbering the people*, p. 195.

[38] See above pp. 327–8.

divided by the average of the two in 1921–30).[39] The true stillbirth rate in early nineteenth-century England will never be known with accuracy, but it is reasonable, if arbitrary, to suppose that it probably lay within, or at least close to, the range suggested by these two estimates.

It is of interest in this connection to note what is known about the level of the stillbirth rate in France and Prussia in the mid-nineteenth century. Von Fircks, writing on behalf of the Prussian statistical service, expressed the view that stillbirth registration was essentially complete by about 1850 in Prussia, though defective in earlier decades. Between 1851 and 1870 the stillbirth rate averaged 40.9 per 1,000 total births. Knodel accepted this judgement initially, but later laid stress on the vivid contrast between the stillbirth rate in Catholic and Protestant areas, attributable to 'a tendency in Catholic areas to treat some stillbirths as if the infant had actually died shortly after birth'. In the sample of settlements whose *Ort-sippenbücher* he analysed, the average stillbirth rate in Protestant villages over the period 1750–1899 was 23.5 per 1,000 higher than in Catholic villages. It is therefore probably safe to assume that the true Prussian national stillbirth rate was as high as 45 per 1,000 or even somewhat higher.[40] French stillbirth registration was also affected by widespread under-registration for much of the nineteenth century. Van de Walle has presented convincing evidence that many departments were delinquent in this regard until *c.*1860. Between 1864 and 1898 the French stillbirth rate averaged approximately 43 per 1,000, though it should be borne in mind that the French definition of a stillbirth may have tended to exaggerate the number of stillbirths.[41] The German and French stillbirth data therefore tend to support the supposition that the English rate was close to 40 per 1,000 in the mid-nineteenth century.

[39] *Norges offisielle statistikk*, XII, tab. 20, pp. 44–7; *Historisk statistik för Sverige*, I, tab. 37, p. 108.

[40] Knodel, *Demographic behavior in the past*, p. 280 and tab. 10.10, p. 281; Knodel, *Decline of fertility in Germany*, tab. 1.6, p. 26.

[41] Van de Walle, *Female population of France*, tab. 2.5, p. 50. The quoted French rate is an approximation made necessary by the fact that van de Walle presented only a table of the distributions of the number of departments with stillbirth ratios of less than 2 per cent, 2.00–3.99 per cent, 4,00–5.99 per cent, and over 6 per cent for successive five-year periods. In order to estimate a rate I have assumed (a) that within each category the average percentage was 1.75, 3.00, 5.00, and 6.50 per cent respectively, and (b) that all departments were the same in population. Dupâquier quotes French rates for 1853 and 1913. In the former year the national stillbirth rate was 38.2 per 1,000 total births; in the latter 42.2 per 1,000 (in this case without data for the department of the Seine). His table also enables rates for urban and rural France to be calculated for the same dates: the urban rate was considerably the higher of the two: in 1853 the urban rate was 49.2 per 1,000, the rural 34.2 per 1,000; in 1913 the two rates were 51.8 and 36.3 per 1,000 respectively (the urban rate again lacking the Seine). These rates suggest a broad stability over the period and certainly no tendency for the stillbirth rate to fall. Dupâquier, 'Pour une histoire de la prématurité', tab. 5, p. 199.

Assuming once again parallelism in the movement of endogenous infant mortality and the stillbirth rate, the latter can now be estimated for seventeenth-century England when the endogenous rate was at its peak. The endogenous rate in the middle and later decades of the seventeenth century was at least 2.5 times its level at the end of the parish register period in 1825–37,[42] and if the stillbirth rate in the latter period lay in the range 40 to 50 per 1,000 total births, then its presumptive level in the seventeenth century would have been between 100 and 125 per 1,000 total births.[43] Even higher stillbirth rates are implied if the calculation were derived from the earliest endogenous infant mortality rate based on the Registrar General's data, but a ratio based solely on reconstitution data seems preferable for this purpose, both *in se* and also because it is sensible to use conservative assumptions in establishing the order of magnitude of the change involved.

An endogenous infant mortality rate of between 80 and 90 per 1,000, such as England experienced in the seventeenth and early eighteenth centuries may appear to be very high when compared with English or Scandinavian rates in the nineteenth century, but there were many areas in which the rate was still higher in the early modern period. For example, the French national rate was 70 per 1,000 in the period 1806–30 although by then infant mortality was far below the levels prevailing in the mid-eighteenth century. Assuming that endogenous mortality formed the same proportion of first month mortality in 1740–9 as it did in the first three decades of the nineteenth century, the endogenous rate in France in the 1740s would have been 116 per 1,000, and in the next two decades 104 per 1,000 in each case.[44]

---

[42] See above, tab. 12.2.

[43] In considering the plausibility of seventeenth-century stillbirth rates in the range 100 to 125 per 1,000, it should be noted that rates approaching this level are not unknown in the twentieth century. The stillbirth rate in Trinidad and Tobago in the period 1920–39 was 68 per 1,000; in British Guiana 76 per 1,000 in 1920–9; while the rate in the principal towns of Ceylon in 1925–39 was 71 per 1,000. The Japanese rate was also very high early in the twentieth century, though here the data reported refer to all foetal deaths and may therefore have included some occurring early in pregnancy: United Nations, *Foetal, infant and early childhood mortality*, I, tab. 2, pp. 78–87. The quoted rates were calculated from the published stillbirth *ratios* (that is, stillbirths per 1,000 *live* births).

[44] Houdaille, 'La mortalité des enfants en Europe', tab. 2, p. 89, tab. 8, p. 104, and tab. G, p. 155. The data in tabs. 2 and 8 enable first month mortality to be calculated for the middle decades of the eighteenth century, while those in tabs. 2 and G permit the percentage of first month mortality which was endogenous to be calculated (over the period 1806–30 this averaged 82.4 per cent). The problems associated with 'ondoyés décédés' remain, of course. The endogenous infant mortality rate in some individual French parishes was far higher than the estimated national rates in the mid-eighteenth century. In Mouliherne in Anjou in the period 1700–90, for example, it was 146 per 1,000, a level closely comparable to that in Crulai in the same era, where it may have lain

Whether the relationship between stillbirths and early infant mortality which held good when the latter was comparatively low also obtained when neonatal mortality was very high cannot be tested rigorously at present, and may never be directly demonstrable for a representative sample of the whole English population, but it represents a neutral assumption given the nature of the two types of mortality. Nor is it at odds with the scraps of empirical information currently available for the later seventeenth century.

Parish registers offer the best hope of direct information about stillbirth rates in the period before the gradual elaboration of a system of civil registration, but most parish registers make only occasional and spasmodic reference to the burial of stillborn children. In a few instances, however, stillbirths were recorded in a more consistent fashion. The Lancashire parish of Hawkshead maintained apparently good registration of stillbirths over a long period of time beginning in the later sixteenth century and ending only in the early eighteenth century, except that it became rather patchy during the Civil War and Commonwealth period. Between 1658 and 1705, a period broadly corresponding to the period of highest endogenous infant mortality, 1,299 children were baptised in Hawkshead, and over the same period a total of 106 children were recorded in the burial register as 'abortive' (or in one instance 'dead borne'), representing a stillbirth rate of 75 per 1,000 total births.[45] There must, of course, be an unresolvable uncertainty about what local practice regarded as an abortive birth, and whether this varied over time.[46] A rate of 76 per 1,000, however, is at least double the rate which probably prevailed in the mid-nineteenth century, given that the national rate was in the region of 40 per 1,000 and that the parish was in an area of very low

in the range 145–60 per 1,000: Lebrun, *Les hommes et la mort en Anjou*, p. 185; Gautier and Henry, *La population de Crulai*, p. 170. However, Gautier and Henry emphasise the difficulties associated with the Catholic practice of baptising a proportion of stillborn children and are inclined only to conclude that *perinatal* mortality was far in excess of 100 per 1,000; ibid., p. 171.

[45] For comparison the case of Catharina Schrader who practised as a midwife in Holland at the end of the seventeenth century and during the first half of the eighteenth century should be noted. She kept a journal of her professional activities and delivered in all about 4,000 babies. Schama notes that 'the average rate of stillbirths – including babies that were dead before labour or died during delivery – ran at around one in thirteen or fourteen and rarely rose above fifteen per cent.' This comment, though rather ambiguously phrased suggests a rate very similar to that found in Hawkshead. Schrader's exceptional skill as a midwife probably helped to keep the stillbirth rate below the level that it might otherwise have reached. Schama, *The embarrassment of riches*, p. 531.

[46] Of the 106 stillbirths, 48 were of indeterminate sex ('a stillborn child of –'), 42 were male, and 16 female. A heavy preponderance of male stillbirths is typical.

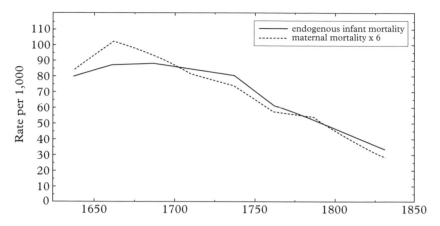

Figure 12.4. *Maternal mortality and endogenous infant mortality in England, 1625–49 to 1825–37*
Source: Wrigley et al., *English population history*, tab. 6.5, p. 236.

mortality.[47] This scrap of empirical evidence, therefore, lends support to the view that stillbirth rates were far higher in the seventeenth century than in Victorian times.

There is one further persuasive, if indirect piece of evidence underwriting the probability that endogenous infant mortality and the incidence of stillbirths moved in parallel. Trends in maternal mortality are likely to be closely linked to those in the incidence of stillbirths, since similar hazards affect both, and if the latter in turn moves in sympathy with endogenous infant mortality, trends in maternal mortality and in endogenous infant mortality should also parallel one another. Figure 12.4 shows that this was the case during the 'long' eighteenth century in England. Maternal mortality rose during the first half of the seventeenth century, reaching a peak in 1650–74, when childbirth was exceptionally dangerous. The risk

[47] Infant mortality was generally very low in this part of Lancashire in the nineteenth century. Hawkshead, a remote highland parish, formed part of the registration district of Ulverston in the early years of civil registration. In the years 1841, 1842, 1845, and 1846, when the Registrar General provided a breakdown of deaths within the first year of life, the overall rate in Ulverston was only 80 per 1,000, and in the first month of life 32 per 1,000. But it was also low in the seventeenth century. During the period 1658–1705, for example, first month mortality in Hawkshead was only a little higher than in Ulverston in the 1840s, at 37 per 1,000. In this instance, therefore, it is not clear that late foetal and immediately postnatal mortality moved in step. Equally, it is quite possible that the boundary between death before and immediately after birth was hard to draw and that it makes better sense to consider a *combined* stillbirth and first month mortality rate, rather than either in isolation. This rate in Hawkshead in 1658–1705, at 110 per 1,000 total births (live and stillborn), was probably roughly double the comparable rate in the 1840s.

of dying from a cause related to pregnancy or childbirth was 17 per 1,000 at each pregnancy, but in the course of the next 150 years the rate fell to little more than a quarter of its peak level.[48] Endogenous infant mortality followed a strikingly similar course, though the absolute rate was about six times higher. Though conclusive evidence about the incidence of stillbirths during this period is lacking, therefore, both direct evidence from other periods and places and indirect evidence for England from the period when the parish registers are the chief source of information about demographic trends provide powerful support for the view that endogenous mortality can be used as a surrogate measure of the stillbirth rate with some confidence.

Stillbirth trends and changes in fertility

The rise in fertility which occurred and the change to be expected as a result of the reduced incidence of stillbirths were of the same order of magnitude. If the stillbirth rate fell from 100 to 40 per 1,000 total births, the live birth rate would have risen by 6.7 per cent,[49] while on the alternative assumption that the stillbirth rate fell from 125 to 40 per 1,000 total births, the rise in the live birth rate would have been 9.7 per cent. The average of the two estimates is 8.2 per cent, a figure identical to that for the peak-to-trough fall in the mean birth interval in table 12.1. Despite the uncertainties surrounding the calculations, the similarity between the scale of the fall in the mean observed birth interval and that implied by the fall in the stillbirth rate encourages a belief that the rise in fertility may be due, not to a smaller average interval between successive conceptions, but to a reduction in the rate at which foetuses were lost during the third trimester of pregnancy.[50]

There is, however, a substantial difficulty with this suggestion. It relates to the timing of the changes which occurred. The mean birth interval began to fall, and therefore fertility began to rise, from about the end of the third quarter of the seventeenth century (table 12.1 and

[48] Wrigley *et al.*, *English population history*, tab. 6.29, p. 313 and fig. 6.22, p. 314. It is of interest to note that both the level and trend of maternal mortality in rural France and in Sweden appear to have been similar to those in England in the later eighteenth century (earlier data are lacking).

[49] A stillbirth rate of 100 per 1,000 total births means that only 900 out of every 1,000 foetuses living at the end of the twenty-eighth week of pregnancy were still living at birth. If the stillbirth rate falls to 40 per 1,000 total births, the number of those surviving to birth will increase to 960, and $100 \times (60/900) = 6.7$.

[50] Indeed, assuming, as is probable, that the rate of foetal loss in the earlier months of pregnancy was also in decline when third trimester loss was falling, it may be that the average interval between conceptions was actually rising even though fertility rates were increasing.

figure 12.1), and although the fall may have continued to the end of the parish register period, it became subdued after the 1780s. Endogenous infant mortality, however, though probably peaking in the final quarter of the seventeenth century, and declining gently thereafter, did not begin to descend sharply until the third quarter of the eighteenth century (table 12.2). Since endogenous infant mortality has been used as an indicator of trends in the stillbirth rate, and the latter in turn as an explanation for the rise in fertility, it would strengthen and simplify the story if the changes in trend in the two measures had coincided more closely.[51] Birth spacing, however, was influenced by many factors other than the stillbirth rate, so that the lack of synchrony is not entirely surprising. Only when a larger body of evidence has been assembled will it be possible to judge how serious this difficulty is.

On the other hand, there are more detailed features of the pattern of change in fertility which reinforce the belief that it was linked to changes in the incidence of stillbirths. The risk of stillbirth rises steadily and steeply with age. The rate for women in their late thirties (35–9), early forties (40–4), and late forties (45–9) may rise to levels as much as twice, three times, and four times that for women in their early twenties (20–4). For example, table 12.6 displays data drawn from the 30-month period from July 1938 to December 1940, a period when the overall stillbirth rate was still as high as 35.9 per 1,000 total births. The overall stillbirth rate for women aged 20–4 was 25.9 per 1,000. In the age group 35–9 this figure had risen to 50.0 per 1,000; in the age group, 40–4, the comparable figure was 68.4 per 1,000; and in the age group 45–9, 94.4 per 1,000. In this example, therefore, the ratios for the older age groups (20–4 = 1.00) were as follows: 35–9, 1.93; 40–4, 2.64; and 45–9, 3.64.

Assuming an equal percentage reduction in the stillbirth rate for each age group, therefore, there will be a more marked rise in age-specific marital fertility rates among older than among younger women, and this pattern is visible in the reconstitution data, as may be seen in table 12.7. Panel A of the table sets out the rates for 1660–1709 and for 1770–1819, corresponding to the period when the mean birth interval was at its longest and to the period when it had largely completed its marked fall. The rates will appear odd in that no data are given for the age group

---

[51] In view of the existence of the concept of perinatal mortality, it might seem natural to consider trends in first week infant mortality as a guide to probable trends in the stillbirth rate, rather than, or at least in addition to, endogenous infant mortality. There are, however, excellent reasons to doubt the reliability of first week mortality data because of the tendency for the birth-baptism interval to increase substantially during the 'long' eighteenth century and because of the complications related to the phenomenon of 'dummy' births. Both these complex questions are fully discussed in Wrigley *et al.*, *English population history*, pp. 110–6.

Table 12.6 *Stillbirth rates by parity and mother's age, England and Wales, July 1938 to December 1940 (rates per 1,000 total legitimate births)*

Mother's age	Parity 0	1	2	3	4	5	6	7	8	9	10 and over	All
under 20	26.8	18.0	36.0	—	—	—	—	—	—	—	—	26.1
20–4	29.1	17.8	22.2	27.8	27.0	26.0	—	—	—	—	—	25.9
25–9	37.7	20.8	23.2	27.7	33.8	34.3	30.0	50.0	—	—	—	30.2
30–4	54.5	26.4	30.2	32.5	34.8	38.3	41.2	39.8	43.0	54.0	59.0	37.8
35–9	77.0	37.7	39.8	45.4	47.8	48.6	47.6	52.0	57.5	59.9	66.0	50.0
40–4	104.8	54.9	55.4	57.5	71.3	66.8	67.5	63.1	66.9	64.0	73.7	68.4
45 and over	123.0	75.0	91.0	97.0	83.0	79.0	85.0	103.0	111.0	88.0	96.0	94.4
All	38.9	24.0	29.5	35.8	42.6	46.1	49.3	53.7	60.7	62.5	73.4	35.9

Note: Figures shown in italics indicate that the rate was based on 200–1, 999 births. Rates based on fewer than 200 births were not entered in the table but their existence is shown by dashes.
Source: Sutherland, *Stillbirths*, tab. XII, p. 26.

Table 12.7 *Age-specific marital fertility (rates per 1,000 woman-years)*

	Panel A						
	Age						
Date	15–9	20–4	25–9	30–4	35–9	40–4	45–9
1660–1709 (1)		329.1	334.6	297.7	228.6	110.0	23.6
1770–1819 (2)		367.1	353.5	292.4	245.5	145.0	18.9
(3) = (2)/(1)		1.115	1.056	0.982	1.074	1.318	0.801
	Panel B						
Wife's age at marriage			1660–1709				
15–9	315.8	329.1	305.5	273.1	205.7	80.2	5.6
20–4		436.1	342.3	290.1	218.4	94.8	8.2
25–9			395.0	311.5	230.7	102.0	22.3
30–4				387.7	250.9	144.3	32.2
35–9					300.7	127.6	42.0
40–4						144.0	58.1
45–9							
			1770–1819				
15–9	507.9	367.1	300.0	287.6	216.4	137.9	12.6
20–4		449.8	371.3	283.4	248.2	143.4	17.6
25–9			438.8	309.4	145.5	135.5	17.9
30–4				441.4	263.4	139.2	25.6
35–9					315.9	212.4	19.1
40–4						158.6	30.8
45–9							24.3

Note: The calculation underlying the rates shown in panel A is explained in the text.
Source: Cambridge Group reconstitutions.

15–9. The reason for this is readily seen in panel B of the table which shows age-specific rates by age at marriage. Rates on the diagonal are best ignored for the present purpose since they were heavily affected by changes in the level of prenuptial pregnancy, itself a fascinating topic but apt to introduce distortion in the present context. The rates shown in the panel A were calculated after excluding the data relating to the rates on the diagonal. Thus, for example, the rate for the age group 25–9 in 1660–1709, 334.6 per 1,000, is calculated from the births and woman-years lived of women who were married at ages 15–9 and 20–4, but *excluding* data for women who married aged 25–9.

The ratios shown on the bottom line of panel A of table 12.7 show that the disparity in rates did not rise evenly across the age groups. In 1770–1819 the ratio was considerably higher than unity in age group 20–4, but little different from unity in the next two age groups, 25–9 and 30–4. But the ratio then rose moderately in the age group 35–9, and in a striking fashion for women aged 40–4, before falling back to less than unity in the final age group, 45–9. There is good reason to pay attention chiefly to the intermediate age groups between the ages of 25 and 44. The rates for the age group 20–4 are based, of course, only on women who married aged 15–9, because 'diagonal' rates are excluded. Since there were relatively few teenage marriages, this represents a slender empirical base. Indeed, if data for women who married aged 20–4 are included in the calculation, after making a rough-and-ready adjustment for the higher level of prenuptial pregnancy in the later period, the resulting overall rates for the age group in the two periods are very similar to one another. The age group 20–4 is therefore best regarded as similar to the age groups 25–9 and 30–4.

A comparable problem affects the rates for the age group 45–9. The absolute number of births occurring in this age group was very small because fertility rates were so low. The rates for 1660–1709 and 1770–1819 were based on only 57 and 64 births respectively, compared with approximately 20 times these totals in the main childbearing age groups from 25 to 39. Only if a very much larger body of data were available, would it be possible to judge with confidence whether the fertility rate in this age group was higher or lower in the later than in the earlier period. It is reassuring to note in this connection that a more formal statistical test confirms that the only rates which in 1770–1819 were significantly different from those in 1660–1709 were the rates for the age groups 35–9 and 40–4.[52]

Whether the increase with age in the ratio between rates in the age groups 25–44 corresponds to what would be expected from the presumed changes in stillbirth levels is not easy to determine. A much larger data base would be needed to establish with confidence the change in the ratio with increasing age of mother, and there must always be a degree of uncertainty about the scale of the rise in the stillbirth rate with age in the past, and especially about whether the steepness of the rise itself varied as a function of the level of the rate. It is, however, clear that the evidence of panel A of table 12.7 tends to support a belief that a fall in the stillbirth rate was the prime cause of the rise in marital fertility in the eighteenth century.

This belief is strengthened by a feature of the more detailed data set out in panel B of table 12.7. In the higher age groups, in which the rates rose

[52] Treating the observations as independent, a difference of proportions test shows that the only difference which were significant at the 5 per cent level were for these two age groups.

the most, the rise in any given age group was greater for long-married women than for those who were only recently married.[53] Marital fertility levels may be viewed as a function of three variables, entry sterility (the proportion of women whose unions are sterile *ab initio*), subsequent sterility (the proportion of women at each age who, once have been fecund, have ceased to be so), and fecund marital fertility (the fertility of women still capable of bearing children). It can be shown that the virtual disappearance of a duration of marriage effect from age-specific rates in the later age groups was principally due to changes in subsequent sterility.[54] The rates in panel B of table 12.7 reflect this phenomenon. In the age groups 35–9 and 40–4 there is a much more pronounced tendency for rates to rise reading down each column in the earlier than in the later period.

Once again the relatively small empirical base presents a problem. The patterns are far less stable than they would be with a larger number of observations. But the phenomenon is clear none the less. For example, if the rate for the age at marriage group 20–4 is used as a base for indexing rates in other age groups in any given column,[55] the difference between the two periods is evident. It makes sense to focus on the age at marriage groups 20–4, 25–9, and 30–4 since far more marriages took place in these age groups than at other ages. If, for reasons already mentioned,[56] the rates on the diagonal and the rates for the age group 45–9 are ignored, then the index numbers for five age group cells in the two periods can be compared (those for women who married when aged 25–9 in the age groups 30–4, 35–9, and 40–4, and those for women who married when aged 30–4 in the age groups 35–9 and 40–4). For each of these cells an index number can be calculated. For example, the fertility rate in 1660–1709 for women aged 30–4 who had married in the age group 25–9 was 311.5 per 1,000 compared with a rate of 290.1 per 1,000 for women of the same age who had married in the age group 20–4, giving an index figure of 107.4 ($100 \times (311.5/290.1) = 107.4$).

The average index figure for the five cells in the earlier period is 117.5 but in the later period only 101.2. Plainly, duration of marriage had a much more muted effect on fertility in the later than in the earlier period. Reference back to table 12.6 suggests the significance of this finding for it will be seen that there was a general if irregular tendency for

[53] Wrigley *et al.*, *English population history*, pp. 392, 398–9, 509–10.
[54] Ibid., tab. 7.7, pp. 386–7 and accompanying text.
[55] The age at marriage group 20–4 is a natural choice as a base because more women married in this age group than in any other and the total of woman-years lived in observation is therefore greater than for other age at marriage groups.
[56] See above pp. 342–3.

rates to rise moving along the rows, though this was much less marked than the rises occurring when moving down the columns. At any given age the stillbirth rate among higher parity women was usually higher than among lower parity women. If the stillbirth rate falls, though the proportional benefit may be the same at all ages and parities, the *absolute* fall will be greater the higher the age and the higher the parity. Long-married women were, of course, on average of higher parity than those who had only been married for a short time, and therefore a lessening of the duration of marriage effect is to be expected if there is a marked fall in the stillbirth rate, and this effect will be more pronounced in the higher age groups.

In general, it seems fair to claim that both the general scale of the changes in fertility which occurred and the pattern of the changes by age and by age at marriage are those which might have been expected on the assumption that the stillbirth rate fell broadly in parallel to the endogenous infant mortality rate. Indeed, viewed in this light, the *absence* of a rise in fertility and a shift in its age pattern would have been surprising.

Stillbirths and fecund marital fertility

A further topic of interest related to the probable incidence of stillbirths in the past concerns the extent to which female fecundity declined with age. In *English population history*, a method of estimating fecund marital fertility rates was described (fecund marital fertility is the fertility of married couples who were still capable of bearing children).[57] The rates for the parish register period as a whole are set out in table 12.8. They refer only to women who were not pregnant at marriage, in order to avoid the misleading inflation of rates in the younger age groups in which most marriages occurred, which would otherwise confuse the issue. The rates in table 12.8 are at their highest in the age group 20–4. The phenomenon of teenage subfecundity is visible in the rates for the age group 15–9. Above the age of 25 the rates fall slowly throughout the balance of the child-bearing age groups.

Since the risk of a foetus being stillborn rises rapidly with age, the extent of the fall in fecundity with age, once the effect of stillbirths has been taken into account, would plainly be less pronounced than when measured by live-born children only. An arbitrary exercise can readily indicate the possible scale of the stillbirth effect. Using the rates in table 12.6 as a rough guide to the relationship between age of mother and the stillbirth rate, let us assume that the *absolute* stillbirth rates by age

---

[57] Wrigley *et al.*, *English population history*, pp. 357–71 and app. 8.

Table 12.8 *Standardised fecund marital fertility of women who were not pregnant at marriage, 1538–1837 (rates per 1,000 woman-years lived)*

Age	(1) Live birth rate	(2) Col. (1) indexed 20–4 = 1,000	(3) Live birth and stillbirth rate combined	(4) Col. (3) indexed 20–4 = 1,000
15–9	378	929	398	928
20–4	407	1,000	429	1,000
25–9	402	988	427	995
30–4	371	912	400	932
35–9	358	880	396	923
40–4	336	826	385	897
45–9	320	786	387	902

Source: The rates in col. 1 are taken from Cambridge Group reconstitutions. Comparable rates, but for the sub-periods rather than for the parish register period as a whole, may be found in Wrigley *et al.*, *English population history*, tab. 7.10, p. 381.

of mother were, on average, over the parish register period as a whole, twice those shown in the table. This enables a new set of rates to be calculated representing the combined live and stillbirth rate. Thus, the stillbirth rate for women aged under 20 in table 12.6 is 26.1 per 1,000 *total* births. Therefore, the fecund marital fertility rate for the age group, 378 per 1,000, should be increased in the ratio $1 + ((26.1 \times 2)/(1,000 - 26.1)) = 1.054$. The combined live and stillbirth rate therefore becomes 398 per 1,000. The resulting set of these rates is shown in column 3 of table 12.8. Both sets of rates are also shown indexed to the highest rate, that for the age group 20–4 (columns 2 and 4).

The contrast between the two sets of index numbers is vivid. There must have been a markedly less pronounced falling off with age in the combined live and stillbirth rate than in the live birth rate alone when stillbirths were common in the past. Indeed, allowing for the higher incidence of foetal loss in the earlier months of pregnancy among older women (that is, before the 28th completed month of pregnancy), the indexed figures shown in column 4 of table 12.8 suggest that conception rates among fecund women were very similar at all ages. This finding, if justified, would also suggest only slight differences in coital frequency by age in the past.

In summary, it appears safe to conclude that there was a large fall in the stillbirth rate in England in the course of the 'long' eighteenth century, and that this in turn caused the mean interval between births to shorten and thus marital fertility to rise, even though the fall cannot be demonstrated directly, and despite the 'timing' issue noted above.[58] As with most historical issues, however, providing an answer to one question immediately raises another in its place. The rise in fertility may be explained by the marked reduction in the stillbirth rate, but what in turn accounts for the improvement in the latter? Since low birthweight babies, especially if they are full-term babies, suffer perinatal mortality rates many times greater than babies born near to the optimum birthweight, and since, further, birthweight is so heavily conditioned by maternal net nutrition, a rise in maternal net nutrition is the most obvious candidate as the cause of the marked reduction in the stillbirth rate.[59]

If improvement in net nutrition lay behind the marked reduction in the frequency of stillbirths, it is highly likely that it was not confined to women but general to the population as a whole. If this were so, *ceteris paribus*, it might be expected to have caused an increase in adult height in both men and women. Fogel's collation of height data from several European countries is consistent with this hypothesis. He found that in the late eighteenth century Englishmen, though not as tall as either Scots or Irish men, and far shorter than men in the newly independent United States, were taller than men in any continental country for which there is evidence.[60] Clear, unambiguous evidence about nutritional levels in the 'long' eighteenth century, and especially about any changes in these levels, is lacking, however. Amongst those who have speculated about the issue, pessimists are perhaps more numerous than optimists. The significance of the topic is indisputable but its resolution remains uncertain.

A comment on another issue to arise from the consideration of stillbirths, however, may not be out of place. The present exercise provides an excellent illustration of the artificiality of the conventional separation of demographic behaviour into fertility, mortality, and nuptiality. In *English population history* the existence of this convention was noted with some regret but little was done to offset it because dealing with the traditional topics occupied so much space.[61] The changes in late foetal mortality, neonatal mortality, and fertility which occurred in England between the late seventeenth and early nineteenth centuries illustrate the importance of eschewing conventional categorisation. The changes were all constituent elements of the same major alteration in the demographic character of the country. Thus, the rise in marital fertility which took

---

[58] See above pp. 339–40.
[59] See above nn. 22 and 24.
[60] Fogel, *Conquest of high mortality*, tab. 4, p. 30 and fig. 5, p. 38. Comparative data on heights within the British Isles *c*.1815 may be found in Floud, Wachter, and Gregory, *Height, health and history*, fig. 5.2, p. 201.
[61] Wrigley *et al.*, *English population history*, pp. 4–6, 550–6.

place is defined as such only because parturition is taken as the beginning of life. If fertility were measured from conception, or indeed from the end of the twenty-eighth week of pregnancy, what has appeared in this discussion as a change in fertility would be treated exclusively as a mortality change.

Conclusion

The most striking feature of the population history of England in the 'long' eighteenth century lies in the fact that during the second half of the seventeenth century the intrinsic growth rate was very close to zero, whereas by the early decades of the nineteenth century it had reached the highest level in national history, at about 0.0171, or 1.71 per cent per annum.[62] The exact scale of the change depends upon whether its measurement is based on, say, decadal data or on the average position over longer intervals of time, but the significance of the increase in the growth rate is clear. Total population rose from a low point of 5.0 millions in 1686 to 11.5 millions in 1821, an increase of about 130 per cent.[63]

The combined contribution of the fall in late foetal and in early postnatal mortality to the overall acceleration in the intrinsic growth rate which took place between c.1680 and c.1820 was substantial. On the assumption that the change in the incidence of stillbirths caused the live birth rate to increase by 8.2 per cent and that endogenous infant mortality fell by 5 per cent,[64] the intrinsic growth rate would have increased from zero to approximately 0.38 per cent per annum, thus accounting for just over a fifth of the acceleration.[65]

This finding is of particular interest if the following set of related assumptions is justified. If it is fair to assume that perinatal mortality is chiefly a function of mean birthweight; that mean birthweight is primarily determined by maternal net nutrition, broadly interpreted to relate to the whole life span of the mother; and that nutrition is closely

---

[62] The intrinsic growth rate over the period 1651–1700 averaged −0.02 per cent per annum. Between 1811 and 1825 the comparable figure was 1.71 per cent per annum; ibid., tab. A9.1, pp. 614–5.

[63] Ibid.

[64] See above p. 339 and p. 324, n. 21.

[65] Modelling the effect of these changes is not a simple exercise, since several other variables will also change. For example, the proportion of women surviving to the mean age at maternity will increase. So also, on certain assumptions about the incidence of stillbirth by age, might the mean age at maternity itself; and so on. No exact, unambiguously correct result is possible. Both formal modelling and simulation were used to examine the issue. The input parameters for the initial population were based on empirical data relating to the later seventeenth century in England when the intrinsic growth rate was very close to zero.

linked to economic conditions, then this component of the accelerating population growth which took place in the 'long' eighteenth century might be regarded as a function of improving economic circumstances.

None of the several steps in the chain of argument is beyond dispute. If they were to prove valid, however, they would represent a more unambiguous linking of economic change and mortality than it has so far proved possible to establish for other components of mortality change in the period. Evidence of close links between economic change and another aspect of demographic behaviour in early modern England has been available for some time. Secular changes in nuptiality closely paralleled changes in real wages, which therefore caused long-term fertility change also to be responsive to economic trends, though in this case the linkage mechanism was social rather than physiological.

A tantalising possibility is suggested when these two pathways by which economic circumstances influenced the population growth rate are considered jointly. If the effect of nuptiality change on the growth rate is added to that brought about by changes in perinatal mortality, it is possible to account for the whole of the acceleration in growth rates during the 'long' eighteenth century. An earlier exercise showed that the change in nuptiality[66] taking place between the late seventeenth century and the early nineteenth century would have increased the intrinsic growth rates from zero to 1.26 per cent per annum, *ceteris paribus*.[67] This change, combined with the increase in the growth rate attributable to the fall in the incidence of stillbirths and in endogenous infant mortality (0.38 per cent per annum), would account for the bulk of the overall increase in the intrinsic growth rate (1.71 per cent per annum).

The foregoing is not intended as an assertion that economic change explains the increase in the rate of growth of population. Such an assertion would be at best premature, at worst wrong-headed. It is notable that the parallelism between economic change and developments in perinatal mortality, which appears to hold good during the 'long' eighteenth century, is much harder to detect in the following century when perinatal mortality improved only marginally in spite of a marked rise in real wages in the half century preceding the First World War. This may be a case where it is easy to mistake coincidence for causation. Moreover, other factors contributed to the increase in the intrinsic growth rate: for example, there was a fall of about 30 per cent in adult mortality between

[66] Nuptiality is used here as an umbrella term intended to encompass a group of variables (age at marriage, proportions marrying, and illegitimacy levels) all closely related to marriage as a social institution in early modern England.

[67] Wrigley and Schofield, *Population history of England*, pp. 265–9.

the mid-seventeenth and the late eighteenth century.[68] And, in any case, it is artificial to ignore the important feedback element between the economic and demographic functioning of society.[69] My purpose extends no further than to show that *if* the various links which have been suggested were in operation, they afford a relatively simple explanation of the great acceleration in the population growth rate.

Even if the several assumptions embodied in this exposition of the possible importance of a falling stillbirth rate in explaining the rise in marital fertility could be shown to be valid, much would still be left unexplained. But the exercise will have served a valuable purpose if it provides a focus for further research into the 'long' eighteenth century, a period during which the differentially rapid rate of population growth in England was so marked, for it was at this time that England gradually ceased to be heavily outranked in population by France, Germany, Italy, and Spain, the major national groupings of continental western Europe, and made rapid progress towards joining them as one of the five largest national populations in the area.[70]

---

[68] Wrigley *et al.*, *English population history*, tab. 6.20, p. 291 and accompanying text. The apparent implication of the introduction of other factors tending to increase the intrinsic growth rate is that the level of some of the quoted variables must have been overestimated since they 'over-explain' the observed rise in the intrinsic growth rate. The apparent implication is not, however, necessarily valid. The changes quoted in the text were trough-to-peak changes, but these changes did not coincide exactly so that their collective effect would not at any given juncture have equalled that suggested by their combined scale.

[69] Wrigley and Schofield, *Population history of England*, ch. 11.

[70] If the population of England (without Wales) is expressed as a percentage of the average of the population totals of France, Germany, Italy, and Spain, its relative size rises from 36 per cent in 1680, to 57 per cent in 1820, and to 92 per cent in 1900; Wrigley, 'Growth of population', tab. 1, p. 122.

13   No death without birth: the implications of English mortality in the early modern period

It is obvious that for most of human history fertility and mortality must have been at closely similar levels. For the former to have fallen short of the latter consistently would have meant extinction, while the opposite case could not have long continued because of the impossibility of increasing food supplies other than very slowly.[1] Man is a slow-breeding animal and, therefore, human mortality was always at a far lower level than in most other animals. There is no reason to suppose that crude birth rates in any large population consistently exceeded about 50 per 1,000. Equally, there can be no reason to believe that crude death rates ever significantly exceeded this level. In individual years and in exceptional circumstances far higher death rates occurred, but even when such mortality surges occurred the usual situation must have been very different. This in turn implies that expectation of life at birth can seldom have been much less than 20 years at birth, and that where this was so, the gross reproduction rate was in the range 3.0–3.5. Those women who survived to the end of the childbearing period bore about seven children on average.[2]

An expectation of life at birth of 20 years represents a drastically more severe mortality regime than that experienced today when expectation of life at birth (e_0) is about 75 years in advanced communities, but even so it is possible to exaggerate the uncertainty of life in such circumstances. Under the age of one, and to a lesser degree under the age of five, life is desperately hazardous. More than half of each new birth cohort dies before reaching their fifth birthday. Thereafter the dangers ease. More than three-quarters of those who celebrate their fifth birthday live to see 20;

---

[1] This generalisation is true only if migration is ignored. For very large units of area or population this is a defensible simplification. In small units, however, relatively large net migration balances may be a longstanding feature of the local situation, and may vitiate the generalisation.

[2] These results follow from stable population theory given that crude birth and death rates were at the level suggested and in the absence of any significant natural increase or decrease.

and of those who see 20 almost a half also reach 50.[3] This represents a disturbing contrast with the healthiest modern states, where more than nine-tenths of each new cohort can expect to survive beyond the end of their fifth decade, compared with only about a sixth where expectation of life at births is only 20 years, but one might well draw still more depressing conclusions about the uncertainty of life in the past from some of the more strongly highlighted descriptions of conditions in earlier centuries.

In any case, the same line of reasoning immediately suggests that in pre-industrial western Europe mortality took a far less heavy toll. The general warrant for this assertion lies in the wide prevalence of the 'European' marriage pattern in Europe north of the Alps and the Pyrenees and west of the Oder. The European marriage pattern was unique, so far as is known, in that the average age at first marriage for women was the mid-20s, and a significant fraction of all women who survived to the end of the child-bearing period never married. This sets a comparatively low upper level to fertility and, on the assumption that growth rates must be close to zero, implies an equally modest level of mortality. For example, if the average age at first marriage for women is 26 and 12 per cent of each cohort never marry, and assuming marital fertility levels similar to those found in England in the seventeenth and eighteenth centuries with a mean age at maternity of 32 years, it can be shown that a stationary population will result from an e_0 in women of about 33 years.[4]

A regime of this 'European' type involves substantially less destructive mortality rates than where e_0 is 20 years. Roughly 85 per cent of all 5-year-olds reach 20, and more than three-fifths of the latter reach 50. The infant mortality rate is about 220 per 1,000 compared with almost 350 per 1,000 in the more severe alternative. In a stationary population with

[3] These estimates were derived from the Princeton model North life tables, combining the l_x values for the two sexes. The information used in constructing these tables all related to nineteenth or twentieth-century populations. More severe levels of mortality than those experienced in the recent past were extrapolated by the authors from these rates. Coale and Demeny, *Regional model life tables.*

[4] The age-specific marital fertility rates used in this illustrative calculation for the five-year age groups 25–9 to 45–9 were 360, 300, 250, 130, and 30 per 1,000. With a mean age of marriage of 26 years, this implies that the average married woman surviving to the end of the childbearing period would have 4.99 children, of which, assuming a sex ratio at birth of 105:100, 2.43 would be female. Allowing for the assumption that 12 per cent of women never marry (and assuming, unrealistically, that there is no illegitimate fertility), the figure of 2.43 for married women is reduced to 2.14 for all women. And it will be found that the proportion of women surviving to the mean age at maternity in the model North life tables, to which English mortality in the early modern period approximated, is such as to imply, with an expectation of life at birth of 32.5 years, that each generation of women were replaced by an equal number in the next generation. For a fuller discussion of the method and assumptions used, with more elaborate model calculations, see Wrigley and Schofield, *Population history of England,* pp. 265–9.

these characteristics, the crude birth and death rates are about 32 per 1,000. In England in the final quarter of the seventeenth century, when the intrinsic growth rate was close to zero, the prevailing crude birth and death rates were approximately at this level.[5]

The 'European' demographic pattern

It is well outside the scope of this essay to attempt to deal *in extenso* with the available evidence of the contrast between the 'European' demographic regime found in western Europe and that found in other parts of Europe, still less with extra-European areas. However, as an illustration of the scale of the differences between eastern and western European countries, consider the data in table 13.1. The data in the top panel relate to the 1870s, the earliest full decade for which national registration data exist for the east European countries. Death rates in the 1870s were about twice as high in the east as in the west, and birth rates were also substantially higher. Rates of natural increase were lower in the eastern countries, except in the case of Russia where the crude birth rate exceeded 50 per 1,000, an exceptional figure. Crude rates are, of course, an imperfect guide to the underlying fertility and mortality conditions, but the contrast is too marked to be attributable to differences in, say, age structure. By the 1870s some decline in mortality had already taken place in western Europe, and indeed the first signs of a secular fall in fertility were visible in places. For England, Norway, and Sweden, however, crude birth and death rates are also available for the second half of the eighteenth century. These are set out in the lower panel of table 13.1. Of the 15 decennial death rates for the three countries all except two lay between 25 and 30 per 1,000, somewhat higher than their rates in the 1870s, but far lower than late nineteenth-century rates in eastern Europe (the two exceptions were both in Norway, in the 1750s and 1790s). The birth rates were normally between 30 and 35, little different from their rates in the 1870s (the exceptions were England 1770–99 and Sweden 1750–9; all four cases lay between 35 and 40).

Using the countries for which data are reproduced in table 13.1 may overstate the extent of the contrast between east and west. For example, crude birth and death rates in France in the later eighteenth century were substantially higher than in England, Norway, or Sweden. Decadal birth rates between 1750–9 and 1790–9 ranged between 36.9 and 40.4 per 1,000; the comparable death rates between 33.3 and 36.3.[6] In eastern

---

[5] They were 31.2 and 30.3, respectively, averaged over five quinquennia from 1674–8 to 1694–8. Wrigley and Schofield, *Population history of England*, tab. A3.1, pp. 528–9.

[6] Henry and Blayo, 'La population de la France de 1740 à 1860', tab. 22, p. 109.

Table 13.1 *Crude birth and death rates (CBR and CDR) in eastern and western Europe (rates per 1,000 total population)*

1870–9	CBR	CDR
England and Wales	35.5	21.6
Norway	30.8	17.1
Sweden	30.4	18.4
Hungary	43.4	40.7
Russia	50.3	36.3
Serbia	40.9	34.5

	England		Norway		Sweden	
	CBR	CDR	CBR	CDR	CBR	CDR
1750–9	33.4	26.1	33.9	24.6	35.8	27.4
1760–9	34.4	28.4	34.7	27.5	34.5	27.5
1770–9	36.2	26.6	30.2	26.0	32.7	29.4
1780–9	36.7	27.7	30.3	25.5	32.5	27.1
1790–9	38.9	26.4	32.9	22.3	33.5	25.3

Sources: For all data in the top panel and for Norway and Sweden in the bottom panel, Mitchell, *European historical statistics*, tab. B6; for England 1750–99, Wrigley and Schofield, *Population history of England*, tab. A3.3, pp. 531–4.

Europe, too, less extreme cases may have existed. The late nineteenth century vital registration data suggest, for example, that birth and death rates in Romania were lower than in Hungary, Russia, or Serbia. But the contrast between western and eastern Europe was marked and the concomitants of the two regimes have wide historical importance.

Since such heavy stress has often been put on the severity of mortality in the past, it is worth noting that dealing in generalities may actually tend to convey too dark an impression even in the case of west European countries. There are two considerations that point to this conclusion so far as early modern England is concerned. First, while in the whole sweep of the historic past it is safe to assume an absence of significant population growth,[7] in early modern England it was unusually rapid, either when compared with earlier periods or with other European countries between

---

[7] Or, more precisely, a rate of growth so slight on average that the demographic characteristics of the population in question must have been barely distinguishable from those of a stationary population.

the sixteenth and nineteenth centuries.[8] Over the quarter-millennium from 1550 to 1800 the annual rate of population growth was about 0.5 per cent per annum: at times it approached 1.0 per cent per annum. Crude birth and death rates were therefore up to 10 per 1,000 per annum apart in the period. In the main the difference from the stationary situation sketched above was due to the existence of higher levels of fertility than those used for purposes of illustration, but in some degree the gap arose because mortality was lower than implied by the e_0 employed to illustrate the stationary case. Expectation of life at birth was lower in the second half of the seventeenth century (when e_0 was similar to that used to construct the stationary case) than in any other comparable period from 1550 to 1850.[9]

Second, mortality at any one time was far from uniform. There were always major regional differences. Low-lying, marshy areas, for example, were very much less healthy than well-drained uplands. More importantly, there was in general a consistent and strong relation between population density and mortality levels. Urban populations, even in market towns of a very modest size, suffered higher death rates than neighbouring rural areas. Large towns such as York, Bristol, Norwich, Newcastle, or, pre-eminently, London, often failed to balance their demographic books. More were buried than were born within city walls and in the surrounding suburbs. Without a steady stream of immigrants many, perhaps most, towns before the nineteenth century would have lost population. Proximity of man to man, impure water, and the inability to remove animal and vegetable waste products, created an environment in which lethal diseases were widely prevalent. Urban mortality rates have proved difficult to measure with precision, but both the urban crude death rates, where they can be estimated, and the available information about age-specific mortality suggest that expectation of life at birth in an urban environment was frequently in the range between 20 and 35 years and sometimes below 20.[10]

---

[8] There are estimates of population totals and population growth rates for all the main west European countries between the mid-sixteenth and early nineteenth centuries in Wrigley, 'Growth of population'.

[9] Detailed information about English crude birth and death rates, gross and net reproduction rates, and expectation of life at birth between 1541 and 1871 may be found in Wrigley and Schofield, *Population history of England*, app. 3, pp. 527–35.

[10] On the unhealthiness of marshy areas generally, and the especially acute problems of malarial areas, see Dobson, 'Population, disease and mortality', chs. 8 and 9, 'The unhealthy marshlands', and 'Mosquitoes and malaria'.

The literature on urban mortality is enormous. Two issues of *Annales de démographie historique,* those of 1962 and 1978, contain substantial sections with a variety of articles on the subject (the sections entitled 'Villes du passé' and Etudes de mortalité', respectively). Similarly, Meyer *et al., Etudes sur les villes en Europe occidentale* contains some

The opposite side of the coin, of course, is that there were many rural areas where mortality levels were substantially better than those that result from a generalised calculation relating to the country as a whole. The proportion of the English population living in towns was very modest in Elizabethan times but rose greatly in the next 200 years. For example, if any settlement with 5,000 or more inhabitants is treated as a town, the urban percentage rose from 8 in 1600 to 28 in 1800.[11] If allowance is also made for the 'weight' of deeply unhealthy rural areas and for the existence of larger areas of relatively high mortality, it will occasion no surprise that death rates in much of the country were substantially lower than in the country as a whole.

The parish of Hartland in Devon is a good example of the modest level of mortality found where conditions were favourable in early modern England. Hartland is situated in the far northwest of Devon, remote from highways, and with the sea on two sides of the roughly square parish. It was a parish with a population varying between about 1,000 and 1,500, largely devoted to agriculture with many scattered farmsteads. It possesses a good parish register, which allowed a family reconstitution study to be carried out. This showed that the age-specific mortality rates up to age 15 suggest an expectation of life at birth of 55 years or more throughout the period from Elizabethan times to the beginning of Victoria's reign.[12]

Of the parishes so far reconstituted, no other has such low mortality as Hartland, but several are only marginally less favourably placed. Since it may occasion some surprise that individual parishes could boast an expectation of life as high in the sixteenth, seventeenth, and eighteenth,

substantive discussion and much bibliographical material. An important new aspect to the discussion of the issue of urban mortality was opened by Sharlin, 'Natural decrease in early modern cities'; but see also Finlay, 'Natural decrease in early modern cities' and van der Woude, 'Population developments in the northern Netherlands'. Among more recent publications, see Landers, *Death and the metropolis*, which throws much light on the experience of London in the 'long' eighteenth century.

[11] Wrigley, 'Urban growth', tab. 7.2, p. 162.

[12] The surviving Hartland parish registers begin in 1558. The family reconstitution exercise was carried down to 1837, the date of inception of a state system of vital registration. The logic of family reconstitution is such that age-specific mortality can be most accurately measured for children up to the age at which they leave home. Estimates of e_0 derived only from death rates up to age 15, however, are unlikely to be subject to wide margins of error because the shape of the mortality curve above 15 years is closely related to its shape below that age. The proportions surviving from birth to age 15, l_{15}, for the successive half-centuries 1600–49 to 1750–99, were 830, 832, 791 and 871.

Note, however, that in the light of more recent work, the assertion that a knowledge of infant and childhood mortality enables prediction of mortality at later ages to be made with confidence now seems mistaken. There was a striking improvement in adult mortality during the eighteenth century, even though childhood mortality showed no change: Wrigley et al., *English population history*, p. 349.

centuries as those attained nationally only about 1920, it is worth examining the considerations that suggest that the reconstitution data are tolerably accurate.

The most plausible reason for supposing mortality to have been underestimated is that the number of deaths occurring in the parish exceeded the number recorded in its registers. If this had happened it is to be expected that it would have affected particularly the recording of the burials of young infants, especially before baptism. Once a child had been baptised, and more especially if it had survived long enough to have acquired social visibility, it is far less likely that, following death, it would not have been accorded normal burial rites and have found a place in the burial register. Infant mortality, in short, might be expected to be underestimated more substantially than mortality at later ages. Infant mortality in Hartland was indeed very low, under 100 per 1,000 in the seventeenth and eighteenth centuries, but its level was just what would be expected from the mortality rates of the age groups 1–4, 5–9 and 10–4 on the assumption that Hartland experienced a mortality regime of the type represented by model North in the Princeton regional tables.[13] In this Hartland's experience was typical of the relative levels of infant and child mortality in the great majority of English parishes. It is worth noting in this regard that *some* English reconstitutions do reveal high rates of infant and child mortality. In Gainsborough, for example, a market town of some size, infant mortality was above 250 per 1,000 in the three successive 50-year periods between 1600 and 1750.[14] Infant mortality rates in general were surprisingly variable in England in the early modern period. Dobson's remarkable study of the 1,185 parishes in Kent, Sussex, and Essex shows this vividly. She found striking differences between rural inland and upland parishes at one extreme and coastal and estuarine marshland parishes at the other. In the former category the five parishes of Ardingly, Framfield, Hever, Shoreham, and Penshurst in the period 1780–1812 the average level of infant mortality was 96 per 1,000 after correction for possible underregistration, while in the latter category the average level of the five parishes of Burnham, East Ham, Strood, Tollesbury, and Southchurch was as high as 410 per 1,000.[15]

---

[13] The model North tables were based on Swedish mortality data between 1851 and 1890 (4 tables), Norwegian data between 1856 and 1880 and again between 1946 and 1955 (4 tables), and an Icelandic life table for 1941–50. Coale and Demeny, *Regional model life tables,* p. 14. Evidence of the good fit between infant mortality rates and the rates for the age groups 1–4, 5–9, and 10–4 in Hartland may be found in Wrigley and Schofield, 'English population history', tab. 14, p. 179, and more generally pp. 175–80.

[14] Ibid., tab. 14, p. 179.

[15] Dobson, *Contours of death,* tab. 4.1, p. 168.

Two further considerations reinforce the view that the low mortality rates found in a number of English reconstitution studies are probably broadly accurate. First, when the state established a vital registration system in 1837 the level of infant mortality found in the published tabulations was normally low in areas where reconstitution studies had suggested low risk to infant life. For example in the Bideford and Holsworthy registration districts, of which in 1841 the parish of Hartland forms part, with 7 per cent of the districts' joint population, the infant mortality rate in 1838–44 was 97 per 1,000.[16] Any underregistration of deaths in the early years of the new state system is thought to have been slight, and this was probably especially true of rural areas. Since mortality improvements in nineteenth-century England were modest until after 1870, the evidence drawn from the early years of state registration affords persuasive support for the credibility of the low infant mortality rates found for earlier periods in some reconstitution studies.[17]

Second, while the mortality rates found in west European reconstitution studies and in other studies that use analogous methods are in general higher than those found in England, high expectations of life and low infant and child mortality rates have come to light at times elsewhere. In Scandinavia infant mortality rates of less than 150 per 1,000 were not uncommon, and there were also parts of Germany and France where such rates were to be found.[18]

Two factors appear to have been especially conducive to low mortality and especially to low mortality early in life. The first has already been touched upon. High population density meant increased exposure to contact with disease carriers; low density usually led to a relative freedom from infection. The second concerns the length and intensity of

[16] *Ninth annual report of the Registrar General*, p. 214. The combined population of the two registration districts in 1841 was 31,934; of Hartland 2,223.

[17] The absence of any substantial improvement in expectation of life at birth in the country as a whole before 1870 may be deceptive. There were probably favourable changes in mortality rates in most types of community but compositional shifts in the population were increasing the proportion living in the least healthy areas as the populations of the cities grew rapidly. For an illuminating discussion of the issue, see Woods, 'The effects of population redistribution'.

[18] For Scandinavia, for example, Brändström and Sundin, 'Infant mortality in a changing society'; Turpeinen, 'Infant mortality in Finland'; for Germany, Imhof, 'Unterschiedliche Säuglingssterblichkeit', and Imhof, 'The amazing simultaneousness of the big differences'. Knodel also identifies some parishes, such as Werdum, where infant mortality was very low; Knodel, 'Natural fertility in pre-industrial Germany'. Low rates may also be found in individual parishes in countries where infant mortality was generally high. For example, in France Galliano's study of 18 parishes near Paris shows that the general level of infant mortality during the period 1774–1794 was fairly high (177 per 1,000) but in Le Plessis, Chevilly, Thiais, and Montrouge the rates were 123, 124, 135, and 139 per 1,000, respectively; Galliano, 'La mortalité infantile', tab. 1, pp. 146–7.

breastfeeding. Where breastfeeding was brief infant mortality was high and marital fertility was also above average because of the relatively short period of amenorrhoea implied by early weaning. Where children were as a rule principally breast-fed until beyond their first birthday, infant mortality was normally much lower and birth intervals were relatively long. In England there is strong indirect evidence that the average duration of breastfeeding was about 15 months, a period sufficiently long to exercise an important influence in keeping infant mortality at a modest level.[19]

A number of reflections suggest themselves in the light of the foregoing.

Why high fertility may result in high mortality

First, while there must have been many populations in pre-industrial times that had no alternative but to seek to sustain high levels of fertility because life was short and uncertain for reasons outside their control, there may have been cases where mortality was well above the 'platform' level set by the nature of the local disease environment because fertility was high. The supposition that where, say, malaria was widely prevalent, the local population would be obliged to accept a low expectation of life and therefore had to foster and sustain social customs such as early and universal marriage, which served to promote high fertility, is neither unfamiliar nor contentious. The alternative was ultimate extinction. Any group that failed to act in this way would in time be replaced by one whose social conventions were better adapted to the exigencies of the local situation. We are less accustomed to consider the possibility that social conventions well suited to coping with high levels of mortality might themselves create the situation to which they were well adapted if the group in question lived in an area in which mortality was *not* necessarily high. This was the kind of circumstance that Malthus had in mind in referring to a 'Chinese' situation, where population was 'forced'.[20]

---

[19] Knodel's classic study of three Bavarian villages in the later nineteenth century showed the striking differences obtaining between places where babies were weaned at birth and those where breastfeeding over six months or more was normal. In Schonberg and Anhausen infant mortality (including stillbirths) was about 400 per 1,000 births (including stillbirths); in Mommlingen about 170. The effect on fertility was also dramatic. Birth intervals in Mommlingen were almost a year longer than in the other two parishes in cases where the preceding child survived; Knodel, 'Infant mortality and fertility'. For the estimation of the average duration of breastfeeding in pre-industrial England, see Wrigley *et al.*, *English population history*, pp. 489–92; Wilson, 'Marital fertility in pre-industrial England, ch. 8, 'Post-partum non susceptibility', pp. 135–54. There is an excellent review of many topics related to breastfeeding and much fascinating empirical data in Vandenbroeke, van Poppel, and van der Woude, 'De zuigelingen- en kindersterfte'.
[20] Malthus, *Essay on population* [1798], pp. 48–9.

The two possible situations are not symmetric. If a population in an area in which environmental influences imposed high mortality failed to produce large families it would die out. If a population, living in an area in which the virulence of local diseases and the nature of other environmental influences on mortality was consonant with a relatively low mortality level, had a higher level of fertility than was 'necessary', it would not, of course, disappear, but might be condemned to lower living standards and harsher conditions of life than would otherwise occur because mortality would rise to match fertility and population totals would be larger than would otherwise have been the case.

The matter can be set out diagrammatically. In figure 13.1(a) the background level of mortality is high, because, say, of the prevalence of insect-borne and parasitic diseases. It is a condition for the successful continuation of population in the area that fertility should match this level. It might perhaps be called the 'West African' situation. (In all the diagrams in figure 13.1 the levels of fertility and mortality shown are intended to capture long-term trends only: they do not therefore reflect the likelihood of notable, and, in the case of mortality, occasionally violent short-term fluctuation.) In figure 13.1(b) we have the 'Chinese' case.[21] The background level of mortality is far lower but fertility is high and invariant, because, say, by social convention all women on or before reaching sexual maturity must be married and are therefore at risk to bear children throughout their fertile lives (though conventions about remarriage may modify this generalisation somewhat). Figure 13.1(c) relates to a third possibility, the west European case. The mortality graph reproduces the curve of 13.1(b), that is we assume that the background level of mortality and the response of mortality to increasing population pressure are the same in both cases. Fertility, however, is lower, because women marry eight to ten years after menarche rather than in rough coincidence with it, and also because a substantial fraction of each cohort, ranging from a tenth up to a fifth or even a quarter, never marry. The mere fact of a lower level of fertility ensures that population growth will cease at a lower total than in 13.1(b); the situation is inherently less 'forced'. But if fertility is also responsive to increasing population pressure, as shown in the f_2 variant, population growth will cease at a still earlier point, perhaps when mortality is scarcely higher than its platform level. Such a situation would obtain, for example, if in a predominantly peasant

---

[21] Malthus was probably mistaken about conditions in China. Although marriage was early and universal, overall fertility rates were not always high because birth intervals within marriage were often substantially longer in Chinese than in European communities. But it is convenient to treat 'Chinese' demography as a limiting case even though empirical reality may have differed from what Malthus supposed.

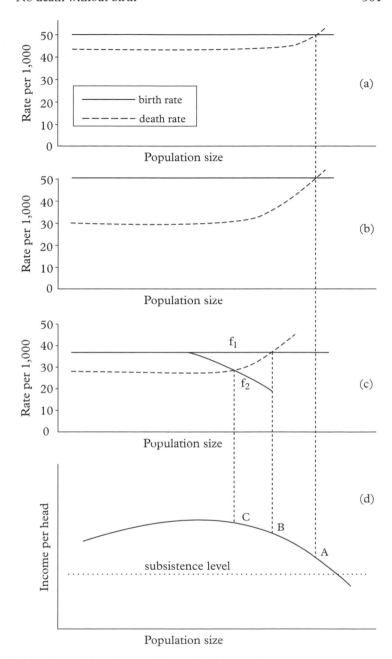

Figure 13.1. *Fertility, mortality, and living standards*

society there were a conventional minimum size of holding regarded as necessary to sustain a family and if marriage were only permitted when a couple could gain access to a holding. The number of marriages in being at any one time would equal the number of 'niches'. As settlement filled the cultivable area with peasant holdings, nuptiality would be progressively reduced and with it fertility also.[22] In a more complex economy where most men were wage earners, similar arrester mechanisms might also exist.[23]

The bottom panel of figure 13.1 shows the implications of these several possibilities for living standards on the assumption that in pre-industrial circumstances a notional optimum population existed, the level of which depended on the prevailing material technology. At this point average real income will be at a peak unattainable at higher population totals, where the tension between production and reproduction pushes living standards down towards subsistence level. It will be seen that both the 'West African' and 'Chinese' examples, though so different in their genesis, result in equally bleak economic prospects for their populations (A in 13.1(d)): they are both 'high-pressure' situations. The west European case is quite different. Having lower fertility is conducive to better living standards (B); having lower fertility that is also sensitive to deteriorating economic conditions may enable an optimum state to be attained, or closely approximated, a 'low-pressure' solution at the opposite extreme from the first two types (C).

Why low fertility may promote rapid population growth

Secondly, we have already noted that population growth rates in early modern England were remarkably high. At first sight this is very surprising, since nuptiality was low and in consequence overall fertility was also generally low, though variable in level because nuptiality fluctuated considerably.[24] Moreover, the proportion of the population living in towns and cities rose rapidly until by 1800 the Netherlands was the only country in Europe more urbanised than England. Urban life was most unhealthy

---

[22] See Ohlin, 'Mortality, marriage and population growth; and Schofield, 'The relationship between demographic structure and environment'.

[23] Malthus discussed this point at length on several occasions. There is an especially interesting analysis of the way in which, in a capitalist economy where most men are wage earners, market mechanisms tend to arrest population growth well before extreme destitution prevails, in Malthus, *Essay on population* [1826], bk 3, ch. 10, 'Of systems of agriculture and commerce combined'.

[24] For two discussions of the evidence for fertility and nuptiality fluctuations in England between the sixteenth and nineteenth centuries, see Weir, 'Rather never than late'; and Schofield, 'English marriage patterns revisited'.

and *ceteris paribus* a high urban proportion might be expected to slow rather than to expedite growth.[25] The fact that growth rates were high though fertility was at modest levels implies that death rates must have been low. Admittedly, a growth rate averaging only 0.5 per cent (5 per 1,000), per annum does not require a large difference between birth and death rates, but it may seem slightly paradoxical that modest fertility and high growth rates should have gone hand in hand. Further reflection suggests a different reaction. A 'low pressure' demographic system such as England had may not only benefit individuals at any given level of population by ensuring that there is less tension between numbers and the resources available for their support than under a 'high pressure' regime, but may also facilitate more rapid long-term growth. It is not difficult to appreciate the potential advantage of a 'low pressure' system in terms of an equilibrium, or static situation, such as that illustrated in figure 13.1, but it may also encourage population growth.

At a given level of material technology, a population with the characteristics of f_2 in figure 13.1(c) will be smaller than populations of the 13.1(a) or 13.1(b) types, but it may none the less enjoy greater potential for growth if it is the case that the higher current level of real incomes stimulates demand for products and services beyond the basic necessities of life, and so fosters developments in secondary and tertiary industry that would otherwise be absent. Primary industry, too, may benefit, for example as a result of the growth in towns brought about by the growing scale and changing structure of aggregate demand. Urban demand, by providing a dependable and expanding market for agricultural produce, may stimulate agricultural improvement very effectively.[26] The productive base of the economy may expand more rapidly as a result, allowing a continuation of population growth which might otherwise not be possible. The significance of low mortality, in other words, may go well beyond the simple arithmetic fact that low death rates make relatively high growth rates more probable. The absence of low mortality does not just have a bearing on the question of growth in demographic terms: it may also be a symptom of an economic, social, or wider environmental context in which the development of the economy in ways likely to encourage growth is difficult or impossible.

---

[25] This is, however, a matter of great complexity. For interesting reflections on this and some cognate issues see de Vries, *European urbanization*, esp. ch. 10, 'Migration and urban growth'.

[26] The classic description of the beneficial possibilities of a positive feedback situation of this type remains that provided by Adam Smith, *Wealth of nations*, I, bk 3, 'Of the different progress of opulence in different nations'.

Mortality decline in Victorian and Edwardian England

Thirdly, improved knowledge of the relatively modest level of mortality in pre-industrial England also throws a new light on change in more recent periods. When McKeown showed that specific medical therapy appears to have made only a limited contribution to the fall in mortality before about 1930, even though the fall had been in train for at least 80 years, it occasioned some surprise.[27] In part the surprise probably reflected the belief that by the early twentieth century expectation of life at birth was at a substantially higher level than any prevailing in earlier centuries. As an observation applied to the national entity, the belief was justified, but inasmuch as remarkably modest mortality prevailed in some communities three or four centuries ago, and perhaps earlier, any surprise may have been misplaced. The reasons for the fall in mortality in the second half of the nineteenth century have yet to be fully clarified[28] and it may therefore be premature to press any parallel with earlier times, but the mere knowledge that expectation of life at birth of up to 50 years was found in some settlements in earlier periods puts the later nineteenth century and early twentieth centuries in a new perspective.

An adequate level of nutrition, a tolerably pure water supply, a fairly low level of contact with serious infectious disease, and an absence of opportunities for the rapid multiplication of disease vectors, such as those afforded by putrescent animal or vegetable wastes, may permit an average life span of half a century even though medical knowledge is slight and medical practitioners may be few and ignorant. Such conditions may arise, as in the case of Hartland, from a combination of remoteness, light population density, and a relatively favourable ratio of agricultural land to mouths in need of food. Equally, the increased wealth of a country that has undergone an industrial revolution may secure the same advantages even for crowded city populations by investment in water supply and sewage systems, combined with cheap transport to link urbanised populations to distant food supplies, and the enforcement by governments of quarantine regulations and by families and local communities of isolation rules for individuals suffering from infectious ailments. Such changes, helped by cheap fuel for domestic heating, more thorough cooking, and more convenient cleansing of clothes and persons, were evidently capable of securing substantial improvements in mortality since comparable

---

[27] McKeown and Record, 'Reasons for the decline of mortality'; McKeown, Record, and Turner, 'An interpretation of the decline of mortality'.

[28] Though matters have improved substantially with the recent publication of Woods, *Demography of Victorian England and Wales*, esp. chs. 5–8.

circumstances arising for different reasons had led to broadly similar low mortality in much earlier times.

Conclusion

Recognition of the immense significance of the west European marriage pattern has transformed work on population history in recent years. It has proved as important for family history, for the study of household composition, for understanding systems of property transmission between the generations, for grasping the significance of the institution of service, and even for certain aspects of economic history, as for understanding the history of nuptiality and fertility.[29] Perhaps, however, its importance for the understanding of the history of mortality has been too little stressed.

The European marriage system is a 'luxury' that pre-industrial populations may frequently have been unable to afford. Where endemic diseases were many and fatal, where epidemic diseases were frequent and devastating, where food supplies were subject to violent and unpredictable fluctuations, or where some combination of these dangers prevailed, early and universal marriage may have been mandatory. Only if a fairly long life-span is attainable is a modest level of fertility feasible, such as tends to follow from the practice of late marriage and frequent celibacy. It would be rash, however, to assume that only in western Europe were the disease environment and agricultural practices such that the platform level of mortality was low. The issue is not capable of demonstration, at least in the present state of knowledge, but it is likely that mortality regimes were frequently 'manufactured' by the social customs, which exercised such a strong influence on fertility levels, and thus indirectly on mortality. Societies that placed a premium on early marriage and high fertility were thereby unwittingly also placing an equal premium on high mortality.[30]

The same point can be made in a different way. If marriage had been early and universal in England and therefore fertility high, there can be no doubt that mortality would have been equally high, or virtually so.

---

[29] See especially, Hajnal, 'European marriage patterns; Laslett, *Household and family in past time*; Wall, *Family forms in historic Europe*; R. M. Smith, *Land, kinship and life-cycle*; Kussmaul, *Servants in husbandry*; and Wrigley and Schofield, *Population history of England*. The list could be very much extended, but a substantial part of the literature available may be found in the bibliographies of these works.

[30] This was a point much stressed by Malthus. For example, in the course of a discussion of the degree of regularity in the paired relationships possible in the triad of births, marriages, and deaths, he remarked, 'The most general rule that can be laid down on this subject is, perhaps, that any *direct* encouragement to marriage must be accompanied by an increased mortality.' He meant, of course, that the births occurring as a result would mostly fail to survive. Malthus, *Essay on population* [1826], I, p. 197.

In one sense, therefore, the low level of death rates in early modern England was the gift of the marriage practices of the day. They were a necessary if not a sufficient condition of low mortality.

It is more than simply a platitude to remark that death is the inevitable consequence of birth. How early death followed birth was, of course, much influenced by the types of disease prevalent in a community; by the extent of social knowledge of ways of treating, avoiding or preventing disease; by a host of social customs that affected the probability of contracting and combating disease;[31] and by economic conditions. But the average lapse of time between birth and death was also conditioned by the level of fertility in the population. High birth rates could not fail, in most traditional societies, to be matched by equally high death rates, or, in other words, by a brief interval between birth and death. Causation might run either way between the two, or in both directions. The same was true of low rates in the two categories.

Accurate information is scarce or non-existent for most countries. Enough has been learned in the last half century to have overturned much of the received wisdom about population history, and to have provoked much speculation about appropriate 'models' of population behaviour, but both additional information and new thinking would be a welcome aid in separating the wheat from the chaff in current theorising. In that spirit it is reasonable to suggest, though difficult to prove (in either the older or newer sense of the word) that, in seeking to understand the notably modest level of mortality in early modern England, one should look as much to the circumstances of birth as to those of death.

---

[31] Probably the most important single social custom influencing mortality was the set of conventions determining the length of breastfeeding and weaning practices. But dietary conventions and taboos; personal and social hygiene; the scope, frequency, and nature of migratory movements; trade and communications; prevailing customs about the scale and usage of space within dwellings; and a host of other such factors also played a part in raising or reducing susceptibility to disease and accident.

14 The effect of migration on the estimation of marriage age in family reconstitution studies

Use of the technique of family reconstitution has provided a wealth of new information about the demography of communities in the past. In spite of this, there has long been a question mark hanging over reconstitution studies because of a particular problem, sometimes referred to as the problem of the reconstitutable minority. Even though it may be possible to obtain unusually detailed information about the lives of some of the inhabitants of a parish in the past, there will always be many others about whom little can be known, at least without the extreme labour of reconstituting a large block of adjacent parishes in order to reduce the problem of 'escapes' through migration.

The problem stems from a feature of reconstitution that is at once a strength and a weakness. Louis Henry turned the product of genealogical work into a source of precise and detailed demographic information by defining clearly the period of time during which an individual who appears on a family reconstitution form (FRF) may properly be regarded as at risk to give birth, to marry, or to die, and thus enabled exact measurements of fertility, nuptiality, and mortality to be made.[1] This constitutes one of the main strengths of family reconstitution. It is balanced by the fact that the accurate definition of periods of risk demonstrated equally clearly that, at least in places where there was a high level of migration into and out of the parish, many individuals who spent part of their lives in a parish could not be regarded as in observation for demographic purposes for much of their sojourn in the parish, and might indeed never enter observation at all. The demographic history of a parish must therefore be based disproportionately on those who spent the whole or most of their

---

[1] The rules which Henry formulated for obtaining unbiased estimates of demographic rates may be found in Fleury and Henry, *Nouveau manuel de dépouillement* and Henry, *Techniques d'analyse en démographie historique*. The period of observation for, say, the measurement of mortality within a given family may well differ from that for fertility. It is perhaps misleading to imply that the rules of observation for nuptiality are analogous to those for fertility and mortality but this is not the place to rehearse such an issue; it has no bearing on the questions treated in this essay.

lives in the parish, rather than upon transients even though transients might form a substantial proportion of the population present at any one time; on 'stayers' rather than 'leavers'; in short upon the reconstitutable minority.

This problem is not equally acute for all types of measurement. It is unimportant, for example, in the study of infant mortality since the great majority of those born in a parish remain in observation during the following year, but it is a much more telling problem where the nature of the measurement depends upon individuals living in a parish continuously over a long span of years. To study completed fertility, for example, requires the continuous observation of women over a period of half a century.

The doubts expressed about reconstitution, therefore, rarely turn on the accuracy of reconstitution but rather on its representativeness. Certainly family reconstitution has given an astonishing impetus to historical population studies since Henry's pioneering work more than 30 years ago, but it has always seemed reasonable to be sceptical about its ability to paint a picture that would hold true for entire communities. If a degree of scepticism seemed justified generally, it was particularly appropriate in the case of England since throughout the whole parish register period the proportion of each rising generation that stayed in its parish of birth has always been modest. Reconstitution, in short, has sometimes been regarded as a fully appropriate technique for studying closed populations but more dubiously so where migration was common.

Ruggles's critique of estimates of marriage age from family reconstitution material

The nature and scale of any distortion resulting from migration and affecting the value of reconstitution studies remained disputable and unclear, however, until Ruggles published an elegant discussion of the question in 1992.[2] It proved of decisive importance in clarifying the issues involved. As with all good work, it is a testimony to its excellence that it should bring into being further work that might not otherwise have been carried out. In this article I shall consider further that part of Ruggles's article in which he dealt with nuptiality, though Ruggles also considered mortality.[3]

Other things being equal, as Ruggles remarks, 'The odds of migrating before marriage are greater for those who marry late than for those who

---

[2] Ruggles, 'Migration, marriage and mortality'.
[3] The issues raised by Ruggles in relation to the measurement of adult mortality are discussed in Wrigley *et al.*, *English population history*, app. 6.

marry early, just because they are at risk of migrating for longer. Thus, late marriages tend to take place after migration and are systematically excluded from analysis.'[4] Average ages at marriage calculated from 'stayers' will therefore be lower than would be the case if 'leavers' were also covered, but the nature of the linkage process in English family reconstitution means that age at marriage is usually known only for the 'stayers'. High levels of adult mortality will have a similar effect in reducing the observed age at marriage below its 'true' level since some of those who die in young adulthood would have married if they had survived.

Ruggles was able to measure the presumptive importance of both effects by conducting a microsimulation exercise in which the population was endowed with demographic characteristics similar to those of the population of England in the early eighteenth century.[5] His assumptions about migration propensities were derived from Souden's work, and are based on the life histories of deponents in ecclesiastical courts in the seventeenth century. The microsimulation showed that the bias introduced by being able to calculate age at marriage only from the 'stayers' was potentially very substantial. For example, in what he defined as the 'medium-migration' variant of his model the difference in mean age at first marriage measured from the whole simulated population, including both those who migrated and those who did not, and the mean age based only on those who stayed in their place of birth and married there was 2.9 years in the case of women and 2.3 years in the case of men.[6]

Ruggles then turned to the question of whether there was as large a bias in English reconstitutions as his microsimulation exercise had shown to be possible *ceteris paribus*. He noted that the simplest way of correcting for any biases was to measure age at marriage among those who had married *and survived* in a parish to age 50. 'The simplest way of correcting the biases is to restrict the analysis to women who are observed locally at age 50, or older. By eliminating those who migrated or died during the marriage years, we eliminate the possibility of censoring.'[7] He showed that if this were done for the 'stayers' in his simulated population the resulting average age at marriage exactly matched that of survivors to age 50 in the whole population consisting of both 'leavers' and 'stayers'. Using data from all 26 reconstitution parishes, he estimated the mean age at first marriage for women in the combined set of parishes as 25.59 years, but the mean age of those women who survived to age 50 as 26.93 years,

---

[4] Ruggles, 'Migration, marriage and mortality', p. 508.
[5] Ibid., pp. 508–10. Souden, 'Pre-industrial English local migration fields'.
[6] Ruggles, 'Migration, marriage and mortality', tab. 4, p. 512.
[7] Ibid., p. 511.

a difference of 1.34 years.[8] This difference is considerable, though less than half the 2.9 years which microsimulation had suggested as likely to arise with moderate levels of migration, other things being equal.

The difference of 1.34 years, however, compounds the effects of migration and mortality, and in this article I shall concentrate exclusively on the former. Although it is true that the loss of individuals from a cohort of women through death, by making marriage impossible for those concerned, will have the effect of reducing the mean age at marriage below its 'true' level, it is rare to a degree for this consideration to be taken into account in measuring age at marriage. The issue should not be ignored in seeking to define 'pure' measures of the nuptiality, but may be ignored in other contexts. Ruggles's conflation of migration and mortality significantly exaggerates the impact of the former. He estimated the mortality effect as 0.7 years for women in his microsimulation. Subtracting this from the overall difference leaves the difference attributable to migration as 0.64 years when using the empirical reconstitution data. This is a far less dramatic statistic than those obtained in the course of the microsimulation exercise. Ruggles himself found the large discrepancy between the two puzzling and speculated that many migration moves may have been linked to marriage (that is, the migration was not independent of marriage). He suggested that if half of all initial moves were linked to marriage the anomaly would largely disappear.[9]

It appears from his article, in short, that migration *can* produce severe distortion in measured marriage age but that the available empirical evidence about its extent suggests that the distortion was far less than might be expected. What follows represents a further contribution to the elucidation of the empirical side of the question and will again concentrate chiefly on the female population. The cogency of Ruggles's logic is not in question.

It is convenient to begin by retracing Ruggles's steps in estimating the extent of the difference between the observed overall average age at marriage and that of those surviving in observation to age 50 or more.

Retracing and extending Ruggles's analysis

The empirical base of Ruggles's work consisted of data drawn from 26 parish reconstitutions held at the Cambridge Group. For each parish he presented two measures of marriage age, which he termed A and B. Measure A was the average age at marriage of all those who married in the

---

[8] Ibid., tab. 5, p. 513.
[9] Ibid., p. 514.

parish in question; measure B the average calculated from the marriages of those for whom there is evidence that they lived beyond the age of 50.[10] It is readily possible to reproduce from the reconstitution data files held at the Cambridge Group the totals and averages in Ruggles's table either precisely or with the tiniest of differences. The mean ages of measure A and B for women, for example, are 25.59 and 26.93 in Ruggles's table, compared with 25.60 and 26.97 when the attempt was made to mirror the exercise he had undertaken (in table 14.1, to avoid misleading precision, the averages are shown only to one place of decimals). It should be noted, however, that Ruggles appears to have obtained his overall averages by weighting the individual parishes means by a measure of parish size based on the number of female births recorded in the parish in question in the reconstitution period.[11] If, alternatively, the weights used are the number of ages at marriage known in each parish (that is, if every age at marriage counts equally with every other) the measure B mean falls to 26.7, though the measure A mean remains unchanged, thus reducing the difference between the two from 1.4 to 1.1 years. This alternative measure will be used in this essay, though the results of using Ruggles's method are also given. For ease of reference the relevant data are set out in table 14.1.

Different ways of calculating means from the same body of data can evidently produce somewhat different results, but there are other changes that it seems proper to make in order to examine the issue further. The changes fall under three heads. The effect of the first is shown on row 2 of table 14.2. It summarises changes which increased the number of cases. They were the following. First, further work on the parish of Birstall increased the number of known female ages at first marriage by 919. This was the largest single change. Second, a redefinition of the period of reliable data that could be secured from the parish of Willingham, a very small parish, increased its total of known marriage ages by 11. Third, an oversight in the original exercise led to the improper exclusion of women for whom there was no date of baptism, but whose date of birth was known. This added a further 248 cases. The remaining 38 cases consist of women who were contracting a first marriage but whose marriage rank was coded in a way which led to their exclusion. The effect of these changes may be appreciated by comparing the first and second rows of table 14.2. It is perhaps fortunate for simplicity of exposition that, although these several changes increase the total of measure A marriages by 1,216, or 8.8 per cent, and measure B marriages by 85, or 2.9 per cent,

---

[10] Ibid., tab. 5, p. 513.
[11] The method of weighting is not specified in the article, but the close similarity in results suggests that this was the method used.

Table 14.1 *Age at first marriage of women in 26 reconstitutions*

Parish	First marriages (1)	Average age (measure A) (2)	Of col. (1) all reaching age 50 (3)	Average age (measure B) (4)	Difference col. (4)–col. (2) (5)	Total of girl children (6)
Alcester	346	27.1	63	29.9	2.8	2,137
Aldenham	395	25.2	79	26.5	1.3	2,413
Ash	559	24.8	113	25.1	0.3	2,708
Austrey	101	27.6	13	28.5	0.9	575
Banbury	1,330	25.7	216	27.5	1.8	7,359
Birstall	2,306	24.5	543	25.3	0.8	8,400
Bottesford	508	26.3	115	27.1	0.8	2,747
Bridford	112	26.4	23	28.8	2.4	615
Colyton	440	27.7	90	30.7	3.0	3,321
Dawlish	366	26.0	73	27.1	1.1	1,264
Earsdon	142	25.8	35	26.7	0.9	586
Gainsborough	1,652	25.5	278	26.9	1.4	8,119
Gedling	570	26.0	153	27.1	1.1	2,304
Great Oakley	53	23.7	5	26.5	2.8	438
Hartland	524	28.3	147	29.7	1.4	1,644
Ipplepen	81	26.2	19	26.6	0.4	350
Lowestoft	348	25.1	81	26.3	1.2	2,269
March	273	25.5	8	31.7	6.2	2,659
Methley	410	26.0	53	26.5	0.5	2,078
Morchard Bishop	789	26.1	280	26.2	0.1	2,605
Odiham	759	25.1	210	25.7	0.6	4,415
Reigate	358	25.2	32	27.2	2.0	1,909
Shepshed	666	25.7	149	26.1	0.4	2,584
Southill	395	24.8	55	25.3	0.5	3,099
Terling	210	24.3	34	24.1	−0.2	1,559
Willingham	90	24.7	15	27.5	2.8	883
All	13,783	25.6	2,882	26.7	1.1	69,040
All weighted by female births		25.6		27.0	1.4	

Source: Cambridge Group reconstitutions.

the difference of means remains almost unchanged, falling from 1.1 to 1.0 years (though, as if to demonstrate the slightness of the change, actually rising very slightly from 1.07 to 1.08 years, if calculated to two places of decimals). The means themselves rose very slightly.

The second step needed to make the comparison of measure A and measure B means as complete and accurate as possible concerns the definition of those surviving to age 50 (and who can therefore be included in measure B). In the original exercise the criterion was taken as a date of end of marriage occurring when the individual in question was above age 50 (that is, either the index individual died above age 50 and thereby brought the marriage to an end or his or her spouse died, but the nature of the information on the FRF left no doubt that the other partner to the marriage survived). It was an unnecessary restriction, however, that the test as originally framed excluded cases where the marriage ended when the index person was under 50 but there is evidence that he or she survived to die above that age. Similarly, evidence of survival to beyond age 50 because the individual in question remarried above that age was ignored, but is a proper reason for inclusion.

The effect of implementing these changes is to be seen in the third row of table 14.2. The changed rules for identifying those reaching age 50 increases their number from 2,967 to 3,806, or by 28 per cent. Since no change is made that affects measure A both the totals of marriages and the mean age at marriage under this head are unchanged, but the mean age at marriage under measure B falls from 26.7 to 26.5 years and the difference in the means falls from 1.0 to 0.8 years. If reference is made to individual parishes, it is apparent that the small fall in the measure B mean is very widespread, occurring in 23 out of the 26 parishes. The fall is almost always small, but it is also markedly consistent.

This was the only modification to the original data that significantly changed the difference of means between measure A and measure B. It seems likely that the original criterion for reaching age 50, that the end of the marriage should occur when the index individual was over 50, introduced a small bias into the result. In the case of women who survived their husbands, it meant that she would only be included if her husband died when she was over age 50 (if he had died when she was under 50, even though she survived to above 50, the case would have been excluded). The ages of spouses are strongly correlated. A man who was, say, age 40 at marriage was more likely to survive from marriage to age 50 or more than a man who married at age 30. The latter, however, was more likely to have a young wife, who, even if she survived his death when she was under 50 and herself reached 50, would be excluded. The rule therefore tended to increase the chance of inclusion of women who

Table 14.2 *Summary measures of marriage age with original and enlarged data sets*

	First marriages (1)	Average age (measure A) (2)	Of col. (1) all reaching age 50 (3)	Average age (measure B) (4)	Difference (col. (4)–col. (2)) (5)	Total of girl children (6)
Original data	13,783	25.6	2,882	26.7	1.1	69,040
Enlarged data set	14,999	25.7	2,967	26.7	1.1	73,789
Changed rules for reaching age 50	14,999	25.7	3,806	26.5	0.8	73,789
Changed censoring rule	10,235	26.0	2,958	26.8	0.8	55,733

Note: For additional details of the make-up of the four data sets shown on successive lines of the table, see associated text.
Source: Cambridge Group reconstitutions.

were above the normal age at marriage relative to those who were below it. Correcting this inaccuracy would therefore tend to reduce the mean of measure B relative to measure A.

The bottom row of table 14.2 shows the effect of making a final change to the original rules. Ruggles excluded the last 50 years of data from each reconstitution to avoid artificially depressing the average age at marriage towards the end of each reconstitution.[12] To have no such rule when marshalling data on a cohort basis, or to have chosen a shorter period, would have allowed young brides and grooms to be accepted into the data set towards the end of a reconstitution but would have caused older brides and grooms to be progressively excluded. However, 50 years is too short a period for the purpose in mind. It avoids the danger of depressing average age at marriage but it means that towards the end of the reconstitution some of those who survive in marriage to age 50 and should be included will nevertheless be excluded since events that would demonstrate their continued presence are excluded from view. Thus, if age at marriage were falling on measure A and also among those who survived to age 50, the latter would not be adequately represented towards the end of the reconstitution because of the 50-year rule. A purist view would be that a period of 100 years should be allowed, but this seems excessively restrictive, and, after some experiment, 85 years was adopted as a suitable censoring period.

To move from 50 to 85 years substantially reduces the number of ages at marriage that can be used, of course. The total of measure A ages at marriage falls by 4,764, or 31.8 per cent, while the measure B total falls by 848, or 22.2 per cent. As was to be expected both means are higher with an 85-year than with a 50-year period of censoring because the years that are additionally excluded fall towards the end of each reconstitution, when age at marriage was falling in England. The difference between the two means, however, remains unchanged at 0.8 years (measured to two decimal places it fell very slightly).[13] For completeness table 14.3 provides information to enable the final position for each parish to be compared with the starting position set out in table 14.1.

---

[12] Ruggles, 'Migration, marriage and mortality'. p. 511, n.10.

[13] The means given in tab. 14.2 were all calculated by giving equal weight to each marriage. If the alternative method used by Ruggles is employed (that is, if the means for each parish are weighted by the totals of female births in each parish), the measure A means comparable to those on the four successive rows of tab. 14.2 are 25.6, 25.7, 25.7, and 25.9 years; the four measure B means are 27.0, 27.0, 26.6, and 26.9 years; and the four differences are 1.4, 1.3, 0.9, and 1.0 years. Both the pattern of change from one set of assumptions to the next and the absolute level of the differences between measure A and measure B means, therefore, are broadly comparable whichever method is employed.

Table 14.3 *Age at first marriage of women in 26 reconstitutions*

Parish	First marriages (1)	Average age (measure A) (2)	Of (col. 1) all reaching age 50 (3)	Average age (measure B) (4)	Difference col. (4)–col. (2) (5)	Total of girl children (6)
Alcester	225	26.2	59	28.5	2.3	1,594
Aldenham	340	25.1	85	26.0	0.9	2,055
Ash	363	25.6	92	25.0	−0.6	2,003
Austrey	73	26.9	15	25.8	−1.1	537
Banbury	999	26.1	251	27.3	1.2	6,667
Birstall	1,853	25.7	494	25.7	0.0	5,839
Bottesford	424	26.5	129	27.1	0.6	2,439
Bridford	94	26.5	22	29.4	2.9	496
Colyton	383	27.8	115	30.0	2.2	3,107
Dawlish	242	26.5	79	27.5	1.0	896
Earsdon	34	25.6	7	26.6	1.0	259
Gainsborough	1,238	25.4	342	26.3	0.9	6,756
Gedling	418	26.6	164	27.4	0.8	1,801
Great Oakley	20	23.8	2	25.5	1.7	229
Hartland	418	28.6	157	29.7	1.1	1,358
Ipplepen	35	27.7	11	30.1	2.4	181
Lowestoft	237	24.8	60	26.1	1.3	1,940
March	196	25.7	5	31.6	5.9	2,009
Methley	324	26.2	69	27.0	0.8	1,733
Morchard Bishop	489	26.1	288	26.2	0.1	1,879
Odiham	684	25.4	227	25.9	0.5	4,231
Reigate	182	24.8	35	26.7	1.9	1,151
Shepshed	433	26.6	151	27.0	0.4	1,892
Southill	301	25.1	49	26.0	0.9	2,664
Terling	151	24.5	32	25.0	0.5	1,324
Willingham	79	24.8	18	26.5	1.7	693
All	10,235	26.0	2,958	26.8	0.8	55,733
All weighted by female births		25.9		26.9	1.0	

Source: Cambridge Group reconstitutions.

Table 14.4 *Age at first marriage of women in 11 reconstitutions: change over time*

Marriages taking place	First marriages (1)	Average age (measure A) (2)	Of col. (1) all reaching age 50 (3)	Average age (measure B) (4)	Difference (col. (4)−col. (2)) (5)
Up to 1699	4,676	26.1	1,305	26.8	0.7
1700 or later	2,791	25.6	981	25.9	0.3

Source: Cambridge Group reconstitutions.

Two further tests of the scale of the difference between measure A and measure B means may be considered: change over time, and the pattern revealed by male, rather than female, first ages at marriages.

Change over time is best measured if the set of parishes is the same in each period. Otherwise any change related to time may be reduced or exaggerated by the effects of compositional change. And any test must be rough and ready since the number of cases is too few to permit extensive subdivision. In table 14.4 the parish register period as a whole is divided into two halves; marriage before and after 1700. The data are drawn from only 11 parishes. The large reduction in the number of parishes from the total of 26 shown in table 14.3 occurs because, although most reconstitutions were continued down to 1837, in many cases the data cease to be reliable after about 1790, and, given the 85-year censoring rule, only those where reliable data continue past 1790 could be included.[14] As a result, whereas there are 10,235 ages at first marriage in table 14.3, there are only 7,467 in table 14.4. Table 14.4 suggests that the difference between measure A and measure B was slightly larger in the earlier than in the later period, but both before and after 1700 the differences are small, in both cases smaller than in the full data set described in table 14.3.

Repeating for men the exercise already carried out for women suggests similar conclusions. The male measure B mean exceeds the measure A mean by 0.7 years, slightly less than in the case of females. The measure A mean is based on a smaller total of cases, 8,001 compared with 10,235 female first marriages, but the measure B mean is based on a somewhat larger number of cases, 3,356 compared with 2,958; 42 per cent of men marrying locally can be shown to have survived beyond age 50 in their parish of birth, compared with only 29 per cent of women. In large part this difference springs from the custom of marrying in the bride's parish

---

[14] The tests for reliability which led to the rejection of much parish data after *c.*1790 are described in detail in Wrigley *et al.*, *English population history*, ch. 4.

even though the couple later settle elsewhere. This both explains the larger total of female first marriage ages and the much lower 'survival' rate.[15]

The measure B mean exceeds measure A by 0.8 years in the case of women and by 0.7 years in the case of men. Since the mortality effect may be expected to cause a measure B mean to exceed a measure A mean by about 0.7 years in the former case and by 0.5 years in the latter case by Ruggles's estimation,[16] it is clear that the scale of any migration effect must be very slight. That there should be so strong a reason in logic for expecting the two measures to differ substantially and so little evidence that they did so in practice may seem puzzling, but before attempting an explanation for the paradox, it is convenient to consider another inference drawn by Ruggles from his data. He devoted two columns in the key table in his article to the percentages of women parish by parish who were included in measure A and measure B.[17]

He derived his percentages by relating totals of known marriage ages in each category to the totals of female births over an appropriate period in each parish. The resulting percentages were low. The overall average given at the foot of each column was 19.90 per cent for measure A, 4.16 per cent for measure B. But this is a rather misleading procedure since each birth cohort was substantially depleted by death before reaching marriageable age. Thus, for example, a girl who died aged 10 can have had no chance of marrying and to include her in the denominator will tend to understate the extent of local marriage among those born in the parish. A more appropriate method of estimating the percentages of local-born who married in the parish is to take as the denominator the number surviving to the mean age at marriage. If this is taken to be 25 years in the case of women, and using level 8 of model North of the Princeton model life tables (e_0 37.5 years),[18] the comparable percentages rise to 34.0 and 7.1 (for men, if mean age at marriage is taken as 27 years, the percentages are 25.5 and 10.7).

The level of these percentages might seem a matter of small significance, but they played a part in convincing Ruggles that the incidence

---

[15] It is worthy of note that inspection of the successive steps by which the original means for men are changed into those described in this paragraph (that is, paralleling for men the steps summarised for women in tab. 14.2) reveals that, as with women, the only change that significantly alters the difference between measure A and measure B means is the change to the criterion for reaching age 50. The same correlation between the ages of spouses that tended to cause the mean age at marriage of women who reached the age of 50 to be exaggerated produced a similar effect in the case of men. Changing the criterion reduced the difference of means from 0.9 to 0.7 years.

[16] Ruggles, 'Migration, marriage and mortality', tab. 4, p. 512.

[17] Ibid., tab. 5, p. 513.

[18] Coale and Demeny, *Regional model life tables*, p. 227.

of migration was very high indeed in English parishes.[19] A more appropriate method of estimating the percentages makes a lower estimate of migration more plausible. It should be recognised, moreover, that even the percentages just given substantially understate the true position. The fact that a marriage remained unlinked to a baptism does not always mean that the bride or groom had been born elsewhere. When reconstitution is done by hand no link is made in cases of 'multiplicity'. Thus to take the two simplest possibilities, if a given baptism can be linked to two marriages, or if the bride on a given FRF can be linked to two or more baptisms, no link is made.[20] The proportion of native brides and grooms is therefore always understated if measured in this fashion. Again, a significant proportion of each birth cohort never married even though surviving throughout the age range within which marriage takes place. This percentage was seldom below 10 per cent and at times rose to 20 per cent or more.[21]

The numbers of marriages of local-born people, therefore, should be related not to all those reaching the mean age at marriage, but to all those who reached this age and married. Making a reasonable allowance for this would raise the measure A and measure B of overall percentages of women who married locally to about 40 and 9 per cent respectively (for men the comparable figures would be 30 and 13 per cent).[22] It is more difficult to quantify the number of cases where no link was made on an FRF because of a 'multiplicity' problem. It varied considerably from parish to parish because in some parishes a relatively high proportion of the population shared a few surnames while in others this was not the case. Clearly, the problem would be much more acute in the former than in the latter type of parish. This factor might well, however, raise the measure A percentage by one or two points, and the measure B percentage proportionately.

However, no plausible adjustments to the percentage of all members of a cohort who were married in their native parish would raise it to the point where fewer than half of all those born in a parish subsequently married elsewhere. Migration was a less dominant experience than is implied in Ruggles's calculations but it was still very common. Why therefore is this

---

[19] Ruggles, 'Migration, marriage and mortality', p. 514.

[20] Different rules apply to reconstitutions carried out by computer. In these cases ambiguities in linkage are resolved and a choice made between alternative possibilities, but there is not enough data as yet to make it possible to estimate the proportion of links that can be made by programs which are not made by hand. All the 26 reconstitutions used in this study were carried out by hand.

[21] Schofield, 'English marriage patterns revisited', tab. 3, p. 14 (and the associated discussion).

[22] The data set out in the second panel of tab. 14.5 show that in the age group 25–9 in 1851 41.3 per cent of the women and 40.2 per cent of the men were local born.

not reflected in a larger difference between the mean ages at marriage of measure A and measure B? Is there other evidence that can be invoked that will shed light on the puzzle? Other evidence exists but, before describing it, it may be helpful to consider a little further the general nature of the problem.

The timing and type of migration

A first point to note is that the mere fact of a high level of migration out of a parish does not necessarily create the effect so elegantly demonstrated in Ruggles's simulation. For example, to take a limiting possibility, if all those who migrate from a parish did so before the beginning of the period of life during which marriage took place, then, however large a proportion they were of the birth cohort, their age at marriage would be identical to that of those who remained behind, *ceteris paribus*. On this assumption, no distortion in the measurement of mean age at marriage will arise from being able to obtain data only from 'stayers'; or, to make the same point in a different way, after making allowance for the effect of mortality, measure A and measure B will produce the same result.

No-one supposes, of course, that all parochial out-migration took this form in early modern England. But neither should its importance be ignored.[23] The institution of service affected the lives of a very high percentage of young people of both sexes in this period. At any one time up to a half of all unmarried adolescents and young adults in the age range from 15 to 24 were out in service and a substantially higher proportion of each generation spent a part of this period in service.[24] A high proportion of those who went into service (or into functional equivalents like apprenticeship) had done so by the age of 18. Detailed evidence on this point for the early modern period is limited, but Wall's study of age at leaving home provides some valuable data bearing on the issue. He was able to assemble data from detailed listings of inhabitants for Swindon (1697), Cardington (1782), Binfield (1801), and Colyton (1841). If the material from the four parishes is consolidated into a single series and the

---

[23] It was not, of course, ignored by Ruggles but his migration schedule may have failed to reflect its scale. Ruggles, 'Migration, marriage and mortality', tab. 2, p. 509.

[24] For example, Laslett has provided some data on the proportion of each age group who were in service separately for men and women. The data are taken from listings of inhabitants of six settlements in the early modern period which, exceptionally, provided information in sufficient detail to enable the incidence of service by age to be studied. The median percentages of those in service in the age groups 15–9 and 20–4 were 35 and 30 for men and 27 and 40 for women. Laslett also provided further detail about the percentages married by sex and age. This makes it possible to calculate the percentages of single persons in service in each age group: these are 35 and 36 per cent for men and 27 and 49 per cent for women in the age groups 15–9 and 20–4. P. Laslett, *Family life and illicit love*, tabs. 1.4 and 1.7, pp. 26–7 and 34.

data for the two sexes merged (the pattern for adolescents of both sexes was similar), 24 per cent of all children aged 15–7 were no longer living at home and 35 per cent of those aged 18–9.[25]

Teenage marriage was almost unknown for men in the past, and few girls were married under the age of 18.[26] The predominant pattern was to enter service in the middle teens and to remain in service until marriage (by convention living-in servants were almost never married).[27] Entering service meant living in another's household, normally under an informal contract of one year's duration. In most cases it appears to have meant departure from the parish of birth, if not initially then by the time the individual in question was of an age to marry.[28] Courtship was often conducted between a man and a woman both of whom were in service when neither was living in his or her own parish. Those women who followed this classical career track were likely to appear as 'leavers' on marrying, but the more prevalent this pattern was, the less likely that there would be a major difference in marriage age between 'leavers' and 'stayers'.

Secondly, migration was a complex phenomenon whose impact on mean age at first marriage may be more ambiguous than is implied in Ruggles's model. Almost all migratory movements involve a return flow and in many cases gross migration is several times as large in volume as net migration. To the extent that a return flow of men and women existed coming back still unmarried to their native parish after a period of residence elsewhere, and on the assumption that some of them later did marry, it would create a counterbalancing factor so far as age at marriage is concerned. Just as those who leave a parish unmarried and subsequently marry must do so on average at a later age than those who do not leave (on *ceteris paribus* assumptions), so those who return still unmarried to a parish after a period away but who later marry will do so at a still higher age than those who left and married away from their parish of birth.

---

[25] Wall, 'The age at leaving home', tab. 3, p. 191.

[26] Over the parish register period as a whole fewer than 1 groom in 100 in bachelor/spinster marriages married before his eighteenth birthday. The comparable figure for brides was between 4 and 5 per 100: Wrigley *et al.*, *English population history*, tab. 5.6, pp. 146–7.

[27] Kussmaul found that the modal age of entry into service in husbandry was 13–4 years, and that 45 per cent of all those who entered service did so between the ages of 13 and 16. Kussmaul, *Servants in husbandry*, p. 70.

[28] Ibid., chs. 4 and 5. Listings of inhabitants with sufficient information to enable this matter to be investigated with precision are extremely rare. The most informative is that of Cardington in the year 1782. Boys and girls in their early or middle teens who were out in service were often resident in Cardington, but as they grew older only an increasingly small minority remained in the parish. Schofield, 'Age-specific mobility', tab. 3, pp. 268–9 and discussion on pp. 270–1.

Thirdly, the existence of an association between migration and marriage, a factor to which Ruggles himself drew attention in seeking to explain the slightness of the difference between his measure A and measure B averages, may have played an important part in explaining the apparently anomalous absence of the pattern suggested by microsimulation. If a chief reason to migrate was to find a partner, or if that partner had already been found and a marriage was imminent, it would not be surprising to find empirical evidence at odds with prediction.

A combination of the three effects just described may easily result in the mean ages at marriage of 'leavers' and 'stayers' being identical, or for that matter producing a reverse gap with 'leavers' marrying earlier than 'stayers'. A very crude and arbitrary example of their joint effect is given in figure 14.1. It is intended to do no more than illustrate the point that these effects can be sufficient to eliminate the marriage age gap between 'leavers' and 'stayers' on broadly plausible assumptions about the parameters involved. The lesson to be drawn from the figure is not that a measurement of marriage age based on 'stayers' is free from distortion, but only that the scale and even the direction of the difference between what can be measured and what one might wish to measure cannot be readily determined *a priori*.

In figure 14.1 matters have been simplified to the point of caricature by ignoring mortality, by assuming that everyone marries, and by restricting all migratory moves to only three points in the history of the birth cohort, at the ages of 18, 23, and 32. At the earliest of these three ages 300 of the members of the cohort leave the parish, say to enter service. Of these, 275 later marry at an average age of 26 years, the average for the cohort as a whole. Of the 700 remaining in the parish 200 have married by the time the cohort is aged 23, and they marry on average at the age of 21.5 years. At this point another mass exodus occurs with 250 of the 500 remaining unmarried women leaving the parish. Of the 250 migrants, 225 marry, again on average at the age of 26, many having been induced to leave by the prospect of marriage. The 250 left behind in the parish, on the other hand, reach the church porch in a more leisurely fashion, marrying on average at age 28. If no further marriages had been contracted the mean age at marriage of 'stayers' (25.1 years) would be somewhat lower than that of 'leavers' (26.0 years). However, 25 of the initial surge of migrants and the same number in the second wave are assumed not to have married while away from their native parish. If, as is assumed in figure 14.1, these 50 migrants return to their native parish in a third return wave of migration at the age of 32 and subsequently marry at an average age of 34, the mean age at marriage of 'stayers' rises to 26.0 years and the two groups therefore have identical ages at marriage.

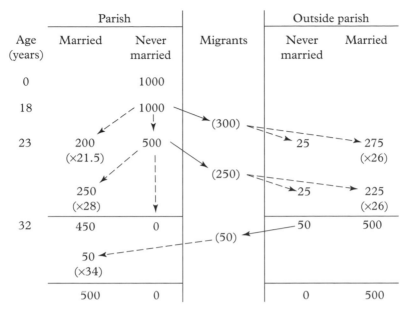

Figure 14.1. *A stylised model of marriage and migration*
Note: Solid lines indicate migratory movement. Broken lines divide those
currently unmarried into those who continue unmarried and those who
marry. The figures in brackets preceded by a multiplication sign indicate
the mean age at marriage of a group of individuals.

Census data and the singulate mean age at marriage

The relevance of this crude and stylised exercise becomes clear if we turn
to evidence drawn from a source that does allow the marriage ages of
'leavers' and 'stayers' to be measured directly. The early English censuses
were sketchy affairs in which the information was collected by parish
overseers: there were no individual household schedules. This changed
in 1841 and the enumerators' books of the next census, held in 1851,
provide information that can be readily adapted to the study of marriage
age. The age, sex, marital status, and place of birth of each individual
was recorded. It is therefore possible to determine what proportion of
men and women had ever been married in each age group, and thus to
calculate the singulate mean age at marriage of 'leavers' and 'stayers' in
each parish.

Table 14.5 contains the results of an exercise carried out on data drawn
from a stratified systematic cluster sample of enumeration districts for
which all personal information relating to individuals present on census

Table 14.5 *Singulate mean age at marriage and proportions never married in 1851 (national sample)*

	Males			Females		
	Local-born	Migrants	All	Local-born	Migrants	All
Proportions never married per 1,000 in the age group						
15–9	984	995	989	971	967	969
20–4	744	759	750	675	686	681
25–9	375	364	369	414	361	383
30–4	254	246	249	310	223	255
35–9	147	133	138	177	137	151
40–4	148	95	114	148	117	128
45–9	139	58	87	187	101	128
50–4	83	145	119	120	83	95
45–54	112	95	101	156	93	113
Totals of individuals in each age group						
15–9	702	595	1,297	783	702	1,485
20–4	570	693	1,263	627	901	1,528
25–9	477	708	1,185	541	768	1,309
30–4	382	615	997	406	695	1,101
35–9	307	540	847	316	607	923
40–4	284	485	769	290	545	835
45–9	223	411	634	214	475	689
50–4	216	304	520	183	396	579

Singulate mean age at marriage

	Males			Females			Number of males	Number of females
	Local-born	Migrant	All	Local-born	Migrant	All		
Small settlements	27.4	27.8	27.6	25.9	26.0	26.0	1,910	1,848
Larger settlements	26.8	26.0	26.3	25.4	26.1	25.9	1,592	1,676
Towns and boroughs	25.6	25.2	25.3	25.6	25.5	25.5	4,010	4,925
All	26.3	26.0	26.1	25.6	25.7	25.7	7,512	8,449

Notes: Small settlements were places with fewer than 2,000 inhabitants; the towns and boroughs category excludes London, while larger settlements consist of places that do not fall into either of the other two categories. The totals in the two final columns of the bottom panel show the total male and female population aged 15–54 in the four categories.

Source: Data kindly provided by Michael Anderson from a random stratified sample of material abstracted from the 1851 census enumerators' returns.

night was put into a machine-readable form. The original exercise covered a 1 in 50 sample of the population of England and Wales in 1851. The data tabulated in table 14.5 relate to about 16,000 individuals forming part of a randomly selected subsample (excluding London) drawn from the full data set.[29] The top panel of the table shows the proportions never married in each age group for the local born, migrants, and the whole population; the middle panel lists the totals of individuals in each age group; while the bottom panel (bottom row) gives the singulate mean age at marriage calculated from the data in the top panel. The bottom panel also gives mean ages for three settlement types into which the sample clusters can conveniently be divided.[30]

It is immediately apparent that there was no significant difference in mean age at marriage between the local born and migrants. The means for these two categories are almost identical for women and only a little further apart in the case of men (where, indeed, the singulate mean age at marriage was *lower* for migrants than for the local born). With minor variations the same is true for each of the three settlement types as for the sample as a whole. The census evidence, therefore, suggests that those who had moved away from their native parish did not marry any later than those who remained at home ('local born' in this context means resident still within two kilometres of the stated birthplace: all others are 'migrants').[31]

In the case of women the census data provide some suggestive, if indirect evidence of the complexity of the relationship between migration and marriage, since the first and second columns of the female section of the top panel of table 14.5 reveal that even though the *ages at marriage* of the local born and migrants were closely similar, the *proportions never marrying* were not. Far fewer migrants had never married by age 50 than local-born women, 9 per cent as compared with 16 per cent.[32] Relatively few women in middle life who were no longer living in their place of birth remained unmarried, but celibacy was much commoner among

---

[29] The selection was done separately for small and larger settlements. The sampling fraction was only half as large for the former as for the latter.

[30] The singulate mean age at marriage was calculated in the manner set out in Shryock and Siegel, *Methods and materials of demography*, I, p. 295 (i.e., taking the proportion never married as the average of the percentages never married in the two age groups 45–9 and 50–4).

[31] All settlements in the data set were given geographical co-ordinates so that a consistent definition of 'local born' is possible.

[32] It may be of interest to note that the mean of the percentages never married in the age groups 45–9 and 50–4 for the 'All' category in tab. 14.5 was 10.3 for men and 11.2 for women. The comparable percentages for the population of England and Wales as a whole at that time were 11.4 and 12.3; Mitchell, *British historical statistics*, ch. 1, tab. 5, pp. 20–2.

'stayers'. It is quite possible that many of the latter had lived away from their birthplace in earlier life but had returned as a result of never having married to live with elderly parents, with siblings, or, if living alone, at least close to surviving kin. There is a hint of this in the slightness of the fall in the proportions never married above the 30–4 age group among the local born. That the fall is irregular is probably a function of the relatively small number of individuals involved and the consequent effects of random variation, but the levelling out in the decline does not reflect, of course, a complete absence of new first marriages in the age range but rather the return to their native heath of women in their later thirties and forties who had not been able to marry and settle elsewhere.[33] Amongst such a group, even though most may have remained unmarried after returning, a few would probably have married. If this was the case, it tends to justify the assumption made in figure 14.1 about the existence and effects of a return migration flow.

The same contrast is not so clearly visible among men. Proportions never married did not differ greatly between the local born and migrants, allowing for the probable presence of random effects in the small numbers who remained unmarried in the higher age groups. Perhaps male migrants who had never married were less attracted or felt less compelled to return to their parish of birth than female migrants. Yet the singulate mean age at marriage of male migrants was much the same as that of the local born. This suggests that other factors, such as migration in large numbers before the age at which marriage first began to be common or a strong association between a migratory move and a subsequent marriage must have operated powerfully.[34]

It would be possible, of course, to calculate singulate mean ages at marriage for each of the 26 reconstitution parishes listed in table 14.1 by tabulating information taken from the relevant enumerators' books. This has not been attempted, partly because of the labour involved, but also because findings based on the 1851 census material can only be authoritative for the last few decades of the parish register period.[35] It is

[33] Inspection of the enumerators' books for individual rural parishes sometimes creates the impression that if one sets aside casual visitors who happened to be in the parish with relations on census night and women who were servants or governesses in the households of clergy and gentry, it was very rare for non-native women who had never married to be present in a parish above the age of about 35.

[34] It is intrinsically likely that the former was a stronger influence among men than women since a male cohort was affected by marriage only at a later age than a female cohort. Given similar age patterns of migration from the parish, therefore, a higher proportion of male than female migrants would have left their native parishes before reaching the bottom end of the age range during which they were at risk to marry.

[35] The materials were to hand, however, to enable the singulate mean age at marriage to be calculated from the 1851 census enumerators' books for Colyton. The Colyton pattern

plausible to argue, however, that a pattern found in deeply rural areas, in market towns, and in large cities in mid nineteenth-century England embraces such a wide range of circumstances that it is likely to have been deeply rooted in social behaviour and therefore of long standing.

Further evidence about marriage age and migration

A partial and indirect test of the situation in earlier centuries is possible. The FRFs from which all reconstitution data are derived may be divided into those in which the age at marriage of neither spouse is known, those where the age of one spouse is known but not that of the other, and those where the ages of both spouses are known. The first category does not concern us in this connection. The last category consists of marriages in which both partners were born in the parish, while the second category comprises cases where one spouse was born in the parish while the other was not.[36] It might be expected that the average age at marriage of husbands and wives in marriages in the last category would be lower than in other cases because in this category both spouses may be presumed to be 'stayers'. Where the age of only one of the two spouses is known, on the other hand, it might be expected that in a substantial proportion of cases the partner whose age is known had left the parish for a period before the marriage took place and had returned in order to be married in his or her native parish. This is particularly likely in the case of the bride, since convention decreed a return to her native parish for the marriage ceremony even though it was no longer where she lived. The age at

---

was very similar to that just described for the national sample. The age at marriage of local-born women was 0.6 years lower than that for migrants to the parish; the male figure was 3.1 years *higher* for the local born. The number of men and women involved was too small to sustain any firm conclusion but the 'migration effect' to be expected from Ruggles's analysis was not visible. Other similar exercises were carried out on census data for parishes that were not reconstituted (Clayworth, Notts.; Grasmere, Westmorland; and a group of 14 contiguous rural parishes in east Norfolk in the hundred of Clavering). All showed inconsequential differences in singulate mean age at marriage between local-born and migrant brides and grooms; and all showed very marked differences in the proportions never married at age 50 between local-born and migrant women. Aggregating all these parishes the overall proportion never married at age 50 was 19 per cent among local-born women, but only 6 per cent among migrant women.

[36] This assertion should be glossed. Marriages in which the age of one spouse is known, but not that of his or her partner, will include a proportion of cases where both partners were born in the parish, but more than one baptism could be linked to one of the spouses and so no link was made.

Table 14.6 *Marriage ages for different categories of marriage*

(1) Both spouses' age at marriage known.
(2) Only one spouse's age at marriage known; some event or events later than the date of marriage recorded on FRF.
(3) Only one spouse's age at marriage known; no event later than date of marriage recorded on FRF.

Males	Average age					Totals		
	(1)	(2)	(3)	(1)–(2)	(1)–(3)	(1)	(2)	(3)
1600–24	27.8	27.4	29.7	0.4	−1.9	207	359	45
1625–49	27.0	27.6	26.4	−0.6	0.6	376	532	39
1650–74	27.2	27.5	29.1	−0.3	−1.9	389	495	48
1675–99	27.7	27.3	28.4	0.4	−0.7	316	459	50
1700–24	27.6	27.5	27.8	0.1	−0.2	404	595	46
1725–49	27.1	27.4	27.7	−0.3	−0.6	430	606	61
1750–74	26.2	26.6	28.4	−0.4	−2.2	531	621	62
1775–99	26.5	26.7	26.7	−0.2	−0.2	457	432	55
Average of the 8 periods				−0.1	−0.9			
Females								
1600–24	25.9	25.4	25.5	0.5	0.4	207	358	181
1625–49	24.9	25.5	26.3	−0.6	−1.4	376	563	252
1650–74	25.3	25.8	26.7	−0.5	−1.4	389	458	236
1675–99	26.1	25.2	26.8	0.9	−0.7	316	401	193
1700–24	26.3	26.1	26.9	0.2	−0.6	404	578	297
1725–49	25.2	25.7	26.8	−0.5	−1.6	430	726	258
1750–74	24.7	26.0	25.9	−0.3	−1.2	531	782	312
1775–99	24.3	24.3	24.8	0.0	−0.5	457	546	229
Average of the 8 periods				0.0	−0.9			

Notes: Since it is necessary to keep a family in observation for a lengthy period in order to determine whether or not any event subsequent to the marriage was registered, only marriages taking place 50 years or more before the end of the reconstitution in a given parish were used in this tabulation; hence the last quarter-century from which such marriages can be drawn is 1775–99. It should be noted that no marriages from Birstall were included in this tabulation, because although the age at marriage of partners to childless marriages is known, the subsequent history of such marriages was not fully recorded in this reconstitution.
Source: Cambridge Group reconstitutions.

marriage of such women, in these circumstances, should be later than that of brides who married men who were also born in the parish in which the marriage was celebrated.

Table 14.6 shows the results of tabulating the data most relevant to this issue. The marriages have been divided into three categories: those where the age of both partners is known; those where the age of only one is known but there is some further information on the FRF (that is, children to the marriage were recorded in the register and so appear on the FRF, or the deaths of one or both spouses occurred in the parish, etc.); and those where the age of only one of the two spouses is known and there was no further information on the FRF (that is, it is to be assumed that the couple left the parish soon after the marriage ceremony).

The revealed patterns are moderately clear and show that there is no trend over time in the scale of the differences between the three series. There was no consistent or significant difference in marriage age either for men or for women between those marriages where both spouses ages were known and those where one only was known but there is evidence that the couple stayed in the parish after the marriage had taken place. But where only one spouse's age was known and the marriage was the last event on the FRF, age at marriage, both in the case of the husband and of the wife, was almost a year greater than in the case of the other two categories. The scale of the difference between this category and the other two fluctuated considerably from one period to the next but in view of the relatively small number of marriages in the third category in the table, it may be prudent to assume that an unchanging pattern of age difference would be visible if the number of cases were larger.

This evidence therefore offers some support for the view that 'leavers' married later than 'stayers', though the difference is much less marked than might have been expected from Ruggles's microsimulation exercise, and it might be thought slightly surprising that there should be no difference at all between the categories shown in columns 1 and 2 in each panel of the table. It remains uncertain, however, how to interpret column 3. In both sexes those who disappear from parish records immediately after marriage are older than other brides and grooms. But the difference may be due to childlessness rather than migration.

In the case of couples to whom children were born and who remained in the parish the interval between a marriage entry and the next family entry in the register was only about a year on average, an interval that represents the elapse of time to the birth of the first child. If every couple had issue the absence of any further information about them following their marriage would be very strong presumptive evidence that they had left the parish and therefore that they were migrants who had returned to their native parish to be married to a 'foreigner'. But some couples had no children and the likelihood of being childless increases steadily with age. Childless couples will not normally occasion any further entry in a parish register after their marriage until one of the two dies, normally many years later. If a small proportion of all column 3 marriages were cases where the couple were childless and remained in the parish but at some much later stage in their lives moved away and died elsewhere, their inclusion in this category might well explain the higher mean age at marriage which characterised it, even though they were 'stayers' rather than 'leavers' (in the sense that the individuals in question may have left the parish only above the age of 50). The data contained in table 14.6 therefore, may well be consistent with a similar age at marriage for both 'stayers' and 'leavers' rather than suggesting a systematic difference between them.

One other feature of table 14.6 also calls for comment. There were five times as many brides as grooms in the category of marriages where the age of only one spouse is known and there are no further recorded events. This strongly underwrites the received wisdom that when a couple who were born in different parishes decided to marry, the ceremony was far more likely to take place in the bride's than in the groom's parish. It also suggests that, at least in the case of the brides in this category, most were indeed 'leavers' who had returned home to marry and then immediately departed once more. But this makes it the more surprising, if Ruggles's argument were correct, that the gap in mean age at marriage between those in column 3 and those in the other two columns was the same for both brides and grooms. If the small number of grooms and an equivalent number of brides were 'stayers', and the great majority of brides were 'leavers', it would be natural to expect that the age gap would be greater for brides than grooms since the former included a far higher proportion of genuine 'leavers'. But the age gap was the same for the two sexes, reinforcing the supposition that there was little or no systematic difference in the marriage patterns of migrants compared to those who did not migrate. The same consideration that tells against migration as an explanation tells also against childlessness, however, so that the similarity between brides and grooms in this category remains puzzling.

The evidence of table 14.6, in summary, gives slightly more ground for suspecting the existence of a 'Ruggles' effect than the evidence of table 14.5, but the evidence is inconclusive. The possibility that the later age at marriage of brides and grooms who were presumptively 'leavers' may have been due to the presence of an unusually high proportion of childless marriages in the category is strengthened by the consideration that this characteristic is stable over time and was still visible in the later decades of the eighteenth century. Since the data taken from the 1851 census seem to provide excellent reason to think that the mean ages at marriage of local-born and migrants were indistinguishable in the first half of the nineteenth century, it is unlikely that the same was not true in the period immediately preceding, which in turn suggests that the differences in marriage age between presumed 'leavers' and 'stayers' do not reflect a genuine difference in the timing of marriage in the two groups.

Conclusion

In the light of all the foregoing evidence it seems fair to claim that ages at marriage obtained in the course of reconstitution using English parish registers, though necessarily based on those who were married in their parish of birth,[37] were broadly representative of all marriages. The marked differences between 'leavers' and 'stayers', which might be expected in view of Ruggles's analysis of the distorting effect of migration on marriage age calculations based only on the latter, are not visible. This may prove an encouragement to those who have invested time and effort in reconstitution work and were uncertain about the status of their results, but it does not detract in any way from the value of the work which Ruggles carried out. It is only because some of the assumptions which he made in setting the parameters for his microsimulation were not valid for early modern England that his expectations were not fulfilled. The force of his logic is unimpaired. The mean ages at marriage of 'leavers' and 'stayers' *happen* to have been closely similar but might have been very different.

It will be instructive to see whether Ruggles's assumptions about the independence of migration and marriage and related matters are met in other populations where migration was common. If so, they will no doubt display the kind of discrepancy between measure A and measure B means that he had anticipated finding in England.[38] By introducing an altogether new and welcome precision into the discussion of these matters, he has opened up a promising field of inquiry into the reasons why his expectations were not borne out by English data. The significance of the institution of service in husbandry and of return migration flows in

---

[37] In some reconstitutions those who carried out the work were able to discover the ages of those who married in 'their' parish but who had been born elsewhere by searching the registers of neighbouring parishes. Such cases, however, were normally only a very small proportion of the total of those marrying in the parish and may be ignored in this context.

[38] Subsequent work has, however, tended to cast further doubt on the validity of Ruggles's argument when confronted with empirical information, even though its logic is sound. For example, Desjardins also found that 'leavers' and 'stayers' married at the same age in French Canada in the seventeenth and eighteenth centuries. This finding is particularly telling since the data at his disposal are notably full and reliable; Desjardins, 'Bias in age at marriage'.

this context, for example, may in future be investigated more effectively in consequence. Since there are excellent reasons for thinking that the level and trend of marriage age were of fundamental importance to general demographic change in England between the reigns of Elizabeth and Victoria, anything which serves to bring the subject more sharply into focus is greatly to be welcomed.[39]

[39] Wrigley and Schofield, *Population history of England*, ch. 10.

15   Demographic retrospective

It is now two decades since the publication of *The population history of England* and more than three decades since the Cambridge Group for the History of Population and Social Structure began the process of garnering the data on which a better description and understanding of the population history of England could be based. The exercise as whole gave rise to two large books and many articles. The original intention in collecting aggregative data from a large number of parishes was to identify those best suited to becoming the subject of a family reconstitution exercise, but in the event, as the volume of aggregative returns grew beyond expectation, thanks to the willing cooperation of many scores of local historians throughout the country,[1] the value of making direct use of these data became more and more evident. An early form of inverse projection was developed to exploit the new opportunities and the results were published in 1981 in *The population history of England*.[2] More than a decade passed before there was a comparable reconstitution volume embodying data drawn from the 26 parishes which had been chosen as promising particularly well for this purpose.[3] The second volume, *English population history*, was published in 1997. The two volumes jointly comprised a far fuller account of the demographic history of England than had previously

---

[1] A total of 230 local historians carried out an aggregative analysis of one or more parish registers on behalf of the Group before the aggregative book was written. A substantial number joined the enterprise thereafter. The total number of parish aggregative analyses returned to the Group exceeded 700, of which 404 were used in Wrigley and Schofield, *Population history of England*. The parishes and names of the volunteers may be found in app. 1 of that work.

[2] The original program is described in ibid., app. 15. A later version of the program, called generalised inverse projection, was used to repeat the exercise after the work on the family reconstitutions which provided the data for *English population history* had been completed. This work caused some of the assumptions embodied in the calculation of birth and death totals to be revised, so that the new exercise used both a modified method and new data. The results may be found in Wrigley *et al.*, *English population history*, tab. A9.1, pp. 614–5.

[3] The tests which led to the selection of the 26 parishes and the characteristics of the individual parishes are described in ibid., chs. 2 and 3.

been available. They were based on two very different methods of using parish register material. Generalised inverse projection (GIP) depends on the counting of births and deaths and converting the resulting aggregative totals into estimates of fertility and mortality, whereas family reconstitution is based on nominal linkage, the articulation of information about individuals to reconstruct the demographic histories of families. This is a convenient moment at which to reflect on the enterprise which produced the two volumes, and especially to consider the validity of the findings published in them.

The fundamental question for consideration is straightforward. Are the findings reliable? And are they representative of national trends? If so, England is in the fortunate position of knowing her demographic history with greater precision and over a longer period than any other country. Moreover, if this were the case, this aspect of her economic and social history in the quarter-millennium from mid-Tudor times would be known in greater detail than any other which can be quantified. The question of the reliability and representativeness of the Group's findings has, of course, been addressed in the past. A substantial part of the original text of both monographs was devoted to these issues. When *The population history of England* appeared in a paperback edition in 1989 an introductory note entitled 'The debate about *The population history of England*' was added to the original text, reviewing the comments and criticisms which had appeared since the publication of the hardback edition eight years earlier. Partly for this reason, but also because family reconstitution generated much more detailed and extensive information, more consideration is given in this essay to the results derived from family reconstitution than to those obtained by GIP. Attention will be focused on the estimates of fertility and mortality; since nuptiality is considered in chapter 14, it is not discussed in this essay.[4]

The demographic findings

The merits and demerits of English parish registers as a data source for demographic history have been explored repeatedly over many decades.[5] It would be otiose to rehearse them at length once again. It is universally agreed, however, that parish registers are very far from being a perfect record of the births, deaths, and marriages which took place locally. Many register books do not survive. Many more have gaps in registration and

---

[4] Some of the ground covered in this essay was previously traversed in Wrigley, 'How reliable?'.

[5] See, for example, the literature cited in ibid., pp. 575–7.

periods of severely deficient registration. At different times and in different places the recording of baptisms fell well short of a complete coverage of parochial births, and the same was true of burials in relation to deaths. Marriages were in no better case. Until Hardwicke's Act both the fact that it was possible to contract a valid marriage in ways which did not contravene the law but which also did not give rise to an entry in the local register, and, from the mid-seventeenth century onwards, the rise of dissent, meant that many unions came into existence without benefit of Anglican registration.[6]

Where a large number of registers are used to provide data, it is normally necessary to make provision to offset registration defects. Extensive corrections and additions were therefore made to the raw aggregative monthly totals of baptisms, burials, and marriages in generating estimated national totals of events for use with generalised inverse projection. Family reconstitution, however, differs somewhat from the general case. The registers used for reconstitution are a tiny minority of registers of the ten thousand ancient parishes of England and are necessarily among the best since only those with continuous registration over a long period and which routinely included a range of information which assists the identification of individuals were considered for such a labour-intensive exercise. In addition to meeting these criteria, moreover, all the registers which were considered for reconstitution were subjected to a number of other tests of the quality and consistency of registration.[7] The question, therefore, is not the completeness of registration in the *average* parish register, but in the *best* registers.

There are a number of ways in which the reliability and representativeness of the results published by the Cambridge Group over the past twenty years can be tested. Four are used in this essay. First, it is illuminating to compare rates derived from English data with those for other countries at similar periods. The Scandinavian countries in particular have been active in recent years in taking advantage of the opportunities afforded by the excellence of their source material to push back the date from which authoritative estimates of fertility and mortality can be made. Such data provide a helpful perspective in judging the plausibility of English rates. Second, there are some demographic characteristics which are largely determined by human physiology. These should be reflected in certain of the tabulations derived from reconstitution data. Their absence or distortion would suggest defective data. Data coverage can also be tested in a similar

---

[6] The exchange of vows before witnesses was sufficient until Hardwicke's Act of 1753 and there were many forms of clandestine marriage: Ingram, 'Spousals litigation', pp. 37–42.
[7] Wrigley *et al.*, *English population history*, chs. 2 and 4.

fashion. It is convenient to consider these two types of test under the same heading. Third, the fertility and mortality estimates obtained by inverse projection and family reconstitution can be compared. This is a searching test since the techniques used in the two exercises are radically different in nature and the data on which they were based had little overlap. Fourth, it is instructive to compare the estimates of fertility and mortality for the latest 'parish register' period with evidence drawn from the early years of civil registration. In addition, to illustrate the effect of making very different assumptions about registration coverage, and taking advantage of the nature of the population balance equation, the implications of Razzell's views about the deficiencies of Anglican registration are reviewed.

These tests are considered in turn in the following sections.

England and Scandinavia

The central direction of the recording and collation of demographic information began early in Scandinavia; in Sweden, for example, in 1749. Data were thus readily available as well as being reliable over an unusually lengthy period, rather as if the Registrar General's office in England had been created a century earlier than was in fact the case. As a result, until after the Second World War the assumptions commonly current about the demographic characteristics of pre-industrial west European populations generally were heavily influenced by the Swedish example. In 1907 Sundbårg, taking advantage of the abundant and accessible Swedish data covering the preceding 150 years, had published his *Bevölkerungsstatistik Schwedens*. In the absence of comparable data for other countries, it was conventional for several decades to assume that events elsewhere shared the Swedish pattern. Recently much further attention has been given to Scandinavian demographic history. Sometimes the sources enable estimates of fertility and mortality to be made from dates in the seventeenth rather than the mid-eighteenth century. In general the demographic histories of the three 'core' countries of Scandinavia bear a strong resemblance to one another. To simplify exposition, only Denmark and Sweden are considered here, but the text would not have needed to be greatly changed if Norway had been chosen.

The population of each of the Scandinavian countries was small, but their growth rates were much higher than those of the larger west European continental countries between the seventeenth and nineteenth centuries. English population growth in the eighteenth century was exceptionally rapid when compared with other countries from the southern shores of the Baltic to the Mediterranean, but its rate of growth was approached more nearly by Scandinavia than by countries elsewhere in

Europe. The population of Denmark in 1834 was 1,231,000. In 1675 it was probably no more than *c*. 550,000, suggesting an increase of about 124 per cent (or about 0.51 per cent per annum).[8] The Swedish population rose from *c*. 1,369,000 in 1700 to 2,888,000 in 1830, a rise of 111 per cent (0.58 per cent per annum).[9] The English population over the same period increased from 5,211,000 to 13,254,000 or by 154 per cent (0.72 per cent per annum).[10] Over the broadly similar period from 1680 to 1820 Spain, Italy, and Germany all grew by between 50 and 65 per cent (about 0.32 per cent per annum), while France and the Netherlands showed more modest growth rates (39 and 8 per cent respectively, 0.23 and 0.05 per cent per annum).[11] Sweden, like England, was experiencing net emigration in this period,[12] so that the intrinsic growth rate must have been somewhat higher than suggested by the annual rate of population growth: Denmark probably enjoyed net immigration in the middle decades of the eighteenth century, partially balanced by net emigration for the following half-century, but the scale of the net flows was modest.[13]

Generalised inverse projection was used to generate estimates of gross reproduction rates and expectation of life at birth from Danish and Swedish birth and death series: these can be compared with the existing GIP estimates for England. In addition it is instructive to compare marital fertility rates for England and Sweden.

Gross reproduction rates and age-specific marital fertility rates

Figure 15.1 plots decennial gross reproduction rates (GRR) in England, Denmark, and Sweden. The bold lines on the graph represent national data; the thinner lines for earlier periods represent estimates based on less complete data. Until *c*. 1760 rates in Denmark and England were broadly similar, though the Danish rate was tending to fall, while the English rate was rising gently. From the mid-eighteenth century onwards the two Scandinavian countries followed the same path, their rates fluctuating without clear trend predominantly in the range 2.10 to 2.30. In this period, in contrast, the English rate rose steeply to a high peak of 2.79 in 1811–20 before falling back to a level close to 2.50 in the middle decades of the nineteenth century.

---

[8] Johansen and Oeppen, *Danish population estimates*, fig. 3, p. 18; Mitchell, *European historical statistics*, tab. B1, p. 29.

[9] Hofsten and Lundström, *Swedish population history*, tab. 1.1, p. 13; Sundbårg, *Bevölkerungsgeschichte Schwedens*, tab. 4, p. 80.

[10] Wrigley *et al.*, *English population history*, tab. A9.1, pp. 614–5.

[11] Wrigley, 'Growth of population', tab. 1, p. 122.

[12] Hofsten and Lundström, *Swedish population history*, tab. 4.1, p. 64.

[13] Johansen and Oeppen, *Danish population estimates*, fig. 4, p. 19.

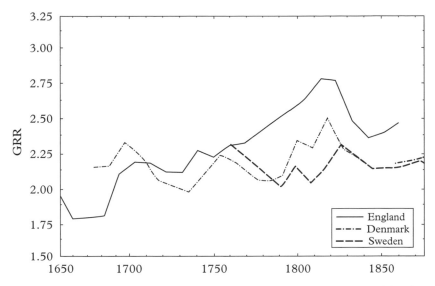

Figure 15.1. *Gross reproduction rates in England, Denmark, and Sweden ('official' national values shown in bold)*
Sources: England: Wrigley *et al.*, *English population history*, tab. A9.1, pp. 614–5. Denmark: Johansen and Oeppen, *Danish population estimates*, fig. 1, p. 11 (a description of the derivation of the totals of births and deaths shown in the figure is given on pp. 4–11). For Danish 'official' values: Andreev, 'Demographic surfaces'. Sweden: *Befolkningsutvecklingen under 250 år. Historisk statistik för Sverige, Demografiska rapporter*, 1999: 2.

The GRR is an informative measure of the level of fertility in the population as a whole, but, since it is heavily influenced by nuptiality, it is not a good guide to the fertility of married women. It is quite possible for a country with high marital fertility to have a lower GRR than another country where marital fertility is lower, if either age at marriage or the proportion never marrying is higher in the first country than the second, or from some combination of the two. The surge in the GRR in England was principally due to increased nuptiality towards the end of the eighteenth century and in the early decades of the nineteenth century. This raises the possibility that, although the GRRs in England and Scandinavia followed different paths, with the English rate rising to a high peak before ending the period much closer to Scandinavian levels, while in Denmark and Sweden the secular trend was broadly flat, age-specific marital fertility rates may have changed little over the century. Table 15.1, which lists marital fertility rates for England and Sweden, and includes a scattering

Table 15.1 *Age-specific marital fertility (rates per 1,000 woman-years)*

	20–4	25–9	30–4	35–9	40–4	45–9	TMFR 20–49
England (1750–99)	419	369	308	243	138	20	7.49
England (1800–24)	425	381	311	255	142	19	7.67
Sweden (1751–1800)	458	379	326	227	122	30	7.71
Sweden (1801–50)	456	374	315	237	130	25	7.69
Heuchelheim (1691–1780)	423	373	316	243	114	15	7.42
Werdum (pre-1850)	449	376	322	256	118	17	7.69
South-west France (1720–89)	410	359	336	257	141	20	7.62

Notes: The English rates for 1750–99 are the average of those for 1750–74 and 1775–99. The Heuchelheim rates are for completed families only. The rates for south-west France were derived from a table which cross-classified age-specific fertility by age at marriage for several time periods; the information contained in the table made it possible to weight the data for separate time periods appropriately and, similarly, to weight by age at marriage groups.
Sources: Wrigley *et al.*, *English population history*, tab. 7.1, p. 355; Knodel, 'Natural fertility in pre-industrial Germany', tab. 3, p. 488; Imhof, 'Structure of reproduction in a west German village'; Sundbärg, *Bevölkerungsgeschichte Schwedens*, tab. 41, p. 121; Henry, 'Fécondité des marriages dans le quart sud-ouest', tab. 1, pp. 978–9.

of German and French examples, shows that there are good grounds for supposing that this was indeed the case. The Swedish national rates make a particularly telling comparison with those for England, since they refer to a national entity and the coverage is thought to be excellent. The English and Swedish total marital fertility rates (TMFR) were virtually identical from the mid-eighteenth to the mid-nineteenth centuries, despite the substantial difference between their GRRs.

The other rates shown in the table are also similar to those in England and Scandinavia. In each case registration coverage is believed to be good, or, if not, as in Henry's study of 10 parishes in south-west France, a series of corrections were made to the observed rate to offset the several causes of under-registration. The rates in Werdum (East Friesland) and Heuchelheim (Hessen) suggest the possibility of a pattern of moderate age-specific rates in much of northern Europe. Marital fertility in south-west France, though resembling the English pattern, was substantially lower than in the other three quarters of the country (France was divided into four quarters by the Institut National d'Etudes Démographiques when analysing its reconstitution fertility data). A fuller comparison of English data with those from other countries or districts, which included a wider range of TMFR levels would be rewarding, but is beyond the scope of this exercise. Table 15.1 shows, however, that marital fertility rates in England resembled those to be found in much of Europe

Age-specific marital fertility rates by single year of age are seldom published but can be highly informative. They are, of course, readily produced from family reconstitution data. The English series bears an almost uncanny resemblance both in level and in shape to those for two non-European populations characterised by natural fertility for which information is available, China in the 1950s and the Cocos-Keeling islands between 1888 and 1947, a resemblance which extended to the details of teenage sub-fecundity and the timing of the peak of fertility in the early twenties.[14]

Razzell's view about the completeness of birth registration in reconstitution parishes has varied over the past three decades. At one point he wrote that 'Wrigley and Schofield's assumption of the absolute accuracy of the parish registers used in their reconstitution work – [in the case of baptism registration] – may be justified.'[15] But this remark was untypical. His general thesis has been that, although the registers used in reconstitution, because of their careful selection, were less defective than most other registers, they still fell well short of achieving a full coverage of births. This claim stemmed principally from a comparison of the information in the 1851 census enumerators' books for a given parish with the Anglican registers of that parish. The former provides a name and age for each individual and lists his or her place of birth. For those born in the parish, its register can then be searched to discover whether there is a matching baptism. Because of the various possible sources of error in both sources, such an exercise has to be conducted with caution, but Razzell showed that there appeared to be numerous instances of missing baptism entries. In his original study, for example, he found that over the period 1761–1800 in the two reconstitution parishes of Colyton and Hartland there were 61 cases out of a total of 229 (27 per cent) where no baptism entry could be found for individuals whose age and

---

[14] Wrigley et al., English population history, fig. 7.6, p. 453. Natural fertility may be defined as existing where married couples do not alter their reproductive behaviour according to the number of children already born. The strengths and weaknesses of the concept are discussed in Wilson, Oeppen, and Pardoe, 'What is natural fertility?'.

[15] Razzell, 'Growth of population', p. 757. It is, incidentally, somewhat cavalier to state that Roger Schofield and I assumed absolute accuracy in the parish registers used for family reconstitution. No such claim was made or would be justified. Our conclusion was that any inaccuracies were minor, but not that the registers were error free. We concluded a lengthy discussion of the problem and of the tests which could be carried by remarking that 'the empirical findings based on the 26 reconstitution parishes are unlikely to be seriously defective', a much more muted claim: Wrigley et al., English population history, p. 118.

place of birth suggested that they were local-born in the period.[16] Four other non-reconstitution parishes were similarly analysed. In two of these (Fordingbridge and Ringwood) the comparable percentage over the same period was 42 per cent, while in two others (Hackney and Kingston) the figure rose to 65 per cent. This appeared to show that reconstitution parishes possessed better registers than other rural parishes and also that there were places where the coverage of events in the parish register was feeble indeed.[17]

Razzell pointed out that even high levels of registration deficiency were not necessarily fatal to the accuracy of reconstitution if failure to register was confined to particular families which might then be excluded from the study, but noted that his evidence showed that 'missing' births were 'distributed more or less randomly amongst all families'.[18] He later agreed that there were aspects of the cross-matching technique he had employed which might have exaggerated the scale of register omissions, but argued that other considerations suggested that the original exercise understated the total of 'missing' entries, and that the one consideration counterbalanced the other, concluding that 'although there are a number of deficiencies and problems associated with the census/baptism comparison method, because of the counter-balancing effects of factors which led to an under-estimation of the N.I.R (not in register) ratio, it provides a very simple standardised way of evaluating the adequacy of particular Anglican baptism registers, as well as forming the basis of a more general assessment of changes in registration accuracy over time'.[19]

It appears reasonable to suppose, in view of the foregoing, that Razzell considers that an omission rate of, say, 27 per cent, the statistic which, in his analysis, characterised Colyton and Hartland in the later eighteenth century, was typical of reconstitution parishes in that period (and indeed, from the general nature of his view about parochial registration, typical also of reconstitution parishes in earlier periods). The implausibility of this view is not difficult to demonstrate. If 27 per cent of births went unregistered, and if this affected all families in a random fashion, then the fertility rates derived from family reconstitution forms should be increased by 37 per cent to make good the difference.[20] Table 15.2 shows the age-specific marital fertility rates based on family reconstitution for the period 1750–99; the same rates increased by 37 per cent

[16] For a different interpretation of the quality of the Colyton baptism register, see Wrigley, 'Baptism coverage'; also Levine, 'Reliability of parochial registration'.
[17] Razzell, 'Baptism as a form of birth registration', tab. 9, p. 130.
[18] Ibid., p. 131.
[19] Razzell, *English population history*, p. 149.
[20] $100/(100-27) = 1.37$.

Table 15.2 *Age-specific marital fertility (rates per 1,000 woman-years)*

	20–4	25–9	30–4	35–9	40–4	45–9	TMFR 20–49
England (1750–99)	419	369	308	243	138	20	7.5
English rates × 1.37	574	506	422	333	189	27	10.2
Bavarian villages (1750–99)	492	534	476	378	200	39	10.6
Hutterite women	550	502	447	406	222	61	10.9

Notes: The English rates are the average of 1750–74 and 1775–99. The three Bavarian villages are Anhausen, Gabelbach, and Kreuth.
Sources: Wrigley *et al.*, *English population history*, tab. 7.1, p. 355; Knodel, 'Natural fertility in pre-industrial Germany', tab. 3, p. 488; Henry, 'Some data on natural fertility', p. 84.

to offset register omissions; the comparable Hutterite rates (the highest known recorded rates); and the rates in three Bavarian villages where most children were weaned at birth (i.e. were never breastfed) and where in consequence marital fertility was exceptionally high. For each set of rates the associated total marital fertility rate is also shown.

The outcome of raising reconstitution fertility rates in the proportion suggested by Razzell produces deeply improbable results. It would suggest that English marital fertility was almost as high as the highest rates ever recorded. The comparison with the Bavarian villages is especially telling. Breastfeeding in England was both widespread and, by modern standards, prolonged. That in spite of this, English women were producing live births at the same tempo as Bavarian women, the great majority of whom did not breastfeed their children at all, is not credible.[21]

The similarity between English marital fertility rates and those in some other countries or communities in the same period (and in other periods in communities not practising family limitation) does not, of course, preclude the possibility of under-registration, though the recorded rates preclude the possibility of under-registration on the scale envisaged by Razzell. The close similarities between England and Scandinavia, however, suggest the likelihood that any shortfall is modest. Later tests will show that it was negligible.[22]

[21] Knodel made use of survey data collected by the Bavarian Statistical Bureau in 1904–7 to show that, in the districts within which his villages lay, 69 and 84 per cent of mothers never breastfed and most of the others had ceased to breastfeed in less than a month. He refers to evidence that this practice was of long standing. Knodel, *Demographic behavior in the past*, p. 543. See also Knodel and van de Walle, 'Breast feeding, fertility and infant mortality'.
[22] See pp. 406–10, 420–2.

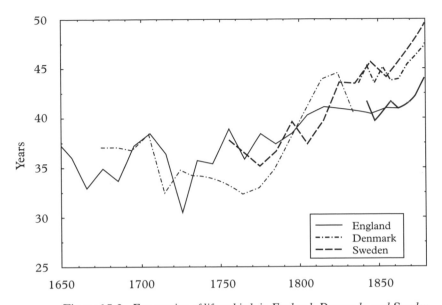

Figure 15.2. *Expectation of life at birth in England, Denmark, and Sweden ('official' national values shown in bold)*
Source: See fig. 15.1. The 'official' values for England were taken from the *Chester Beatty life tables.*

Mortality

Scandinavian countries also afford a valuable initial test of the plausibility of the estimates of English mortality in the early modern period, both because their data are of excellent quality and because Scandinavian demographic regimes appear to have had many characteristics also found in England. Figure 15.2 plots trends in expectation of life at birth for England, Denmark, and Sweden. The lines in bold in this figure and the next indicate 'official' national data.

The Danish series begins with the decade 1670–9. Between then and the end of the eighteenth century the mortality experience of Denmark and England was similar apart from a period between the 1750s and the 1780s. Expectation of life at birth in the two countries in the successive quarter centuries from 1675–99 to 1775–99 was as follows (the Danish figure is given first in each case): 36.0, 34.8 (1675–99); 36.2, 37.0 (1700–24); 33.4, 33.5 (1725–49); 32.6, 37.7 (1750–74); 36.1, 37.9 (1775–99). Thereafter Denmark drew well ahead of England. The English e_0, though higher than in the past showed little upward trend, but in Denmark it improved markedly and its trend was much more decidedly upward. Sweden and England are almost indistinguishable from one another in the second half of the eighteenth century, but after the turn of the century the improvement in e_0 in Sweden resembled that in Denmark.

Attempting to account for mortality differentials between countries in the past is hazardous: the result is seldom convincing. Two comments, however, may be borne in mind when comparing the mortality histories of Denmark and England in the 'long' eighteenth century. The first is that Denmark, in common with other Scandinavian countries, was not free from sharp mortality crises until the last decades of the eighteenth century. There were several years in the second half of the eighteenth century when the number of deaths soared above the total of births, notably in 1763–4, and 1772–3. There were 21 years in all during the century when deaths exceeded births. In England, in contrast, the last period in which there were more deaths than births was in the two-year period 1741–2 (in the century as a whole there were 8 such years; 1712, 1720, 1727–30, and 1741–2).[23] Increasing freedom from such episodes in England played a part in creating a mortality difference in favour of England, an aspect of European mortality history to which Flinn drew attention a quarter of a century ago.[24] The second consideration may have been equally significant, though the danger of assuming causation because of coincidence needs no stressing. Kjaergaard has described the widespread evidence of progressive environmental degradation in Denmark from the sixteenth century until the later eighteenth century.[25] Matters were at their worst in the first half of the eighteenth century, and improved rapidly towards its end. England appears to have been largely free from this scourge, in part because of its very different pattern of energy use to which Kjaergaard draws attention.[26] The striking achievements of English agriculture in increasing both output per acre and output per man simultaneously in the early modern period also played a part in avoiding the stresses to which Denmark was subject, but from which she made a swift recovery in the course of the eighteenth century, assisted, it has been argued, by a series of agricultural reform measures, beginning with the freehold legislation of 1769. Apart from the period of divergence in the eighteenth century, however, a general similarity in the mortality history of the two countries, both in level and in trend, is evident.

After 1800 the failure of England to match the improvement in expectation of life taking place in the two Scandinavian countries may well reflect the stress of rapid urbanisation. Woods has shown how it is possible

---

[23] Johansen, *Danish population history*, p. 43.
[24] Flinn, 'The stabilization of mortality'.
[25] Kjaergaard, *The Danish revolution*.
[26] Ibid., ch. 4, esp. pp. 116–29.

for mortality to improve in each settlement type (village, small town, city, metropolis) but without any improvement in the national figures because of the differentially rapid growth of population in the settlement types with the highest death rates.[27]

As with fertility, so with mortality. Demonstrating that there was a general similarity in the mortality characteristics of the populations of England and Scandinavia does not provide proof that the English estimates are reliable. The comparison is worthwhile, however, in that it shows that countries in which the original data are believed to be well recorded and tolerably complete displayed very similar demographic patterns and trends to those to be found in England over a period of two centuries.

Reproductive physiology and data coverage

Birth interval data

Birth intervals in a population which does not practise family limitation are strongly influenced by reproductive physiology which gives rise to distinctive patterns in their frequency distribution. This enables the completeness of birth registration to be tested. One such test provides compelling evidence of the general completeness of birth coverage in the reconstitution data set. The evidence is a by-product of the measurement of fecundability. The concept of fecundability refers to the probability of conceiving in the course of a single monthly cycle on the part of women who are capable of conceiving. Its measurement from birth interval data usually presents fewest problems when analysing the distribution of birth intervals between marriage and first birth. If there were no sexual intercourse before marriage, women would first become exposed to the risk of conception only after their marriage; none would be pregnant at marriage or engaged in breastfeeding at that time. In these circumstances the distribution of intervals to first birth can be analysed to yield an estimate of fecundability. Later in marriage there will be long periods when a woman is not capable of conceiving because of pregnancy, as a result of a miscarriage, or because she is amenorrhoeic as a result of breastfeeding. It has commonly been supposed, therefore, that the measurement of fecundability is not feasible except when using first birth intervals.

At first sight this appears to put the accurate measurement of fecundability beyond reach using English reconstitution data. Pregnancy before marriage was common in early modern England. It reached a peak

---

[27] Woods, 'The effects of population redistribution'.

towards the end of the eighteenth century when about a quarter of all first births occurred outside marriage and a further quarter, though the birth was post-marital, were conceived before the marriage took place.[28] It proved possible, however, both to overcome the problems of pre-marital sexual activity in estimating fecundability from the distribution of the interval between marriage and first birth, and also to use birth interval data to estimate fecundability later in marriage. In both cases the analysis suggested that the level of recognisable fecundability in early modern England was about 0.25 (that is about one quarter of married women who were capable of conceiving did so in the course of a monthly cycle).[29] The spread of estimates of fecundability in other European populations in the past suggests that England was close to or somewhat above the average[30] (a relatively high level of fecundability does not necessarily imply comparably high marital fertility, of course, if breastfeeding is widespread and prolonged, as was the case in England).[31] In this context, however, it is not the level of fecundability itself which is primarily important, but a feature of the distribution of birth intervals from which fecundability is inferred.

In summary, the argument is this. Long intervals should be rare in populations not practising contraception if registration is satisfactory. At the level of fecundability found in early modern England, the percentage of birth intervals greater than a given length can be estimated from fecundability models such as that of Bongaarts.[32] Using this model, Wilson estimated that the percentage of birth intervals of greater than 60 months in early modern England may be expected to be about 2 per cent.[33] As the revised estimates of fecundability for England presented in *English*

---

[28] Wrigley, 'Marriage, fertility and population growth', pp. 160–2.

[29] Recognisable fecundability, as the term suggests, excludes cases where an egg has been fertilised but lost in the first months of pregnancy, often without the loss being noticed. It was defined by Bongaarts as 'the probability of a conception which is recognised as the end of the conception cycle by the nonoccurence of the menstruation': Bongaarts, 'Estimation of fecundability', p. 646.

[30] Wilson, 'Determinants of marital fertility', tab. 8.4, p. 219 provides details of fecundability estimates for a range of German, French, and Flemish communities in the eighteenth and nineteenth centuries.

[31] On the estimation of the length of breastfeeding in England, see Wrigley *et al.*, *English population history*, pp. 489–91. Using different methods, Wilson concluded that the average probably lay between 14 and 18 months; Wilson, 'Determinants of marital fertility', pp. 222–4 (fig. 8.6, p. 222 is especially striking). For estimates of recognisable fecundability in French and German parish populations in the eighteenth century, see Bongaarts, 'Estimation of fecundability', tab. 2, p. 652 and Knodel and Wilson, 'Fecundity in German village populations', tab. 8, p. 69.

[32] Bongaarts, 'Estimation of fecundability'.

[33] He based the figure of 2 per cent both on the use of Bongaarts's model in conjunction with his estimate of fecundability and on evidence from other historical populations: Wilson, 'Marital fertility in pre-industrial England', p. 112. The model itself is described in ibid., app. 4.

population history are slightly higher than Wilson's earlier estimate of this variable, the related percentage is slightly lower, about 1.8 per cent.[34] Lest it be supposed that the percentages produced using Bongaarts' model bear little relationship to those observed empirically, it is worth noting that the work of Knodel and Wilson shows that the predicted and observed percentages of birth intervals greater than 60 months in German villages populations in the eighteenth and nineteenth centuries were very similar to each other.[35]

In England, because so many women were pregnant at marriage or already breastfeeding a child born before marriage, the interpretation of the distribution of the intervals between marriage and first birth, the usual data source for the estimation of fecundability, is not straightforward, though the evidence is not at odds with the assumption that no more than 2 per cent of such intervals exceeded 60 months in length.[36] Fortunately, the evidence from later in marriage is more clear-cut and points to excellent birth coverage. It is very difficult to suppose that the recording of baptisms (births) in reconstituted families was other than virtually complete. If there were underregistration, long intervals would be more common than predicted by the model since some intervals that were apparently between successive births would actually refer not to intervals between *a* and *b* but to intervals between *a* and *c,* with *b* missing from the record.

The possibility of estimating fecundability later in marriage stems from the fact that when an infant death occurred the mother was again exposed to the risk of pregnancy. This did not happen instantly, especially if the child died soon after birth. When this happened the after-effects of giving birth were superimposed upon those of the cessation of breastfeeding, and as a result the peak in the distribution of the next following birth is relatively flat topped,[37] but in cases where the child died between the age of three months and the end of his or her first year of life

---

[34] The revised English figure lies in the range 0.25 to 0.27: Wrigley *et al., English population history*, tab. 7.40, pp. 474–5 and associated text, and p. 499 where the reason for a slightly higher figure than that arrived at from the data in tab. 7.40 is discussed. The revised English figure is the same as that for 14 German villages in 1800–24, for which the predicted proportion of birth intervals of 60 months or greater using Bongaarts' method of estimation is 1.8 per cent: Knodel and Wilson, 'Fecundity in German village populations', tab. 7, p. 68 and tab. A2(1), p. 82.

[35] Ibid., tab. A2(1), p. 82.

[36] Wrigley *et al., English population history*, pp. 467–72. The measurement of fecundability using English parish register data is far from straightforward, whether in relation to the interval to first birth or later in marriage. There is a lengthy discussion of the issues involved in ibid., pp. 464–501. It is not possible within the compass of this essay either to describe the estimation method fully or to do justice to the complexities of the topic.

[37] Ibid., p. 484.

(3–11 months), the distribution of the interval to the next birth, in cases where the next birth was conceived after the death of the preceding child (the great majority), was remarkably similar to the distribution of intervals from marriage to first birth, except that the peak month occurred in the twelfth rather than the tenth month, suggesting that normal ovulation took a few weeks to become re-established after the death of the earlier child.[38]

The striking fact, so far as the issue of registration completeness is concerned, is very simple. There were 3,379 birth intervals occurring 9 months or more after the preceding child died aged 3–11 months. Of these only 1.1 per cent were greater than 60 months in length.[39] This figure is actually somewhat lower than the figure to be expected at the level of fecundability prevailing in early modern England, which, as already noted, is about 1.8 per cent, encouraging the belief that very few births went unregistered in the reconstitution parishes. If there had been any considerable number of 'missing' births, of cases where the next child recorded after child a was not child b but child c (or even child d or later, if the 'missing' births happened to follow one another), it is to be expected that there would have been a significantly higher percentage of intervals which were apparently greater than 60 months in length. This can be tested using the reconstitution data set. If births within the set are removed at random, it is self-evident that birth intervals will lengthen. For example, if 25 per cent of births are removed, and therefore a much increased proportion of the birth intervals become a–c (or a–d, a–e, etc.) intervals rather than a–b intervals, the total of birth intervals occurring 9 months or more after the death of the preceding child aged 3–11 months falls to 2,192 and the percentage of intervals greater than 60 months rises to 5.6 per cent, a level five times greater than that found before the births were depleted in this fashion.[40] Razzell has suggested

---

[38] The patterns of birth intervals in question may be seen in ibid., fig. 7.9, p. 485.

[39] Ibid., tab. 7.41, p. 498. The totals were obtained by adding together both cases where the wife's age was known and where it was not known (the rate was much the same in both categories). Note that last birth intervals, which are, on average, substantially longer than the average, were excluded in this exercise as inappropriate in the calculation of fecundability.

[40] The births which were deleted in this exercise (25 per cent of the total) were identified by giving each birth a one in four chance of being selected using a random number generator. Note that the total of birth intervals falls by 35 per cent rather than 25 per cent. This occurs because the total of birth intervals falls by the same number as the reduction in the total of births but the proportional fall is greater: thus, for example, if there are four lamp posts, there will be three intervals between them, but if one lamp post is removed, the number of lamp posts falls by 25 per cent, but the number of intervals falls by 33 per cent. I am greatly indebted to Ros Davies for carrying out this further exercise.

that about one-third of all births escaped registration in parish registers generally, and that even in reconstitution parishes where coverage was better than the average, the proportion escaping registration was about one quarter.[41] If this were indeed the case, it is difficult to avoid the conclusion that the percentage of very long birth intervals would be far higher than the observed percentage.[42] It is incumbent on anyone who favours the view that many births escaped recording in the reconstitution parishes to account for the marked paucity of long birth intervals since analysis shows that, if registration were defective, long birth intervals would be much more frequent than appears in the empirical record.

Sterility

Another aspect of reproductive physiology which also provides a searching test of the reliability of reconstitution data relates to sterility. At some point in the lifetime of every woman she will become incapable of conceiving a child. The likelihood that this has occurred rises exponentially with age from a very low figure for women in their teens (a small minority of women, of course, were infecund throughout life). The incidence of sterility (the reciprocal of fecundity) can be measured, in a population which does not practise contraception within marriage, by calculating the percentage of completed marriages (marriages which endure beyond the wife's fiftieth birthday) which produce no children. If the marriages are divided into those contracted when the wife was aged 15–9, 20–4, and so on, the increase of sterility with age can be established (since the available historical data relate to married couples rather than individuals, it would be more accurate to refer to sterile couples rather than to sterile women). Figure 15.3 shows that during the parish register period from 1538 to 1837 sterility was less than 3 per cent among marriages contracted when the wife was a teenager, rising exponentially to reach about 70 per cent among couples who married when the wife was aged 40–4 (the vertical scale is logarithmic). The figure also plots comparable data from six other populations in which there is believed to have been little or no restriction of fertility within marriage, which were collated by Pittenger when constructing his model of the progression of sterility

---

[41] The estimate of one-third may be found in Razzell, 'Baptism as a form of birth registration', p. 145. When he later reviewed his earlier conclusions, he found little reason to change them; idem, *English population history*, ch. 5. The attribution of the lower figure for reconstitution parishes is described on pp. 401–2; see also p. 433.

[42] Reducing the number of births by 25 per cent was deliberately conservative in this regard: if the number is reduced by 30 per cent, for example, the number of birth intervals longer than 60 months rises to 6.8 per cent of the birth interval total.

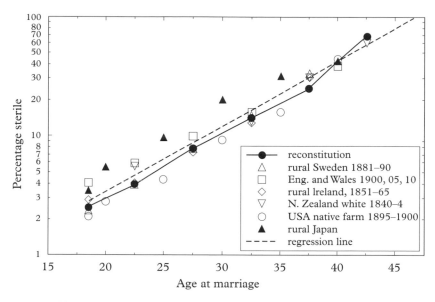

Figure 15.3. *The increase of sterility with age*
Source: Wrigley *et al.*, *English population history*, fig. 7.2, p. 395.

with age.[43] The English data conform closely to the regression line representing the average experience of the other populations. Agreement between the expected and the empirical is further testimony to the quality of baptism coverage. In the higher age at marriage groups in particular, where offspring were necessarily few in number, any significant under-registration of births would increase the proportion of apparently sterile couples, but the graph does not suggest this. In the age at marriage group of women 35–9 the percentage sterile is below expectation (as measured by the regression line); in the age group 40–4 it is above expectation, but neither should be regarded as significant since the number of marriages on which the percentages were based was small in both cases (in 82 per cent of all marriages the bride was aged 20–34).

Infant and child mortality

The reliability of estimates of mortality early in life can be checked by a method which resembles that used to monitor fertility data, though this test relates to the precision and coverage of the data rather than to the physiological attributes of the population.

[43] Pittenger, 'An exponential model of female sterility'.

If there is a failure to register deaths, infant deaths are likely to suffer most of all, and especially infants in the first days and weeks of life. Public baptism symbolised, among other things, entry into the local community. Thereafter death was much less likely to pass unrecorded. But an infant dying before baptism (or, indeed, perhaps after a private baptism) was at greater risk to slip the net.[44] Equally, if it is demonstrable that such deaths were well recorded, it is unlikely that there will have been serious deficiencies in recording deaths at greater ages. It is therefore fortunate that an effective test of the coverage of deaths in infancy in the burial registers of reconstitution parishes is possible. It depends upon the fact that baptisms can be divided into three categories according to the subsequent fate of the child: those cases where it is known that the child died before his or her first birthday; those where the child is known to have survived his or her first birthday; and those where the fate of the child is unknown. Where the number of cases is sufficiently large, this enables the quality of the registration of infant deaths to be tested rigorously. Fortunately, the reconstitution data set includes tens of thousands of baptisms which qualify for use in this connection.

The argument is this. In a parish in which registration was complete, all the 'fate unknown' cases would relate to children who survived infancy but who subsequently emigrated from the parish before their marriage or death, events which would have given rise to an entry in the register if they had occurred locally. Therefore, the birth intervals following such baptisms should resemble the birth intervals following a birth where the child is known to have survived infancy because of a later event linked to the baptism. If, however, a proportion of the children in question had died in infancy but without any record of the burial surviving, the mean and distribution of the birth intervals in the case of 'fate unknown' children would differ from the mean and distribution of those 'known to have survived', because birth intervals which followed the death of the preceding child in infancy were much shorter than those following a child who survived. In early modern England, when an infant died young the interval to the next birth was about 8 months shorter on average than when he or she survived.[45] This was principally because breastfeeding prolonged amenorrhoea, and children were breastfed on average for about 19 months in early modern England.[46] The cessation of breastfeeding brought about by the infant death therefore made the mother likely to conceive again much

[44] There is a fuller discussion of delayed baptism and of its possible effect on registration completeness in Wrigley and Schofield, *Population history of England*, pp. 96–7.

[45] Wrigley *et al.*, *English population history*, tab. 7.35, pp. 438–9. The interval was a little shorter in the case of parity 1 births and a little longer for all higher parities, with the overall average difference about 8.4 months.

[46] Ibid., pp. 489–91.

sooner than if she were still breastfeeding. Birth intervals in the 'known to have died' category therefore have a very different distribution from those in the 'known to have survived' group. Formal statistical testing using the Kolmogorov–Smirnov (KS) test makes it possible to establish whether or not the 'fate unknown' and the 'known to have survived' categories of birth intervals differ from one another. If they do, there will be reason to doubt the completeness of coverage of infant burials: if they do not, it is likely that registration was effectively complete.[47]

The three panels of figure 15.4 display the frequency distribution of birth intervals of varying lengths for the three types of birth interval. Between them the panels cover the whole parish register period. It might seem sensible to avoid subdividing the period as a whole in this fashion since this must reduce any random effects obscuring the underlying pattern. But there are decisive reasons against this strategy. By the end of the parish register period birth intervals were significantly shorter than at its beginning, falling by 7 per cent between 1650–79 and 1800–37.[48] This in turn means that comparing means and distributions in the three categories over the period as a whole will tend to produce a misleading result. The 'fate unknown' category was a substantially larger fraction of the total of cases at the end of the period than at its beginning, and, since birth intervals in general were becoming shorter, this must tend to reduce the mean length of the 'fate unknown' category relative to the 'known to have survived' category over the 250-year period as a whole. Within the three sub-periods, however, birth interval distributions changed little and the relative size of each category was stable. The mean birth interval in 1550–99 for the two types were: 30.41 (died over 1 year), and 30.51 months (age at death unknown). The comparable means for 1600–1749 were 30.46 and 30.45 months; and for 1750–1837 29.14 and 29.23 months. KS shows that there is no reason to reject the null hypothesis that in the two later sub-periods the birth intervals in the two categories came from the same population, especially as, against expectation, in the last period the mean interval in the case of 'fate unknown' category was actually the higher of the two. The issue is more open for the earliest period and it is possible, though not certain, that in the sixteenth century some infant deaths went unregistered.[49] This test, therefore, shows how

[47] The technical issues concerning types of birth intervals which can properly be included in this test are discussed in ibid., p. 103.

[48] The mean birth interval fell over this period from 32.9 to 30.6: ibid., tab. 7.36, p. 447.

[49] In the earliest period the test barely fails to reject the null hypothesis that the two samples were drawn from identical populations at the 5 per cent level of significance. In the two later periods the test provides no reason to doubt that the samples were drawn from the same population. Details of the KS tests and a general discussion of the data and their implications are to be found in ibid., pp. 102–6.

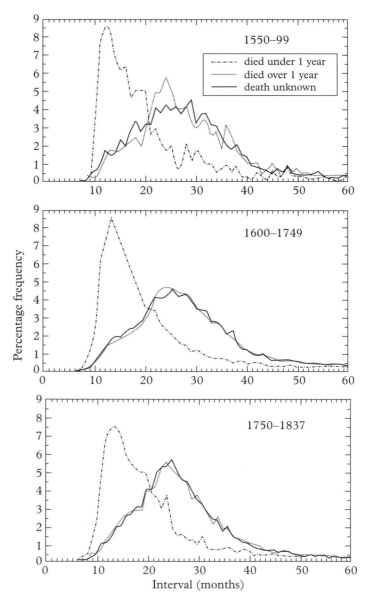

Figure 15.4. *The distribution of birth intervals where the previous child died under one, where the previous child survived, and where the fate of the previous child is unknown*
Source: Wrigley *et al.*, *English population history, fig.* 4.2, p. 104.

difficult it is to entertain serious doubts about the completeness of the registration of infant deaths in the reconstitution data: and, since infant deaths were more likely to be omitted from a parish register than later deaths, confidence in death registration generally is strengthened.

Generalised inverse projection and family reconstitution

A further important test of the Cambridge Group's findings is to discover whether the results obtained by inverse projection and family reconstitution are consistent with each other. This test is straightforward in relation to mortality since both methods yield estimates of expectation of life at birth and of partial life expectancies (similar comparisons of fertility estimates are not feasible because the two techniques do not produce directly comparable data: GIP-generated fertility rates refer to the whole female population, both married and unmarried, whereas family reconstitution only yields estimates of fertility within marriage). Before making any comparisons, however, it is important to note that agreement between results obtained by the two techniques is not preordained either because they draw upon the same body of original data or by their intrinsic nature.

The aggregative data used to construct the estimates published in the *Population history of England* were taken from 404 parish registers. The reconstitution data which formed the basis of *English population history* came from only 26 parishes. Neither data set included any London parishes, but aggregative data were 'corrected' to offset this defect.[50] Of the 26, 14 had been used in the earlier, aggregative study.[51] These, therefore, were the only 'overlap' parishes. If one were to draw a series of samples of parishes at random from the set of 404, each consisting of 14 parishes, and then add 12 others from outside the 404 to form groups of 26 parishes, many of the resulting groups would diverge widely in character and in demographic history from the national aggregative sample of 404 parishes. If the aggregative and reconstitution results run in parallel, in other words, their similarity cannot be attributed to a common data source, and the claim that reconstitution results, though derived from a modest data base, are representative of the country as a whole is enhanced. Equally important, however, in testing both sets of results, is the fact that the two techniques differ fundamentally. Generalised inverse projection makes use of totals of births and deaths in conjunction with

---

[50] Wrigley and Schofield, *Population history of England*, pp. 77–88.
[51] The parishes in question were Alcester, Aldenham, Banbury, Bottesford, Colyton, Earsdon, Gainsborough, Gedling, Hartland, Odiham, Reigate, Shepshed, Southill, and Willingham.

a terminal census containing age data. It depends on counting totals of events. Family reconstitution uses nominal record linkage to reconstruct the demographic histories of families, full or partial. The former makes use of all the recorded birth (baptism) and death (burials) events recorded in a register. The latter, because of the complex rules which determine for how long a given family is 'in observation' for the measurement of a particular phenomenon (say, infant mortality, or age-specific marital fertility), makes use of varying, and often quite small proportions of the total of events of a given type recorded in a register. The two techniques have been described in detail elsewhere.[52] Reflection will show that they are so different in nature that there is no reason to expect them of necessity to produce similar estimates of fertility and mortality, even when using a common data source, and still less when the data sources are different.

Mortality: expectation of life at birth and partial life expectancies

Both family reconstitution and GIP provide estimates of expectation of life at birth and of partial life expectancies and it is therefore readily possible to discover how closely they are in agreement. Figure 15.5 gives a visual impression of the similarity of the estimates derived by the two methods.

The top panel of the figure presents estimates of expectation of life at birth (e_0); the middle panel the partial life expectancy from birth to age 15 ($_{15}e_0$); and the bottom panel a series of partial life expectancies between 25 and 45, 45 and 65, and 65 and 85 ($_{20}e_{25}$, $_{20}e_{45}$, and $_{20}e_{65}$). Partial life expectancies specify the number of years lived between two ages. For example, if death rates were zero between the ages of 25 and 45, a group of 1,000 individuals would accumulate a total of 20,000 years lived between these two ages, and $_{20}e_{25}$ would be 20.0, but if $_{20}e_{25}$ were, say, 17.5, a comparable group of 1,000 individuals would accumulate the lower total 17,500 years lived over the same age span.

The first two panels show decennial estimates, the third uses quarter-century periods. The dotted sections of the reconstitution line in the top panel indicate that complete data for some age groups were not available and that some age-specific rates were therefore obtained by estimation.[53]

---

[52] Wrigley, 'Family reconstitution; Oeppen, 'Back projection and inverse projection' and 'Generalized inverse projection'.

[53] For a description of the methods used in deriving estimated rates, see Wrigley *et al.*, *English population history*, pp. 281–2 and app. 6.

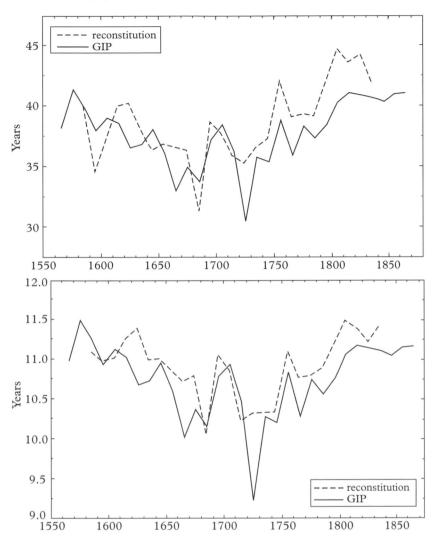

Figure 15.5. *Estimates of expectation of life at birth and of partial life ex-*
pectancies from family reconstitution and by generalised inverse projection: top
panel e_0; middle panel $_{15}e_0$; bottom panel $_{20}e_{45}$, $_{20}e_{45}$, and $_{20}e_{65}$.
Note. The same data were used as given in the source note, but in the
original figures some data were quinquennial, some decennial, and some
referred to 25-year century periods. In this figure in the first two panels
all data are decennial; in the third panel the data refer to 25-year periods.
Source: Wrigley *et al.*, *English population history*, figs. 8.3 and 8.4,
pp. 541 and 543.

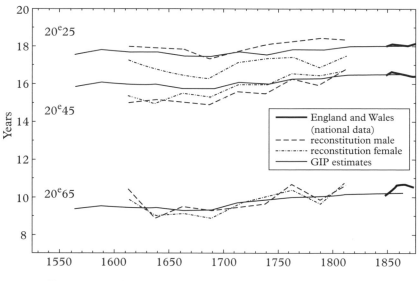

Figure 15.5. *Continued*

The top panel shows that both the level and trend in e_0 are similar in the two series except for the tendency of the reconstitution line to drift above the GIP line after *c.* 1750. The middle panel showing $_{15}e_0$ displays the same pattern and provides a clue to the reason for the drawing apart of the two sets of estimates. The reconstitution estimates rise above those from GIP because childhood mortality, especially $_4q_1$, is lower in the reconstitution series than in its comparator, a point further examined below.[54] One other feature of the top two panels may be noted. One prominent feature of the GIP estimates, the very marked deterioration in mortality in the late 1720s, is absent from the reconstitution data. It would seem that, fortuitously, the reconstitution parishes largely escaped the heavy mortality that affected a substantial proportion of all English parishes in this period.[55]

The third panel brings to light some points of great interest. GIP produces estimates of mortality only for the two sexes combined, but reconstitution allows the two to be treated separately, and the third panel takes advantage of this fact. GIP distributes deaths among the several

[54] See pp. 422–3 below.
[55] In 1727/8 and 1728/9, the two years when mortality rates were highest during the crisis of the late 1720s, the proportion of parishes in which there was a detectable local crisis was 28.2 and 28.5 per cent respectively. Wrigley and Schofield, *Population history of England*, tab. A10.2, p. 653. The years in question run from July to June. The definition of a local 'crisis' is described in ibid., pp. 646–9.

age groups in a manner which reflects the characteristics of the Princeton model North life table, using a Brass single parameter system.[56] Model North is based on data taken from the later nineteenth century onwards.[57] Reconstitution data show that mortality in England only came to conform closely to the North pattern in the course of the eighteenth century. Before then adult mortality was much more severe relative to infant and child mortality than would be expected from the age-specific rates in model North.[58] Moreover, the data on which model North was based refer to a period after maternal mortality had fallen far below the level of earlier centuries. It is not therefore surprising that the partial life expectancies $_{20}e_{25}$ show that a combined sex mortality level would be somewhat below the GIP figure in the first half of the period rising to equality towards its end, nor that the female figure is well below that for men but with some tendency for the gap to close, in part due to the marked improvement in maternal mortality during the 'long' eighteenth century (see figure 15.6 below). In later middle age ($_{20}e_{45}$), after the perils of childbirth, partial life expectancies are much the same for men and women, though now with a slight female advantage. More striking is the steady rise in the reconstitution estimates relative to that from GIP, reflecting the very marked fall in adult relative to infant and child mortality between the late seventeenth and the early nineteenth centuries. Partial life expectancy for the elderly ($_{20}e_{65}$) was similar for men and women, and the reconstitution and GIP estimates agree closely.

The fact that the mortality history of England revealed by GIP and that obtained by reconstitution resemble each other is reassuring to both exercises. It is highly improbable that they would agree closely by chance and likely that both are close to the truth.[59]

Reconstitution and early civil registration

Civil registration began in England in 1837. At the end of the parish register period a further test is therefore possible since the inception of civil registration means that the Registrar General's *Annual reports* provide a new point of comparison. The 26 parishes mirrored closely the economic and demographic characteristics of the country as a whole, though this similarity was the product of chance rather than conscious design.[60] It is

---

[56] See Wrigley *et al.*, *English population history*, pp. 516–20.
[57] Coale and Demeny, *Regional model life tables*, pp. 13–4.
[58] Wrigley *et al.*, *English population history*, pp. 348–50.
[59] There is a fuller discussion of this issue in ibid., pp. 541–4.
[60] The evidence for this assertion may be found in ibid., pp. 41–70. It should be noted that, because reconstitution began and ended at differing dates in the 26 parishes, there

therefore instructive to compare the reconstitution data with the national data collected by the Registrar General.

Fertility estimates

The Registrar General interested himself so little in fertility that, although totals of births were published, his returns do not contain breakdowns that enable age-specific marital fertility rates to be calculated. At first sight this might seem to prohibit an effective comparison of the fertility patterns found by family reconstitution with any that might be derived from the state's new vital registration system. However, it is feasible to combine vital registration material with census data to enable an indirect comparison to be made. The 1851 census tabulates the population by sex, age, and marital status. Therefore, it is possible to estimate the number of legitimate children who would have been born to married women at that time if the levels of marital fertility found in the reconstitution populations had prevailed nationally.

Column 1 in table 15.3 lists the annual totals of legitimate births in England in 1849–53, and their average number centring on the census year, 1851. Column 2 shows the totals of married women in each five-year age group in 1851, while columns 3 and 4 show the age-specific marital fertility rates derived from reconstitution data for the two periods 1700–49 and 1780–1829. Since the coverage of events in parish registers declined with the advent of civil registration, it is not possible to make a meaningful comparison of data from the two sources for exactly the same period. The half-century 1780–1829 is separated on average by 45 years from 1851, but represents the closest comparison period which is conveniently possible. Since it was a period of high marital fertility, an earlier half-century period, when marital fertility was somewhat lower, is also included for comparative purposes. Applying the rates for these two periods to the totals of married women, totals of births can then be calculated which may be compared with the average number registered nationally in the years centring on 1851. The birth totals shown in the lower half of the table reveal that those resulting from the use of reconstitution-based age-specific marital fertility rates exceed those recorded by the new civil registration system by 10 per cent (1780–1829), or by 6 per cent (1700–49).

The difference between the observed and calculated totals may in principle be attributable to a fall in marital fertility occurring in the early

was only a limited period during which data were drawn from the full set of parishes. The methods used to overcome any difficulties arising from this inconvenient fact are described in ibid., especially pp. 24–8 and app. 7.

Table 15.3 *A comparison of totals of births obtained by applying the age-specific marital fertility rates (ASMFRs) derived from reconstitution data to census totals of married women in 1851 compared with birth totals recorded by the Registrar General in 1849–1853*

	Legitimate births (1)	1851 Census: married women		Reconstitution ASMFRs (per 1,000 woman-years)	
			(2)	1700–49 (3)	1780–1829 (4)
1849	505,167	15–9	21,301	15–9	323	532
1850	518,718	20–4	253,996	20–4	419	429
1851	538,971	25–9	424,004	25–9	374	390
1852	546,227	30–4	439,820	30–4	320	312
1853	537,275	35–9	394,793	35–9	249	255
Total	2,646,358	40–4	350,088	40–4	127	148
1849–53 average	529,272	45–9	280,632	45–9	23	23

Average annual total of legitimate births 1849–53	529,272 (a)
Total of births if 1700–49 reconstitution ASMFRs had prevailed among married women in 1851	561,843 (b)
Total of births if 1780–1829 reconstitution ASMFRs had prevailed among married women in 1851	581,822 (c)

Ratio (b)/(a) = 1.062   **Ratio (c)/(a) = 1.099**

Note: The totals of births recorded by the Registrar General and the census totals refer to England only, rather than to England and Wales.
Source: Wrigley *et al.*, *English population history*, tab. 7.38, p. 463.

decades of the nineteenth century, to the early deficiencies in civil registration, to the reconstitution parishes having fortuitously high marital fertility, or to a combination of these possible causes. Estimates of the scale of early under-registration in the civil registers suggest that this may have been the most important single factor. Farr, Glass, and Teitelbaum each made estimates of the ratio between an estimated 'true' total of births and the registered totals for the two decades 1841–51 and 1851–61. Assuming that for the reference period of table 15.3 the appropriate ratio is the mean of the two decadal figures, the three men considered the ratio to be 1.047, 1.060, and 1.0445 respectively. A comparable exercise undertaken to produce data for inverse projection suggested a figure of

Table 15.4 *Comparison of reconstitution mortality estimates with the third English life table (1,000q$_x$)*

	Third English life table 1838–54	Reconstitution data 1825–37
${}_1q_0$	149.5	151.7
${}_4q_1$	133.7	98.3
${}_5q_5$	46.6	34.7
${}_5q_{10}$	25.6	34.7
${}_{10}q_5$	71.0	68.2
${}_{15}q_0$	315.4	287.2

Note: The reconstitution mortality rate ${}_1q_0$ is an overall rate including illegitimate children.
Sources: Wrigley *et al.*, *English population history*, tabs. 6.2 and 6.10, pp. 219 and 250–1. The q_xs of the third English life table were calculated from the l_xs in Registrar General, *Supplement to sixty-fifth annual report*, pt 1, tabs. H and I, pp. xlviii–li.

1.058.[61] If these estimates are of the right order of magnitude, there is very close agreement between the reconstitution estimates and the civil registration data, and it is plain that this test counts against the view that there was a significant under-registration of births in the reconstitution parish registers.

Mortality

William Farr, conscious of the deficiencies of civil registration in its early decades, went to much trouble to try to ensure that the third English life table, which drew upon data for the 17-year period 1838–54, was authoritative. Its accuracy is widely acknowledged except for the higher age groups where the reported rates are improbably low.[62] Table 15.4 compares the life table death rates based on reconstitution data with those taken from the third English life table.

---

[61] The estimates made by Farr, Glass, Teitelbaum, and Wrigley and Schofield are set out in Wrigley and Schofield, *Population history of England*, tabs. A8.3 and A8.4, p. 635. In these four exercises, the estimated true totals for the decade 1841–51 exceed the registered totals by between 6.1 and 7.8 per cent, while for 1851–61 the differences range between 2.8 and 4.9 per cent.

[62] The rates are too low because of progressively greater overstatement of age in the higher age groups in mid-nineteenth century censuses: R. Lee and Lam, 'Age distribution adjustments for English censuses': see also Wrigley and Schofield, *Population history of England*, app. 14.

The infant mortality rate derived from the pooled data of the reconstitution parishes for 1825–37 is slightly higher than that in the third English life table. The childhood mortality rates for the age range between the first and fifteenth birthday ($_{14}q_1$), in contrast, were 18 per cent lower in the reconstitution estimates than in the national data. The two rates were 195.2 and 159.8 per 1,000. This difference is due almost entirely to the much higher rate in the age group 1–4 in the third English life table. Apart from this age group there is close agreement between the two sets of rates. It is possible that in this respect the reconstitution parishes are unrepresentative of the national pattern, perhaps because they include no parishes from major urban areas in which early childhood mortality was severe (the birth and death totals used in GIP included both significant proportion of 'urban' events and a correction designed to offset the absence of London parishes from the data set).[63] This consideration very probably accounts for the difference between the two rates. The issue is uncertain, however, since there is persuasive if indirect evidence that early childhood mortality was rising rapidly in the second quarter of the nineteenth century. Swedish data illustrate the point effectively. In Sweden the ratio of $_1q_0$ to $_4q_1$ fell from almost 2:1 early in the nineteenth century to only about 1.2:1 c. 1850 before rising again to its former level by the end of the century. During the first quarter of the century and again after the mid-century when the level and trend of the ratio can be plotted for both England and Sweden, there was a close correspondence between the experience of the two countries.[64] If the same held true during the second quarter of the century in England, the anomaly would disappear or be much attenuated. Given that the reconstitution data centre on a date 15 years earlier than the comparable data for the civil registration data, the interpretation of the contrast in rates remains unclear. Nevertheless, it is probable that the $_4q_1$ reconstitution rates understate the national rate in this period, though only further investigation will settle the issue.

In this connection, it is noteworthy that one-to-one comparisons of individual parishes and their respective registration districts normally show strong similarities in both infant and child mortality rates. These rates can be calculated for registration districts for a few years in the 1840s and compared with the reconstitution rates for 1825–37. The registration district was, of course, a much bigger unit than the parish, but, perhaps surprisingly, the comparison reveals that in most cases there is a close agreement between the pattern of infant and child rates in individual parishes and those in the registration districts in which they were

---

[63] Ibid., pp. 45–56, 77–83.
[64] Wrigley et al., English population history, fig. 6.8, p. 259 and associated text.

situated.[65] In the case of the eight reconstitution parishes whose registers were reliable until 1837, a comparison with the registration districts in which they were situated showed, for example, that after adjustment of the rates to allow for the fact that reconstitution data exclude illegitimate births and deaths but the state registration included all births and deaths, the average infant mortality rate in the eight parishes differed by only 4 per cent from the average rate in the eight districts. The mean absolute discrepancy in the paired infant rates was 8 per 1,000. Since the infant rate is the rate most sensitive to underregistration, this is a notable result. The childhood rates in the registration districts were generally, though not invariably, the higher of the two, and the differences were again most marked in $_4q_1$ but because of the issue outlined in the last paragraph, the interpretation of the difference is unclear.[66]

Because deaths early in life are thought more likely to be absent from any registration system than those of adults, infant and child mortality rates have often come under close scrutiny. Razzell, for example, takes issue with the infant and child mortality findings from reconstitution, considering them much too low. It is particularly important for him to establish this point, given that, as will become apparent, his adult mortality estimates are not dissimilar to those of the Cambridge Group and that he views fertility levels as broadly unchanging during the period of accelerating population growth in the eighteenth and early nineteenth centuries. Thus a major improvement in infant and child mortality rates is necessary to account for the acceleration in population growth. Since the reconstitution evidence suggests only a modest improvement in mortality during the eighteenth century, the logic of his position commits him to the view that parochial registration coverage improved in the course of the century, thus cloaking the scale of the improvement. He envisages as probable, for example, an infant mortality rate between 250 and 340 per 1,000 in the seventeenth and early eighteenth centuries.[67]

[65] Ibid., tab. 4.3, p. 93 and, more generally, the discussion on pp. 93–7.

[66] Ibid., pp. 95–6. A similar exercise was carried out by Huck using infant mortality data from nine industrial parishes in the midlands and the north (Walsall, Handsworth, West Bromwich, Sedgeley, Armley, Wigan, Ashton-under-Lyne, Great Harwood, and Denton) for the period 1831–6. He compared the infant mortality rates calculated from parish register data with those for 1839–46 taken from the Registrar General's returns for the five registration districts in which the parishes were situated. In general, the parish register-based rates agreed well with the civil registration data. The former had been corrected where the level of endogenous mortality seemed suspiciously low, but the scale of the correction was modest, averaging only 15 per 1,000 over the nine parishes: Huck, 'Infant mortality in nine industrial parishes'. See also Galley, *Demography of early modern towns*, fig. 7.7, p. 186.

[67] Razzell, 'Growth of population', p. 757. His later discussion of the same issue suggests that he now inclines to a lower figure, probably about 250 per 1,000. Razzell, 'Eighteenth-century English population growth', pp. 486–94.

The strength of the evidence against the view that infant deaths were widely missed in the parish registers has already been rehearsed.[68] If infant mortality had indeed been at a level of *c.* 300 per 1,000 in this period, moreover, it would have been far out of line with experience in other countries whose later mortality history is like that of England. But it is worth noting that, ironically, one element in Razzell's discussion of the issue tells against his general thesis rather than favouring it. It concerns the fall in endogenous infant mortality in the eighteenth century, itself a matter of the greatest interest.

The picture obtained from reconstitution data shows little change in mortality in the 'long' eighteenth century from the end of the first month of life until the age of 15, although there is a very marked improvement in adult mortality. It is this absence of improvement in mortality early in life which limits the overall contribution of mortality to the rising growth rate. However, mortality in the first month of life fell markedly. Endogenous infant mortality, which is confined to the first month, fell from 88 per 1,000 in 1650–99 to 33 per 1,000 in 1825–37, whereas exogenous infant mortality rose from 88 to 111 per 1,000 over the same period. First month mortality (which includes all endogenous mortality and some exogenous deaths) fell from 107 to 49 per 1,000.[69] Since infant deaths are more prone to underregistration, and also because the average delay between birth and baptism was increasing during the eighteenth century (an unbaptised child who died was less likely to have his or her death entered in the burial register than one who had been baptised), it is evidently possible that the sharp fall in endogenous mortality is spurious, due to more and more young deaths being omitted from the parish registers. The clearest evidence that the fall is genuine lies in the close similarity between the endogenous rate taken from reconstitution material and the rate calculated from the early *Annual reports* of the Registrar General. The national rate in the early 1840s was 28 per 1,000 compared to a reconstitution rate of 33 per 1,000 for 1825–37.[70] There is, however, also strong supporting evidence in the fact that the maternal mortality rate fell in parallel with the endogenous infant rate, as might be expected since many of the dangers were common to both mother and child. The closeness of their relationship both in the parish register period and more recently is illustrated in figure 15.6.

[68] See above pp. 411–5.

[69] Endogenous infant mortality refers to deaths from the birth trauma, prematurity, and inherited defects; exogenous infant mortality to deaths from infection, accident, and neglect. Wrigley *et al.*, *English population history*, tab. 6.4, p. 226 and tab. 6.5, p. 236.

[70] Ibid., fig. 6.5, p. 232 and the related discussion on pp. 231–5.

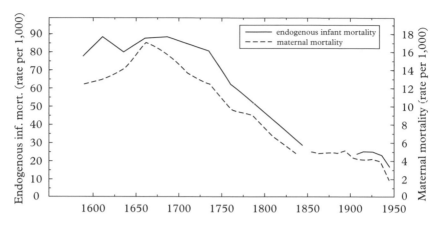

Figure 15.6. *Maternal mortality and endogenous infant mortality in England, 1580–99 to 1940–9*
Source: Wrigley *et al.*, *English population history*, tab. 6.5, p. 236; Loudon, *Death in childbirth*, app. 6, tab. 1, pp. 542–3; *Supplement to the twenty-fifth annual report of the Registrar General*, p. vii; *Registrar General's statistical review of England and Wales 1960*, III, Commentary, tab. LII, p. 113.

Razzell commented that it was 'impossible to say whether the Cambridge Group's finding of a sharp fall in neo-natal mortality is reliable' but implies that the rate was probably understated.[71] Questioning the scale of the fall in endogenous mortality, however, implies a difficulty with his wider argument which obliges him to expect improved death coverage in the burial registers. But if endogenous deaths were falling *less* rapidly in reality than would appear from reconstitution tabulations, this must mean that registration was deteriorating rather than improving, at odds with the view that the reverse was happening. It is worth stressing that the endogenous rate for the last quarter of the seventeenth century, at 88 per 1,000, is high compared with many of those calculated from parochial registration in other countries. This is precisely the category of infant deaths which is most likely to remain unrecorded, since all take place very soon after birth, and the mere fact of such a high rate in the reconstitution tabulations in itself provides a good reason to doubt whether any under-registration of infant deaths could be other than trivial in a period in which Razzell viewed death coverage as especially poor.

[71] Razzell, 'Eighteenth-century English population growth', p. 487.

Adult mortality

If infant deaths were well recorded in the reconstitution registers, it would be surprising if that were not also the case with adult deaths. Any doubts about adult rates are therefore likely to be focused elsewhere, on such matters as the danger that rates based exclusively on married people are not representative of the population as a whole, or the ability of the techniques employed to allow for the fact that many individuals were in observation in the parish for part of their adult lives but died elsewhere.[72] Independent evidence about adult mortality rates is not abundant and such evidence often refers to limited groups, such as the peerage or members of a tontine. Nevertheless a comparison between the later years of parochial registration and the third English life table is again feasible; and it is convenient to add to this comparison a review of the evidence assembled by Razzell from which estimates of mortality over part of the adult age span can be made.

In the later years of the parish register period adult mortality rates derived from reconstitution data were notably similar to those in the third English life table (ELT). For technical reasons, the parish register data can only be used down to 1809.[73] A comparison of the age-specific mortality rates for the 5-year age groups from 25–9 to 80–4 for the period 1750–1809 obtained by reconstitution with the comparable rates in the third English life table reveals that the late eighteenth-century rates were on average 4 per cent higher than the national rates in the period 1838–54 until the age of 75 (table 15.5). Above that age the third ELT rates were the higher. The periods covered are too widely spaced for this to constitute decisive evidence of registration completeness, but, once more, the outcome does not suggest concern that reconstitution estimates were defective. The stability of the ratios shown in the final column is also instructive, suggesting that the technique used to estimate adult mortality from reconstitution data produces credible results. Since the technique is complex, this is a reassuring outcome.[74]

A striking improvement in adult mortality is one of the most notable features of the reconstitution mortality tabulations.[75] Translated into Princeton model life table terms, the reconstitution data suggest that adult mortality moved from the equivalent of level 5 in model North in the period 1640–89 to the equivalent of level 9 in 1750–1809, or a rise

---

[72] The complexities of dealing with this problem and a description of the solution adopted may be found in Wrigley *et al.*, *English population history*, app. 6.
[73] The reasons for this restriction are described in ibid., pp. 598–600.
[74] Ibid., app. 6.
[75] Ibid., tab. 6.20, p. 291.

Table 15.5 *Adult mortality (sexes combined): reconstitution data and the third English life table (ELT) compared (1,000 q_x)*

	Reconstitution data 1750–1809	Third English life table extended 1838–54	
	(1)	(2)	(1)/(2)
25–9	49.4	47.8	1.033
30–4	53.7	52.5	1.022
35–9	62.4	58.4	1.069
40–4	68.3	66.2	1.031
45–9	88.4	76.8	1.150
50–4	99.9	94.1	1.062
55–9	123.0	123.3	0.998
60–4	171.3	171.2	1.000
65–9	238.5	243.8	0.978
70–4	376.4	352.1	1.069
75–9	438.2	483.1	0.907
80–4	598.2	620.9	0.964

Note: The rates in col. 1 were derived from the male and female rates given in Wrigley *et al.*, *English population history*, tab. 6.26, p. 303, on the assumption that the ratio of the l_x's for each sex in each age group was the same as in the third ELT, and assuming a sex ratio at birth of 105.

Sources: Col. 1: Cambridge Group reconstitutions. Col. 2: from 25–9 to 45–9, taken from the third ELT, Wrigley and Schofield, *Population history of England*, tab. A14.1, p. 709; from 50–4 to 80–4 extended from Princeton model North tables in the manner described in ibid., pp. 711–3.

of 10 years (each successive level yields an e_0 2.5 years greater than the next lower level in this system). Indeed, the improvement from its worst level in the 1680s is the equivalent of a gain in e_0 of over 15 years.[76] This stands in stark contrast with the limited improvement in mortality under the age of 15. The scale of the reduction was especially dramatic in the

[76] Ibid., p.282. Razzell is a little disingenuous over the scale of improvement in adult mortality in the reconstitution tabulations. He quotes a passage which, he claims, summarises the new findings about e_{25} as showing an increase of 3 or 4 years in the seventeenth and eighteenth centuries, a figure much lower than some alternative estimates which he quotes. But on the same page from which the quotation is taken there is a passage which runs, 'if adult mortality data were the sole guide to mortality change in England in the later seventeenth and eighteenth centuries, the rise in e_0 would appear to have been very sharp and pronounced, at least 10 years, and possibly more than 15 years, depending on whether the estimate was based on lengthy period, or from the trough to the later eighteenth-century plateau'. Razzell, 'Eighteenth-century English population growth', p. 495. If e_0 had indeed changed so greatly it would, *ceteris paribus*, have increased the intrinsic growth rate by between 0.75 and 1.00 per cent per annum, thus accounting for a large fraction of the acceleration which took place.

case of maternal mortality which fell from 17.0 per 1,000 birth events in 1650–74 to only 4.7 per 1,000 in 1825–37.[77]

Razzell made much of the evidence to be gleaned from marriage licences when arguing for a major improvement in adult mortality. He believed that this finding was at odds with Cambridge Group estimates. There is, however, it transpires, broad agreement between the evidence assembled by Razzell and the Cambridge Group adult mortality estimates, though Razzell believed otherwise. A reconsideration of his findings may clarify matters.

The information contained in marriage licences can be used to specify the proportion of cases where the father was still living at the time of his daughter's marriage. Several of Razzell's tabulations were based on the frequency of such cases where the bride was a spinster under the age of 21. For example, he analysed data for two areas; London, and the Home Counties and environs of London. In both areas between the mid-seventeenth century and the late eighteenth or early nineteenth century there was a substantial rise in the proportion of cases in which the father was still living when his daughter married. His analyses may be summarised as follows: in London over this period the percentage of surviving fathers rose from 53.1 to 64.5; in the Home Counties and the environs of London from 57.1 to 68.1.[78]

It so happens that a direct comparison with reconstitution results over an approximately similar time span is readily feasible, since male adult mortality q_xs were calculated for the periods 1640–89 and 1750–1809. Thus, reconstitution data can be converted into a form which mimics the survivorship percentages in the marriage licence material by calculating male survivorship over the same life span. A comparison of these two sets of estimates is especially apt since both refer to married men rather than to the adult male population generally. The average age at marriage of women who married under 21 was almost exactly 19.5 years.[79] Mean age at maternity in the reconstitution data was about 33 years in the earlier period but had fallen to just over 31 years in the later period.[80] The age gap between grooms and brides where both were marrying for the first time was about 2 years in the early and middle decades of the seventeenth century but declined to about 1.5 years thereafter, but mean

---

[77] Wrigley et al., English population history, tab. 6.29, p. 313.

[78] For the earlier period these are the weighted averages of the figures for 1600–51 and 1661–99, and for the later period the weighted averages of those for 1750–89 and 1840–9. Razzell, 'Eighteenth-century English population growth', tab. 10, p. 497.

[79] The average age of brides marrying before their 21st birthday in bachelor/spinster marriages in 1625–74 was 19.4 years, and in 1750–99 19.5 years: Wrigley et al., English population history, tab. 5.6, pp. 146–7.

[80] Ibid., p. 534.

age at paternity was greater than these age gaps would suggest since there were many marriages in which the groom was not a bachelor. The age gap in widower/spinster and widower/widow marriages was much wider than in bachelor/spinster marriages and such marriages greatly outnumbered bachelor/widow marriages. The commonest category was widower/spinster marriages where the age gap was about 10 years, and since brides in this category were less than 30 years old on average throughout the parish register period, and often bore several children, mean age at paternity must make allowance for this.[81] On the assumption that the mean age at paternity was 37 in the earlier period and 34 in the later period, the proportion of married men surviving to age 56.5 and age 53.5 respectively (that is, mean age at paternity plus 19.5 years in each case) can readily be calculated. The percentages in question are 60.4 and 72.1.[82]

The proportionate improvements in mortality in the marriage licence and reconstitution data are very similar, although the absolute survival percentages are significantly lower in London than in the reconstitution-based estimate, as might be expected, and slightly lower in the case of the Home Counties and the environs of London, which again is not surprising.[83] Any conclusion based on these survival percentages must be tentative. The validity of any comparison depends, in effect, on the

---

[81] Ibid., tab. 5.7, p. 149.

[82] The percentages were calculated from the q_xs in ibid., tab. 6.26, p. 303. It may be of interest to note that the survivorship percentages for London imply, by comparison with the Princeton model North life tables, that London moved from c. level 3 to c. level 5.5; the Home Counties and the environs of London from c. level 4 to c. level 7; while the reconstitution data imply a move from c. level 5 to c. level 9.

[83] Razzell also published an analysis of marriage licence data for East Kent. This showed a much more striking improvement in mortality, from a paternal survivorship of 54.8 per cent to 75.9 per cent, calculated in the same way (in this case the weighted averages of 1619–46, 1661–76, and 1677–1700 for the earlier period, and of 1751–79 and 1780–1809 for the later period); Razzell, 'Growth of population', tab. 6, p. 761. I have not included this analysis with those for London and for the Home Counties and the environs of London, however, since it is difficult to interpret and may be unreliable. There are two problems. First, two different paternal survivorship percentages are quoted for women marrying under the age of 21 in the period 1619–46 (58.2 per cent in tab. 5, p. 760; 53.33 per cent in tab. 6, p. 761, the former based on 280 cases, the latter on 1,275). This makes for confusion, but a second problem is more puzzling. In tab. 5, in addition to the paternal survivorship percentage for brides under 21 (58.2), a comparable percentage is given for the fathers of brides aged 21–5 (42.1). This suggests that whereas 58.2 per cent of fathers whose daughters averaged about 19.5 years of age survived to authorise the marriage, only 42.1 per cent did so when their daughters were on average 23 years old. Assuming that age at paternity and age of daughter at marriage are not correlated, this in turn implies, on the assumptions set out above in the main text, that between the ages of 56.5 and 60 (37 + 19.5 and 37 + 23) mortality was sufficiently severe to move very quickly from a survivorship of 58.2 per cent to one of only 42.1 per cent. This is scarcely credible. It implies a wastage of 28 per cent of fathers in a span of 3.5 years in their later fifties (100 − (42.1/58.2 × 100) = 27.7). A survivorship of 58.2 per cent from

assumption that those marrying by licence, if not a random sample of brides, were tolerably representative of the population at large. It may be, however, that families which had lost the father were more likely (or indeed less likely) to resort to marriage by licence than others; or that marriage by licence was socially selective in a manner which affected any comparison with the population at large; or that either of these variables, and others which might be listed, changed over time. However, in so far as the comparison is valid, it is reassuring. There seems little reason to suppose that the evidence relating to male adult mortality drawn from marriage licences and that drawn from reconstitution are at odds.

Razzell's alternative scenario

Between the mid-sixteenth and mid-nineteenth centuries the population of England grew faster than that of neighbouring countries on the continent. The contrast was often marked. For example, in 1550 the French population was more than five times as large as the English (17 and 3 millions respectively). By 1850 the ratio had changed radically. The population of France was then 36 millions: that of England 17 millions. The ratio between the two populations had changed from 5:1 to 2:1.[84] The bulk of the gain relative to other countries occurred after 1700.

The work of the Cambridge Group has suggested that the marked acceleration in growth which took place in this period was chiefly due to a rise in fertility, which in turn was largely due to a fall in the age at marriage. Declining mortality also made a substantial contribution to this acceleration but the rise in fertility was the stronger influence, roughly in the ratio of 2:1.[85] Before the publication of *The population history of England*, most, though not all scholars, had supposed that mortality

37 to 56.5, expressed in Princeton model North terms, lies between level 4 and level 5. The expected proportion surviving from 37 to 60 at the same mortality level, however, is approximately 49.6 per cent, a far cry from the reported 42.1 per cent. The wastage in model North terms is less than 15 per cent, rather than 28 per cent. It seems highly probable that either the quoted survivorship percentage for fathers of brides under 21 is too high, or that the percentage for fathers of brides aged 21–5 is too low, or possibly that a powerful distorting factor is at work. For example, brides may have been increasingly likely to marry by licence as they grew older if their father was no longer living.

[84] Mitchell, *European historical statistics*, tab. B1, p. 30; Wrigley, *People, cities and wealth*, tab. 9.1, p. 216; Wrigley *et al.*, *English population history*, tab. A9.1, pp. 614–5.

[85] In the period 1651–1700 the intrinsic growth rate in England averaged almost exactly 0.00. In 1811–25 it reached a peak of 1.71 per cent per annum. Over the same period e_0 rose from 34.9 years to 40.9 years while the GRR increased from 1.97 to 2.82. The relative contribution of fertility and mortality to the increase in the intrinsic growth rate can be estimated from these data, and shows that fertility contributed slightly more than twice as much as mortality to the increased intrinsic growth rate. The data are taken from ibid., tab. A9.1, pp. 614–5.

decline was the principal agent in causing the rate of growth to increase.[86] This is still the view of Razzell, who has been persistently critical of the findings of the Cambridge Group, both those produced by inverse projection and those resulting from family reconstitution. In both cases it is Razzell's view that the deficiencies in Anglican parochial registration vitiate the findings. At several junctures the difficulty of accepting his principal thesis about the dominance of mortality changes in determining growth rates has been exposed. The preceding sections of this essay provide reasons for accepting the general soundness of the findings of the Group obtained both from reconstitution and generalised inverse projection. This in turn supports the revised view of the demographic changes which produced accelerated growth in the 'long' eighteenth century, but it may be of interest to consider the implications of Razzell's alternative suggestions taken as a whole.

First, the nature of the population balance equation should be noted. The equation specifies the nature of a necessary internal consistency in the demographic attributes of any given population between any two successive dates: it takes the form $P_2 = P_1 + B - D + I - E$ (where P_1 and P_2 represent the population at two successive dates, and B, D, I, and E represent the totals of births, deaths, immigrants and emigrants between the two dates). The equation implies that if one or more of the variables in question is changed there must be related changes in one or more of the other variables to preserve the identity which it expresses. If, for example, the population total at the later of the two dates is raised, there must be an increase in the previously assumed total of births; a decrease in the total of deaths; an increase in net migration; or some combination of the three. Or, to take another possibility, if it is held that the number of births occurring between two dates has been underestimated, this must imply raising the previously accepted estimates of the population total at the end of the period; or lowering the estimation of its size at the beginning of the period; or, if the population totals are known to be accurate, increasing the number of deaths by the same number as the total of births has been raised; or, some other change or combination of changes which preserves internal consistency. The equation makes it clear that to propose a change in any one of the constituent variables of the equation must imply change in one or more of the other variables. GIP exemplifies the operation of the population balance equation in the sense that the estimates of population totals, fertility, mortality, and net

[86] A notable exception was Habakkuk whose thoughtful contribution to the debate half a century ago played an important part in reviving the debate about the proximate causes of the acceleration in population growth: Habakkuk, 'English population in the eighteenth century'.

migration which it generates are constrained to be internally consistent. The estimates may be in error because of flaws in the input data, or for a variety of other reasons, but by construction all the demographic estimates must be mutually consistent.

If Razzell's estimates of the shortfall between registered events and those which actually occurred are used to produce revised totals of births and deaths, GIP can then be employed to discover both how different the population history of the country would have been on his assumptions and to test whether his assumptions are compatible with each other. His early work provides alternative estimates of the crude birth rate in the first four decades of the nineteenth century, 1801–41. They are somewhat higher than those produced by GIP from the Cambridge Group's estimates of birth and death totals. For the four decades they are (comparable GIP-derived rates in brackets): 41.4 (37.8), 42.0 (39.3), 40.1 (38.8), and 35.9 (35.7).[87] His general view, based on the comparison of census entries with baptism registers for 45 parishes, was initially that about one-third of all births were omitted from baptism registers, and when he returned to the issue at a later date he came to much the same conclusion.[88] The nature of the census/baptism register comparison precluded making estimates before 1760 using this method (because there were very few survivors in 1851 who had been born before 1760), but between 1760 and the end of the parish register period in 1837 the proportion of births missing from the baptism registers fluctuates in a band fairly close to one-third.[89] For want of any direct estimate and in line with Razzell's view about the general deficiencies of parochial registration, it is reasonable to suppose that the same level of omission occurred before 1760. It is therefore readily possible to generate birth totals for the whole parish register period, though with less certainty before 1760 than afterwards. After 1801 the totals were obtained by relating the birth rates quoted to the midpoint population totals for each decade: before 1801 the recorded baptism totals were multiplied in the ratio 3:2.[90]

Generating a comparable series for deaths is more problematic. As with births, there is a basis for the calculation of totals of deaths after 1801,

---

[87] Razzell, 'Baptism as a form of birth registration', tab. 17, p. 138; Wrigley *et al.*, *English population history*, tab. A9.1, pp. 614–5.

[88] Razzell, 'Baptism as a form of birth registration', p. 145 and Razzell, *English population history*, ch. 5.

[89] Razzell, 'Baptism as a form of birth registration', tab. 8, p. 129.

[90] The baptism totals may be found in Wrigley and Schofield, *English population history*, tab. A4.1, col. 5, pp. 537–44. They were therefore the same as the baptism totals which were used to generate the demographic estimates in the book, though the inflation factors which converted the baptism totals into estimated birth totals were, of course, very different from those chosen by Razzell.

since Razzell offered estimates of the percentages of deaths omitted from Anglican registers for the four decades from 1801 to 1841 as 34.1, 38.8, 28.3, and 15.7 respectively.[91] He suggested that 'burial registration gradually improved throughout the seventeenth and early eighteenth century – the omission rate declining from 34 per cent to 25 per cent – which was followed by a period of overall stability for the rest of the eighteenth and early nineteenth centuries'.[92] He went on to suggest that the situation was much the same for both adults and children. These estimates, however, were based on work on reconstitution parishes, so that they probably represent a lower bound to his estimate of the extent of underregistration in parish registers generally. Nevertheless, in generating a death series to parallel the birth series for the period before 1801, these inflation factors were used, in the absence of estimates for parish registers generally. Thus burial totals before 1600 were inflated in the ratio 100/66 and between 1720 and 1800 by 100/75, while in between 1600 and 1720 the inflation ratio was reduced in each quinquennium to produce a smooth decline between the two plateaus.

The birth and death series produced in this fashion represent only one possible interpretation of Razzell's conclusions about the scale of underregistration in different periods, but they permit the study of the implications of this interpretation of his assumptions since GIP is able to convert them into estimates of population size, expectation of life at birth, the gross reproduction rate, net migration, and so on. Exactly the same GIP system was used in generating the results based on Razzell's assumptions as had been used to generate the Cambridge Group estimates, including the use of the same algorithm to estimate 'smoothed' net migration rates.[93] The results are shown in figures 15.7, 15.8, and 15.9.

The impossibility of accepting the combination of assumptions made by Razzell is immediately clear in the figures. Figure 15.7, for example, plots the course of the GRR. In the nineteenth century Razzell's estimates and those published in *The population history of England* are, not surprisingly, in close agreement, but, moving backwards in time from 1800, Razzell's figure rises to more than 5.0 *c.* 1700, and, after a dip in the mid-seventeenth century, rises steeply once more to average 5.4 in

[91] Razzell, 'Baptism as a form of birth registration', tab. 18, p. 139. Razzell offered two sets of correction percentages in this table. They differ only marginally, but his discussion suggests that he regarded burial/death estimates as less well founded than the corresponding baptism/birth series.

[92] Razzell, 'Eighteenth-century English population growth', p. 480.

[93] I am much indebted to Jim Oeppen for carrying out this exercise and for advice about the interpretation of the results.

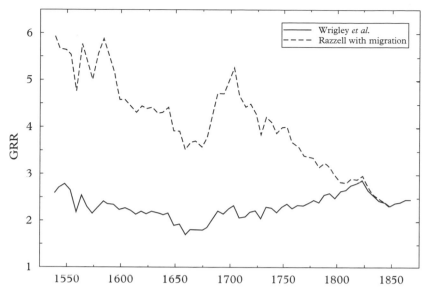

Figure 15.7. *Gross reproduction rates: Cambridge Group and Razzell*
Sources: Cambridge Group rates; Wrigley *et al.*, *English population history*,
tab. A9.1, pp. 614–5. Razzell's rates; see text.

the sixteenth century. Since the GRR expresses the number of daughters
each woman would have in the absence of any loss of life before the end
of the fertile period, a figure as high as 5.4 would require each woman on
average to produce 11 children. Even if marriage were both universal and
took place at a very early age, this would be an astonishingly high figure.
In a society where a significant proportion of women never married and
where the average age at marriage was in the mid-twenties, it is not credible. Even Hutterite levels of marital fertility would not suffice to reach
this level in a population with English nuptiality patterns (see table 15.2
above).

With fertility as high as that suggested by figure 15.7, it necessarily
follows that mortality must also be very high if population growth were to
remain in bounds, and figure 15.8 reflects this necessity. In the course of
the eighteenth century there is indeed a massive improvement in mortality
in conformity with Razzell's general thesis. Expectation of life at birth
rises markedly, from little more than 24.2 years in the first decade of
the eighteenth century to about 33.4 years in the first decade of the
nineteenth century. In the seventeenth century mortality is crippling. In
the half century 1641–90, for example, e_0 averages only 19.4 years. An
expectation of life at this level would imply a crude death rate in excess

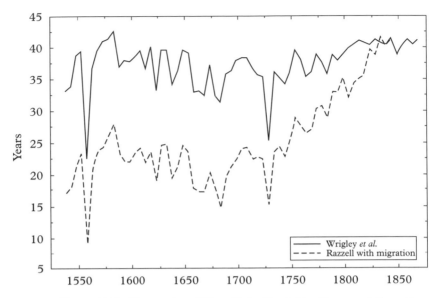

Figure 15.8. *Expectation of life at birth: Cambridge Group and Razzell*
Sources: See fig. 15.7.

of 50 per 1,000. Although most pre-industrial populations experienced occasional years in which mortality reached this level, and some cities were sufficiently unhealthy to have caused crude death rates to average 50 per 1,000 or more over long periods, no large European population was ever subjected to such a drastic toll.

Figure 15.9 shows the path of population growth, consonant with the fertility and mortality estimates produced by GIP. The eye immediately notes that the gap between the Razzell-based estimates and those of the Cambridge Group is widest in the late seventeenth century. Since the vertical scale is logarithmic, this implies that the relative difference between the two estimates is at its greatest in this period. In 1686 the Razzell line results in a population total of only 3.54 millions, 30 per cent lower than the Cambridge Group estimate of 5.04 millions. Before the mid-seventeenth century the gap is stable (that is the percentage difference between the two estimates at any given date remains much the same). The rapid widening of the gap in the eighteenth century is due to the greater inflation of baptisms than burials during the eighteenth century. An increased birth surplus moving backward in time has the opposite effect from its effect moving forward in time (GIP takes a known population total and structure at an end point and infers earlier populations from

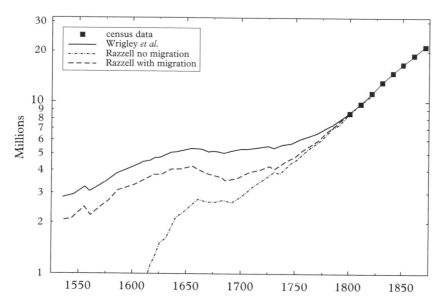

Figure 15.9. *English population totals: Cambridge Group and Razzell*
Sources: See fig. 15.7.

preceding streams of births and deaths).[94] The enhanced birth surplus
in the eighteenth century therefore implies a rapid decrease in population
moving backwards in time where a birth surplus moving forward in time
would imply rapid increase. The stabilisation in the relative gap between
the two series before the late seventeenth century is not a function of the
similarity in the inflation ratios for baptisms and burials over this period.
It is due to the very high level of net emigration which the program is,
in effect, forced to generate in order to avoid a population implosion.
During the sixteenth century the annual net emigration rate averages just
over 6 per 1,000, declining to *c.* 4 per 1,000 at the end of the seventeenth
century, and to only a little more than 1 per 1,000 about 1800. The final
figure is quite plausible, especially in view of the fact that deaths of men
at sea or in warfare abroad will be interpreted by the program as emigration, but a rate as high as 6 per 1,000 is deeply implausible two
centuries earlier.[95] Yet the imbalance between the birth and death totals resulting from Razzell's assumptions in effect forces emigration to

---

[94] See Oeppen, 'Generalized inverse projection'.
[95] Note that the net emigration rate would have to be much higher still to produce the
substantially higher population totals in the sixteenth and seventeenth centuries which
have been common ground amongst those who have studied English population history
from Rickman onwards.

substitute for deficient deaths. To underline this point, figure 15.9 also shows the path of population growth in a closed population using the same birth and death totals (that is, allowing no migration and deriving the totals by successively adding the deaths and subtracting the births occurring in each quinquennium backwards from 1871).

The population balance equation, therefore, mediated through GIP, strongly reinforces reservations about the credibility of Razzell's assumptions about the phasing and scale of deficiencies in Anglican parochial registration. Just as it is incumbent on anyone attempting a reconstruction of the demographic history of England to ensure that its constituent elements are consonant with each other, so it is important that the same should hold good for alternative schema.

Conclusion

The roll call of those who have interested themselves in English population history is long and distinguished. Participants in the debate over the last two centuries have disagreed about many things, but surprisingly little about the simplest and most fundamental of all demographic statistics, the size of the population and its change over time. The remarkable initiative taken by Rickman in 1836 in assembling returns of annual totals of baptisms, burials, and marriages from all parishes whose registers began before 1600 provided him with a vast body of empirical data. The totals were for three-year periods at intervals throughout the parish register period. The analysis of these data published in the 1841 census suggested that the population in 1570, the earliest date for which information had been collected, was about 3.7 millions, that it rose substantially to more than 5.1 millions by 1630 but thereafter changed little until the end of the seventeenth century before accelerating sharply during the eighteenth century to reach about 8.6 millions in 1801.[96] Later estimates have varied somewhat from those of Rickman, but chiefly within a range of plus or minus 10 per cent from his figures. All the estimates give rise to similar trends over time.[97] The road travelled is not in dispute. Disagreement has been confined to the means of locomotion. Were the slow, secular swings between growth and stasis principally due to fluctuations in mortality or in fertility, and, if the latter, was this in turn the result of changes in the incidence and timing of marriage with little or no change in marital fertility, or was it due to other factors? The answers to these questions revealed

---

[96] Wrigley and Schofield, *Population history of England*, tab. A5.2, p. 574 and tab. A5.3, p. 577 and accompanying text.
[97] Ibid., app. 5.

by the work of the Cambridge Group for the History of Population and Social Structure over the past 35 years have been described elsewhere and it would be otiose to rehearse them here. Some of the findings were novel. Many were derived by methods which were complex and often not readily comprehensible. While it may be true that the complexity was unavoidable, this cannot have increased confidence in the findings on the part of many of those who had a keen interest in the outcome but felt difficulty in assessing its authority. This essay represents an attempt to allay the doubts and hesitations which, understandably, were not uncommon.

The doubts fell chiefly under two heads, reliability and representativeness. In relation to the first, the evidence provided by the tests described in this essay seems clear cut. There is good reason to have confidence in the estimates of fertility and mortality based on reconstitution data, and chapter 14 showed the same to be true for nuptiality. By implication, since the results obtained by generalised inverse projection closely resemble those obtained by reconstitution, this tends also to give further support to the former. Representativeness is less easy to monitor than reliability as far as the reconstitution data are concerned (the problem is much more tractable in relation to inverse projection[98]). It was discussed at length in *English population history*.[99] There the occupational structure of the reconstitution parishes was described and it was compared with that of the country as a whole. In addition, the secular trends in the aggregative totals of baptisms, burials, and marriage in the reconstitution parishes were compared with those in the parishes from which national totals of births, deaths, and marriages were derived in *The population history of England*. The following passage summarises the conclusion reached: 'Overall, a comparison of the behaviour of totals of events drawn from the reconstitutions with the template provided by the totals of events in the set of 404 parishes is encouraging. Like the earlier analysis of occupational data from the 1831 census, it underwrites the belief that, though as a result of serendipity rather than initial design, it is reasonable to regard any findings – as likely to reflect national characteristics.'[100]

Establishing similarity between the occupational structure of the reconstitution parishes and that of the country as a whole, and between aggregative patterns in the two bodies of data, is valuable but speaks only indirectly to the question of whether the demographic measures derived from either reconstitution or inverse projection capture national characteristics. The only direct test possible relates to the 'join' between fertility

---

[98] Ibid., ch. 2.
[99] Wrigley *et al.*, *English population history*, ch. 3.
[100] Ibid., p. 70.

and mortality estimates from the end of the parish register era and national returns under the new civil registration system. The test is not ideal since the deterioration in parochial registration coverage which occurred with the inception of civil registration makes it impossible to compare results from the two sources over the same time period. Nor is the test meaningful for inverse projection results based on the aggregative returns from the 404 parishes since the national birth and death series derived from the aggregative returns are constrained to join smoothly with the early civil registration totals. Therefore, the estimates of the gross reproduction rate and of expectation of life at birth produced by GIP are bound to be in close conformity with comparable data based on the *Annual reports* of the Registrar General. A comparison of reconstitution estimates with early civil registration material, on the other hand, has point. The two sources were in close agreement over fertility estimates and, in general, over mortality, though early childhood mortality, $_4q_1$, in the early nineteenth century may well be have been below the national level in the reconstitution parishes.[101]

Unambiguous precision is, and will remain, beyond reach. The most that is attainable is to reduce the margins of uncertainty which surround almost all attempts to quantify economic, social, and demographic behaviour in past centuries. It is idle to expect that all doubts will be quelled by an exercise of the sort represented by this essay, which is not without its *longueurs*. I hope, nonetheless, that the balance between those who are prepared to accept the account of the population history of England developed by the Cambridge Group and those who remain in doubt may be shifted further in favour of the former by this essay. If so, it will have served its purpose.

[101] See p. 423 above.

Bibliography

SECONDARY SOURCES

Abrams, P., 'Towns and economic growth: some theories and problems', in P. Abrams and E. A. Wrigley, eds., *Towns in societies: essays in economic history and historical sociology* (Cambridge, 1978), pp. 9–33.

Allen, R. C., 'Economic structure and agricultural productivity in Europe, 1300–1800', *European Review of Economic History*, 3 (2000), pp. 1–26.

Andreev, K. F., 'Demographic surfaces: estimation, assessment and presentation, with application to Danish mortality, 1835–1995' (PhD thesis, University of Southern Denmark, 1999).

Armstrong, W. A., 'The use of information about occupation', in E. A. Wrigley, ed., *Nineteenth-century society: essays in the use of quantitative methods for the study of social data* (Cambridge, 1972), pp. 191–310.

Ashton, T. S., *The industrial revolution 1760–1830* (Oxford, 1948).

An economic history of England: the 18th century (London, 1955).

Bairoch, P., *Cities and economic development: from the dawn of history to the present* (Chicago, 1988).

Bairoch, P., Batou, J., and Chèvre, J., *La population des villes européennes. Banque de données et analyse sommaire des résultats* (Geneva, 1988).

Benaerts, P., *Les origines de la grande industrie allemande* (Paris, 1933).

Berg, M. and Hudson, P., 'Rehabilitating the industrial revolution', *Economic History Review*, 2nd ser., 45 (1992), pp. 24–50.

Berry, B. J. L., *Geography of market centers and retail distribution* (Englewood Cliffs, N J, 1967).

Blayo, Y., 'La mortalité en France de 1740 à 1829', *Population*, 30, special number (Nov. 1975), pp. 123–42.

Bongaarts, J., 'A method for the estimation of fecundability', *Demography*, 12 (1975), pp. 645–60.

Booth, C., 'Occupations of the people of the United Kingdom, 1801–81', *Journal of the Statistical Society*, 49 (1886), pp. 314–435.

Bourgeois-Pichat, J., 'La mesure de la mortalité infantile', *Population*, 6 (1951), pp. 233–48, 459–80.

Brändström, A. and Sundin, J., 'Infant mortality in a changing society. The effects of child care in a Swedish parish 1820–1894', in A. Brändström and J. Sundin, eds., *Tradition and transition*, Studies in microdemography and social change, no. 2 (Umeå, 1981), pp. 67–104.

Brewer, J., *The sinews of power: war, money and the English state 1688–1783* (London, 1989).

Burns, C. M., *Infant and maternal mortality in relation to size of family and rapidity of breeding* (Newcastle, 1942).

Cameron, R., 'The industrial revolution, a misnomer', in J. Schneider, ed., *Wirtschaftskräfte und Wirtschaftswege*, vol. V (Stuttgart, 1981), pp. 367–76.

Campbell, B. M. S., Galloway, D., Keene, D., and Murphy, M., *A medieval capital and its grain supply: agrarian production and distribution in the London region c. 1300*, Historical Geography Research Series no. 30 (1993).

Campbell, D. M. and MacGillivray, I., 'Outcome of twin pregnancies', in I. MacGillivray, D. M. Campbell, and B. Thompson, eds., *Twinning and twins* (Chichester, 1988), pp. 179–202.

Cannadine, D., 'The present and the past in the English industrial revolution', *Past and Present*, 103 (1984), pp. 131–72.

Chambers, J. D., *The workshop of the world. British economic history from 1820 to 1880* (London, 1961).

The Chester Beatty Institute serial abridged life tables, compiled by R. A. M. Case, C. Coghill, J. L. Harley, and J. T. Pearson (London, 1962).

Chisholm, M., *Rural settlement and land use*, 3rd edn (London, 1979).

Christaller, W., *Die zentralen Orte in Süddeutschland: eine ökonomisch-geographische Untersuchung über die Gesetzmässigmeit der Verbreitung und Entwicklung der Siedlungen mit städtischen Funktionen* (Jena, 1933).

Clapham, J. H., *An economic history of modern Britain*, 3 vols., 2nd edn reprinted (Cambridge, 1950–1).

Clark, C., *The conditions of economic progress* (2nd edn, London, 1951).

Clark, P. and Souden, D., eds., *Migration and society in early modern England* (London, 1987).

Coale, A. J. and Demeny, P., *Regional model life tables and stable populations* (Princeton, 1966).

Cobbett, W., *Cottage economy*, first pub. 1822 (Oxford, 1979).

Cole, W. A., 'Factors in demand 1700–80', in R. Floud and D. McCloskey, eds., *The economic history of Britain since 1700*, vol. I (Cambridge, 1981), pp. 36–65.

Cook, E., *Man, energy and society* (San Francisco, 1976).

Cottrell, F., *Energy and society: the relation between energy, social change, and economic development* (New York, 1955).

Cowley, Abraham, *The complete works in verse and prose of Abraham Cowley*, ed. A. B. Grosart, 2 vols. (Edinburgh, 1881).

Crafts, N. F. R., 'Patterns of development in nineteenth century Europe', *Oxford Economic Papers*, 36 (1984), pp. 438–58.

British economic growth during the industrial revolution (Oxford, 1985).

Crouzet, F., 'Towards an export economy: British exports during the industrial revolution', in F. Crouzet, *Britain ascendant: comparative studies in Franco-British economic history* (Cambridge, 1990), pp. 213–61.

Davies, M. L., ed., *Maternity: letters from working women* (1915; repub. with new introd. by G. Dallas, 1978).

Deane, P., 'The British industrial revolution', in M. Teich and R. Porter, eds., *The industrial revolution in national context* (Cambridge, 1996), pp. 13–35.

Deane, P. and Cole, W. A., *British economic growth 1688–1959: trends and structure* (Cambridge, 1962).

Desjardins, B., 'Bias in age at marriage in family reconstitutions: evidence from French Canadian data', *Population Studies*, 49 (1995), pp. 165–9.

De Vries, J., *The Dutch rural economy in the Golden Age 1500–1700* (New Haven and London, 1974).

European urbanization 1500–1800 (Cambridge, Mass., 1984).

'The industrial revolution and the industrious revolution', *Journal of Economic History*, 54 (1994), pp. 249–70.

'Dutch economic growth in comparative historical perspective, 1500–2000', *De Economist*, 148 (2000), pp. 443–67.

De Vries, J. and van der Woude, A., *The first modern economy: success, failure and perseverance of the Dutch economy, 1500–1815* (Cambridge, 1997).

De Zeeuw, J. W., 'Peat and the Dutch Golden Age: the historical meaning of energy availability', *A.A.G. Bijdragen*, 21 (1978), pp. 3–31.

Dobb, M., *Studies in the development of capitalism* (London, 1946).

Dobson, M. J., 'Population, disease and mortality in southeast England, 1600–1800' (unpub. DPhil thesis, University of Oxford, 1982).

Dobson, M. J., *Contours of death and disease in early modern England* (Cambridge, 1997).

Dupâquier, J., 'Pour une histoire de la prématurité', *Annales de démographie historique, 1994* (Paris, 1994), pp. 187–202.

Dyer, C., 'The consumer and the market in the late middle ages', *Economic History Review*, 2nd ser., 42 (1989), pp. 305–27.

Eversley, D. E. C., 'The home market and economic growth in England 1750–80', in E. L. Jones and G. E. Mingay, eds., *Land, labour and population in the industrial revolution* (London, 1967), pp. 206–59.

Falkus, M. E. and Jones, E. L., 'Urban improvement and the English economy in the seventeenth and eighteenth centuries', *Research in Economic History*, 4 (1979), pp. 193–233.

Farr, W., *Vital statistics* (London, 1885).

Finlay, R., 'Natural decrease in early modern cities', *Past and Present*, 92 (1981), pp. 169–74.

First and second prayer books of Edward VI, introd. D. Harrison (Everyman's Library, London, 1968).

Fisher, J. C., *Energy crises in perspective* (New York, 1974).

Fleury, M. and Henry, L., *Nouveau manuel de dépouillement et d'exploitation de l'état civil ancien* (3rd edn, Paris, 1985).

Flinn, M. W., 'The stabilization of mortality in pre-industrial western Europe', *Journal of European Economic History*, 3 (1974), pp. 285–318.

The history of the British coal industry, vol. II, 1700–1830: the industrial revolution (Oxford, 1984).

Floud, R., Wachter, K., and Gregory, A., *Height, health and history: nutritional status in the United Kingdom, 1750–1980* (Cambridge, 1990).

Fogel, R. W., *The conquest of high mortality and hunger in Europe and America: timing and mechanisms*, Working paper series on historical factors in long run growth, no. 16, National Bureau of Economic Research (Cambridge, Mass., 1989).

Galley, C., *The demography of early modern towns: York in the sixteenth and seventeenth centuries* (Liverpool, 1998).

Galliano, P., 'La mortalité infantile dans le banlieue sud de Paris à la fin du XVIIIe siècle (1774–1794)', *Annales de démographie historique* (1966), pp. 130–77.

Gautier, E. and Henry, L., *La population de Crulai: paroisse normande* (Paris, 1958).

Glass, D. V., *Numbering the people. The eighteenth century population controversy and the development of census and vital statistics in Britain* (Farnborough, 1973).

Golas, P. J., *Mining* in *Science and civilisation in China*, ed. J. Needham, V, pt XIII (Cambridge, 1999), pp. 186–201.

Goubert, P., *Beauvais et le Beauvaisis de 1600 à 1730*, 2 vols. (Paris, 1960).

Gough, R., *The history of Myddle*, ed. D. Hey (Harmondsworth, 1981).

Grantham, G., 'Divisions of labour: agricultural productivity and occupational specialization in pre-industrial France', *Economic History Review*, 46 (1993), pp. 478–502.

Grigg, D., *The dynamics of agricultural change: the historical experience* (London, 1982).

Haggett, P., *Locational analysis in human geography* (London, 1965).

Habakkuk, H. J., 'English population in the eighteenth century', *Economic History Review*, 2nd ser., 6 (1953), pp. 117–53.

Hajnal, J., 'European marriage patterns in perspective', in D. V. Glass and D. E. C. Eversley, eds., *Population in history* (London, 1965), pp. 101–43.

Hart, N., 'Famine, maternal nutrition and infant mortality: a re-examination of the Dutch hunger winter', *Population Studies*, 47 (1993), pp. 27–46.

Harte, N. B., 'The economics of clothing in the late seventeenth century', *Textile History*, 22 (1991), pp. 277–96.

Hazlitt, William, *The complete works of William Hazlitt*, ed. P. P. Howe, 21 vols. (London and Toronto, 1930–4).

Henry, L., 'Some data on natural fertility', *Eugenics Quarterly*, 8 (1961), pp. 81–91.

'Fécondité des mariages dans le quart sud-ouest de la France de 1720 à 1869', *Annales E.S.C.*, 27 (1972), pp. 612–40 and 977–1023.

Techniques d'analyse en démographie historique (Paris, 1980).

Henry, L. and Blayo, Y., 'La population de la France de 1740 à 1860', *Population*, special number, 30 (1975), pp. 71–122.

Himmelfarb, G., *The idea of poverty: England in the early industrial age* (London, 1984).

Hoffman, W. G., 'The take-off in Germany', in W. W. Rostow, ed., *The economics of take-off into sustained growth* (London, 1963), pp. 95–118.

Hofsten, E. and Lundström, H., *Swedish population history: main trends from 1750 to 1970*, Urval no. 8, Skriftseries uitgiven av Statistiska centralbyrån (Stockholm, 1976).

Holderness, B. A., 'Prices, productivity, and output', in *The agrarian history of England and Wales*, VI, *1750–1850*, ed. G. E. Mingay (Cambridge, 1989), pp. 84–189.

Hoppit, J., 'Counting the industrial revolution', *Economic History Review*, 2nd ser., 43 (1990), pp. 173–93.

Hoppit, J. and Wrigley, E. A., 'Introduction', in J. Hoppit and E. A. Wrigley, eds., *The industrial revolution in Britain*, vol. II in R. A. Church and E. A. Wrigley, eds., *The industrial revolutions* (Oxford, 1994), pp. ix–xl.

Hoselitz, B. F., 'Generative and parasitic cities', *Economic Development and Cultural Change*, 3 (1954–5), pp. 278–94.

Hoskins, W. G., 'The rebuilding of rural England, 1570–1640', *Past and Present*, 4 (1953), pp. 44–59.

Houdaille, J., 'La mortalité des enfants en Europe avant le XIX siècle', in P.-M. Boulanger and D. Tabutin, eds., *La mortalité des enfants dans le monde et dans l'histoire* (Liège, 1980), pp. 85–118.

Huck, P., 'Infant mortality in nine industrial parishes in northern England, 1813–1836', *Population Studies*, 48 (1994), pp. 513–26.

Imhof, A. E., 'Structure of reproduction in a west German village 1690–1900', in S. Åkerman, H. C. Johansen, and D. Gaunt, eds., *Chance and change: social and economic studies in historical demography in the Baltic area* (Odense, 1978), pp. 23–32.

'Unterschiedliche Säuglingssterblichkeit in Deutschland, 18. bis 20. Jahrhundert – warum?, *Zeitschrift für Bevölkerungswissenschaft*, 7 (1981), pp. 343–82.

'The amazing simultaneousness of the big differences and the boom in the nineteenth century – some facts and hypotheses about infant and maternal mortality in Germany, eighteenth to twentieth century', in T. Bengtsson, G. Fridlizius, and R. Ohlsson, eds., *Pre-industrial population change: the mortality decline and short-term population movements* (Stockholm, 1984), pp. 191–222.

Ingram, M., 'Spousals litigation in the English ecclesiastical courts c.1350–c.1640', in R. B. Outhwaite, ed., *Marriage and society: studies in the social history of marriage* (London, 1981), pp. 35–57.

Innis, H., *The fur trade in Canada: an introduction to Canadian economic history* (New Haven, Conn., 1930).

Jackson, R. V., 'Government expenditure and British economic growth in the eighteenth century: some problems of measurement', *Economic History Review*, 2nd ser., 43 (1990), pp. 217–35.

'What was the rate of economic growth during the industrial revolution?', in G. D. Snooks, ed., *Was the industrial revolution necessary?* (London and New York, 1994), pp. 79–95.

James, P., *The travel diaries of Thomas Robert Malthus* (Cambridge, 1966).

Population Malthus: his life and times (London, 1979).

Johansen, H. C., *Danish population history 1600–1939* (Odense, 2002).

Johansen, H. C. and Oeppen, J., *Danish population estimates 1665–1840*, Danish Center for Demographic Research, Research report 21 (Odense, 2001).

Jones, E. L., 'The reduction of fire damage in southern England', *Post-Medieval Archaeology*, 2 (1968), pp. 140–9.

'Agriculture 1700–80', in R. Floud and D. N. McCloskey, eds., *The economic history of Britain since 1700*, vol. I (Cambridge, 1981), pp. 66–86.

Jones, E. L. and Falkus, M. E., 'Urban improvement and the English economy in the seventeenth and eighteenth centuries', *Research in Economic History*, 4 (1979), pp. 193–233.

Kander, A., *Economic growth, energy consumption and CO_2 emissions in Sweden 1800–2000*, Lund Studies in Economic History 19 (Stockholm, 2002).

Kindleberger, C. P., *Economic development*, 2nd edn (New York, 1965).

King, G., *Natural and political observations and conclusions upon the state and condition of England 1696*, reprinted in *The earliest classics: John Graunt and Gregory King*, with an introd. by P. Laslett (Gregg International, 1973).

Kjaergaard, T., *The Danish revolution 1500–1800: an ecohistorical interpretation* (Cambridge, 1994).

Kline, J., Stein, Z., and Susser, M., *Conception to birth: epidemiology of prenatal development* (New York, 1989).

Knodel, J., 'Infant mortality and fertility in three Bavarian villages: an analysis of family histories from the nineteenth century', *Population Studies*, 22 (1968), pp. 297–318.

'Breast feeding and population growth', *Science*, 198 (1974), pp. 1111–5.

The decline of fertility in Germany, 1871–1939 (Princeton, 1974).

'Natural fertility in pre-industrial Germany', *Population Studies*, 32 (1978), pp. 481–510.

Demographic behavior in the past: a study of fourteen German village populations in the eighteenth and nineteenth centuries (Cambridge, 1988).

Knodel, J. and Hermalin, A. I., 'Effects of birth rank, maternal age, birth interval and sibship size on infant and child mortality: evidence from 18th and 19th century reproductive histories', *American Journal of Public Health*, 74 (1984), pp. 1098–106.

Knodel, J. and van de Walle, E., 'Breastfeeding, fertility, and infant mortality: an analysis of some early German data', *Population Studies*, 21 (1967), pp. 109–32.

Knodel, J. and Wilson, C., 'The secular increase in fecundity in German village populations: an analysis of reproductive histories of couples married 1750–1899', *Population Studies*, 35 (1981), pp. 53–84.

Kussmaul, A., *Servants in husbandry in early modern England* (Cambridge, 1981).

A general view of the rural economy of England 1538–1840 (Cambridge, 1990).

Landers, J., *Death and the metropolis: studies in the demographic history of London 1670–1830* (Cambridge, 1993).

Laslett, P., 'Size and structure of the household in England over three centuries', *Population Studies*, 23 (1969), pp. 199–223.

'Introduction: the history of the family', in P. Laslett and R. Wall, eds., *Household and family in past time* (Cambridge, 1972), pp. 1–89.

ed., *Household and family in past time* (Cambridge, 1972).

'Clayworth and Cogenhoe', in P. Laslett, *Family life and illicit love in earlier generations* (Cambridge, 1977), pp. 50–101.

Family life and illicit love in earlier generations (Cambridge, 1977).

Lebrun, F., *Les hommes et la mort en Anjou aux 17e et 18e siècles* (Paris, 1971).

Lee, C. H., *British regional employment statistics 1841–1971* (Cambridge, 1979).
'The service sector, regional specialization, and economic growth in the Victorian economy', *Journal of Historical Geography*, 10 (1984), pp. 139–55.

Lee, J. Z. and Wang Feng, *One quarter of humanity: Malthusian mythology and Chinese realities, 1700–2000* (Harvard, 1999).

Lee, R. and Lam, D., 'Age distribution adjustments for English censuses, 1821 to 1931', *Population Studies*, 37 (1983), pp. 445–64.

Leridon, H., *Human fertility* (Chicago, 1977).

Levasseur, E., *La population française*, 3 vols. (Paris, 1889–92).

Levine, D., 'The reliability of parochial registration and the representativeness of family reconstitution', *Population Studies*, 30 (1976), pp. 107–22.
Family formation in an age of nascent capitalism (New York, 1977).
'Production, reproduction and the proletarian family in England 1500–1851', in D. Levine, ed., *Proletarianization and family history* (London, 1984), pp. 87–127.

Lösch, A., *Die räumliche Ordnung der Wirtschaft* (Jena, 1940).

Loudon, I., *Death in childbirth, an international study of maternal care and maternal mortality 1800–1950* (Oxford, 1992).

McCloskey, D., '1780–1860: a survey', in R. Floud and D. McCloskey, eds., *The economic history of Britain since 1700*, 2nd edn, vol. I (Cambridge, 1994), pp. 242–70.

McCulloch, J. R., *A statistical account of the British Empire*, 2 vols. (London, 1837).

Machin, R., 'The great rebuilding: a reassessment', *Past and Present*, 77 (1977), pp. 33–56.

McKendrick, N., 'The consumer revolution of eighteenth-century England', in N. McKendrick, J. Brewer, and J. H. Plumb, eds., *The birth of a consumer society: the commercialization of eighteenth-century England* (London, 1982), pp. 9–33.

McKendrick, N., Brewer, J., and Plumb, J. H., eds., *The birth of a consumer society: the commercialization of eighteenth-century England* (London, 1982).

McKeown, T. and Record, R. G., 'Reasons for the decline of mortality in England and Wales during the nineteenth century', *Population Studies*, 16 (1962), pp. 94–122.

McKeown, T., Record, R. G., and Turner, R. D., 'An interpretation of the decline of mortality in England and Wales during the twentieth century', *Population Studies*, 29 (1975), pp. 391–422.

Maddison, A., *Phases of capitalist development* (Oxford, 1982).
The world economy: a millennial perspective (OECD, 2001).

Malthus, T. R., *An essay on the principle of population as it affects the future improvement of society with remarks on the speculations of Mr Godwin, M. Condorcet and other writers* [1798], in *The works of Thomas Robert Malthus*, ed. E. A. Wrigley and D. Souden (London, 1986), vol. I.
An investigation of the cause of the present high price of provisions [1800], in *The works of Thomas Robert Malthus*, ed. E. A. Wrigley and D. Souden (London, 1986), vol. VII.
An essay on the principle of population; or a view of its past and present effects on human happiness; with an inquiry into our prospects respecting the future removal or mitigation of the evils which it occasions (London, 1803).

A letter to Samuel Whitbread, Esq. M.P. on his proposed bill for the amendment of the poor laws [1807], in *The works of Thomas Robert Malthus*, ed. E. A. Wrigley and D. Souden (London, 1986), vol. IV.

An inquiry into the nature and progress of rent, and the principles by which it is regulated [1815], in *The works of Thomas Robert Malthus*, ed. E. A. Wrigley and D. Souden (London, 1986), vol. VII.

Population [1824], in *The works of Thomas Robert Malthus*, ed. E. A. Wrigley and D. Souden (London, 1986), vol. IV.

An essay on the principle of population; or a view of its past and present effects on human happiness, 6th edn [1826], in *The works of Thomas Robert Malthus*, ed. E. A. Wrigley and D. Souden (London, 1986), vols. II and III.

Principles of political economy considered with a view to their practical application, 2nd edn [1836], in *The works of Thomas Robert Malthus*, ed. E. A. Wrigley and D. Souden (London, 1986), vols. V and VI.

Marx, K., *Capital: a critical analysis of capitalist production*, ed. F. Engels, trans. S. Moore and E. Aveling from the 3rd German edn (2 vols., 1887).

Marx, K. and Engels, F., *The Communist manifesto*, trans. S. Moore (London and Chicago, 1996).

Mathias, P., 'The social structure in the eighteenth century: a calculation by Joseph Massie', in P. Mathias, *The transformation of England: essays in the economic and social history of England in the eighteenth century* (London, 1979), pp. 171–89.

The first industrial nation, 2nd edn (London, 1983).

Mathias, P. and O'Brien, P. K., 'Taxation in England and France 1715–1810', *Journal of European Economic History*, 5 (1976), pp. 601–50.

Mendels, F. F., 'Proto-industrialization: the first phase of the industrialization process', *Journal of Economic History*, 32 (1972), pp. 241–61.

Meyer, J., Lottin, A., Poussou, J. P., Soly, H., Vogler, B., and van der Woude, A., *Etudes sur les villes en Europe occidentale, milieu due XVIIIe siècle à la veille de la révolution française*, 2 vols. (Paris, 1983).

Mill, J. S., *Principles of political economy with some of their applications to social philosophy*, introd. V. W. Bladen, textual ed. J. M. Robson, 2 vols. (Toronto, 1965).

Mitchell, B. R., *European historical statistics 1750–1975*, 2nd edn rev. (London, 1981).

British historical statistics (Cambridge, 1988).

Mitchell, B. R. and Deane, P., *Abstract of British historical statistics* (Cambridge, 1962).

Mokyr, J., *The lever of riches: technological creativity and economic progress* (Oxford, 1990).

'Editor's introduction: the New Economic History and the industrial revolution', in J. Mokyr, ed., *The British industrial revolution: an economic perspective* (Boulder, San Francisco, and Oxford, 1993).

Mooney, G., 'Stillbirths and the measurement of urban infant mortality rates c. 1890–1930', *Local Population Studies*, 53 (1994), pp. 42–52.

Muldrew, C., *The economy of obligation: the culture of credit and social relations in early modern England* (London, 1998).

Nef, J. U., *The rise of the British coal industry*, 2 vols. (London, 1932).

Netting, R. M., *Balancing on an Alp: ecological change and continuity in a Swiss mountain community* (Cambridge 1981).

North, D. C., *Structure and change in economic history* (New York, 1981).

O'Brien, P. K., 'European economic development: the contribution of the periphery', *Economic History Review*, 2nd ser., 35 (1982), pp. 1–18.

'The political economy of British taxation, 1660–1815', *Economic History Review*, 2nd ser., 41 (1988), pp. 1–32.

Oeppen, J., 'Back projection and inverse projection: members of a wider class of constrained projection models', *Population Studies*, 47 (1993), pp. 245–67.

'Generalized inverse projection', in D. S. Reher and R. Schofield, eds., *Old and new methods in historical demography* (Oxford, 1993), pp. 29–39.

Ohlin, G., 'Mortality, marriage and population growth in pre-industrial populations', *Population Studies*, 14 (1961), pp. 190–7.

Ormrod, D., 'Dutch commercial and industrial decline and British growth in the late seventeenth and early eighteenth centuries', in F. Krantz and P. M. Hohenberg, eds., *Failed transitions to modern industrial society: Renaissance Italy and seventeenth-century Holland* (Montreal, 1975), pp. 36–43.

Overton, M., *Agricultural revolution in England: the transformation of the agrarian economy 1500–1850* (Cambridge, 1996).

Patten, J., 'Changing occupational structures in the East Anglian countryside, 1500–1700', in H. S. A. Fox and R. A. Butlin, eds., *Change in the countryside* (London, 1979), pp. 103–21.

Phelps Brown, E. H. and Hopkins, S. V., 'Seven centuries of building wages', *Economica*, 23 (1955), pp. 195–206.

'Seven centuries of the prices of consumables, compared with builders' wages', *Economica*, 24 (1956), pp. 296–314.

A perspective of wages and prices (London, 1981).

Pimentel, D., 'Energy flow in the food system', in D. Pimentel and C. W. Hall, eds., *Food and energy resources* (London, 1984), pp. 1–24.

Pittenger, D. B., 'An exponential model of female sterility', *Demography*, 10 (1973), pp. 113–21.

Plutarch, *The rise and fall of Athens: nine Greek lives*, trans. I. Scott-Kilvert (Harmondsworth, 1960).

Pollard, S., 'Labour in Great Britain', in P. Mathias and M. M. Postan, eds., *The Cambridge economic history of Europe*, vol. VII, pt I (Cambridge, 1978), pp. 97–179.

'The industrial revolution: an overview', in M. Teich and R. Porter, eds., *The industrial revolution in national context* (Cambridge, 1996), pp. 371–88.

Rappaport, S., *Worlds within worlds: structures of life in sixteenth century London* (Cambridge, 1989).

Razzell, P. E., 'The evaluation of baptism as a form of birth registration through cross-matching census and parish register data', *Population Studies*, 26 (1972), pp. 121–46.

'The growth of population in eighteenth-century England: a critical reappraisal', *Journal of Economic History*, 53 (1993), pp. 743–71.

Essays in English population history (London, 1994).

'The conundrum of eighteenth-century English population growth', *Social History of Medicine*, 11 (1998), pp. 469–500.

Ricardo, D., *On the principles of political economy and taxation* in *The works and correspondence of David Ricardo*, I, ed. P. Sraffa with the collaboration of M. H. Dobb (Cambridge, 1951).

Rich, E. E., *Hudson's Bay Company, 1670–1870*, 3 vols. (New York, 1960).
Montreal and the fur trade (Montreal, 1966).

Rogers, J., *Family reconstitution: new information or misinformation?* Reports from the Family History Group, Department of History, Uppsala Univ., no. 7 (Uppsala, 1988).

Rosso, P. and Cramoy, C., 'Nutrition and pregnancy', in M. Winick, ed., *Nutrition: pre- and postnatal development* (New York, 1979), pp. 133–228.

Rostow, W. W., *The process of economic growth*, 2nd edn (Oxford, 1960).

Rozman, G., 'Urban networks and historical stages', *Journal of Interdisciplinary History*, 9 (1978), pp. 65–91.

Ruggles, S., 'Migration, marriage and mortality: correcting sources of bias in English family reconstitutions', *Population Studies*, 46 (1992), pp. 507–22.

Schama, S., *The embarrassment of riches* (London, 1987).

Schofield, R. S., 'Age-specific mobility in an eighteenth century rural English parish', *Annales de démographie historique, 1970* (Paris, 1971), pp. 261–74.
'The relationship between demographic structure and environment in pre-industrial western Europe', in W. Conze, ed., *Sozialgeschichte der Familie in der Neuzeit Europas* (Stuttgart, 1976), pp. 147–60.
'English marriage patterns revisited', *Journal of Family History*, 10 (1985), pp. 2–20.

Sen, A., *Poverty and famines: an essay on entitlement and deprivation* (Oxford, 1981).

Shammas, C., *The pre-industrial consumer in Britain and America* (Oxford, 1990).

Sharlin, A., 'Natural decrease in early modern cities: a reconsideration', *Past and Present*, 79 (1978), pp. 126–38.

Shryock, H. S. and Siegel, J. S., *The methods and materials of demography*, 2 vols. (Washington, D.C., 1971).

Sieferle, R. P., *The subterranean forest: energy systems and the industrial revolution* (Cambridge, 2001).

Sjoberg, G., *The preindustrial city: past and present* (Glencoe, Ill., 1960).

Slicher van Bath, B. H., *Een samenleving onder spanning. Geschiedenis van het platteland in Overijssel* (Assen, 1957).

Smith, A., *An inquiry into the nature and causes of the wealth of nations*, 5th edn, ed. E. Cannan, 2 vols. (Chicago, 1976: orig. pub. 1904).

Smith, R. M., ed., *Land, kinship and life-cycle* (Cambridge, 1985).
'Human resources', in G. Astill and A. Grant, eds., *The countryside of medieval England* (Oxford, 1988), pp. 188–212.
'Demographic developments in rural England 1300–48', in B. M. S. Campbell, ed., *Before the Black Death: studies in the 'crisis' of the early fourteenth century* (Manchester, 1991), pp. 25–77.

Snell, K. D. M., 'Agricultural seasonal employment, the standard of living, and women's work in the south and east, 1690–1860', *Economic History Review*, 2nd ser., 34 (1981), pp. 407–37.

Snooks, G. D., 'Great waves of economic change: the industrial revolution in historical perspective, 1000 to 2000', in G. D. Snooks, ed., *Was the industrial revolution necessary?* (London and New York, 1994), pp. 43–78.

Souden, D. C., 'Pre-industrial English local migration fields' (unpub. PhD thesis, University of Cambridge, 1981).

Spufford, M., *The great reclothing of rural England: petty chapmen and their wares in the seventeenth century* (London, 1984).

'The cost of apparel in seventeenth-century England, and the accuracy of Gregory King', *Economic History Review*, 53 (2000), pp. 677–705.

Stevenson, R. L., 'El Dorado' in *Virginibus Puerisque* (London, 1947), pp. 137–42.

Stone, R., 'Some seventeenth century econometrics: consumers' behaviour', *Revue Européenne des Sciences Sociales*, 26 (1988), pp. 19–41.

'Gregory King and the development of economic statistics', in R. Stone, *Some British empiricists in the social sciences 1650–1900* (Cambridge, 1997), pp. 71–115.

Some British empiricists in the social sciences 1650–1900 (Cambridge, 1997).

Sundbärg, G., *Bevölkerungsgeschichte Schwedens, 1750–1900* [Stockholm, 1907], reprinted with preface and vocabulary in English, Urval, no. 3 (Stockholm, 1970).

Sutherland, I., *Stillbirths: their epidemiology and social significance* (London, 1949).

Tafari, B., 'Low birth weight: an overview', in D. B. Jelliffe and E. F. P. Jelliffe, eds., *Advances in international maternal and child health*, I (Oxford, 1981), pp. 105–27.

Tawney, A. J. and Tawney, R. H., 'An occupational census of the seventeenth century', *Economic History Review*, 5 (1934), pp. 25–64.

Tawney, R. H., *Religion and the rise of capitalism: a historical study* (London, 1926).

Thirsk, J., *Economic policy and projects: the development of a consumer society in early modern England* (Oxford, 1978).

Thomas, B., 'Escaping from constraints: the industrial revolution in a Malthusian context', *Journal of Interdisciplinary History*, 15 (1985), pp. 729–53.

Thomas, D. S., *Social and economic aspects of Swedish population movements 1750–1933* (New York, 1941).

Tillott, P. M., 'Sources of inaccuracy in the 1851 and 1861 censuses, in E. A. Wrigley, ed., *Nineteenth-century society: essays in the use of quantitative methods for the study of social data* (Cambridge, 1972), pp. 82–133.

Tooke, T., *A history of prices and of the state of the circulation*, 6 vols. (London, 1838–57).

Tranter, N. L., 'The labour supply 1780–1860', in R. Floud and D. McCloskey, eds., *The economic history of Britain since 1700*, vol. I (Cambridge, 1981), pp. 204–26.

Turpeinen, O., 'Infant mortality in Finland 1749–1865', *Scandinavian Economic History Review*, 27 (1979), pp. 1–21.

Unger, R. W., 'Energy sources for the Dutch golden age: peat, wind and coal', *Research in Economic History*, 9 (1984), pp. 221–53.

Vallgårda, S., 'Trends in perinatal death rates in Denmark and Sweden, 1915–40', *Paediatric and Perinatal Epidemiology*, 9 (1995), pp. 201–18.

Van de Walle, E., *The female population of France in the nineteenth century* (Princeton, 1974).

Van der Woude, A., 'Population developments in the northern Netherlands (1500–1800) and the validity of the "urban graveyard" effect', *Annales de démographie historique 1982* (Paris, 1982), pp. 55–75.

Van der Woude, A., Hayami, A., and de Vries, J., eds., *Urbanization in history: a process of dynamic interactions* (Oxford, 1990).

Vandenbroeke, C., van Poppel, F., and van der Woude, A., 'De zuigelingen- en kindersterfte in Belgie en Nederland in seculair perspectief', *Tijdschrift voor Geschiedenis*, 94 (1981), pp. 461–91.

Vaughan, W. E. and Fitzpatrick, A. J., eds., *Irish historical statistics. Population, 1821–1971* (Dublin, 1978).

Ville, S., 'Total factor productivity in the English shipping industry: the northeast coal trade, 1700–1850', *Economic History Review*, 2nd ser., 39 (1986), pp. 355–70.

Von Thünen, J. H., *The isolated state*, Eng. trans. of *Der isolierte Staat in Beziehung auf Landwirtschaft und Nationalökonomie*, ed. and trans. P. Hall (Oxford, 1966).

Voth, J., 'Time-use in eighteenth-century London: some evidence from the Old Bailey' (unpub. DPhil thesis, University of Oxford, 1996).

Wall, R., 'The age at leaving home', *Journal of Family History*, 3 (1978), pp. 181–202.

ed., *Family forms in historic Europe* (Cambridge, 1983).

Ward, W. P., *Birth weight and economic growth* (Chicago, 1993).

Weatherill, L., *Consumer behaviour and material culture in England, 1660–1750* (London, 1988).

Weir, D., 'Rather never than late: celibacy and age at marriage in English cohort fertility, 1541–1871', *Journal of Family History*, 9 (1984), pp. 341–55.

White, L. P. and Plaskett, L. G., *Biomass as fuel* (London, 1981).

Wilson, C., 'Marital fertility in pre-industrial England, 1550–1849' (unpub. PhD thesis, University of Cambridge, 1982).

Wilson, C., 'The proximate determinants of marital fertility in England 1600–1799', in L. Bonfield, R. M. Smith, and K. Wrightson, eds., *The world we have gained: histories of population and social structure* (Oxford, 1986), pp. 203–30.

Wilson, C., Oeppen, J., and Pardoe, M., 'What is natural fertility? The modelling of a concept', *Population Index*, 54 (1988), pp. 4–20.

Woods, R., 'The effects of population redistribution on the level of mortality in nineteenth-century England and Wales', *Journal of Economic History*, 45 (1985), pp. 645–51.

The demography of Victorian England and Wales (Cambridge, 2000).

Wrigley, E. A., 'Family reconstitution', in E. A. Wrigley, ed., *An introduction to English historical demography* (London, 1966), pp. 96–159.

'A simple model of London's importance in changing English society and economy 1650–1750', *Past and Present*, 37 (1967), pp. 44–70.

'The process of modernization and the industrial revolution in England', *Journal of Interdisciplinary History*, 3 (1972), pp. 225–59.

'Baptism coverage in early nineteenth-century England: the Colyton area', *Population Studies*, 29 (1975), pp. 299–316.

'Parasite or stimulus: the town in a pre-industrial economy', in P. Abrams and E. A. Wrigley, eds., *Towns in societies. Essays in economic history and historical sociology* (Cambridge, 1978), pp. 295–309.

'Marriage, fertility and population growth in eighteenth-century England', in R. B. Outhwaite, ed., *Marriage and society: studies in the social history of marriage* (London, 1981), pp. 137–85.

'The growth of population in eighteenth-century England: a conundrum resolved', *Past and Present*, 98 (1983), pp. 121–50.

'Elegance and experience: Malthus at the bar of history', in D. Coleman and R. Schofield, eds., *The state of population theory: forward from Malthus* (Oxford, 1986), pp. 46–64.

'Some reflections on corn yields and prices in pre-industrial economies', in E. A. Wrigley, *People, cities and wealth: the transformation of traditional society* (Oxford, 1987), pp. 92–130.

'The classical economists and the industrial revolution' in E. A. Wrigley, *People, cities and wealth: the transformation of traditional society* (Oxford, 1987), pp. 21–45.

'Urban growth and agricultural change: England and continent in the early modern period', in E. A. Wrigley, *People, cities and wealth: the transformation of traditional society* (Oxford, 1987), pp. 157–93.

People, cities and wealth: the transformation of traditional society (Oxford, 1987).

Continuity, chance and change: the character of the industrial revolution in England (Cambridge, 1988).

'Energy availability and agricultural productivity', in B. M. S. Campbell and M. Overton, eds., *Land, labour and livestock: historical studies in European agricultural productivity* (Manchester, 1991), pp. 323–39.

'Society and the economy in the eighteenth century', in L. Stone, ed., *An imperial state at war: Britain from 1689 to 1815* (London, 1994), pp. 72–95.

'How reliable is our knowledge of the demographic characteristics of the English population in the early modern period?', *Historical Journal*, 40 (1997), pp. 571–93.

Wrigley, E. A. and Schofield, R. S., *The population history of England, 1541–1871: a reconstruction* (paperback edn with new introd., Cambridge, 1981).

'English population history from family reconstitution: summary results 1600–1799', *Population Studies*, 37 (1983), pp. 157–84.

Wrigley, E. A., Davies, R. S., Oeppen, J., and Schofield, R. S., *English population history from family reconstitution 1580–1837* (Cambridge, 1997).

Young, A., *Travels in France and Italy during the years 1787, 1788 and 1789*, Everyman's Library (London and Toronto, n.d.).

OFFICIAL PUBLICATIONS

1811 Census, Enumeration abstract, *Parliamentary Papers*, 1812, XI.
1821 Census, Enumeration abstract, *Parliamentary Papers*, 1822, XV.

1831 Census, Enumeration abstract, I and II, *Parliamentary Papers*, 1833, XXXVI and XXXVII.

1841 Census, Enumeration abstract, *Parliamentary Papers*, 1843, XXII.

1841 Census, Occupation abstract, *Parliamentary Papers*, 1844, XXVII.

1851 Census, Population tables, II, Ages, condition, occupations and birthplace of the people, vols. I and II, *Parliamentary Papers*, 1852–3, LXXXVIII.

1861 Census, General report, *Parliamentary Papers*, 1863, LIII.

1861 Census, Population tables, II, Ages, civil condition, occupations and birthplaces of the people, *Parliamentary Papers*, 1863, LIII.

1871 Census, vol. III, Civil condition, occupations and birthplaces of the people, *Parliamentary Papers*, 1873, LXXI.

Annual reports of the Registrar General.

Befolkningsutvecklingen under 250 år. Historisk statistik för Sverige, Demografiska rapporter (Statistiska centralbyrån, Stockholm, 1999).

Historisk statistik för Sverige, del. I, Befolking 1720–1967 (Statistika centralbyrån, Stockholm, 1969).

Norges offisielle statistikk, XII, 245, *Historiske statistikk* 1968 (Oslo, 1969).

Registrar General's statistical review of England and Wales.

United Nations, Department of Social Affairs, Population Division, *Foetal, infant and early childhood mortality*, I, *The statistics* (New York, 1954).

Index